P9-BAW-305

THE CENTURY SOCIAL SCIENCE SERIES

Social Legislation

The life of the law has not been logic: it has been experience. The felt necessities of the time, the prevalent moral and political theories, intuitions of public policy, avowed or unconscious, even the prejudices which judges share with their fellow men, have had a good deal more to do than the syllogism in determining the rules by which men should be governed. The law embodies the story of a nation's development through many centuries, and it cannot be dealt with as if it contained only the axioms and corollaries of a book of mathematics. In order to know what it is, we must know what is has been, and what it tends to become. We must alternately consult history and existing theories of legislation. But the most difficult labor will be to understand the combination of the two into new products at every stage. The substance of the law at any given time pretty nearly corresponds, so far as it goes, with what is then understood to be convenient; but its form and machinery and the degree to which it is able to work out desired results depend very much upon its past.

OLIVER WENDELL HOLMES, JR.
from *The Common Law*

Social Legislation

HELEN I. CLARKE
University of Wisconsin

SECOND EDITION

New York

APPLETON-CENTURY-CROFTS, INC.

645-7

Library of Congress Card Number: 57-6100

PRINTED IN THE UNITED STATES OF AMERICA

E 19775

To

MY PARENTS

FOREWORD

In this second edition of *Social Legislation,* the author is careful to point out that her book deals only with selected phases of social legislation. However, I think most people would probably agree that she has selected the two most important phases of social legislation, as we use that term in this country: namely, legislation concerned with family relationships and income maintenance. So far as I know, no other book on social legislation attempts to cover both.

The discussion of family law is especially comprehensive. The discussion of legislation dealing with income maintenance covers not only the evolution of the poor law but the public assistance and social insurance features of the Social Security Act.

This book is not only useful as a textbook or reference book for university students, both undergraduate and graduate, interested in social work and the social sciences. It is a book which should be read by professional social workers and lay persons already engaged in social welfare activities, whether under public or private auspices.

The caseworker who might be expected to be more interested in family relationships will find the discussion of income maintenance fully as interesting and valuable. Likewise, the person engaged in the administration of social insurance, who might be expected to be more interested in income maintenance, will find the discussion of family law very much worth his while. Caseworkers are constantly confronted with family problems arising out of insufficient family income. The administrators of Old-Age and Survivors Insurance and of veterans' benefits, for example, are constantly obliged to make decisions involving guardianship for hundreds of thousands of children and other persons entitled to benefits.

Everyone interested in understanding the significance of the growing responsibility of the modern democratic state for promoting the general welfare will find reading the first chapter a particularly rewarding experience. This chapter provides the reader with a splendid vantage point from which to survey and appraise social legislation, since it deals with such stimulating subjects as the police power, the welfare state, theories of constitutional law, and the common law.

As this book clearly shows, we have made considerable progress during the last twenty-five years in developing the necessary social organization and social instrumentalities designed to promote the general welfare of the citizens of this country. The Social Security Act, enacted in 1935, probably represents the most important single piece of social legislation in the history of our nation. Of even greater significance than the particular provisions of the Social Security Act is the fact that it is no longer attacked as "creeping socialism" but recognized as the necessary buttress of a free-enterprise system.

Although we can be gratified at the social progress represented by the Social Security Act, we cannot afford to be complacent. The Social Security Act needs to be improved in many ways in order to provide basic protection against all of the major economic hazards that can cause widespread destitution and suffering. I am confident that the next edition of this book will record many changes in the Social Security Act, just as this edition has done, because this act is both a symbol and a practical expression of the simple but never ending quest of our American democracy—the quest for social justice.

ARTHUR ALTMEYER

PREFACE

This second edition of *Social Legislation* offers an up-to-date-analysis of the legal relationships of husband, wife, and the state; parent, child, and the state; and needy persons and the state. It is primarily concerned with public policy as defined by legislatures, but it also considers the effects of judicial decisions upon such policy and some of the administrative problems associated with its implementation.

As one who has taught social work courses for a long time, including one on social legislation, the author has observed that many students are interested in the problems of marriage, divorce, adoption, illegitimacy, juvenile delinquency, poverty, sickness, but know next to nothing about their legal ramifications. Many colleges offer courses in social security, social insurance, labor legislation, public administration; but few courses, except perhaps those in law schools adequately cover legislation on the first two of the three subjects included in this study. Perhaps this book will serve as an incentive for the development of courses in aspects of social legislation over and above those now available. Perhaps, too, it will be used as a reference in social science courses employing various approaches to the analysis of social problems. It should have value for laymen seeking sociolegal information on specific subjects. In her classroom teaching, the author supplements *Social Legislation* with two mimeographed volumes of judicial decisions which she places in the hands of students. These cases do much to vitalize and illuminate the systematic discussions of the book. Students should be encouraged to make frequent use of such cases and to familiarize themselves with the statutes of the various jurisdictions involving the issues under consideration.

Since this book deals with so wide a range of subject matter, it is obvious that no single topic is exhaustively treated. There are, for example, countless books that deal with marriage and divorce from the specific perspective of the lawyer, theologian, sociologist, economist, anthropologist, historian, and so forth. *Social Legislation,* however, attempts to give the reader, and particularly the undergraduate social science student, an introduction to (1) the constitutional framework of social legislation; (2) the author's point of view on the role of the state in determining policy for the general welfare; (3) the historical background of much modern legislation; (4) federal and state laws on the subjects chosen for discussion; (5) judicial decisions and administrative actions on the same subjects; (6) inadequacies and needs, opportunities and methods for improvement of social legislation.

Some of the materials of this study, as of any book dealing with current problems, are dated. Facts and figures, laws and opinions are inevitably of a given moment. They may be of the past or the present, or they may be more or less accurate predictions of the future. Many of them may be history by the time of publication. This does not mean that the discussion is outmoded or irrelevant. Rather, it provides the student with information to which he can add, and about which he can form, his own beliefs and values.

There have been thousands of legislative enactments, judicial opinions, administrative rulings since 1940, when the first edition of *Social Legislation* was published. However, most of the basic legal principles under discussion in the following pages had been established at that time. This revised edition records the progress that has been made in the enactment and administration of public policy since the earlier publication. Many obsolescent measures have been superseded by improved provisions. Policies and practices established in some jurisdiction or other have been adapted and applied elsewhere. New practices have been conceived and established. Perhaps one illustration of the definition, modification, and limitation of policy will suffice to show tremendous but nevertheless incomplete movement. In 1935 Congress provided for two social insurances. One, old-age insurance, was exclusively a federal program, and the other, unemployment compensation, a federal-state co-operative venture. Over the intervening years federal and state legislatures have greatly modified these programs. The fundamental policy was established in 1935, namely, that it was legitimate for the federal government to provide for the general welfare through social insurances formerly considered a matter for the states or for private business. Congress has not yet extended the insurance principle to include health and comprehensive disability insurance legislation. When and if it does, it will enlarge the social insurance principle and the constitutional precept that the federal government may act in new or adapted ways for the general welfare.

Although exponents of the "welfare state" as it is defined in this book do not have to evangelize in the same way as they did in the 1890's or 1930's, there is no justification for apathy or complacency. If we are to preserve the best of the past and present and to achieve improvements in the future, we cannot rest. There will continue to be disagreements about whether any unit of government and which unit of government should assume responsibility for various aspects of the general welfare; whether particular legislation violates constitutional principles; whether too much power is flowing to the center; whether individual initiative and enterprise will be sapped by subsidies and benefits. We can be equally sure that we in the United States, and with gathering momentum the peoples of the world, will keep on struggling for policies and programs which are conducive to a better life.

Large sections of *Social Legislation* have been rewritten. A few chapters have required less revision than others, since they are primarily historical in content. The introductory chapter on the legal background of social reform has been elaborated. Some sections of Part I, "Marriage, the Family, and the State," have been rewritten entirely. Chapter 3, which deals with English common law and statutory history as it concerns the family, has been brought up to date. Chapters 4, 5, and 6 on marriage and divorce in American jurisdictions have been expanded, and the two chapters dealing with planned parenthood and sterilization have been changed extensively to include recent developments and data.

In Part II, most chapters have been greatly revised or completely rewritten. Chapter 9, "Rights and Duties of Parents," has been amplified to include recent legislative and judicial modifications, as have the chapters on guardianship, child welfare services, adoption, and children of unmarried parents. The chapter formerly entitled "Juvenile and Domestic Relations Courts" has been expanded to three chapters on youthful offenders and the special court systems and facilities that are being established to cope with the problems of juvenile delinquency.

Part III, "The Dependent and the State," has undergone substantial reorganization. The background chapter on the secularization of relief has been extended to include not only the progress in social assistance programs made by individual countries but the impetus and guidance provided these countries by the activities of the United Nations. The history of English social security has been brought up to the present and includes a discussion of the radical changes in England's social policies and programs since World War II.

The material on the development of relief, assistance, and insurance programs in this country has been thoroughly reorganized with a view toward emphasizing those aspects which most directly affect and interest the American people today. The historical sections have been consolidated to present a briefer though adequate picture of social assistance during the first century of this nation's existence. The chapter on emergency relief measures now contains an evaluation of some of the programs instituted in the 1930's and their effect on subsequent legislation. The last four chapters are devoted entirely to an analysis of the Social Security Act. Chapters 22 and 23 discuss the assistance and service programs, with particular attention to provisions for the aged. Chapters 24 and 25 deal with the insurance programs: the former with the OASI and the recent disability insurance provisions; the latter with the unemployment compensation program. All four chapters present not only the development and current content of the act but some of the issues that will require legislative consideration in the future.

The author wishes to express her appreciation to the many persons in and out of the state of Wisconsin who have taught her so much about social legislation. She is grateful for the opportunity she has had to serve on local and state committees concerned with legislation. They have given her the opportunity to discuss existing and desirable public services and to learn how politicians, laymen, and professional social workers can and must co-operate if the general welfare is to be advanced. Among the invaluable committee contacts have been those with laymen, so considered by this writer since they are outside the professional practice of social work. These include Mrs. William Hastings, Mrs. Harrison Garner, Mrs. Otto Falk, Joseph Mire, Howard Brown, and Lowell Frautschi. It is people such as these who serve as liaison between the citizenry and the administrators and as pressure and veto sources. She values greatly her contacts with public welfare administrators who have had the challenging and often thankless task of putting into effect the innumerable and complicated laws enacted by federal, state, county, and municipal governing bodies. Among such persons are Dorothy Waite, Cynthia Stokes, Mary Weaver, Margaret McDowell, Mary Schuster, Amy Weinstock, Sydney Miller, Morris Hursh, George Keith, Joseph Wilson, John Mannering, Thomas Lucas, Sr., John Tramburg, Fred DelliQuadri. She cannot adequately thank Wisconsinites, Edwin E. Witte and Arthur A. Altmeyer, representatives of the highest type of public servants, for the inspiration and encouragement they have afforded her and many others. She wants further to acknowledge the services of numerous librarians. These include Mrs. Ellen Commons, librarian of the U.S. Department of Health, Education, and Welfare, the staffs at the Wisconsin Historical Library, University of Wisconsin Library, and the Wisconsin Law Library, and Miss Alice Vincent, librarian of the Wisconsin Department of Public Welfare. She particularly wants her students to know how much she has benefited by their discerning questions and eager interest. Lastly, the author wishes to express particular gratitude to Mrs. Catherine Pieper, who has copied the manuscript numbers of times, who has been a most responsible proofreader and, best of all, an encouraging and patient friend.

HELEN I. CLARKE

CONTENTS

FOREWORD vii

PREFACE ix

Introduction

CHAPTER

1. Legal Background 3

PART I

Marriage, the Family, and the State

2. The Family: Early History 27
3. The Family: English Common Law and Statutory History . 53
4. Marriage in American Jurisdictions I 73
5. Marriage in American Jurisdictions II 96
6. Divorce in Modern American Jurisdictions 117
7. Planned Parenthood 152
8. Sterilization 187

PART II

Parent, Child, and the State

9. Rights and Duties of Parents 215
10. Guardianship of Children 256
11. Child Welfare Services 280
12. Adoption 308
13. Children of Unmarried Parents 339
14. Youthful Offenders and the Juvenile Court I 368
15. Youthful Offenders and the Juvenile Court II 384
16. Youthful Offenders and the Juvenile Court III 409

PART III

The Dependent and the State

17. The Secularization of Relief 437
18. English Social Security Policies 465
19. General Assistance Legislation I (in the United States) . . 486
20. General Assistance Legislation II (in the United States) . . 501
21. Emergency Legislation for Unemployment Relief (in the United States) 524
22. Old-age Assistance (Social Security Act) 552
23. Other Assistance and Service Programs (Social Security Act) 580
24. Old-age and Survivors Insurance and Disability Insurance (Social Security Act) 607
25. Unemployment Compensation (Social Security Act) . . . 625

TABLE OF CASES 643

INDEX 651

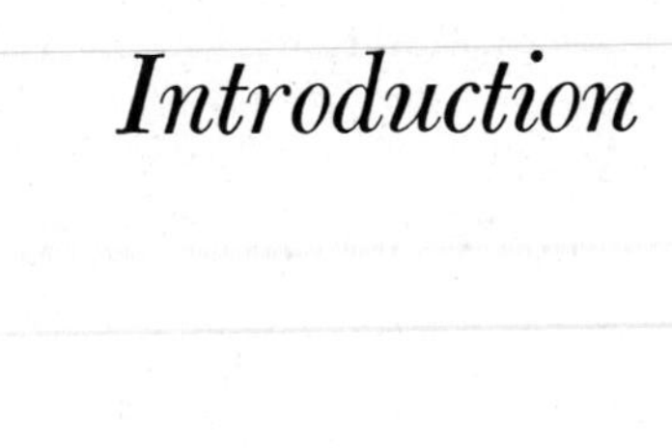

Introduction

CHAPTER 1

Legal Background

INTRODUCTION

In this book we shall be concerned with (1) common-law theories and rules, legislative enactments, and judicial decisions, prescribing and limiting the authority of the state over persons in certain relations with each other and to the state; (2) historical backgrounds of social legislation; and (3) administrative resources and processes for carrying out legislatively determined policy. The major portion of the book will be devoted to the first concern. It is important, however, that we know something of the origins and background of our law and of the family. In this chapter we shall introduce the student to the study of selected phases of social legislation through a review of the purpose of law, the form of American government, and the origins of Anglo-Saxon law. In the next two chapters we shall discuss early and more recent family customs and how they affect and are affected by law. Throughout the book we shall refer to administrative agencies and some of their pertinent activities.

THE PURPOSE OF LAW

"The law is a method of making decisions, of disposing finally of controversies, of settling human problems."[1] It is the system for the just regulation of men's conduct in their relation with each other, the community, and with the state. It is composed of (1) rules as laid down by the law-making bodies, the legislatures; and (2) principles which are derived from the experience of the judicial profession in the administration of justice. The former can be termed the written law; and the latter, the unwritten law, since, though it is expressed in judicial decisions, it derives from tradition and precedent.

Law is one of the most important methods of social control. Except for a Robinson Crusoe, every individual today touches the law at many points from birth to death and even prior to birth and after death. The as yet unconceived child is protected by marriage license laws requiring his potential parents to meet certain physical and social requirements.

[1] John S. Bradway, *Law and Social Work* (Chicago, University of Chicago Press, 1929), p. 49; see also, John C. Gray, *The Nature and Sources of the Law*, 2d ed. (New York, Macmillan, 1921), ch. 1.

The conceived but unborn child is affected by statutory provisions concerning prenatal examinations of his mother. The state requires that at birth his eyes shall be treated as a protection against blindness and that his birth and its legitimacy or illegitimacy shall be recorded. At the other end of the life cycle are statutes prescribing methods for disposing of the deceased individual's body, reporting and recording his death, and directing how his personal and real property may or shall descend.

The state protects rights and imposes duties simultaneously. Every person must pay taxes, keep the peace, obey the laws of the land, and, if necessary, give his life for his country. Reciprocally, he is entitled to an education; to an orderly community; to protection from contagious diseases and impure foods and drugs; to medical care under some conditions, especially if he has inadequate income to provide for himself; to fair wages and to decent working conditions, including the right to speak for himself through his duly selected labor organization representatives; to leisure and to resources for enhancing its significance; to speak his mind about his government; and to elect his spokesmen and policy makers.

In the early days of civilization, altercations between persons or groups were settled by battle. Governmental agencies, gradually created by law, became the instruments for maintaining peace and order within a state. For centuries these agencies made little or no effort to obtain the facts in an altercation but settled the dispute by the methods of oath, ordeal, fire, and battle. *Order* not *justice* was the motive of those attempting to dispose of the situation. Later, added to this primary function of government was that of protecting and enforcing rights and duties of individuals, and thus we have the introduction into legal theory of the concept of individual justice. The enactment of statutes and the creation of governmental agencies for the purpose of protecting *groups* of persons with special needs or of increasing the *social* as contrasted with *individual* welfare are largely a twentieth-century phenomenon, with the momentum starting at the beginning of the nineteenth century. This phase of law we today call *social legislation.* The term was first used in connection with Bismarck's achievements in Germany during the 1880's in obtaining legislation providing for social insurance against sickness, accident, invalidity, and old age. Some persons limit the meaning to legislation enacted for the benefit of disadvantaged groups; others extend it to legislation enacted for the general welfare. We shall use the term in both senses.

Legal interest in the group is manifested through what is called *public law,* by which lawyers mean that branch of law which is concerned with the state in its sovereign or political capacity. Legal concern for the individual is expressed through *private law,* by which is meant that part of the law which is administered between person and person and which is concerned with the rights and duties of individuals as individuals rather than as members of a group. In this book we are primarily concerned with public law or with the growth of the concern of the state for the general welfare. Sometimes, however, it will be necessary to discuss the rights and duties of individuals so that we may be aware of their fundamental rights and so that we may concretely observe the growth of the concern of the state with social well-being.

Although extensive enactment of social legislation is recent, that is not to say that outstanding examples have not appeared in the course of human history. For example, there are parts of the Code of Hammurabi among the Babylonians that can be labeled "social." The concept of criminal guilt was outlined, the *lex talionis* being the dominating feature in the penalties. Marriage and inheritance customs were defined.[2] Solon's Reforms in Greece attempted to prevent workers and small farmers from mortgaging their persons and bodies as security for debt. The Roman Twelve Tables, though they were harsh laws in many respects, gave substantial consideration to family relations, husband and wife, parent and child, guardian and ward. By the first century B.C. Rome had a system of dispensing bread and wine to the poor, which, although not intended as a poor-relief measure, had some of the same effects.

Among the Hebrews the Mosaic Code laid down religious and moral commandments which had the force of law. Under Diocletian the Roman Empire attempted to project governmental control into the economic life of the people by a regulated price-fixing. Benevolent despots, such as Frederick the Great of Prussia and Catherine the Great of Russia, put through legislation in an effort to improve the condition of the peasants of their respective countries. On the whole, the legislative efforts of governments in the past to improve the social and economic welfare of their peoples have been sporadic and sustained only for short periods, after which there have often been strong reactions, with sometimes but a segment of the advancement retained.

The impetus for the extensive enactment of social legislation began with the Industrial Revolution, when the law which had grown out of the feudal system proved inadequate to meet new conditions. This movement in England can be said to start with the enactment in 1802 of the Health and Morals of Apprentices Act.

THE POLICE POWER AND THE SOCIAL SERVICE STATE

Although there were benevolent and humanitarian persons in all western countries who, during the nineteenth century, sought to remedy many of the ills which were inevitable in a new economic society, their efforts were delayed and forestalled by the prevalence of a *laissez-faire* philoso-

---

[2] See several articles on "Law" (Primitive, Cuneiform, Greek, Roman, etc.), in *Encyclopaedia of the Social Sciences* (1933), Vol. 9, pp. 202–267.

phy. If reduced hours and increased wages were advocated, the stock reply was that only through free competition could the world's goods best be produced and distributed. If women wanted social and political freedom, they were told that they needed the protection of men, who in feudal times had fought to protect the fair sex; if they wanted economic freedom, they were warned that their place had always been the home and they had no right to expect an equal place with men in the wage-earning world.

With aggravation and acceleration of unequal conditions, modification of old patterns had to occur, or rebellion and revolution were inevitable. New conditions created new needs and caused a new philosophy to emerge. Basic to this philosophy was the belief in man and democracy as contrasted with a belief in rank and aristocracy. This is the theory of political democracy, or the control of government by the people rather than by a few persons with property and rank. If early nineteenth-century philosophy was that of individualism, free competition, *laissez faire*, and governmental "hands-off," it can be said that twentieth-century American philosophy is characterized by a belief in the value of every personality, by a concern for the welfare of the people generally, and by governmental participation in the achievement of reasonable security and happiness here and now for all. Legally, this theory gets expression through the doctrine of the "police power," which permits the state not only to prevent unfortunate occurrences but to compel positive action for the general welfare.

THE POLICE POWER

That which we in the United States call *police power* has always existed and is a function of government everywhere.[3] The word *police* in its Greek origin means "of or pertaining to an organized community." In its Roman origin it means "the condition of the state," and in the age of Augustus the Romans established a police system for the maintenance of law and order in the community or state. The particular phrase, "the police power," seems not to have occurred until Chief Justice John Marshall used it in 1827, when he held that the removal of dangerous explosives "unquestionably remains, and ought to remain, with the state as a branch of the police power."[4]

Under our system of government by which the federal government has only those powers which are delegated to it and the states have all others

---

[3] Walter H. Hamilton and Carlton C. Rodee, "Police Power," *Encyclopaedia of the Social Sciences* (1934), Vol. 12, pp. 190–193; Ernst Freund, *The Police Power, Public Policy, and Constitutional Rights* (Chicago, University of Chicago Press, 1904); J. M. Mathews, *American State Government*, rev. ed. (New York, Appleton-Century-Crofts, 1924).

[4] *Brown* v. *Maryland*, 12 Wheat. 419 (1827).

except those prohibited to them, the police power is a function of the states. The federal government exercises it only as an incident to its powers of taxation, interstate commerce, eminent domain, etc. Nowhere is the police power mentioned in the Constitution. It has been defined hundred of times by the courts, but it still remains a flexible, constantly changing and enlarging concept. It is universally conceded to include everything essential to the public safety, health, morals, and general well-being of the people and to justify the destruction or abatement of whatever may be regarded as a public nuisance.

Under this power it has been held that the State may order the destruction of a house falling to decay or otherwise endangering the lives of passers-by; the demolition of such as are in the path of a conflagration; the slaughter of diseased cattle; the destruction of decayed or unwholesome food; the prohibition of wooden buildings in cities; the regulation of railways and other means of public conveyance, and of interments in burial grounds; the restriction of objectionable trades to certain localities; the compulsory vaccination of children; the confinement of the insane or those afflicted with contagious diseases; the restraint of vagrants, beggars, and habitual drunkards; the suppression of obscene publications and houses of ill fame; and the prohibition of gambling houses and places where intoxicating liquors are sold. Beyond this, however, the State may interfere wherever the public interests demand it, and in this particular a large discretion is necessarily vested in the legislature to determine, not only what the interests of the public require, but what measures are necessary for the protection of such interests. . . . To justify the State in thus interposing its authority in behalf of the public, it must appear, first, that the interests of the public generally, as distinguished from those of a particular class, require such interference; and, second, that the means are reasonably necessary for the accomplishment of the purpose, and not unduly oppressive upon individuals.[5]

In other words, inherent in the sovereignty of the state is the power of the legislature to act for the protection of the general welfare. The police power in reality includes all those powers, not otherwise defined, which have for their purpose the protection of the public rather than private interests. If we take such a broad definition, it can be said that the police power is also a federal function even though the federal government must exercise it circuitously through some other function. This interpretation was definitely stated by Commons and Andrews: [6]

Hereafter, for our purposes, in speaking of the police power, we shall use the term in this broad sense, to imply all the powers of government, whether state or federal, whether of police, taxation, or interstate commerce, in so far as they are used to justify that inadequate extension of power for some newly recognized public purpose.

This position on the existence of a federal as well as a state police power has strong opponents and proponents. Many judges and lawyers,

[5] *Lawton* v. *State*, 52 U.S. 133 (1894).

[6] John R. Commons and John B. Andrews, *Principles of Labor Legislation* (New York, Harper, 1927), p. 17.

teachers and students, administrators and politicians vehemently argue that the federal government was not intended to exercise this power of sovereignty; that this residual power belongs with the states; that when the federal government exercises a police power it is usurping powers reserved to the states; that if functions which are not clearly authorized by the Constitution are required of the federal government they should come into existence only after constitutional amendment. Many others from the same walks of life contend that our forefathers meant the principles of the Constitution, especially those stated in the great ambiguous and undefined phrases, to be continuously interpreted and reinterpreted in order that government may keep step with the times; that it is the duty of the courts to uphold the actions of legislative and executive branches of government unless such actions are clearly unconstitutional; that the prolonged process of amending the Constitution is required only when clear violation of the Constitution is likely.

Congress has enacted many laws dealing with lotteries, infectious diseases of men, animals and plants, narcotics, obscene literature, food and drugs, contraceptives, convict-made goods, prize-fight films, extortion and blackmail, stolen automobiles, kidnaping, the white slave traffic, poverty. These statutes involve matters which clearly appear to be for the health, safety, morals, welfare of the public, all aspects of the police power and therefore reserved to the states. However, modern systems of production and distribution, transportation and communication necessitate country-wide as opposed to local and state-wide controls. Through the exercise of its interstate commerce, post office, tax and general welfare powers, Congress attempts to meet conditions with which the separate states are inadequate to deal. The courts, and ultimately the United States Supreme Court, often have to decide whether, in the enactment of such laws, Congress is exercising its constitutionally conferred authority or is stepping on the toes of states' rights. Sometimes the laws are held to be constitutional and sometimes not. Let us illustrate.

The first federal child labor law enacted in 1917 was declared unconstitutional by the Supreme Court in 1918.[7] The law forbade the use of the channels of interstate commerce for the shipment of childmade goods. The majority of the Court held that the goods themselves were not harmful so could not be kept out of the channels of interstate commerce, that the regulation of the conditions of manufacture belonged with the states. Justice Holmes, in a biting minority decision, argued the validity of the statute. There was, he said, no infringement on states' rights, since the states could continue to regulate their domestic commerce as they chose, but when they placed their goods in the channels of interstate commerce

[7] *Hammer* v. *Dagenhart,* 247 U.S. 251 (1918). For additional discussion of this case, see below, Ch. 11.

a federal matter was involved. Thirty-three years later, in *United States* v. *Darby*, the Court reversed this decision and took the position earlier advocated by Justice Holmes. The Darby case tested the constitutionality of the Fair Labor Standards Act which, among other things, forbade the shipment in interstate commerce of goods made in establishments oppressively employing children.[8] The Court held that Congress could exercise its power to prevent the use of interstate commerce as an instrument of competition in the distribution of goods produced under substandard labor conditions, since such competition is injurious to commerce and the states. The labor itself might be a local transaction, but since it directly affects interstate commerce Congress has the right to regulate it.

The tax and welfare section of the Constitution, like the commerce clause, has frequently been used to widen the powers of the federal government to act for the public interests. The first paragraph of Article I, section 8 reads: "The Congress shall have power to lay and collect taxes, duties, imports and excises, to pay the debts and provide for the common defense and general welfare of the United States . . ." Over the years there has been extensive debate in and out of courts as to whether Congress has the power to collect taxes "in order to" provide for the general welfare or whether it has an independent welfare power. If Congress has an independent welfare power, why did the writers of the Constitution bother to enumerate specific powers? If it has only the power to levy taxes "in order to" promote the general welfare, what limits are imposed upon the power and when can taxes be levied for this purpose?

In 1937 Justice Cardozo used the tax and welfare clauses to uphold the legality of the federal Social Security Act enacted in 1935. The unemployment insurance provisions of the act were tested in *Steward Machine Company* v. *Davis*.[9] The constitutionality of Title IX, "Tax on Employers of 9 or More," and Title III, "Grants to States for Unemployment Compensation Administration," were at issue. Justice Cardozo concentrated his attention on the tax provisions and held Title III uncontroversial, as it involved no appropriation of public monies. His main concern was whether Congress, in imposing taxes and acting for the general welfare, had deprived the states of political powers reserved to them by the Tenth Amendment. He reasoned that the problem of unemployment had become national in scope and that there was need for help from the national government if people were not to starve.

It's too late today for the argument to be heard with tolerance, that in a crisis so extreme the use of the monies of the nation to relieve the unemployed and their dependents is a use for any purpose narrower than the promotion of the general welfare. . . . The *parens patriae* has many reasons—fiscal and eco-

---

[8] 312 U.S. 100 (1941).
[9] 301 U.S. 548 (1937). See Ch. 22, for further discussion of these cases.

nomic as well as social and moral—for planning to mitigate disasters that bring these burdens in their train.

He repudiated the idea that there had been a usurpation of state powers and affirmed the judgment of the lower court that Title IX was constitutional.

On the same day, in *Helvering* v. *Davis*,[10] Justice Cardozo gave his decision which upheld titles VIII and II of the Social Security Act pertaining to social insurance for the aged. Title VIII, regarding taxes for old age insurance, being analagous to IX, providing taxes for unemployment compensation and settled in the Steward Machine Company case, he easily disposed of. Title II, "Federal Old Age Insurance Benefits," occupied his attention. He held that the scheme of benefits created by that title was not in contravention of the Tenth Amendment. Congress, he said, may spend money in aid of the general welfare, even though there have been great statesmen who have stood for the opposite. Although this interpretation of the spending power is conceded, there remain unsettled difficulties. The line, he continued, must still be drawn between one welfare and another, between particular and general welfare. Where this line shall be placed cannot be known through a formula in advance of the event. There is a middle ground or a penumbra in which discretion is great. That discretion, however, is not confided to the courts but belongs to Congress, unless the choice is clearly wrong and is a display of arbitrary power. Nor is the concept of general welfare static. Needs that were narrow or parochial a century ago may be interwoven in our day with the well-being of the nation. What is critical or urgent changes with the times. Moreover, the separate states cannot possibly deal with old age effectively. Whether wisdom or unwisdom resides in the scheme of benefits of Title II is not for the Court but for Congress to say. The concern of the Court is with power, not wisdom.

Perhaps these illustrations will suffice to show that there is such a thing as a federal police power; that Congress seeks and finds authority in the Constitution to enact legislation for the public good; and that the courts often have to determine whether Congress has acted legally.

In concluding this brief statement concerning the meaning of police power and the need for its exercise by the federal government, we wish to point out that numerous methods for implementing it are employed by federal and state governments. These methods include licensing, publicity, security or bond, registration and reports, inspection and search, prohibition and exclusion, demolition and destruction. We shall not attempt a description of each of them, since they are more or less familiar to the reader.

---

[10] 301 U.S. 619.

THE SOCIAL SERVICE STATE

The twentieth century has seen such an expansion in the exercise of the police power, or something analogous to it, to achieve the greatest good for the greatest number that we can safely say that we now have a state one of the primary purposes of which is to render social services. This kind of state is often called a *social service* or *welfare* state. Many shades of meaning are given these terms. Sometimes they are used interchangeably and sometimes distinctions are made between them. In the latter case one or the other is often given a more favorable connotation. For example, some persons derogatorily label the present-day British state a "welfare state" in contrast with ours which, with more approval, they designate a "social service state." These people appear to imply that the British government has usurped too much power. For example, it has arrogated to itself too much public ownership of basic resources and provided too many social services, such as universal free medical care. The inference seems to be that aspects of our social service state are desirable, necessary, and legitimate. But we better watch out, or the "government," especially the federal branch of the government, will seize too many powers and become authoritarian, socialist, communist, undemocratic, and un-American.

In this book we shall use the terms *welfare* and *social service* state interchangeably to mean one with the power to act for the well-being of the people generally or for designated groups needing special protection. Both the federal and state governments have the power to act for the welfare of their citizens. Both will continue to meet needs as they arise. Many governmental compulsions, prohibitions, and services rejected yesterday are taken for granted today. We can anticipate that each significant new proposal to expand the police power will bring debate, resistance, compromise. That process will continue. There are no final answers to such questions as: What is the general welfare? What functions can best be performed by the individual for himself and what by the state? Which welfare or service functions belong to the federal and which to state government?

To citizens of the United States, even though complete agreement on such questions cannot be achieved, a theoretical answer is possible. Its logic is as follows: the government, federal and state, emanates from the people and changes its purpose and structure in response to their will; modern conditions require that the welfare of groups of persons and of society as a whole be a primary consideration of government; hence, it is the will of the people that government, given form and function through law, shall have a social purpose and program. We, the people, continue to want the form of government that is an expression of ourselves; and one of these expressions is a government performing social service functions. We differ among ourselves as to what is best for us, but we will determine by political processes what we want and must have.

THEORIES OF CONSTITUTIONAL LAW

Since social legislation must be tested by the same constitutional standards as all other types of legislation, it is important to know at what points it comes into conflict with the principles of constitutions and constitutional law. It is necessary, therefore, to observe (1) what a constitutional government is; (2) the theory of judicial review; (3) our dual system of government; and (4) the significance of the provisions of our federal and state constitutions on "due process of law" and "the equal protection of the laws," and that section which requires that each state give "full faith and credit" to the acts of another state. In our above statement on police powers we somewhat incidentally referred to some of these matters. Here we shall discuss them in a more systematic way.

THE NATURE OF A CONSTITUTIONAL GOVERNMENT

Both England and the United States have a constitutional form of government. England has no formal written constitution. Its constitution is said to be unwritten in the sense that it has never been assembled into one organized document. The English constitution is made up of all the various outstanding English royal grants, charters, and declarations, such as the Magna Charta, the Bill of Rights, the Petition of Rights, all English statutes, and the court decisions. Taken together they make up the basic law of the land.

On the other hand, in the United States the federal government and the various states all have written constitutions drafted by a convention, adopted by the people, and subject to amendment only in a prescribed manner. Some of the main differences between a written and unwritten constitution are: [11]

1. The former gathers into one instrument the whole of the basic law of the land; the latter is found in the separate acts of the executive and the legislature and in custom.
2. The former is either granted by the rules of the people or ordained by them; the latter is evolved gradually and is contributed to by all the branches of government.
3. The former is a creation or a product; the latter is the result of growth.
4. The former can be altered only by formal action; the latter grows and expands to meet new needs.
5. The former cannot be changed or set aside except by those who created it, the people; the latter can be changed at any time by the lawmaking body.

---

[11] Henry C. Black, *Handbook of American Constitutional Law,* 4th ed. (St. Paul, Minn., West Publishing Co., 1927), pp. 5–7.

A constitution enunciates the principles upon which the government of a particular state is founded. It secures the liberties of the people; it regulates the division of sovereign powers; it describes the structure, organization, and functions of that government and the manner in which the functions are to be performed. The Constitution of the United States is the supreme law of the land. In practice, a distinction is drawn between basic laws called *constitutions* and those called *statutes*. Both are laws in a broad sense, but constitutions and statutes differ in a number of respects: [12]

1. Constitutions are adopted by the whole people who are to be governed by them; whereas statutes are enacted by the representatives of the people in an organized legislative body.
2. Constitutions can be modified or added to only by those who formulated them; statutes can be changed by succeeding legislatures, usually by a bare majority vote.
3. Constitutions provide the basic principles of government; statutes to a large extent regulate current conduct.

In the United States, our federal and state constitutions are grants of power to those charged with the task of government, but they are not grants of rights and freedom to the people. The people adopt constitutions in order to protect their *pre-existing rights*. Constitutions define and guarantee rights, but they do not create them. The theory is that all power, all rights, and all authority reside in the people before they adopt a constitution.[13] The people create the constitution, and they put into it what they deem necessary for the full enjoyment of life, liberty, property, and human happiness. It is for these reasons that constitutions contain "bills of rights," which are nothing more than formal declarations of the fundamental, natural, civil, and political rights of the people. It was the lack of a bill of rights in the federal Constitution that caused some of the hesitancy in its adoption, and it was only after a promise was made to take care of this defect by amendment that the ratification by the necessary number of states was procured. Early in George Washington's administration a number of amendments were added, the first ten of which constitute the federal Bill of Rights.

THE THEORY OF JUDICIAL REVIEW

The federal Constitution declares that it shall be the supreme law of the land. This supremacy means that it must endure and be respected as the paramount law at all times and under all circumstances. The governmental agency which maintains it as the supreme law of the land is the judicial system. The Constitution does not give the courts the power to

[12] *Ibid.*, pp. 3, 4.
[13] *Ibid.*, pp. 7, 8.

declare legislative acts unconstitutional in so many words, but this power can be reasonably implied. The earliest case in which an act of Congress was weighed by the United States Supreme Court was in 1796.[14] In this decision the court upheld a statute laying a direct tax upon carriages. In 1803 in *Marbury* v. *Madison,* Chief Justice Marshall forcefully stated the theory of the power of judicial review. His reasoning was as follows: [15]

1. a written constitution is a superior obligation and consequently any acts contrary to it must be invalid;
2. a written constitution with limitations on the powers of government necessitates the exercise of judicial review;
3. the oath of judges to support the Constitution requires them to follow it and disregard conflicting statutes;
4. legislative acts contrary to the Constitution are *ipso facto* void, and therefore the courts are bound to disregard them.

This doctrine of judicial review is one of the distinguishing characteristics of our American system of government. In England, parliamentary action is final. However, under our system even though a statute is in violation of a provision of the Constitution, it is not void *per se,* but it is voidable only at the instance of some person whom it affects injuriously. The courts have no inherent power to render advisory opinions or to initiate actions for the purpose of determining questions of constitutionality. Before they can determine such questions, there must be an actual *bona fide* piece of litigation before them in which the question of constitutionality inheres. If after due consideration of an actual justiciable case the courts find a given statute to be clearly in contravention of the Constitution, they may and must pronounce it a nullity. This power of judicial review is not a veto power, nor is it a supervisory power over legislation; it is simply the power to ascertain what the law is in the situation before it.[16] Most courts have the right to determine questions of constitutionality, but it is the United States Supreme Court which has final authority on the federal Constitution and the state supreme courts on the state constitutions. Once those courts have spoken upon given questions their decisions become precedent and binding upon all lower courts.

Both federal and state courts have held many pieces of social legislation unconstitutional. This is particularly true in the field of labor legislation.[17] Although the courts must uphold legislation unless it is clearly unconstitutional, it is inevitable that judicial opinions should reflect the beliefs of the judges. It is theoretically true that ours is a government of

---

[14] *Hylton* v. *U.S.,* 3 Dall. 171 (1796).
[15] 1 Cranch 137, 2 L. Ed. 60 (1803).
[16] Black, *op. cit.,* pp. 54–55.
[17] For this history, see such books as Commons and Andrews, *op. cit.*

laws and not of men; nevertheless, it is practically true, as Chief Justice Hughes said, "the Constitution is what the judges say it is." Legislation for the benefit of groups of underprivileged persons has often been thrown out by the courts, because the opinions of the judges were a reflection of current and prevailing thinking and were built on a *status in quo* philosophy. Minority opinions sometimes express liberal viewpoints which eventually become majority opinions. Inevitably there is a lag between conditions needing change and enactments of legislatures and decisions of judges that effect change.

OUR DUAL SYSTEM OF GOVERNMENT

In our discussion of the police power we referred to the fact that under the federal Constitution certain powers are delegated to the federal government and certain others are reserved to the states. The constitutional authority for this distribution of authority is found in the Tenth Amendment, which reads: "The powers not delegated to the United States by the Constitution, nor prohibited by it to the States are reserved to the States." The power of Congress to pass any given law must be found in some express grant of authority given to it by the Constitution or be implied in the authority given to it. As we pointed out above in our discussion of police power, Article I, section 8, lists the major powers of Congress. The last clause, sometimes called the "elastic" or "necessary and proper" clause, gives Congress the power "To make all laws which shall be necessary and proper for carrying into execution the foregoing powers, and all other powers vested by this constitution in the government of the United States, or in any department or officer thereof." This clause enables Congress to expand the functions of the federal government to meet the needs of changing times.

Since the states possess "reserved" powers, it is commonly said that the state governments may do all those things which are not delegated by the Constitution to the national government. If the question as to the validity of federal action is raised, the power must be shown to exist in the Constitution; but if the question of the validity of state action is raised, it is not the justification but the prohibition which must be shown. That is, state action is presumed to be warranted until the objector has been able to point out the specific provision of either the federal or the state constitution with which it is incompatible; but the converse is true in regard to federal legislation.

There are many times when it is not clear whether a particular activity is the function of the federal or the state governments or both. In fact, ever since the foundation of the Union, two schools of thought have existed as to the nature and boundaries of federal and states' rights. According to one school, the federal Constitution is to be subjected to a strict construction in respect to the powers granted to the national government and to a liberal interpretation for the preservation of the autonomy of the states. According to the other school, the rules of interpretation are to be reversed. One group contends that the government of the Union shall be strictly held to the exercise of the powers expressly granted to it, and that its province and jurisdiction shall not be enlarged by implication. The other group asserts that the true theory of our government and institutions is such a construction of the Constitution as will give the federal government the largest measure of power which is compatible with the continued and useful existence of the states. By this group, the nation is regarded as the only sovereign power; it contends that the central government shall be accorded all those rights and powers which will enable it to discharge its function and to maintain its place among the nations of the world.

Although the two theories of construction, strict and liberal, persist, it is now quite generally agreed that both the several states and the federal government are supreme, each within its own appropriate sphere; that the rights of the individual states and the federal government are equally necessary and must be accommodated each to the other. Those statesmen who act on this theory are doing all they can to develop a co-operative relationship between the federal and the state governments.

Our constitutions, federal and state, provide not only for a division of authority between these two units of government but for a separation of powers. The executive, the legislative, and the judicial functions of government are familiar to all and in this connection need no detailed discussion. Legislative bodies enact the laws which are carried out by the executive branch. The judiciary settles controversies; it determines whether the facts brought before it come under the laws, and in this connection it may be necessary for the court to find unconstitutional the statute under which the action was brought. Of recent years there has been a rapid growth in the administrative functions of government, sometimes called a fourth branch of government. With the expansion of government supervision and control of many activities and relationships, it is impossible for legislative bodies to foresee every development and to limit and define every kind of governmental action. Hence our lawmaking bodies create boards, commissions, bureaus, and departments, define their general policies, and give them broad authority to discover conditions and to make rules to meet these discoveries.

CONSTITUTIONAL QUESTIONS

Due Process of Law. The very fact that the police power, which is the legal source for so much of our social legislation, is indefinable makes it inevitable that the courts often have to determine whether a particular statute has overstepped the bounds of the legitimate exercise of the police power and violated some fundamental constitutional right. When the constitutionality of social legislation is challenged, it is most often over the question of taking life, liberty, or property without due process of law, although the clauses pertaining to equal protection of the laws and full faith and credit are also invoked. Due process clauses appear in both the Fifth and Fourteenth amendments to the federal Constitution. The due process clause of the Fifth Amendment is a prohibition upon Congress and the federal government. That in the Fourteenth Amendment applies to the states and provides that no state shall deprive any person of life, liberty, or property without due process of law. All state constitutions have practically identical clauses.

The requirement of due process of law has come down to us through English constitutional history. The concept, if not the words, appeared in the Magna Charta (1215), which declared "that no freeman shall be taken or imprisoned, or disseized or outlawed, or banished or anyways destroyed, nor will we (the king) pass upon him or commit him to prison, unless by the legal judgment of his peers or by the law of the land." The "law of the land" and "due process" are synonymous. Through the centuries the content of due process has been enlarged. In the days of the Magna Charta it was most often invoked in situations where judgments were given without trial. In 1776 the American colonies fought because earlier they had been deprived of due process of law in the "taxation without representation" actions of the mother country.

In the twentieth century due process, although incapable of exact definition, has two broad meanings: (1) proper and fair procedure, and (2) proper and fair law. By fair procedure we mean the administration of equal laws according to well-recognized rules not violative of the fundamental principles of private rights by a competent tribunal having jurisdiction of the case and proceeding upon due notice and fair hearing. By proper and fair law we mean laws whose very substance is just and reasonable. After the Civil War the Fourteenth Amendment was added to the Constitution on the theory that the freed slaves needed not only adequate procedural or adjective law but adequate substantive law or law which in and of itself was fair and just. It was believed that if such a responsibility were not imposed upon the Southern states, they would not act so as to protect the life, liberty, and property of the Negro.

Due process of law to the man on the street means that he will get a "square deal" if for any reason he has to appear before a court. He is aware of only half the meaning of this fundamental phrase. Due process means a fair trial *and* reasonable action. Police power means the general welfare or public purpose.

Equal Protection of the Laws. Another constitutional prohibition which has sometimes been invoked to invalidate social legislation, particularly in the labor field, is that part of the Fourteenth Amendment which prescribes that no state shall deny any person within its jurisdiction the equal protection of the laws. This means that each state is required to give equal protection and security to all under like circumstances to the end that no greater burden shall be laid on one than on others in the same circumstances. The basic object of this clause is to prevent arbitrary discrimination and class legislation not founded on legal and reasonable grounds of distinction.[18] The equal protection clause is a limitation on state action only and not on the legislative power of Congress. Under this provision, it has been held, for example, not to be an unreasonable classification to require an antenuptial physical examination of men and not of women. Very often, social legislation which is challenged on the ground of the lack of due process is also condemned because it denies the equal protection of the laws.

Full Faith and Credit. In their relations with each other the states are in somewhat, although not altogether, the same position as independent nations. Every state is sovereign and independent within its sphere of government. The statutes of one state have no legal effect outside the boundaries of that state. When a resident of Iowa commits an offense in Nebraska, he is, of course, dealt with under the laws of Nebraska. The states, however, are not absolutely independent of each other. Article IV, section 1, of the federal Constitution provides: "Full faith and credit shall be given in each state to the public acts, records, and judicial proceedings of every other state. And the Congress may by general laws prescribe the manner in which such acts, records, and proceedings shall be proved, and the effect thereof." This means that the statutes, and so forth, of one state shall be given the same effect in the courts of another state as they would have at home.

If there were not such a full faith and credit provision in the federal Constitution, the statutes, judgments, and decrees of each state would be treated as those of a foreign state or country, and their effect would have to be determined by the principles of international law. Under our federal system of government, peace and good will between states are promoted by this theory of reciprocity. This is in contrast with what prevails, let us say, in Europe, where each country is autonomous and settles its disputes with other countries by international law and often by war. Although each state gives full faith and credit to the public acts, records, and judicial proceedings of every other state, the circumstances under which and the extent to which the behavior of individuals under the laws of one state are bound to be recognized in another state is the subject of "conflict of laws," one of the most baffling and confusing phases of law and one which receives much attention in law schools. For example, is Alabama bound to consider legitimate the children of a miscegenous marriage contracted legally, let us say, in Massachusetts when under the laws of Alabama there could be no mixed marriage and children of such a mating would be illegitimate?

---

[18] *State* v. *R.R. Com. of Wis.*, 174 Wis. 458, 183 N.W. 687 (1921).

The federal courts have been very liberal in their interpretation of the meaning of the full faith and credit clause of the Constitution, giving the states considerable latitude to determine what acts of persons performed under the laws of one jurisdiction shall receive recognition within another jurisdiction. It is not within our competence to delve into the intricacies of the subject of conflict of laws. We shall, however, give it some further attention in the chapters on marriage and divorce.

FORMULATION OF STATUTES

It is self-evident that if our legislators, many of whom before election had never looked inside a statute book, are to enact laws which are constitutional, they need the help of expert draftsmen and research workers. It is the function of legislators to find the policy which they wish to enact into law; it should be the function of experts to draw up the statute so that it is clear, concise, accurate, and not in conflict with other statutes or with the Constitution. One jurist has said the following about the task of bill-drafting: "I will venture to affirm that what is commonly called the *technical* part of legislation is incomparably more difficult than what may be called the *ethical*. In other words, it is far easier to conceive justly what would be useful law than so to construct that same law that it may accomplish the design of the lawgiver." [19]

The legislative reference library, bill-drafting bureaus, and the office of the reviser of statutes are all agencies for facilitating the enactment of sound and well-drawn statutes. The legislative library is a research agency that gathers information on subjects of interest to legislators and helps them assemble these data into well-drawn bills. In some states there is a separate bureau for bill drafting. Several states also have revisers of statutes whose duty it is to revise, consolidate, and abbreviate the statutes. Their revisions are required to be submitted to the legislatures for approval. These three agencies can do much to improve the quality of our legislation.

THE COMMON LAW

Since so much of our legislation and judicial decision derives from, or is in derogation of, the common law, it behooves us to review briefly the history of the common law.[20] The law of the United States is not something that developed by accident and chance; rather it is a part of and an

---

[19] Quoted in Robert Luce, *Legislative Procedure* (Boston, Houghton Mifflin, 1922), p. 566.

[20] This history has been taken from Charles A. Huston, *Modern American Law* (Chicago, Blackstone Institute, 1914), Vol. 1, Pt. 2, pp. 93–165; see also, Roscoe Pound, *Readings on the History and System of the Common Law*, 2d ed. (Boston, Boston Book Co., 1913); Roscoe Pound, *The Spirit of the Common Law* (Boston,

outgrowth of the English law brought over to this country in the seventeenth century by the colonists.

Prior to the invasion of England by William the Conqueror (A.D. 1066), there existed an established system of Anglo-Saxon courts which were communal in character. They were not specialized tribunals, and their members were not lawyers. They were popular assemblies which carried on the functions of government. They considered disputes arising in their own membership and often rendered judgment by acclamation. There was no central court which regularly administered a law common to the whole country, but the land was covered with an intricate network of competing courts which sought to maintain order but which rendered little real justice to individuals.

The policy of the first Norman kings was to disturb the existing order as little as possible. However, William did establish a court of his own which eventually crowded out all others, native and Norman alike. This early body was called the *Curia Regis*. It was not set up as a court of general jurisdiction for the purpose of administering justice to all, but to exercise jurisdiction over matters directly affecting the dignity and the proprietary rights of the crown and over matters involving the king's own tenants. Not for some time after the Conquest did men begin to consider it the duty of the sovereign to dispense justice to all his people, and it was even longer before a single court, wielding the entire judicial power and exercising authority over the whole community, was conceived as either possible or desirable.

In the reign of Henry II (1154–1189), the policy in respect to the king's court was radically altered. Disorder throughout the realm was great, and it became necessary to establish a strong centralized organization of the government to maintain the supremacy of the king. Henry found the king's court the most effective means for securing this end. He offered the use of his court to the whole body of the people for litigation of virtually all kinds. A great number of writs were formulated for the sake of drawing into the royal court causes which, in the old order, were brought only in the communal and the feudal courts. The result was that Henry placed royal justice at the disposal of anyone who could bring his case within a certain formula, and greater uniformity in the administration of justice resulted.

Gradually, in its period of greatest expansion the common law began to ossify. This was partly due to the fact that the barons and lords were jealous of the power exercised by the king's appointees, who were generally his favorites. The surest safeguard against favoritism was to adhere to the strict, definite, and rigid rules provided by the statutes and the

---

Marshall Jones, 1921); Oliver Wendell Holmes, Jr., *The Common Law* (Boston, Little, Brown, 1949).

earlier decisions. Thus, the administration of justice became more and more formal.

The fourteenth and fifteenth centuries were periods of great political, social, and economic change with tremendous problems of adjustment; and so far as the common law was concerned, the way had been closed by which new conditions could be met. A resource was found, however, in the judicial functions of the king's chancellor. He, as the chief secretary of the king, issued the various writs, and, gradually, he began to exercise extraordinary justice in special cases which called for the summary and powerful sanction of the king. The chancellor's power in time was extended to those situations not covered by common-law processes. The common law had not evolved remedies for every wrong, although it was one of the maxims of the common-law courts that there was a remedy for every wrong. It was to supplement these deficiencies that the Chancery successfully developed its characteristic equity jurisdiction. Equity was free to interfere in all those cases where, because of the rigid rules of common law, justice was not possible. In time, the relief granted in those special cases where the common-law rule was inadequate became the usual form in which the chancellor's equitable powers were exercised. The field of his jurisdiction came to be conceived as compelling conduct in accord with what good conscience required.

At first the procedure in Chancery was simple, inexpensive, and arbitrary. Upon considering the petition or bill, as it was called, which invoked the chancellor's justice, he issued the famous *subpoena*, which required the person complained of to appear before him in person to answer the bill on pain of forfeiting a hundred pounds. When the defendant appeared, the chancellor himself examined the defendant under oath and without giving a jury trial to him. The greatest benefit the chancellor introduced in procedure was in the kinds of relief that he could award the successful plaintiff. A common-law judgment was an exceptionally rigid thing, absolute in terms, and could not be conditioned upon the performance of some future act. Chancery, as a court of conscience, vindicated the rights of the plaintiff by compelling the defendant to perform his specific duty under penalty of imprisonment for contempt of court in case of failure to do so. It ordered him to do the very act he was under duty to do; furthermore, if he were recalcitrant, it threw him into prison and kept him there until he was ready to perform his duty according to the chancellor's decree. Thus the Chancery not only could redress past injuries but, by means of its characteristic weapon, the injunction, could prevent threatened injuries. By the decree of specific performance it could secure to the plaintiff a relief often more adequate than money compensation.

Gradually, through a long series of political and social struggles, the practice developed, especially after the Reformation, of appointing lawyers as lord chancellor. These men were less daring than their predecessors, who had often been scholars and clerics, in the exercise of their discretion in determining what constituted conforming to good conscience. Being common-law lawyers, they gradually developed rigidity in their practices. Equity, then, ceased to be a simple system of interference with the ordinary course of administration of justice under the common law and itself became a part of that system, co-ordinate with it and supplementing it in many cases, although running counter to it in some. This, then, is a brief and simplified history of the common law up to the union of equity and law actions into a single court, as has been accomplished by statute in American states and by the Judicature Act of 1873 in England.

In 1722 the Judicial Committee of the Privy Council, which, under the British system of colonial government prevailing in the seventeenth and eighteenth centuries, had control of the American colonies, laid down as a rule of English law

> that if there be a new and uninhabited country found out by English subjects, as the law is the birth-right of every subject, so wherever they go they carry that law with them, and hence such new-found country is to be governed by the laws of England; though after such country is inhabited by the English, acts of Parliament made in England, without naming the foreign plantations, will not bind them.

This ruling, although it is only a practical application of the principles of international law, states clearly the prevailing doctrine as to the relation of the American to the English common law. Following the American Revolution, many states proceeded to provide by statute that the common law of England should be the basis of their law, and even in the absence of express legislation, the same doctrine was assumed in practice. In Wisconsin, for example, by force of Article XIV, section 13, of the state constitution, "Such parts of the common law as are now in force in the territory of Wisconsin, not inconsistent with this Constitution, shall be and continue part of the law of this State until altered or suspended by the legislature."

In concluding this statement on the development of the common law it can be stated that the common law is custom as defined by the courts; theoretically the courts do not *create* the common law but merely *find* and *define* it. In pronouncing an opinion they draw from the great reservoir of custom, tradition, mores. The basic principles of the common law were collected by Blackstone in his *Commentaries on the Laws of England* about ten years before the American Revolution. The common law is found in court decisions which are recorded in hundreds of volumes known as *reports*. Usually only the decisions of the higher appellate courts are printed. Despite the enactment of thousands of statutes, a very large part of our law today is that of court decisions.

It is because the common law was not solicitous of the social needs of groups of people but was concerned with the legal rights and duties of individuals to each other that it has been necessary to enact so much social legislation, much of it not declaratory of, but in derogation of, the common law. The common law reduced the wife and child to a state resembling slavery. The doctrine of primogeniture left all but the eldest son without assurance of support. Under the rule of *caveat emptor,* the buyer was required to beware, a good enough theory undoubtedly when purchasing was done at arm's length. The fellow servant, assumption of risk, and contributory negligence doctrines prevailed in the relation of master and servant. The common law assumed no responsibility for the poor person in dire distress. In other words, as Freund points out, the common law did not keep pace with changing ideals. It was emphatic in maintaining order and authority, but it showed little interest in relieving social weakness and inferiority. Hence the need for social legislation, certain aspects of which we shall presently survey and digest.

SUMMARY AND CONCLUSIONS

The increase in the number of governmental agencies which provide service for individuals and groups is a characteristic of the twentieth century. The depression of the 1930's, two world wars, and a "cold war," brought in their wake myriads of agencies, some permanent and some temporary, for improving economic and social conditions. The federal government has increasingly accepted responsibility for enlarging the "public welfare." It has done this through the exercise of an authority which Commons and Andrews call the "police power." Lawyers say it is a power analogous to the police power, and one which is exercised as an incident to some other power, as the tax and general welfare, postal, interstate commerce powers.

For purposes of distinction we can say that the copious social legislation enacted by both the federal and state governments is primarily concerned with *economic* or *social* conditions. If the former, it includes price-fixing statutes, antitrust laws, regulation of co-operatives, chain-store regulations, "blue-sky" laws, small-loan laws, zoning regulations, and laws dealing with industrial relations. These subjects are extensively discussed in books on business and labor law. If the latter, it includes statutes dealing with such matters as marriage and divorce, limitation of size and quality of family, definitions of parental responsibility and the extent to which the state can interfere between parent and child, provisions for the poor when in need of public assistance, and social insurance. In this book we shall review statutes concerning this second group of subjects, with the exception of those pertaining to social insurance, which are only partially discussed in connection with the analysis of the

Social Security Act, since they have been so extensively and expertly treated in numerous books on social insurance.

The federal government has not found the authority to enact legislation on all economic and social problems. For example, it has no power to pass laws on the subjects of marriage, divorce, and sterilization, although it has the authority through its interstate commerce and postal powers to enact legislation preventing the distribution of contraceptive information and materials. Much recent federal social legislation has derived its authority from the taxing and spending powers. Regardless of the source of the power, both federal and state governments have lately enacted innumerable statutes affecting the public welfare. With certain more or less arbitrarily selected phases of social legislation, the balance of this book will be concerned.

Selected References

BEARD, Charles A., *Public Policy and the General Welfare* (New York, Farrar and Rinehart, 1941).

BRADWAY, John S., *Law and Social Work* (Chicago, University of Chicago Press, 1929).

COMMONS, John R., and ANDREWS, John B., *Principles of Labor Legislation* (New York, Harper, 1927).

FELLMAN, David, ed., *Readings in American National Government* (New York, Rinehart, 1950).

FENN, Percy T., *The Development of the Constitution* (New York, Appleton-Century-Crofts, 1948).

FREUND, Ernst, *The Police Power, Public Policy, and Constitutional Rights* (Chicago, University of Chicago Press, 1904).

GLUECK, Sheldon, ed., *The Welfare State and the National Welfare* (Cambridge, Addison-Wesley, 1952).

GRAY, John C., *The Nature and Sources of the Law*, 2d ed. (New York, Macmillan, 1921).

HOLMES, Oliver Wendell, Jr., *The Common Law* (Boston, Little, Brown, 1949).

HURST, James Willard, *The Growth of American Law* (Boston, Little, Brown, 1950).

POUND, Roscoe, *The Spirit of the Common Law* (Boston, Marshall Jones, 1921).

RADIN, Max, *The Law and You* (New York, New American Library, 1948).

SCHLESINGER, Arthur M., *The American as Reformer* (Cambridge, Harvard University Press, 1950).

TRUMAN, David, *The Governmental Process* (New York, Knopf, 1951).

U. S. Commission on Intergovernmental Relations, *A Report to the President for Transmittal to the Congress* (Washington, D.C., G.P.O., 1955).

WILSON, Woodrow, *The State*, special ed. (Boston, Heath, 1918).

The student should also consult the Constitution of the United States of America, constitutions of individual states, and federal and state statutes.

PART I

Marriage, the Family, and the State

CHAPTER 2

The Family: Early History

INTRODUCTION

The family, created by marriage, is undoubtedly the most basic as well as the oldest social institution.[1] Authorities point out that the family is both resistant and responsive to social changes; that like old man river, it just keeps rolling along.[2] Marriage, in the legal sense, is an act that places a man and woman under legal and social obligations to each other.[3] In a broader sense, marriage is a social institution, defined by Westermarck:

> as a relation of one or more men to one or more women which is recognized by custom or law and involves certain rights and duties both in the case of the parties entering the union and in the case of the children born of it. These rights and duties vary among different peoples and cannot, therefore, all be included in a general definition.[4]

If this comprehensive definition of marriage is used, marriage and the family become almost identical social institutions. In this and the next chapter it is our purpose to trace summarily the growth and development of the social and legal aspects of marriage, divorce, and other family relationships from early historic times down to the present.

The degree of social regulation of marriage and the family has varied in different situations and at different times. Family custom and law have had to be adjusted many times to changing social conditions.[5] For

---

[1] "Family," *Encyclopaedia Brittanica* (1952), Vol. 9, pp. 59–62; John A. Ryan, "Family," *Catholic Encyclopedia* (1909), Vol. 5, pp. 782–785; Margaret Mead, "Family, Primitive," *Encyclopaedia of the Social Sciences* (1931), Vol. 6, pp. 65–67; Carl Brinkman, "Family, Social Aspects," *Encyclopaedia of the Social Sciences* (1931), Vol. 6, pp. 67–70; J. H. S. Bossard, ed., *Annals of the American Academy of Political and Social Science: Toward Family Stability* (November, 1950), Vol. 272.

[2] Carle C. Zimmerman, "The Family and Social Change," *Annals of the American Academy of Political and Social Science* (November, 1950), Vol. 272, pp. 22–29.

[3] Willystine Goodsell, *A History of Marriage and the Family* (New York, Macmillan. 1935).

[4] Edward Westermarck, *A Short History of Marriage* (New York, Macmillan, 1926), p. 1.

[5] Stuart Queen and John B. Adams, *The Family and Various Cultures* (Philadelphia, Lippincott, 1952); Carle C. Zimmerman, *Family and Civilization* (New York, Harper,

instance, not so long ago in the occidental world, custom as well as law definitely limited the sphere of activity for a married woman. The community expected her to confine her activities to her home and family, and any departure from such a design of life was looked upon with disapproval. In much of the western world the status of a married woman is more or less equal to that of her husband. In Fascist countries a reversion to the old family pattern occurred. In Soviet Russia the position of all women in every sphere of activity approaches identity, if it is not identical, with that of men. As changes in the economic and social life of the world occur, the status of women, especially married women, will necessarily undergo modification.

Another of the noticeable changes in family custom and law is the basis for contracting marriage. In the United States voluntary choice and affection are today regarded as the only justifiable foundations for marriage. Not only are they considered the only reasonable conditions for entrance into marriage but also for its continuance. Research workers point out that the regulatory devices of voluntary choice and affection bring about stable marriage relationships and that marriages of affection and companionship are usually more happy than those of romance and infatuation.[6] The law, which for some time has accepted voluntary choice as a condition of valid marriage, is now in the process of recognizing that the absence of voluntariness and of affection are valid conditions for its discontinuance, as, for example, when what amounts to incompatibility becomes a ground for divorce in some jurisdictions. It also recognizes alienation of the affection of a husband or wife as an offense, even though such is not accompanied by adultery.

Customs and the law do not change abruptly or radically; reforms come about slowly and emerge out of what has gone before. Much of our modern family custom and law have their roots in the past, and it is to those origins that we now turn. We shall observe, for example, that many of our statutory provisions on marriage and divorce derive from the Roman Catholic church, and, further, that the phenomenon of children's rights to the protection of the state is of fairly recent origin.

1947); Ernest R. Groves, Edna L. Skinner, and Sadie J. Swenson, *The Family and Its Relationships* (Philadelphia, Lippincott, 1948); Ernest R. Groves and W. F. Ogburn, *American Marriage and Family Relationships* (New York, Holt, 1928); Ernest W. Burgess and Harvey J. Locke, *The Family from Institution to Companionship* (New York, American Book Co., 1945); Judson T. Landis and Mary G. Landis, eds., *Readings in Marriage and the Family* (Englewood Cliffs, N.J., Prentice-Hall, 1952).

[6] Ernest W. Burgess and Paul Wallin, *Engagement and Marriage* (Philadelphia, Lippincott, 1953); Paul Wallin, "Marriage Adjustment and Engagement Adjustment," in Landis and Landis, *op. cit.*, pp. 114–120; Ernest W. Burgess and Leonard S. Cottrell, Jr., *Predicting Success or Failure in Marriage* (Englewood Cliffs, N.J., Prentice-Hall, 1939).

MARRIAGE AND THE FAMILY AMONG PRIMITIVE PEOPLES

Numerous theories concerning the origin of marriage have been offered.[7] According to some students of the subject, sexual desire is not stable enough to form a basis for a permanent union between a man and a woman. Most students are agreed that the origin or source of that permanent union, marriage, is probably found in the need of the newborn infant and his mother for protection. It has been suggested that this permanent union, which existed for the care of infant and mother, was eventually embedded in the culture, and thus marriage evolved into a social institution.

In the beginning, therefore, it was the family that created marriage. Both primitive marriage and divorce in the very earliest periods were informal agreements resting upon the consent of the man and woman concerned. As society became more complex and as recognition of genealogical relationships developed, marriage became a relationship between kin groups as well as between two individuals. Regulation from the group began to appear and prevented the individual from doing as he or she pleased. In nearly every part of the primitive world, nearness of relationship restricted one in the choice of his mate. This rule, which demands that an individual must find a mate outside of his own group, is called exogamy.

In primitive society brides were acquired in various ways. Though marriage by capture existed, it was not so common as the early literature on the subject has suggested. By far the most common way of acquiring a bride was by purchase. In some regions women were sold outright; in others, there was only the appearance of purchase, since the price offered for the bride was balanced by an equivalent gift or dowry. Among primitive peoples marriage was usually regarded as a private contract and therefore could be dissolved at the will of both parties or, in some instances, of only one party, usually the man. Sterility was almost everywhere an adequate cause for divorce.

In most primitive groups the presence of children operated against widespread divorce, regardless of legal rights. Woman's status varied in different tribes and in different situations. Nevertheless, it is known that the position of women was generally not so desirable as that of men, except in those tribes that were definitely matriarchal. In some tribes woman was a chattel; in others, although she was free, she had no rights over property or over her person. Yet, as with us, the individual woman,

---

[7] Robert H. Lowie, *Primitive Society* (New York, Boni and Liveright, 1925), pp. 15–17; Goodsell, *op. cit.*, pp. 3–4; George Eliot Howard, *A History of Matrimonial Institutions* (Chicago, University of Chicago Press, 1904), Vol. 1, p. 222.

because of a forceful and magnetic personality, was often the dominant person in her household.

In a society based upon hunting or primitive agriculture or where war was carried on by hand-to-hand methods, it was natural that the functions of woman should be associated with childbearing and care of the home.[8] Physical survival depended upon male prowess. Even under a tribal social system in which name, rank, and property descended through the mother, women did not hold a dominant and superior position. Under such a system it was the woman's brother or father who directed the affairs of the household and, in turn, the community. Children, too, were regarded as property and were under the control of the father, whose power over them, in many groups, extended to the taking of life and the right to sell into slavery.

MARRIAGE AND THE FAMILY UNDER ANCIENT GREEK CIVILIZATION

THE NATURE OF THE GREEK FAMILY [9]

The Greek family was essentially patriarchal in character; that is, it was governed by the father or the oldest male member of the family. His will served as the law of the group. There was a basic difference between the source of patriarchal power in the Greek family as compared with the Hebrew. In the case of the Hebrews the father was the absolute monarch in his own right; he patterned his government after that of the all-powerful Jehovah. The Greek father, however, derived his power from the fact that he was the trustee of the family estates and the priest of the domestic worship of ancestors. It was the family, and not the patriarch, that operated as the unit of power in Greece. The power of the father was derivative and not inherent in himself.

The patriarch controlled and regulated the economic affairs of the family; he served as its protector in time of danger. But a large part of his power within the family accrued to him by virtue of the fact that he was the priest of all the religious ceremonies within the family circle. The Greeks were given to ancestor worship, and it was this institution that played a large part in welding the family into a close-knit unit carrying on its domestic and religious affairs around the family altar. In the central court of the Greek home stood the altar of Zeus, protector of the family group. It was here that the father, as priest of his household, offered sacrifices to the family gods.

Membership in the Greek family was founded not only upon the

---

[8] Margaret Mead, "Woman, Position in Society, Primitive," *Encyclopaedia of the Social Sciences* (1934), Vol. 15, pp. 439–442.

[9] Goodsell, *op. cit.*, pp. 82–84.

bonds of blood relationship but upon two other factors as well: (1) sharing the worship of the family gods and (2) coming under the power of the family head. A son who had been emancipated by the father from his control no longer shared in the affairs of the family. The same was true of a daughter; when she married she became a part of the family circle of her husband.

THE POWERS OF THE GREEK FATHER [10]

The Greek patriarch possessed far-reaching powers over the members of his family. It is true that these powers were derived from the family itself; nevertheless, in the exercise of his powers, his authority was complete. Before the time of Solon's reforms (621 B.C.), the father had the right to sell both his sons and daughters. Such sale perhaps was not outright but was more likely a transfer of the child's labor and services as the child remained under the father's authority for all family purposes. Partly as a result of the work of such reformers as Solon, the sale of the daughter was forbidden and later also the sale of the son.

The Greek father held a peculiar power at the birth of his children. It was his prerogative to accept or reject the child and condemn it to exposure if it was a weakling or if there was likelihood of acquiring too many daughters. It was his privilege to bestow both son and daughter in marriage. He could emancipate his son and deprive him of the privileges of the family circle. In the earlier stages of Greek history, it is quite likely that the father exercised patriarchal power over his son as long as he lived. By the time of Solon, the son on reaching his majority was freed from the domination of his father and came into certain legal rights and powers of his own.

THE STATUS OF THE GREEK WIFE [11]

The powers of the Greek husband over his wife were no less than those exercised over his children. Since it was fundamental that the family survive, he could cast her aside for failure to bear children. The dowry brought by an Athenian wife became the husband's property during his lifetime. He had the right to any separate earnings which his wife might acquire by her own labor. She was under his jurisdiction almost completely; she could not leave the home without his permission. When the Athenian wife became a widow, she did not become free but fell under the guardianship of some man selected by her husband. She was not even given the legal custody of her children; they, like herself, passed into the care and custody of the appointed guardian. The life of a well-born Athenian woman was narrow and restricted. In the words

---

[10] *Ibid.*, pp. 84–85.
[11] *Ibid.*, pp. 85–87.

of Menander, "The life of a respectable woman is bounded by the street door."

THE PLACE OF THE CHILD IN THE GREEK FAMILY [12]

The birth of a child was often a joyful event in the Greek family. If the baby were a boy, an olive wreath was attached to the door to symbolize the public honors which might become his. If the newcomer were a girl, a strip of wool was fastened to the entrance to represent the household activities to which a good part of her life would be devoted. On the seventh day after the child's arrival, a special ceremony was held for the purpose of inducting the infant into family membership. It was on this occasion that the father exercised his prerogative of determining whether or not the child was to continue to live. If he was satisfied with his offspring, he made a formal declaration accepting the responsibility of bringing up the child; if the child was a weakling, the father might decline to accept him and order him exposed to the elements. Exposure was sanctioned by law but was probably not often practiced.

The title to family property was held by the father. On his death it passed to the eldest son, and the other children had no share in the estate. In no case could a married daughter inherit, since she ceased to be a member of her father's family at the time of her marriage. In Sparta, however, women were in a position to take lands and personal property by inheritance.

MARRIAGE AMONG THE ANCIENT GREEKS [13]

Marriage among the Greeks was a sacred ceremony, for by means of the bonds of matrimony the family was perpetuated, inheritance was prescribed, and worship of the family gods and ancestors was assured. In some Greek city-states the man who did not marry lost certain rights. The ceremonies of marriage consisted of the betrothal and the nuptials. Betrothal was really a marriage agreement arrived at by the parents without the voluntary consent of the prospective bride and groom. Money matters occupied an important place in the betrothal negotiations and in the final contract. The amount of the bride's dowry was settled, and provision was made for its payment and for its return in case the wife was divorced without good cause. The betrothal was purely a business proposition and was not accompanied by religious rites.

The nuptials, however, were more religious in character. On the day selected for the wedding there were extensive ceremonies. In the morning the bride and groom bathed in water from a sacred stream. Late in the day the groom went to the home of the bride. Each guest was given

---

[12] *Ibid.*, pp. 84–85, 106–107.
[13] *Ibid.*, pp. 88 ff.

a cake. The bride's father offered sacrifices to the gods and handed over his daughter to the groom. These religious ceremonies were entirely private, the father himself serving as the priest. The marriage was substantially an interfamily affair in which the state took no part.

DIVORCE IN ANCIENT GREECE [14]

Perhaps by the beginning of the historic period, divorce had begun to appear as a legal means of severing the marriage relation. Much greater rights in respect to divorce were given to the husband than to the wife. There were two grounds upon which a Greek husband was justified in seeking a separation from his wife, barrenness and adultery. Since the fundamental purpose of marriage was to produce offspring and to perpetuate the family, naturally barrenness was a reason for severing the marriage tie.

The Greeks looked upon a wife's adultery with much severity. If caught in the act, the paramour might be put to death by the husband. If the husband allowed the heat of his anger to cool, probably he was not permitted to kill his wife. It was his privilege to inflict severe physical punishment upon her and keep her in confinement. On the other hand, the Greek woman had very few rights to divorce. Adultery by her husband was not a sufficient ground, unless his conduct inflicted hardship upon the family and unless he treated her with extreme cruelty. Even then the task of obtaining the divorce was not an easy one, for she had to appear before a high official with a written complaint. In Greece, then, divorce was considered more or less a private and family affair and essentially the prerogative of the husband. The granting of divorce was not under the jurisdiction of the state except in the case of the wife's adultery.

MARRIAGE AND THE FAMILY UNDER EARLY ROMAN CIVILIZATION

THE NATURE OF THE EARLY ROMAN FAMILY (753–202 B.C.) [15]

Before the Punic Wars the family in Rome was strongly patriarchal. The early Roman family consisted of the father, mother, children, grandchildren, and slaves, and, as such, it served as a legal, religious, and economic unit. The patriarch was vested with all the religious rights as priest of the family worship. He also possessed all the legal rights and was the only person recognized by law. As a legal person he was the sole owner of the family property. In contrast to Greece, the *potestas* of the father over all male adult members was permanent, and it continued so long as the

[14] *Ibid.*, pp. 98–101.
[15] *Ibid.*, pp. 115–116.

pater lived. The family was a strongly knit unit, for in those days there was no place for the individual outside of the family group. The Roman family was in reality a small state, and so it continued until the early years of the empire.

THE POWERS OF THE EARLY ROMAN FATHER [16]

The power of the father, *patria potestas,* over his children extended to life and death and was recognized by the laws of the Twelve Tables (completed about 450 B.C.). In one respect only was his power limited: if a child committed a grave offense, the patriarch had to call together his adult male relatives and confer with them before passing judgment. But even if the majority of his relatives differed with him, he still remained free to pass judgment. Such a procedure was also followed if a wife was accused of a serious offense; if a husband discovered his wife had committed adultery, however, he was free to kill her at once. By a ceremony of emancipation (a fictitious sale) a son could be set free from the authority of his father, but since sons were highly valued, this seldom occurred. Even after marriage a son remained under the power of his father, and not until his father's death could he control his own property and earnings or make a will.

THE STATUS OF THE EARLY ROMAN WIFE [17]

The legal power which the Roman husband held over his wife was called *manus.* During the first five centuries of Roman history, woman had few, if any, legal rights. She could not control property and was not recognized as a person by law. Even that which she brought with her from her father's house became the property of her husband. The Roman woman at marriage went from the *potestas* of her father to that of her husband. He had the jurisdiction to sit in judgment of her when she committed serious offenses. If she committed a capital offense, he might, after a discussion with the family council, condemn her to death. If he were to discover her in the act of adultery, it was his privilege to put her to death at once. In lesser matters he possessed the authority personally to chastise and correct her.

In spite of the way in which the Roman wife was hedged about by the authority of her husband, in early times she stood in a position of complete social equality and held a place of dignity and honor within the family and the state. She was the mistress of her household. She was not nearly so confined as her Greek sister. She attended public and social events with her husband. She was guardian of the family honor; she served as the co-partner of her husband in the education of their children and acted as a priestess at the family altar beside her husband in the ad-

---

[16] *Ibid.*, pp. 117–118.
[17] *Ibid.*, pp. 118–120.

ministration of religious rites. She was both honored and subordinated; she was highly respected, and yet she was given no tangible legal rights.

THE PLACE OF THE CHILD IN THE EARLY ROMAN FAMILY [18]

The child played a more vital part in the Roman than in the Greek family. It was perhaps true that the Romans, like the Greeks, practiced child exposure, although there is reason to believe that it was not so prevalent in Rome as in Greece. Usually nine days after the birth of the infant a ceremony took place which was celebrated as a family festival. On this occasion the father lifted the child from the floor, gave it a name, and received it into the family. In the early Roman home, both father and mother assumed the entire task of educating youth. The mother nursed and brought up her own offspring. The boys were first instructed by the mother and later by the father. They were given a practical education and one that prepared them for active citizenship. Every boy visited the forum, usually in company with his father, and was instructed in the laws of the Twelve Tables. He heard the addresses of the political leaders of his day. He visited the senate and the courts of law and thus learned his government and politics at first hand.

With respect to the right of the Roman son and daughter to inherit property it seems safe to say that the following rules prevailed: (1) All persons actually under the *potestas* of the father at the time of his death shared equally in all his property. (2) The widow enjoyed the right of inheritance on an equal footing with her sons and her unmarried daughters. (3) The eldest son shared in the inheritance to no greater extent than his younger brothers. (4) A married daughter was deprived of all right to share in her father's estate.

MARRIAGE AMONG THE EARLY ROMANS [19]

At the time that the Twelve Tables were enacted, the almost invariable custom was to contract marriage with *manus* (hand or bond). A marriage with *manus* put the wife under the power of her husband. Since at all times an unmarried daughter was legally under the power of her father, marriage for a woman consisted of severing that slavelike relationship with her father and assuming the same type of relationship with her husband. She passed out of her original family and lost all rights of inheritance in it. The consent of the father to the marriage of children under his power was essential. In fact, the control of the father over his children was so great that it extended to the right of life and death.

---

[18] *Ibid.*, pp. 120–121, 129–131.

[19] James Bryce, *Studies in History and Jurisprudence* (New York, Oxford University Press, 1901), p. 787. Quotations from this work are by permission of The Clarendon Press, Oxford, England.

Any property the wife brought with her from the home of her father belonged to her husband. Her subjection to him was practically absolute. In return she was supported by her husband and at his death was entitled to a share of his property as one of his family heirs. The creation of the *manus* relationship between husband and wife could be made by the use of three formalities: *confarreatio, coëmptio,* and *usus. Confarreatio* was a religious ceremony; *coëmptio* (or mock purchase), a purely civil one. *Usus* was an ancient custom lacking both "religious sanction and ceremonial dignity." It automatically created the *manus* relationship after a woman had lived with her husband for a year without being absent from his home for more than three consecutive nights. Marriage contracted by *usus* is probably analogous to the modern common-law marriage, or a marriage contracted privately by two persons.

DIVORCE IN ANCIENT ROME [20]

The right of divorce belonged exclusively to the husband. The wife had no power to institute or prevent divorce. The husband was permitted to repudiate his wife for three causes: adultery, preparing poisons, and the falsification of keys. Except in the case of adultery, the husband had to confer with his own and his wife's male relatives concerning the divorce. Divorce, though legally unrestricted for the male, was restrained by public opinion and property considerations, either the property the wife had brought to her husband at the time of her marriage or that which he would have to forfeit if he divorced her. The marriage of *confarreatio* was dissolved by a religious ceremony, *coëmptio* and *usus* marriages by mock sales. Thus the wife was freed from the *manus* of her husband and returned to her father's home. Divorces were few during this period.

MARRIAGE AND THE FAMILY IN THE LATER ROMAN WORLD (202 B.C.–A.D. 500)

CHANGES IN MARRIAGE.[21]

In the period after the Punic Wars free marriage gradually replaced marriage with *manus.* Slowly woman developed equality on the legal side as well as on the social side. By the time of Julius Caesar (102–44 B.C.), marriage with *manus* and the legal act placing the wife under the husband's control had almost completely disappeared. In this period, just before the appearance of Christianity, legislation governing both marriage and divorce contains much of our present marriage doctrine.

---

[20] Bryce, *op. cit.,* p. 800; James P. Lichtenberger, *Divorce* (New York, McGraw-Hill, 1931), p. 40; Goodsell, *op. cit.,* pp. 125–127; Stephen Pfeil, "The Law of Marriage," *Encyclopedia Americana* (1951), Vol. 18, pp. 313–318.

[21] Goodsell, *op. cit.,* pp. 135–138.

The general characteristics of this legislation were stated by Bryce as follows: [22]

The conception of the marriage relation is an altogether high and worthy one. A great jurist defines it as a partnership in the whole of life, a sharing of rights both sacred and secular. The wife is the husband's equal. She has full control of her daily life and her property. . . .

The marriage relation is deemed to be wholly a matter of private concern with which neither the state nor the Church has to concern itself. . . .

The marriage relation rests entirely on the free will of the two parties. If either having promised to enter it refuses to do so, no liability is incurred. If either desires to quit it, he or she can do so. Within it, each retains his or her absolute freedom of action, absolute disposal of his or her property.

Compulsion in any form or guise is utterly opposed to a connexion which springs from free choice and is sustained by affection only.

A formal betrothal, *sponsalia,* usually preceded the actual wedding. The betrothal, however, created no legal right, and no legal action lay upon it analogous to that which English and American law allows in a breach-of-promise suit. In this period both the husband and wife were two distinct legal persons. Each had complete control over his or her property, yet the practical needs of a joint household made necessary a plan for the expenses of such a household.

It was customary for the wife to bring land or goods with her. This property, which was for the support of the couple and their children, was called the *dos. Dos* should not be confused with the English word *dower,* for dower describes the right of a wife who survives her husband to have a share in his estate. Various rules existed regarding the *dos,* especially in the case of divorce. An old Roman custom prohibited either the husband or wife from giving gifts to each other. This custom was to protect a husband or wife from being "bullied" out of his or her separate property. It evolved from a view taken by jurists that affection must not be abused so as to obtain favors and that if the parties to a marriage were permitted to make gifts, the omission to make such gifts might lead to the dissolution of the marriage. By the time of Justinian (A.D. 527–565), Roman marriage laws were well settled.

CHANGES IN THE IMPORTANCE OF THE ROMAN FATHER [23]

With the decline of the power of the husband over his wife, there followed a similar weakening of the control of the father over his children. Legislation appeared restricting the rights of a father. For instance, about A.D. 200 a father's power over his son was limited to moderate chastisement. The right of sale was restricted to young children, and then only in case of necessity. The head of the family, however, was still regarded as

---

[22] Bryce, *op. cit.,* pp. 798–799.
[23] Goodsell, *op. cit.,* pp. 138–139.

owner of all the earnings and acquisitions of his children except those obtained through military service.

CHANGES IN THE STATUS OF WOMEN [24]

The Punic Wars (264–249 B.C.; 219–202 B.C.) resulted in considerable change in the legal and social status of both women and children. While the men were fighting, the management of their affairs was left to their women. Upon the return of the men, these women did not willingly give up their activities. This, and the situation that grew out of the fact that as a result of the successful wars wealth began to flow into Rome and accumulate in certain families, caused the old system to undergo modifications. Fathers became unwilling to give to their daughters at marriage a rich dowry which would immediately pass to the control of the daughter's husband. Thus, the custom grew up of contracting marriage without *manus,* which left the wife, after her marriage, under the control of an appointed guardian. Consequently, women, not legally under the authority of their husbands and possessing large dowries, began to demand from their husbands and the community a larger amount of freedom in controlling their own persons and property. The Roman wife during the late Roman period was probably more independent, legally and socially, than was a wife in any period in the occidental world until the last fifty years.

Although the Roman woman had gained considerable legal and social independence during the period following the close of the Punic Wars, with the rise of Christianity there developed a tendency to restrict her legal and social rights again. Jesus, during his lifetime, expressed no new ideas with respect to the position of woman, but the Apostle Paul advocated that woman take a subordinate position to man and this became the prevailing attitude of early Christian leaders. This belief was probably an outgrowth, in part, of the attitude of the early Christians to sex activity, which was considered carnal, and women, the chief vehicle of sin. The weakening of the power of a father over his children, unlike that of a husband over his wife, continued after the rise of Christianity; by the time of Justinian, a father's rights over his children were considerably restricted.

DIVORCE UNDER THE ROMAN EMPIRE [25]

In this period, divorce, like marriage, was an informal transaction based on the desires of either party. Though easy to obtain, divorce, at first, was

---

[24] William Lecky, *History of European Morals from Augustus to Charlemagne* (New York, D. Appleton, 1906), Vol. 2, pp. 302 ff.; Bryce, *op. cit.,* pp. 791–798.

[25] Bryce, *op. cit.,* pp. 794 ff.; Goodsell, *op. cit.,* pp. 144–147; J. B. Bury, *A History of the Later Roman Empire* [A.D. 395–A.D. 800] (London, Macmillan, 1889), Vol. 1, pp. 17–24.

rare. Records indicate that the first instance of divorce in Rome was in the case of a certain Spurius Carvilius Ruga, who in 231 B.C. divorced his wife, although fond of her, on account of her sterility. However, by the second century B.C., divorce had become common in the Roman Republic, being one of the characteristics of a general decline of morals and manners. Though public opinion, on the whole, sanctioned divorce, restrictive legislation began to appear. Augustus, during his reign (27 B.C.–A.D. 14), was so alarmed at the increase in divorce that he required the party desiring the divorce to declare his intent in the presence of seven witnesses. Although similar legislation continued down to the time of Justinian, the number of divorces did not seem to decrease appreciably.

Not until after the widespread acceptance of Christianity was there a decrease in divorce. Very early, Christianity looked upon the marriage union as permanent and sacred. However, the Christian emperors of the Roman Empire did not dare outlaw divorce altogether but attempted to deal with the problem by regulatory legislation. Penalties were levied on the party blamed for the divorce. If the wife were to blame, she lost part of the *dos;* if the husband, he was forced to forfeit part of his property. The custody of the children was always given to the father out of respect for his paternal power.

The early church accepted the Roman doctrine that marriage required nothing more than the free consent of the two parties to make it a lawful union. Marriage thus informally contracted continued to be recognized by the church down to 1545–1563, when, at the Council of Trent, certain changes were made in the canon law relating to matrimony. Slowly the doctrines of the church worked themselves into those of the state. Church law finally assumed exclusive jurisdiction over complete areas of activity, one being matrimony. This was true not only of the Roman Empire but of the whole of western Christendom. Such a development was made easy for the church from the fifth century onward because of the many barbarian invasions of the Roman Empire and the lack of stable civil authority.

MARRIAGE AND THE FAMILY AMONG THE TEUTONIC PEOPLES

MARRIAGE [26]

Western marriage custom and law have been influenced by early Teutonic customs as they existed before they were modified and changed by Christianity. Before Christian influences became strong, wife capture

[26] Sir Frederick Pollock and F. W. Maitland, *The History of English Law Before the Time of Edward I* (Cambridge, University Press, 1911), Vol. 2, p. 364; Goodsell, *op. cit.*, pp. 198–199.

was not an uncommon practice among Germanic tribes. However, during the first century of the Christian era this custom had been displaced by another practice known as wife purchase. This was really the purchase of the *mund* or protectorship over a woman. Apparently women were openly bought in marriage up to the tenth century. Under such a system there must have been little true affection between spouses. Among the Anglo-Saxons in England during the ninth century the law actually fixed the price of a woman sought in marriage. That price was three hundred shillings. However, in most of Europe, the sale and purchase of the bride had ceased by about the tenth or eleventh century. Under the wife-purchase agreement the man became the woman's elder, but, unlike the early Roman custom, the bond between her and her blood kinsman continued.

FORMS OF CONTRACTING MARRIAGE [27]

Among the early Teutonic peoples marriage consisted of two parts; the *beweddung*, or betrothal, and the *gifta*, or marriage ceremony itself. At first the *beweddung* was merely a sale and consisted of the payment by the bridegroom of the *weotuma* to the bride's father or guardian. By the sixth century the payment of the *weotuma*, the full price of the bride at the betrothal, had been replaced by the payment of a small sum, the *arrha*, to the bride's father or guardian as a guarantee of full payment at the time of the nuptials. In time the *arrha* was paid to the bride herself. The modern engagement ring has evolved from this custom.

By the tenth century the purchase money, the *weotuma*, was being transformed into a legal obligation of the bridegroom to make a settlement on his wife payable to her after his death. The *weotuma* gradually merged with the morning gift and became a regular legal provision for the widow. Originally the morning gift was a voluntary gift given to the bride on the morning following the nuptials, depending on whether or not the bridegroom was pleased with her. As the *weotuma* decreased in importance, the morning gift increased; finally, the two merged into one and became the direct predecessor of the modern dowry. The second part of the ceremony was the *gifta*, or the actual giving of the bride by her father or guardian to the bridegroom. As in modern times, this act was accompanied by ceremony and solemnity. Uncertainty exists as to whether marriage in the legal sense began with the betrothal or with the nuptials.

Originally, the father could betroth his daughter against her will. This power of the father was first weakened by granting the daughter a veto on the choice of her bridegroom. Gradually, the situation reversed

[27] Howard, *op. cit.*, Vol. 1, pp. 258–268; Goodsell, *op. cit.*, pp. 199–203.

itself until it was the father who was granted the veto power. Naturally enough, it was the widow, in the case of a second marriage, who first emancipated herself from the control of her parental guardian regarding her choice of a mate. With the right of self-betrothal, the bride and the bridegroom also gained, slowly to be sure, the right of *self-gifta.* At a later date this custom of *self-gifta,* which church doctrine accepted, caused confusion in both civil and church courts.

POWERS OF THE TEUTON FATHER [28]

Though the power of a father over his children did not compare with that granted the old Roman father, it was great. A child was considered his father's *mund,* or ward. The power of the father did not continue indefinitely, since, after attaining a certain age, children became independent. This age of majority varied at different periods and for different purposes. Probably the same rules applied to both males and females.

POSITION OF WOMEN [29]

For the most part Teutonic women were under the control of their husbands. Nevertheless, since a woman did not become a legal member of her husband's family but remained a member of her own, her husband was not responsible for her debts or conduct. In fact, at the woman's marriage it was customary for her kin to give security to answer for her conduct during her married life. As a correlative of this practice, when injury was perpetrated upon the wife, the fines were payable to her family and not to her husband. Women were not persons in the legal sense, for a father, brother, or guardian answered for them in the courts and paid their fines.

The Teutonic husband had full power personally to chastise his wife and only in case of unwarranted cruelty which resulted in serious bodily injury or in case of unreasonable divorce would her kindred step in and give her protection or sue for a fine. The wife was bound to strict obedience of her husband. She had the right to ownership of certain kinds of property, among which were (1) the bride price, after it had become the custom to pay it to her rather than to her father, (2) the morning gift, and (3) the *gerade.* The *gerade* consisted of household linen, furniture, money, and even poultry or sheep she had tended before her marriage. Practically all of the Teutonic tribes excluded women from the ownership of land.

---

[28] W. S. Holdsworth, *A History of English Law* (London, Methuen, 1923), Vol. 2, pp. 97–99.

[29] Goodsell, *op. cit.,* pp. 203–210.

DIVORCE [30]

The folk laws of most of the Teutonic tribes made provision for some kind of divorce. Among the Burgundians in France, divorce by mutual consent was permitted, which was due undoubtedly to a measure of Roman influence. Most of the codes drew a sharp distinction between the effects of adultery when committed by the husband as compared with the same act committed by the wife. A married man might be slain if discovered in the act. His crime was not one of unfaithfulness to his wife but the violation of the rights of another husband. On the other hand, an adulterous wife could be led through the streets of her home village and beaten until lifeless. There seems to have been a tendency to restrict the grounds upon which a man might divorce his wife, as barrenness, gluttony, drunkenness, and quarrelsomeness were not sufficient reasons. In their treatment of the divorce problem the Visigoths were more progressive than some tribes, as they restricted the husband's right to divorce to the cause of adultery, and they granted the wife the same privilege if the husband indulged in two unfaithful experiences.

HEBREW INFLUENCES ON MARRIAGE AND THE FAMILY

THE CHARACTER OF THE ANCIENT HEBREW FAMILY [31]

Hebrew marriage doctrine and family law are laid down in the Torah and Talmud. The former is that law which, according to tradition, Moses received from Jehovah at Mount Sinai. The Talmud consists of commentaries on the Torah written by a number of learned rabbis and judges. The early Hebrew family was of the patriarchal type, but it was not so strong an example of this kind of family organization as that exhibited in early Rome. The isolated pastoral life of each family group caused the owner of the flock to subordinate all members of the group to his control. This meant that wives, children, daughters-in-law, slaves, and strangers were all under the patriarch's absolute control.

The Hebrew wife was far from a free person. All her life she was under the control of some male. Only the widowed mother, who went into her son's home on the death of her husband, had any semblance of freedom and independence. The Hebrews honored and respected their mothers, whereas their wives and concubines were often looked upon as property. There is no historical evidence that the patriarch had the power of life and death over his wives except in case of adultery.

---

[30] *Ibid.*, pp. 210–212.
[31] *Ibid.*, pp. 53 ff.

Hebrew children were under the discipline of the father, whose authority extended to life and death, at least in the early patriarchal days. Later, there is biblical evidence that the Israelites were forbidden to burn their children on the altars of Molech.[32] The power of the Hebrew patriarch was restricted in at least two other respects: (1) he was specifically prohibited from making his own daughter a prostitute; (2) he could not sell her to a foreigner.[33]

MARRIAGE LAWS AND CUSTOMS [34]

Marriage was regarded more as a family matter than a personal one. The validity of Hebrew marriages depended upon certain conditions, such as legal age, consent, and avoidance of prohibited marriages. In Leviticus and Deuteronomy we find prohibitions against marrying within certain degrees of relationship. The Hebrews developed the institution of the *levirate,* which provided for the marriage of a widow to her deceased husband's brother.[35] This custom may, in part, have grown out of a desire to keep the property of a family intact. Such a marriage could be evaded by the brother, but only at considerable loss of social prestige. It has also been customary among the Jews for a man to marry his deceased wife's sister. In England such a marriage was invalid until 1907 when the Deceased Wife's Sister Marriage Act became law; and not until 1921 was a law passed that permitted a man to marry his deceased brother's widow.[36]

Hebrew law required the consent of the parties to a marriage. This concept, accepted by Christianity, is basic in existing marriage doctrine. If consent were forced, the marriage could be declared null and void. Neither idiots nor the insane were regarded by Jews as capable of consent. This concept, along with the prohibition of marriage between near relatives, probably contains the seed of some of our eugenic legislation. The consent of the parents was a legal requirement of a valid marriage, if the parties to the marriage were not of legal age. Talmudic law fixed the legal age of contracting marriage at puberty, the end of the eleventh year for females, and the thirteenth for males.

DIVORCE

The restrictions upon the right of the Hebrew patriarch to divorce his wife were very few, even down to the begining of the Christian era. The

---

[32] Lev. 18:21.
[33] Lev. 19:29.
[34] Goodsell, *op. cit.*, pp. 61–70; Earle Bennett Cross, *The Hebrew Family* (Chicago, University of Chicago Press, 1927), pp. 151–166.
[35] Gen. 38:11.
[36] Deceased Wife's Sister's Marriage Act, 1907, 7 Edw. VII, c. 47; Deceased Brother's Widow's Marriage Act, 1921, 11–12 Geo. V, c. 24.

Mosaic law provided that if a wife proved unsatisfactory in her husband's eyes because of "some uncleanness in her, then let him write her a bill of divorcement, give it in her hand and send her out of his house." [37] But even before Christ, some of the prophets had voiced serious objection to the doctrine of divorce. About the first century of the Christian era two schools of thought seemed to have crystallized among the Hebrews with respect to the correct interpretation of the biblical expression, "some uncleanness." One group interpreted it loosely so as to give the husband unlimited freedom of divorce. The other school construed the words more strictly, and contended that they meant some serious moral fault, thereby curtailing the right of the husband to obtain a divorce. However, by the third century the Hebrews began to disapprove of divorce except upon certain serious grounds, such as adultery, flagrant disregard of moral decency, refusal to cohabit for one year or more, and change in religion. Physical disabilities, such as leprosy and inability to bear children, were also considered adequate grounds upon which to seek divorce.

In early patriarchal days the Hebrew wife possessed no right to divorce whatever except in one situation: where a bondswoman had been brought up by her master as a wife or concubine, she was permitted to go free if he failed to provide for her.[38] She was not to receive any money, but her husband had to give her a bill of divorcement. There are those who believe that this provision was the embryo from which sprang the later right of the Hebrew free wife to demand divorce upon certain grounds. There is no certain proof that free wives had the right to divorce until after the Roman conquest of Palestine (about 65 B.C.). As a result of the influence exerted by Roman law and custom, the Hebrew married woman's right to divorce became more common. There was one check upon her ability to secure a divorce. She was required to ask her husband to write her a *get* or bill of divorcement. If he refused to grant the bill, she encountered serious difficulty in winning her freedom.

CHRISTIAN INFLUENCES ON MARRIAGE

THE DEVELOPMENT OF CATHOLIC MARRIAGE DOCTRINE [39]

Church attitudes toward marriage and divorce derive in large part from the preachings of Christ's disciples, which, in turn, are the result of their

---

[37] Deut. 24:1.

[38] Exod. 21:7–11.

[39] "Marriage," *Encyclopaedia Brittanica* (1952), Vol. 14, pp. 940–950; "Law of Marriage," *Encyclopaedia Brittanica* (1952), Vol. 14, pp. 950–955; several articles on "Marriage," *Catholic Encyclopedia* (1910), Vol. 9, pp. 691–715; Sidney B. Fay, "Marriage," *Encyclopaedia of the Social Sciences* (1933), Vol. 10, pp. 146–154; William Smith and Samuel Cheetham, eds., "Marriage," *Dictionary of Christian Antiquities* (Hartford, J. Burr Publishing Co., 1880), Vol. 2, pp. 1092–1114; Stephen Pfeil, "The Law of Marriage," *Encyclopedia Americana* (1951), Vol. 18, pp. 313–318.

early experiences and their resistance to prevailing depravity. According to Matthew: [40]

> Ye have heard that it was said, Thou shalt not commit adultery: but I say unto you, that every one that looketh on a woman to lust after her hath committed adultery with her already in his heart. And if thy right eye causeth thee to stumble, pluck it out, and cast it from thee: for it is profitable for thee that one of thy members should perish, and not thy whole body be cast into hell. And if thy right hand causeth thee to stumble, cut it off, and cast it from thee: for it is profitable for thee that one of thy members should perish, and not thy whole body go into hell. It was said also, Whosoever shall put away his wife, let him give her a writing of divorcement: but I say unto you, that every one that putteth away his wife, saving for the cause of fornication, maketh her an adulteress: and whosoever shall marry her when she is put away committeth adultery.

St. Paul, whose attitudes toward sex and sin have had so marked an effect upon church doctrines and practice, wrote to the Corinthians: [41]

> Now concerning the things whereof ye wrote: It is good for a man not to touch a woman. But, because of fornications, let each man have his own wife, and let each woman have her own husband. Let the husband render unto the wife her due: and likewise also the wife unto the husband. The wife hath not power over her own body, but the husband: and likewise also the husband hath not power over his own body, but the wife. . . .
>
> But I say to the unmarried and to widows, It is good for them if they abide even as I. But if they have not continency, let them marry: for it is better to marry than to burn. But unto the married I give charge, *yea* not I, but the Lord, That the wife depart not from her husband (but should she depart, let her remain unmarried, or else be reconciled to her husband); and that the husband leave not his wife. . . .

The early church was forced to accept existing temporal marriage customs and laws. It had to content itself with giving its blessing to marriages and to enforcing rules regarding marriage disabilities, such as those arising from affinity or nearness of kin.[42] At an early date, wherever the Christian church existed, a priestly benediction was given in connection with betrothals and nuptials. At a later period there is evidence that the bride and groom went to church on the day following the bridal night to attend a special bride mass and to receive the blessings of a priest. The blessings did not in any way add to the validity of the marriage but were received by all good Christians as a matter of religious duty. By the tenth century the marriage ceremony, though still a private temporal transaction, was taking place just outside the church door in the presence of a priest, who did not, however, perform the ceremony. Following a lay ceremony at the church door, the couple immediately entered the church for the bride mass and to receive the blessings of the clergy.

---

[40] Matt. 5:27–33.
[41] I Cor. 7:1–12.
[42] Howard, *op. cit.*, Vol. 1, pp. 291–309.

In time an elaborate ritual conducted by a priest, not merely in his presence, developed out of the earlier informal lay ceremony that took place outside the church door; and the clergy gradually appropriated the old function of the father to give his daughter in marriage. Remnants of the old custom of a father giving his daughter in marriage appear in the marriage rituals of today. This function of the father diminished in importance as it became acceptable for a third person other than the father or for the parties themselves to perform the marriage ceremony. Undoubtedly the church made an effort to acquire this function in order to gain control of the nuptial celebration and hence to give religious form to an institution believed by it to be sacred. The church may also have visualized some of the evils of private unions, if the presence of the father or guardian of the bride at the marriage ceremony was no longer required.

Through such an evolution, the marriage ceremony became religious in nature and a function of the clergy. Not until 1164, in the fourth book of Peter Lombard's *Sentences,* was there a clear formulation of the now recognized seven sacraments, marriage being the last to be accepted.[43] This formulation was later approved by the Council of Florence in 1439 and by the Council of Trent in 1543–1563. The doctrine of the sacramental nature of marriage means that God has joined together two persons whose marriage bond thus becomes indissoluble. These concepts, like many others of the church, were slowly accepted. As on most of the Continent, ecclesiastical authority in matrimonial matters was established in England between the seventh and twelfth centuries. By the end of the twelfth century, the doctrine that marriage was a sacrament was firmly established in England and Europe.

Canonists have espoused various theories at different times concerning the formation of the marriage bond. At first they accepted the Roman idea that marriage began with physical union, *copula carnalis;* but during the early Middle Ages (A.D. 395–815) they emphasized the desirability of a priestly benediction given in connection with the marriage ceremony. If the nuptials were thus solemnized, the marriage was valid, even if not followed by physical union.

By the twelfth century canonists again favored the idea that a valid marriage did not exist until after actual wedded life, and any promises made before were considered void.[44] Before the end of the century, however, theologians had developed and gained acceptance of a doctrine as to when a valid marriage existed that almost proved disastrous to the security of the marriage bond. The essence of this doctrine was that

---

[43] Baptism, confirmation, Holy Eucharist, penance, extreme unction, orders, and matrimony; Howard, *op. cit.,* Vol. 1, pp. 332–334; Augustinus Lehmkuhl, "Sacrament of Marriage," *Catholic Encyclopedia* (1910), Vol. 9, pp. 707–715.

[44] Howard, *op. cit.,* Vol. 1, pp. 334–336.

marriage outside the church could be one of two kinds: *sponsalia per verba de futuro* or *sponsalia per verba de praesenti*. The former was a promise for future joining in marriage; the latter was a present agreement that a man and woman were taking each other for husband and wife. It was valid, even though not followed by *copula carnalis,* and was sustained by canon law against a subsequent marriage performed with due publicity by a priest.

These two forms of marriage have historically been referred to as common-law marriage. American jurisdictions, which today accept the common-law marriage, have rejected the *de futuro* marriage. The church considered the informal marriage valid but illegal. This meant that all the rights and duties attendant upon marriage accrued and that an indissoluble contract existed but that ecclesiastical penalties were imposed upon the parties since the church had not blessed or created the union. In its efforts to keep people out of "sin" and to avoid "bastardizing" children, the church presumed everything it could in favor of lawful matrimony. This distinction between valid and legal marriages as propounded by theologians of the twelfth century is still made by the Roman Catholic church and by some other churches, notably the Church of England and the Episcopalian church in the United States.

The evils of private marriage, often called clandestine marriage because so many irregular and temporary unions were formed in its name, prevailed everywhere in medieval times and later. Martin Luther commented thus on the situation: [45]

> They have played a regular fool's game with their *verbis de praesenti vel futuro.* With it they have torn apart marriages which were valid according to their law and those which were not valid they have bound up. . . . Indeed I should not myself know how a churl would or could betroth himself *de futuro* in the German tongue, for the way one betroths himself means *per verba de praesenti,* and surely a clown knows nothing of such nimble grammar as the difference between *accipio* and *accipiam;* therefore, he proceeds according to our way of speech and says, "I will have thee," "I will take thee," "thou shalt be mine."

Local ecclesiastical courts were kept busy devising penalties in an effort to put a stop to private, secret marriage agreements. The church hierarchy also attempted to abate the evil. The Lateran Council in 1215, through the efforts of Pope Innocent III, made mandatory banns or proclamations of an intention to marry if heavy ecclesiastical penalties were not to be inflicted, but it did not make them essential to a valid marriage. It was not until the Council of Trent that a solution to the private marriage problem was reached. It provided that all marriages would be null and void for both civil and ecclesiastical purposes if they were not celebrated in the presence of witnesses and a represent-

---

[45] Martin Luther, "Von Ehesachen," *Werke,* Erlangen ed., Vol. 23, pp. 102, 103, quoted in Howard, *op. cit.,* Vol. 1, p. 341.

ative of the church. This action proved effective on the continent, since in most of the western world the church had exclusive jurisdiction over matrimonial matters.

The church took this position not only to secure religious blessings on every marriage but to prevent the many scandals arising out of uncertain marriage contracts. It was also decreed at this time that the old requirement of publication of banns be everywhere enforced. They were still unessential to a valid marriage, but ecclesiastical penalties were imposed on those persons who did not meet the requirements. These decrees represent an attempt by the church to adjust its doctrine to existing social conditions. They were not accepted in England, and, consequently, the many evils growing out of privately contracted and secret marriage agreements continued there until 1753, when Parliament passed the Hardwicke Act.

CHRISTIAN INFLUENCES ON DIVORCE

THE DEVELOPMENT OF CATHOLIC FORMS OF DIVORCE [46]

The early Christians accepted the current pagan ideas concerning the private and secular character of marriage. The same is true with respect to their early attitudes toward divorce. For several centuries the Christians recognized the right of married persons to dissolve their marriage without interference from either church or state. By the fifth century the Christian attitude toward divorce had begun to change substantially. For a number of centuries, divorce was condemned and strictly forbidden. The dogma of the church, enforced by threats of excommunication and from the membership of the "saved," had a tremendous effect in restricting divorce. However, under the stress and needs of everyday life the theologians were forced to devise means of granting divorce, but they had to be in harmony with the existing Christian doctrine of matrimony.

By the tenth century the church was allowing two types of divorce: *divortium a vinculo matrimonii,* from the chains of matrimony, and *divortium a mensa et thoro,* from bed and board. The former was used to designate the nullification of a marriage which had been void or at least voidable from the beginning on account of some impediment.[47]

[46] Howard, *op. cit.,* Vol. 1, pp. 51–60; Pollock and Maitland, *op. cit.,* Vol. 2, pp. 393 ff.; Goodsell, *op. cit.,* pp. 211–215, 221–224; Smith and Cheetham, *Dictionary of Christian Antiquities,* pp. 1092–1114; Walter G. Smith, "Divorce" *Catholic Encyclopedia* (1909), Vol. 5, pp. 54–69; "Divorce," *Encyclopaedia Brittanica* (1952), Vol. 7, pp. 453–461; Frank H. Hankins, "Divorce," *Encyclopaedia of the Social Sciences* (1931), Vol. 5, pp. 177–184.

[47] A void marriage is a marriage contract that because of some impediment is *ipso facto* void; a voidable contract is one that must be declared null and void by a court.

This type of so-called divorce is akin to our present annulment; it permitted remarriage. *Divortium a mensa et thoro* was a judicial separation of husband and wife which left the marriage bond untouched. Canon law permitted such a separation on three grounds: adultery, "spiritual adultery," the meaning of which is not clear, and cruelty. This type of so-called divorce permitted neither the man nor the woman to remarry. The church sanctioned two exceptions to the rule that genuine marriage could never be dissolved. A Christian abandoned by an infidel spouse was allowed to remarry because, according to church doctrine, it was the unbeliever and not the Christian who dissolved the marriage. The second exception permitted the dissolution of a marriage if one of the parties took holy orders. Dissolution of marriages was also within the papal power of dispensation.

The granting of divorce *a vinculo*, or the annulling of marriage, became a flourishing business for the church. Marriage was strictly forbidden within seven degrees of relationship, both of consanguinity and affinity. Even spiritual relationships, or those acquired at baptism, served as barriers to legal marriage. A case has been reported in which a marriage was pronounced null because the husband had stood godfather to the cousin of his wife.[48] Only the most astute of ecclesiastical scholars were able to unravel the complicated system of canonical disabilities arising from relationship. At the beginning of the sixteenth century so extensive was the casuistry concerning marriage that it has been said that for a fat fee a canonical flaw could be found in almost any marriage. Though the many scandals arising out of divorce *a vinculo* or annulment have long disappeared, the doctrine of annulment permitting remarriage is maintained by the Roman Catholic church.

CONFLICT BETWEEN ECCLESIASTICAL AND TEMPORAL COURTS

In England, during late Anglo-Saxon times and part of the first century after the Norman conquest, the adjudication of matrimonial matters took place largely in the temporal courts. However, by the close of the twelfth century, the church had acquired undisputed jurisdiction in such causes. It had developed its own system of courts, and these tribunals administered canon law, which included the regulation of marriage. Under this jurisdiction the ecclesiastical courts decided questions relating to the celebration of marriage, the capacity of parties to marry, and the legitimacy of children. However, the common-law courts were not completely ousted from matters touching upon the marriage relation since that part of the marriage law affecting the property rights of the two

[48] Lecky, *op. cit.*, Vol. 2, p. 194.

parties continued within their jurisdiction. Very often in determining such questions as the right of a woman to dower and the rights of inheritance where the testator left no will, they had to decide whether or not there had been a marriage.

For some time the common-law courts were not jealous of the acquisition of jurisdiction over matrimonial matters by the church courts. In fact, the common-law courts very often sought the aid of the church judge in determining whether a litigant was legitimate or whether there had been a valid marriage upon which the common-law court could determine property rights.[49] As time went on, however, the common-law courts became less willing to do this, and a conflict developed along two lines: over the right to hear and determine matrimonial matters in the first instance, and over the principles of substantive law that should govern in these cases. We shall not discuss the first of these conflicts here. It grew out of the desire of the church courts to retain as much of their jurisdiction as they could and the tendency of the common-law courts to expand their judicial field as much as possible.

The struggle in the substantive field has greater importance for us. Frequently the common-law courts laid down rules of substantive law at variance with those of the canon law, which was more liberal in its attitude as to what was necessary to consummate a valid marriage. This attitude was evidenced in a leading case that was decided in the reign of Stephen. Richard de Ansty prosecuted a lawsuit that grew out of divorce pronounced in 1143 under the authority of a papal rescript. The church court decided that a church-celebrated marriage, of which a child was born, was to be set aside in favor of an earlier marriage consummated by the mere exchange of consenting words. The result of this suit in the ecclesiastical courts indicates what was to become a characteristic doctrine of the canon law.[50]

The common-law courts took a stricter view of what was necessary to constitute a valid marriage. They were interested in curbing clandestine marriages which grew out of the scholastic dogma that mere consent secretly expressed in the present tense constituted a valid marriage, and they attempted to accomplish this by making the acquisition of certain property rights depend upon the publicity of the espousals. A widow, for instance, could not recover her dower in the common-law court unless the nuptials had taken place publicly before the church door. What common-law courts demanded as a basis for determining the various property rights growing out of the marriage relation was not so much a religious ceremony as publicity of the nuptials.

Only the church courts could decide whether a valid marriage existed,

---

[49] Pollock and Maitland, *op. cit.*, Vol. 2, p. 367.
[50] Howard, *op. cit.*, Vol. 1, pp. 351–352.

but the common-law courts could determine the kind of contract upon which the marriage was based; that is, whether or not there had been a *de facto* marriage or merely a marriage *de jure*. If proof existed that a marriage had been contracted and consummated as a result of a public ceremony at a church door or the publication of banns, that marriage was declared by the common-law courts to be a *de facto* marriage. They then proceeded to determine property rights on the basis of such a marriage. If the proof submitted in the common-law courts showed that the marriage was privately and secretly contracted, it was pronounced *de jure* marriage, and the common-law courts could and often did ref to grant the widow of such a marriage her dower, or they withheld the children of such a marriage the right to inherit their father's p erty.[51]

These differences between the two systems of courts as to the stantive requirements of marriage naturally led to further conflicts jurisdiction. Out of the confusion resulting from the doctrine o *praesenti* marriages, the annulling of marriages, and the friction bet the ecclesiastical and temporal courts, measures for reform eme Efforts were made to formulate a plan by which religious doct could be adjusted to new conditions of life. The Council of Trent, w it decreed publicity for marriages, attempted to make such an adj ment, but England rejected this principle.

THE REFORMATION

The Reformation, at least on the Continent, changed more profound than any other reform movement the then-existing ideas concerning th nature of marriage and related matters, though it was years before tha influence was definitely felt in legislation.[52] It was essentially a religi movement opposed to the centralization of ecclesiastical power in pope at Rome. It succeeded in destroying the monopolistic position of Catholic church, which thus became one of many Christian groups stead of *the* one.

Martin Luther, the most important single figure of the Reformati is responsible for abandonment of the concept that marriage is a sac ment. As late as 1519 Luther declared that marriage was a sacrame but in the very next year and again in 1539 he retracted this doctri His expressions concerning the sacramental nature of marriage seeming contradict themselves for, on the one hand, he declared that though

[51] *Ibid.*, pp. 355–356.

[52] *Ibid.*, pp. 370–392; Heinrich Böhmer, "Luther in the Light of Recent Research," *The Christian Herald*, trans. Carl F. Huth, Jr. (New York, 1916), pp. 146–155; H. Richard Niebuhr, "Reformation," *Encyclopaedia of the Social Sciences* (1934), Vol. 13, pp. 186–194; Goodsell, *op. cit.*, pp. 266–268.

marriage was not technically a sacrament, it was a holy and a most spiritual status ordained and founded by God. On the other hand, he advised the clergy not to meddle with matrimonial questions unless requested by the state, because marriage was a temporal, worldly thing which did not concern the church. Two conditions probably accounted for the apparent contradiction in Luther's thinking: (1) the many scandals connected with the sacerdotal celibacy of the clergy; and (2) the many evils growing out of church doctrine and ecclesiastical law. By denying the sacramental nature of marriage, the way was paved to trans- the jurisdiction over matrimonial subjects to civil courts.

ther proclaimed the right of priests to marry and, at the same time, tress on the purity and holiness of marriage as an institution. He f married a nun in 1525. On the continent, especially in Germany, of the Protestant leaders agreed with Luther as to the nature of ge. With his reaction against celibacy, many did not agree. Most reform groups agreed that the abuses arising out of the law of den degrees and other canonical impediments ought to be remedied; iere was much divergence of opinion as to the precise reform d. Unfortunately, almost none of the ideas of the Reformation were ssed in legislation or judicial decree. Consequently, although beliefs rning the fundamental nature of marriage had changed, specific ation in accordance with new concepts failed to gain support or take until a later date.

For Selected References, see those following Chapter 3.

but the common-law courts could determine the kind of contract upon which the marriage was based; that is, whether or not there had been a *de facto* marriage or merely a marriage *de jure*. If proof existed that a marriage had been contracted and consummated as a result of a public ceremony at a church door or the publication of banns, that marriage was declared by the common-law courts to be a *de facto* marriage. They then proceeded to determine property rights on the basis of such a marriage. If the proof submitted in the common-law courts showed that the marriage was privately and secretly contracted, it was pronounced a *de jure* marriage, and the common-law courts could and often did refuse to grant the widow of such a marriage her dower, or they withheld from the children of such a marriage the right to inherit their father's property.[51]

These differences between the two systems of courts as to the substantive requirements of marriage naturally led to further conflicts over jurisdiction. Out of the confusion resulting from the doctrine of *de praesenti* marriages, the annulling of marriages, and the friction between the ecclesiastical and temporal courts, measures for reform emerged. Efforts were made to formulate a plan by which religious doctrines could be adjusted to new conditions of life. The Council of Trent, when it decreed publicity for marriages, attempted to make such an adjustment, but England rejected this principle.

THE REFORMATION

The Reformation, at least on the Continent, changed more profoundly than any other reform movement the then-existing ideas concerning the nature of marriage and related matters, though it was years before that influence was definitely felt in legislation.[52] It was essentially a religious movement opposed to the centralization of ecclesiastical power in the pope at Rome. It succeeded in destroying the monopolistic position of the Catholic church, which thus became one of many Christian groups instead of *the* one.

Martin Luther, the most important single figure of the Reformation, is responsible for abandonment of the concept that marriage is a sacrament. As late as 1519 Luther declared that marriage was a sacrament; but in the very next year and again in 1539 he retracted this doctrine. His expressions concerning the sacramental nature of marriage seemingly contradict themselves for, on the one hand, he declared that though

[51] *Ibid.*, pp. 355–356.

[52] *Ibid.*, pp. 370–392; Heinrich Böhmer, "Luther in the Light of Recent Research," *The Christian Herald*, trans. Carl F. Huth, Jr. (New York, 1916), pp. 146–155; H. Richard Niebuhr, "Reformation," *Encyclopaedia of the Social Sciences* (1934), Vol. 13, pp. 186–194; Goodsell, *op. cit.*, pp. 266–268.

marriage was not technically a sacrament, it was a holy and a most spiritual status ordained and founded by God. On the other hand, he advised the clergy not to meddle with matrimonial questions unless requested by the state, because marriage was a temporal, worldly thing which did not concern the church. Two conditions probably accounted for the apparent contradiction in Luther's thinking: (1) the many scandals connected with the sacerdotal celibacy of the clergy; and (2) the many evils growing out of church doctrine and ecclesiastical law. By denying the sacramental nature of marriage, the way was paved to transfer the jurisdiction over matrimonial subjects to civil courts.

Luther proclaimed the right of priests to marry and, at the same time, laid stress on the purity and holiness of marriage as an institution. He himself married a nun in 1525. On the continent, especially in Germany, most of the Protestant leaders agreed with Luther as to the nature of marriage. With his reaction against celibacy, many did not agree. Most of the reform groups agreed that the abuses arising out of the law of forbidden degrees and other canonical impediments ought to be remedied; but there was much divergence of opinion as to the precise reform needed. Unfortunately, almost none of the ideas of the Reformation were expressed in legislation or judicial decree. Consequently, although beliefs concerning the fundamental nature of marriage had changed, specific legislation in accordance with new concepts failed to gain support or take form until a later date.

For Selected References, see those following Chapter 3.

immediate impetus being Henry VIII's demand for a divorce. As a result of Henry's inability to secure a divorce from Katherine of Aragon in the ecclesiastical courts, he took the matter into his own hands and prosecuted his suit in the court of the archbishop of Canterbury, where he obtained sanction for his divorce.

The successful attempt of Henry to thrust aside the divorce doctrine of the church had far-reaching results. Having considered the consequences of the divorce upon the relations of pope and king, the Parliament which sat from 1529–1536 threw off all papal jurisdiction over the English church by legislating the obedience of the clergy to the king, who thus became the head of the Church of England. In 1532, Parliament passed the Act of Submission of the Clergy, which declared that no new canons could be passed by convocation without the king's consent and that those in existence had to receive his approval.

CIVIL MARRIAGE UNDER CROMWELL [4]

Unfortunately, the Established Church of England did not legislate against secret and privately contracted marriages, as the Roman Catholic church did, so England continued to suffer from all the evils attendant on these marriages. In 1540, Henry VIII attempted to restrict the validity of such marriages by decreeing that those solemnized by the church should be recognized over against those not thus celebrated or those privately contracted. The law was repealed by his successor, Edward VI, and consequently the old conditions remained unchecked. In 1538, Henry succeeded in having a law passed requiring that each parish keep records of the births, deaths, and marriages within the parish. Such records have been kept in many parishes in England from that date.

During the protectorship of Oliver Cromwell (1653–1658) the doctrines of the Reformation were partly incorporated into legislation with the passage of the Civil Marriage Act of 1653, which made a civil marriage ceremony obligatory for all. The act provided that after proper publication of banns, a certificate was to be obtained by the couple from the parish registrar. The marriage ceremony was performed upon the couple's presentation of the certificate to a justice of peace of the same county, city, or town where the publication of banns had taken place. The ceremony consisted merely of an expression of mutual consent accompanied by the clasping of hands.[5] If either party were under

---

[4] George Eliot Howard, *A History of Matrimonial Institutions* (Chicago, University of Chicago Press, 1904), Vol. 1, pp. 361 ff.; Willystine Goodsell, *A History of Marriage and the Family* (New York, Macmillan, 1934), pp. 263–265.

[5] Howard, *op. cit.*, Vol. 1, p. 419: "I, A. B., do here in the presence of God the Searcher of all Hearts, take thee, C. D. for my wedded wife; and do also in the presence of God, and before these witnesses, promise to be unto thee a Loving and Faithful Husband. The woman . . . promising to be his 'Loving, Faithful, and Obedient wife.'"

twenty-one, proof of parental consent was to be presented to the justice of peace. This statute was significant not only because judicial authority over matrimony was vested in civil law but because such authority was placed in the hands of local judges. After the restoration of King Charles in 1661, the Act of 1653 and other supplementary legislation were repealed. At the same time, opponents of the Civil Marriage Act made an unsuccessful attempt to have all marriages performed under the act declared null and void. Not until nearly a century later was a statute again passed that prescribed a definite form for contracting marriage. This was the Hardwicke Act, which we shall discuss shortly.

THE STRUGGLE FOR REFORM [6]

Although clandestine marriages had been common in the seventeenth century, they increased to such an extent in the eighteenth that the many scandals resulting therefrom made apparent to everyone the need for reform. As early as the reign of William II (1689–1702) an act was passed which attempted to enforce a law requiring a small duty on marriage licenses and imposing a fine of one hundred pounds on any person who married couples without such a license.

The law was easily evaded, for at that time certain chapels were exempt from the control of the bishops. These so-called lawless churches became known as places where an unmarried couple of legal age could be united in matrimony without preliminary formalities. The greatest scandal in this respect grew out of the irregular marriages performed in the Fleet Prison, where clergymen, imprisoned for debt, started their infamous trade of publicly advertising their willingness to unite persons in matrimony for a small sum and of marrying couples without requiring banns or licenses. Though additional legislation continued to be passed, imposing cash penalties on persons performing irregular marriages, it seems to have been completely inoperative. Fleet marriages were performed on a large scale until 1753.

At that time, on the motion of Lord Bath, the House of Lords decided to bring a "bill for the better preventing of clandestine marriage." The drafting of the bill was assigned to twelve judges, but their product was so imperfect that the chancellor, Lord Hardwicke, revised it thoroughly. The bill was quickly passed by the Lords, but in the House of Commons it met considerable opposition. The arguments in support of the measure were direct, practical, and convincing, while those against it were, especially in the light of modern experience and knowledge, either forced or frivolous.

Sponsors of the act focused attention on the many scandals and hardships

---

[6] Howard, *op. cit.*, Vol. 1, pp. 435–448; Goodsell, *op. cit.*, pp. 333–336.

caused by clandestine marriages and argued that their bill provided an effective remedy for those hardships. That remedy, they stated, was publicity which could be secured only by insisting upon banns or by requiring licenses, securing parental consent in certain situations, and following this by a public marriage ceremony; such action should be necessary to a valid marriage.

Opponents changed every argument for the bill into a fault and interpreted the motives of the proponents as being aristocratic. Private, secret marriage contracts were elevated practically to the position of offering the chief security of a democracy. It was stated that the bill, if passed, would discourage marriage among the working classes, as it would make solemnization of the ceremony so slow and expensive that many persons would prefer to remain single or to live together without marriage. The opponents climaxed their arguments by treating publicity in the forming of a marriage contract as improper and an unjustifiable violation of modesty. According to Nugent, one of those who argued against the measure, "it is certain that proclamation of banns and a public marriage ceremony is against the genius and nature of our people; and a young fellow does not like to be exposed so long beforehand to the jeers of all his companions." [7]

THE HARDWICKE ACT [8]

After a long and stormy debate the bill was finally passed by the Commons on July 6, 1753. The Hardwicke Act provided that all marriages except those of Quakers, Jews, and members of the royal family were to be solemnized only after publication of banns or the securing of a license and a ceremony performed in an Anglican church by Anglican clergymen in the presence of two or more witnesses. Parental consent was necessary for the marriage of persons under twenty-one. No license, with some exceptions, was to be issued without four weeks' residence in the parish of one of the parties. Performing marriage ceremonies in any other manner was made punishable by fourteen years transportation, and the marriages so solemnized were null and void. The clergy were required to keep registers, and the falsifying or destroying of these records was punishable by death.

Although the general effect of the Hardwicke Act was good, it created a great deal of adverse feeling since it was most intolerant toward all non-Anglicans with two exceptions. Yet every attempt to amend the statute to gain relief for the large group of non-Anglicans failed until 1836, when a bill was passed permitting civil marriage for those unwilling to accept the established rites.[9] Simultaneously, a bill was passed creating a system

---

[7] Quoted in Howard, *op. cit.*, Vol. 1, p. 458.
[8] Hardwicke Act, 1753: 26 Geo. II, c. 33.
[9] 6 and 7 Wm. IV, c. 85.

of civil registration of births, deaths, and marriages which has since functioned.[10]

These two laws and the Hardwicke Act, with a few later modifications and additions, constitute the present law of England relating to the celebration and registration of marriage. English marriage history ended, as it began, in a civil rather than a religious contract, but in a public and formal rather than in a private and informal contract. The state succeeded in imposing upon that civil contract the condition of publicity, a task which the English church earlier attempted but failed to accomplish.

DIVORCE

The Catholic church and the Church of England have historically recognized two forms of divorce, annulment and separation, only the former permitting remarriage. The common-law courts had no jurisdiction over the actual granting of divorces, but they did have jurisdiction over property rights of the persons concerned. After some wrestling with the problem, the lawyers of the common-law courts developed the principle that divorce *a vinculo* deprived the widow of her dower but that divorce *a mensa et thoro* did not. Later, under Edward I, a statute was passed which punished with the loss of dower the woman who eloped and then continued to live with her adulterer, unless her husband voluntarily received her back again and became reconciled with her. In situations of these kinds the common-law courts with their juries took it upon themselves to inquire into the facts of such elopement and adultery for the purposes of determining property rights.[11]

Though frequent efforts were made to change and reform the old Catholic ecclesiastical law of divorce, it remained in full force, except for an occasional short period, well into the nineteenth century. Henry VIII appointed a commission to compile and prepare a new body of ecclesiastical law which would be in harmony with the views of the new English church. It drew up the famous *Reformatio Legum* (Reform of Ecclesiastical Laws). By its provisions, separation from bed and board was abolished, and complete divorce was granted by the ecclesiastical courts on the grounds of adultery, desertion, absence, cruelty, an attempt upon the life of one spouse by the other, and deadly hatred between the spouses. The innocent party to a divorce could marry, but the guilty party was subjected to penalties. The consent of the parent or guardian was necessary to a valid marriage of persons of a certain age.

Although the *Reformatio Legum* reflected prevailing English Protestant opinion, it never became law. Henry died before the commission made

---

[10] *Ibid.*, c. 86.
[11] Pollock and Maitland, *op. cit.*, Vol. 2, p. 392.

a final report. Despite the fact that Edward VI, Henry's successor, ratified the report, the House of Commons refused to make it law, objecting to spiritual jurisdiction of any kind, whether by Catholic or Protestant church.[12] During the reign of Edward and for some years subsequently, divorces were granted by ecclesiastical courts in accordance with the *Reformatio Legum,* the doctrines of which were sustained in 1546 by both ecclesiastical and civil authorities in the case of Lord Northampton, who, after obtaining an ecclesiastical court separation from his first wife, contracted a second marriage. Shortly afterward a commission of delegates, headed by the archbishop of Canterbury, declared the second marriage valid because the first contract had been destroyed by the wife's infidelity. In 1559 the decision was confirmed by an act of Parliament, which declared the marriage valid "by the law of God—any decretal, canon ecclesiastical, law, or usage notwithstanding." For awhile thereafter marriages were freely contracted after obtaining a divorce from an unfaithful spouse.[13]

No one questioned the rights of the divorced parties to remarry until 1602, when the Star Chamber, in the Foljambe case, pronounced invalid a second marriage which had been contracted after a divorce *a mensa et thoro* had been obtained from an ecclesiastical court. The chamber declared that marriage was indissoluble by English law and that no court had the power to dissolve a valid marriage. A royal decree the next year revived the old canons concerning absolute indissolubility, and thereafter there could be no marriage following a decree *a mensa et thoro.* Thus, though custom had for a period established the validity of a second marriage contracted by a person who had obtained a decree *a mensa et thoro,* this decision was successful in re-establishing the old ecclesiastical law regarding the absolute indissolubility of marriage.[14]

After the decision of the Foljambe case there developed the practice of obtaining divorce by special acts of Parliament. This procedure had been suggested by previous instances of legislative intervention in matrimonial matters, as in the case of Lord Northampton, whose second marriage was declared valid by an act of Parliament. Howard, in reviewing the instances of parliamentary divorce during the entire period in which the system was in existence, found that in no case was a divorce sought without the charge of adultery. It is interesting to note that in only three or four instances were divorce acts passed upon the request of a woman, and in each of these cases infidelity on the part of the husband was attended by other offenses.

Before a parliamentary divorce could be obtained, it was necessary

---

[12] S. B. Kitchen, *A History of Divorce* (London, Chapman and Hill, 1912), pp. 175–179; Howard, *op. cit.,* Vol. 2, pp. 77–80.
[13] Howard, *op. cit.,* Vol. 2, pp. 80–81.
[14] *Ibid.,* pp. 82–84.

to secure a common-law judgment of adultery and a divorce *a mensa et thoro* from the ecclesiastical courts. Obviously the costs of securing such a divorce were prohibitive for any but the rich. The injustice of this system is illustrated by an 1845 case of a poor man who had committed bigamy. His defense was that when he married his second wife he had in reality no wife, for his first spouse had robbed and deserted him and was then living with another man. Justice Maule imposed only light penalties on the man and ironically commented: [15]

> But, prisoner, you have committed a grave offense in taking the law into your own hands and marrying again. I will now tell you what you have done. You should have brought an action into the civil court, and obtained damages, which the other side would probably have been unable to pay, and you would then have had to pay your own costs, perhaps £100 or £150. You should then have gone to the ecclesiastical court, and obtained a divorce *a mensa et thoro* and then to the House of Lords, where, having proved that these preliminaries had been complied with, you would have been enabled to marry again. The expenses might amount to 500 or 600 or perhaps £1000. You say you are a poor man, and you perhaps do not possess as many pence. But, prisoner, you must know that in England there is not one law for the rich and another for the poor.

THE ENGLISH DIVORCE ACT OF 1857 [16]

The scandal growing out of this system of divorce was finally remedied by the Divorce Act of 1857, which was furiously opposed in Parliament on religious grounds. This parliamentary action followed upon the 1853 report of the first of three royal commissions on marriage and divorce. By the act the entire jurisdiction in matrimonial matters, which had heretofore belonged to the spiritual courts, except that part of the law relating to the granting of marriage licenses, was transferred to a new civil court, "The Court for Divorce and Matrimonial Causes." The court was empowered to grant a divorce to men on account of the adultery of their wives. However, wives were not granted divorces on account of the adultery of their husbands unless such had been accompanied by cruelty. This aspect of the law was subsequently amended, and since 1923 adultery of either spouse has been a recognized ground for a divorce petition.

The 1857 law prescribed that a divorce judgment should always be a decree *nisi,* that is, it was not to be absolute until after six months. A divorced person, whether guilty or innocent, was by this law permitted to marry again; but no clergyman of the "United Church of England and Ireland" could be compelled to solemnize the marriage. Should he refuse, he could not legally prevent a brother minister from using his church for the celebration.

---

[15] Cited by William Lecky, *Democracy and Liberty* (New York, Longmans, Green, 1903), Vol. 2, pp. 201–202.

[16] 20 and 21 Vict., c. 85; Goodsell, *op. cit.,* pp. 445–455.

This law further permitted the granting of "judicial separations" to either the husband or wife on the ground of adultery, cruelty, or two year's desertion. After a separation, the wife had all the rights of a single woman with respect to the control of her property and the power to contract or sue. It also recognized what is commonly called "magisterial separation," which was a legal method for protecting a deserted wife's acquired earnings or property from seizure by her husband or by his creditors. This provision had real significance at that time, for a married woman without a separate estate had practically no property rights during her husband's entire lifetime.[17]

The following excerpt describes the attitude of many clergymen to the 1857 Divorce Act: [18]

It is a very serious aggravation of the mischief of the state that the Divorce Act has compromised the church. Nothing, indeed, can be more clear and certain than the law of the church of England. She has always consistently maintained, as the office for Holy Matrimony emphatically lays it down, that death alone can dissolve a true marriage. Yet the Act of 1857, whilst it releases any individual priest from the obligation to officiate in case of a person divorced for adultery, gives him no such exemption in the case of the "innocent party." Although the law of the Church expressly forbids a priest to accord the nuptial benediction whilst the guilty party, though separated, is still living, the state law will try to force him to do so. And what seems even more humiliating, if he himself refuses to pronounce what in such a case are "mocking words," "those whom God hath joined let no man put asunder," the Act of Parliament orders that, in the forcible words of the Report (a report of the New York Convocation, Episcopal Church) "he shall hand over his church to be desecrated and his parishioners to be scandalized by the blasphemous performance of this farce by some other minister hired for a guinea or two, if any base enough to perform it can be found." Truly the injustice and oppression of these enactments are such as we ought not endure. If left unrepealed they are certain eventually to lead—nay, they ought to lead—to most serious conflicts between Church and State, between the civil and the ecclesiastical law. . . . Those who are content to be absolved from their marriage vows by mere state intervention may surely be contented with a merely legal union, and should resort to the registrar's office.

Periodically, the English church has made efforts to adjust its doctrines to those held by the state; for example, in 1932 the convocations of Canterbury and York sanctioned the appointment of joint committees on "The Church and Marriage." It was thought by many that through this committee, the church might make a significant restatement of its position regarding divorce, but the committee's majority report in 1935 recommended no change in church doctrine regarding the nature of marriage and advised that under no circumstance should the remarriage of anyone who has a spouse still living be solemnized in the church. In 1937 the world witnessed a public discussion of this issue in the case of the mar-

---

[17] Howard, *op. cit.*, Vol. 2, pp. 104–114.

[18] Quoted from an article which appeared in the *Guardian* in 1894, by H. Luckock, *The History of Marriage* (London, Longmans, Green, 1895), pp. 238–239.

riage of the now Duke and Duchess of Windsor. The Duke, even though then King Edward VIII and nominal head of the Church of England, was, unlike Henry VIII, not able to disregard ecclesiastical law and still maintain his throne.[19]

RECENT CHANGES IN ENGLISH DIVORCE LAW

No essential change was made in the divorce law of England until 1937. Although the 1912 majority report of the Second Royal Commission on Divorce and Matrimonial Causes, appointed by Edward VII in 1909, favored increasing the grounds for divorce, providing court facilities throughout the country for divorce cases with low incomes, giving the courts power to declare marriages null and void when there was unsound mind, epilepsy, or specific disease, Parliament made no changes in the divorce law until 1923. In that year it equalized the law between men and women but did not extend the grounds for divorce. Almost annually thereafter a divorce bill proposing to reform the existing law was introduced in Parliament. Finally, in 1937, under the leadership of Alan Patrick Herbert, a reform bill was passed. Herbert, a professional writer, in his novel *Holy Deadlock,* had effectively satirized the English law of divorce. He carried to Parliament his battle against Britain's anachronistic divorce law and, in his book *The Ayes Have It,* described the bitter battle involved in securing the passage of modernized legislation. By the 1937 law, grounds for divorce by either husband or wife now include adultery, desertion for three years preceding the petition, cruelty, and unsound mind with continuous care and treatment for five years preceding the petition.[20] The wife can secure a divorce on the additional grounds that since marriage her husband has been guilty of rape, sodomy, or bestiality. A petition for divorce cannot be presented to the High Court at the date of prosecution unless three years have passed since marriage.

In 1951 King George VI appointed the Third Royal Commission on Marriage and Divorce, whose 300,000-word, 405-page report was not issued until 1956.[21] The commission recommended a slight easing of Britain's divorce laws. The unanimous recommendations included three new grounds for divorce:

1. Willful refusal by a spouse to consummate the marriage (previously a ground for nullity).
2. Acceptance by a wife of artificial insemination by a donor without her husband's consent.

---

[19] "The King, The Cabinet, and The People," *The Political Quarterly* (January–March, 1937), pp. 1–6; "The Church and Divorce," *The Spectator* (June 14, 1935), pp. 1005–1006.

[20] 1 Edw. VIII and 1 Geo. VI, c. 57; see also, Hansard's *Parliamentary Debates* (London, 1886), Vol. 307, col. 135, no. 5.

[21] "Easing Divorce Urged in Britain," *New York Times* (March 21, 1956); *Royal Commission on Marriage and Divorce Report: 1951–55,* Cmd. 9678 (London, Her Majesty's Stationery Office, 1956).

3. The fact that a spouse is a mental defective who has been continuously detained for five years and whose recovery from violent or dangerous propensities is improbable.

The commission split on the question of whether divorce should be granted on the ground that both parties to a marriage agreed it had irretrievably broken down. Except for one dissenting vote, the commission agreed that grounds for divorce should be limited to matrimonial offenses, thus excluding such factors as incompatability. In other words, the commission rejected the doctrine of "breakdown of marriage" and retained that of "matrimonial offense." Measures to equalize treatment of men and women in divorce proceedings, including the proposal that men receive the right to ask alimony, was unanimously approved. The commission warned that there is real danger that the conception of marriage as a lifelong union of one man and one woman may be abandoned. It reported that the number of marriages in England and Wales ending in divorce had increased from .2 per cent in 1911 to 6.7 per cent in 1954. There were about 640 divorces in England and Wales in 1911 against 27,471 in 1954. The real remedy against divorce lies in broad education, which would heighten the individuals' sense of responsibility toward marriage and the community. What Parliament will do with the proposals of the royal commission remains to be seen.

THE LEGAL POSITION OF WOMEN

In few societies have women been legally equal to men.[22] Married women have often been at even more of a disadvantage than their unmarried sisters, or *femmes soles.* The sphere of married women has generally been considered the home, where she was expected to be subservient to her husband and to the father of her children but where it was her duty to assume responsibility for the development and preservation of peace and harmony.

Sometimes women, married and unmarried, through their salons, their personal associations, and their writings have achieved notable fame. Fannie Burney, Mary Wollstonecraft, Hannah More, Fanny Kemble, Caroline Norton, Elizabeth Barrett Browning, and Marian Evans, better known as George Eliot—all English women of the eighteenth and nineteenth centuries—exerted great influence over various phases of the life of the times, despite the fact that their legal position was inferior. Less

[22] "Legal Position of Women," *Encyclopaedia Brittanica* (1952), Vol. 23, pp. 704–708; Edward F. Donovan, "Legal Rights of Women," *Encyclopedia Americana* (1951), Vol. 29, pp. 457–458; Louise M. Young, ed., *Annals of the American Academy of Political and Social Science: Women's Opportunities and Responsibilities,* Vol. 251 (May, 1947); U.S. Department of Labor, Women's Bureau, *Women's Bureau Conference: The American Woman, Her Changing Role* (Washington, D.C., G.P.O., 1948), Bull. No. 224.

than a hundred years ago the English wife had few legal rights. Today women, including married women, in both England and the United States, have approximately equal legal rights with men.

Although unmarried women often have had a legal status unequal to that of their fathers and brothers, the greatest inequalities, at least in English law, have been those of married women. The English law pertaining to married women was a relic of the feudal period. As the military tenure of land became common, woman's position declined, due to the fact that the fighting services of men were more needed and hence more valuable than the domestic services of women. Also, suitors of noble women often performed feudal services for their fathers to obtain the dowry, and, having married the daughters, maintained that they had earned rights to the property.[23] This meant that in time married women lost their legal identity in that of their husbands.

Blackstone described the position of married women which had existed from feudal times as follows: "By marriage, the husband and wife are one person in law; that is, the very being or legal existence of the woman is suspended during the marriage, or at least is incorporated or consolidated into that of her husband, under whose wing, protection and cover she performs everything." [24] This legal unity persisted until the late nineteenth century. The great body of principles governing the relation of husband and wife, including property rights, is found in the decisions of the common-law courts. With the twelfth century, and for several centuries thereafter, the ecclesiastical courts, upon the death of one of the parties, determined the rights of succession to personal property; but the common-law courts determined the rights of inheritance to real property.[25] Let us see what some of these rights of husbands and wives were.

THE WIFE'S LAND [26]

Early in its history the English law rejected the principle of community ownership of the family property. It preferred to place the ownership of particular property with particular individuals, although it did later work out legal theories whereby persons could own land in common with others or jointly with others. Marriage had an effect upon the lands which the wife held in *fee simple* [27] before and after matrimony; the husband

---

[23] Goodsell, *op. cit.*, pp. 224 ff.

[24] Sir William Blackstone, *Commentaries on the Laws of England in Four Books* (Philadelphia, Rees, Welsh and Co., 1897), Bk. 1, ch. 15, p. 442.

[25] Pollock and Maitland, *op. cit.*, Vol. 2, p. 339.

[26] *Ibid.*, pp. 399 ff.; W. S. Holdsworth, *A History of English Law* (London, Methuen, 1923), Vol. 3, pp. 525 ff.

[27] A freehold estate of inheritance, absolute and unqualified; the owner is entitled to the entire property, with unconditional power of disposition during his lifetime and descending to his legal heirs upon his death intestate, *Black's Law Dictionary*, 3d ed. (1933), p. 761.

acquired an estate which lasted throughout the period of the marriage. This estate gave him the right to enjoy rents and profits of the land, and, moreover, he could alienate these profits without his wife's concurrence. If a child were born to them, the husband became a *tenant by the curtesy*, that is he had an estate which endured for the whole of his life, and he was also given the right to alienate this interest without the consent of his wife. The wife, however, during the continuance of the marriage had no power to convey her own land without her husband's consent. Though the husband was given wide powers over the land and the wife was denied the same, he was never considered as being solely seised of the land but rather seised in the right of the wife. Where there was a lawsuit concerning the wife's land, both husband and wife were required to be before the court, and a default of one of them was equivalent to the default of both.

THE WIFE'S CHATTELS

The husband's right over the wife's personal property was almost unlimited. After the close of the thirteenth century the common law put the absolute property in the wife's chattels with the husband. He was entitled to take them into his own possession and alienate them if he wished. He was privileged to sue for all debts owed to her, and he could do this without her concurrence. Whatever he brought under his control became his absolutely, and he could dispose of it during his lifetime or by will. Upon his death, the wife became entitled to all personal property and debts owed to him which he had not reduced to his possession. The wife's paraphernalia, that is her dress and personal ornaments, ordinarily survived to her, unless the husband had alienated them. She was not permitted to make a will without his consent.

THE WIFE'S RIGHT TO CONTRACT AND TO DOWER [28]

The married woman could not contract in her own behalf. This disability was not a personal one but was based on the idea that she had no property that she could deal with freely. It was not permissible for her to perform duties of a legal character. She could not act as the executor of an estate; nor could she act as an agent for her husband. It was her right, however, to pledge her husband's credit to procure necessaries for the household. The common-law principle was well defined that if a husband wrongfully deserted his wife and left her without means of support, she became his "agent of necessity" and could pledge his credit for necessaries.

The widow's right to dower at common law seems to have grown out

---

[28] Holdsworth, *op. cit.*, Vol. 3, pp. 528–530; Pollock and Maitland, *op. cit.*, Vol. 2, pp. 432–433.

of the custom whereby the bridegroom endowed his bride with a gift at the church door. He might endow her with particular lands, but if no particular lands were bestowed, he endowed her with one third of the land in his possession at the time of the espousal. In the early days the dower rights did not include lands which the husband acquired after marriage, but during the thirteenth century the wife's right was extended to include all the land of which he was possessed during his lifetime, unless she accepted less at the church door. Later, the law provided that she was entitled to one third of the lands of which her husband had been seised in fee at any time during the continuance of the wedded state. This became the settled view of the common law.

THE HUSBAND'S PROPERTY RIGHTS [29]

In respect to all his own lands, the husband had the right to appear in court alone. This was true, even though the lands were subject to the wife's right of dower. After the twelfth century it became well settled that he could not convey good title to his land without his wife's consent. If he did convey it to a third person without having her join in the execution of the deed, the grantee from the husband held the land subject to the wife's dower rights, which she could enforce against the land upon the death of her husband. The common law did not assure any part of the husband's personal property to the widow. He could bequeath it all away from her by will; he could sell it all during his lifetime, and after his death it could be taken for his debts.

Another property advantage that accrued to the husband was his right to a tenancy by the curtesy. This right arose where a man married a woman who owned lands in fee simple and had by her a child who was born alive and who was capable of being her heir. If these requirements concurred, then upon the death of his wife it was his privilege to hold her lands for the duration of his life as a tenant by the curtesy. This right, once it had attached, endured even though the child later died or became of age and even though the husband married a second time. This very liberal right was based on the theory that the father had the duty to support the child and that he ought to have the profits of the wife's land to aid him in that duty.

THE HUSBAND'S LIABILITY [30]

Although the husband at common law had many advantages over his wife in relation to property, he also had to assume certain liabilities. While the marriage lasted, he was liable to the whole extent of his

---

[29] Pollock and Maitland, *op. cit.*, Vol. 2, p. 421; Blackstone, *Commentaries*, Vol. 2, p. 126.

[30] Pollock and Maitland, *op. cit.*, Vol. 2, pp. 402–403.

property for the debts incurred by his wife and the wrongs committed by her before and after marriage. If a third party wished to recover for injuries committed by the wife, he had to bring the action against both husband and wife as codefendants. After the death of the husband, his estate was no longer liable for his wife's wrongs, and she became liable alone. After her death, the husband became liable for her wrongs as her administrator but only to the extent of the property that came into his possession as her administrator.

EARLY PROTECTION GIVEN BY EQUITY COURTS

By the eighteenth century an English matron through the chancery courts had greatly enlarged personal and property rights. The unmarried woman received little legal attention during the period of medieval history; apparently she could manage her personal property as could a male. In order to assure the benefactor, usually the father, that gifts to a woman before or after marriage were hers and not her husband's, the practice of appointing a trustee for her protection was developed in the equity court. The result was that the property especially designated for the use of the wife and under the management of a trustee became her separate property and was not subject to the wishes or actions of her husband.

Although a married woman could thus deal freely with her separate property, it was often possible for a husband to get property away from his wife by persuasion. To offset this possibility, it became customary to introduce into marriage settlements a clause known as the *restraint on anticipation* which made it impossible for a woman during her married life to alienate property settled on her or to charge it with debts. Consequently, even though a married woman could not exercise full rights as an owner of property, she was protected against anyone desiring to take her separate property from her. In respect to her separate property, a married woman was in equity almost in the same position as an unmarried woman. Her contractual and testamentary capacities, however, were limited to her separate property.

This situation created inequality between the position of the poor and rich. Women with marriage settlements, usually women from well-to-do families, could retain ownership of all property possessed by them at the time of their marriage or acquired after marriage. On the other hand, women who married without a settlement, usually working-class women, were deprived of any small amount of property which they might acquire and, more important, of their earnings. This condition of inequality between rich and poor woman continued until the nineteenth century.

MARRIED WOMEN'S RIGHTS BY STATUTE

Few efforts were made, except through equity, to remedy the position of all married women with respect to personal and real property until after the middle of the nineteenth century. As the number of married women employed in the new factory system increased, the injustice of their legal position concerning their person, property, and earnings attracted public attention. The Divorce Act of 1857 guaranteed the property rights of a deserted wife, but nothing was done by Parliament for all married women until the passage in 1870 of the first Married Woman's Property Act.[31] The bill was most unsatisfactory; instead of placing a married woman in the position of a *femme sole,* the statute, based upon the principles of equity with regard to separate property of married women, merely secured for every married woman as her separate property her earnings and certain investments.

This halfway measure can be explained by the fact that though considerable objection existed in Parliament to a complete change in the legal position of woman in relation to her property, opposition did not extend to a statute that did no more than give to every married woman the same rights that some married women acquired under a marriage settlement. In addition, wealthy members of Parliament were unwilling to give up the techniques used in the courts of equity to protect the fortunes of well-to-do women against fortune-seeking husbands. Such protection would have been abolished had a statute been passed placing all married women in the position of *femmes soles* with regard to their property. An act, passed in 1882, made *all* the property of a married woman her separate property.[32] Since that date, married women of England have been able to hold and dispose of all of their real and personal property as freely as single women.

MOTHER AND CHILD AT COMMON LAW

The English married woman, legally dominated by her husband, was also subordinate to him in regard to their children. Although the father had extensive rights concerning his children, he at no time possessed the *patria potestas* of the Roman father. The infant was subject to special disabilities, but he was also accorded many privileges. A legitimate child, in contrast with the "bastard," had extensive personal and property rights. During the nineteenth century, when legislation for the benefit of women, both rich and poor, was passed, many new theories concerning the rights of mothers and of children in relation to each other were incorporated into statutes. This is a story for another chapter.

---

[31] 33 and 34 Vict., c. 93.
[32] 45 and 46 Vict., c. 75.

The position of women in the United States has never been so unfavorable as in England, although many of the same restrictions did exist and many of the same common-law theories were applied. By legislation, constitutional enactment, and judicial decision most of these legal handicaps have been removed. In the field of labor law there is a considerable body of legislation which discriminates in favor of women.[33] Many women's and labor organizations favor such protection. The main argument of these groups is based upon the biological characteristics of women. Those groups opposed to preferential legislation for women, particularly the National Woman's Party, are strong proponents for an equal rights amendment to the Constitution providing that "Equality of rights under the law shall not be denied or abridged by the United States or by any state on account of sex." Their main argument stems from their belief that women can and do perform the same functions as men and, like men, should be permitted to bargain for themselves. When in 1920 the Nineteenth Amendment to the federal Constitution was finally ratified by the required three fourths of the states, women were in the same position as men to select their governmental servants and hence to affect public policy.[34] That amendment reads: "Rights of citizens of the United States to vote shall not be denied or abridged by the United States or by any state on account of sex."

According to a memorandum issued by the secretary general of the United Nations, of eighty countries polled in 1954 only sixteen still withheld all political rights from women. The lands in which women could neither vote nor hold office were Afghanistan, Cambodia, Egypt, Ethiopia, Honduras, Iran, Iraq, Jordan, Laos, Libya, Liechtenstein, Nicaragua, Paraguay, Saudi Arabia, Switzerland, and Yemen. Twenty-four governments have granted either full or limited voting rights to women since the United Nations Charter was signed in 1945.[35]

The above abbreviated statement of the legal status of women at common law and by statute is included, along with a somewhat longer review of marriage and divorce developments in the ancient and modern western world, so that the reader may have an over-all view of the evolution of family law. It is not our intent in succeeding chapters to review further the American history of the legal status of women.

---

[33] "Women in Industry," *Encyclopaedia of the Social Sciences* (1934), Vol. 15, pp. 451–459; Margaret Perry Bruton, "Present-Day Thinking on the Woman Question," *Annals of the American Academy of Political and Social Science*, Vol. 251 (May, 1947), pp. 10–16; U.S. Department of Labor, Women's Bureau, *State Laws of Special Value to Women: January 1, 1950* (Washington, D.C., G.P.O., 1950); "The Legal Status of Women," *The Book of the States: 1954–55* (Chicago, Council of State Governments, 1955), Vol. 10, pp. 319–322.

[34] Dorothy Kenyon, "Woman Suffrage," *Encyclopedia Americana* (1951), Vol. 29, pp. 445–456.

[35] *New York Times* (August 28, 1954); see also, Dorothy Kenyon, "United Nations Commission on Status of Women," 33 Women Law. J. 37–44 (1947).

SUMMARY AND CONCLUSIONS

In the last two chapters we have reviewed some of the customs and laws of several societies pertaining to the family. It has been our purpose, first, to show how regulations affecting the family grow out of a particular culture and in turn contribute to the making of that culture; second, to indicate that family law responds to the needs and pressures of the time, often with a notable cultural lag; and, third, to place American family law in an historical setting, since so much of present-day belief and practice is rooted in this history.[36]

The greatest *single* influence upon family custom and law in the occidental world has been Christianity, at first through the disciples and their followers, then the Catholic church, and, later, through other denominations also. In its early days the church was largely responsible for the abatement of the mutilations and cruelties, indecencies and immoralities of the Roman world. It incorporated the concept of the sacredness of marriage into its doctrine and practice. Since marriage was a sacred institution and a man and a woman were made husband and wife through God's blessing, there could be no separation in order to permit remarriage if the first marriage was valid. Luther believed that marriage was holy, but he upset the idea of its sacramental nature and did not consider women the tools of the devil nor sex indecent. Marriage and divorce legislation today reflects in varying degrees the influences of Christianity as interpreted primarily by the Catholic church, the Church of England, and those Protestant groups which still derive their attitudes toward marriage and family from the period of the Reformation.

The basic changes in family law observed in this and the preceding chapter can be summarized as follows:

1. The informal and private marriage contract has been replaced by the formal and public contract.
2. In primitive days the community recognized the civil marriage ceremony; later the church, with the inclusion of marriage among the sacraments, favored the church ceremony. In modern times, with separation of church and state and the increase of sects and denominations, the civil ceremony is again recognized, and either an ecclesiastical or civil ceremony is legal.
3. For centuries the church attempted and to a considerable degree succeeded in regulating the conditions for entry into matrimony. What the church at one time had almost exclusive jurisdiction over, the state now regulates through licensing, solemnization, recording procedures, and civil court processes.
4. The dissolution of marriage, especially if there are children, has always been frowned upon. The church refused to permit remarriage after a valid first

[36] William F. Ogburn, "The Changing Functions of the Family," in Judson T. Landis and Mary G. Landis, eds., *Readings in Marriage and the Family* (Englewood Cliffs, N.J., Prentice-Hall, 1952), pp. 18–21; Ernest W. Burgess, "The Family in a Changing Society," in Landis and Landis, *op. cit.*, pp. 21–26.

marriage, although at one time it freely permitted annulments, after which remarriage could take place. In the last several centuries both the Catholic church and the Church of England have persistently fought efforts to liberalize divorce provisions. With great variation between American jurisdictions, divorce is now generally granted, at least for adultery, desertion, and cruelty by either spouse.

5. As the position of woman has become economically more important, her legal position has changed. In democratic countries she generally has the same right to dispose of her property and her earnings as her father, brother, or husband; her person is hers and not her husband's; and she is equally entitled with her husband to the custody and control of their children. She encounters considerable protective legislation in the labor field. She has the same rights as the male to vote and hence to select her public servants.

The student of society is thoroughly aware that many activities formerly performed by the family are today carried on by other private and public agencies and institutions. The economic, status-giving, educational, protective, religious, and recreational functions are performed, in considerable part, by industry, public schools, the church, and commercial recreation. The affectional function remains the primary responsibility of the family, as no adequate substitute has been found for marital and parental love. This means that legislative bodies have the responsibility of enacting laws to protect individuals and families for the ultimate benefit both of themselves and of the state, and judges have the obligation to interpret the law so as to achieve the results intended in a democracy. Hence, legislation is needed which, among other things, prevents the formation of undesirable families and the hasty dissolution of families; protects the members of the family and their relationships; and provides administrative and supervisory services for the protection of individuals and of the state.

Selected References

ANSCHEN, Ruth N., ed., *The Family: Its Function and Destiny* (New York, Harper, 1949).

BLACKSTONE, Sir William, *Commentaries on the Laws of England in Four Books* (Philadelphia, Rees, Welsh and Co., 1897), Bk. 1, ch. 15.

BOSSARD, J. H. S., ed., *Annals of the American Academy of Political and Social Science: Toward Family Stability*, Vol. 272 (November, 1950).

BURGESS, Ernest W., and COTTRELL, Leonard S., Jr., *Predicting Success or Failure in Marriage* (Englewood Cliffs, N.J., Prentice-Hall, 1939).

———, and LOCKE, Harvey J., *The Family from Institution to Companionship* (New York, American Book Co., 1945).

———, and WALLIN, Paul, *Engagement and Marriage* (Philadelphia, Lippincott, 1953).

ELLIS, Albert, and DOORBAR, Ruth R., "Classified Bibliography of Articles, Books, and Pamphlets on Sex, Love, Marriage, and Family Relations, Published During 1952," *Marriage and Family Living*, Vol. 15, No. 2 (May, 1953), 156–175.

GOODSELL, Willystine, *A History of Marriage and the Family* (New York, Macmillan, 1934).

GROVES, Ernest R., SKINNER, Edna L., and SWENSON, Sadie J., *The Family and Its Relationships* (Philadelphia, Lippincott, 1948).

HARPER, Fowler V., *Problems of the Family* (Indianapolis, Bobbs-Merrill, 1952).

HILL, Reuben, *Families under Stress* (New York, Harper, 1949).

———, and DUVALL, Evelyn, *When You Marry* (Boston, Heath, 1953).

HOLDSWORTH, W. S., *A History of English Law* (London, Methuen, 1923).

HOWARD, George Eliot, *A History of Matrimonial Institutions* (Chicago, University of Chicago Press, 1904).

LANDIS, Judson T., and LANDIS, Mary G., eds., *Readings in Marriage and the Family* (Englewood Cliffs, N.J., Prentice-Hall, 1952).

LECKY, William, *History of European Morals from Augustus to Charlemagne* (New York, D. Appleton, 1906).

LICHTENBERGER, James P., *Divorce* (New York, McGraw-Hill, 1931).

MACKAY, Richard V., and MANDELL, Irving, *Law of Marriage and Divorce Simplified*, 2d ed. (New York, Oceana, 1951).

National Council on Family Relations, *Marriage and Family Living* (quarterly).

POLLOCK, Sir Frederick, and MAITLAND, F. W., *The History of English Law before the Time of Edward I* (Cambridge, University Press, 1923).

QUEEN, Stuart, and ADAMS, John B., *The Family in Various Cultures* (Philadelphia, Lippincott, 1952).

Royal Commission on Marriage and Divorce Report: 1951–1955, Cmd. 9678 (London, Her Majesty's Stationery Office, 1956).

SMITH, William, and CHEETHAM, Samuel, eds., *Dictionary of Christian Antiquities* (Hartford, J. Burr Publishing Co., 1880), 2 vols.

TRUXAL, Andrew G., and MERRILL, Francis E., *The Family in American Culture* (Englewood Cliffs, N.J., Prentice-Hall, 1947).

U.S. Interagency Committee on Background Materials for the National Conference on Family Life, *The American Family: A Factual Background* (Washington, D.C., G.P.O., 1949).

U.S. National Office of Vital Statistics, *Summary of Marriage and Divorce Statistics, U.S.: 1950.* Vital Stat. Spec. Repts., Nat'l. Summaries: 1952, Vol. 37, No. 3 (Washington, D.C., G.P.O., 1952).

VERNIER, Chester G., *American Family Laws* (Stanford, Cal., Stanford University Press, 1931).

WESTERMARCK, Edward, *A Short History of Marriage* (New York, Macmillan, 1926).

YOUNG, Louise M., ed., *Annals of the American Academy of Political and Social Science: Women's Opportunities and Responsibilities*, Vol. 251 (May, 1947).

ZIMMERMAN, Carle C., *Family and Civilization* (New York, Harper, 1947).

———, *The Family of Tomorrow* (New York, Harper, 1949).

The student should also consult the Bible and the following encyclopedias: *Catholic Encyclopedia, Encyclopedia Americana, Encyclopaedia Brittanica,* and *Encyclopaedia of the Social Sciences.*

CHAPTER 4

Marriage in American Jurisdictions I

WHAT IS MARRIAGE?

Attitudes toward and customs affecting marriage, divorce, and the family from one country or state to another and from one period to another were presented in the preceding two chapters. In this and the next two chapters it is our purpose to review the high spots of American marriage and divorce legislation and judicial decision. It is impossible to state a simple American law of marriage and divorce, since no two states are in agreement. It is possible and feasible, however, to summarize some of the present provisions of statutes, their similarities and dissimilarities, to refer to leading cases, to indicate trends in family law, and to emphasize points where change seems desirable.

CONCEPTS AND DEFINITIONS [1]

Courts and legislatures have met with much difficulty in defining marriage since it may be looked upon as a contract, a status, a relationship, or an institution. It is important to know what its nature is, for many legal rights and duties are dependent upon a definition. Blackstone, in his treatise on the common law, considered marriage a "civil contract." He pointed out that the law treated marriage as it did all other contracts and permitted it to be good where the parties were willing, able, and did contract. What the courts seem to mean when they describe marriage as a contract is that for the marriage to be binding in law upon the parties, numbers of the same requisites are necessary as in the case of an

---

[1] Chester G. Vernier and others, *American Family Laws* (Stanford, Cal., Stanford University Press, 1931–1938), Vol. 1, with 1938 suppl.; John W. Morland, *Keezer on the Law of Marriage and Divorce,* 3d ed. (Indianapolis, Bobbs-Merrill, 1946), with suppl. to 1950; "Marriage," 35 Am. Jur. (with cumulative suppl. to 1952) 173–381; "Marriage," 55 C.J.S. 804–954; Joseph W. Madden, *Persons and Domestic Relations* (St. Paul, Minn., West Publishing Co., 1931); James W. Schouler, *Marriage, Divorce, Separation, and Domestic Relations,* 6th ed. (Albany, N.Y., Matthew Bender and Co., 1921), Vols. 1 and 2; Morris Ploscowe, *Sex and the Law* (Englewood Cliffs, N.J., Prentice-Hall, 1951), ch. 1; Harriet F. Pilpel and Theodora Zavin, *Your Marriage and The Law* (New York, Rinehart, 1952); Fowler V. Harper, *Problems of the Family* (Indianapolis, Bobbs-Merrill, 1952).

ordinary contract. There must be an offer and an acceptance, a consent or a meeting of minds, and a consideration or the promise to perform various duties and obligations—all elements of a contract, which are as necessary to establish a valid marriage as they are to consummate a binding business contract.

The Missouri Supreme Court has said that marriage may be defined as the civil status of one man and one woman, capable of contracting, united by contract and mutual consent for life, for the discharge to each other and to the community of the duties legally incumbent on those whose association is founded on the distinction of sex.[2] The Indiana Supreme Court has defined it to be a union of one man and one woman to the exclusion of all others, so long as they both shall live, by an obligation which they cannot by their own will dissolve, but which can be severed only by the authority of the state.[3]

A famous Utah case, which denied Mormons the right to practice polygamy, definitely emphasized that in our civilization and under our law the distinguishing feature of marriage is that it is a relation that can exist between only one man and one woman at any one time, and that once a man and woman have taken each other as husband and wife, they are possessed of something more than a private covenant.[4] They are in a new relationship and they have acquired a new status which can be changed only by the state itself.

From time to time our courts have shown how marriage differs from an ordinary contract and have indicated when it is not to be considered as such. This idea is expressed in an early opinion of the Supreme Court of Maine: [5]

> When the contracting parties have entered into the married state, they have not so much entered into a contract as into a new relation, the rights, duties, and obligations of which rest not upon their agreement, but upon the general law of the state, statutory or common, which defines and prescribes those rights, duties, and obligations. They are of law, not of contract. It was of contract that the relation should be established, but, being established, the power of the parties, as to their extent or duration, is at an end. Their rights under it are determined by the will of the sovereign as evidenced by law. . . .
>
> It is not then a contract. . . . It is rather a social relation, like that of parent and child, the obligations of which arise not from the consent of concurring minds—but are the creation of the law itself.

An early New York decision recognized that marriage, though a civil contract for certain purposes, was not consequently synonymous with "contract" as employed in the common law or statutes. The court reasoned that marriage more nearly resembled an "institution" regulated and controlled by public authority upon the principles of public policy

---

[2] *State* v. *Bittick*, 103 Mo. 183, 15 S.W. 325 (1891).
[3] *Rocke* v. *Washington*, 19 Ind. 53, 81 Am. Dec. 376 (1862).
[4] *Riddle* v. *Riddle*, 26 Utah 268, 72 Pac. 1081 (1903).
[5] *Adams* v. *Palmer*, 51 Me. 480 (1863).

for the welfare of the community.[6] The United States Supreme Court, in the leading case of *Maynard* v. *Hill,* held that marriage is not an ordinary contract.[7] In that case, the Oregon territorial legislature had granted a divorce to one, Maynard, by a private legislative act. It was claimed that under the Constitution the legislature had no right to impair the obligations of the marriage contract. The Court held otherwise and in substance said: marriage is not a contract within the meaning of the prohibition of the federal Constitution against the impairment of contracts by state legislatures; the types of contracts sought to be protected by this clause are contracts by which perfect rights, certain, definite, and fixed private rights of property, are vested. The Court further observed that when text writers, courts, and legislatures termed marriage a "civil contract" they did so for the purpose of pointing out that it was a civil and not a religious institution and that a religious ceremony was not necessary for its solemnization.

Although a marriage contract resembles a private contract, there are several ways in which it materially differs:

1. Once the relation has been established, the parties cannot by their own voluntary acts change or rescind it. It becomes a legal status that can be severed only by laws and acts of the state itself; whereas in the case of the private contract, the parties can modify or restrict it, enlarge it, or entirely release it by their mutual acts and consents.
2. Tests of capacity to contract marriage differ from those applied to ordinary contracts. Thus, infants who may not make a binding contract in the business world may enter into a valid marriage above certain age limits.
3. Most private contracts do not result in relationships which become permanent upon the making of the agreement, as they can be severed by the acts and consent of the parties without the consent of the state.

In the private contract the parties can specify the length of time the agreement shall endure, and they can state in advance the conditions under which it shall terminate. In the marriage contract the parties cannot agree in advance that the marriage shall continue for a specified time or so long as the parties shall find it agreeable; nor can they agree upon certain damages which shall go to the injured party if they separate. It was so held in a Colorado case. A doctor and a woman agreed to enter into the relationship of marriage and remain married so long as it was satisfactory to both parties and to their mutual happiness. They stipulated that at any time they wished, they could separate on the condition that the husband pay the wife one hundred dollars per year for each year that they remained together and such payment was to release the husband from any further liability. The court held that the agreement was void as against public policy and said: [8]

---

[6] *Wade* v. *Kalbfleisch,* 58 N.Y. 282 (1874).
[7] 125 U.S. 190, 8 Sup. Ct. 723 (1887).
[8] Estate of Duncan, *Popham* v. *Duncan,* 87 Colo. 149, 285 Pac. 757 (1930).

The antenuptial contract was a wicked device to evade the laws applicable to marriage relations, property rights, and divorces, and is clearly against public policy and decency. It was nothing more, in effect, than an attempt, on the part of the deceased, in whose favor the contract was drawn, to legalize prostitution under the name of marriage, at the price of $100 per year. It was the establishing of a companionate marriage, to exist only so long as neither party objected to a continuance.

About half the states have express statutes relating to the nature of marriage.[9] A considerable number of these jurisdictions declare it to be a "civil contract"; several call it a "personal relation growing out of a civil contract."

COMMON-LAW MARRIAGE IN ENGLAND AND THE UNITED STATES

COMMON-LAW MARRIAGE IN ENGLAND

Marriage in the United States today is largely regulated by statute, but in so far as it is not, the English common law prevails. Common-law marriage, as we learned in the preceding chapter, did not depend for its validity upon any religious or civil ceremony but could be entered into by the mere consent of the parties. If, at the time of making the contract, the parties were willing to contract, able to contract, and did contract in the proper forms required by law, the marriage was recognized as valid and binding in the eyes of the courts.

As a general proposition, all persons are able to enter into the marriage contract unless they are under some particular disability or incapacity. At common law these disabilities were of two sorts: (1) those which were canonical and which were sufficient under the canon law to invalidate the marriage in the church courts, and (2) those which can be classed as legal disabilities. Blackstone pointed out that canonical disabilities made the marriage voidable but not *ipso facto* void in the common-law temporal courts.[10] They were not treated as void in the common-law courts until a specific decree of nullity had been issued. Disabilities of this character included precontract, consanguinity or relation by blood, affinity or relation by marriage, and certain corporal infirmities.

Legal disabilities rendered an attempted marriage void *ab initio* and not merely voidable. If any persons attempted to unite in marriage under these legal incapacities, the union was meretricious. A type of legal disability was *prior marriage,* that is, having another husband or wife living. This rendered a second marriage absolutely void for all purposes.

---

[9] Morland, *op. cit.,* p. 7; Vernier, *op. cit.,* Vol. 1, p. 51.

[10] Sir William Blackstone, *Commentaries on the Laws of England in Four Books* (Philadelphia, Rees, Welsh and Co., 1897), Bk. 1, pp. 434–436.

Want of age was another form of legal disability and was sufficient to avoid all other contracts because of the immaturity of the judgment of the parties. For the same reason it was also sufficient to avoid marriage contracts. The age of capacity for boys at common law was fourteen, and for girls, twelve. They could consent to marry at an age as early as seven, but such a marriage was imperfect and inchoate and could be avoided by the parties when they reached the ages of twelve and fourteen. This they could do without any pronouncement of divorce in the spiritual courts. In the strict common law, however, if the parties married below the age of consent and then continued to live together after reaching that age, there was no necessity to remarry for the original marriage was affirmed.

A third kind of legal disability was *want of consent of the parents.* At both the canon and the common law if the parties themselves were above the age of consent, no further concurrence on the part of anyone was necessary. Later, by statute, a female child under a specified age could not marry without the consent of her parents, and the man who took her in marriage without such consent was subject to a fine.

Finally, *want of reason* presented the fourth type of legal disability. If either of the parties did not possess the requisite amount of reason, the attempted marriage was absolutely void. Blackstone's justification for this rule was that the persons concerned were unable to exercise proper judgment in choosing their mates and in making the decision to be joined in marriage, and not that they lacked the physical and mental capacity to carry on the relationship.

Not only must the parties be *willing* and *able* to contract, but they must contract in the forms and with the solemnities recognized by law. We have already seen how under both the ecclesiastical and the common law a simple private contract of marriage was valid and binding. Contracts made *per verba de praesenti* and *per verba de futuro* were recognized as valid. We must remember, however, that for the purpose of determining the right to dower and the right of children to inherit land, the common-law courts required more than did the ecclesiastical courts in the way of publicity so that the community might know the true relationship of the parties. Nevertheless, marriages *de praesenti* and *de futuro* were recognized in England down to the passage of the Hardwicke Act, which did not apply to the English colonies beyond the seas or to Ireland and Scotland where the common-law marriage remained valid for many years afterward. This situation brought to the English courts on appeal from lower Scotch and Irish jurisdictions those cases involving issues of the validity of common-law marriages.

Though Blackstone laid down with a certain positiveness what had been a valid common-law marriage, the English temporal courts were not so positive in their pronouncements. In fact, by the middle of the nineteenth century the English House of Lords, acting in the capacity of an appellate court, injected both confusion and misunderstanding into what was believed to have been the law before the passage of the Hardwicke Act.

The English ecclesiastical courts seem to have had no serious difficulty in deciding what was required to constitute a valid marriage before the act of 1753. The reader should recall that the church courts retained jurisdiction over all matrimonial questions until after 1857. More than fifty years after the Hardwicke Act went into effect, one of the higher English church courts had the opportunity to review and restate the old marriage law. In the celebrated case of *Dalrymple* v. *Dalrymple,* heard in the consistory court of London in 1811, the ecclesiastical judges had to determine the validity of a Scotch marriage *per verba de praesenti,* which had not been celebrated by or in the presence of a priest "in orders." [11] The judges, after a careful survey of the canon law, held in a lengthy opinion that a marriage *per verba de praesenti* was valid at the old canon law of England and Scotland. They admitted, however, that the common-law courts required more than words of the present tense to establish a marriage on which real property rights were to be based.

In spite of this decision, the English House of Lords seems to have reached an historically incorrect result when the same question came before it in 1843 in the case of *Regina* v. *Millis.*[12] That case involved the validity of a marriage in Ireland in which the ceremony was performed by a Presbyterian minister, not a priest in orders, and the parties entered a present contract of marriage. The husband of this marriage later went to England and married again. In 1842 he was indicted for bigamy; but on appeal the House of Lords found him not guilty of the charge, since the first marriage was not valid because a union of present consent was not a full and complete marriage unless made in the presence and with the intervention of a minister in holy orders. Thus, according to this decision, that which had been the common law for centuries was not to be the common law. The House of Lords had an opportunity to correct the decision in 1861, but it chose to follow the principle of *stare decisis* and held to the ruling of the Millis case.[13]

COLONIAL MARRIAGE CUSTOMS AND REGULATIONS [14]

The early colonists brought with them their family customs and law. The New Englanders brought the ideas and doctrines of the Reformation; the southern colonists, those of the Church of England; and the middle

[11] 2 Hagg. Const. 54, 161 Eng. Rep. 665 (1811).

[12] 10 Clark and Finnelly 532, 8 Eng. Rep. 844 (1843).

[13] *Beamish* v. *Beamish,* 9 H. of L. 274, 11 Eng. Rep. 735 (1861).

[14] George Eliot Howard, *A History of Matrimonial Institutions* (Chicago, University of Chicago Press, 1904), Vol. 2, pp. 121–238; Arthur W. Calhoun, *A Social History of the American Family* (Cleveland, Ohio, Arthur H. Clark Co., 1917), Vol. 1.

colonists, those of several different countries. In the middle colonies the customs of the Dutch, who came from Holland, where optional civil marriage had been sanctioned since 1658, and the simple religious ceremony of the Quakers were equally acceptable. Naturally, the customs and law brought to the colonies did not long remain unchanged; the pioneer environment necessitated changes, and the very isolation of the new world afforded an opportunity to reform or even discard outworn traditions.

EARLY MARRIAGE LAWS IN NEW ENGLAND [15]

From the very beginning of the settlement of New England, many matters which in England had been under the jurisdiction of the church were given to civil bodies. For a long time the church congregation and the town meeting were practically identical, but authority was almost always exercised in the name of the latter. This was true in matters pertaining to matrimony. Marriage was declared to be not a sacrament but a civil contract in which the intervention of the clergy was unnecessary. In this respect the New England colonies were more than a century ahead of their mother country.

At first, the solemnization of marriage by a civil officer was sustained only by public opinion. In 1646 the colony of Plymouth passed the first New England statute requiring that all marriages be celebrated before a justice of the peace or other magistrate. Other New England colonies did likewise shortly thereafter. Toward the close of the seventeenth century there began a movement for the renewal of the use of religious rites in the solemnization of marriage. A 1692–1693 Massachusetts law authorized both clergymen and justices of the peace to perform the marriage ceremony. This statue was soon adopted in other colonies, and gradually the religious marriage ceremony prevailed. This principle of equality between civil and religious marriage celebrations is one of the outstanding characteristics of our present marriage legislation.

EARLY MARRIAGE LAWS IN THE SOUTHERN COLONIES [16]

In the southern colonies, where the Church of England was established, the doctrine that marriage was a sacrament was predominant. In Virginia, in 1660–1661, the religious marriage ceremony, according to the rites of the Church of England, was prescribed by law. It was not until 1784, shortly after the close of the American Revolution, that the colony by statute even partially abandoned the principle of ecclesiastical marriage. A law was passed in that year which granted power to the courts to

---

[15] Howard, *op. cit.*, Vol. 2, pp. 124–143; Frank G. Cook, "Marriage Celebration in the Colonies," *Atlantic Monthly* (March, 1888), pp. 350–362.

[16] Howard, *op. cit.*, Vol. 2, pp. 228–247.

nominate certain laymen to perform marriage ceremonies in the remote frontier sections of Virginia where there were no clergymen. Before this time important advance was made in two particulars: (1) the lay courts had gained functions which in England belonged to the church courts; (2) beginning in 1631, legislation had been passed embodying all the essential features of the later English Hardwicke Act. The requirements of banns or licenses, parental consent, certification, and registration were all carefully defined by statute. Thus, the many evils which might have grown out of the common-law consent system of marriages were avoided, and the usual results of a civil marriage system were obtained.

At the time of the Revolution, everywhere in the South, except in Maryland, the optional civil ceremony was legally or practically recognized under certain conditions. Maryland early adopted a policy of toleration and recognized as legal either the religious or civil ceremony. There followed a bitter struggle for supremacy in the colony among the followers of the Church of England, Catholics, and Quakers. In 1777 the victorious Anglican group enacted a law which recognized as valid the religious marriage only, with the exception of Quakers, who were permitted to use a lay celebration. Clergymen from all denominations were permitted to celebrate marriages. There still seem to be three states which, with some exceptions, require a religious ceremony: Maryland, West Virginia, and Delaware.[17]

EARLY MARRIAGE LAWS IN THE MIDDLE COLONIES [18]

In the middle colonies, where no religious or political group gained control, tolerance for both the religious and lay ceremony existed. Pennsylvania, settled by Quakers, held from the beginning that the regulation and the protection of marriage belonged to civil authority. In New Netherlands it was required that all marriages be celebrated by a minister of the Dutch Reformed church. In 1664, after England had gained control of the colony, both lay and religious marriage ceremonies were equally valid. Laws were passed in all the middle colonies providing for banns, public posting of intention or securing a license to marry, and registration.

From this brief discussion it is apparent that the American colonists on the whole adopted certain principles of marriage legislation: (1) the optional religious or civil ceremony, (2) the rejection of private contract marriage, and (3) the use of publicity methods, such as banns, licenses, parental consent, and registration. Thus, by the early part of the

[17] Richard V. Mackay and Irving Mandell, *Law of Marriage and Divorce Simplified,* 2d ed. (New York, Oceana, 1951), p. 37; Martindale and Hubbell, *Law Directory* (Summit, N.J., Martindale and Hubbell, 1956), Vol. 3.

[18] Howard, *op. cit.,* Vol. 2, pp. 315–327.

eighteenth century the foundation of our present marriage statutes had been laid.

COMMON-LAW MARRIAGE IN THE UNITED STATES

The old common-law marriage by consent did not gain wide recognition in the American colonies, in spite of the fact that it was an accepted type of marriage in England at the time that a large share of the early colonists migrated to America. Common-law marriages in the United States became prevalent later on. Strangely, this phenomenon occurred after England had definitely abolished common-law marriage in 1753, thirty years before we became independent of her.

There was no outstanding early decision which paved the way for the acceptance of the common-law doctrine of marriage. It was given impetus in this country by Chancellor Kent in 1809. At that time he was judge in a New York court and the case of *Fenton* v. *Reed* came before him. In his decision he threw out an *obiter dictum,* which he later reaffirmed in his famous commentaries, to the effect that marriage was a civil contract which could be entered into by mutual consent just like any other contract. He said: "A contract of marriage made *per verba de praesenti* amounts to an actual marriage and is as valid as if made *in facie ecclesiae.*" [19] Kent thereby sowed the seeds for a rule which was adopted by one court after another throughout the country. Undoubtedly, this was done in part to protect the persons and property involved.

In 1810 the Massachusetts Supreme Court had an opportunity to pass upon the validity of a common-law marriage in the face of a statute which regulated marriage but which contained no express prohibition against the private marriage. This court held it invalid, maintaining that when civil government had established regulations for the due celebration of marriage, it was the duty of all citizens to conform to the regulations, otherwise the vilest seduction could be practiced under the pretext of marriage. The court said: "If this be not a reasonable inference, fruitless are all the precautions of the legislature. In vain do the laws require a previous publication of banns, or the assent of parents or guardians of young minors, or prohibit a justice or minister from solemnizing the marriage without these prerequisites." [20]

During the nineteenth century, one state court after another took a position opposite to that of Massachusetts and upheld common-law marriage as long as there was no express prohibition against it in the statutes. By 1877 even the United States Supreme Court had succumbed to the doctrine. In the case of *Meister* v. *Moore* it held that common-

---

[19] 4 Johns 52 (N.Y. 1809).

[20] *Town of Milford* v. *Town of Worcester,* 7 Mass. 48 (1810).

law marriages were valid as long as there was no express mandate against them. The Court made it clear that though most states had statutes regulating the celebration of marriage, the age of the persons marrying, etc., they were merely directory to magistrates, clergymen, and the parties. In the absence of any positive statute declaring all marriages not celebrated in a prescribed manner void, such marriages were legal. In the words of the Court: "As before remarked, the statutes are held merely directory; because marriage is a thing of common right; because it is the policy of the state to encourage it, and because, as has sometimes been said, any other construction would compel holding illegitimate the offspring of many parents conscious of no violation of law." [21]

DEFINITIONS OF COMMON-LAW MARRIAGE IN THE UNITED STATES

Our courts have generally held with the English courts that a present agreement or consent to become husband and wife is a valid common-law marriage.[22] A few jurisdictions have required more than "a present taking" and have held that cohabitation is necessary in addition to present consent.[23] Some courts have expressly stated that cohabitation is not necessary to perfect a marriage *de praesenti*.[24]

On the matter of what is necessary to constitute present consent, there are courts which have said that no express words are needed. It must appear either from the words or conduct of the parties that marriage was intended.[25] Further, it has been held that "repute" or public recognition of the marital contract is not essential.[26] It has even been held that the parties need not be in the presence of each other at the time the agreement is entered into, but the marriage may be consummated by letter where the parties are in different jurisdictions.[27] Our federal courts have gone so far as to recognize a common-law marriage by proxy between a woman in Portugal and a man in Pennsylvania.[28] The result of these diverse opinions has been uncertainty between and within jurisdictions as to what a common-law marriage is.

---

[21] 96 U.S. 76 (1877).

[22] *Fisher* v. *Fisher,* 250 N.Y. 313, 165 N.E. 460 (1929); *Dumaresly* v. *Fishly,* 10 Ky. 368 (1820).

[23] *Grigsby* v. *Reib,* 105 Tex. 597, 153 S.W. 1124 (1913); *Herd* v. *Herd,* 194 Ala. 613, 69 So. 885 (1915).

[24] *Great Northern R.R. Co.* v. *Johnson,* 254 Fed. 683, 166 C.C.A. 181 (1918); *Port* v. *Port,* 70 Ill. 484 (1873); *Hulett* v. *Carey,* 66 Minn. 327, 69 N.W. 31 (1896).

[25] *In re Wittick's Estate,* 164 Iowa 485, 145 N.W. 913 (1914); *State* v. *Hansbrough,* 181 Mo. 348, 80 S.W. 900 (1904).

[26] *In re Peter's Estate,* 73 Colo. 271, 215 Pac. 128 (1923).

[27] *Mathewson* v. *Phoenix Iron Foundry,* 20 Fed. 281 (1884); *Great Northern R.R. Co.* v. *Johnson,* 254 Fed. 683, 166 C.C.A. 181 (1918).

[28] *Ex parte Suzahana,* D.C. 295 Fed. 713 (1924).

The *de futuro* marriage has not been recognized in the United States to any appreciable extent. In fact, some states expressly refuse to recognize such marriages. There seems to be no clear decision in the United States that an engagement to marry and no more, though followed by intercourse, constitutes a common-law marriage.[29] It is contended that if *de futuro* marriages were valid, there could be no such thing as seduction under a promise of marriage, for the intercourse would then make the persons man and wife.[30] The prevailing American rule seems to be that an agreement to marry in the future, followed by sexual intercourse, is not a valid common-law marriage unless the cohabitation is understood by the parties as a present acceptance of the married state.[31]

PRESENT ATTITUDES TOWARD COMMON-LAW MARRIAGE

On the whole, sociologists, lawyers, religionists, and social workers are opposed to common-law marriages. Howard said of them: "Practically all the hardship and social anarchy of the common law at its wickedest survive in our common law marriage . . . a creation which legalizes and virtually invites impulsive, impure, and secret union." [32] Pollock and Maitland wrote: "The one contract, which to our thinking should certainly be formal, has been made the most formless of all contracts." [33] As early as 1892 the American Bar Association recommended that some ceremony, formality, or written evidence be positively required for a binding and valid marriage, and, in 1911, the National Conference of Commissioners on Uniform State Laws advocated that the states abolish common-law marriages.[34]

Tolerance of common-law marriage defeats the effectiveness of reforms contemplated by social legislation. For example, such acceptance renders inoperative provisions for premarital examination and for licensing restrictions. The Veterans' Administration, the U.S. Department of Health, Education, and Welfare, and state departments of industrial relations and of public welfare many times encounter administrative problems as they attempt to determine which spouses and their children are eligible for certain benefits. The pioneer conditions which fostered and justified common-law marriage in the United States have disappeared. It has been

---

[29] Madden, *op. cit.*, pp. 57–58; Morland, *op. cit.*, p. 37.

[30] *Cheney* v. *Arnold*, 15 N.Y. 345, 69 Am. Dec. 609 (1857).

[31] *In re Danikas' Estate*, 76 Colo. 191, 230 Pac. 608 (1924).

[32] Howard, *op. cit.*, Vol. 3, p. 222.

[33] Sir Frederick Pollock and F. W. Maitland, *The History of English Law Before the Time of Edward I* (Cambridge, University Press, 1923), Vol. 2, p. 367.

[34] Otto E. Koegel, *Common Law Marriage and Its Development in the U. S.* (Washington, D. C., John Byrn and Co., 1922), p. 167; see also, Mary E. Richmond and Fred S. Hall, *Marriage and the State* (New York, Russell Sage Foundation, 1929), pp. 370–371; Vernier, *op. cit.*, Vol. 1, pp. 106–109.

said that today the clerk's office is available to all and that none is beyond the sound of church bells. From the standpoint of public morals and policy there seems to be no reason for perpetuating the common-law marriage.[35] Nevertheless, there are still sixteen jurisdictions which sanction common-law marriage.[36]

THE FAILURE TO CONSUMMATE MARRIAGE: BREACH-OF-PROMISE SUITS

THE NATURE AND ORIGIN OF BREACH-OF-PROMISE SUITS [37]

A breach-of-promise suit is handled in court like a violation of a contract. In the early common law there is no record of breach-of-promise suits. It was not until 1638 that the English common-law courts recognized the right of a person injured by the breaking of a promise of marriage to bring such an action.[38] Even then the common-law courts had some difficulty with the problem, because the contract to marry was based upon a spiritual consideration over which the ecclesiastical courts had jurisdiction. This doctrine that the ecclesiastical courts had jurisdiction over breach-of-promise matters became firmly established after the decision in *Holcroft* v. *Dickenson*,[39] which contained the first full discussion of the subject and paved the way for reliance upon the doctrine in both England and America.

Apparently, before the development of the common-law right to damages, the ecclesiastical courts supplied a remedy in the nature of *specific performance*. These courts, by the use of religious pressure, compelled the consummation of *de praesenti* and *de futuro* marriages in face of the church, which, according to Pollock and Maitland, was not specific performance in the common-law and equity sense but rather the forcing of persons already married to celebrate their marriage again at the church door. As early as 1651 English equity courts refused to decree specific performance of a promise to marry on the grounds of public

---

[35] Morland, *op. cit.*, p. 59; Vernier, *op. cit.*, Vol. 1, pp. 106–109. See also, *In re Robert's Estate*, 58 Wyo. 438, 133 Pac. 2d, 492 (1942), for a long historical discussion of the common-law marriage. Here, the Wyoming court abrogated common-law marriages and held its marriage laws mandatory.

[36] Martindale and Hubbell, *op. cit.*, Vol. 3: Alabama, Florida, Idaho, Indiana, Iowa, Kansas, Michigan, Mississippi, Ohio, Oklahoma, Pennsylvania, Rhode Island, South Carolina, South Dakota, Texas, and the District of Columbia.

[37] Morland, *op. cit.*, ch. 7; "Breach of Promise of Marriage," 8 Am. Jur., 845–883; Donald Slesinger, "Breach of Marriage Promise," *Encyclopaedia of the Social Sciences* (1930), Vol. 2, pp. 688–689; W. J. Brockelbank, "The Nature of the Promise to Marry," 41 Ill. L. Rev. No. 1, 1–26 (1946–1947).

[38] *Stretcher* v. *Parker*, 1 Rollis Abr. 22 (1638).

[39] 124 Eng. Rep. 933, Carter 233 (1672).

policy.[40] In the United States it was not until the 1930's that there began to be legislative restrictions on this action. In France and other civil-law countries the right to bring an action for breach of promise does not exist.

THE ELEMENTS OF DAMAGE

The plaintiff, usually the woman, no matter how much she may have suffered, has no remedy without the promise to marry, unless her injury was caused by particular wrongs or tortious acts of the defendant not connected with any promise. Where there has been a promise and a breach of that promise, the courts have developed rules of law that permit very substantial recoveries in many cases.[41] The issue of damages is decided by the jury under proper instructions from the judge.[42] All courts grant without question that the plaintiff is entitled to recover such financial outlays as she reasonably made in reliance upon the defendant's promise, such as for a trousseau if her wedding day was agreed upon. There are courts which have gone further and permitted her to have a recovery such as would make her pecuniary condition as good as that she would have had if the contract to marry had been carried out.[43] Some courts hold that the jury may take into consideration the plaintiff's loss of opportunity during her engagement to contract a suitable marriage with another man.[44] In assessing damages the jury may also give weight to other factors, including injury to the plaintiff's health caused by the defendant's failure to perform the agreement to marry.[45]

There are certain kinds of acts committed by the defendant which may be weighed by the jury to increase damages or to justify the assessment of punitive damages. Punishment and not compensation is the legal theory back of the levy of aggravated damages. Some of the types of circumstances which have been held to aggravate damages are:

1. Seduction under the promise of marriage with or without causing pregnancy.
2. Pregnancy as a result of seduction accompanied by such a promise.
3. Slanderous and libelous statements by the defendant with respect to the plaintiff in his defense of the action.
4. The manner in which the defendant committed cruel, wanton, and insulting acts or words in the perpetration of the breach.

---

[40] *Baker* v. *Smith,* 82 Eng. Rep. 729, Style 295 (1651).

[41] R. S. Bauer, *Essentials of Law of Damages* (Chicago, Callaghan Co., 1919), p. 282.

[42] *Hahn* v. *Bettingen,* 81 Minn. 91, 83 N.W. 467 (1900).

[43] *Mabin* v. *Webster,* 129 Ind. 430, 28 N.E. 863 (1891); *Lawrence* v. *Cook,* 56 Me. 187 (1868).

[44] *Hively* v. *Golnick,* 123 Minn. 498, 144 N.W. 213 (1913).

[45] *Hahn* v. *Bettingen,* 81 Minn. 91, 83 N.W. 467 (1900); *Ruben* v. *Klemer,* 44 R.I. 4, 114 Atl. 131 (1921).

5. The fact that the defendant made his promise without any intention of fulfilling it.

There are also some circumstances which tend to mitigate or lessen damages. One of the most common grounds relied upon is the bad character and unchaste conduct of the plaintiff, on the theory that if she is that type of person her sense of humiliation and loss of reputation will not be great.[46] An offer to marry the woman, if made in good faith, may lessen the damages.[47] The wealth of the defendant also affects the amount.

PRESENT ATTITUDES TOWARD SUITS FOR BREACH OF PROMISE [48]

There is no doubt that the privilege of bringing actions for breach of promise has been much abused. The newspapers frequently carry stories of sensational suits brought against wealthy men quite obviously for the anticipated pecuniary results. Occasionally, the demands are for hundreds of thousands of dollars and, more rarely, for millions of dollars. The facts show that numbers of men become involved in situations of which advantage can be taken by unscrupulous women; they also show that numbers of women are encouraged to enter into compromising relationships with the expectation of marriage to follow. Some men and some women may be foolish or vicious; some may be sincere but mistaken. However, these facts doubtfully justify breach-of-promise suits. If the woman has become pregnant, the courts are available for paternity and support actions. Little real justice will be accomplished by an exposure of personal affairs to the courts for financial rewards.

One authority has written that the breach-of-promise action "which has survived through no merit of its own, is anomalous and out of date and represents a distinct cultural lag in an age when women are becoming increasingly independent economically." [49] The policy of the law allowing actions for breach of promise has been condemned by many. The following objections are raised: [50]

1. It is often used as an instrument of blackmail and is not applied for a just cause. Too often it is used by designing females as a source of revenue rather than as proper compensation for the loss suffered.
2. It is unfortunate to give publicity to sordid and unhappy love affairs.
3. In practice it is available to one sex only.

---

[46] *Young* v. *Corrigan*, 208 Fed. 431 (1912).

[47] *Kurtz* v. *Frank*, 76 Ind. 594 (1881).

[48] Nathan P. Feinsinger, "Legislative Attack on 'Heart Balm,'" 33 Mich. L. Rev. 979–1009 (1935); Nathan P. Feinsinger, "Current Legislation Affecting Breach of Promise to Marry, Alienation of Affections, and Related Actions," 10 Wis. L. Rev. 417–430 (1935).

[49] Slesinger, *loc. cit.*, Vol. 2, p. 688.

[50] Vernier, *op. cit.*, Vol. 1, pp. 26–27.

4. The measure of damages often turns out to be unjust because juries are gullible.
5. Engaged persons should be free to correct mistakes.

Apropos of this last point, it is pertinent to comment that a function of the engagement period is the opportunity it affords the parties to become better acquainted. It offers a means of discovering whether the relationship has those attributes likely to contribute to permanency. Certainly an anomaly exists in breach-of-promise situations, which penalize a person who has decided that he does not wish to enter into a permanent relationship found beforehand to be unworkable!

Among those who are antagonistic to breach-of-promise suits are persons who advocate a complete abolition of the cause of action, and those who maintain that the evils which have crept into these suits can be eliminated by proper legislation so as to preserve the cause of action in all cases where it is truly justified. Some of the suggestions advanced include:[51]

1. Require written evidence of the engagement to marry.
2. Provide that actions for seduction be brought in separate suits.
3. Regulate more carefully the types of evidence admissible and require corroboration.
4. Limit damages to material loss incurred on the faith of the promise.

Numbers of states have abolished causes of action for breaches of promise.[52]

One of the strong early legal objections to abolition of breach-of-promise suits was that of unconstitutionality. It was thought by some persons that statutes forbidding breach-of-promise suits violated the constitutional prohibition against the impairment of the obligation of contracts and the due process clause of the Fourteenth Amendment. These claims were tested in 1936 when the constitutionality of the New York statute was challenged. In the case of *Fearon* v. *Treanor* the statute was upheld.[53] The New York Court of Appeals pointed out that marriage is a unique contract in which the state has an interest, and, as such, does not come within the prohibitions of the contract clause of the Constitution. This opinion is in accordance with those reviewed earlier in this chapter, which maintain that in some respects marriage is like a contract and in some it is not. The court reasoned further that such statutes do not violate due process because the state has complete power to change or even destroy a common-law right of action. Hopefully more states will pass legislation denying "heart balm" suits.

---

[51] Vernier, *op. cit.*, Vol. 1, p. 29.
[52] Morland, *op. cit.*, p. 197; Pilpel and Zavin, *op. cit.*, p. 4.
[53] 272 N.Y. 268, 5 N.E. 2d 1815 (1936).

STATUTORY REGULATION OF MARRIAGE: LICENSES, SOLEMNIZATION, RECORDING

THE REQUIREMENT OF A MARRIAGE LICENSE

Legislatures have recognized that if they are to protect the interests of the state, they must enact administrative regulations to control who enters into marriage and the circumstances under which it takes place. An Indiana court expressed this point of view as follows: [54]

> the relations, duties, obligations, and consequences flowing from the marriage contract are so important to the peace and welfare of society as to be subject to legislative control. The legislature may prescribe who may marry; the age at which they may marry; the procedure and form essential to constitute marriage; the duties and obligations created by marriage; the effect on the property rights of the parties; and the causes which shall be regarded as sufficient for its dissolution.

For centuries the publication of banns gave interested parties a chance to interfere if the contemplated marriage contravened the sanctions of the period. Banns are still used by some religious groups, but marriage license laws furnish the legal means of control. Licensing attempts to catch errors before committed; it determines by administrative process the elements of invalidity which can be corrected after marriage only by judical process.[55]

All the states outline a course of procedure which, if taken by a man and a woman who are competent to marry, will make them husband and wife.[56] These statutes usually provide for the giving of advance notice of intention to marry and for the issuance of a license by some authorized officer. The two main purposes of license laws are to give the state a method of withholding permission for marriage and to obtain marriage statistics. The license laws usually prescribe: (1) that a license shall be obtained for a valid marriage; (2) the form and content of the application, and by whom and where it shall be issued; and (3) the substantive regulations as to the qualifications of the parties.

Although all American jurisdictions have license laws, the license is not always essential to a valid marriage. Some laws are "mandatory" in that they require a license as a prerequisite to a valid marriage; others are merely suggestive of the proper ways and means of getting married, and are therefore said to be "directory." Many of the steps specified by

[54] *Wiley* v. *Wiley,* 75 Ind. App. 456, 123 N.E. 252 (1920); see also, *Town of Milford* v. *Town of Worcester,* 7 Mass. 48 (1810); *Maynard* v. *Hill,* 125 U.S. 190, 8 Sup. Ct. 723 (1887).

[55] Geoffrey May, *Marriage Laws and Decisions in the United States* (New York, Russell Sage Foundation, 1929), pp. 12–13.

[56] Madden, *op. cit.,* pp. 48–49.

the statutes are relatively unimportant, and to allow an innocent omission to invalidate a marriage would, in many instances, produce unfairness and needless hardship. Often legislatures insert in the statutes various "saving clauses" which provide that if certain kinds of omissions and mistakes are made, they shall be considered immaterial or may be remedied. For example, a marriage is usually considered valid when two individuals believe themselves to have been married by one who is authorized to perform the ceremony but who in reality is not.

BY WHOM ISSUED [57]

The duty of issuing licenses is delegated to a local officer. There is great diversity as to where the parties must apply for the license. Some states allow them to apply in any county in the state; others, in the county where either party resides; others, where the woman resides, or if both are non-residents of the state, where the marriage is to take place. Facts which the issuer of licenses must ascertain concerning the parties are of two main classes: those which are required primarily for complete and accurate records, such as the names of the parties, residence and occupation, time of the proposed marriage, parental names and address; and, more important, those which must be proved in order that the legality of the marriage may be established, such as ages, race, relationship to each other if any, the status of any former marriages of the parties, the existence in either party of venereal disease, insanity, epilepsy, imbecility, feeble-mindedness, habitual criminality, tuberculosis.

Many license issuers are perfunctory in the administration of these functions, and, practically speaking, it is often the applicants who decide their own fitness for marriage.[58] The responsibility of the official issuing the license should be more than routine law enforcement. He should be charged with the duty of making reasonable inquiry regarding the identity of the parties and their capacity to marry, and, further, he should be subject to a penalty for issuing a license improperly.[59]

Numerous suggestions have been made for improving the administration of license issuance, among which are: [60]

1. A central state agency should be required to draft license manuals to aid local officers to understand their duties and the nature of the law.
2. When issuers discover parties attempting to violate the law, they should be required to report such violations to proper county prosecuting officers.
3. Both candidates should be required to appear when application for the license is made, and one applicant should not be permitted to vouch for the other.

---

[57] Vernier, *op. cit.*, Vol. 1, p. 60.

[58] Fred S. Hall, "Marriage and the Law," *Annals of the American Academy of Political and Social Science* (March, 1932), Vol. 160, pp. 113–114.

[59] Schouler, *op. cit.*, Vol. 2, p. 1463.

[60] Richmond and Hall, *op. cit.*, ch. 3.

4. Verification of the statements of the candidates should be required under oath and penalty.

5. Documentary proof of the age of minors and written proof of parental consent should be required in all doubtful cases.

6. Proof of residence should be required.

7. Refusal of licenses should be reported to neighboring license issuers with the reasons therefore.

8. Licenses should be issued only during regular office hours except in grave emergencies.

THE REQUIREMENT OF ADVANCE NOTICE [61]

When the license system was first invoked, the task of getting a license was an over-the-counter transaction; no advance notice was required, and the license could be used immediately upon receipt. In 1858 Maine passed the first law requiring an advance notice of intention to marry; now, over half the jurisdictions have this type of statute. Advance-notice statutes are of two kinds: one requires a lapse of from one to five days from the time of making application to the issuance of the license; the other requires that the license be issued at once but that a period of time shall elapse before it can be used. The second method is less desirable, for the reason that obliging officiants can perform the ceremony at once and then postdate the marriage certificate. The first method decreases the number of marriage candidates who come in from other states and apply for licenses, reduces the number of hasty marriages, and prevents the consummation of illegal unions, since definite disqualifications may be brought to light during the intervening period.

The greatest value of advance notice lies in the opportunity for cooling off. The five-day notice gives the opportunity to the more thoughtful one of any two persons contemplating marriage to consider and possibly to reconsider. The prevention of deliberate fraud is important, but far more important, both for the protection of the state and the welfare of the individual, is the chance for this additional though brief time for second and more mature thought.

WHO MAY SOLEMNIZE AND THE FORM OF CEREMONY

The statutes provide that either civil or religious officials may perform the marriage ceremony. They usually require that the ceremony be performed before witnesses and that the officials have proper credentials. Most statutes provide that any one of a number of persons may officiate at a marriage. Among those listed are governors, mayors, any judge of a court of record, any justice of the peace or magistrate, or any person commissioned by the court. The largest number of civil marriages are performed by justices of the peace. One New England town is reported to

[61] Vernier, *op. cit.*, Vol. 1, p. 54, with 1938 suppl., p. 10.

have had twenty-one justices, some of whom held the office merely for the marriage fees. There are a good many "marrying justices" who have the business organized as a fee racket, perhaps even guaranteeing to marry the parties in a certain number of minutes. One justice in a marriage-market town had the following on his business card: [62]

> If a man loves a girl, that's his business.
> If a girl loves a man, that's her business.
> If they want the knot tied, that's my business.

Even among religious officiants there are a goodly number of "marrying parsons." Included in the reforms which have been suggested for the solemnization of marriage are: [63]

1. The number of civil officiants should be greatly reduced.
2. The more populous cities and counties should set up central marriage bureaus, as has already been done in New York and Chicago with some measure of success.
3. Civil officiants should be denied the personal right to collect fees, all of which should be turned over to the local government.

The statutes do not attempt to impose detailed rules as to the form of the religious marriage ceremony, for such requirements would probably run counter to the constitutional guarantee of religious freedom. Over half the jurisdictions have not attempted to legislate on the subject at all. Some statutes provide that the parties shall declare in the presence of the solemnizing officer that they take each other to be husband and wife, and a few specify that this declaration must be made in each other's presence. The majority of states require the presence of witnesses.[64] There seems to be no legal reason why each state should not require its *civil* officiants to follow some prescribed form of ceremony which would make the civil ceremony less perfunctory and more meaningful.

RECORDING OF MARRIAGE LICENSES AND CERTIFICATES

The return and recording of marriage licenses and certificates are important aspects of administrative procedures for the regulation and control of marriage. All American jurisdictions have recording statutes of one kind or another.[65] In most states the license-issuing official is required to make a record of this fact. Unless this is done, if the required certificate is not returned, there is no record of the marriage. Such recording does not necessarily mean that the marriage is finally celebrated, but it does give the state notice that a marriage is expected to occur.

The marriage certificate not only furnishes evidence of marriage to

[62] Richmond and Hall, *op. cit.*, p. 232.
[63] *Ibid.*, pp. 236–241.
[64] Vernier, *op. cit.*, Vol. 1, pp. 92–93.
[65] *Ibid.*, 145–160

the parties themselves, but when filed with the state as part of its permanent records, it becomes an important factual and evidential document, as well as a source for social statistics. About half the states provide that a copy of the certificate shall be furnished to the parties. In a smaller number of states the officiant is under a positive duty to deliver a certificate to the bride and groom. About half the states require the return of the license to the official issuing the license, and somewhat more than half require that the local recording officer shall transmit a copy of his record to the appropriate state bureau or officer.[66]

STATUTORY REGULATION OF MARRIAGE: CHILD MARRIAGES

MINIMUM AGE REQUIREMENTS [67]

All the states have statutes containing provisions as to the age requirements of parties contracting marriage. We have seen that at common law, males of fourteen and females of twelve could contract a legal marriage; all marriages under the age of seven were absolutely void and required no court action to annul them. The parties under the age of consent could avoid the marriage upon reaching the age of fourteen or twelve. If they did not do so, and confirmed the marriage by continuing to live together after reaching the age of consent, the marriage was valid. All but a few jurisdictions have enacted legislation requiring the attainment of a higher age than that required at common law before a valid marriage can be contracted. The statutory minimum marriage age varies, with a few exceptions, from sixteen to eighteen for boys and from fourteen to sixteen for girls. Table 1 shows the age of consent for males and females in forty-eight states and the District of Columbia.[68]

The right to disaffirm a marriage on the ground of nonage is not always limited to the party who was under the age of consent where the other party was of suitable age, but it may extend to the latter also. The courts take the position that the right to disaffirm such a marriage is limited to the parties to the marriage unless otherwise specifically provided by statute.[69] Many statutes do not provide for disaffirmance by others than the parties themselves, and, as a result, society and the parents are often powerless to avoid the marriage.

---

[66] *Ibid.*

[67] *The Book of the States: 1954–55,* (Chicago, Council of State Governments, 1955), Vol. 10, p. 323; Morland, *op. cit.,* ch. 9; Mary E. Richmond and Fred S. Hall, *Child Marriages* (New York, Russell Sage Foundation, 1925); Vernier, *op. cit.,* Vol. 1, pp. 115–119; Madden, *op. cit.,* pp. 28–32.

[68] *The Book of the States: 1954–55,* Vol. 10, p. 323.

[69] *Niland* v. *Niland,* 96 N.J. Eq. 438, 126 Atl. 530 (1924).

Table 1
AGE OF CONSENT

Male	*No. of States*
Common law (14 yrs.)	7
15	2
16	10
17	2
18	27
20	1
Female	
Common law (12 yrs.)	7
14	9
15	7
16	25
18	1

Some laws give the courts discretion to annul child marriages. For example, in a 1924 New York case action for annulment of marriage was brought by an infant through her guardian *ad litem*. The court, after reviewing the facts, which showed that the plaintiff was fifteen years old when married and the defendant twenty-one and that the latter had plainly taken advantage of the innocence of the plaintiff, decided for annulment. It said: [70]

> It is apparent, from the evidence in the case, the conduct of the defendant, the extreme youth of the plaintiff, and this defendant's worthless character, evidenced by his conduct, that there was no such real unity of lives and of spirit as to constitute a real state of matrimony. . . . I have no hesitation in this case in exercising the power within my discretion which is conferred upon the court by the statute. The marriage contract between the parties should be annulled.

Newspapers frequently publish sensational stories of child marriages. One such story was illustrated by a picture of a twelve-year-old mother recuperating from the birth of twin boys. Another gave a follow-up report on the marriage of a nine-year-old Tennessee girl, about whose marriage a shocked America read in 1937. A reporter who visited her thirteen years later found her to be a strapping, hard-working, apparently happy young woman. This particular child marriage was, in part, responsible for the raising of the minimum marriage age in Tennessee. In another child marriage situation involving an action for annulment by the mother of the girl, the court is reputed to have told the thirty-two-year-old groom that he could keep his twelve-year-old bride. "I believe," he said, "society, law, and everyone concerned will be better served by the court's refusing to annul this marriage," because to annul it would

[70] *Kellogg* v. *Kellogg*, 203 N.Y. Supp. 757, 122 Misc. and Rep. 734 (1924).

result in turning the child out of house and home with no place to go. Obviously, what the child bride needed was the help of a children's agency which could look into and contribute to her needs.[71] The evils of child marriage are too obvious to require extensive discussion. The weight of medical opinion is against the marriage of either sex at puberty and against the marriage of girls under sixteen. Most married children cannot adequately assume the responsibilities of the marriage state or the care of offspring.

THE REQUIREMENT OF PARENTAL CONSENT

At common law, if the parties were over the minimum age at which they themselves could consent to marriage, the consent of parents or guardians was not necessary. However, modern American statutes in all jurisdictions now require that minors above their own age of consent, but below a certain age, must formally secure the consent of parents or guardians. The great majority of states fix the age of parental consent for males at twenty-one and for females at eighteen. Table 2 below shows the distribution for forty-nine jurisdictions.[72]

Table 2

Age below Which Parental Consent Is Required

Male	*No. of States*
Below 21	42
Below 18	3
Below 20	1
Not reported	3
Female	
Below 18	35
Below 21	13
Not reported	1

The form of parental consent varies. In most states it must be either by personal appearance or in writing, and if the latter, usually under oath. Numbers of child marriages occur with parental consent, as when the daughter is pregnant or has been assaulted, or where the parents have romantic ideas or wish to absolve themselves of further financial and personal responsibility. Enforcement is usually secured by making such consent a prerequisite to license issuance, and the burden of obtaining the facts is placed upon the license officer. For violations the license officer is subject to a penalty, usually a fine. Failure to secure parental consent does not generally affect the validity of the marriage but imposes a penalty upon the license clerk. Few license clerks are prosecuted, and

[71] *Capital Times*, Madison, Wis. (June 26, 1937).

[72] *The Book of the States: 1954–55*, Vol. 10, p. 323; Vernier, *op. cit.*, Vol. 1, pp. 119–128.

very few are found to have had the intent to violate the law. Parents cannot obtain the annulment of their child's marriage contracted without parental consent unless statutes give them that right.[73]

In addition to raising the age of personal and parental consent in those jurisdictions where they are still too low, the following suggestions have been made for preventing child marriages:

1. Proof of age should be strengthened.
2. Both candidates should be required to apply for the license.
3. Gretna Greens should be put out of existence by accepting the provisions of uniform legislation and by forbidding the contracting of marriage outside the state for the purpose of evading the prohibitions of the state of residence, one of which should be age of consent.

For Selected References, see those following Chapter 5.

---

[73] *State ex rel. Scott* v. *Lowell et al.,* 78 Minn. 166, 80 N.W. 877 (1899).

CHAPTER 5

Marriage in American Jurisdictions II

STATUTORY REGULATION OF MARRIAGE: PHYSICAL, MENTAL, RACIAL RESTRICTIONS

PROHIBITED MARRIAGES GENERALLY

From the earliest times various peoples and states have seen fit to prohibit the marriage of certain persons under certain conditions. The social theories which have been back of these prohibitions are not always apparent. Very often, and regardless of what may have been the original purpose of such prohibitions, they were enforced by religious sanction. Whether the Old Testament Hebrews and the early Christians, for example, prohibited the marriage of close relatives for social and religious reasons or, in part, for what we today call eugenic reasons is not clear. Much of our recent restrictive legislation undoubtedly has both a social and a eugenic purpose.[1]

In the following discussion we shall deal primarily with prohibitory marriage laws. First, we shall review those where the primary aim is to limit the procreation of the undesirable and unfit or to restrain marriages between races. Our legislatures have attempted to accomplish this through statutes prohibiting the marriage of those who are mentally defective, insane, or epileptic; those who are closely related; those with certain physical diseases and defects; and those of different races. In these situations marriage is not permitted with those who are considered unfit, or at least not until the unfitness has been removed. Second, we shall look at marriages which are prohibited upon legal, religious, or moral grounds. Such marriages include those perpetrated by fraud, duress, or mistake; those which are bigamous or polygamous in character; and those contracted in violation of the required waiting period after divorce. The purposes behind these two groups of prohibited marriages are not mutually exclusive.

[1] H. S. Jennings, "Eugenics," *Encyclopaedia of the Social Sciences* (1931), Vol. 5, pp. 617–621.

THE INSANE, FEEBLE-MINDED, AND EPILEPTIC [2]

The prohibition of marriage on account of insanity derives from two theories, one legal, and the other scientific. Since the law at many points looks upon marriage as a civil contract to which the parties must give their real consent, there can be no valid marriage if either party is mentally incapable of giving consent. The scientific reason for prohibiting the marriage of those who are mentally incapable is the desire to save the family and society from unnecessary burdens. The majority of states have enacted specific statutes on the matter and have sought to prevent the marriage of the insane and feeble-minded by one of two methods: (1) by prohibiting the issuance of licenses and imposing fines for violation; (2) by declaring such marriages void and making them the basis for an annulment. Some authorities feel that the latter method is the stronger. However, in the majority of those states where such marriages are void by statute they turn out to be voidable only. In reality, very few such marriages are set aside.

Most statutes do not define who are incompetent persons; the courts have to settle the problem. Some states prohibit or render void marriages of persons who are "incapable of consenting for want of sufficient understanding"; a number prohibit the marriage of "the insane"; some include "idiots" and some "imbeciles"; others cover "those who are feeble-minded" or "persons of unsound mind"; some mention "lunatics"; a few include "persons unable to contract." The courts, whether discussing the problem at common law or under the statutes, are strongly legalistic in their treatment of the question, partly because they have no adequate scientific definition as to what is insanity, lunacy, or mental incompetency. To them the issue is the capacity of the parties to contract at the time of the marriage.

In a Wisconsin case on this subject the court said: [3]

> and as was held in *Hempel* v. *Hempel,* 174 Wis. 332, 121 N.W. 74, that the test of mental capacity was not whether the parties were of sufficient mentality to measure up to the responsibilities incurred by bringing offspring into the world, but the true test was whether there was understanding and mental capacity sufficient to realize what was then being done and consenting thereto.

Here, the party was held mentally capable of entering into marriage, although a few years before he had been found mentally incompetent to manage his estate. The insanity or incompetency must exist at the time

---

[2] John W. Morland, *Keezer on the Law of Marriage and Divorce,* 3d ed. (Indianapolis, Bobbs-Merrill, 1946), ch. 8; "Marriage," 35 Am. Jur. (with cumulative suppl. to 1952), 247–261; Richard V. Mackay and Irving Mandell, *Law of Marriage and Divorce Simplified,* 2d ed. (New York, Oceana, 1951).

[3] *Roether* v. *Roether,* 180 Wis. 24, 191 N.W. 576 (1923); *Lewis* v. *Lewis,* 44 Minn. 124, 46 N.W. 323 (1890).

of the marriage to avoid it, and neither prior insanity nor subsequent insanity is sufficient,[4] although some courts hold it proper for the jury to consider prior and subsequent mental incompetency as bearing on the question of the mental condition at the time of the marriage.

The courts hold that feeble-mindedness or mere defect or weakness of mind does not constitute a basis for annulling a marriage unless the person has not sufficient mental capacity to give an intelligent consent. At present there does not seem to be any satisfactory means of preventing the marriage of mentally defective persons, even though the statutes prohibit such marriages, since there is no generally accepted psycholegal definition of feeble-mindedness. When all the states have competent state psychologists and psychiatrists, when definitions of defect are generally recognized, when registration of mentally inadequate and incompetent persons is required, when marriage license clerks are furnished such lists and are forbidden to issue licenses to persons whose names appear thereon, and when a state agency is required to see that the law is enforced, some control of this problem may be expected! It must be acknowledged that even if it were possible to prevent the marriage of the subnormal, such problems as illegitimate pregnancy would not necessarily be avoided.

At common law, the marriage of insane and feeble-minded persons was null and void on the theory that from the beginning there was a want of capacity to contract and that no binding contract had ever come into existence. Of course, only those obviously insane or mentally deficient were affected. If a sentence of nullity were pronounced, it was merely the declaration of an accomplished fact. Upon occasion the courts did declare marriages void on the theory that although a declaration of nullity was not necessary, it was sounder practice to make such a declaration. "The fitness and propriety of a judicial decision, pronouncing the nullity of such a marriage, is very apparent and is equally conducive to good order and decorum, and to the peace and conscience of the party." [5]

Under statutes where marriages of the insane and feeble-minded are declared void but which provide judicial action for the annulment, there is usually an enumeration of the persons by whom, and the conditions under which, an action for annulment may be brought. If the competent spouse is not included in the enumeration, he does not have the right to have the marriage annulled.[6] Some statutes give the party *compos mentis* the right to annulment if he did not know of the condition at the time of marriage. Under this type of statute it is necessary to go through the formal annulment proceeding.

---

[4] *Nonnemacher* v. *Nonnemacher*, 159 Pa. 634, 28 Atl. 439 (1894).
[5] *Wightman* v. *Wightman*, 4 Johns 343 (Ch. N.Y. 1820).
[6] *Hoadley* v. *Hoadley*, 244 N.Y. 424, 155 N.E. 728 (1927).

About one third of the jurisdictions prohibit the marriage of epileptics.[7] Several allow epileptics to marry if the female is above forty-five years of age; and a few permit the marriage of hereditary epileptics if they have submitted to an operation for sterilization. Geneticists today do not justify this type of restrictive legislation, since they cannot demonstrate that epilepsy is an inherited malady. There has been conflict as to whether or not the marriage of an epileptic in violation of a statute is void or voidable. A case of this kind came before the Wisconsin Supreme Court. The marriage statute of that state then provided that no epileptic person was capable of contracting marriage. Here, the wife was an epileptic, and both husband and wife knew of the condition before marriage. After her death, a third party challenged the right of the husband to act as administrator of his wife's estate. The court held that the marriage of epileptics was void and not merely voidable, for if the legislature had intended such marriages to be voidable, it would doubtless have provided a means for avoiding them.[8] In 1953 the Wisconsin legislature abolished the statutory provision prohibiting the marriage of epileptics and legalized all earlier marriages of epileptics if otherwise valid and legal.[9]

Statutes which forbid marriages of the insane, feeble-minded, and epileptic have prevailingly been held constitutional. For example, in the leading case of *Gould* v. *Gould* the court made the following statement concerning the constitutionality of the Wisconsin statute prohibiting the marriage of epileptics: [10]

> That epilepsy is a disease of a peculiarly serious and revolting character, tending to weaken mental force, and often descending from parent to child, or entailing upon the offspring of the sufferer some other grave form of nervous malady, is a matter of common knowledge, of which courts will take judicial notice. . . . One mode of guarding against the perpetuation of epilepsy obviously is to forbid sexual intercourse with those afflicted by it, and to preclude such opportunities for sexual intercourse as marriage furnishes. To impose such a restriction upon the right to contract marriage, if not intrinsically unreasonable, is no invasion of the equality of all men before the law, if it applies equally to all, under the same circumstances, who belong to a certain class of persons, which class can reasonably be regarded as one requiring special legislation either for their protection or for the protection from them of the community at large. It cannot be pronounced by the judiciary to be intrinsically unreasonable if it should be regarded as a determination by the General Assembly that a law of this kind is necessary for the preservation of public health, and if there are substantial grounds for believing that such determination is supported by the facts upon which it is apparent that it was based.

---

[7] Morland, *op. cit.*, p. 268; Chester G. Vernier and others, *American Family Laws* (Stanford, Cal., Stanford University Press, 1931–1938) Vol. 1, pp. 199–203.

[8] *King* v. *Cannon*, 221 Wis. 322, 266 N.W. 918 (1936).

[9] Wis. Stat., 1953, c. 245.03(1), 245.035.

[10] *Gould* v. *Gould*, 78 Conn. 246, 61 Atl. 604 (1905).

CONSANGUINITY AND AFFINITY [11]

The church early prohibited marriages when the relationship between the parties was close. The prohibited degrees of relationship were of two kinds: those based on blood relationship or descent from a common ancestor, consanguinity; and those based upon relationship through marriage, affinity. Today, where there is no statute to the contrary, consanguinity and affinity, being canonical disabilities, render the marriage merely voidable and not void. All American statutes prohibit marriage with one's mother or father, grandmother or grandfather, sister or brother, aunt or uncle, niece or nephew. There is less agreement on other relationships, but over half the states prohibit the marriage of first cousins.[12] Relatives of the half blood are brought within the prohibitions of some states.

It is impossible to say with any degree of positiveness what effect the statutes and courts in the various jurisdictions give to marriages in violation of these prohibitions.[13] Several jurisdictions have statutes which positively declare that marriage between close relatives is void *ab initio* without further legal procedure. A few have statutes which clearly provide that marriages within the prohibited degrees of consanguinity are void only from the time they are annulled by a judicial proceeding. Statutes in the other jurisdictions are confused, and the courts are called upon to interpret them.

According to English canon law, relationship by affinity was as much an impediment to marriage as consanguinity. In the United States, about one half the states have prohibitions on the subject.[14] There is a tendency to give less and less weight to affinity as a ground for prohibiting marriage, and, certainly, if we look at the problem objectively, there are no sound moral or physiological reasons to forbid such marriages. In the absence of statutes prohibiting them, the courts have generally refused to follow the English law. As early as 1837, the Vermont Supreme Court definitely ruled that it was permissible for a man to wed his deceased wife's sister.[15] In a more recent Iowa case, a man was permitted to marry his wife's daughter by a previous marriage.[16]

---

[11] Morland, *op. cit.*, ch. 11; Vernier, *op. cit.*, Vol. 1, pp. 173–187.

[12] Morland, *op. cit.*, p. 222: Arizona, Arkansas, Colorado, Delaware, Idaho, Illinois, Indiana, Iowa, Kansas, Louisiana, Michigan, Minnesota, Mississippi, Missouri, Montana, Nebraska, Nevada, New Hampshire, North Dakota, Ohio, Oklahoma, Oregon, Pennsylvania, South Dakota, Utah, Washington, West Virginia, Wisconsin, Wyoming.

[13] *Arado* v. *Arado,* 281 Ill. 123, 117 N.E. 816 (1918).

[14] Morland, *op. cit.*, pp. 220–221: Alabama, Connecticut, Delaware, District of Columbia, Georgia, Iowa, Kentucky, Maine, Maryland, Massachusetts, Michigan, Mississippi, New Hampshire, Oklahoma, Pennsylvania, Rhode Island, South Carolina, South Dakota, Tennessee, Texas, Vermont, Virginia, West Virginia.

[15] *Blodget* v. *Brinsmaid,* 9 Vt. 27 (1837).

[16] *Back* v. *Back,* 148 Iowa 223, 125 N.W. 1009 (1910); *Kelly* v. *Neely,* 12 Ark. 657 (1852).

VENEREAL AND OTHER DISEASES

A fairly recent development in the field of prohibited marriages is restriction on account of disease. Persons most commonly made subject to restrictions are those with venereal disease. A few states forbid the marriage of persons with tuberculosis and with other transmissible diseases. It is apparent that the marriage of these persons, regardless of the inheritability or transmissibility of the disease, is bound to have serious consequences for the husband and wife, for their children, and for society as a whole. Whether or not alcoholism is a disease, and despite the verdict that it is undoubtedly not inherited, a few states prohibit the marriage of alcoholics, obviously for social and economic reasons.

Since the venereal diseases have afforded an important cause of mortality and morbidity in the United States, medical men and sociologists have given much consideration to their control. The development of new drugs in the decades of the 1940's and 1950's has done much to mitigate the dangers of these diseases. Prohibition of the marriage of venereally diseased persons is part of the movement for their reduction. In 1913 Wisconsin passed the first permanent law requiring premarital examinations for venereal disease. It provided that all male applicants for a marriage license be examined by a licensed physician and that no license be issued unless the applicant was found free from acquired venereal diseases. Wassermann tests were not compulsory. The act also made provision for penalties for the improper issuance of medical certificates and marriage licenses.

The original law was hotly contested, but in 1914 the Wisconsin Supreme Court upheld its constitutionality. The court said: [17]

> The power of the state to control and regulate by reasonable laws the marriage relation, and to prevent the contracting of marriage by persons afflicted with loathsome or hereditary diseases, which are liable either to be transmitted to the spouse or inherited by the offspring, or both, must on principle be regarded as undeniable. To state this proposition is to establish it. Society has a right to protect itself from extinction and its members from a fate worse than death. If authority be needed to support this proposition, reference may be made to Freund on Police Power #124 and cases there cited.

It further held that the law was not an unreasonable restriction upon the inalienable right of marriage; that it did not impair the inherent right to enjoy life, liberty, and the pursuit of happiness; and that it did not interfere with religious freedom. The court pointed out certain weaknesses in the law, and in 1915 the legislature heeded these suggestions and amended the law in a number of respects. It was almost a quarter of a

---

[17] *Peterson* v. *Widule*, 157 Wis. 641, 147 N.W. 966 (1914); "Constitutionality of Eugenic Marriage Laws," 27 Harv. L. Rev. 573 (1914); "Wisconsin Marriage Law Upheld," 13 Mich. L. Rev. 39 (1914); "Eugenics and Modern Law," 32 Ill. L. Rev. 327 (1937).

century before both males and females were required to have premarital examinations for venereal disease.[18] The present Wisconsin law provides that all male applicants for marriage licenses shall, at any time within fifteen days prior to such application, be examined as to the existence or nonexistence of any venereal disease and recognized clinical tests shall be applied on the discretion of the examining physician.[19] State laboratories are available for use when requested by the physician. In addition, both parties to a proposed marriage shall, within fifteen days prior to making application for a license to marry, submit to and be given the Wassermann or other standard blood test for syphilis. No license shall be issued without a physician's certificate showing that he believes the applicant to be free of diseases. Penalties are imposed upon violators of the provisions.

The restrictive laws of numbers of states are relatively ineffectual. Some states do not require all marriage-license applicants or even all male applicants to present medical certificates of their freedom from disease. Some merely forbid the marriage of venereally diseased persons. Some require the license candidates to take an oath that they are not venereally diseased. Others require the applicants, if they have ever been so afflicted, to present medical certificates showing freedom from the disease. The fact that the parties may go to another state to escape the requirement and that such evasions apparently do not injure the validity of the marriage when the parties return to their home state destroys much of the effectiveness of these clauses. In a leading Wisconsin case the court held that a marriage contracted outside of the state in violation of the eugenic and license provisions of the law was valid. The court here said: [20]

> The requirement of the antenuptial physical examination . . . is made obligatory only upon him who is an applicant for a marriage license, and this must be construed to refer to the applicant for a marriage license within this state for a marriage ceremony to be solemnized here.
>
> The eugenic marriage law, therefore . . . which provides for the obtaining by any male applicant for a license who had ever been afflicted with a venereal disease of a proper certificate as to a complete cure, does not make null or void the outside marriage and does not "disable or prohibit," within the meaning of the term as used in sec. 2330 m, persons otherwise competent and capable of contracting a valid marriage who do so contract without the state.

In 1956 forty states had laws requiring serological testing and/or examinations for syphilis as a prerequisite to the issuance of a marriage license.[21] Laws which require examinations of both parties for venereal disease and compulsory laboratory tests are clearly the most effective.

---

[18] Wis. Stat., 1937, c. 245.10(5).
[19] Wis. Stat., 1953, c. 245.10.
[20] *Lyannes* v. *Lyannes,* 171 Wis. 381, 177 N.W. 683 (1920).
[21] *Social Hygiene News,* Vol. 31, No. 2 (February, 1956).

In those states merely requiring a premarital examination, there may be inadequacies of the following types in the legislation and its administration:

1. Examinations may not be required of women. There is no sound reason why this should be.
2. Medical examinations are often perfunctory and superficial. Laboratory tests should be required.
3. Statutory fee limitations encourage doctors to make hasty examinations. Public examiners might be designated for all examinations or for some defined classes of persons. Free Wassermanns might also be provided.
4. The laws are often evaded through out-of-state marriages. In those states already having laws forbidding certain kinds of out-of-state marriages, there should be an extension of the prohibition to include those persons seeking to evade the venereal disease provisions.

Although there are many respects in which eugenic marriage laws can be improved, they have undoubtedly contributed much to general health and social welfare. Among the benefits may be enumerated the following:

1. A large number of men, particularly, have received warning as to the dangers of venereal infection at a time when they are most likely to pay attention to it.
2. Men considering marriage have been encouraged to make sure they are fit, even before applying for the medical certificate.
3. Undoubtedly many marriages have been postponed when the required examination showed an infection.

IMPOTENCY [22]

For centuries impotency has been recognized as a ground for annulling marriages. Impotence is the physical incapacity for sexual intercourse. The mere fact that one of the parties to the marriage is incapable of procreating and that the condition is incurable is no ground for annulling a marriage, for capacity to copulate, not fruitfulness, is the test. The existence of the incapacity at the time of marriage, since it was a canonical disability allowed by the ecclesiastical courts to prevent fornication and adultery, renders such a marriage merely voidable during the lifetime of the parties and only by decree of a court. The marriage may be ratified by continuing to live with the spouse after discovery of the disability.[23]

It is interesting, since impotency has so long been recognized as a reason for avoiding a marriage, that less than half the states have specific legislation upon the subject.[24] The statutes agree that such a condition at

---

[22] Vernier, *op. cit.*, Vol. 1, pp. 196–198; Joseph W. Madden, *Persons and Domestic Relations* (St. Paul, Minn., West Publishing Co., 1931), pp. 36–38; 35 Am. Jur. 256.

[23] *Kirschbaum* v. *Kirschbaum*, 92 N.J. Eq. 7, 111 Atl. 697 (1920); *G______* v. *G______*, 67 N.J. Eq. 30, 56 Atl. 736 (1903).

[24] Harriet F. Pilpel and Theodora Zavin, *Your Marriage and the Law* (New York, Rinehart, 1952), pp. 257–258; Vernier, *op. cit.*, Vol. 1, pp. 197 and table, 242–246.

the time of marriage is a ground for annulment. In a few states the courts have held that a marriage can be annulled for impotency, even in the absence of a statute so authorizing. In well over half of the states impotence is a ground for absolute divorce, either as a substitute for an annulment or as a concurrent remedy.[25] Generally, the statutes require that the condition shall have existed at the time of marriage.

MISCEGENATION [26]

At common law and in England today, there is no impediment to marriage based upon race, color, religion, or social rank. In the United States, if there is no prohibitory statute, it is legal for persons of different races to intermarry. Miscegenous marriages are prohibited by statute in over half the states. Marriage of Negroes and whites is forbidden in Alabama, Arizona, Arkansas, Colorado, Delaware, Florida, Georgia, Idaho, Indiana, Kentucky, Louisiana, Maryland, Mississippi, Missouri, Montana, Nebraska, North Carolina, North Dakota, Oklahoma, Oregon, South Carolina, South Dakota, Tennessee, Texas, Utah, Virginia, West Virginia, and Wyoming. These, it will be observed, are southern, border, or western states. It is extremely difficult to determine who is a Negro because of mixture of stocks. Some states attempt statutory definition by providing that a person is a Negro who has one eighth or more of Negro blood. Some simply make a blanket prohibition, and the courts have to decide.[27] Marriage is further prohibited in some states between whites and Indians, Malayans, Chinese, Japanese, and Hindus. Some states prohibit the marriage of whites with anyone but whites. In states with miscegenous marriage laws the marriage is usually considered void, the children illegitimate, and the relationship a crime, even a felony.

The constitutionality of statutes forbidding miscegenous marriages has been upheld. For example, an Alabama court in 1877 held that an act punishing parties to miscegenous marriages was not in violation of the civil rights section of the federal Constitution. The court found no discrimination against Negroes in the law, since it applied equally to both races. Although marriage is a civil contract, it is one of a peculiar character and one over which the state may exercise a considerable measure of control, as, for example, deciding who may be permitted to enter such a contract. Whether or not a state feels the need of legislation forbidding marriage between two races depends in large part upon the proportions and conditions of the two races in that state. The Alabama court argued as follows: [28]

---

[25] Vernier, *op. cit.,* Vol. 2, pp. 38–42.

[26] Morland, *op. cit.,* ch. 10.

[27] *Dillon* v. *Dillon,* 60 Ga. 204 (1878); Charles S. Mangum, Jr., *The Legal Status of the Negro* (Chapel Hill, N.C., University of North Carolina Press, 1940).

[28] *Green* v. *State,* 58 Ala. 190 (1877); see also, *Scott* v. *State,* 39 Ga. 321 (1869).

It is, also, a fact not always sufficiently felt, that the more humble and helpless families are, the more they need this sort of protection. Their spirits are crushed, or become rebellious, when other ills besides those of poverty, are heaped upon them. And there are (we presume) but few localities anywhere in the United States, in which the conviction has not obtained, and been approved by minds the most sedate, that the law should absolutely frustrate and prevent the growth of any desire or idea of such an alliance . . . Manifestly, it is for the peace and happiness of the black race, as well as of the white, that such laws should exist. And surely there can not be any tyranny or injustice in requiring both alike to form this union with those of their own race only, whom God hath joined together by indelible peculiarities, which declare that He has made the two races distinct.

The California court in 1948 gave a more liberal opinion.[29] Involved was a proceeding in mandamus to compel the county clerk of Los Angeles County to issue a certificate of registry and a license to marry to a white woman, Andrea Perez, and to a Negro man, Sylvester Davis. The clerk refused to issue the certificate and license, invoking the civil code which provided that all marriages of white persons with Negroes, Mongolians, members of the Malay race, or mulattoes were illegal and void and which prohibited the issuance of a license to marry to such persons. The Supreme Court held that the statute violated the equal protection of the laws clause in the Fourteenth Amendment of the United States Constitution by impairing the right of individuals to marry on the basis of race alone and by arbitrarily and unreasonably discriminating against certain social groups. In a concurring opinion one of the justices stated:

The freedom to marry the person of one's choice has not always existed and evidently does not exist here today. But is not that one of the fundamental rights of a free people? . . . If the right to marry is a fundamental right, then it must be conceded that an infringement of that right by means of a racial restriction is an unlawful infringement of one's liberty. It is immaterial that perhaps only a few would wish to marry persons not of their own race or color. It is material that the few who do so desire have the right to make that choice. It is only ignorance, prejudice and intolerance which denies it.

Although there is no scientific proof that intermarriage of the black or yellow and white races brings about racial deterioration, such is prevailing opinion in some areas of the country; and it is an argument employed by legislatures and courts for the prohibition and denial of miscegenous marriages.[30] Perhaps the California decision forecasts a more scientific and humane trend.

---

[29] *Perez et al.* v. *Lippold,* 32 Calif. 2d 711, 198 Pac. 2d 17.

[30] Innumerable popular and scientific writings provide authority for this statement. See such articles by recognized anthropologists as E. A. Hooton, "When Races Intermarry," *Nation* (July 25, 1928), p. 84; F. Boas, "Fallacies of Racial Inferiority," *Current History* (February, 1927), p. 676; M. J. Herskovits, "Race Crossing and Human Heredity," *Scientific Monthly* (December, 1934), p. 540.

STATUTORY REGULATION OF MARRIAGE: LEGAL, RELIGIOUS, MORAL RESTRICTIONS

FRAUD, DURESS, MISTAKE, JEST [31]

In most jurisdictions there are civil or criminal statutes or both on the effect of fraud, duress, and mistake on the marriage contract. A number of states provide that a marriage so induced is voidable at the suit of the innocent party, and almost half provide that where fraud has been present the marriage may be annulled. Under the common law, as well as under the statutes, marriage induced by one of these conditions is merely voidable and not absolutely void and can be avoided only by the innocent party. Probably the most common ground for annulment is fraud. As the statutes do not define these terms, it remains for the courts to determine just what situations make the marriage voidable. They say that to affect the validity of the marriage, the fraud must relate to some fact essential to the marriage relation, but the courts do not agree upon what these essentials are. It has been well recognized judicially that no misrepresentation as to fame, fortune, rank, or character constitutes ground for annulment,[32] although there are authorities who hold that in extreme cases misrepresentation as to character may constitute the required ground, especially if the victim is very young and the mismating would be shocking.[33] Modification of this general rule is taking place in some jurisdictions. In at least two states, California and New York, annulment is often used as a substitute for divorce. In 1948 annulments in California constituted somewhat more than one ninth of all legal marriage dissolutions. In New York the proportion of the total was even larger. From 1940 to 1948 the annulments in New York State constituted almost one third of all annulments in the nation.[34] This is due to the fact that the state grants divorce for adultery only and annulment for eight different grounds, some of which are ill defined. It seems clear that the majority of annulments furnish a means to evade strict divorce laws.[35] Some undoubtedly serve to satisfy religious objections to divorce.

---

[31] Morland, *op. cit.*, pp. 269–276; Vernier, *op. cit.*, Vol. 1, pp. 223–228, and 1938 suppl., p. 25; Madden, *op. cit.*, pp. 9–22.

[32] *Reynolds* v. *Reynolds*, 3 Allen 605 (Mass. 1862); *Hawkins* v. *Hawkins*, 142 Ala. 571, 38 So. 640 (1904).

[33] *Brown* v. *Scott*, 140 Md. 258, 117 Atl. 114 (1922).

[34] Kingsley Davis, "Statistical Perspective on Divorce," in Judson T. Landis and Mary G. Landis, *Readings in Marriage and the Family* (Englewood Cliffs, N.J., Prentice-Hall, 1952), p. 337.

[35] A. E. Hotchner, "The New Annulment Racket," *This Week* (January 21, 1951); Richard H. Wels, "New York: The Poor Man's Reno," 35 Cornell L. Q. 303–326 (1950); Pilpel and Zavin, *op. cit.*, pp. 266–274.

Misrepresentation as to age usually will not entitle the injured party to have the marriage set aside,[36] nor will antecedent unchastity. If the husband had intercourse with the wife before marriage, the fact that she was pregnant by another does not constitute a basis for annulment, for he would be barred from raising the question by his own fault and by his negligence in not ascertaining the facts. There are, however, some cases where annulment was granted in which the wife induced the marriage by representing to the husband that she was pregnant by him when, in fact, she was pregnant by another.[37] Where pregnancy before marriage is concealed from the husband who has not had previous improper relations with the wife, the courts hold that there are grounds for an annulment, provided the discovery is followed by a cessation of cohabitation.[38] In a Wisconsin case, the court annulled a marriage in which the wife had concealed from her husband the fact that she had a venereal disease. The court maintained that the existence of the disease was so dangerous to the health of the husband that it practically prevented the enjoyment of his marital rights.[39]

The courts have some difficulty in defining the character of the duress which will make a marriage voidable. Stated generally, the consent to marriage obtained by such physical force or threats of violence as to overwhelm the will and compel the consent of one of the parties is sufficient to render the marriage voidable.[40] Where a man is maliciously arrested for seduction and bastardy and then marries the complainant to avoid imprisonment, he acts under such duress as will render the marriage voidable.[41]

The existence of mistake may render a marriage voidable at the option of the mistaken party. However, the mistake must go to the essence of marriage, such as mistake as to the sex of the other party. Marriages contracted in jest are generally voidable.

MULTIPLE MARRIAGES [42]

Under the common law it was legally possible to have but one husband or one wife at any given time, so the existence of a valid, undissolved prior marriage by either of the parties was an impediment to another marriage. An effort at a second marriage while a binding pre-existing

[36] *Williams* v. *Williams,* 71 Misc. 590, 130 N.Y. Supp. 875 (1911).
[37] *Gard* v. *Gard,* 204 Mich. 255, 169 N.W. 908 (1918).
[38] *Harrison* v. *Harrison,* 94 Mich. 559, 54 N.W. 275 (1893).
[39] *C______* v. *C______,* 158 Wis. 301, 148 N.W. 865 (1914).
[40] *Shoro* v. *Shoro,* 60 Vt. 268, 14 Atl. 177 (1888).
[41] *Shoro* v. *Shoro,* supra; contra, *Jacobs* v. *Jacobs,* 146 Ark. 45, 225 S.W. 22 (1920).
[42] Vernier, *op. cit.,* Vol. 1, pp. 214–223; Madden, *op. cit.,* p. 39; 55 C.J.S. 831–839; 35 Am. Jur. 271–282; Morland, *op. cit.,* pp. 271–277.

marriage was still in force was absolutely null and void from its inception without the decree of a court. The offspring of the void marriage were illegitimate. In England, as early as 1604, there was a statutory provision making bigamy a felony, unless the former spouse had been continuously away for "seven years beyond the seas" or "absent for seven years and not known to be living." Similar statutes have been passed in many American jurisdictions. Bigamous marriages are both criminally and civilly condemned by all fifty-one jurisdictions. There are two rules of general application: (1) Whoever has a spouse living and marries another without a divorce or annulment is guilty of the crime of bigamy, usually made a felony. (2) Bigamous marriages are invalid, often being void without court action.

Criminal statutes on bigamy do not necessarily have any direct effect upon the question of the validity of bigamous marriages, yet they do have important indirect effects. The severe penalties imposed are a factor in securing the enforcement of prohibitions against plural marriages. The majority of statutes declare that bigamous marriages are nullities. The other states obtain the same results by less positive legislation or by judicial decision. A number of jurisdictions do not specify in definite terms whether such unions are void or merely voidable. It seems strange, in view of the prevailing objection to bigamous marriages, that only a minority of ten states declare that they are void without any legal process. A few states permit bigamy to become a ground for absolute divorce, thus providing for the legitimacy of the children.

It is well settled in the United States that the possession of two or more wives cannot be justified or excused on religious grounds. This argument was attempted before the United States Supreme Court by one who professed the Mormon faith when that problem was still causing trouble in Utah. The Court in substance said that a person cannot justify what otherwise amounts to bigamy by proof that his plural marriage was sanctioned by his religious belief. The professed doctrines of religious belief cannot be superior to the law of the land. Laws are made for the government of actions, and although they cannot interfere with religious beliefs and opinions, they may interfere with practices. Criminal intent will be implied when a man has one wife living and marries another believing that he has such a right under the doctrines of his religion.[43]

Several states have enacted statutes to meet the problems arising in what are known as Enoch Arden marriages, those contracted in the absence of a spouse supposed to be dead but who sooner or later returns. For example, they may provide that when a former spouse has been absent and unheard of for a given number of years, the second marriage shall be voidable only, and shall remain valid unless the first

[43] *Reynolds* v. *U.S.*, 98 U.S. 145, 25 L. Ed. 344 (1878).

spouse reappears and institutes an action for annulment.[44] There are differences between states as to how long the absent spouse must have been away before a valid marriage can be contracted, what constitutes absence, and the effect of a second marriage after the absent spouse returns.

THE VALIDITY OF PROHIBITED MARRIAGES AND CONFLICT OF LAWS

PROTECTION OF CHILDREN OF NULL AND VOID MARRIAGES

A serious social problem appears when children are born of null and void marriages. At common law they were "bastards." Fortunately, the severity of the common law has been tempered by modern legislation, although the bias against certain types of prohibited marriages and the legitimizing of the issue is still strong. In the absence of statutes to the contrary, the common-law doctrine prevails that children of null and void marriages are illegitimate. Most jurisdictions have passed legislation modifying the common law to some extent.[45] The most common form of statute is the one which provides that children of marriages null in law are legitimate.[46]

THE VOID OR VOIDABLE NATURE OF PROHIBITED MARRIAGES [47]

There is great legal confusion as to which marriages are absolutely void and which are merely voidable. This confusion arises in large part because of statutory ambiguity or confusion and because of the inconsistency of the courts in their use and definition of the terms *void* and *voidable* and in their opinions as to whether judicial action is necessary to set aside a void marriage as well as one that is merely voidable.

In law, any act which is void is null and ineffectual; it has no legal force or binding effect. On the other hand, an act which is voidable is one which may be declared void; it is not void in and of itself.[48] As applied to marriage, the distinction between void and voidable grew out of the fact that the ecclesiastical courts established certain canonical

---

[44] *In re Del Genovese's Will*, 120 N.Y. Supp. 1121, 136 App. Div. 894 (1909).

[45] Vernier, *op. cit.*, Vol. 1, pp. 230–235, and 1938 suppl., pp. 26, 27.

[46] "What Constitutes Marriage Within the Meaning of A Statute Legitimating Children of All Marriages Null in Law," 84 A.L.R. 499 (1933).

[47] Morland, *op. cit.*, ch. 14; Vernier, *op. cit.*, Vol. 1, pp. 239–282; James W. Schouler, *Marriage, Divorce, Separation, and Domestic Relations*, 6th ed. (Albany, N.Y., Matthew Bender and Co., 1921), Vol. 2, pp. 1343–1357; "Particular Disqualifications, Impediments, and Grounds for Annulment," 35 Am. Jur. 234–282.

[48] *Black's Law Dictionary*, 4th ed. (1951), p. 1746.

disabilities to entering matrimony, such as precontract, consanguinity, affinity, and impotency, and these rendered the attempted marriage voidable only. The civil disabilities, such as want of age, idiocy, lunacy, and fraud, were dealt with by the common-law courts and were generally treated as rendering a marriage void.

Since a void marriage is a nullity, it has been said by the courts that a marriage void in its inception does not require the judgment of a court to restore the parties to their original rights. However, though no court action under the common law was necessary as far as the parties themselves were concerned, the courts recognized a broad power to challenge void marriages in a direct or collateral action where the fact of marriage was material.

Today the language of the statutes is often not clear; some say that certain marriages are void, some say null and void, some impose a prohibition, as "no marriage shall be contracted" or "it shall not be lawful for any person." The necessity of court action to annul a marriage depends upon the wording of the statutes, and if the statutes are not clear in their intent, the courts hold that they must act before the marriage is a nullity. The courts often say that no sentence of nullity on a void marriage is necessary, yet for the sake of the good order and decorum of society, it is expedient that the validity of the marriage be ascertained and determined by a competent judicial body.[49] If the statutes merely prohibit a marriage, the courts are more apt to hold it voidable than if the law declares it absolutely void or null and void.

A voidable marriage is one which may be avoided by one of the parties, usually the one who has been injured or the party for whose protection the law was enacted. A voidable marriage is regarded as valid until the nullity has been declared in the proper proceeding.[50] It cannot be collaterally attacked, and the action must be brought during the lifetime of the parties.[51] At common law a void marriage makes cohabitation at all times unlawful and illegitimizes the children; a voidable marriage protects intercourse between the parties for the time being; furnishes to each the incidents of survivorship, such as curtesy and dower; and protects the children from the stigma of illegitimacy. As soon as the sentence of nullity is pronounced, the shield of the law falls, and the marriage is void from the beginning. Voidable marriages can be ratified and affirmed, which is not true of void marriages.

All American jurisdictions have legislation affecting grounds for annulment, but they show great variation as to what the grounds are and,

---

[49] *Hawkins* v. *Hawkins*, 142 Ala. 571, 38 So. 640 (1904); *Wightman* v. *Wightman*, 4 Johns 343 (Ch. N.Y. 1820).

[50] *In re Gregorson*, 160 Calif. 21, 116 Pac. 60 (1911); *State* v. *Smith*, 101 S.C. 293, 85 S.E. 958 (1915).

[51] 35 Am. Jur. 219–234; Schouler, *op. cit.*, Vol. 2, p. 1353.

as has been said, whether or not court action is necessary. The most uniformly adopted grounds are nonage and incapacity. A number of jurisdictions have no specific statutes on annulment for nonage, but often the courts rely upon the general statutes defining the marriageable age for infants. At common law a marriage of persons under seven was a nullity; over that age and under the age of consent it was not void but voidable and could be affirmed or disaffirmed at the age of consent. Generally under our statutes today, a marriage in which one of the parties is under the statutory age of consent but who is competent by common law is voidable only and is valid for all civil purposes unless annulled by judicial decree. As a general rule, persons who marry without the consent of their parents do not render their marriages void.

At common law the marriage of mentally incompetent persons was absolutely void; some statutes declare them so today, although some render them only voidable. Under the statutes or by court decision physical incompetency generally renders marriage merely voidable. The statutes in some jurisdictions make the intermarriage of persons of different races absolutely void. Unless expressly forbidden by statute, consanguineous marriages within the levitical degrees are generally not void but voidable. At common law and under many statutes a bigamous marriage is null and void. By great weight of judicial authority, as well as under the statutes, marriages procured by fraud, duress, and mistake are merely voidable. Terms are undergoing redefinition in a number of states.

Admitting exceptions, several conclusions concerning void and voidable marriages can be drawn:

1. Statutes often do not state clearly whether prohibited marriages are void or voidable. If they are merely prohibited, and not clearly designated as null and void, the courts may treat them as voidable.
2. If the marriage is voidable, a court action is necessary to set it aside.
3. Where a marriage is void at common law or under a statute, there seems to be a question as to whether a decree of nullity is necessary to set it aside. There is common-law authority holding that no sentence of nullity is necessary, but most courts recommend a judicial determination of the question as being the better practice.
4. A void marriage may be annulled after the death of the parties, whereas a voidable one can be attacked during their lifetime only. A void marriage may be challenged in a direct or collateral proceeding where the fact of a valid marriage may be material; but a voidable marriage can, as a general rule, be attacked only in a direct proceeding.
5. A voidable marriage can ordinarily be ratified or affirmed. This is not true of the void marriage.

There is a commendable statutory tendency to make court action necessary for setting marriages aside. Although this increases the litigation on family matters, it gives the courts a chance to ascertain the facts and, in many instances, to protect the family. Undoubtedly, in some types of situations discretion should be given the courts to decide whether even though a prohibition has been violated, it would be better to keep the family intact.

CONFLICT OF MARRIAGE LAWS [52]

In Chapter 1 we pointed out that the fundamental law of the United States is the federal Constitution which divides the powers between the federal and state governments. The federal Constitution provides that "full faith and credit shall be given in each state to the public acts, records, and judicial proceedings of every other state" and, at the same time, each state is sovereign as regards those powers which the federal Constitution has given to it. Since there are great differences in legislation between states, many difficulties are encountered in the efforts of each state to give full faith and credit to the statutes, records, and judicial proceedings of every other state and, at the same time, protect its own sovereignty. The subject of conflict of laws is one for lawyers; only a brief statement of problems and principles will be attempted here.

Marriage and divorce statutes differ so greatly from state to state that the problem of conflict of laws frequently arises in the courts. They have to decide what law shall govern: that of the domicile of both parties; that of the domicile of either; that of the state where the marriage was contracted; or that of some third state where the question arose. Some of the specific questions which occur include: Was there a valid marriage when the residents of one state went to another state to celebrate it? Is a marriage which is good in the home state valid in another state? Shall a divorce granted in one state always be recognized in another? Did the state granting divorce have jurisdiction over the parties?

Generally speaking, the courts hold that the validity of a marriage is governed by the law of the place where it is entered into or celebrated. It follows that as a general proposition, a marriage valid at the place of celebration will be recognized as valid everywhere, though it would be invalid if celebrated in the domicile of both parties or of one of them. Conversely, where the marriage is invalid by the law of the place of celebration, it cannot be considered valid by the law of the domicile of either party. However, there are important exceptions. Since the evasion statutes, if there are any, are inexplicit, the courts have to decide what statutory marriage provisions can or cannot be evaded. They usually hold that out-of-state marriages in violation of the *directory* laws of the state of domicile are valid in the home state. On the other hand, out-of-state marriages in violation of the *prohibitory* laws are often held to be invalid

[52] Herbert F. Goodrich, *Conflict of Laws* (St. Paul, Minn., West Publishing Co., 1927); Joseph H. Beale, *The Conflict of Laws* (New York, Baker Voorhis, 1935), Vol. 2, pp. 666–702; Schouler, *op. cit.*, Vol. 2, pp. 1493–1502; Morland, *op. cit.*, pp. 16–21.

in the home state. To illustrate: The marriage license, certificate, and solemnization provisions which impose an obligation upon certain persons to carry out the law do not have extraterritorial effect. The laws expressing Christian principles and the morality of the community, such as polygamy and incest laws, and those defining local public policy, such as miscegenation and remarriage-after-divorce laws, generally do have extraterritorial effect.

UNIFORM MARRIAGE LAWS [53]

Many people are deeply concerned with the great diversity in marriage and divorce legislation between states and the extensive evasion of the provisions of the stricter states. We have observed, for example, that some states still recognize the anachronistic common-law marriage and others do not; some have excellent license laws and others do not; some require physical examinations before marriage and others do not. Various suggestions have been offered as to methods of producing greater uniformity between states in their marriage legislation. Two of these are an amendment to the federal Constitution and the enactment of uniform laws.

Since authority to regulate marriage and divorce problems derives from the police power of the states and Congress has no power to regulate such matters, it has been suggested that an amendment be added to the federal Constitution. Senator Capper of Kansas (deceased) introduced into Congress in 1921 his first resolution on the subject. It read: "Congress shall have power to establish and enforce by appropriate legislation uniform laws as to marriage and divorce: Provided, that every state may by law exclude, as to its citizens duly domiciled therein, any or all causes for absolute divorce in such laws mentioned." Similar resolutions have subsequently been introduced into Congress without success.

The National Conference of Commissioners on Uniform State Laws have spearheaded the effort to secure uniform marriage and divorce legislation with the hope of preventing some of the confusion resulting from evasion. In 1911 they adopted a uniform marriage-license act with provisions concerning such items as definition of the essential elements of a marriage contract; manner of contracting marriage; consent of parents or guardians of minors; requirement of a marriage license in all cases; manner of issuing the license; manner of recording the certificate of marriage; fees; penalties; prohibition of common-law marriages; and legitimization of children. We have seen that every state has license laws but that they differ greatly in provisions. Only two states adopted the commissioners' measure: Massachusetts in 1911 and Wisconsin, with some modifications, in 1917.

---

[53] "History of Efforts to Secure a Uniform Law on Marriage and Divorce," *Congressional Digest* (June–July, 1927), pp. 183–186; N. Ruth Wood, "Marriage and Divorce Laws," 33 Women Law. J. No. 1, 23–32 (Spring, 1947), contains a chronological history of the uniform marriage and divorce law movement.

In 1912 the commissioners adopted a uniform marriage evasion act which was designed to keep any person residing and intending to continue to reside in a given state who was disabled or prohibited from contracting marriage under the laws of that state from going to another state to evade the laws of the home state. The act made such marriages null and void and imposed upon the license clerk the obligation of determining whether the applicant was evading the marriage laws of his state of residence. Many states have enacted marriage-evasion acts of one kind or another, but only five accepted the commissioners' law: Vermont, Massachusetts, Louisiana, Illinois, and Wisconsin. On the theory that uniform acts can be effective only if they have widespread adoption, the commissioners withdrew both the license and evasion acts in 1943.[54]

In 1950 the commissioners adopted another marriage-license act, this time called the "Uniform Marriage License Application Act."[55] It was their intent to limit the act to three narrow purposes: (1) to make all marriage-license applications matters of public record; (2) to provide for a waiting period between the filing of the application and the issuance of the license, leaving the length of the period to the discretion of each state; and (3) to require a blood test as a prerequisite to the acceptance and filing of the application. In a prefatory note to the statement of the provisions of the act, the commissioners commented:[56]

> It is apparent that all three of the requirements embodied in the Act are socially desirable. Particularly in view of the high ratio between marriages and divorces, it is obvious that many marriages are being contracted in haste and repented at leisure. On the other hand, uniformity of legislation between the states with respect to other requirements for the issuance of marriage licenses does not appear to be particularly desirable. Examples of this are the age required of the applicant before the license will be issued without the consent of the parents and the age at which the consent of the parents is required. Because of varying social conditions throughout the country, the fixing of these ages may vary considerably from state to state.

It seems clear that every state ought to exert greater control over marriage by adequate license and evasion acts. The former will do much to eliminate meretricious marriages within the state, and the latter to simplify the problem of conflict of laws. The regulation of family law, especially of marriage and divorce law, does not legally or socially belong with Congress but with the states.

---

[54] *Handbook of the National Conference of Commissioners on Uniform State Laws: 1943,* p. 147.
[55] *Ibid.* (1950), pp. 242–244.
[56] *Ibid.* (1950), p. 242.

SUMMARY AND CONCLUSIONS

At best, the state can do little to make marriage a socially beneficent institution. But even in the area where legal control is possible, legislatures, reflecting public opinion, are unwilling to pass laws which, if properly enforced, would help to protect the family. If the parties to the marriage, their children, and the community are to be protected from hasty and unwise unions, more attention must be given both to training for family life and to proper legal control. The diversity in statutes between states, the uncertainty as to the intent of legislatures in many instances and the consequent problems handed to the courts, the significance of court decisions in clarifying or laying down the law, and the variation between jurisdictions in court decisions have been discussed in this chapter. Numerous suggestions for modifications of the statutes have also been offered.

In summary, the most important measures for improving the legal control of marriage seem to this writer to be:

1. The complete abolition of common-law marriage and breach-of-promise suits.
2. Clarification of which marriages are void and which are voidable.
3. Enactment of uniform license and evasion laws.
4. Requirement that those officials who issue licenses shall be under some form of state supervision and that proof of age and parental consent shall be submitted to these officials.
5. Requirement of premarital physical examinations to include the Wassermann and other laboratory tests for both men and women, and the further requirement that marriages contracted in violation of these provisions shall be void.
6. A statutory definition of feeble-mindedness and insanity when psychiatrists reasonably agree upon one.
7. The legitimization of children of void marriages where this is not yet true.

Selected References

ALEXANDER, Paul W., and others, *Conference on Divorce,* The Law School of the University of Chicago Conference Series (Chicago, 1952), No. 9.

BISHOP, J. P., *New Commentaries on Marriage, Divorce, and Separation* (Chicago, T. H. Flood, 1891), Vol. 1, Bk. 3.

BLACKSTONE, Sir William, *Commentaries on the Laws of England in Four Books* (Philadelphia, Rees, Welsh and Co., 1897), Bk. 1.

BOSSARD, J. H. S., ed., *Annals of the American Academy of Political and Social Sciences: Toward Family Stability,* Vol. 272 (November, 1950).

BRECKINRIDGE, S. P., *The Family and the State* (Chicago, University of Chicago Press, 1934).

CALHOUN, Arthur W., *A Social History of the American Family* (Cleveland, Arthur H. Clark Co., 1917), Vol. 1.

DESPERT, J. Louise, *Children of Divorce* (New York, Doubleday, 1953).

Divorce: A Re-examination of Basic Concepts, 18 L. and Contemp. Prob. (1953), pp. 1–106.

ERNST, Morris L., and LOTH, David, *For Better or Worse* (New York, Harper, 1952).

HARPER, Fowler V., *Problems of the Family* (Indianapolis, Bobbs-Merrill, 1952).

HENDERSON, James M., and others, *Nelson on Divorce and Annulment,* 3d ed. (Chicago, Callaghan Co., 1945), 3 vols., with 1952 cumulative suppl.

HOWARD, George Eliot, *A History of Matrimonial Institutions* (Chicago, University of Chicago Press, 1904).

MACKAY, Richard V., and MANDELL, Irving, *Law of Marriage and Divorce Simplified,* 2d ed. (New York, Oceana, 1951).

MADDEN, Joseph W., *Persons and Domestic Relations* (St. Paul, Minn., West Publishing Co., 1931).

MANGUM, Charles S., Jr., *The Legal Status of the Negro* (Chapel Hill, N.C., University of North Carolina Press, 1940).

MORLAND, John W., *Keezer on the Law of Marriage and Divorce,* 3d ed. (Indianapolis, Bobbs-Merrill, 1946), with 1950 suppl.

PILPEL, Harriet F., and ZAVIN, Theodora, *Your Marriage and the Law* (New York, Rinehart, 1952).

PLOSCOWE, Morris, *Sex and the Law* (New York, Prentice-Hall, 1951).

POLLOCK, Sir Frederick, and MAITLAND, F. W., *The History of English Law before the Time of Edward I* (Cambridge, University Press, 1923), Vol. 2.

RICHMOND, Mary E., and HALL, Fred S., *Marriage and the State* (New York, Russell Sage Foundation, 1929).

SCHOULER, James W., *Marriage, Divorce, Separation, and Domestic Relations,* 6th ed. (Albany, N.Y., Matthew Bender and Co., 1921), Vols. 1 and 2.

U.S. Interagency Committee on Background Materials for the National Conference on Family Life, *The American Family: A Factual Background* (Washington, D.C., G.P.O., 1949).

VERNIER, Chester G., and others, *American Family Laws* (Stanford, Cal., Stanford University Press, 1931–1938), Vol. 1, and 1938 suppl.

The student should also consult statutes, judicial decisions, articles in the various law encyclopedias, and the following references: *American Jurisprudence, Corpus Juris Secundum,* and *Uniform Laws Annotated.*

CHAPTER 6

Divorce in Modern American Jurisdictions

INTRODUCTION

It has been said that divorce, or the formal dissolution of marriage, is, in any society, a corollary of the theory and practice of marriage, that it is a direct measure of marital stability, and that it is designed primarily to relieve the hardships imposed in individual cases by the customary marriage rules.[1] Attitudes toward marriage and divorce are conditioned by the past and especially by the forces of religion. During the last half century or more the law, as well as public opinion, has begun to look upon marriage as a human rather than a religious institution, with the result that we hear expressed such diametrically opposite opinions as: (1) No one should seek or obtain a divorce, since marriage is a sacred institution; anyone who wishes a divorce should be able to obtain one, since marriage is a civil and human institution. (2) Divorce should be available to the innocent party only when adultery has been committed; divorce should be available on a number of grounds with adequate procedure to protect the family and the state. (3) No one should be permitted to contract a second marriage while the first spouse lives; after the divorce both innocent and guilty parties should be permitted to remarry.

Courts within the same state differ substantially in their opinions on separation and divorce. A judge in Wisconsin was heard to say that he does everything in his power to prevent divorces because he personally disapproves of them. Another judge within the same state grants divorce on the slenderest grounds.

EARLY DIVORCE IN THE UNITED STATES

DIVORCE IN THE NEW ENGLAND COLONIES

From the beginning the colonists treated marriage as a civil contract. The same influence that established the civil marriage in New England

---

[1] Frank H. Hankins, "Divorce," *Encyclopaedia of the Social Sciences* (1931) Vol. 5, pp. 177–184.

also worked for a liberal policy regarding divorce. For the most part, the doctrines of the *Reformatio Legum* were put into practice. In almost all the colonies the canonical decree *a mensa et thoro* was entirely abandoned. Dissolution of the marriage bond was granted in the colonies for such causes as desertion, cruelty, and adultery. Generally, the husband and wife were dealt with as equals before the law. In Massachusetts, as in most of the colonies, neither causes for, nor kinds of, divorce were defined by statute. Because of this lack of positive legislation, harmony in judicial practices concerning divorce did not always exist. Governor Thomas Hutchinson (1711–1780), who presided in the divorce court of Massachusetts for many years, summarized the policies used in granting divorces during the colonial period as follows: [2]

> In matters of divorce they left the rules of the canon law out of the question; with respect to some of them, prudently enough, I never heard of a separation, under the first charter, a *mensa et thoro*. Where it is practiced the innocent party suffers more than the guilty. In general, what would have been cause for such a separation in the spiritual courts was sufficient, with them, for a *divorce a vinculo*. Female adultery was never doubted to have been sufficient cause; but male adultery, after some debate and consultation with the elders, was judged not sufficient. Desertion of a year or two, when there was evidence of a determined design not to return, was always good cause; so was cruel usage of the husband. Consanguinity they settled in the same degrees as it is settled in England and in the Levitical laws.

DIVORCE IN THE SOUTHERN AND MIDDLE COLONIES [3]

In the southern colonies, English law and custom with respect to divorce and separation generally prevailed. In England the ecclesiastical courts had jurisdiction in such matters, but the southern colonies, like all the others, never established such courts; nor did they give jurisdiction with respect to the dissolution of marriage to any other court. Therefore, though parties could and did separate by mutual consent, neither divorces nor legal separations were granted during the colonial period.

The middle colonies also adopted a conservative policy toward divorce. In New York, under Dutch rule, a divorce was occasionally granted by the civil courts. When the colony came under the rule of England, theoretically at least, the English law concerning divorce was adopted, but, as in the southern colonies, ecclesiastical courts were not established, and no court was given jurisdiction. Consequently, as in the South, neither divorces nor legal separations were granted. In Pennsylvania, though a statute passed in 1682 recognized absolute divorce on the ground of adultery, no

---

[2] Thomas Hutchinson, *The History of the Colony and Province of Massachusetts Bay*, ed. Lawrence Shaw Mayo (Cambridge, Harvard University Press, 1936), Vol. 1, p. 375.

[3] George Eliot Howard, *A History of Matrimonial Institutions* (Chicago, University of Chicago Press, 1904), Vol. 2, pp. 366–389.

tribunal was ever empowered to grant the divorce, and the law was a dead letter. Absolute divorces, however, could be granted in Pennsylvania by legislative act, but there is no evidence to show that they were at all common. By the early part of the eighteenth century the foundation of our marriage law had been laid, but a fundamental doctrine of divorce had not been developed.

LATER DEVELOPMENTS IN AMERICAN DIVORCE LAW

After the colonies became the United States, legislative divorce by private statute continued to be the practice for more than half a century. It was not until legislatures conferred divorce jurisdiction upon the courts that they became active in this field. Gradually, the statutes defined the grounds for divorce and bestowed divorce jurisdiction upon both the ordinary law and the equity courts. As early as 1785 Pennsylvania enacted a statute providing a number of grounds for divorce, both from bed and board and from the bonds of matrimony. Georgia, Mississippi, and Alabama were among the first states to do away with individual divorces by legislative act. By the middle of the nineteenth century, legislative divorce had disappeared in most American jurisdictions.

DISTINCTIONS BETWEEN ABSOLUTE AND PARTIAL DIVORCE AND ANNULMENT

Today, the states make provision for the absolute or partial dissolution of marriage by complete divorce, by partial divorce, sometimes called legal separation, and by annulment. The basis of this differentiation was derived from the English common and canon law which we have earlier described. In England the term *divorce* was used broadly to apply both to the decrees of nullity of marriages and to decrees of separation. In the United States the term applies to decrees dissolving the effect of a valid marriage, although the statutes in a few states confuse the terms by allowing "divorce" for causes such as fraud, duress, and impotency, which in sound theory are really grounds for a decree of nullity.

Absolute divorce or *divorce a vinculo matrimonii* is the legal separation of man and wife effected for cause by the judgment of a court totally dissolving the marriage relation. It operates upon a perfectly valid marriage and is grounded upon causes which have developed subsequent to the marriage ceremony. It absolutely releases the parties from the obligations of matrimony and is the only real "divorce."

Legal separation is partial or qualified divorce for cause by the judgment of a court, and the parties are forbidden to cohabit. It does not effect the basic obligations of the marriage, and under it there is no right to remarry. It grew out of the old ecclesiastical *divorce a mensa et thoro,* and some statutes still use those terms.

A decree of annulment, the *divorce a vinculo matrimonii* of the ecclesiastical courts, means that no marriage ever occurred. Hence, neither party ever acquired any marital rights, and upon the issuance of the decree the parties return to the *status in quo* at the time of marriage. No property rights accrue, and in the absence of a statute to the contrary, children are illegitimate.

LEGISLATIVE REGULATION OF DIVORCE: JURISDICTION AND PROCESS

DIVERSITY OF STATUTES [4]

All American jurisdictions grant absolute divorce, South Carolina being the last state to do so. There is agreement among the states upon one ground only, adultery. There are eight main causes for granting divorce; thirty or more minor grounds are recognized by one or more jurisdictions. In addition to the differences as to causes, there are variations in respect to jurisdiction, domicile or residence, the time required for various steps in connection with procuring the divorce, notice and service of papers, the effects of foreign divorces, alimony and property, custody and support of children, remarriage, and appeals.

JURISDICTION TO GRANT DIVORCE [5]

The jurisdiction to grant divorce is wholly statutory, and legislatures have bestowed that right upon designated courts. As a general rule, statutes confer upon the courts power to grant divorces only when one or both parties is resident in the state. Probably the most common requirement is that the plaintiff shall be domiciled in the state where he brings his action. Ordinarily, the place where the cause for the divorce arose has no legal significance, so there is no jurisdiction to grant a divorce for an offense committed within the state if the domicile of the parties is in another state. As a general rule, the statutes require a definite period of residence

---

[4] For exhaustive discussion of divorce, see James M. Henderson and others, *Nelson on Divorce and Annulment,* 3d ed. (Chicago, Callaghan, 1945), Vols. 1–3, with 1952 cumulative suppl.; John W. Morland, *Keezer on the Law of Marriage and Divorce,* 3d ed. (Indianapolis, Bobbs-Merrill, 1946), with suppl. to 1950; Joseph W. Madden, *Persons and Domestic Relations* (St. Paul, Minn., West Publishing Co., 1931); James W. Schouler, *Marriage, Divorce, Separation, and Domestic Relations,* 6th ed. (Albany, N.Y., Matthew Bender and Co., 1921), Vols. 1 and 2; *Divorce,* 17 Am. Jur. (with cumulative suppl. to 1952), 192–583; *Divorce,* 27 C.J.S. 513–1306; Chester G. Vernier and others, *American Family Laws* (Stanford, Cal., Stanford University Press, 1931–1938), Vol. 2 and 1938 suppl. See also, Morris Ploscowe, *Sex and the Law* (Englewood Cliffs, N.J., Prentice-Hall, 1951), chs. 2 and 3; Harriet F. Pilpel and Theodora Zavin, *Your Marriage and the Law* (New York, Rinehart, 1952), Pt. 4; Fowler V. Harper, *Problems of the Family* (Indianapolis, Bobbs-Merrill, 1952), ch. 7.

[5] Vernier, *op. cit.,* Vol. 2, pp. 5–7; Madden, *op. cit.,* pp. 312, 313; Schouler, *op. cit.,* Vol. 2, p. 1736. See also, *The Book of the States: 1954–55* (Chicago, Council of State Governments, 1955), Vol. 10, p. 324, for residence period by state.

within the state before a person has a right to bring an action or the court has the right to hear it. The period varies from six weeks in Idaho, Nevada, and the Virgin Islands, sixty days in Wyoming, ninety days or three months in Arkansas, Florida, and Utah, to five years in Massachusetts. Twenty-eight jurisdictions require one year, the most common requirement.

It should be noted that courts interchangeably use the terms *domicile* and *residence,* as we have done. Strictly speaking, domicile is where one is, intends to remain, and, if away, the place to which he intends to return. Residence is where one actually is. Domicile seems to be what the courts are really interested in. The Williams II case, to which we shall presently refer, established the doctrine that fraudulently claimed domicile is not enough to give the foreign court that jurisdiction which shall receive full faith and credit in the home state. Jurisdiction, in other words, depends upon domicile, or at least residence *animo manendi,* of one of the parties.

PROCESS AND PLEADINGS AS A BASIS FOR OBTAINING JURISDICTION [6]

In divorce actions, as in any other civil action, there must be service of process upon the defendant according to the trial practice rules of the state in order to give the court jurisdiction to hear and determine the particular case. Generally, the law provides for two methods of service of process, actual and constructive. Actual or personal service of process is made by reading the original process to the defendant or by delivery to him of a copy. Constructive or substituted service of process is made by leaving a copy of the process at the defendant's residence when he is absent or by posting or publishing notice of the pendency of the suit and mailing a copy of the notice posted or published to the defendant if his post office address is known.

In divorce actions constructive service gives the court jurisdiction over the marital *status* or *rem* but not over the person of the defendant unless he chooses to appear. In some states a divorce can be obtained against a nonresident by constructive service of process, the statutes so authorizing, because of the *in rem* nature of the action. However, if the plaintiff wishes to obtain a judgment for alimony or a judgment affecting property rights, personal service is required. This is because the court has no right or power to order a person to pay a sum of money unless he is within the jurisdiction of the court and has personally been served with a summons and complaint. When he is within the borders of the state and has been served in person, then the court has acquired jurisdiction of his person and can hand down a personal judgment against him ordering him to pay

[6] 17 Am. Jur. 295–318; Schouler, *op. cit.,* Vol. 2, pp. 1764–1774; Morland, *op. cit.,* ch. 46.

a sum of money. As a general rule, the statutory requirement as to service of process in divorce actions, which includes several minor processes, must be strictly complied with or the decree will be looked upon as void.

The complaint, petition, or libel, as it is variously called, is a statement of the facts which constitute the plaintiff's cause of action. It should therefore state all the facts essential to establish the cause of action. The defendant may "answer" the complaint within a stated period of time, in which case he or she will deny the allegations of the plaintiff and attempt to show that no grounds for divorce actually exist; or "demur" to the complaint if the facts as stated in the complaint fail to state a cause of action; or "answer" and ask for a divorce in a cross bill or cross complaint if such a practice is provided by statute. Usually the plaintiff must be present in person at the trial. In most divorce actions the defendant does not put in an appearance.

LEGISLATIVE REGULATION OF DIVORCE: GROUNDS

GENERAL

Each state has the right to prescribe the grounds upon which divorce may be granted within its borders. As a rule, the courts will grant divorce only for some cause named by statute, and the general attitude of the courts and legislatures is that the marriage relation should be dissolved only for grave and substantial causes specifically stated in the law.[7] Once an innocent plaintiff has proved a ground for divorce prescribed by statute, he is entitled to the divorce as a matter of law.[8] Although the court is interested in reconciliation, the protection of the family and the marriage relationship, and perhaps in delaying trial or holding up a decree, the attitude of the courts has become more practical in recent years. One court frankly stated that society is not interested in perpetuating a status out of which no good can come and from which harm may result.[9] There are a few states which, by statute, have given the courts discretionary power to grant divorces for causes not specifically provided by statute.

ADULTERY[10]

Adultery is the voluntary sexual intercourse of a married man or woman with a person other than the offender's spouse. Today, statutes in

[7] *Trenchard* v. *Trenchard,* 245 Ill. 313, 92 N.E. 243 (1910); *Alexander* v. *Alexander,* 140 Ind. 555, 38 N.E. 855 (1894); Lottie Friedler, "Divorce Laws," 33 Women Law. J., No. 1, 32–36, contains enumeration of causes for divorce by state.

[8] *Miles* v. *Miles,* 137 Mo. App. 38, 119 S.W. 456 (1909).

[9] *Lingner* v. *Lingner,* 165 Tenn. 525, 56 S.W. 2d 749 (1933).

[10] Vernier, *op. cit.,* Vol. 2, pp. 18–24; Morland, *op. cit.,* ch. 18; Richard V. Mackay and Irving Mandell, *Law of Marriage and Divorce Simplified,* 2d ed. (New York, Oceana, 1951), pp. 69–71; Henderson, *op. cit.,* Vol. 1, ch. 5; Vol. 3, chart 612.

all jurisdictions make adultery a ground for divorce. Almost without exception there is no distinction between the rights of a husband and a wife. Generally adultery need not be "habitual."

An examination of the decisions will give some notion of what adultery is. A man may be guilty of adultery, even though the offense was committed with a woman who was stupefied with liquor at the time,[11] or where the act was committed without the consent of the woman.[12] It has been said that if a man chooses to marry an unchaste woman with full knowledge of her unchastity, he cannot obtain a divorce for her subsequent adultery, but this is not true. The true test is not knowledge of previous conduct but a violation of the conditions of the marriage after it has been entered into. Even though a man had illicit sexual relations with his wife before marriage and married her while she was an inmate of a house of prostitution, those facts do not vitiate his right to a divorce for her refusal to leave the house and to discontinue her adulterous acts.[13] Voluntary separation does not grant a license to commit adultery, and it is generally held that under such circumstances the innocent party may have a remedy against the other by way of divorce.[14]

Adultery may be proved by circumstantial evidence, but the courts often say that it must be of a "clear and positive" nature.[15] The defendant is entitled to the same presumption of innocence as in criminal cases.[16] It is not necessary to prove the defendant guilty of adultery "beyond a reasonable doubt," but it is sufficient if he is found guilty by a "clear preponderance of the evidence." [17] In proving adultery where the parties are not caught, two elements are required: the opportunity to commit the act and the inclination to commit it. For example, if a man takes a woman to a hotel and retires with her to a room for the night, that is usually sufficient to prove both the opportunity and inclination to commit adultery.[18]

CRUELTY [19]

Cruelty is a cause for divorce in most jurisdictions. The terms commonly used in the statutes are *cruelty, extreme cruelty,* and *cruel and inhuman treatment.* No exact, all-inclusive definition of legal cruelty can be given. The courts generally content themselves with determining whether the facts in the particular case constitute cruelty. The early de-

---

[11] *Commonwealth* v. *Bakeman,* 131 Mass., 577, 41 Am. Rep. 248 (1881).

[12] *State* v. *Henderson,* 84 Iowa 161, 50 N.W. 758 (1891).

[13] *Roote* v. *Roote,* 33 App. D.C. 398, 23 L.R.A. (N.S.) 240 (1909).

[14] *Watts* v. *Watts,* 160 Mass. 464, 23 L.R.A. 187 (1894).

[15] *Taft* v. *Taft,* 80 Vt. 256, 67 Atl. 703 (1907).

[16] *German* v. *German,* 137 Md. 424, 112 Atl. 789 (1921).

[17] *Neff* v. *Neff,* 96 Conn. 273, 114 Atl. 126 (1921).

[18] *Kerr* v. *Kerr,* 134 App. Div. 141, 118 N.Y. Supp. 801 (1909).

[19] Vernier, *op. cit.,* Vol. 2, pp. 25–29, and 1938 suppl., p. 40; Mackay and Mandell, *op. cit.,* pp. 69–71; Morland, *op. cit.,* ch. 21; Henderson, *op. cit.,* Vol. 1, ch. 6.

cisions required physical violence upon the person with danger to life or health. This attitude was strongly voiced by the Michigan supreme court in an early opinion. It said:[20]

> The law does not permit courts to sever the marriage bond and to break up households, merely because the parties, from unruly tempers or mutual wranglings, live unhappily together. It requires them to submit to the ordinary consequences of human infirmities, and of unwise selections, and the misconduct which will form a good ground for a legal separation must be very serious, and such as amounts to extreme cruelty, entirely subverting the family relations, by rendering the association intolerable.

There are some courts which still cling to this point of view. A single act of violence ordinarily will not serve as a ground for divorce if it is committed in a heat of passion and there is no likelihood that it will be repeated.[21] However, if the single act was very severe and involved malice, it might be sufficient cause.[22] Again, where one of the parties commits a series of less serious acts, and there is a likelihood that they will be continued, even though no one of the acts would be sufficient by itself, the cumulative effect of the acts is cruelty.[23]

Although few states make mental cruelty a ground for divorce by the express words of their statutes, the courts in many jurisdictions accept it as a valid cause. When the mental injury is such that it preys upon the mind and undermines the health, though the suffering is caused by words or conduct unaccompanied by an act of physical violence, the result is bodily harm, and therefore the conduct producing the mental suffering is legal cruelty.[24] In other words, without entirely repudiating the early theory that the injury must be physical, some courts admit that legal cruelty may come about from continuous nagging and abuse, humiliating insults, and other mean and annoying conduct which cause mental suffering and consequent ill health.[25] The chain of causation is indirect, but the ultimate result is an injury to health. Under the indirect injury to health doctrine, divorces have been granted on the ground of cruelty for harsh and humiliating language or demeanor;[26] for the wife's or husband's constant nagging;[27] for making false charges of infidelity,[28] for such things as the husband telling the wife of his love for someone else;

---

[20] *Cooper* v. *Cooper*, 17 Mich. 205 (1868).

[21] *Hastings* v. *Hastings*, 147 Md. 177, 127 Atl. 743 (1925); *Johnson* v. *Johnson*, 80 N.H. 15, 112 Atl. 399 (1921).

[22] *French* v. *French*, 4 Mass. 587 (1808); *Anderson* v. *Anderson*, 68 Calif. App. 218, 228 Pac. 215 (1924).

[23] *Gibbs* v. *Gibbs*, 18 Kan. 419 (1877).

[24] Madden, *op. cit.*, p. 271.

[25] *Pearson* v. *Pearson*, 230 N.Y. 141, 129 N.E. 349 (1920); *Bailey* v. *Bailey*, 97 Mass. 373 (1867); *Freeman* v. *Freeman*, 31 Wis. 235 (1872).

[26] *Koehler* v. *Koehler*, 137 Ark. 302, 209 S.W. 283 (1919).

[27] *Barngrover* v. *Barngrover*, 57 Calif. App. 43, 206 Pac. 461 (1922).

[28] *Eward* v. *Eward*, 72 Ind. App. 638, 125 N.E. 468 (1919).

for unfounded accusations of crime and misconduct; for studied vexations and deliberate insults; and for stopping payment on checks and destroying credit. Excessive sexual demands by the husband upon the wife is not an uncommon ground for divorce.[29] The courts of some states have granted divorce on the ground of cruelty for the denial of reasonable intercourse for an extended period, such as twelve years.[30]

DESERTION [31]

Most jurisdictions grant divorce for desertion. The specified period of desertion varies from a few months to five years, the usual period being one year. It is variously designated as *willful desertion, willful and malicious desertion,* and *utter and continued desertion.* Before desertion becomes a legal ground for divorce, certain elements must be present: [32]

1. A cessation of cohabitation.
2. Desertion for the period prescribed by statute.
3. An intention to abandon.
4. Want of consent on the part of the party abandoned.
5. Unjustifiable abandonment.

There is no simple or uniform statutory definition of desertion as a cause for divorce. Many courts hold that if the husband drives his wife away from him, his conduct will amount to desertion as clearly as if he had left her.[33] When either spouse, after having been gone for some time, offers in good faith to return but is rejected, the absence will not amount to desertion unless such rejection is justified.[34] There must be an intention to abandon.[35] The intent to abandon need not be shown by direct evidence but may be inferred from the circumstances, as when there is long absence without justifiable cause.[36] Desertion must be without the consent of the abandoned spouse. If there is a separation by consent, either expressed in the words of the parties or inferred from the acts of the parties, desertion cannot be relied upon as a cause for divorce.[37] The abandonment must be unjustifiable. If either spouse is guilty of such misconduct as to create proper grounds for the other's departure, the latter's absence will not make out the necessary desertion.[38] The question often arises as to what kind of conduct is sufficient justification for one spouse

---

[29] *Mayhew* v. *Mayhew,* 61 Conn. 233, 23 Atl. 966 (1891); *Griest* v. *Griest,* 154 Md. 696, 140 Atl. 590 (1927).

[30] *Nordlund* v. *Nordlund,* 97 Wash. 475, 166 Pac. 795 (1917).

[31] Vernier, *op. cit.,* Vol. 2, pp. 31–38, and 1938 suppl., p. 41; Mackay and Mandell, *op. cit.,* pp. 69–71; Morland, *op. cit.,* ch. 22; Henderson, *op. cit.,* Vol. 1, ch. 4.

[32] Madden, *op. cit.,* p. 276.

[33] *Reynolds* v. *Reynolds,* 224 Ky. 668, 6 S.W. 2d 1078 (1928).

[34] *Provast* v. *Provast,* 71 N.J. Eq. 204, 75 Atl. 1101 (1906).

[35] *Williams* v. *Williams,* 130 N.Y. 193, 29 N.E. 98 (1891).

[36] *Morrison* v. *Morrison,* 20 Calif. 431 (1862).

[37] *Turner* v. *Turner,* 187 Calif. 632, 203 Pac. 109 (1921).

[38] *Warner* v. *Warner,* 54 Mich. 492, 20 N.W. 557 (1884); *Leonard* v. *Leonard,* 174 Iowa 734, 156 N.W. 803 (1916).

to leave the other.[39] There is serious conflict on this question, and some courts stand strictly upon the principle that nothing but conduct which is a ground for divorce will justify one spouse in leaving the other.[40]

IMPOTENCE [41]

Ordinarily, if impotence exists at the time of the marriage it is a ground for annulment. However, more than half of the states make it a cause for absolute divorce, either as a substitute for annulment or as a concurrent remedy. The statutes are vague or silent on a number of points. In several states the word is used without any attempt at definition. Numbers of states do not prescribe when the impotence must exist. Some specify that it must exist at the time of the marriage and when the action is brought. Under the decisions impotence usually means the inability to copulate and not sterility; it must be incurable and generally must exist both at the time of the marriage and at the time the action is brought.

CONVICTION FOR CRIME [42]

Imprisonment or conviction of crime is a cause for divorce in most jurisdictions. Again, the statutes are vague on many important points. They use varying language to describe the ground, such as "conviction of crime," "conviction and sentence," or "sentence followed by imprisonment." In about a third of the jurisdictions the "crime" must be a felony, and in some it is by inference a felony. There is great variation as to the length of the sentence and the place of punishment, as in "state prison," in "penitentiary," or in "any county jail in or out of this state or in any state." It has been held that it is of no consequence that a sentence is reduced below the specified period by an allowance of time for good behavior; it will not destroy the effect of the initial conviction and imprisonment as a ground for divorce.[43] It has also been held that if a woman knowingly marries a felon, she cannot afterward set up his conviction as a ground for a divorce.[44]

HABITUAL DRUNKENNESS [45]

Habitual drunkenness is a ground for divorce in the majority of American jurisdictions. The statutes do not as a general rule define drunken-

---

[39] *Lyster* v. *Lyster,* 111 Mass. 327 (1873).

[40] *Arnaboldi* v. *Arnaboldi,* 101 N.J. Eq. 126, 138 Atl. 116 (1927).

[41] Vernier, *op. cit.,* Vol. 2, pp. 38–42; Mackay and Mandell, *op. cit.,* pp. 69–71; Morland, *op. cit.,* ch. 24; Henderson, *op. cit.,* Vol. 1, pp. 326–333.

[42] Vernier, *op. cit.,* Vol. 2, pp. 42–48, and 1938 suppl., p. 42; Mackay and Mandell, *op. cit.,* pp. 67–71; Morland, *op. cit.,* ch. 20; Henderson, *op. cit.,* Vol. 1, pp. 320–326.

[43] *Oliver* v. *Oliver,* 169 Mass. 592, 48 N.E. 843 (1897).

[44] *Caswell* v. *Caswell,* 64 Vt. 557, 24 Atl. 988 (1892).

[45] Vernier, *op. cit.,* Vol. 2, pp. 48–53, and 1938 suppl., p. 42; Mackay and Mandell, *op. cit.,* pp. 69–72; Morland, *op. cit.,* ch. 23; Henderson, *op. cit.,* Vol. 1, ch. 7.

ness, although they often require that it be "habitual." It is well recognized that excessive indulgence in intoxicating drinks as a fixed habit is habitual drunkenness, and this is true even though there may be intervals when the party refrains entirely from the use of intoxicating liquors.[46] The courts have held that neither occasional drunkenness [47] nor habitual but moderate use of liquor will constitute a ground for divorce.[48] A wife cannot set up habitual drunkenness as a cause if at the time of the marriage she had full knowledge of the existence of the habit.[49]

NONSUPPORT [50]

Over half the jurisdictions make nonsupport a ground for divorce. According to most of the statutes, the nonsupport must have continued for a definite period of time, ranging from sixty days to two years, one year being common and some states specifying no definite period. The courts usually lay down the additional requirement that the husband must have been able to support the wife before his failure to support becomes a ground for divorce.[51] Sometimes this provision is laid down in the statute.

INSANITY [52]

It is well recognized that insanity at the time of the marriage affects its validity, and in most jurisdictions this is a statutory ground for annulment. In the absence of a statute expressly permitting it, divorce cannot be decreed for insanity arising after marriage.[53] Some who oppose divorce for insanity occurring after marriage do so on the theory that divorce should be granted only because of some fault on the part of the defendant. Those who favor it do so on the ground that insanity is not one of the risks and consequences which society ought to compel the well spouse to bear. American legislatures have been reluctant to make insanity after marriage a ground for divorce. About half the jurisdictions, however, permit divorce for idiocy or insanity. Under these statutes it is a common requirement that the insanity shall have existed for a definite period of time, which varies from two to more years, five years being the most usual. The statutes usually specify that the spouse must have been de-

---

[46] *Garrett* v. *Garrett,* 252 Ill. 318, 96 N.E. 882 (1911).

[47] *Smith* v. *Smith,* 172 Mich. 175, 137 N.W. 644 (1912).

[48] *Bain* v. *Bain,* 79 Neb. 711, 113 N.W. 141 (1907).

[49] *McNabb* v. *McNabb,* 182 Iowa 1143, 166 N.W. 457 (1918).

[50] Vernier, *op. cit.,* Vol. 2, pp. 54–58; Mackay and Mandell, *op. cit.,* pp. 69–71; Morland, *op. cit.,* ch. 29.

[51] *Shelhart* v. *Shelhart,* 195 Mich. 144, 161 N.W. 843 (1917); *Seigmund* v. *Seigmund,* 46 Wash. 572, 90 Pac. 913 (1907).

[52] Vernier, *op. cit.,* Vol. 2, pp. 58–64, and 1938 suppl., pp. 43–45; Mackay and Mandell, *op. cit.,* pp. 69–71; Morland, *op. cit.,* ch. 26; Henderson, *op. cit.,* Vol. 1, pp. 333–338; Joseph Simon, "Shall the Incurably Insane Be Divorced?" 65 N.J.L.J. 61 (1942).

[53] *Pile* v. *Pile,* 94 Ky. 308, 22 S.W. 215 (1893); *Cain* v. *Milburn,* 192 Iowa 705, 185 N.W. 478 (1921).

clared incurably insane and that he must be confined in an asylum or institution.

MISCELLANEOUS [54]

Divorce is granted for numerous miscellaneous reasons, such as living apart a given number of years, conviction of crime before marriage, crimes against nature, infecting spouse with venereal disease, habitual use of drugs, habitual indulgence in violent temper. Of particular interest are provisions in a few states allowing divorce for incompatibility of temper. Of interest, too, is a general clause in the statutes of a few states which gives the courts a wide discretion to grant divorce for grounds not specifically indicated by statute.[55] In Washington the statute permits divorce for any cause deemed sufficient by the court if it is satisfied that the parties can no longer live together.[56]

LEGISLATIVE REGULATION OF DIVORCE: DEFENSES

GENERAL AND SPECIAL DEFENSES [57]

The defenses to actions for divorce may be classified as general and special. The general defenses belong to the parties as litigants and are such as may arise in any lawsuit. The special defenses have been developed to protect all those likely to be affected by the dissolution of a marriage. It is the policy of the law to encourage the continuance of the marriage relation once it has been brought into existence. The law, therefore, encourages the defense of divorce actions. There are four generally accepted special defenses: collusion, connivance, condonation, and recrimination. A fifth, a statute of limitation, is found in some jurisdictions. A majority of the jurisdictions have statutes on one or more of the defenses. A small proportion have legislation which covers all of these main defenses, and about the same number have no statute on any of them. This latter situation does not mean that the defenses are lacking but that they are supplied by the courts under the common law.

COLLUSION [58]

Collusion is any agreement between the parties by which they endeavor to obtain a divorce by an imposition on the court. Its essence is fraud upon the court. As demonstrated by cases, this fraud may appear

---

[54] Vernier, *op. cit.*, Vol. 2, pp. 64–72, and 1938 suppl., p. 46.
[55] Madden, *op. cit.*, p. 293.
[56] *Bickford* v. *Bickford*, 57 Wash. 639, 107 Pac. 837 (1910).
[57] Vernier, *op. cit.*, Vol. 2, pp. 72–92; Morland, *op. cit.*, ch. 33; Henderson, *op. cit.*, ch. 9.
[58] Madden, *op. cit.*, p. 298; Vernier, *op. cit.*, Vol. 2, pp. 75–77.

in at least three forms: (1) by the commission of an offense for the purpose of obtaining a divorce, (2) by the introduction of false evidence of an offense not actually committed, and (3) by suppression of a valid defense.

The courts have had ample opportunity to describe what facts amount to collusion. Some courts have held that any agreement between the husband and wife whereby they attempt to obtain a divorce by imposing upon the court is collusion.[59] There are those courts which have gone further and have maintained that where the parties act in concert, even though there are valid grounds for divorce, there is such collusion as will prevent the granting of the divorce. In 1910 the New Jersey court advocated this interpretation: [60]

> What is termed "collusion" in divorce suits is a definite kind of agreement by parties concerning the divorce. If collusion is to be limited (as some definitions would limit it) to "a corrupt bargain to impose a case upon the court," that is, either by the suppression of evidence, or by the manufacture thereof, then, each case where there was an agreement between the parties would have to be investigated to see whether such agreement came within the interdiction of the definition of collusion. But if collusion is given an ampler definition, so as to include any agreement between the parties as a result of which no defense shall be made, then the case will not be investigated after the ascertainment that there is such an agreement, because that agreement itself would be within the definition of collusion and would defeat the suit.

From the administrative point of view there is an argument in favor of this interpretation, for it leaves out the elements of uncertainty and thus makes the task of the courts easier. However, this is fortunately not the generally accepted interpretation of collusion, and the majority of courts do permit agreements on some questions connected with the divorce suit. It is well recognized that it is collusion for the parties to agree that one of them shall institute suit for divorce for a cause which does not exist, although they may have some other valid ground.[61] The courts have no difficulty in finding collusion where the evidence makes it clear that the parties suppressed pertinent and material facts.[62] There is no collusion where one party takes advantage of a matrimonial offense of the other as a ground for divorce, even though the offense was committed by the other in the hope that such advantage would be taken.[63] The mere fact that both parties strongly desire divorce will not in itself make the suit collusive.[64] It is also fairly well recognized that an agreement about

[59] *Squier* v. *Squier,* 99 Vt. 452, 134 Atl. 529 (1926); *Lanktree* v. *Lanktree,* 42 Calif. App. 648, 183 Pac. 954 (1919).
[60] *Sheehan* v. *Sheehan,* 77 N.J. Eq. 411, 77 Atl. 1063 (1910).
[61] *Stokes* v. *Anderson,* 118 Ind. 533, 21 N.E. 331 (1888).
[62] *Griffiths* v. *Griffiths,* 69 N.J. Eq. 689, 60 Atl. 1090 (1905).
[63] *Wiemer* v. *Wiemer,* 21 N.D. 371, 130 N.W. 1015 (1911).
[64] *McCauley* v. *McCauley,* 88 N.J. Eq. 392, 103 Atl. 20 (1918).

a property settlement on the possibility that a divorce might be granted is not necessarily collusive.[65]

Since the very essence of collusion is fraud upon the court and the law, collusion is not a defense which will be brought out by the parties themselves unless one of them repents and discloses it; therefore, unless it is made the duty of some public official, comparable to the king's proctor in England, to guard against it, the existence of collusion will be brought to light only through ignorance, accident, or clever cross-examination. Because of this situation, large numbers of divorces are procured through collusion every year. The courts are not primarily to blame for this phenomenon, since it is physically impossible for them to carry on extensive investigation outside the courtroom.

CONNIVANCE [66]

Connivance is the corrupt consenting by one married person to the marital offenses and acts of the other. The theory back of the connivance doctrine is that one who has consented to an act or wrong cannot be said to be injured by it and therefore should not be given the privilege of taking advantage of it as a ground for divorce. From the cases it seems that connivance appears most often in connection with adultery. A husband's connivance at his wife's adultery has often been held a bar to a divorce for the particular act connived at.[67] Some courts have gone further and have held the husband guilty of connivance for subsequent acts of adultery by the wife with either the same or another person on the theory that by his consent in the first instance, he paved the way for further iniquitous conduct.[68] Where the husband has connived at one act of adultery and later discovers that his wife had previously committed adultery of which he had no knowledge, some courts have held that he would not be barred from seeking divorce for the first adultery; but as one court has said: [69]

> The character of the connivance under some circumstances may be so open, gross, and revolting, that the court may find that no injury has been done the husband, and that therefore there is nothing to redress, that the husband has entirely abandoned all right to claim that his wife should be chaste, and that he has thus consented to her prior adultery. He may come before the court with such impure hands, that, upon the soundest considerations of public policy, his divorce should be refused.

---

[65] *Jarrard* v. *Jarrard,* 116 Wash. 70, 198 Pac. 741 (1921); *Doeme* v. *Doeme,* 96 App. Div. 284, 89 N.Y. Supp. 215 (1904); there are cases contra, however.

[66] Madden, *op. cit.,* p. 294; Vernier, *op. cit.,* Vol. 2, pp. 77–79.

[67] *Delaney* v. *Delaney,* 71 N.J. Eq. 246, 65 Atl. 217 (1906); *Armstrong* v. *Armstrong,* 45 Misc. Rep. 260, 92 N.Y. Supp. 165 (1904).

[68] *Hedden* v. *Hedden,* 21 N.J. Eq. 61 (1870); *Woodward* v. *Woodward,* 41 N.J. Eq. 224, 4 Atl. 424 (1886).

[69] *Morrison* v. *Morrison,* 142 Mass. 361, 8 N.E. 59 (1886).

Passive conduct on the part of one spouse has been held as much a bar as active consent,[70] but usually the courts require more.

CONDONATION [71]

Condonation is the forgiveness of a marital offense constituting a ground for divorce. California, which has a well-drafted law on the subject of condonation, defines it to mean "conditional forgiveness of a matrimonial offense constituting a cause of divorce." It further names the three elements of condonation: (1) knowledge on the part of the condoner of the facts constituting a cause for divorce, (2) reconciliation and remission of the offense by the injured party, (3) restoration of the offending party to all marital rights. This statute has put together some of the principles governing condonation which have been laid down by the courts. It is to the courts, however, that we must still look for our understanding of the doctrine of condonation.

It is necessary to look into the cases to see what offenses may be condoned, what is necessary to constitute condonation, and what are the effects of the condonation. That the doctrine applies to adultery is too well recognized to discuss. It applies to cruel and inhuman treatment and perhaps to every other offense that constitutes a ground for divorce.[72] An offer to forgive is not condonation unless it is accepted and acted upon by the other party,[73] nor is the mere writing of letters in affectionate terms by the aggrieved spouse to the guilty one.[74] Sexual intercourse with knowledge of a prior offense is the type of conduct which will make a case of condonation.[75] Formal forgiveness is not essential to condonation, for the forgiveness may be implied from the conduct of the parties. There can be no condonation without knowledge of the offense committed, so that continued cohabitation cannot be construed as forgiveness if there is no realization that an offense has been committed.[76]

RECRIMINATION [77]

Recrimination is a counter charge that the complaining party has also been guilty of an offense constituting a ground for divorce. Adultery may always be offered as a defense, and in most states any conduct which is

---

[70] *Cairns* v. *Cairns*, 109 Mass. 408 (1872).

[71] Madden, *op. cit.*, p. 300; Vernier, *op. cit.*, Vol. 2, pp. 79–82; Henderson, *op. cit.*, Vol. 1, ch. 11.

[72] *Clague* v. *Clague*, 46 Minn. 461, 49 N.W. 198 (1891).

[73] *Quarles* v. *Quarles*, 19 Ala. 363 (1851), *Anderson* v. *Anderson*, 89 Neb. 570, 131 N.W. 907 (1911).

[74] *Lundy* v. *Lundy*, 23 Ariz. 213, 202 Pac. 809 (1922).

[75] *Rogers* v. *Rogers*, 67 N.J. Eq. 534, 58 Atl. 822 (1904).

[76] *Rogers* v. *Rogers*, 122 Mass. 423 (1877).

[77] Madden, *op. cit.*, p. 305; Vernier, *op. cit.*, Vol. 2, pp. 82–88; Henderson, *op. cit.*, Vol. 1, ch. 10.

recognized by statute as a ground for divorce may be offered in recrimination. The doctrine of recrimination is grounded on the old equity theory that one who asks relief must come into court with clean hands and that divorce laws are made to give relief to the innocent and not to the guilty party.[78]

There are several kinds of recrimination statutes. By the first type the defendant is allowed to recriminate by proving that the plaintiff was guilty of the "same crime or misconduct." A second type allows recrimination by showing that the plaintiff was guilty of an equal wrong. A statute of this kind makes for absurd and unsound comparisons. A third type merely limits the defense to matters which constitute grounds for divorce. The general rule is that in cases where the defense of recrimination is shown, the courts will refuse to grant either party a divorce. However, in 1934, Nevada by statute adopted the "comparative rectitude" theory. The statute provides that in an action for divorce when it shall appear to the court that both parties have been guilty of wrongs which constitute grounds for divorce, the court shall not for this reason refuse divorce, but in its discretion may grant a divorce to the party least in fault.[79] Kansas and Oklahoma appear to have similar statutory provisions.[80]

The courts show variation in their interpretation of what constitutes recrimination. Since there are jurisdictions which maintain that the recrimination must be in like kind to the cause upon which the demand for the divorce is based, drunkenness and extreme cruelty, for example, cannot be set up in recrimination to adultery.[81] In the absence of clear statutes on the point the more generally accepted rule of the courts is that any cause for divorce recognized by statute may be set up by way of recrimination to any other ground for divorce. Under this rule recrimination on the ground of cruelty may be set up as a defense to a divorce for adultery,[82] and, similarly, desertion may be an adequate defense to an action for divorce on the ground of adultery.[83]

STATUTES OF LIMITATION [84]

A statute of limitation imposes a time limit within which an action for divorce can be brought. The statutes vary considerably. In several jurisdictions the period of limitation applies to all causes for divorce; in several others it applies only to divorce for adultery; in a few only certain

[78] *Hoff* v. *Hoff*, 48 Mich. 281, 12 N.W. 160 (1882); *Blankenship* v. *Blankenship*, 52 Nev. 48, 280 Pac. 97 (1929).
[79] Vernier, *op. cit.*, 1938 suppl., pp. 48–49.
[80] Morland, *op. cit.*, p. 568.
[81] *Bast* v. *Bast*, 82 Ill. 584 (1876).
[82] *Pease* v. *Pease*, 72 Wis. 136, 39 N.W. 133 (1888).
[83] *Young* v. *Young*, 94 N.J. Eq. 155, 119 Atl. 92 (1922).
[84] Vernier, *op. cit.*, Vol. 2, pp. 89–92; Morland, *op. cit.*, pp. 562, 563.

causes are affected by the statute. The period within which the action must be brought varies from a few months to several years. Usually the period begins from the time of the commission of the act or from the time of the discovery of the wrongful conduct which constitutes the ground for divorce. *Laches,* or unreasonable delay in suing, may justify a court in denying relief and dismissing the action. The courts, however, do not mean to imply that the parties must rush their family difficulties into court.[85]

JUSTIFIABILITY OF DEFENSES

It seems incredible to those who believe that marriage is a human institution and that its primary values are to be derived from respect, companionship, and love of children, that all these defenses are allowed to impede divorce. Unwise and hasty entry into marriage should be blocked by carefully drawn statutes; community resources should be available to assist married persons in their adjustments; and if reasonable compromises cannot be achieved, dissolution of the marital tie should be possible. To force the parties to lie concerning their behavior, or one party to connive at the adultery of the other, is a travesty on justice. Likewise, it would be ludicrous, were it not so unjust and unsocial, to penalize forgiveness and to deny a decree because both parties, instead of just one, have been guilty of offenses. Some authorities believe that legal defenses in divorce actions should be abolished. If this were done, the divorce counsel, whose functions we shall presently discuss, could devote most of his time to the social rather than the legal situation. He would then be primarily a social worker rather than a lawyer and prosecutor.

THE DIVORCE COUNSEL

Because of the interest of the state in maintaining the marriage institution, it is sometimes said that an action for divorce is a triangular suit involving husband, wife, and the state. The state is also interested in protecting the interests of persons not before the court. The plaintiff and defendant are usually represented by private attorneys; the state, in most jurisdictions, is represented merely by the court, with no resources for extramural inquiry. In ordinary civil litigation, collusion is practically unknown. On the other hand, in divorce litigation it is common knowledge that the parties often do everything in their power to evade the requirements of the statutes and resort to perjury and fraud to accomplish their ends. This is especially true in uncontested suits, which make up a large proportion of all divorce litigation.[86] If the adversary or litigious

[85] *Tufts* v. *Tufts,* 8 Utah 142, 3 Pac. 309 (1892).

[86] Schouler, *op. cit.,* Vol. 2, pp. 1732–1734; 17 Am. Jur. 294–295; Vernier, *op. cit.,* Vol. 2, pp. 92–98.

theory of divorce actions continues, and, unfortunately, it seems likely that it will for a long period, there ought to be resources to protect the interests of the state. The duty of supplying this protection should not be left to the already overburdened courts alone, but should be delegated to some agency which has the time and the opportunity to look into the affairs of the parties outside the courtroom. This agency should have the power to make reports and recommendations to the court.

In England, since 1860, the interests of the state have been protected by the king's proctor. His main duties are (1) to intervene after a decree *nisi,* (2) to instruct and counsel at any stage of the litigation when so directed by the court, and (3) to take steps involving investigation and recommendations when collusion is suspected. The basic theory of the divorce counsel or proctor is that he acts as a special agent of the state to protect the community against too easy dissolution of the family and also assists in obtaining justice for the parties. In most American jurisdictions, in the absence of statutes creating such an agency, the court before which the proceedings are pending represents the interests of the state and is charged with the duty of protecting those interests.[87] It has been held that the attorney general, district attorney, or other public officer is not permitted to intervene in behalf of the state, unless specifically authorized by statute to do so.[88]

About half the jurisdictions provided by statute for an officer comparable to the king's proctor.[89] There are great differences between the states as to when he may intervene, what he is called, what his duties are, and what his compensation is. The official named to perform this function may be an attorney appointed by the court, the district attorney, a probation officer, the attorney general, or some other person. The duties of such officers vary. In several states he intervenes only in cases where insanity is a ground for divorce, and in a few, when the defendant defaults, when there are minor children, or in all divorce actions. In some jurisdictions he simply represents the defendant who is absent by default or incapable because of insanity; in others he ascertains whether the grounds are legal and sustained by proof; in still others he merely investigates and reports to the court or acts in the discretion of the court.

Whether or not his functions are more than perfunctorily performed depends upon the statutes, the interest of the court, and the competence of the counsel. If defenses in divorce actions were modified or abolished entirely, the functions of the divorce counsel would change. He would then primarily attempt to assist with social adjustment and to protect the rights of the parties rather than to block divorce because of legal techni-

---

[87] *Blank* v. *Nohl,* 112 Mo. 159, 20 S.W. 477 (1892).

[88] *State ex rel. Fowler* v. *Moore,* 46 Nev. 65, 207 Pac. 75 (1922).

[89] Vernier, *op. cit.,* Vol. 2, p. 94, and 1938 suppl., p. 49.

calities. Modification of the functions of the divorce counsel and abolition of the defenses are not likely to occur until public pressure demands that state legislatures adopt divorce statutes incorporating principles and practices geared to the requirements of modern society. This will necessitate dropping the theories that one of the parties is guilty, that two parties are in contention, and that the state, through its courts, must prevent dissolution of marital ties except upon the strictest legal evidence. It will mean the establishment of family courts with diversified and highly skilled personnel whose function will include reconciliation, protection of legal rights, and recommendations for dissolution.[90]

RIGHTS OF DIVORCED PARTIES

TO REMARRY [91]

Since absolute divorce terminates the relationship of the parties as married persons and restores both parties to the status of single persons, either party is competent to contract a new marriage with a third person in the absence of statutory prohibition to the contrary.[92] About three quarters of the American jurisdictions, by express statute, limit the right of divorced persons to marry again. The statutes vary as to whether they apply (1) equally to both guilty and innocent parties; (2) to the guilty party only; or (3) to both, but more drastically to the guilty party. They also vary in their methods of limiting a second marriage by (1) granting an interlocutory decree or one which postpones the granting of the final decree for some period of time; (2) declaring that remarriages within a certain period of time after the divorce shall be null and void; and (3) imposing a penalty. The statutory limitation, whether imposed upon both parties or only upon the guilty one, varies greatly in time, the total spread being a matter of months to life for the guilty party. In some states the court has the option of determining the waiting period, which varies from a short period to life; and in some the guilty party, if guilty of adultery, cannot marry the paramour during the life of the innocent party.

Rationalization for the waiting period is based upon two assumptions: (1) that opportunity for reconciliation is afforded, and (2) that hastily contracted and ill-considered new marriages will be avoided.[93] To many authorities in the field of family relations a waiting period of several months or a year for both parties seems reasonable. Others believe that the waiting period induces hasty divorce actions, reduces the interest of

---

[90] Royal D. Rood, *Matrimonial Shoals* (Detroit, Detroit Law Book Co., 1939).

[91] Vernier, *op. cit.*, pp. 172–179, and 1938 suppl., p. 58; Henderson, *op. cit.*, ch. 20.

[92] *Barber* v. *Barber,* 16 Calif. 378 (1860); *Baughman* v. *Baughman,* 32 Kan. 538, 4 Pac. 1003 (1884).

[93] Pilpel and Zavin, *op. cit.*, pp. 322–327.

the state in reconciliation, and encourages illicit relations or migratory marriage with evasion of the laws of the state of domicile. Regardless of which position is taken, forbidding remarriage for a long period of time or completely is vindictive and imposes a restraint that encourages violation and evasion of the law.

ALIMONY [94]

In Blackstone's time in cases of divorce *a mensa et thoro,* the law allowed alimony to the wife. It was that allowance which was made to her for her support out of the husband's estate and was settled at the discretion of the ecclesiastical judge on consideration of all the circumstances of the case. Except for parliamentary divorce, the only kind of divorce was from bed and board. Since it did not affect the husband's right to the absolute ownership of his wife's chattels, to collect her earnings, and to the sole use of her hands during coverture, it, of course, was necessary to make provision for her, which was generally about a third of her husband's income. When, in 1857, Parliament passed an act authorizing absolute divorce in restricted circumstances, it also provided alimony for the wife. By that time the English wife had some rights to her own property, so the courts had the new problem of considering what support was reasonable for the husband to furnish the wife. In a case arising shortly after the passage of the act the court said: "I consider . . . that the wife ought not to be left destitute; on the other hand I think it would not be politic to give to wives any great pecuniary interest in obtaining a dissolution of the marriage tie." [95]

Today alimony, strictly speaking, is an enforcement of the husband's obligation to support the wife. Every jurisdiction granting absolute divorce has some kind of statute authorizing the court to provide for the support of the wife in divorce actions. Under ecclesiastical law alimony was a money judgment against the person of the husband and was payable in installments; so alimony, strictly speaking, is a money decree. Most of the states have statutes of this kind, although a number authorize an award of alimony out of the husband's property. Some jurisdictions follow the rule of the ecclesiastical courts and do not permit a guilty wife, usually when she is an adulteress, to receive alimony.

The determination of the amount of the alimony generally is left to the courts' discretion.[96] In arriving at a just award the courts take into consideration such factors as the health of the parties, their earning power,

---

[94] Madden, *op. cit.,* pp. 319–330; Vernier, *op. cit.,* Vol. 2, pp. 259–321; Morland, *op. cit.,* chs. 37–41; Henderson, *op. cit.,* Vol. 2, chs. 14–18; "Alimony and Other Allowances," *Divorce and Separation,* 17 Am. Jur. sec. 14; *Alimony,* 6 L. and Contemp. Prob. (Spring, 1939), entire issue.

[95] *Fisher* v. *Fisher,* 2 Swab. and Tr. 410.

[96] Vernier, *op. cit.,* Vol. 2, p. 283.

age, ability to pay, and station in life. Frequently, the courts are called upon to revise their awards. A majority of jurisdictions have specific statutes making provision for the right to revise.[97] In those states where there is no statutory provision for revision, the courts seem to have the power to place a reservation in their decrees allowing for change in the award at a later date if the circumstances warrant it.[98] Such conditions as remarriage and change in finances warrant reconsideration of the amount.

A decree for alimony is as much a judgment creating an obligation or debt as is any other judgment for money. Accordingly, a wife awarded alimony occupies the position of a judgment creditor of her ex-husband, and, as such, she is entitled to avail herself of all the remedies given to a judgment creditor.[99] In some respects she is in an even stronger position than the ordinary judgment creditor, for the statutes may provide that the husband can be punished for contempt of court if he fails to obey the court's order to pay, and he may actually be confined to jail. This is a common mode of alimony enforcement,[100] both under the statutes and at common law.

Most jurisdictions have specific statutes on enforcement of alimony decrees.[101] These fall conveniently into three classes:

1. Those dealing with security for the husband's performance. When the decree is handed down, the husband may be compelled to give some security to insure that he will pay or, if he defaults, that the wife will be amply protected. He may be required to put up a bond or furnish sureties or give a lien or mortgage on particular property.

2. Those dealing with specific enforcement measures. Here, the statutes authorize the courts to order the whole sum due upon the husband's default in paying any alimony installment; the court may seize particular property for the wife's benefit; there may be execution on, and sale of, certain property; or there may be punishment for contempt.

3. Those conferring as broad powers on divorce courts as are possessed by courts of equity. Here, the statutes allow the courts to use any and all remedies available in equity, and the court may go so far as to have a receiver or a trustee appointed to take over and manage the husband's property and pay the income to the wife.

Some of these remedies seem to put the husband at the mercy of his divorced wife. It is probable that many wives of well-to-do husbands do obtain divorces for the sake of the alimony. On the other hand, the courts often protect the divorced husband, leaving the wife and children with inadequate support. Every lawyer handling divorce cases and all social

---

[97] *Ibid.*, Vol. 2, p. 261, and 1938 suppl., pp. 64–65.

[98] 17 Am. Jur. 491–492.

[99] *Ibid.*, pp. 501, 502.

[100] *Selph* v. *Selph*, 27 Ariz. 176, 231 Pac. 921 (1925); *Staples* v. *Staples*, 87 Wis. 592, 58 N.W. 1036 (1894).

[101] Vernier, *op. cit.*, Vol. 2, pp. 290–302.

workers are well acquainted with the husband who does not pay his alimony because he "skips," or because he remarries, or because his earnings are inadequate.

Strictly speaking, alimony to the husband is a misnomer, since it is a substitute for his common-law duty to support his wife, and she owes no such duty to him. Today, a considerable number of jurisdictions have laws which grant alimony to husbands under certain conditions. In a sizeable number the courts are given the power to divide the property of both parties between them, without regard to the owner, on the basis of the facts in each case.[102] This trend seems sound in view of married women's property acts and equal-rights laws.

Apparently all jurisdictions with perhaps the exception of Tennessee have made provision for temporary alimony and suit money to the wife. Temporary alimony, or alimony *pendente lite,* is an allowance ordered by the court to be paid by the husband to the wife for her support during the pendency of the divorce action, whether the suit is brought by herself or by the husband. In 1935 Illinois enacted a law providing for the allowance of temporary alimony to the husband. The making of the award and the amount are in the discretion of the court in all jurisdictions.

RESUMPTION OF MAIDEN NAME

Most divorce courts are authorized by statute to allow a woman to resume her maiden name or that of a former husband if she asks for it in her petition. At common law she can assume her maiden name or any other which does not interfere with the rights of others. Probably most women with children choose not to drop their husband's name. It is doubtless also true that many professional women prefer to resume their maiden name.

CUSTODY OF CHILDREN [103]

Divorce, when there are children of the marriage, is often particularly unfortunate. The courts are confronted with the necessity of determining which of the parties to the marriage shall have custody of the offspring and whether custody shall be total or partial and divided. Today, the decision regarding custody is based upon the welfare of the child, often an exceedingly difficult matter to decide when both parents can give emo-

[102] *Ibid.,* Vol. 2, pp. 303–309, and 1938 suppl., pp. 67, 68.

[103] *Ibid.,* Vol. 2, pp. 191–215; Morland, *op. cit.,* ch. 42; Henderson, *op. cit.,* Vol. 2, ch. 15; "Custody and Support of Children," *Divorce and Separation,* 17 Am. Jur., sec. 15; J. Louise Despert, *Children of Divorce* (New York, Doubleday, 1953); Kingsley Davis, "Children of Divorce," in Judson T. Landis and Mary G. Landis, *Readings in Marriage and the Family* (Englewood Cliffs, N.J., Prentice-Hall, 1952), pp. 351–360.

tional security, wise guidance, and a good home. In the absence of social service facilities, the court cannot be expected to determine soundly for the benefit of all of the parties and particularly for the welfare of the children. Some commentators recommend that the matter of custody, when it is contested, be referred to juvenile courts. The problem of custody will be discussed further in Chapter 9.

CONFLICT OF DIVORCE LAWS

THE MATTER OF JURISDICTION [104]

The most complex of all legal problems in connection with divorce is that of "foreign divorce." The questions that arise in connection with the conflict of divorce laws are so numerous, complex, and technical, and their treatment by the courts is so confused, that the most this chapter can hope to do is to indicate some of the confusion and to present some general conclusions of textbook writers. Such a discussion is attempted, incomplete as it must necessarily be, because of the importance of the social problems resulting from the uncertainty as to whether or not there actually has been a divorce granted. The matter of jurisdiction is the basis of the problem of conflict of laws in divorce, and it is a general rule that jurisdiction depends on the domicile of the parties. In order to give the court jurisdiction, at least one party must be domiciled in the state where action is brought; but what constitutes domicile and when it is established are sticklers.

Until the first of the famous Williams cases was decided by the United States Supreme Court, the equally famous Haddock case established the rule that a state requiring *in personam* divorce actions need not, although it could if it chose, recognize a divorce of a foreign jurisdiction when there was no jurisdiction obtained over the defendant but merely one over the *status* or *rem*. The doctrine of the Haddock case prevailed from 1906 until 1942, when the Williams I case established another rule.

PRINCIPLES [105]

A simplified statement concerning several domiciliary and jurisdictional requirements of the full faith and credit clause of the Constitution

---

[104] Morland, *op. cit.*, ch. 35; Henderson, *op. cit.*, Vol. 3, ch. 33; "Foreign Divorce and Alimony Decrees" 17 Am. Jur. 556–582, sec. 18; Madden, *op. cit.*, pp. 312–319; Hamilton Vreeland, *Validity of Foreign Divorces* (Chicago, Callaghan Co., 1938); Robert M. Bozeman, "The Supreme Court and Migratory Divorce: A Re-examination of an Old Problem," 37 A.B.A.J. 107 (1951); William G. Ruymann, "The Problem of Migratory Divorce," 37 A.B.A.J. 12 (1951); Pilpel and Zavin, *op. cit.*

[105] A considerable portion of this discussion is taken from *Miscellaneous Acts,* 9 U.L.A. 364–375 (1951).

as currently interpreted by the United States Supreme Court on divorce jurisdiction follows:

1. Jurisdiction to entertain a suit for divorce is confined to a state in which at least one of the parties to the marriage is domiciled.[106]

2. A decree of divorce containing a finding that the jurisdictional requisite of domicile exists is entitled to full faith and credit in other states.[107]

3. But such a decree obtained upon a false representation of domicile is not entitled to full faith and credit, and the lack of jurisdictional prerequisite may be shown in a proceeding in another state despite the recital in the decree of the existence of domicile.[108]

4. However, a defendant who personally appears in the original suit and obtains the divorce on cross petition, or one who answers denying the plaintiff's domicile in the state of the forum and is present at the trial, taking some part therein, may not be permitted thereafter to contest the validity of the divorce upon the ground of plaintiff's want of domicile.[109]

CASES

The two Williams cases, commonly referred to as Williams I and Williams II, from which three of these principles are derived, involved two North Carolina couples. O. B. Williams, father of four children, and Lillie Hendrix, a married woman, both long-time residents of their state, decided that they wanted to marry each other. They went to Nevada and established the required six weeks' legal residence, after which each filed suit for divorce upon grounds of "extreme mental cruelty." Immediately upon the granting of the second of the two divorces, Mr. Williams and Mrs. Hendrix were married and returned at once to their home state. North Carolina officials, incensed at the new marriage, brought a criminal action against the new spouses for bigamous cohabitation. It was necessary for the courts to determine whether the Nevada divorce was good and hence required to be recognized in North Carolina. If so, there was a legal marriage and, of course, no bigamy. The North Carolina courts convicted the defendants and sentenced them to prison. The state courts based their decisions that there was not a legal divorce upon the fact that Nevada never obtained jurisdiction over the defendants. Notice was served upon them, but they were never personally served within the jurisdiction of the Nevada court and never voluntarily brought themselves under the jurisdiction of that court.

The case was taken to the United States Supreme Court, which reversed the judgment of the North Carolina courts and its own earlier ruling established in the famous Haddock case. The facts in this 1906

---

[106] *Williams* v. *N. Car.,* 65 Sup. Ct. 1092, 325 U.S. 226 (1945).

[107] *Williams* v. *N. Car.,* 63 Sup. Ct. 207, 317 U.S. 287 (1942).

[108] *Williams* v. *N. Car.,* 65 Sup. Ct. 1092, 325 U.S. 226 (1945).

[109] *Sherrer* v. *Sherrer,* 68 Sup. Ct. 1087, 334 U.S. 343 (1948); *Coe* v. *Coe,* 68 Sup. Ct. 1094, 334 U.S. 378 (1948).

case were that a husband left his wife and the matrimonial domicile in New York and moved to Connecticut.[110] There, he sought and obtained a divorce. His wife was constructively served with notice, but she was never personally under the jurisdiction of the Connecticut court. Many years later the wife sought and obtained in the New York courts a legal separation and an order for alimony from her husband, who, according to the laws of Connecticut, was no longer her husband. The Supreme Court had to decide whether a divorce obtained in Connecticut with jurisdiction over a part of the marital status, an action *in rem*, was entitled to recognition in New York, which maintained the right to require that a divorce granted by a foreign jurisdiction must have been obtained by acquiring personal jurisdiction over the defendant, especially when the rightful matrimonial domicile was in New York. The Court held that the divorce was valid under the laws of Connecticut but that New York had a right to insist, if it wished, upon personal service and personal jurisdiction.

It was upon the rule established by the Haddock case that the North Carolina courts decided that the Williams marriage, following a Nevada divorce without acquiring personal jurisdiction over the defendants who remained in North Carolina, was bigamous. The United States Supreme Court reversed itself in the Williams I case and established another doctrine, the second stated above. Thenceforth, individuals living in states which did not recognize *in rem* divorce actions of foreign jurisdictions were in violation of the full faith and credit provisions of the federal Constitution.

The citizens of North Carolina, still irate over the deliberate and flagrant evasion of their statutes, brought a second action for bigamous cohabitation, and this time both the state and the United States Supreme Court ruled the Nevada divorce did not have to be recognized in North Carolina and, hence, the new Mr. and Mrs. Williams were bigamists. The argument made by the state was that Mr. Williams and Mrs. Hendrix fraudulently established domicile in Nevada. The United States Supreme Court held that Nevada had the right, if it chose, to define domicile for divorce purposes as six weeks' residence. But a divorce granted in a foreign jurisdiction, where the parties went for the purpose of evading the laws of their home state, established a short period of residence, married, and returned at once to the home state, was not entitled to full faith and credit. North Carolina was not required to recognize the Nevada divorce and marriage. The couple was guilty of bigamy. The third of the above principles was established.

The fourth principle grew out of two cases decided by the United States Supreme Court in 1948. We shall refer to only one of them, the

---

[110] *Haddock* v. *Haddock*, 201 U.S. 562.

Sherrer case, as the situation and rule of law in the Coe and Sherrer cases are similar. In the Sherrer case a wife went from her Massachusetts home to Florida and sued for a divorce in a Florida court after the expiration of the ninety-day period of residence required by the Florida law. Her husband, who was notified, was represented by counsel and he himself appeared. She was given the divorce. He was given the custody of the two children except for summers. She at once married a man from Massachusetts who had followed her to Florida. After a short time the newly married couple returned to Massachusetts, and the first husband there instituted proceedings attacking the Florida decree on the ground that the wife had no domicile in Florida and, consequently, the Florida court had no jurisdiction.

Justice Vinson ruled for a majority Court that the requirements of the full faith and credit clause barred the husband from attacking the divorce on the assertion of deprivation of due process. The husband had had his day in court. When in court, although he denied the allegations, including his wife's Florida residence, he had accepted the divorce provisions without cross-examination and rebuttal or appeal to the courts. The Florida court had had jurisdiction both of subject matter (the *rem*) and of parties (the *personam*).

Justice Frankfurter wrote a long and scholarly minority dissenting opinion, in which he maintained that a person had no right to play ducks and drakes with the state laws of Massachusetts by leaving the state just long enough to obtain a divorce and then by returning. He derided "quickie divorces" and the establishment of "sham domicile." Under such circumstances, in his opinion, there was no violation of the full faith and credit clause when the state of genuine domicile refused to recognize the foreign divorce, even though the defendant had been in court. Since domestic relations are reserved to the states under our federal Constitution, uniformity of laws in this field is difficult of achievement, but it is not, wrote Justice Frankfurter, the prerogative of the Supreme Court to attempt some degree of uniformity by doing away with high standards of some states in favor of low standards of others.

UNIFORM DIVORCE LAWS

Unless the states adopt uniform rules on the matter of divorce jurisdiction, there is little help for the prevailing legal confusion between states. Considerable interest has been shown by groups of lawyers and others in remedying the confusion in divorce law, but not enough to achieve any degree of uniformity. Several significant efforts have been made to achieve greater uniformity in divorce legislation. We shall not again discuss the movement for constitutional amendment, for that was done in the last chapter.

In 1906 a National Congress on Uniform Divorce Laws held a meeting, the result of which was the drafting of a uniform annulment of marriage and divorce act. This act was approved in 1907 by the National Conference of Commissioners on Uniform State Laws. It provided for annulment of marriage and for divorce from bed and board, fixed the grounds for divorce, and covered the matter of jurisdiction and the force and effect of foreign divorce.[111] It was accepted by just three states: Delaware and New Jersey in 1907, and Wisconsin in 1909. In 1927 the conference came to the conclusion that the matter of divorce should be reconsidered. In 1930 the commissioners finally agreed upon an act which eliminated all provisions of the earlier act except those pertaining to jurisdiction and to the question of full faith and credit. In essence it provided that for full faith and credit to be given to out-of-state divorces, jurisdiction should not be exercised unless (a) the defendant was domiciled in the state where action was brought or the state was the state of matrimonial domicile, or (b) the complainant had a separate domicile in the state (the defendant being domiciled out of the state). Domicile must have been for one year. The only state accepting the act was Vermont, which passed such a law in 1931 and repealed it in 1933. A small number of states, on their own, enacted laws attempting to clarify this subject of jurisdiction and comity between states. In 1943 the commissioners withdrew the act, declaring it obsolete.[112]

In 1948 a new act, the uniform divorce recognition act, was approved by the commissioners.[113] They observed that the act took its inception from public dissatisfaction over "migratory divorce." This wave of reaction

> is bearing fruit in agitation for transfer of control over divorce to the National government since the states have been unable to unite upon proposals for uniform divorce legislation. It seems obvious, however, that national jurisdiction over the termination of marriage must entail assumption of control over the entire institution. The prospect of centralization thus presented is out of harmony with American practice and involves such grave problems that it ought to be avoided if relief can be secured in any other way.

The act was framed on the theory that it is desirable to discourage migration in pursuit of divorce; that specific statutory refusal to recognize extrastate divorces obtained by domiciliaries of the state enacting the statute will reduce tourist divorce seeking; and that recognition of extrastate divorces obtained by domiciliaries should be refused except as specifically required by the United States Constitution. The proposal was intended to preserve to each state the authority to determine the marital status of its domiciliaries. It was not a measure to better the

---

[111] *Handbook of the National Conference of Commissioners on Uniform State Laws: 1930,* pp. 498–502.

[112] *Ibid.,* p. 151.

[113] 9 U.L.A. 364–375 (1951).

marriage or divorce laws, substantive or procedural, of the several states.

The essential provisions of the act are as follows: [114]

Validity of Foreign Decree. A divorce from the bonds of matrimony obtained in another jurisdiction shall be of no force or effect in this state if both parties to the marriage were domiciled in this state at the time the proceeding for the divorce was commenced.

Evidence of Domicile. Proof that a person obtaining a divorce from the bonds of matrimony in another jurisdiction was (a) domiciled in this state within twelve months prior to the commencement of the proceeding therefor and resumed residence in this state within eighteen months after the date of his departure therefrom, or (b) at all times after his departure from this state and until his return maintained a place of residence within this state, shall be *prima facie* evidence that the person was domiciled in this state when the divorce proceeding was commenced.

Uniformity of Interpretation. The act shall be so interpreted and construed as to effectuate its general purpose to make uniform the laws of those states which enact it.

Up to 1953 no state had accepted the exact provisions of the act although some states, as Wisconsin, seem earlier to have enacted laws containing the essential provisions of the uniform act.

Other groups have been concerned with the achievement of uniform divorce laws. Among such is the National Association of Women Lawyers. A bill was drafted by a committee drawn from that organization and from the Chicago Bar Association. The proposed bill adopts what its proponents term a "therapeutic approach" to the divorce problem; otherwise, say its supporters, it represents a restatement and codification of the best case and statutory law in the forty-eight states. The evils which it seeks to correct are enumerated in the declaration of policy which reads as follows: [115]

SECTION 2 (Declaration of Policy)

a. WHEREAS, due to the divergent social attitudes and requirements of the several states, the laws of divorce are most confusing, unsatisfactory and not uniform in application among the several States, so that subsequent remarriages are frequently of questionable validity and rights in property are often clouded, and

b. WHEREAS, the continuation of a marriage between two parties which has become unbearable to the parties, may be unfair to the children, if any, and may be of no value to the State, and

c. WHEREAS, a Decree of Divorce ought to be granted by the Court when in its sound discretion it finds that there is no reasonable possibility of recon-

---

[114] *Ibid.*, pp. 373–374.

[115] "Toward Uniform Divorce Laws," 38 Women Law. J. 15–20 (1952); Michael Levin, "Proposed Uniform Divorce Bill," 39 Women Law. J. 3–4 (1953); see also, Morris Ploscowe, "The Failure of Divorce Reform," 13 Ohio S.L.J. 3–12 (1952), and Paul W. Alexander, "Public Service by Lawyers in the Field of Divorce," 13 Ohio S.L.J. 13–21 (1952).

ciliation of the parties, and that the welfare of the parties (husband, wife, children, if any) will be promoted by the divorce, and

d. WHEREAS, a uniform divorce law embodying uniform requirements will tend to correct the evils outlined above and effectuate this policy,

THEREFORE, the ________ declares that it is its purpose to correct the evils outlined above by enacting this law.

The suggested bill makes no change in legal process and procedures except that the proceedings commence with a petition which is styled "In the matter of the family of John and Mary Doe" and the hearing cannot be set before at least thirty days after filing of petition. The right to trial by jury is preserved. The committee made an attempt to reconcile conflicting views in connection with residence and domicile by sharply defining domicile to mean "the place where one resides with an unqualified intention of so residing for an indefinite period of time, and without any intention of returning to any former residence, or to remove elsewhere." The grounds for divorce are included in five general classifications: mutual fidelity, mutual respect, mutual right of *consortium,* mental capacity, sexual incapacity. These five causes embrace the usual grounds found in most states, such as adultery, cruelty, legally adjudicated mental illness continuing for three years, impotency which has existed from the time of marriage, willful desertion, habitual drunkenness, and imprisonment. There are provisions for the use of social agencies and prehearing conferences closed to the public and conducted on the basis of mediation rather than contest.

The group took care to restate the best law of the country on such matters as custody and maintenance of children, alimony and property rights, costs, expenses, and fees. It made attempts (1) to resolve the contradictory rules and decisions of courts in connection with modification of decrees after divorce because of changed circumstances, such as economic, remarriage, or death; and (2) to achieve some measure of uniformity by the provision that decrees and orders of sister states shall be given the same force and effect as decrees of the instant state. The proposal permits remarriage immediately after the entry of a decree of divorce.

Exponents of the bill argue that the therapeutic approach means that parties should be able to come to court not for a fight but for help. Legal machinery, they believe, should be available for the purpose of healing and curing. Divorce courts, like juvenile courts, should endeavor to ascertain the cause of breakup and should seek remedies. Under the proposed bill of this group the court has the right to terminate the marital status only upon the ultimate showing that a particular family cannot achieve good family relationships. There should be no surgery until every avenue of treatment has been explored. This bill represents only one of the many efforts to improve marriage and divorce legislation. It is improbable that any state will pass such a proposal. Rather, some of its remedies may be adopted piecemeal fashion by one or another state.

LIMITED DIVORCE AND SEPARATION [116]

Divorce *a mensa et thoro* was granted by the ecclesiastical courts of England. It destroyed the rights of cohabitation, but left the parties with no right to marry again. The wife did not regain her property which had gone to her husband by reason of the marriage. If either spouse took another mate, a charge of adultery could be brought. This form of divorce was responsible for much unhappiness and injustice. There seems little reason for its existence today. However, about half the jurisdictions grant limited divorces. This number does not include those states which allow a suit for separate maintenance or alimony without divorce. In the absence of express statutory authority to grant limited divorces, the courts will not grant them. They are not granted for causes which are not designated in the statutes, and, frequently, either an absolute or a partial divorce can be obtained for the same cause. Causes include adultery, cruelty, desertion, intoxication, insanity, impotency, and nonsupport.

No effort will be made here to summarize the statutory material on divorce from bed and board. Suffice it to say that the laws on defenses are incomplete, and it is often impossible to tell whether the statutes on defenses to divorce are to apply also to partial divorce. Jurisdiction to grant limited divorce is completely dependent upon statutory provisions. The laws are "particularly incomplete" in their definition of procedure. In the absence of statutory provisions, a limited divorce does not change the property rights of either person. Generally, the courts are given the same powers concerning the custody and maintenance of children as in absolute divorce.

Under the ecclesiastical and common law an agreement between husband and wife to live apart was void. A good number of the states have specific legislation relating to separation agreements between husband and wife. These laws generally agree that husband and wife cannot, by any contract with each other, alter their legal relations except as to property, and they may make provision for the support of either of them and of their children during the separation.

Where the husband deserts or lives apart from his wife and children, his duty of support can be enforced. A majority of jurisdictions have

---

[116] This summary is taken from Vernier, *op. cit.*, Vol. 2, pp. 341–464, 467–516, and Vol. 3, pp. 112–138; Morland, *op. cit.*, chs. 15, 16, 17; "Separation Agreements," 17 Am. Jur., sec. 17.

statutes giving a *civil* remedy for support or maintenance. In several jurisdictions relief is authorized by judicial decisions. Most states have *criminal* statutes relating to support of abandoned wives and children. The primary purpose of these criminal laws is to punish; fortunately the statutes of most jurisdictions authorize releasing the husband on probation upon his promise to furnish proper support.

The uniform desertion and nonsupport act, formulated by the National Conference of Commissioners on Uniform State Laws in 1910, was adopted by twenty-four jurisdictions. This act made it a punishable offense for a husband to desert or willfully neglect or refuse to provide for the support and maintenance of his wife in destitute or necessitous circumstances, or for a parent to fail in the same duty to his child under sixteen years of age. The defects of the 1910 act were that it attempted to impose the enforcement of the duties of support through the criminal law only and made no reference to enforcement as against husbands and fathers who fled from the state.

With the increasing mobility of the American population the problem of interstate enforcement of the duties of support became acute. In June, 1949, the Social Security Administration announced that the total bill for aid to dependent children, where the father was absent and not supporting, was approximately $205 million a year. A deserting husband going to another state was beyond the reach of agencies in the state where he had abandoned his family. Welfare departments were often prevented from enforcing the duty of support in the state where the husband could be found because of court decisions holding that the duty existed only as to obligees within the state. The means of criminal enforcement against the out-of-state husband was also ineffectual. Charges could be brought against the fleeing husband, but he had to be returned for trial to the state where the offense was committed. Extradition was expensive and technical, and it was often impossible to prove that the man had fled from justice or his legal duties.

As a result of such problems the commissioners in 1950 adopted a uniform reciprocal enforcement of support act and, in 1952, amended it.[117] The act attempts to improve and extend by reciprocal legislation the enforcement of duties of support through both the criminal and civil law. Its provisions are in addition to remedies already existing for the enforcement of duties of support within the state. The act, among other improvements, covers details of what is known as "the two-state proceeding," by which the judge in the home state before whom a simple

[117] *Handbook of the National Conference on Commissioners on Uniform State Laws: 1952* (Baltimore, The Lord Baltimore Press, 1952), pp. 291–306; see also, Wis. Stat. 1953, c. 52.10, "Uniform Reciprocal Enforcement of Support Act," for essential provisions of the law adopted by the commissioners; 10 U.L.A. (1922 and 1952 Cumulative Annual Pocket Part for annotations on original act). For further discussion of the act, see Chs. 9, 13, and 20 of this book.

petition is brought sends the petition to a court of the responding state to which the husband has fled or in which he has property. If that court finds that a duty of support exists, it may order the defendant to furnish support, and it has the right to insist upon compliance. This court has the duty to transmit to the initiating court any payments it receives, and the initiating court, in turn, disburses the payments. In the provisions on civil enforcement, the duties of support are those now existing in the several states. The act, in other words, does not attempt to dictate to the states what duties shall be enforced. For example, some states enforce a duty to illegitimate children; a large number require children to support their parents; about one fourth require support between brothers and sisters; somewhat more require a wife to support a husband under some circumstances.

SUMMARY AND CONCLUSIONS

Clearly, the United States has a divorce problem. High divorce figures prove the point. The number of divorced persons in 1890 per 100 married persons was 0.54, and in 1949, 2.82, an increase of 521 per cent. The average number of divorces per 100 marriages was 5.56 during the 1880–1890 decade and 25.89 in the 1940–1950 decade, an increase of 466 per cent.[118] Each year we grant about 400,000 divorces and annulments. Some nine thousand people go to Nevada every year to get divorces. There are about 7,000,000 divorced spouses in our country at any given time. Some 300,000 children yearly are affected.[119] Nobody knows when the peak figure will be reached. Was it reached in 1946 with forty divorces per 100 marriages, or over 600,000 divorces? The rising rate of divorce characterizes all countries encountering industrial-urban development. The rate of increase, however, is not uniform. Italy, Spain, and Ireland apparently do not permit absolute divorce. Although the recent rate of increase in divorce for England and Wales far exceeds that of any other European country, the United States' rate is many times greater. Significant as is the divorce situation, it should be noted that the rising divorce rate has not meant, as is so commonly believed, a corresponding rise in the number of broken families. This seems to be true, although we do not accurately know the combined frequency of annulment, desertion, and informal separation. The rate is kept lower than might otherwise be the case by the decline in mortality to compensate for the increase in divorce and by the tendency of most divorced persons to remarry.

Are we to become disillusioned and discouraged by this phenomenon

[118] Kingsley Davis, "Statistical Perspective on Divorce," in Landis and Landis, *op. cit.*, pp. 333–338.

[119] Pilpel and Zavin, *op. cit.*, p. 297.

of broken families in our modern industrial world? Although the answer is no, we are not, by so saying, relieved of a grave responsibility to find out why there are so many divorces, annulments, separations, and desertions, and what remedies are available. Many explanations are given, and many proposals of what to do are offered. Some people hope to improve the situation by re-emphasizing the religious nature of marriage; some by tightening the divorce statutes; some by liberalizing divorce statutes and tightening marriage statutes; some by placing greater emphasis upon the social obligations of marriage; some by greatly expanded family education and counseling; some by changed and improved legal and judicial systems. Clearly, there is no single answer, and certainly consternation, condemnation, panic, panaceas will not solve the problem.

One of the most active exponents of modified legal and judicial procedure is Paul W. Alexander, Judge of the Court of Common Pleas, Lucas County (Toledo, Ohio), a family court handling many types of cases, including divorce. Judge Alexander refers to our present divorce situation in such terms as "our legal horror, divorce,"[120] or "the follies of divorce."[121] He condemns our anachronistic principles and practices of guilt and contest, limited causes, defenses, uncertain rules of domicile, and the restrictive and legalistic functions of the court. He believes that what people need in divorce courts is not more hell but more help! He therefore favors the establishment of family courts with broad jurisdiction, operating like the best of the juvenile courts. The purpose of such courts would be to help people come to sound decisions concerning the present and future of their marital relationships. This would mean abolishing statutory provisions concerning grounds, defenses, divorce counsels, advocacy and contention, except over such matters as money rights and custody of children. Further, it would mean modernization of equipment and personnel.

The proposal that there be developed a unified family court is of concern to many groups, including those mentioned above, and to such others as the American Bar Association and the Interprofessional Commission on Marriage and Divorce Laws, which is chaired by Judge Alexander. It is encouraging to know that groups like these are studying means of relieving the present "imbecilic" legal situation of which, according to Judge Alexander, every honest lawyer is ashamed. The present atmosphere of hypocrisy and lies on which the lawyer and his clients operate is not, he believes, conducive either to preservation of the family or to respect for the laws of a democracy. Perhaps such a commission, although it lacks official sanction, can facilitate extensive and objective consideration of the legal aspects of the problem, which, in some parts

---

[120] *National Parole and Probation Association Yearbook: 1949*, pp. 138–152.
[121] 36 A.B.A.J. 105–108 ff. (1950).

of the country, is blocked by citizen indifference or religious opposition. It may also be able to encourage formulation of official federal and state commissions to study our marriage and divorce problems.[122]

In the meantime, numbers of legal changes can be considered by those jurisdictions in need of them. We suggest the following:

1. The liberalization of the grounds of divorce in order to eliminate lying, collusion, fraud.
2. The change of procedure so that private affairs are not emblazoned from the housetops.
3. The abolition of divorce *a mensa et thoro* with its train of immoral consequences.
4. The elimination of breach-of-promise actions and the resulting possibility of blackmail.
5. The use of the interlocutory decree, thus discouraging hasty divorces and providing opportunity for reconciliation.
6. The abolition, or at least the recasting, of the defense statutes.
7. The abolition of discrimination between the sexes as to causes for divorce.
8. The disuse of the term "guilty spouse," since there are many other causes than adultery for divorce.
9. The granting of alimony to the defendant when justified.
10. The adoption of uniform provisions on the subject of jurisdiction and comity of states.

Those fatalists who believe that the institution of marriage is in the process of dissolution and that many, if not most, future marriages will go on the rocks know little history. Further, they have little understanding of the inevitability of change and the capacity of human institutions to adapt and adjust. The permanency of marriage does not rest upon the external power of church or state. Marriages endure because of their own intrinsic character. To compel persons to remain married because of archaic religious beliefs or anachronistic statutes is almost as abhorrent as wife capture and slavery. It seems clear that the institution of marriage will endure, that it will make adaptations to rapidly changing social and economic conditions, and that divorce will continue to be a method of achieving some measure of adjustment when marriage is a failure. To make and keep marriages that are happy and socially useful is the desire of all students of society and lovers of mankind. So, also, is it the

---

[122] Pilpel and Zavin, *op. cit.*, pp. 303–306; Paul W. Alexander, "Family Life Conference Suggests New Judicial Procedures and Attitudes Toward Marriage and Divorce," 32 J. Am. Jud. Soc. 38 (1948); "Symposium on Divorce," U. Ill. L. Forum, Vol. 1949, No. 3, pp. 547–711; "Symposium on the Law of Divorce," 28 Iowa L. Rev. 179–340 (1943); John S. Bradway, "Domestic Relations," 44 Mich. L. Rev. 1052–1089 (1946); Wood, "Marriage and Divorce Laws," 33 Women Law. J. 23 (1947); Paul W. Alexander and Dorothy Dunbar Bromley, "We Can Clear up Our Divorce Tangle," *This Week* (November 21, 1948); Thomas F. Walker, "Our Present Divorce Muddle: A Suggested Solution," 35 A.B.A.J. 457 (1949); Randolph Ray, *Marriage Is a Serious Business* (New York, Whittlesey House, 1944).

wish of many to provide methods of dissolution when the marriage is demoralizing and when the parties involved seek its termination.

For Selected References see those at the end of Chapter 5.

CHAPTER 7

Planned Parenthood

INTRODUCTION

The planned parenthood movement includes four aspects: conception control or, in common parlance, "birth control"; treatment for infertility; research in human reproduction; education for marriage and parenthood.[1] Leaders in the movement have a twofold interest: first, the health and well-being of individuals and families, and, second, the world-wide population problem. In connection with the first they are concerned that every family shall have the opportunity (1) to plan its size and to space its children in such a way as to protect the health of the mother and child, (2) to preserve or improve its economic status, and (3) to increase the happiness and satisfactions involved in having children. This was the original interest of Mrs. Margaret Sanger, who established the first birth-control clinics in this country. Advocates also wish to facilitate the development of resources for those unfortunate spouses unable for one reason or another to have children. In connection with the second interest, that of population control, supporters point out the suffering of parents and children in many parts of the world where the standards of living are unbelievably low and the death rate of mothers and children incredibly high. They wish to relieve this intolerable human situation. Further, they want to protect the world's resources from depletion by rapid and uncontrolled population increases. For these two basic reasons proponents of planned parenthood have placed major emphasis upon contraception or birth control. So shall we in this chapter. And like them, we shall also give consideration to aspects of the movement involving treatment for infertility and to research and counselling.

DEFINITION OF BIRTH CONTROL

Historically the size and quality of the family, and also of the general population, have been both consciously and unconsciously, purposely and accidentally, controlled by such forces and measures as war, infanticide and euthanasia, neglect, pestilence, famine, celibacy, abortion, castration, delayed marriage, sex taboos, perversions, and vice. Civilized and

[1] David Loth, "Planned Parenthood," *Annals of the American Academy of Political and Social Science,* Vol. 272 (November, 1950), p. 95.

planned methods include institutional segregation, restrictive marriage laws, eugenics, education, improvement of environment, sterilization, and birth control. It is our purpose in the next two chapters to discuss the last two methods of regulating family size, of limiting the total population, and of influencing its quality.

The term *birth control* was coined by Mrs. Margaret Sanger and her friends at the time she was editing *The Woman Rebel* (1914), the first magazine in the United States published for the purpose of agitating for popular education in relation to the problem of contraception.[2] The term is generally used to apply to practices designed to prevent conception by the employment of mechanical, chemical, and other means, although the word *contraception* would be more accurate. In its wider connotation, birth control, contraception, includes the diversity of practices referred to above.[3] For our purpose birth control does not imply these broad meanings but "the conscious control of the birth rate by means that prevent conception. The essential facts are: First, it is the prevention of conception, not the interruption of pregnancy after conception has taken place. Second, it is control, not necessarily limitation." [4]

HISTORICAL BACKGROUND

DEVELOPMENT OF SCIENTIFIC INFORMATION

Though numbers of methods of birth control have been known and used for centuries, the birth-control movement, which has become the planned parenthood movement, is of recent origin. Reports are available showing the efforts among primitive tribes to avoid pregnancy. That many of the methods employed were ineffective and sometimes dangerous is clear from the literature of anthropologists and historians. The desire to prevent conception seems to have been present in all civilizations at all times. Even in the densely populated oriental countries of Japan, China, and India, which have stressed family solidarity and ancestor worship, the *desire* for prevention is old.

Efforts of individuals to plan their own families started with infanticide and abortion, but there are evidences of contraceptives being used as long ago as 1850 B.C.[5] A contraceptive formula was found in the Petri papyrus of that date. Beginning with the fourth century B.C., Greeks and Romans

[2] Margaret Sanger, *My Fight for Birth Control* (New York, Farrar and Rinehart, 1931), pp. 80–83; Lawrence Lader, *The Margaret Sanger Story* (New York, Doubleday, 1955).

[3] Frank Hankins, "Birth Control," *Encyclopaedia of the Social Sciences* (1930), Vol. 2, pp. 559–565.

[4] Margaret Sanger, "Birth Control," *State Government* (September, 1934), p. 187.

[5] This early history is taken from *Birth Control, U.S.A.: Highlights of the Program* (New York, Planned Parenthood Federation, 1952).

followed the Egyptians in recommending birth control. We find contraceptive measures described in the Hebrew Tosephta Niddah of A.D. 230. In India the Kama-Sutra of the early fourth century described chemical and occlusive methods. Persian literature has numbers of descriptions of contraceptive methods from A.D. 923 onward. Italian-born St. Thomas Aquinas condemned birth control as "against nature and therefore morally wrong," indicating that the practice flourished in the thirteenth century.

Until very recently, contraceptive techniques have been largely accidental since so little was scientifically known of reproduction processes. What is new is not the desire for prevention but effective, harmless means of achieving it on a widespread scale.[6] From the dawn of history *coitus interruptus* seems to have been common practice. Chemicals have long been used. As early as the sixteenth century we find reference to the use of the sheath. In 1838 Friedrich Adolph Wilde, and in 1882 Wilhelm P. J. Mensinga, invented occlusive diaphragms which revolutionized medical contraceptive practice. Today the most scientific methods include chemicals and occlusives, although the most widely used are chemicals and sheaths.

The scientific search for easier, cheaper, safer methods moves on apace. Press reports tell of experiments on human subjects testing the contraceptive properties of lithospermum, a widespread weed, varieties of which grow the world over. Primitive man was well aware of the contraceptive possibilities of lithospermum long before scientists conducted laboratory experiments. The Shoshones and other American Indian tribes have been using an extract made from this weed for generations. They have also used other herbs for the same purpose. In fact, at least one hundred different herbs with some indication of contraceptive effect have been identified. Scientists report that lithospermum is just one of twenty or more current research leads meriting further study.[7]

A conference of scientists, physicians, and pharmacists convened in 1952 by the Planned Parenthood Federation of America, considered, among other matters, research leads for control of fertility. During the course of the meetings attention was given to anti-enzyme phosphorylated hesperidia studies, which, as a means of contraception, have been widely publicized.[8] At the diamond jubilee meeting of the American Chemical Society in September, 1951, James Conant, then president of

---

[6] Norman E. Himes, *Medical History of Contraception* (Baltimore, Williams and Wilkins, 1936), p. 185; see also, Marie Stopes, *Contraception: Its Theory, History, and Practice*, 4th ed. (London, Putnam, 1934).

[7] *Planned Parenthood News*, No. 3 (Spring, 1953).

[8] "New Horizons in Fertility Research," *Planned Parenthood News*, No. 1 (Fall, 1952).

Harvard University, stated that by 1961 biochemists will have made available cheap and harmless antifertility compounds to be added as one sees fit to the diet. He predicted, perhaps overconfidently, that as the twentieth century draws to a close, the attitude of the religious leaders of the world will have completely altered on the subject without any diminution of religious feeling.

ENGLISH DEVELOPMENTS

Medical discussion of contraception is old, but the economic and social justifications known as neo-Malthusianism are of the nineteenth century. The source of the modern planned parenthood movement can be found in the population doctrines of Malthus and in the propaganda methods of Place. In 1798, Malthus first published his theory that population has a tendency to increase beyond the means of subsistence and, hence, the excessive reproductive rate of human beings is the primary cause of poverty. The obvious outgrowth of the theory is that checks must be found to restrain the growth in population. Malthus proposed moral restraint. Francis Place was not the first to discuss the techniques of contraception, but he seems to have been the first to start an organized attempt to educate the masses. He holds the same position in social education on contraception that Malthus holds in the history of general population theory.[9] Place did much to put birth control on the map.

In 1822, Place published his "Illustrations and Proofs of the Principle of Population," the first English discussion on population to propose contraceptive measures as a substitute for Malthus' moral restraint. He also circulated thousands of handbills calling attention to the need of contraceptive instruction. He gave greater emphasis to economic than to medical reasons for restraint. Although he and his disciples suffered abuse, there was no legal interference with their birth control activities. With the passage of the Reform Bill in 1832, the new Poor Law in 1834, and Malthus' death the same year, the clamor for social reform abated and interest in birth control declined. There was little formal activity in this field until two American pamphlets by Robert Dale Owen and Dr. Charles Knowlton were reissued in England.

The American birth-control movement dates from about 1830. In that year Robert Dale Owen published his *Moral Physiology,* the first publication in America on birth control, the chief method recommended being *coitus interruptus.* In 1832 Knowlton anonymously published his *Fruits of Philosophy,* in which he advocated douching as the most effective method for birth control. About 10,000 copies of the latter book were

---

[9] Himes, *op. cit.,* p. 212. Much of the historical material in this chapter is taken from Himes's book and Hankins, *loc. cit.*

sold in the United States up to 1839. By 1834 it had been reprinted in England, and between that date and 1876 about 42,000 copies had been sold.

It was not until the Bradlaugh-Besant trial in 1877–1879 that Knowlton's pamphlet achieved notoriety. The facts in this famous case can be briefly summarized. Henry Cook of Bristol was convicted of interleaving obscene pictures with a Charles Watts' edition of Knowlton's pamphlet and, as a consequence, was sentenced to two years imprisonment at hard labor. Charles Watts, the London publisher, was thereupon prosecuted; he pleaded guilty and was let off easily. Charles Bradlaugh and Annie Besant, workers in the Free-thought movement, believed the pamphlet decent and useful and decided upon a test case to settle the legality of its sale. They especially organized the Free-thought Publishing Company for reprinting it. The London police were notified of the time and place of its distribution, whereupon these two were arrested and tried. The case finally reached the Court of Queen's Bench (high court of justice) where it was dismissed on a technicality because specific evidence of obscenity was not included.

At about the same time another prosecution accentuated interest and increased the dissemination of birth-control information among the masses. Edward Truelove, a Free-thought publisher, was arrested in 1877 for publishing and exhibiting in his shop window Owen's *Moral Physiology* and another somewhat similar tract. The prosecution argued that the pamphlet would have an injurious effect on the minds of the young and that such an influence was intended by the author and publishers. Truelove was convicted, and a sentence of four months in prison and a fine was imposed.

The effect of these two trials was great, and through them the attention of millions was drawn to the need for, and methods of, contraception. The Bradlaugh-Besant trial established the legality of the general free distribution of medical information on contraception. It led to the development of a succession of organizations concerned with various aspects of birth control. Today, England has many public and private centers dispensing information about planned parenthood.

INTERNATIONAL DEVELOPMENTS [10]

Following the Bradlaugh-Besant trial of 1877 and the organization of the Malthusian League in England, the birth-control movement became world-wide. Leagues were formed for propagandist purposes in Holland (1885), France (1895), Germany (1899), Bohemia (1901), Spain (1904), Brazil (1905), Belgium (1906), Cuba (1907), Switzerland (1908), Sweden (1911), Italy (1913), and Mexico (1918). At present, some

[10] Hankins, *loc. cit.*, pp. 559–565.

countries officially encourage planned parenthood, although others deliberately seek curtailment.[11] Here, we refer briefly to a few developments in countries other than the United States.

In the Scandinavian countries there is a liberal government position on birth control. In Norway the only restriction is a prohibition of the display or advertising of anything which offends public taste. Numbers of cities run tax-supported centers, and voluntary centers are found, too. The Swedish National League for Sex Education celebrated its twentieth anniversary in 1953. The Swedish government constantly consults the league, which runs numbers of centers. It is compulsory for apothecaries to keep contraceptives in stock. In Denmark a 1937 law provided for the establishment of birth-control clinics by local authorities in co-operation with the state. Strong opposition blocked the carrying out of this provision, and, as a result, it is private practitioners who are the main dispensers of advice and information on birth-control matters.

The Canadian law on contraception reflects the efforts of the government to reconcile two widely different cultures, French and English. The advertising and sale of contraceptives and literature on birth control are expressly forbidden in accordance with Catholic tradition. On the other hand, the British and Protestant traditions are recognized by a subsection of the law which states that no one shall be convicted of any offense if he proves that the public good was served by his alleged acts and that no excess in the acts alleged existed beyond what the public good required. The judge alone determines "the public good." After about half a century of this statute it is reported that there has been only one prosecution, and it resulted in an acquittal.

Congested and poverty-ridden countries like India and Japan are actively promoting resources for planned parenthood; in fact, these two countries are leading the world in sponsorship of contraceptive measures.[12] Birth control in Japan is legal for physical or economic reasons at full discretion of physicians. The lack of an ideal contraceptive is making abortion, now legalized, a national health problem. From more than 600,000 abortions in 1951, the 1952 estimate jumped to 1,500,000. Japan is attempting to combat the great increase in abortions by a vigorous campaign for birth control. In India the five-year plan passed by Parliament in 1952 emphasized the urgency of the problem of family planning and population control. The second five-year plan contemplates opening 1,100 health centers in Indian villages at an estimated cost in

---

[11] The following materials on international developments are, taken for the most part from *Around the World News of Population and Birth Control*, Nos. 1–15 (1952–1953), published by the International Planned Parenthood Federation.

[12] "Family Planning Gains in Far East," *New York Times* (May 26, 1953); *Chicago Daily News* (September 9, 1955); S. Chandrasekhar, *Population and Planned Parenthood in India* (London, Allen and Unwin, 1955); personal correspondence with Planned Parenthood Federation of America, Inc. (December 29, 1955).

excess of $6,000,000. These clinics will not only provide child welfare and maternity benefits but will also bring knowledge of family planning to the intensely religious and conservative village folk. India is one of the few countries in the world to adopt birth control as a deliberate policy of government. Officials admit, however, that not even the fringe of the health and population problems has so far been touched. Recent developments in Communist China indicate that the government is retracting its position against birth control. The birth-control program there is primarily pushed by such organizations as the All China Federation of Women. Recent and apparently well-substantiated reports indicate that several hundred thousand dollars worth of contraceptives have been moving into China from Hong Kong each year. This could hardly occur without approval of the government.

Soviet Russia's early birth-control activities were put into effect not through the spread of knowledge regarding contraception but through the practice of abortion.[13] So many abuses resulted from the 1926 legalization permitting the interruption of pregnancies that in 1936 the U.S.S.R. enacted legislation forbidding most abortions and increasing material aid to women in childbirth and with large families. In 1955 the Soviet Union again legalized abortions. One clear aim of the new edict was to avert harm caused to the health of women by abortions obtained outside medical establishments. The operation may be carried out only in hospitals and other medical establishments as provided by the Soviet ministry of health. Henceforth, according to the edict, the state will rely on education and propaganda to encourage motherhood and to prevent unnecessary abortions. By the end of 1955 the Soviet government's drive to step up the birth rate through bachelor's taxes, family allotments, and other devices seems to have met with marked success. In fact, the annual population increase more than offset the wartime depopulation. According to a Russian doctor visiting London in 1952, the practice of birth control is illegal except for medical reasons, and no birth control clinics exist.

Numbers of other countries discourage birth-control practices, and, in some instances, forbid dissemination of contraceptive information and materials. Catholic countries in general, such as France, Belgium, Italy, and Eire, restrict or prohibit the use of contraceptives. In France measures suppressing and prohibiting contraceptives go back as far as the second half of the nineteenth century. Birth control is illegal except by doctor's prescription and for open sale of *condoms* regarded as prophylactics. Numbers of countries, including France and Belgium, encourage

---

[13] *New York Times* (December 1, 1955); A. Sauvy, "Doctrine Sovietique en Matiere de Population," *Revista Italiana di Demografia e Statistica,* Vol. 2, No. 4 (December, 1948), p. 475; citation included in personal letter to author from the Planned Parenthood Federation of America, Inc. (May 20, 1953).

an expanding birth rate through family allowances. In Belgium birth control is illegal except for open sale of prophylactics. In Italy birth control is illegal. However, the birth rate is declining, despite all government measures to the contrary. In Germany the pattern of family limitation began late but spread rapidly. By 1930 a strong movement for birth control existed, but Hitler's population program, like Mussolini's, had nationalistic expansion and the stimulation of high birth rates as its goals. So the birth-control movement was quashed. There has, however, been a postwar renaissance of the movement in Germany, at least in western Germany.[14]

There have been several international conferences for planned parenthood. At a 1952 Bombay conference the International Planned Parenthood Federation was formed. Five hundred delegates from fourteen nations attended the Indian conference, which created the new federation and appointed as joint presidents Lady Rama Rau of India and Mrs. Margaret Sanger. The new organization has three regional offices, one for Asia in India, one for Europe in London, and one for North America in New York. The significance of these international conferences is great. They highlight the great desire of overpopulated countries for reduction in their birth rates and for raised standards of living. They demonstrate the desire of the people for inexpensive and adequate forms of birth control. They indicate the concern of officials for the private and public development of resources for planned parenthood. They reveal the belief of many religious groups that there is nothing irreligious in the practice of artificial birth control. Dr. S. Radhakrishnan, vice-president of India, scholar, philosopher, and spiritual leader, in his opening speech to the Bombay conference, said:

> We have today two thousand, five hundred million human beings in this world. We now talk about human rights. The Bill of Human Rights has been adopted by the United Nations and UNESCO. In other words, we wish to protect children; to give them all the facilities of food, clothing, shelter, medicine, education, etc. We have committed ourselves to this doctrine of human rights. People are not prepared to accept an axiomatic poverty, misery, starvation, and other things. We are committed to a social welfare state. . . . The question is sometimes raised whether it is not true that God sends children into this world and that we should not interfere with the will of God. I may tell you that if God has given us any intelligence, He has given it to us to be used. Intelligence is a Divine gift which we must use . . . . it cannot be argued that God is an external despot. He is present in the innermost depth of your being, and when He tells you and prompts you, or when He asks you to use your intelligence in a fair-minded, objective, honest way, you are being asked to use the gift of God for purposes of human welfare.

---

[14] Information from personal letter to author from the Planned Parenthood Federation of America, Inc. (May 20, 1953); see also, Vera Houghton, "Birth Control in Germany," *Eugenics Review*, Vol. 43 (1952), pp. 141–142.

International diplomats are vitally concerned with population problems and hence with methods of birth control. Thus far the World Health Organization seems able to encourage birth control solely through the rhythm method.

In the United States numerous nineteenth-century writers, in addition to Owen and Knowlton, gave momentum to the birth-control movement in both its medical and social aspects. The so-called Comstock law of 1873 prohibiting the distribution of contraceptive information through the mails hampered the movement. The legal history of birth control in the United States centers around this law, which associates contraception with indecency and obscenity. In no other country is contraceptive information considered obscene.[15] Our legal history on this subject consists largely of attempts by various groups to repeal or modify the Comstock law or to find a legal way to get around that and similar state legislation.

ATTITUDES TOWARD AND ARGUMENTS PERTAINING TO BIRTH CONTROL

During the first quarter of the twentieth century the United States witnessed a stormy battle over the idea that it is the legal right of married individuals to receive information and advice from professional personnel concerning contraceptives. Individual liberties as well as the general welfare were involved, at least so thought the advocates of the birth-control movement. Except for the Roman Catholic church, this is today the prevalent opinion in the United States.

RELIGIOUS ARGUMENTS: CATHOLIC POSITION

The principal opposition comes from the Roman Catholic church, which argues that children constitute the natural, religious, and socially necessary culmination of marriage and furnish invaluable life discipline. Since Thomas Aquinas, Catholic theologians have condemned the prevention of conception by unnatural or artificial means and use as one of their authorities the biblical story of Onan:

> And Er, Judah's first born, was wicked in the sight of the Lord; and the Lord slew him. And Judah said unto Onan: "Go in unto thy brother's wife and perform the duty of a husband's brother unto her, and raise up seed to thy brother!" And Onan knew that the seed would not be his; and it came to pass, whenever he went in unto his brother's wife, that he used to spill it on the ground, lest he should give seed to his brother. And the thing which he did was evil in the sight of the Lord; and He slew him also.[16]

---

[15] Mary Ware Dennett, *Birth Control Laws: Shall We Keep Them, Change Them, or Abolish Them?* (New York, Hitchcock, 1926), p. 28.

[16] Gen. 38:7–10.

Catholics have interpreted this to mean that the Lord punished Onan because he practiced *coitus interruptus* rather than because he refused to perform the levirate marriage.[17]

The papal encyclical, "*Casti connubii,*" of December 31, 1931, rejects contraception. It states: [18]

> And now, Venerable Brethren, we shall explain in detail the evils opposed to each of the benefits of matrimony. First consideration is due to the offspring, which many have the boldness to call the disagreeable burden of matrimony and which they say is to be carefully avoided by married people not through virtuous continence (which Christian law permits in matrimony when both parties consent) but by frustrating the marriage act. Some justify this criminal abuse on the ground that they are weary of children and wish to gratify their desires without their consequent burden. Others say that they cannot on the one hand remain continent nor on the other can they have children because of the difficulties whether on the part of the mother or on the part of family circumstances.
>
> But no reason, however grave, may be put forward by which anything intrinsically against nature may become conformable to nature and morally good. Since, therefore, the conjugal act is destined primarily by nature for the begetting of children, those who in exercising it deliberately frustrate its natural power and purpose sin against nature and commit a deed which is shameful and intrinsically vicious.
>
> Small wonder, therefore, if Holy Writ bears witness that the Divine Majesty regards with greatest detestation this horrible crime and at times has punished it with death. As St. Augustine notes, "Intercourse even with one's legitimate wife is unlawful and wicked where the conception of the offspring is prevented. Onan, the son of Juda, did this and the Lord killed him for it."
>
> Since, therefore, openly departing from the uninterrupted Christian tradition some recently have judged it possible solemnly to declare another doctrine regarding this question, the Catholic Church, to whom God has entrusted the defence of the integrity and purity of mortals, standing erect in the midst of the moral ruin which surrounds her, in order that she may preserve the chastity of the nuptial union from being defiled by this foul stain, raises her voice in token of her divine ambassadorship and through Our mouth proclaims anew: any use whatsoever of matrimony exercised in such a way that the act is deliberately frustrated in its natural power to generate life is an offence against the law of God and of nature, and those who indulge in such are branded with the guilt of a grave sin.

The official position of the Catholic church on the subject of artificial birth control is reiterated by the American hierarchy. For example, Father Francis J. Connell stated in 1939 that the Catholic church can never change its stand on this matter. If the human race exists ten thousand years hence, no matter what changes have taken place in the social, economic and scientific spheres, the Catholic church will still be preach-

---

[17] Himes, *op. cit.*, p. 71.

[18] "Encyclical Letter on Christian Marriage by Pope Pius XI," in *Four Great Encyclicals* (New York, Paulist Press, 1931), pp. 90–96; *Catholic Action* (January, 1936), pp. 3–4; Hankins, *loc. cit.*, p. 563.

ing the same doctrine on birth control that it now teaches.[19] In a 1951 book, *Moral Problems in Social Work,* the author, in his discussion of birth control, in substance stated that the primary consideration of the church concerning this subject is that artificial birth control is intrinsically wrong, that it is wrong from its very nature and not wrong because the Catholic church says so. The church merely teaches that it is intrinsically immoral, that is, immoral from its very nature and hence wrong for Catholic and non-Catholic alike. The church passes some laws which bind only her own members, but in this case it does not matter whether the client is Catholic or non-Catholic, in good health or in poor health; the use of contraceptives is an offense contrary to natural law.[20]

In 1932 Dr. Leo J. Latz published *The Rhythm Theory of Sterility and Fertility in Women* with ecclesiastical approval. This book recognizes the value of child spacing and recommends the "safe period" as the alternative to artificial contraceptives.[21] This liberalized stand of the Catholic church was welcomed by many Catholics and Protestants alike. In 1951 the Pope, apparently alarmed by the spread of birth control and "licentiousness" in modern society, issued a proclamation to members of the Catholic Union of Obstetricians holding a congress in Rome on the subjects of abortion, artificial insemination, sterilization, and birth control. His position on the use of the rhythm theory was that husbands and wives may enjoy their matrimonial rights on days of natural sterility, but if the "connubial act" is performed only on those days, then the behavior of the couple must be examined more closely. If both participants deliberately avoid their duty of procreation while fully satisfying their sensuality, they sin against the essence of marital life.[22]

RELIGIOUS ARGUMENTS: NON-CATHOLIC POSITION

The attitude of Protestant and other non-Catholic groups is more sympathetic. In 1931 liberal Protestants expressed their beliefs in a report by the committee on marriage and home of the Federal Council of the Churches of Christ in America, which is here quoted in part: [23]

This committee is strongly of the opinion that the church should not seek to impose its point of view as to the use of contraceptives upon the public by legis-

---

[19] Francis J. Connell, "Birth Control: The Case for the Catholic," *Atlantic Monthly,* Vol. 144 (July–December, 1939), pp. 468–473.

[20] Charles R. McKenney, *Moral Problems in Social Work* (Milwaukee, Wis., Bruce Publishing Co., 1951), ch. 14; see Paul Blanshard, *American Freedom and Catholic Power* (Boston, Beacon Press, 1949), especially ch. 7, for refutation of this point of view.

[21] Chicago, Latz Foundation, 1932; Irving F. Stein and Melvin R. Cohen, "An Evaluation of the Safe Period," *Journal of American Medical Association* (January 12, 1938), pp. 257–261.

[22] "Pope Strengthens Procreation View," *New York Times* (October 30, 1951).

[23] "Birth Control: Protestant View," *Current History* (April, 1931), p. 97, contains the full text of the report.

lation or any other form of coercion; and especially should not seek to prohibit physicians from imparting such information to those who in the judgment of the medical profession are entitled to receive it. . . . A majority of the committee holds that the careful and restrained use of contraceptives by married people is valid and moral. They take this position because they believe that it is important to provide for the proper spacing of children, the control of the size of the family, and the protection of mothers and children, and because intercourse between mates, when an expression of their spiritual union and affection, is right in itself.

Planned parenthood was endorsed in 1952 at the eleventh biennial convention of the American Lutherans' Conference in Minneapolis. In a report prepared by its Commission on Social Relations the following statement appeared: [24]

When practiced in a spirit of love, of freedom and of stewardship accountability to God, the conscientious planning for the number and spacing of their children may bring the Christian husband and wife a sense of peace, of joy, and of contentment over their partnership with God in this creation of each new life entrusted to them.

In March, 1953, the Pennsylvania League for Planned Parenthood launched a program to educate student ministers in Protestant theological seminaries in problems of modern family life. The lecture course came about as the result of a ministerial meeting addressed by Dr. Abraham Stone, then vice-president of the Planned Parenthood Federation of America and one of the nation's leading marriage counselors.[25] These are a few of the many illustrations of the widespread acceptance of planning for parenthood by non-Catholic religious groups.

MEDICAL ARGUMENTS

Medical opinion, on the whole, strongly supports the view that maternal and infant health is greatly aided by a considerable period between births. Various authorities have stated that in consideration of the mother's health, as well as that of the infant, there should be an interval of at least one and preferably two years between pregnancies. Psychiatrists have long recognized the emotional maladjustment connected with the fear of pregnancy. Birth-control advocates argue that if physicians freely give information to their patients, the number of abortions each year in the United States will decrease. Abortion operations, in general, are prohibited by law except for therapeutic reasons, but many illegal operations are performed by "quacks" under unfavorable medical conditions, and many are induced by women themselves. Death often results. Establishing the legal right of married persons to receive contraceptive information will not entirely do away with abortions and ma-

[24] *Around the World News of Population and Birth Control,* No. 12 (February, 1953).

[25] *Planned Parenthood News,* No. 3 (Spring, 1953).

ternal deaths resulting therefrom; however, it undoubtedly will lessen the number.

General understanding of the close association between the problems of excess fertility, infant and maternal morbidity and mortality, and standards of living is increasing. The public health aspects of childbearing are twofold: the prevention of disease associated with childbearing, and the effort to raise general standards of health by lowering excess population pressures and improving standards of living. Numbers of studies show the correlation between the prevalence and effectiveness of contraception, socioeconomic class, and health problems. Raymond Pearl made such studies in the 1930's. Others were made in the 1940's in such localities as Indianapolis, Ind., Spartanburg, S.C., and Logan County, W.Va.[26]

For years the American Medical Association practically ignored the medical aspects of birth control. Not until 1937, following liberal judicial interpretation by federal courts, did birth control become a matter for the official and scientific concern of the A.M.A. In that year the association accepted three principles: (1) that the A.M.A. make clear to physicians their legal rights in this matter; (2) that the A.M.A. undertake research concerning contraceptive materials and methods; (3) that through medical schools the A.M.A. promote education on the subject.[27] Following adoption of these principles, the executive committee of the Catholic Hospital Association met and discussed the position of the A.M.A. Subsequently, it requested that the A.M.A. state more precisely its attitude toward birth control and, in so doing, give consideration to the moral as well as the legal aspects.[28]

SOCIAL AND ECONOMIC ARGUMENTS

Proponents of birth control state that the legal right to learn about and use contraceptives will enable married couples to avoid having more children than they can decently support. The small earner in the United

---

[26] Regine K. Stix, "The Place of Fertility Control in Public Health," *American Journal of Public Health,* Vol. 36, No. 3 (March, 1946); see also, Raymond Pearl, "Contraception and Fertility in 4945 Married Women," *Human Biology,* Vol. 6, No. 2 (May, 1934), pp. 355–401; P. K. Whelpton and Clyde V. Kiser, "Determinants and Control in Human Fertility," *Annals of the American Academy of Political and Social Science* (January, 1945), pp. 112–122; F. W. Notestein and Clyde V. Kiser, "Factors Affecting Variations in Human Fertility," *Social Forces,* Vol. 14, No. 1 (October, 1935), pp. 32–41; C. V. Kiser and P. K. Whelpton, "Social and Psychological Factors Affecting Fertility," *Milbank Memorial Fund Quarterly,* Vol. 21, No. 3 (July, 1943), pp. 221–280.

[27] "Report of Committee on Contraception of A.M.A.," *Journal of Contraception* (June–July, 1937), pp, 123–125; Prentiss Willson, "Victory with Reservations," *Journal of Contraception* (June–July, 1937), pp. 125–127; "American Medical Association Action on Prevention of Contraception and Other Problems" *Journal of American Medical Association* (June 26, 1937), p. 2204; "Report of Reference Committee and Executive Session," *Journal of American Medical Association* (June 26, 1937), pp. 2217–2218.

[28] Alphonse M. Schwitalla, "The American Medical Association and Contraception," *Hospital Progress* (July, 1937), pp. 219–224.

States should be given an opportunity to maintain a reasonable minimum standard of living for his family, and he should not have to accept public assistance in order to do so. The necessity of accepting financial assistance often could be prevented if the wage earner and his wife could plan and control the size of their family. Children whose parents are dependent upon public assistance start life at a disadvantage, economically and socially.

A considerable number of people have the idea that "procreation becomes the first concern of families when they are accepted for relief." [29] This belief is due to the confusion of two different problems: one is concerned with the level or status of fertility in relief families; the other with changes in fertility associated with the fact of dependency. That dependency causes changes in fertility has not been proved. However, it has been established that the birth rate is higher for families receiving public assistance than for comparable families not requiring help.[30] Although no study seems to have been made which shows that the birth rate rises when families get public help, it is clear that the burden for the taxpayer increases because some large families must accept assistance and because already large families, carrying on their pattern of rapid reproduction, grow larger. Contraceptives should be available to these families, and they should be encouraged to curtail the size of their families so that an unnecessary tax burden shall not be imposed upon those who have small incomes and who choose to limit the size of their families. It may be that some of these families do not have the will or the intelligence to limit the number of births, but many more undoubtedly have both the desire and the intelligence to do so.

POPULATION DATA AND ARGUMENTS

Many believers in the birth-control movement are vitally interested in long-time planning of the size, quality, and distribution of the population. This is not the place for a long discussion of the complex and immensely important population problem; but a few facts and opinions are introduced so that the student may be aware of population trends and the necessity for correlation of the birth-control and population movements. Neither "population pressure" nor "race suicide" should be the bogey of any nation.

The most ominous force in the world today, next to the atom bomb,

---

[29] Corrington Gill, "Study of the Three Million Families on Relief in October, 1933," (Washington, D.C., Works Progress Administration, 1934), pp. 25–36; Frank W. Notestein, "The Fertility of Populations Supported by Public Relief," *Milbank Memorial Fund Quarterly* (January, 1936), pp. 37–49.

[30] Samuel A. Stouffer, "Fertility of Families on Relief," *Journal of the American Statistical Association* (September, 1934), pp. 295–301, and "Trends in the Fertility of Catholics and Non-Catholics," *American Journal of Sociology* (September, 1935), pp. 143–166; U.S. National Resources Committee, Science Committee, *The Problems of a Changing Population* (Washington, D.C., G.P.O., 1938), ch. 5.

is uncontrolled fertility.[31] This is the statement of Robert Cook, a distinguished geneticist and student of population problems. The crisis in human fertility is world-wide. It is composed of two aspects: How many people? What kind of people? [32] Today, there are nearly 2,500,000,000 human beings in the world, and the number is increasing by some 68,000 or more every twenty-four hours. Between 1850 and 1940 the population of the earth doubled. In the last three hundred years it increased from 500,000,000 to 2,500,000,000. Yearly it increases some 20,000,000. It is predicted that by 1980 there will be a world population increase of 1,500,000,000. Distribution of these increases is not equal. In many areas that are already densely populated the growth is most rapid. In only a few is the population decreasing in size or remaining stable, as in France, Sweden, and Ireland. In Puerto Rico, Egypt, India, Japan, China, Russia, and Greece there are more hungry mouths than can be, or at least are, fed. Even where unchecked fertility has not forced a scramble for survival, there is misplaced and badly distributed fertility. This phenomenon Cook dubs "biological erosion." [33]

The high death rate has been an important factor in keeping the world's population in some kind of equilibrium. It is estimated that 100 million people starved to death in China alone during the past century. Within the last hundred years man has begun to invent vaccines, aseptic surgical and obstetrical techniques, scientific methods of fertility control, antibiotics, and to impose public health and sanitation measures which have greatly improved the processes of death control. The tendency for death rates to decline but for birth rates to increase has created a world overflowing with people, some two billion of whom are estimated to be half starved.[34] The power to defer death brings with it grave responsibilities. On a global basis, what Malthus predicted would happen is happening, namely, that the increase in population is far greater than in food production.

An alarming aspect of this problem in the minds of such men as Cook, Fairfield Osborn,[35] and William Vogt,[36] is the prodigally wasteful use of the world's resources. This wastage has been occurring long before there is any indication that invention of synthetic foods will adequately supplement natural resources for billions yet to be born. Millions have died of starvation, and millions more will. They must starve, according to Vogt, as sacrifices on the twin altars of uncontrolled human reproduction and uncontrolled abuse of the land's resources.[37] Mankind has backed

---

[31] Robert C. Cook, *Human Fertility* (New York, William Sloane Associates, 1951), p. 5.

[32] *Ibid.*, p. 334.

[33] *Ibid.*, p. 5.

[34] *Ibid.*, p. 321.

[35] Fairfield Osborn, *Our Plundered Planet* (Boston, Little, Brown, 1948).

[36] William Vogt, *Road to Survival* (New York, William Sloane Associates, 1948).

[37] Vogt, *op. cit.*, p. 225.

itself into an ecological trap by excessive breeding and abuse of the land. By a lopsided use of applied science the world has been living on promissory notes, and now, all over the globe, the notes are falling due.[38] Ecological health for the world requires (1) wise use of irreplaceable resources, and (2) adjustment of the demand to the supply either by accepting less food per capita or by maintaining less people.[39] Fairfield Osborn comments that the tide of the earth's population is rising and the reservoir of the earth's living resources is falling. Technologists may create artificial substitutes for natural substance, and new areas, such as those in tropical or subtropical regions may be adapted to human use. These kinds of resources and developments, however, cannot be expected to offset the present terrific attack upon the natural life-giving elements of the earth. There is only one solution. Man must co-operate with nature, temper his demands, and conserve the natural living resources in a manner that alone can provide for the continuation of his civilization.[40]

Many natural scientists and population experts believe that population planning here and now is necessary if this planet is not to face greater disaster than it has known. This cannot be done by any nation alone. It must be done by intergovernmental planning. It places a heavy responsibility upon the United Nations, which should encourage (1) planned parenthood clinics, including birth control and sterilization counsel and research; (2) conservation of natural resources; and (3) invention and production of new resources to meet the needs of an expanding population.[41]

POPULAR ATTITUDES

Prevailing attitudes toward birth control are favorable. Numbers of popular polls, publications, and speeches show this to be true. Several illustrations are here included.

In 1938 the *Ladies' Home Journal* conducted such a poll. It showed that 79 per cent of the women in the United States approve the use of birth-control methods. Of the Catholic women participating in the poll, 51 per cent declared themselves in favor of some form of control.[42] A 1940 Gallup Poll revealed that 77 per cent of the American public favored inclusion of birth-control service under government health auspices. A *Fortune* magazine poll in 1942 showed that 85 per cent of women in the childbearing ages questioned were in favor of medically approved birth-

---

[38] *Ibid.*, p. 284.
[39] *Ibid.*, p. 265.
[40] Osborn, *op. cit.*, p. 201.
[41] Guy Irving Burch and Elmer Pendell, *Human Breeding and Survival* (Baltimore, Penguin Books, 1947), pp. 128, 129.
[42] Henry F. Pringle, "What Do the Women Think about Birth Control?" *Ladies' Home Journal* (March, 1938), p. 12.

control information being made available to all married women; 69 per cent of the Catholic women questioned concurred in the opinion. In 1935 the National Broadcasting Company ended radio censorship of birth control by broadcasting the address of a member of Congress from Oregon, preceding the "Birth Control Comes of Age" dinner commemorating the twenty-first anniversary of the movement. In 1938 *Fortune* magazine printed, and later published in pamphlet form, "The Accident of Birth," the first comprehensive survey of the birth-control industry, which was doing a yearly business of $250,000,000. In 1942 the National Association of Broadcasters informed radio stations that there was nothing in its code which would bar discussion of birth control from the air. Following this, a larger number of radio broadcasts of national conferences, forums, and programs were initiated by local groups. In the same year the National Negro Advisory Council of thirty-five Negro leaders was formed to initiate an educational program on the urgent need for child spacing among Negroes to combat the high disproportionate infant and maternal death rates.

From 1946 to 1952 annual Lasker awards were given to various persons associated with the birth-control movement, including Margaret Sanger. In 1948 William Vogt's *Road to Survival* brought a flood of publicity to the planned parenthood movement and acquainted the man on the street with the fact that population control is his concern. In 1949 a documentary film, "A Planned Parenthood Story" was issued. In March, 1953, the University of Chicago Round Table presented world planned parenthood leaders in an NBC broadcast entitled "Three Billion People." The panel discussion was recorded in November, 1952, during the International Planned Parenthood Conference at Bombay, India.[43]

A survey of 138 magazines from January, 1951, to the fall of 1952 spotted 241 articles dealing in whole or in part with some phase of planned parenthood.[44] Although a large number of these articles were favorable to planned parenthood, there were some which were exceedingly energetic in their opposition. For example, in 1951 the *Reader's Digest* published three articles: two favorable and one unfavorable. The unfavorable article was the condensation of a letter from Douglas J. Murphy, then president of the Co-ordinating Committee of Catholic Lay Organizations. He strongly criticized the magazine for its article on Margaret Sanger and included numbers of quotations from Catholic periodicals vehemently condemnatory of voluntary parenthood and the *Reader's Digest*.[45]

[43] *Planned Parenthood News,* No. 3 (Spring, 1953).

[44] *Planned Parenthood News,* No. 1 (Fall, 1952).

[45] "The Catholic Case Against Margaret Sanger," *Reader's Digest,* Vol. 59, No. 356 (December, 1951), pp. 139–142.

POSITIONS OF COUNCILS OF SOCIAL AGENCIES

In 1953 the Health and Welfare Council of New York City, the Planned Parenthood Federation, and the Catholic church became involved in a controversy of country-wide significance. The facts, widely publicized in the New York press and throughout the country, were as follows. The Roman Catholic dioceses of New York and Brooklyn threatened withdrawal from the Welfare and Health Council of New York City if the New York Planned Parenthood Federation was admitted. This organization had been a member of the Health Council of Greater New York. With the merger of the Health and the Welfare councils, new applications from some agencies were required. The New York Planned Parenthood Federation was one of these and the only agency whose application for membership the board rejected. A citizens' committee for planned parenthood was formed, headed by the distinguished Protestant clergyman, Dr. Harry Emerson Fosdick. Among its members were such prominent persons as the Reverend John Haynes Holmes, Eleanor Roosevelt, and Bruce Barton. Finally, after several months of hearings and community wide discussion, the Welfare and Health Council voted 317 to 259 to admit the Planned Parenthood Federation. The following day fifty-three Catholic agencies resigned from the council.[46]

In the winter of 1953 the Pennsylvania League for Planned Parenthood conducted a study of the acceptance and rejection of planned parenthood groups in health and welfare councils. A questionnaire was sent to the councils of social agencies in the fifty-two communities where a Planned Parenthood Federation affiliate enjoyed membership. Responses were received from thirty-six councils. Outstanding in the conclusions were (1) general agreement that Planned Parenthood membership in local councils had no effect upon public support of the other member agencies; (2) indications that in a majority of these communities affiliate and Catholic agencies maintained side-by-side membership without disruptive effect; (3) a small number of withdrawals by Catholic agencies because of Planned Parenthood membership. Four communities reported that Catholic agencies had withdrawn from the council, but one such withdrawal was later reversed at the request of a joint Protestant-Catholic committee of citizens.[47]

---

[46] *Planned Parenthood News,* No. 2 (Winter, 1953); articles in the *New York Times* during the first half of 1953.

[47] *Planned Parenthood News,* No. 2 (Winter, 1953).

FEDERAL LEGISLATION

INFLUENCE OF ANTHONY COMSTOCK

American legislation against the spreading of birth-control information and the dissemination of contraceptive articles grew out of a drive against obscenity. In 1873 Anthony Comstock, a crusader against indecency and obscenity, was instrumental in framing and securing the passage of the first federal birth-control law. The bill was delayed in hearings and passage because of a great congressional scandal over the operations of the Credit Mobilier, a joint-stock company organized to finance the building of the Union Pacific Railroad which was accused of offering bribes to prominent Republicans.[48] This may, in part, be the reason for the passage of the Comstock Act with little discussion and apparently with no realization of the implications of the phrase "for the prevention of conception." At any rate, in 1873 a bill was passed prohibiting the mailing of obscene matter within the United States, including the District of Columbia and the territories, and classifying prevention of conception with obscenity.

Almost immediately Comstock was appointed special agent of the Post Office Department. He was also secretary of the Society for the Suppression of Vice in New York State and had the power to require the assistance of New York police forces in the enforcement of laws for the suppression of the circulation of obscene literature and articles of indecent and immoral use. For many years he energetically, even fanatically, lectured against indecency and conducted inspections, arrests, and prosecutions. Comstock was largely responsible, therefore, for the passage of a federal law which forbade the circulation of pornographic literature and which associated contraceptives and indecency. It is probable that it was his intention merely to prohibit *indecent* use of contraceptives. The *Congressional Globe* (now called the *Congressional Record*) reveals that the original draft of the law exempted information concerning prevention of conception given by a physician in good standing and in good faith. The fact remains, however, that Congress passed a law closing the mails to contraceptive literature and materials and that this law was the starting point for additional prohibitory legislation.

At present, federal statutes concerning birth control (1) identify contraceptive information with obscenity and prohibit the mailing of such; (2) prohibit the importation and transportation by any express company or other common carrier of obscene books or things designated, adapted, or intended for preventing conception; (3) prohibit the circulation of obscene literature, including that concerning the prevention of concep-

---

[48] Heywood Broun and Margaret Leech, *Anthony Comstock* (New York, Albert and Charles Boni, 1927), pp. 79 ff.

tion; and (4) prohibit the importation of obscene books and articles for the prevention of conception. In all of these statutes, birth control is identified with obscenity.[49]

INFLUENCE OF MARGARET SANGER, MARY WARE DENNETT, AND OTHERS

Except for the attention attracted by Comstock to the obscenity provisions of the federal laws, relatively little was heard of them until 1914 when Mrs. Sanger, a nurse who had seen the results of excessive child-bearing, resolved that women should have knowledge of contraception.[50] In 1913 she made a trip to Europe, seeking scientific contraceptive information to bring back to the United States. On her return in 1914 she agitated for birth control and the repeal of the Comstock Act through the medium of a magazine which she founded, *The Woman Rebel.* Shortly after the publication of the magazine she was notified by postal officials that it contained material prohibited by the federal laws and was, therefore, unmailable. She continued to print and distribute the magazine, and indictments on nine counts were made against her. Instead of defending her case on the date set by the court, Mrs. Sanger went to Europe in order to obtain more information and to have more time to prepare an adequate and intelligent defense of her activities. Upon her return she was not given the opportunity to present her defense, for the case was dismissed without a hearing. From then on, Mrs. Sanger continued her fight for legal distribution of birth-control information and materials. She and another outstanding advocate of planned parenthood, Mrs. Mary Ware Dennett, organized groups designed in one way or another to facilitate the development of clinics and to repeal or modify restrictive legislation. As these groups accomplished or failed to accomplish their purposes, they gave way to other and more needed organizations. Today the Planned Parenthood Federation of America, Inc. exists as a strong national organization largely because of the pioneer work of Margaret Sanger and a few other fearless women. It is essentially an educational and research organization.[51]

To date, efforts to modify or repeal federal legislation on contraception have been unsuccessful. Testimony given before congressional commit-

---

[49] The federal statutes providing for contraception are found in two distinct portions of the United States Code. The first two of these sections are part of Title 18: Crimes: ch. 71: Obscenity; the third is contained in Title 19: Customs Duties; 18 USC §1461, 18 USC §1462, 19 USC §1305. See also, Fowler V. Harper, *Problems of the Family* (Indianapolis, Bobbs-Merrill, 1952), pp. 327–329, for excerpts from statutory provisions.

[50] Margaret Sanger, *Margaret Sanger: An Autobiography* (New York, Norton, 1938), ch. 9, and *My Fight For Birth Control,* pp. 62–95; Lawrence Lader, *op. cit.*

[51] For this development see Sanger, *Autobiography,* and Mary Ware Dennett, *op. cit.*

tees on "doctors only" bills showed the type of arguments given by both proponents and opponents.[52] Most of the arguments *for* the bill were lucid, logical, humanitarian, scientific, and given by doctors, nurses, social workers, mothers. Most of the arguments *against* it were religious and moral, given by a few doctors and many religionists. This law, thoughtlessly and stupidly passed in 1873, remains with us to be violated even by many adherents of the groups strongest opposed to change. Congressional modification of the law in the immediate future seems doubtful. In fact, the need for change is lessened because judicial interpretation has liberalized its provisions.

STATE LEGISLATION

After the passage of the Comstock Act by Congress, many of the states passed similar legislation identifying birth control with obscenity. In 1955 nineteen states neither prohibited nor restricted the dissemination of birth-control information.[53] Twenty-nine states had restrictive legislation. Fourteen had statutes restricting the distribution and dissemination of information on the prevention of conception but expressly exempting medical practice. Thirteen states had statutes aimed at the indiscriminate advertising and distribution of information regarding the prevention of conception but exempting medical practice by implication or construction. The restrictive laws of Massachusetts and Connecticut defy classification and will be referred to presently in our discussion of state judicial decisions. The New York statute relating to indecent articles and contraception was enacted almost in its present form in 1881 and included a provision for the exemption of physicians. In only one state, Connecticut, is the *use* of contraceptives prohibited. Obviously, this law is not enforced; nor is it possible to think of an adequate method of enforcement. The legislation applying to the District of Columbia has been virtually nullified by federal judicial decision. Most statutes restricting the free movement of contraceptive literature and materials have various types of exemptions, such as provisions allowing medical schools, physicians, and druggists to disseminate contraceptive information and materials.

---

[52] U.S. Senate, *Hearings Before a Subcommittee of the Committee on the Judiciary*, 72d Cong., 2d sess. on S. 4436 (May 12, 19, 20, 1932); *Hearings Before a Subcommittee of the Committee on the Judiciary*, 73d Cong., 2d sess. on S. 1842 (March 1, 20, 27, 1934).

[53] *The Legal Status of Contraception* (New York, Planned Parenthood Federation of America, 1953); The nineteen states are Alabama, Florida, Georgia, Illinois, Kentucky, Maryland, New Hampshire, New Mexico, North Dakota, Oklahoma, Rhode Island, South Carolina, South Dakota, Tennessee, Texas, Utah, Vermont, Virginia, and West Virginia. Correspondence with the Planned Parenthood Federation of America, Inc. (December 21, 1955), indicates that so far as the organization knows the 1953 figures are still accurate.

The various national birth-control organizations have intermittently given their assistance to modification or repeal of state legislation. Their efforts were sporadic, for they came to realize that federal prohibitory legislation curtailed state activities and state courts often patterned interpretation of state obscenity and birth-control laws on decisions of the federal courts. Hence the emphasis of those organizations gradually shifted to modification or repeal of federal statutes. With the decision in 1936 that the federal statutes cannot be construed to prevent the importation of contraceptive articles for lawful use, there is less likelihood that federal statutes will be used as models for state laws, and with the liberalization of federal judicial opinion, there is greater possibility of liberal construction by state courts of those statutes limiting the dissemination and use of contraceptives. Consequently, emphasis again needs to be placed on change of some of the state laws or upon securing liberal judicial decisions in the state courts modeled after those of the federal courts.

JUDICIAL DECISIONS

We have seen that birth-control leaders have been unsuccessful in their efforts to modify or repeal those parts of the federal laws that concern contraception. Judicial decisions have had the effect of modifying these laws. It is significant that from the judiciary, the branch of government usually considered most conservative, has come the legal recognition of the right under existing prohibitory statutes to distribute, receive, and use contraceptive information.

FEDERAL COURTS

In the main, the cases taken into the courts fall into two categories, some falling into both: (1) those pertaining to the legality of mailing, transporting, importing books, circulars, and similar material about birth control or where contraceptives can be obtained; (2) those pertaining to the definition of contraceptives and the mailing, transporting, and importing of these articles. A review of some of the decisions will show modifications in the interpretation of the statutes.

In 1873, almost immediately upon the passage of the Comstock Act, two defendants were separately indicted in the federal courts, one of them for depositing in the mails a certain powder designed and intended for preventing conception or causing abortion, and the other for depositing an advertisement giving information where certain contraband articles could be obtained. The court in this case, usually referred to as the Bott case, said that both incidents were in violation of the law and that there was no defense for the first in the fact that the materials would not have the effect advertised. "The unlawful act of depositing contraband matter, coupled with the intent to deposit such matter, constitutes the crime." [54]

As more persons became interested in limiting the size of their families, a number of commercial concerns undertook to manufacture contraceptive devices.[55] It was inevitable that for one reason or another some of these establishments should be drawn into the courts.[56] The holding of the Bott case was maintained by the federal courts until 1930, when two commercial manufacturers of contraceptive devices tangled. The Youngs Rubber Corporation began in 1916 to sell and ship packages of prophylactic rubber articles for the prevention of disease, and in 1926 it began to use the trademark "Trojan" to which it was exclusively entitled. This corporation alleged that the C. I. Lee Company had infringed upon its registered trademark. The Lee Company denied using a restricted trademark in interstate commerce and set up as affirmative defenses the illegality of the Youngs Rubber Corporation's business and the illegality of its trademark.

The court said: [57]

> Taken literally, this language (U.S.C.A. title 18 Paragraph 334, 396) would seem to forbid the transportation by mail or common carriage of anything "adapted," in the sense of being suitable or fitted, even though the article might also be capable of legitimate uses and the sender in good faith supposed that it would be used only legitimately. Such a construction would prevent mailing to or by a physician of any drug or mechanical device "adapted" for contraceptive or abortifacient uses, although the physician desired to use or to prescribe it for proper medical purposes. The intention to prevent a proper medical use of drugs or other articles merely because they are capable of illegal uses is not lightly to be ascribed to Congress. Section 334 forbids also the mailing of obscene books and writings; yet it has never been thought to bar from the mails medical writings sent to or by physicians for proper purposes, though of a character which would render them highly indecent if sent broadcast to all classes of persons. . . . It would seem reasonable to give the word "adapted" a more limited meaning than that above suggested and to construe the whole phrase "designed, adapted or intended" as requiring an intent on the part of the sender that the article mailed or shipped by common carrier be used for illegal contraception or abortion or for indecent or immoral purposes. However, we do not find it necessary to decide this question in the present case.

The soundness of the reasoning of the Youngs Rubber Corporation opinion was referred to in the 1933 case of *Davis* v. *United States*.[58] The appellants here were charged with mailing nonmailable matter and de-

---

[54] *United States* v. *Bott, United States* v. *Whitehead,* 24 Fed. 1204 (1873).

[55] Elizabeth H. Garnett, "Birth Control's Business Baby," *New Republic* (January 17, 1934), p. 270.

[56] See, for example, *Ackley* v. *United States,* 200 Fed. 217 (1912).

[57] *Youngs Rubber Corp.* v. *C. I. Lee Co.,* 45 Fed. 2d 103 (1930).

[58] 62 Fed. 2d 473 (1933).

positing for carriage with an express company articles condemned by statute. The court held that the essence of a crime under the statute was the intent to use for condemned purposes the articles described in the circulars, which were mailed and shipped in interstate commerce, whereas here they were intended for a legal purpose, the prevention of disease. The Youngs Rubber Corporation and Davis cases established the precedent that under certain circumstances contraceptive materials and literature could lawfully be shipped and sent through the mails.[59]

Many cases have been taken into the federal courts on alleged violation of the statutory provisions prohibiting mailing, shipping, and importing obscene and immoral literature. Two of these cases received considerable attention, in part because of the identity of the defendants. In *United States* v. *Dennett,* the facts were that the defendant, Mrs. Mary Ware Dennett, actively identified with the birth-control movement, had been denied use of the mails to send a copy of "The Sex Side of Life," a pamphlet originally written for her sons. She used them anyway, and while so doing, sent one to a decoy. When the case was brought to trial, the lower court held the book obscene, but the higher court reversed the judgment. It seemed incredible to Mrs. Dennett and to many others that the postal authorities could ban so decent and dignified a publication if there were not some personal and emotional antagonism against the writer. In the case of *United States* v. *One Obscene Book, Entitled "Married Love,"* written by Dr. Marie Stopes of England, also an ardent proponent of birth control, the court held that the book was indecent and could not be brought into the country.[60]

In *United States* v. *Clarke* the jury held that a pamphlet on the subject of venereal disease was obscene, the question of whether or not the author was a doctor being immaterial.[61] In *Bours* v. *United States* a doctor was convicted by a lower court for illegally using the mails, among other things, to announce that if an operation were necessary to save life he would perform it.[62] However, the Circuit Court of Appeals held that the indictment was fatally defective in charging that the physician in his letter to the mother of an illegitimately pregnant daughter intended to give illegal information, for the facts did not justify this conclusion. These cases show the extreme difficulty of determining what is indecent and obscene, the variation in definition depending often upon time, judge, and jury.

Few cases have reached the federal courts in which action has specifically been taken against printed material on the subject of contraception, especially if written for doctors. In *United States* v. *Pupke* the

---

[59] 39 Fed. 2d 564.
[60] 48 Fed. 2d 821 (1931).
[61] 38 Fed. 732 (1889).
[62] 229 Fed. 960 (1915).

indictment brought under the conception portion of Section 3893 of the revised statutes was demurred to and the demurrer sustained.[63] In a 1913 case the defendant was indicted on thirteen counts regarding the misuse of the mails for sending information on where, how, when, and from whom contraceptive information and materials could be obtained. The court allowed several of the counts.[64] Another book by Dr. Stopes entitled *Contraception* gave a court in 1931 the opportunity to liberalize its opinion regarding what was legal under the statutes. This book, designed for doctors, was held to be neither obscene nor immoral, and by this decision doctors were assured access to scientific information.[65]

In a 1938 case a federal circuit court held that doctors were not the only persons who could lawfully receive contraceptive literature. Here the United States appealed from two decrees of the lower court for dismissing libels of information against two publications concerning contraception: *Parenthood, Design or Accident,* a book mailed from Great Britain, and copies of a magazine, *Marriage Hygiene,* mailed from British India. One of the claimants was Norman E. Himes, to whose writings we have referred in this chapter. He was the American editor of the magazine published in India. The government's contention in these two cases was that although Section 305 did not in so many words forbid the importation of contraceptive literature, Section 593 (b), another provision of the Tariff Act, did. The circuit court held that the tariff act did not apply and ruled that *Marriage Hygiene* was to be released to Mr. Himes as one "qualified" to receive it but that although *Parenthood, Design or Accident* could not be forfeited, it could not be released to Nicholas, the other claimant, because there was nothing in the record regarding his qualifications to receive birth-control literature. Neither man was a physician.[66]

The most important decision affecting birth control was made in 1936. In this case the facts were that a package of pessaries had been sent from Japan to Dr. Stone, a New York physician, who intended to prescribe them where it was not desirable for a patient to undertake a pregnancy. The court held that the Tariff Act of 1930 could not be construed so as to prevent the importation of articles for the prevention of conception when intended for lawful use.[67] Justice Hand said, that the design of the Comstock law, in his opinion, was not to prevent the importation, sale, or carriage by mail of things which might intelligently be employed by conscientious and competent physicians for the purpose of saving life or

[63] 133 Fed. 243 (1904).
[64] *U.S.* v. *Currey,* 206 Fed. 322 (1913).
[65] *U.S.* v. *One Book Entitled "Conception,"* 51 Fed. 2d 525 (1931).
[66] *U.S.* v. *One Book, Nicholas, Claimant* and *U.S.* v. *Certain Magazines, Himes, Claimant,* 97 Fed. 2d 510 (1938).
[67] *U.S.* v. *One Package,* 86 Fed. 2d 737 (1936).

promoting the well-being of their patients. The decision in this case is clearly logical and right. For years, the mails and other common carriers have been freely used to transport scientific literature on therapeutic abortions, even though the laws specifically penalize persons unlawfully performing abortions. The courts have never construed the federal statutes to mean that publication and mailing of scientific texts on abortion are unlawful. The same line of reasoning is applicable to birth control.

Another important legal victory for birth control was a 1939 Puerto Rico decision.[68] The federal judge acquitted six directors of the Puerto Rico Maternal and Child Health Association who had been indicted under the 1873 federal statute for disseminating contraceptive information. The court held that this statute applied to Puerto Rico and that anyone prescribing contraceptives merely to prevent birth would be acting illegally, but that "contraceptives may have a lawful use and the statutes prohibiting them must be read as prohibiting them only when they have an unlawful use." The way was thus opened for the operation of birth-control clinics by the insular health department under the act passed in 1937 by the insular legislature.

It is gratifying that the federal courts have finally interpreted the laws to mean that it was not the intent of Congress to stifle the publication of scientific information on birth control or the legitimate receipt and distribution of materials. There can be no doubt that contraceptive literature and articles can be imported, transported, or mailed if the person receiving them is "qualified." Physicians and other qualified persons now have access to birth-control books and materials.

STATE COURTS

We have observed that some states have no specific laws on the subject of contraception; others have a variety of legislation, some enforceable and some not. One of the earliest cases, if not the earliest one, regarding the legality of birth-control clinics arising under state laws was purposely precipitated in the New York courts by Mrs. Sanger. In 1916 she opened a clinic in a New York area called Brownsville. Shortly after the opening, the police raided the clinic. As a result, Mrs. Sanger and Mrs. Ethel Byrnes, one of her associates, who was also her sister and a nurse, were sentenced to the workhouse for thirty days. They were charged with violating Section 1142 of the Penal Code of the state of New York designed to prevent dissemination of birth-control information. Mrs. Sanger appealed her case, but the appeal was denied. The court stated that Mrs. Sanger could not operate a birth-control clinic under the existing laws of the state of New York, since only a licensed physician could legally prescribe contraceptives for the cure or prevention of disease and

---

[68] *U.S.* v. *Dr. José Belaval,* D.C. Puerto Rico, 1939 (unreported).

she was not a physician.[69] The constructive accomplishment of this decision was a definition of "disease," the prevention or cure of which by a physician permitted the use of contraceptive techniques. In the words of the court: [70]

> This exception in behalf of physicians does not permit . . . advice to patients irrespective of their condition, but it is broad enough to protect the physician who in good faith gives such help or advice to a married person to cure or prevent disease. "Disease," by Webster's International Dictionary, is defined to be "an alteration in the state of the body, or of some of its organs, interrupting or disturbing the performance of the vital functions and causing or threatening pain and sickness; illness; sickness; disorder."
>
> The protection thus afforded the physician would also extend to the druggist, or vendor, acting upon the physician's prescription or order.

In 1923 Mrs. Sanger opened another clinic in New York City with a licensed physician in charge. After six years of successful operation, a police raid again occurred and members of the staff were arrested for violating the same statute for which Mrs. Sanger and Mrs. Byrnes had been convicted in 1918. A contraceptive device had been prescribed for, and sold to, a policewoman who had entered the clinic as a decoy. The issue at the trial again involved the definition of "disease." [71] The doctors from the clinic maintained that they had prescribed contraceptives for the purpose of avoidance of disease, for the policewoman had indicated that she was the mother of three children, aged one, three, and five, and that she wished to prevent another pregnancy. Medical authorities testified that the chances of good health for a fourth child would be greater if such child were born at least two years after its predecessor. In this instance there was a likelihood of poor health for the mother and child if another pregnancy followed too quickly. Dr. Stone, director of the clinic, and her co-workers were released, and the interpretation of "disease" was further enlarged.

The decisions of the courts of Massachusetts and Connecticut are in reverse of the trend established by federal courts. The Massachusetts law provides that whoever sells, lends, gives away, exhibits, or offers to sell, lend, or give away any drug, medicine, instrument, or article whatsoever for the prevention of conception shall be punished for a felony. In a 1938 case four defendants, a doctor, a nurse, and two social workers, were operating a charitable clinic in Salem called the North Shore Mothers' Health Office. The defendants claimed that the statute did not apply to drugs and so forth intended for contraceptive use which were prescribed by a duly qualified physician for preservation of life or health and ac-

---

[69] Sanger, *My Fight for Birth Control,* pp. 125–160; see also, Sanger, *Autobiography,* chs. 17 and 18.

[70] *People* v. *Sanger,* 222 N.Y. 192, 118 N.E. 637 (1918).

[71] In the Magistrate's Court, 2d District of Manhattan, on May 14, 1929 (unreported).

cording to generally accepted medical practices. The court held that the law contained no exception, that the words were plain, unequivocal, and peremptory, sweeping, absolute, and devoid of ambiguity; that they were directed with undeviating explicitness against the prevention of conception by any of the means specified; and that no judicial interpretation could except physicians under the statute.[72] Thus, in 1938 the Massachusetts court refused to define contraception to permit prescription by physicians for medical reasons. The United States Supreme Court declined to review the decision of the Massachusetts court, and shortly thereafter the defendants appeared in court and paid their fines of $200 each. Efforts to secure modification of the Massachusetts statute so as to permit medical exemptions have thus far been unsuccessful. The overwhelming majority of the "no" vote comes from predominantly Catholic Boston, Lowell, and Fall River.

The Connecticut birth-control law passed in 1879 reads:

> Any person who shall use any drug, medicinal article or instrument for the purpose of preventing conception shall be fined not less than fifty dollars or imprisoned not less than sixty days nor more than one year or be both fined and imprisoned.[73]
>
> Any person who shall assist, abet, counsel, cause, hire or command another to commit any offense may be prosecuted and punished as if he were the principal offender.[74]

Between 1879 and 1939 there were no legal developments. The matter first came up when two doctors and a nurse attached to the Waterbury Clinic were arrested for violating the law. The court held that there was no implied exception in the law which would permit a doctor to prescribe contraceptives for a patient, at least in the absence of anything beyond danger to the general health of the patient.[75] The law was further tested in 1942. Dr. Wilder Tileston, a gynecologist and obstetrician connected with Yale University Medical School, brought an action against Abraham S. Ulman, the state's attorney for New Haven County. The physician alleged that he intended to give contraceptive advice to three patients suffering from various diseases and that he was threatened with arrest if he so prescribed. The court held in a three to two decision that no exception of any kind could be read into the Connecticut law, even where life or serious injury to health was involved.[76] The United States Supreme Court dismissed an appeal on a narrow procedural issue.

The Planned Parenthood League of Connecticut introduces a bill to

---

[72] *Commonwealth* v. *Gardner, and three other cases,* 300 Mass. 372, 15 N.E. 2d 222 (1938).

[73] General Statutes of Conn., Revision of 1949, Vol. 3, c. 423, sec. 3101.

[74] General Statutes of Conn., Revision of 1949, Vol. 3, c. 433, sec. 8875.

[75] *State* v. *Nelson,* 126 Conn. 412, 11 Atl. 2d 856 (1940).

[76] *Tileston* v. *Ulman,* 129 Conn. 84, 26 Atl. 2d 582 (1942).

correct this situation in every session of the legislature.[77] Up to 1953 it had introduced fourteen such bills. Therapeutic abortion is legal in Connecticut, as is sterilization in specific cases. It is almost impossible to get a state's attorney to enforce the present birth-control law. Hence the citizenry has taken the law into its own hands, but with the possibility of blackmail hanging over physicians. In March, 1953, numbers of prominent men made a demand on the governor that the law be enforced or repealed, stating that it seemed inconceivable that the legislative body should repeatedly vote to retain a law which the executive branch of the government makes no effort to enforce. Perhaps the "enforce or repeal" cry will be "the Achilles heel." It remains to be seen what the courts of Massachusetts and Connecticut will do if and when a woman patient brings an action against government officials for depriving her of her due process rights to medical treatment. In the meantime in these two states the sale of contraceptives as preventatives of disease proceeds, but medical prescription for those who most need the service is banned.

ARTIFICIAL INSEMINATION

An aspect of the planned parenthood movement which, as yet, has received little judicial attention but considerable legal comment is artificial insemination.[78] Statistics show that there are over two million couples who are unable to conceive children in the normal way. For some of these persons who prefer not to adopt children artificial insemination provides a method of obtaining children. Probably something over 10,000 women throughout the United States have achieved at least one pregnancy by this method. Occasionally, a second or even a third pregnancy has been so induced. There are two different types of situations in which a wife may have a baby by artificial insemination. One is with the semen of the husband, who, for one reason or another, may be incapable of normal impregnation. This is called artificial insemination homologous, AIH. The other is artificial insemination by a donor, AID. Artificial insemination often is employed because the husband is sterile; but it may also be used because of the wife's inabilities. Legal commentators seem to feel that legal problems will be infrequent and relatively simple if

[77] Personal correspondence with the Planned Parenthood League of Connecticut, Inc. (May 29, 1953).

[78] "Artificial Insemination," 35 Cornell L.Q. 183–186 (1949); 12 Modern L. Rev. 384–387 (1949); Murray Russell, "Artificial Insemination," *Journal of American Medical Association* (1950), pp. 144, 461; "Artificial Insemination versus Adoption," 34 Va. L. Rev. 822 (1948); "Artificial Insemination—Its Socio-Legal Aspects," 33 Minn. L. Rev. 145–156 (1949); Watson Davis, "10,000 Test-Tube Babies," *Science Digest,* Vol. 34, No. 6 (December, 1953), pp. 36–38; Harriet F. Pilpel and Theodora Zavin, *Your Marriage and the Law* (New York, Rinehart, 1952), ch. 8; Morris Ploscowe, *Sex and the Law* (Englewood Cliffs, N.J., Prentice-Hall, 1951), ch. 4.

AIH is practiced. They predict that there will be some acute problems reaching the courts with AID. So far, there have been very few reported cases.

In 1948 the New York courts established the legitimacy of a child born to a woman artificially impregnated with a donor's semen and with the husband's consent. Here, the divorced wife contended that her husband was not entitled to visitation of their child on the ground that the child was not his. The court held that he was entitled to visitation and that the child was legitimate, since his legal status was the same as that of a child born out of wedlock who by law becomes legitimate upon the marriage of the parents. The court commented further: [79]

> The court does not pass on the legal consequences in so far as property rights are concerned in a case of this character; nor does the court express an opinion on the propriety of procreation by the medium of artificial insemination. With such matters the court is not here concerned; the latter problem particularly is in the fields of sociology, morality, and religion.

In the Canadian case of *Oxford* v. *Oxford* artificial insemination was held to be adultery.[80] Here, the wife brought suit for alimony on the ground that her husband refused to take her back after a temporary separation. He brought a countersuit for divorce on the ground of adultery, charging that his wife had had a child by another man. Evidence showed that the pregnancy resulted from artificial insemination without the husband's knowledge or consent. The court observed that if this was not adultery, it was a monstrous conclusion; if such a thing had never before been declared to be adultery, then on the grounds of public policy, the court should now declare it such. The court said:

> In my judgment, the essence of the offense of adultery consists not in the moral turpitude of the act of sexual intercourse, but in the voluntary surrender to another person of the reproductive powers or faculties of the guilty person; and any submission of those powers to the service or enjoyment of any person other than the husband or the wife comes within the definition of adultery. . . . Sexual intercourse is adulterous because in the case of the woman it involves the possibility of introducing into the family of the husband a false strain of blood. Any act on the part of the wife which does that would, therefore, be adulterous.

In an English case the wife sought a decree of nullity of marriage because of the impotency of her husband.[81] The court had to decide whether she lost her right to an action for annulment on the ground of failure to consumate the marriage, since she had permitted herself to be inseminated with the semen of her husband who was psychologically impotent. The court held that the wife, by her conduct, had not appro-

---

[79] *Strnad* v. *Strnad*, 78 N.Y. Supp. 2d 390, 190 Misc. 786.
[80] Ont. L.R. 15, 58 D.L.R. 251 (1921).
[81] *R. E. L.* v. *E. L.* (1949), Probate 211.

bated the abnormal and incomplete marriage and that a decree of nullity was not barred because the child of the marriage would be bastardized if her petition were granted.

In the latter months of 1954 newspapers carried such headlines as "Artificial Insemination Illegal Unless Donor, Recipient Wed."[82] In the Chicago case to which the headlines referred, the judge ruled that human artificial insemination is illegal, except when donor and recipient are married to each other, and that children conceived by sperms other than those of the mother's legal mate are illegitimate. Such insemination, with or without the consent of the husband, is contrary to public policy and good morals and constitutes adultery on the part of the mother. This ruling was made in a divorce action brought by the wife. It was made on her petition that she be given sole custody of her son and that her husband be denied visits to the child.

These cases illustrate the types of legal problems which have come before the courts when AIH or AID is involved. Undoubtedly courts will encounter numbers of problems in the immediate future, especially in AID cases. In 1954 the Chicago Bar Association ordered a study of artificial insemination with a view to recommending a law to the legislature.[83] The committee planned to call physicians and lawyers for discussion of such matters as:

1. The rights and liabilities of doctors performing the insemination.
2. Determining whether or not the donor or the husband is the child's legal father or whether the mother becomes the sole natural parent.
3. The adulterous or nonadulterous nature of artificial insemination.
4. The effect of husband's consent and the binding qualities of such a contract.
5. The husband's obligation of support with and without consent and in the absence of formal adoption.
6. The inheritance rights of the baby born of artificial insemination.

Despite religious and other opposition, there will undoubtedly be an increase in the use of artificial insemination. Eventually, legislatures will have to decide whether the process is legal or illegal.[84] It seems clear to this writer that AIH should be legal and so, too, should AID with the husband's consent. A child born of AID should be deemed the legitimate child of the husband and wife and a stranger at law to the donor. Statutes should restrict the process to authorized medical practitioners. Records of the consent of the husband and wife and of the genetic characteristics of the donor should probably be required, but the identity

---

[82] *Capital Times*, Madison, Wis. (December 13, 1954).

[83] *Ibid.* (October 25, 1954).

[84] "Artificial Insemination—Its Socio-Legal Aspects," 33 Minn. L. Rev. 104 (1949). In May, 1956, according to newspaper accounts, Pope Pius XII told delegates to the World Fertility Congress that artificial insemination for human beings is not morally permissible.

of the donor should not be recorded. Birth records should show the child to be the legitimate child of the husband and wife.

CENTERS AND CLINICS

In 1953 the Margaret Sanger Research Bureau of New York rounded out thirty years of service. More than 136,000 women had registered with this earliest American birth-control clinic, and over a million letters had been answered. It is directed as a demonstration and research center by Dr. Abraham Stone, author, with his deceased wife, of the best seller, *A Marriage Manual.* Hundreds of physicians, both American and foreign, have trained at the center. More than 2,000 couples had taken advantage of the fertility service of the center. In 1952 there were sixty-six fertility services in thirty-seven states and the District of Columbia. Thirteen of these centers were sponsored by affiliates of the Planned Parenthood Federation of America and most of the others were conducted by hospitals.

Today, there are more than five hundred birth-control clinics in the United States, about two hundred of which are operated by affiliates of the Planned Parenthood Federation of America. The rest are connected with hospitals or with public health departments of the several states in which family planning is part of the public health program. North Carolina was, in 1937, the first of several southern states to initiate such a program with the backing and guidance of the Planned Parenthood Federation of America. The clinics in these southern states are supported by public health departments and make up about half the total number of clinics in the country.[85]

The Maternal Health Association of Cleveland was one of the first planned parenthood centers to establish a specialized marriage counseling service. From the inception of the child-spacing clinics in 1928 the clinicians and nurses were aware that such a medical setting offered a unique opportunity to help men and women understand the physical and emotional relationships of marriage. With growth in demands from the community the association engaged workers, known as marriage counselors, whose professional experience is social work. The patients represent all social and economic levels. The fees for each interview are arranged in terms of the economic circumstances of the patients. Although the marriage counseling service is designed primarily to help people with sexual problems in marriage, it is recognized that multiple factors enter into the picture which must be considered in treatment. The Maternal Health Association of Cleveland believes that the counseling service is a link in the process of forging strong marriages.[86]

---

[85] Personal correspondence with the Planned Parenthood Federation of America, Inc. (May 20, 1953).

[86] *Planned Parenthood News,* No. 2 (Winter, 1953).

Many organizations and agencies throughout the country are experimenting with the development of counseling services to stablize marriages. Sometimes these services are extended to patients in planned parenthood clinics, as in Cleveland. Sometimes they are provided by churches, social agencies, or general hospitals and clinics which provide birth-control information if indicated, or which refer the client to the resource that can furnish it. All serious students of family relationships continuously seek methods by which family life can be stabilized. Control of conception, remedying conditions of infertility, and counseling are all involved in this process.

SUMMARY AND CONCLUSIONS

In many parts of the world, and for the most part in the United States, the dissemination and use of contraceptive information is accepted without particular comment or alarm except by the Catholic church. A recent manifestation of religious support for planned parenthood was given in May, 1956, when the Methodist church, the largest Protestant denomination in the United States, endorsed the principle of planned parenthood at its quadrennial General Conference. With increased public acceptance of the desirability of the dissemination of birth-control information, and with the sanction of the judiciary in many situations, the effects of prohibitory federal legislation on the subject have been largely nullified. So far as federal laws are concerned, physicians can now legally give contraceptive advice to "specific patients." Many doctors are giving such advice through birth-control clinics, some of which are tax supported.

When Margaret Sanger began to draw attention to the need for birth control by her militant methods, leaders in the field insisted upon the repeal of all legislation prohibiting the dissemination and use of contraceptives. After a time emphasis was placed upon securing modified legislation permitting the medical profession to dispense scientific information. Since the courts have given a liberal interpretation to the federal laws and recognize that contraceptive literature and articles may have a lawful use, the primary emphasis of the movement is no longer legal but educational and medical. An exception is in Massachusetts and Connecticut, where the state courts have held that birth-control information and materials may not be dispensed, even by doctors for medical reasons.

The story told in this chapter must be discouraging to believers in democracy. It seems incredible that the greatest democratic country in the world could unthinkingly pass an unsound law in 1873 and almost a century later still have it on the statute books. However, it is just because the United States is a democracy that such a predicament exists. Legislators, responsive to the will of their constituents, have hesitated to incur the antagonisms of organized opposition. The federal courts, wherein judges are appointed rather than elected by the people, the institution of government considered least responsive to the wishes of the public, have been the means of liberalizing this obsolescent legislation. The pressure of public opinion and the availability of scientific information have had their influence upon our jurists, who do not fear the electorate, rather than upon our legislators, who must answer to their constituents.

It seems reasonable to assume that the following developments will occur:

1. Growth in the number of public and private clinics will continue, and more and more doctors will dispense better scientific information to patients who seek it.
2. Those states with legislation out of line with trends will continue to seek ways of modification.
3. Scientific study of ways of improving contraceptive methods will continue and so, too, will research into ways of encouraging fertility and of assuring effective artificial insemination.
4. A slow diminution in organized religious resistance to the movement can be expected to occur as population pressures increase and scientific information is more accessible.
5. The problems of world population in relation to natural resources will appear increasingly important, and efforts to disseminate scientific contraceptive information over the globe will increase.

Selected References

BLANSHARD, Paul, *American Freedom and Catholic Power* (Boston, Beacon Press, 1949).

BOYLAN, Marguerite T., *Social Welfare in the Catholic Church* (New York, Columbia University Press, 1941).

BROUN, Heywood, and LEECH, Margaret, *Anthony Comstock* (New York, Albert and Charles Boni, 1927).

BURCH, Guy Irving, and PENDELL, Elmer, *Human Breeding and Survival* (New York, Penguin Books, 1947); originally published under the title *Population Roads to Peace or War.*

CHANDRASEKHAR, S., *Population and Planned Parenthood in India* (London, George Allen and Unwin, 1955).

DENNETT, Mary Ware, *Birth Control Laws, Shall We Keep Them, Change Them, or Abolish Them?* (New York, Hitchcock, 1926).

———, *Who's Obscene?* (New York, Vanguard Press, 1930).

FLETCHER, Joseph, *Morals and Medicine* (Princeton, N.J., Princeton University Press, 1954).

HARPER, Fowler V., *Problems of the Family* (Indianapolis, Bobbs-Merrill, 1952).

HIMES, Norman E., *Medical History of Contraception* (Baltimore, Williams and Wilkins, 1936).

———, *Practical Birth Control Methods* (New York, Modern Age Books, 1938).

LADER, Lawrence, *The Margaret Sanger Story: And the Fight for Birth Control* (New York, Doubleday, 1955).

LOTH, David, "Planned Parenthood," *Annals of the American Academy of Political and Social Science* (November, 1950), Vol. 272, p. 95.

MCCORMICK, C. O., "Planned Parenthood: Road to National Health and World Peace," *J. Indiana St. M.A.*, Vol. 41 (January, 1948), pp. 81–87.

MCKENNEY, Charles R., *Moral Problems in Social Work* (Milwaukee, Bruce Publishing Co., 1951), under imprimatur of archbishop of Catholic church in Milwaukee.

NAISSMITH, Grace, "The Racket in Contraceptives," *American Mercury,* Vol. 71, No. 319 (July, 1950), pp. 3–14.

"Note, Judicial Regulation of Birth Control Under Obscenity Laws," 50 Yale L.J. 682 (1941).

OSBORN, Fairfield, *Our Plundered Planet* (Boston, Little, Brown, 1948).

OSBORN, Frederick, *Preface to Eugenics* (New York, Harper, 1940).

PILPEL, Harriet F., and ZAVIN, Theodora, *Your Marriage and the Law* (New York, Rinehart, 1952).

Planned Parenthood Federation of America, Inc., *The Legal Status of Contraception* (New York, 501 Madison Ave., 1952).

PLOSCOWE, Morris, *Sex and the Law,* (Englewood Cliffs, N.J., Prentice-Hall, 1951).

SANGER, Margaret, *Margaret Sanger: An Autobiography* (New York, Norton, 1938).

———, *My Fight for Birth Control* (New York, Farrar and Rinehart, 1931).

"Some Legislative Aspects of Birth Control Problems," 45 Harv. L. Rev. 723 (1932).

STONE, Abraham, "Planned Parenthood Around the World," *Marriage and Family Living,* Vol. 15, No. 2 (May, 1953), pp. 98–101.

VOGT, William, *Road to Survival* (New York, William Sloane Associates, 1948).

The student should also consult pertinent statutes, judicial decisions, and issues of the *United Nations Demographic Yearbook.*

CHAPTER 8

Sterilization

INTRODUCTION

In the preceding chapter we observed that the size and quality of both the family and the general population have been controlled in numerous ways, some accidental and some deliberate, some beneficial and some adverse. Birth control is an important factor in the reduction of the birth rate. Sterilization has had no appreciable effect upon the population curve, even in Germany where, under the Nazis, sterilization was more extensively and viciously practiced than anywhere else in the world. The fundamental purposes of the sterilization movement are eugenic and social, the former being first in historical sequence. Its primary aim is not to reduce the birth rate but to improve the inborn quality of future generations, physically and mentally. *Eugenic* is the term given to that aspect of the sterilization movement concerned with reducing inherited disabilities in man.[1] Sterilization operations are performed for two other reasons: penal and therapeutic. Few operations are performed for penal reasons; many, but how many no one knows, are done for therapeutic reasons.

Methods of sterilization have been known for centuries. The most primitive is castration, which was often used as a means of insult and punishment or for unsexing harem attendants (eunuchs) and choir boys. Castration has been considered a cruel and inhuman operation for many years. Resistance to this particular operation has been so great that opposition has carried over to the present humane and simple operations, which do not impair the sex life and personality but do destroy the reproductive life. Although sterilization has been known for a long time in many forms, concerted efforts to increase its use as a eugenic and social measure are recent.

[1] H. S. Jennings, "Eugenics," *Encyclopaedia of the Social Sciences* (1931), Vol. 5, pp. 617–621.

STERILIZATION IN FOREIGN COUNTRIES

ENGLAND

The sterilization movement has had greater impetus in the United States than in any other country except Germany, and more experimentation with legislation to validate this operation has occurred in this country than elsewhere. England, which has secured much social legislation in advance of the United States, has no sterilization law. Between 1905 and 1909, a royal commission for the care and control of the feebleminded studied the incidence and problems of feeble-mindedness. In 1924 another group appointed by the chief medical officer of the Ministry of Health and taking its name from the chairman, Mr. A. H. Wood, studied the same problem and reported in 1929. The findings of these two groups yielded data admitting of comparison, some of which had a bearing on sterilization. In 1930, shortly after the appearance of the Wood Report, the Eugenics Society, headed by Major Leonard Darwin, son of the great Charles, formulated its proposals for legalizing sterilization. The society advocated changes not as a money-saving device but as an auxiliary to segregation, holding that it was an appropriate measure for those defectives who could live in the community.

In 1932 a deputation of representatives of important organizations requested the minister of health to appoint an impartial official committee to study sterilization. This suggestion was accepted, and a departmental committee of eight persons, under the chairmanship of Mr. L. G. Brock, was appointed. The report of the committee was published two years later.[2] It condemned compulsory sterilization but recommended that voluntary sterilization be legalized for mental defectives, for those suffering from mental disorders, and for persons suffering from, or believed to be carriers of, grave physical disabilities which have been shown to be transmissible.

Unfortunately, the legislative proposals of the Brock Committee never received parliamentary approval. Since then, with the war years in between, sterilization proposals as such have elicited little public interest, although the problem of mental deficiency does. Sterilizations on therapeutic grounds are performed every day in England, but the physician who wants to undertake an operation for eugenic grounds is in a potentially hazardous position.[3] One physician, Dr. C. P. Blacker has suggested that five-purpose parenthood clinics be set up as part of a family welfare

---

[2] Great Britain, Parl. Papers, 1933–1934, Vol. 15, Cmd. 4485, p. 5; Great Britain, Board of Control, Committee on Sterilization, *Report of the Departmental Committee on Sterilization* (London, His Majesty's Stationery Office, 1934).

[3] C. H. Rolph, "Sterilisation and the Law," *New Statesman and Nation*, Vol. 39 (June 3, 1950), pp. 626–627. and *ibid.* (June 17, 1950), p. 684.

service within the National Health Service.[4] These clinics would provide marriage guidance, premarital examinations, eugenic diagnosis to include sterilizations where indicated, birth control, and treatment of infecundity. Since Britain is a comprehensively insured country and has a universal health service, its figures on mental and physical, curative and custodial health problems are carefully scrutinized both within and without the country. The burden of mental disorders is among the heaviest the state faces, so it is possible that sterilization soon will be seriously considered as a means of reducing costs of care for certain forms of mental disability.

GERMANY

The German law, which was passed in 1933 and which went into effect in 1934, was considered by experts at that time to be the best drawn of any sterilization statute. Its essential points were proposed and considered several years before the Nazi regime was entered upon. A translation of some sections of the law reads: [5]

> Those hereditarily sick may be made unfruitful (sterilized) through surgical intervention when, following the experience of medical science, it may be expected with great probability that their offspring may suffer severe physical or mental inherited damage.
>
> The hereditarily sick, in the sense of this law, is a person who suffers from one of the following diseases: Inborn feeble-mindedness, schizophrenia, circular insanity, hereditary epilepsy, hereditary Huntington's chorea, hereditary blindness, hereditary deafness, severe hereditary physical deformity. Further, those may be made unfruitful who suffer from severe alcoholism.

Provisions were made for trial, appeal, and administration of the law. Applications were to be passed upon by hereditary health courts consisting of three judges, two of whom were required to be physicians. An appeal could be taken from any of the lower, or hereditary health courts, to the higher courts, or courts of appeal. Opponents to sterilization did not need to be operated upon if they were kept in institutions without cost to the state, a provision designed to please the Catholic church.

One investigator estimated that up to July, 1935, approximately 15,000 sterilizations had been performed.[6] Thereafter, Nazi edicts made data on the subject unavailable. Estimates of the number of sterilization opera-

---

[4] Charles Paton Blacker, *Eugenics: Galton and After* (London, Duckworth, 1952).

[5] W. W. Peter, "Germany's Sterilization Program," *American Journal of Public Health* (March, 1934), pp. 187–191; Hans Harmsen, "The German Sterilization Act of 1933," *Eugenics Review*, Vol. 46, No. 4 (January, 1955), pp. 227–232; Charles Paton Blacker, " 'Eugenic' Experiments Conducted by the Nazis on Human Subjects," *Eugenics Review*, Vol. 44 (1953), pp. 9–19.

[6] Marie E. Kopp, "Legal and Medical Aspects of Eugenic Sterilization in Germany," *American Sociological Review* (October, 1936), pp. 761–770; Clifford Kirkpatrick, *Nazi Germany: Its Women and Family Life* (Indianapolis, Bobbs-Merrill, 1938).

tions performed upon Nazi victims vary. There may have been several hundred thousands. The world has seen the danger of placing sterilization or any similar power in the hands of hatemongers.[7] It must be admitted, of course, that the most carefully drawn statute, even though it assures due process of law to the individual, is capable of misuse under administrators who have no respect for constitutional processes. This is hardly a justifiable argument against the adoption of a sterilization program in a democratic country. There seems little likelihood that the United States will encounter misuse of this tool, first, because of our form of government, and, second, because to date there are no indications that such laws will be other than sparingly applied.

OTHER COUNTRIES

The committee of the American Neurological Association, making its report on sterilization in 1936, noted laws on this subject in effect in Alberta and British Columbia, Danzig, Denmark, Estonia, Finland, Germany, Norway, Sweden, Switzerland, and in Vera Cruz, Mexico.[8] Others are presently interested. The laws of foreign countries differ as much as do those in the various jurisdictions of the United States. We shall refer to developments in a few countries.

The Swedish statute of 1941, replacing an earlier law, regulates the grounds for sterilization of legally competent persons, that is, those capable of giving consent. Further, it orders that if any of the indications listed apply to a person who, for reasons of mental disturbance, lacks the capacity of giving valid consent, the operation may be performed without his consent. Sterilization is principally voluntary, although those who lack mental capacity for giving consent may be sterilized without it.

The Swedish law recognizes two general indications: the eugenic and social and a special medical one applicable only to women. Not only can persons with transmissible mental difficulties be sterilized but also those with serious diseases and defects. Those who are unfit to take care of children because of their asocial way of life may be sterilized. This classification includes severe alcoholism, incorrigible vagrancy, or serious criminality. The medical indication refers to women who require and consent to sterilization in order to prevent pregnancy which would seriously endanger life or health. The law prescribes that sterilization shall be carried out with permission of the board of health except for certain medically indicated cases, as when a women who is capable of giving consent requires sterilization to prevent pregnancy which would

---

[7] Moya Woodside, *Sterilization in North Carolina* (Chapel Hill, N.C., University of North Carolina Press, 1950), p. 24; Albert Deutsch, *The Mentally Ill in America*, 2d ed. (New York, Columbia University Press, 1949), p. 376.

[8] American Neurological Association, *Eugenical Sterilization* (New York, Macmillan, 1936), pp. 20–23.

cause serious damage to her life or health. In such cases the statute requires that the doctor who performs the operation and another doctor in a public medical position declare why the sterilization is performed. The law specifically excludes sterilization for therapeutic indications, meaning diseases of the sex organs necessitating operations causing sterility.

From 1935 to 1948, 15,519 sterilizations were carried out under the law. The number of women sterilized was almost four times as large as the number of men. More than half of all cases involved mental deficiency. The second largest category was that of women exhausted through many childbirths. The law was applied to approximately one in every 3,000 persons. The Swedish law secures the right to everyone legally qualified for sterilization. It offers protection to the physician, who otherwise would act at his own risk if he acted at all. It promotes lawful sterilizations by authorizing them and prevents unlawful ones by withholding the right to them. The law is an integral part of the comprehensive social organization of Swedish society to protect the size, quality, and welfare of its population.[9]

The first Danish sterilization law was passed in 1929 and replaced in 1935.[10] The statute provides that after due application a person may be sterilized for social reasons. With regard to mentally normal individuals, it is required that particular indications be present, especially inherited predispositions. Concerning mentally abnormal individuals who are not feeble-minded, it is provided that the operation shall be a benefit to the person involved. A 1934 law concerning the feeble-minded includes directions on sterilization. Such persons may be sterilized when there are social reasons against having offspring, for example, when they are adjudged to be so defective as to be incapable of adequately providing for or educating children. Application for sterilization under both statutes must be made to designated public officials, and individual rights are carefully protected. Between 1929 and 1945 approximately 3,600 persons were sterilized. Of this number about 2,800 were feeble-minded. The ratio of women to men for the feeble-minded was 1,909 to 894, and for the others 664 to 141.

India and Japan are vitally interested in sterilization and in birth control. India's first five-year plan, adopted in 1952, provides that government hospitals and health centers may give advice on methods of family limitation.[11] If a physician feels that a woman patient cannot undergo again the strain of pregnancy without danger to health, it is his duty to

[9] Philipp Weintraub, "Sterilization in Sweden: Its Law and Practice," *American Journal of Mental Deficiency,* Vol. 56, No. 2 (October, 1951); reprinted by Human Betterment Association of America, Inc., 32 West 58th St., New York.

[10] Tage Kemp, "Danish Experiences in Negative Eugenics, 1929–45," *Eugenics Review,* Vol. 38, No. 4 (January, 1947); reprinted by Birthright, Inc. (subsequently Human Betterment Association of America, Inc.), Pub. No. 7.

[11] Report of Consulate of India in New York City to the Human Betterment Association of America, Inc., contained in personal letter to author (May 29, 1953).

give such advice as is necessary to prevent conception. In these circumstances he is justified in suggesting such chemical, mechanical, or biological methods of contraception or sterilization as are indicated. Although there is no sterilization legislation in India, there is governmental recognition of its need. Planned parenthood clinics under governmental auspices provide free sterilization operations for members of the army when medically indicated. These services are primarily available in the large cities, like Bombay, Delhi, and Calcutta. The government also provides sterilization operations without charge for poor couples with large families when medically indicated. The number of these operations is infinitesimal.

Japan adopted a eugenic protection law in 1948, since amended.[12] The object of the law is to prevent the increase of inferior descendants from the eugenic standpoint and to protect the life and health of mothers. Sterilization and artificial interruption of pregnancy or abortion are both allowed. In the year 1952 when something like 1.5 million abortions occurred, only about 22,000 sterilizations were officially reported. Less than 1 per cent of the operations were on males. Japan's concern with population control is shown in its legal and medical provisions for birth control, sterilization, and abortion. Until there are more adequate facilities for birth control and sterilization there will doubtless be excessive and unfortunate reliance upon abortions.

Puerto Rico, with its rapidly expanding population and excessive poverty, is more than mildly interested in sterilization and birth control, both of which under some circumstances are legal.[13] The country's death rate has dropped 50 per cent, and its birth rate has doubled since 1898 when it became an American colony. These phenomena are believed to be the result, in part at least, of United States government measures designed to be helpful to the economic welfare of the colony. We saw in the last chapter that birth control in Puerto Rico is restricted under the law to women with medical problems. Many Puerto Rican women seek sterilization as a surer method of preventing enlargement of their families.

---

[12] Personal correspondence with Human Betterment Association of America, Inc. (May 29, 1953); Irene Tauber and Marshall Balfour, "Control of Fertility in Japan," *Milbank Memorial Fund Quarterly* (January, 1952); "Free Japan," *U. S. News and World Report* (September 12, 1952).

[13] William Vogt, *Road to Survival* (New York, William Sloane Associates, 1948), pp. 76, 77; Robert Cook, *Human Fertility* (New York, William Sloane Associates, 1951), ch. 2, which tells the story of America's contribution to the population problems of Puerto Rico.

REASONS FOR STERILIZATION

DEFINITION OF STERILIZATION

Sterilization has been defined to mean a method of preventing parenthood without destroying the sexual life of the individual.[14] The usual methods are the cutting of the *vas deferens* in the male and the Fallopian tubes in the female, that is, vasectomy and salpingectomy. These two operations do not involve cruelty, do not lower sexual power for gratification, and do not cause a change in personality or psychic mutilation. Several sterilization statutes provide for the use of the two abovementioned operations. Sterilization is not castration, which does destroy the sexual life.

In general, sterilization advocates favor its application to persons with diagnosed inherited mental and physical inadequacies. Some favor it for the feeble-minded and mentally ill where no history of inheritance is indicated but where social adjustment is unlikely; some for socially inadequate persons with no pronounced physical or mental defect. There is difference of opinion as to the extent to which sterilization should be applied to the mentally diseased and also as to whether the operation should ever be compulsory or always voluntary. In other words, even among those who advocate sterilization, there is disagreement as to the groups for whom such treatment is biologically and socially reasonable and desirable.

THE EUGENIC REASON

Proponents of *eugenic* sterilization sometimes argue that mental disease and mental defect, epilepsy, and criminality are on the increase and that strict control of the propagation of this part of our population is not only advisable but necessary. Some studies indicate that these conditions are not really increasing but only that more cases are being brought to light, so that the figures, though showing an increase in actual numbers, do not represent an absolute increase.[15] It is also contended that those who are mentally defective and diseased propagate at a greater rate than the normal population and, consequently, that there will be an increasing proportion of these groups in the population. However, some believe that facts do not validate the contention that the fertility rate of these classes is higher than that of normals. If the feeble-minded produce larger families than normals, the increase must be among the higher-grade and

---

[14] Frederick W. Brown, "Eugenic Sterilization in the United States," *Annals of the American Academy of Political and Social Science* (May, 1930), p. 22.

[15] American Neurological Association, *op. cit.*, pp. 24–58; Deutsch, *op. cit.*, ch. 17, pp. 354–386.

borderline persons, since the low-grade and many medium-grade individuals are sterile. It seems likely to some students that the reproductive rate for all feeble-minded may not be greater than for the normal population but that the reproductive rate for the higher range is considerably greater. At any rate, it is this group which creates many of our acute community problems, as the other two groups are more frequently institutionalized or more closely protected by their families.

Even if it were proved—and satisfactory and conclusive proof has not yet been furnished—that the percentage of mental defect and disease is not increasing and that the birth rate of the mentally deficient is no higher than the birth rate of the normal population, and even if it were shown that only a small percentage of feeble-mindedness and mental disease is inherited, there would still be need to control the population selectively. To many people the costs of caring for the socially ineffectual and the personal and social tragedies involved in their inadequacies seem to be sufficient justification for curtailing procreation of persons in these groups.

THE PENAL REASON

The *penal* aim of sterilization has received many attacks. Application of the old saw, "Make the punishment fit the crime," is particularly ridiculous so far as crime and sterilization are concerned. The idea that an individual who has stolen or been abusive or committed sex crimes, such as indecent exposure, rape, or sodomy, will pass this behavior on to his children through the germ plasm and that he, therefore, should be deprived of his procreative faculties is absurd. Also, since sterilization does not affect sex desires and impulses, there is no reason to believe that this operation will curtail sex crimes. Therefore, sterilization for punishment or for prevention of the transmission of criminal characteristics is unjustified. It can be argued, though, that sterilization for some criminals is desirable, since such persons are not likely to be adequate parents. Under such circumstances sterilization is for social and not punitive reasons.

The statutes have not always been clear as to whether sterilization of criminals was for eugenic, social, or punitive reasons. Several states have or have had statutes providing for the sterilization of sex or other offenders. California abolished such a provision in a 1951 statute which, in effect, set up procedural provisions for three classes of institutionalized persons: (1) those afflicted with transmissible mental disease; (2) those with mental deficiency; (3) those with marked departure from normal mentality.[16] The state of Washington's statutory provisions regarding criminals were held constitutional in 1912. In 1921 the Washington legislature

[16] S. 730 (1951), California Stat., chap. 552 or *Welfare and Institutions Code Annotated*, sec. 6624.

passed another law providing for sterilization only for eugenic or therapeutic purposes, but for procedural reasons it was declared unconstitutional. Today, the state of Washington has no sterilization law. The Iowa and Nevada statutes were held unconstitutional in 1914 and in 1918.[17] Oklahoma's Habitual Criminal Sterilization Act was held constitutional by the state high court in 1941 and unconstitutional by the United States Supreme Court in 1942.[18]

THERAPEUTIC AND SOCIAL REASONS

Apparently there is no vehement objection to medical or therapeutic sterilization from any group except the Catholic church under some conditions. The Catholic position seems to be that an operation, such as an hysterectomy, from which sterilization incidentally results is legitimate but not a sterilization operation performed for such a medical reason as a heart condition of the mother. There is no agreement among sterilization proponents as to what is therapeutic. Is multiparity a reason, and if so, how many children must a woman have had? Is Caesarian birth a reason, and if so, how many operations must there have been? Are heart, diabetic, kidney, lung diseases justification? Must the sex organs themselves be diseased? Must there be a eugenic as well as a medical purpose or vice versa? How sick must a person be? Can disease be interpreted as liberally as was the case for birth control when the New York court interpreted it to include promotion of health? Can the operation be used as a form of birth control or voluntary family limitation? These are some of the problems upon which there is no agreement between doctors and hospitals and upon which state legislation gives inadequate answers. In many situations where there is a medical problem two results are simultaneously obtained through sterilization: the health of the mother is protected, and the birth of children who might be neglected and become family and community problems is prevented.

A considerable number of people support the idea of sterilization for social and economic reasons. They maintain that some individuals with poor physical or mental health or who are incompetent might well be sterilized. The aim is to prevent the birth of children for whom the parents cannot decently provide and whom society may have to support and protect. Although contraceptive information should be available to this group, it is desirable also that a more certain method of control be available.

---

[17] J. H. Landman, *Human Sterilization* (New York, Macmillan, 1932), table, pp. 294–299.

[18] *Skinner* v. *State,* 189 Okla. 235, 115 P. 2d 123 (1941), 316 U.S. 535 (1942).

RELIGIOUS POSITIONS

Organized opposition to sterilization comes largely from the Catholic church and has been expressed in the encyclical letter of Pope Pius XI referred to in the last chapter. In that letter he stated: [19]

> Finally, that pernicious practice must be condemned which closely touches upon the natural right of man to enter matrimony but affects also in a real way the welfare of the offspring. For there are some who oversolicitous for the cause of eugenics, not only give salutary counsel for more certainly procuring the strength and health of the future child—which, indeed, is not contrary to right reason—but put eugenics before aims of a higher order, and by public authority wish to prevent from marrying all those whom, even though naturally fit for marriage, they consider, according to the norms and conjectures of their investigations, would, through hereditary transmission, bring forth defective offspring. And more, they wish to legislate to deprive these of that natural faculty by medical action despite their unwillingness; and this they do not propose as an infliction of grave punishment under the authority of the state for a crime committed, nor to prevent future crimes by guilty persons, but against every right and good they wish the civil authority to arrogate to itself a power over a faculty which it never had and can never legitimately possess.
>
> Those who act in this way are at fault in losing sight of the fact that the family is more sacred than the State and that men are begotten not for the earth and for time, but for Heaven and eternity. Although often these individuals are to be dissuaded from entering into matrimony, certainly it is wrong to brand men with the stigma of crime because they contract marriage, on the ground that, despite the fact that they are in every respect capable of matrimony, they will give birth to defective children only, even though they use all care and diligence.

Father Joseph Fletcher, professor of pastoral theology and Christian ethics at the Episcopal Theological School in Cambridge, Mass., presents arguments for sterilization from a Protestant point of view and seeks to refute the position of the Catholic church.[20] His arguments are essentially the same as those presented by most advocates of sterilization and we shall not here repeat them.

Proponents of sterilization statutes have attempted to satisfy religious opposition by offering to exempt persons with such objections if institutional arrangements are made for their care. Bills in Wisconsin and New Jersey to make such exceptions were defeated by religious opposition. Since the Catholic church believes that sterilization is forbidden by natural and sacred law, it is clear why it does not condone a sterilization program for anyone. Its conviction is a matter of faith rather than of reason or science.

---

[19] "Encyclical Letter on Christian Marriage by Pope Pius XI," in *Four Great Encyclicals* (New York, Paulist Press, 1931), pp. 90–96; Charles R. McKenney, *Moral Problems in Social Work* (Milwaukee, Wis., Bruce Publishing Co., 1951), ch. 10; Paul Blanshard, *American Freedom and Catholic Power* (Boston, Beacon Press, 1949), ch. 7.

[20] *Morals and Medicine* (Princeton, N.J., Princeton University Press, 1954), ch. 5.

DATA CONCERNING STERILIZABLE GROUPS

THE MENTALLY DEFICIENT

Accurate data concerning the amount of feeble-mindedness and mental deficiency are difficult to obtain because of the absence of uniform definitions for the terms describing mental conditions. Mental deficiency is often used synonymously with feeble-mindedness; in legal practice the two are frequently used interchangeably. Some authorities use the term *feeble-minded* to include also the mentally retarded having borderline intelligence. Extensive use of mental tests is responsible for this broader interpretation of the term *mental deficiency* to include both the feeble-minded and the intellectually subnormal. Feeble-mindedness may mean a subnormal intellect according to psychometric tests, or it may mean such an intellect *plus* social inadequacy.

The mentally deficient have been classified as idiot, imbecile, and moron. These three groups are today usually referred to as low-, medium-, and high-grade defectives. There is no accurate information on the number of defectives in our society for several reasons. Many persons with limited intellectual ability make reasonable adjustments to their environments and are not diagnosed as defective. Then, too, there are differences of opinion as to the lines of demarcation between the lower limit of normal intelligence and defectiveness, although an IQ of 70–75 is generally used as the dividing line. Figures of institutionalized defectives represent only a portion of the total. A general and probably conservative estimate is that about 1 per cent of the population is mentally defective.[21]

Various estimates have been made as to the percentage of feeble-mindedness caused by heredity.[22] Few students place this at less than 50 per cent, and some as high as 80 to 90 per cent. It is estimated that almost 90 per cent of inheritable mental defect is transmitted through carriers, that is, persons who are not themselves defective. We have at present no means of discovering who these carriers are. It has been said that should all the feeble-minded be sterilized at once the number in the next generation would be reduced only about 11 per cent. There are persons who still have the idea that Mendelian laws of inheritance can be expected to apply more or less infallibly to human propagation and that sterilization of all those now discovered to be feeble-minded will clear the world of defective strains. Biologists and geneticists have refuted these ideas, which were so widely promulgated in the beginning of the twentieth cen-

[21] James V. Lowry, "Mental Health," *Social Work Year Book: 1954,* pp. 346–355; "Health, Education, and Welfare of Mentally Retarded Children," *Social Legislation Information Service,* 84th Cong. (September 30, 1955), No. 33, entire issue.

[22] Deutsch, *op. cit.,* p. 374; James V. Lowry, "Mental Hygiene," *Social Work Year Book: 1951,* pp. 320–330; *This Is Your Concern* (New York, Human Betterment Association of America, 1951).

tury. They have taught us that the mode of transmission of feeble-mindedness is not clear. There is no single hereditary character causing feeble-mindedness; it is caused by many factors, both hereditary and environmental, which, in an interaction process, determine mental characteristics.

Although scientists are not clear about the laws of inheritance as applied to mental disability, they have established that there are hereditary factors at work. We are all familiar with the Carrie Buck type of family, which gave Justice Holmes the opportunity to make his *bon mot:* "Three generations of imbeciles are enough." Mental characteristics run in families, as do brown eyes or kinky hair. It is shortsighted social policy to permit academic theories of heredity to interfere with sterilization of persons obviously inheriting their defects. It can be argued with considerable validity, however, that there is not ample biological reason at present for extending the compulsory features of sterilization laws to include carriers. The committee on sterilization of the American Neurological Association favored sterilization for inherited feeble-mindedness but not when it is environmental in origin, and not, by implication, for carriers. It stated: [23]

> There need be no hesitation in recommending sterilization in the case of feeble-mindedness, though it need not, of course, be urged in the case of those conditions which are definitely of environmental origin. Though we hesitate to stress any purely social necessity for sterilization, it is obvious that in the case of the feeble-minded there may be a social as well as a biological situation of importance. Certain of the feeble-minded can only, under the most favorable circumstances, care for themselves, and a family of children may prove an overwhelming burden. However, in a world which has much low-grade work to be done, there is still room for the people of low-grade mentality of good character.

At present, most sterilization statutes apply only to the feeble-minded who are in public institutions; few states extend the law to include the feeble-minded in the population at large. This is much the larger group, and sterilization should certainly be available for it. Generally, sterilization operations should be performed upon institutionalized persons only if they are to be discharged or paroled. Parole plans should be put into effect only if there is good reason to believe that the parolees can make reasonably good social adjustment and supervisory resources are available. Perhaps every legally determined feeble-minded person should remain all his life under the permanent supervision of the state. This would not mean institutionalization but skillful supervision given according to the needs of the feeble-minded individual. Such a proposal, of course, is unlikely and, for the present, impractical.

Today, all over the country, parents of mentally retarded children have joined together in an attempt to serve their own and their children's

---

[23] Reprinted from American Neurological Association, *Eugenical Sterilization* (New York, Macmillan, 1936), p. 180, by permission of The Macmillan Company.

interests. In a 1953 pamphlet, "Parents of Retarded Children," the Human Betterment Association of America, Inc., summarized what is now known of the special problems of retarded young people and suggested sterilization as one practical solution. The pamphlet made it clear that the decision as to which young people of subnormal intelligence are sterilized should be based on professional estimates of the degree of retardation and the adjustment potential of the individual. Undoubtedly, most parents of mentally defective children are unaware of the benefits their children could reap from sterilization. Certainly most of their children under our present statutes will not be candidates for sterilization unless they are institutionalized, and then, as figures show, only a very small number will be afforded an opportunity for the operation.

THE EPILEPTIC

Heredity as a factor in epilepsy is given less emphasis today than when the sterilization movement started. Epilepsy, strictly speaking, is not a mental disease but a group of disorders having as a common symptom a generalized or local convulsion which may or may not be associated with a temporary loss of consciousness. The frequency of epilepsy is not accurately known, but a conservative estimate is three per 1,000.[24] When epileptics are institutionalized they are unfortunately often placed with the mentally defective with whom they do not necessarily belong. Drugs, and in some cases operations, have been beneficial. If and when sterilization is applied to epileptics, it should be done for social rather than eugenic reasons and certainly on a voluntary basis. As we pointed out in Chapter 5, some states provide that epileptics shall not marry unless sterilized. A few, such as Wisconsin, are repealing legislation imposing special restraints upon epileptics as a class.

THE MENTALLY DISEASED

The size of our mentally diseased population as reflected in hospital figures has greatly increased. In 1880 the total number of patients in public mental hospitals was less than 41,000. At the end of 1950 it was well over half a million, about 85 per cent of whom were in state hospitals. Over 250,000 patients each year are admitted to hospitals, and a somewhat smaller number discharged; so that in a period of one year about 900,000 different individuals are in mental hospitals.[25] The National Association for Mental Health in 1954 reported that in 1953, 750,000 persons were cared for daily in mental hospitals, about 50 per cent of the patients in hospitals of all types.[26] During that same year about 2,500,000

[24] Lowry, *loc. cit.*, pp. 346–355.
[25] *Ibid.*, pp. 346–355.
[26] *New York Times* (October 25, 1954).

men, women, and children were being treated in mental hospitals, at psychiatric clinics, or in the offices of private pyschiatrists. Multiple causes are responsible for this increased number of mental and emotional maladies, including better diagnoses, more institutional facilities, and a higher percentage of older persons in the population who are susceptible to certain types of mental disorders, such as arteriosclerosis. Obviously, costs of caring for these mentally ill persons are tremendous. Figures on size of the problem and costs indicate need for improved and expanded methods of prevention and care of mentally ill persons. One method which has been sparingly used is sterilization.

The sterilization committee of the American Neurological Association made it clear that inheritance is no factor in certain mental diseases, such as alcoholic psychosis and senile psychosis, but that in other diseases, such as dementia praecox and manic-depressive psychosis, there are hereditary factors at work. The literature led the committee to the conclusion that whatever the hereditary factors are, they are not Mendelian.

Although this committee found no cause for undue alarm regarding the problem of procreation by defective and diseased persons, it did recommend sterilization under the following circumstances: (1) in selected cases of certain diseases with the consent of the patient or of those responsible for him; those diseases are Huntington's chorea, hereditary optic atrophy, familial cases of Friedreich's ataxia, and certain other disabling degenerative diseases recognized to be hereditary; (2) dementia praecox; (3) manic-depressive psychosis; and (4) epilepsy, mainly on social rather than biological grounds.

The committee was unequivocal in its insistence that sterilization for all groups should be voluntary, should be applicable to patients in and out of institutions, that the machinery for administering any sterilization law should be by boards experienced in the problems involved, that adequate legal protection should be given such boards and the surgeons carrying out the recommendations, and that extensive and prolonged research on the inheritance of mental and physical characteristics should be conducted.[27]

STERILIZATION LEGISLATION AND JUDICIAL DECISION

COMPULSORY AND VOLUNTARY STERILIZATION [28]

Sterilization statutes provide for either voluntary or compulsory sterilization or a combination of both. Voluntary sterilization does not legally

[27] American Neurological Association, *op. cit.*, ch. 11.

[28] "Voluntary Sterilization: A Symposium," *Eugenics Review*, Vol. 43 (January, 1952), pp. 180–184; Manfred S. Guttmacher and Henry Weihofen, *Psychiatry and the Law* (New York, Norton, 1952), ch. 8, pp. 187–204.

mean the private and confidential submission of a patient to a surgical operation; it means, rather, that the execution of the sterilization law cannot be effected until the patient and/or his legal guardian consent. Compulsory sterilization is the coercive sterilization of selected patients at large or in an institution, whether they and/or their legal guardian consent to the operation or not. In such instances, after an administrative order for sterilization has been made, appeal can be taken to a court.

Whether legislation provides for compulsory or voluntary sterilization, the number of persons actually sterilized is an infinitesimal proportion of those covered by law. This means that administrative officials apply the law as though it were voluntary and then most cautiously. Only a few states at one time or other have provided exclusively for voluntary sterilization.[29] In those states, no matter what the diagnosis and advice of the authorities, human sterilization could not be performed unless consent was procured. In 1953 Minnesota and Vermont were the only states providing exclusively for voluntary sterilization.

STERILIZATION LEGISLATION

In 1897 the first sterilization bill—really a castration bill—was introduced into the Michigan legislature, but it failed of passage. In 1905 the Pennsylvania legislature passed a sterilization statute, but it was vetoed by the governor. In 1899 Dr. Harry Sharp of the Indiana State Reformatory began to sterilize inmates of his institution with their consent but without statutory sanction. Not until 1907 did Indiana pass a sterilization statute, the first in the United States. In 1921 the Indiana law was declared unconstitutional. Subsequent legislation has been passed which is valid. Since 1907, thirty-two states have passed sterilization laws. In 1955 twenty-seven states had sterilization laws.[30] Georgia, in 1937, was the last state to enact legislation.

In general, and with many variations, sterilization statutes include the following provisions: [31]

1. A statement of objectives, as, for example, whether or not the

[29] Richard C. Donnelly, *Legal Bibliography on Sterilization, through September, 1954* (New York, Human Betterment Association of America, 1954); J. H. Landman, *Human Sterilization* (New York, Macmillan, 1932), p. 279, and table, pp. 308, 309.

[30] *Sterilizations Reported in the United States to January 1, 1956* (New York, Human Betterment Association of America, 1956), lists these as Alabama, Arizona, California, Connecticut, Delaware, Georgia, Idaho, Indiana, Iowa, Kansas, Maine, Michigan, Minnesota, Mississippi, Montana, Nebraska, New Hampshire, North Carolina, North Dakota, Oklahoma, Oregon, South Carolina, South Dakota, Utah, Vermont, Virginia, West Virginia, Wisconsin. The Alabama law, inoperative since 1935, is still on the statute books.

[31] *Digest of U. S. Sterilization Statutes as of October, 1951* (New York, Human Betterment Association of America, 1951), Pub. No. 34; *A Suggested Sterilization Bill* (New York, Human Betterment Association of America, n.d.), Pub. No. 20, and *Outline of Suggested Sterilization Bill* (New York, Human Betterment Association of America, n.d.), Pub. No. 20A.

operation is recommended for the best interests of society and of the individual, for hereditary, medical, eugenic, or social reasons.

2. Classifications of persons covered, such as the mentally deficient or the feeble-minded, the mentally ill, epileptic, criminal, physically disabled and incapacitated. We have already pointed out that there is little reason to include epileptics unless they are mentally handicapped or transmitters of mental disability. Justifiable argument for sterilization of this class of individuals rests only upon social grounds in the absence of additional defects. We have also discussed the undesirability of sterilizing criminals for punitive reasons. If they are to be sterilized, the operation should be performed only because they, like epileptics, have additional mental or social difficulties. Provision for sterilization of criminals or habitual criminals is still included in several states. This seems to be true in Delaware, Idaho, Iowa, Nebraska, Oregon, and for sex offenders in Idaho, Iowa, Michigan, Nebraska, Oregon, and Utah.[32] Close inspection of the laws is necessary to determine whether sterilization is for punishment or for eugenic reasons. There is adequate reason for sterilizing selected persons with physical defects and disease. In most instances there should be no element of compulsion, or if there is, sterilization should be carried out only when there is a clear-cut history of actual inheritance, as with hemophilia and deaf-mutism.

3. Institutionalized and noninstitutionalized individuals. All laws cover certain groups of institutionalized persons, and eight states provide for sterilization of some classes of noninstitutionalized individuals.[33] It seems clear that sterilization laws should be sufficiently comprehensive to include numbers of groups of noninstitutionalized persons for the obvious reason that most people who need or want sterilization live outside institutions. Whether or not these operations should only be performed with official sanction or under some or all circumstances on a purely private basis is a matter for policy decision.

4. Procedure. Procedural provisions are crucial, since in the absence of well-drafted legislation courts may hold the patient to be deprived of due process and equal protection of the laws. Included in the procedural provisions are such items as who shall or may originate the action. In the case of institutionalized patients this is generally the superintendent or physician in the institution. Statutes also include provisions concerning notice, consent, hearings, appeals, authorization, and penalties.

---

[32] *Digest of U. S. Sterilization Statutes as of October, 1951;* see also, Harriet F. Pilpel and Theodora Zavin, *Your Marriage and the Law* (New York, Rinehart, 1952), ch. 13; Marian S. Olden, "Present Status of Sterilization Legislation in the United States," *Eugenical News,* Vol. 1 (March, 1946), pp. 3–14.

[33] Delaware, Idaho, Iowa, Michigan, North Carolina, Oregon, South Dakota, and Utah, from *Sterilizations Reported in the United States to January 1, 1955* (New York, Human Betterment Association of America, 1955). Pilpel and Zavin, *op. cit.,* ch. 13, p. 205, do not include Utah.

5. The administrative agency. In some states a special eugenics or other board is established. Boards are variously composed of physicians and administrators. In some states the authorizing agency is the state department of welfare. Although some laws do not provide for appeal from the order of the agency to the courts, this protection should be included.

6. Protection of administrators and physicians. Numbers of laws provide that those who carry out the provisions of the act shall be exempt from civil or criminal liability. Some statutes specifically exclude doctors performing sterilization operations for therapeutic purposes.

7. Type of operation. Many states exclude or prohibit castration for sterilization purposes. When operation type is designated, vasectomy and salpingectomy are most often mentioned. Not every one yet understands that these two operations have a very different effect upon the patient than does castration, for only the latter changes the sex characteristics of the patient.

8. Records. For research purposes, if for no other, careful records should be kept. What is included in the records is usually determined by administrative officials.

9. Appropriations. Unfortunately, many of the states provide such small amounts of funds for carrying out this function that the number of operations performed is negligible. For example, in 1955 the state of Wisconsin provided $500.00.[34]

10. Compulsory, voluntary, private nature of the operation. In effect, the statutes are administered as though they were voluntary. There seems little logical or valid reason why for some classes of inherited defects there should not be provisions for compulsory operations. Since the statutes contain almost nothing concerning private operations, it is impossible to do more here than to emphasize the importance of clarifying what conditions may or shall exist in order to authorize private sterilization and what protections are afforded doctors and others participating in the process.

JUDICIAL DECISIONS

On twenty-three reported occasions the constitutionality of sterilization statutes of fifteen states has been tested.[35] On eleven occasions they were

[34] Wis. Stat., 1955, c. 20.670(3).

[35] Landman, *op. cit.*, pp. 204–299. They were held unconstitutional in New Jersey (1913), Iowa (1914), Michigan (1918), twice in New York (1918), Nevada (1918), Indiana (1921), Oregon (1921), North Carolina (1929), Oklahoma by U.S. Supreme Court (1942), Washington (1942). They were declared constitutional in Washington (1912), Michigan (1925 and 1926), twice in Virginia (1925), U.S. Supreme Court for Virginia (1927), Kansas (1928), Utah (1929), Idaho (1931), California (1939), Oklahoma (1941), Washington (1942). See table in "Court Decisions on Eugenic Sterilization," *Eugenic Sterilization in the U.S.: A Comparative Summary of Statutes and Review of Court Decisions,* Public Health Reports (Washington, D.C., G.P.O.,

declared unconstitutional, once in the United States Supreme Court; and on twelve others, once in the United States Supreme Court, they were held constitutional.

The statutes have been challenged on the grounds of whether (1) they were within the police power of the state, (2) there was unequal protection of the law, (3) there was lack of due process of law, (4) there was cruel and unusual punishment, and (5) in one instance, the law was a bill of attainder, defined to be a legislative act inflicting punishment without a judicial trial.[36]

The leading case of *Buck* v. *Bell*, decided in 1927 in the United States Supreme Court, committed us to a policy of human sterilization and established the constitutionality of well-drawn compulsory laws. In this instance Carrie Buck, a feeble-minded white woman, was committed to a Virginia state institution. She was the daughter of a feeble-minded mother in the same institution and the mother of an illegitimate feeble-minded child. At the time of the trial Carrie was eighteen years old.

In rendering his decision, Justice Holmes uttered the famous words: "We have seen more than once that the public welfare may call upon the best citizens for their lives. It would be strange if it could not call upon those who already sap the strength of the State for these lesser sacrifices, often not felt to be such by those concerned, in order to prevent our being swamped by incompetents." [37] He further stated that a sterilization law does not embody unjust classification, even though the statutes may apply exclusively to defective dependent persons within institutions; all legislation is classificatory, but only that which is unreasonable and capricious is so unjust as to be called unconstitutional.

Statutes which are carefully drawn after the general model of the Virginia statute, with particular attention paid to the procedural provisions, will hereafter, it seems, be considered constitutional. Although well-drawn sterilization legislation is constitutional, a 1929 Utah decision makes clear that officials must be careful to determine who comes within the provisions of the act.[38] In the Utah case no evidence was presented to prove that the person for whom sterilization was proposed came under

---

1940), suppl. No. 162, p. 41, for citations and holdings of state and federal courts on *eugenic* but not on *punitive* sterilization legislation. Additional information secured by correspondence from Human Betterment Association of America, Inc.

[36] Landman, *op. cit.*, pp. 112–121, 294–299; Walter Wheeler Cook, "Eugenics and Euthenics," 37 Ill. L. Rev. 287–332 (1943); Hon. Edward Leroy van Roden, "Sterilization of Persons as Punishment for and Prevention of Crimes," 23 Temple L.Q. 99–106 (1949); Abraham Myerson, "Certain Medical and Legal Phases of Eugenic Sterilization," 52 Yale L.J. 618–633 (1943).

[37] *Buck* v. *Bell, Superintendent*, 143 Va. 310 (1925), 274 U.S. 200 (1927).

[38] *Davis, Warden* v. *Walton*, 74 Utah 80, 276 Pac. 921 (1929); see also, Landman, *op. cit.*, pp. 99–104.

the law, as it was not shown that he had inherited undesirable mental characteristics.

CRIMINAL LIABILITY

In most jurisdictions the extent of a physician's liability in connection with sterilization performed outside the provisions of the statutes and that of the spouse or guardian who gives consent is apparently undetermined and uncertain. Provisions are usually incorporated into the laws absolving from criminal and civil liability those who perform any operation under conditions specified by statute.

The question has been raised as to whether there might be criminal liability in situations resulting in death or mayhem of a patient operated upon outside the specific provisions of the law. In the latter case, since practically all of the states have definitions of the crime of mayhem in their codes, these definitions would determine whether the sterilization operation was mayhem and, therefore, whether or not it constituted criminal liability. Many of the definitions of mayhem require intent to maim, premeditated design, unlawful and malicious removal of, disabling, disfiguring, or rendering useless a member of the human body. In the old English common law consent of the injured in this type of operation did not act to prevent criminal liability. It is doubtful if a modern sterilization operation would be classified as mayhem. So far as we can determine, nowhere in England or the United States has a case been reported holding sterilization to constitute mayhem.[39] In 1938 the Wisconsin attorney general ruled that statutes prohibiting mayhem were not applicable to sterilization operations performed for the benefit of a patient's health or with his consent. If performed without the patient's consent, however, it might constitute criminal assault and therefore possibly result in criminal action.[40]

Several states have enacted legislation in regard to private operations. One group of states provides that nothing in the law shall be construed as preventing any physician from giving medical treatment for sound therapeutic reasons, which treatment might involve the nullification or destruction of reproductive functions. The other group has enacted statutes which provide that sterilization performed otherwise than in accordance with the law shall be illegal. Unless penalties are provided, this is probably at most a provision designed to avoid civil liability.

---

[39] Justin Miller and Gordon Dean, "Civil and Criminal Liability of Physicians for Sterilization Operations," 16 A.B.A.J. 158–161 (1930); 87 A.L.R. 242; Richard C. Donnelly, "Liability of Physicians for Sterilization in Virginia," *Virginia Medical Monthly* (January, 1951), pp. 24–27, and "Queries and Minor Notes," *Journal of American Medical Association,* Vol. 141 (September–December, 1949), 810–811.

[40] Ops. Atty. Gen., June 25, 1938, p. 416.

This prohibition appears to mean that any sterilization operation in private practice for eugenic or social reasons is illegal.

CIVIL LIABILITY

Though operations of various types have resulted in the nullification of reproductive functions, as far as could be discovered by Miller and Dean in 1930, no patient had brought civil suit against a doctor.[41] At least two cases have occurred since then, one in Minnesota and one in California.

In 1934 a Minnesota man, having been informed that childbirth would be dangerous for his wife, was advised by a surgeon that a sterilization operation (vasectomy) upon himself would protect his wife against further pregnancies. The operation was performed, was declared successful, and the man resumed marital relations with his wife. Although his wife thereafter became pregnant, she survived the pregnancy and delivery without injury. A suit for damages on a breach of warranty was brought against the surgeon on the ground that the operation performed did not fulfill the surgeon's promise.[42] Paradoxically, the defense argued that a sterilization operation on contract, based on an illegal act, was void. The court held that "the contract to perform sterilization was not void as against public policy, nor was the performance of the operation illegal on that act." It is well to note that the operation was clearly for medical reasons. The court expressed no opinion as to what the policy might have been had there been no medical necessity. However, authorities are of the opinion that in states that have no penal provision prohibiting sterilization, the consent of the party to the operation, as in the Minnesota case, will excuse the surgeon from liability for damages provided the operation was performed without negligence.[43]

In a 1936 California situation both civil and criminal actions were involved. The plaintiff in the civil case had been given a Binet Test and was found to have an IQ of about 70. Her mother thereupon asked two San Francisco surgeons to sterilize her for eugenic reasons, and they did so when she was twenty years old. When she came of age she brought suit for damages against her mother, and the case was settled out of court. The prosecuting attorney in San Francisco also brought the surgeons to trial on the criminal charge of mayhem. The judge ruled that (1) it was not against the law to perform a sterilization operation in California; (2) as the girl was a minor, the mother had a legal right to consent to any legal operation on her behalf; (3) there was no evidence of negligence, fraud, or other complicating factor. The court threw the case out on the ground that the evidence of the prosecution did not show that

[41] Miller and Dean in 16 A.B.A.J. 158–161 (1930).

[42] *Christensen* v. *Thornby*, 192 Minn. 123, 255 N.W. 620 (1934); 93 A.L.R. 573.

[43] Arthur J. O'Keefe, "Contracts—Sterilization—Public Policy," 8 So. Calif. L. Rev. 250 (1935).

a crime had been committed. "It appears, therefore, that the legal situation is pretty clear in California, and presumably the situation would be the same in any state which had no law against sterilization in private practice . . . which means any state except Connecticut, Kansas, and Utah."[44]

Some ten years earlier, in 1928, the Wisconsin attorney general ruled the opposite. He was asked whether the Wisconsin General Hospital might legally perform an operation on a sixteen-year-old girl with a mentality of nine and a half years who was about to be married. The father was dead and the mother and fiancé consented. The attorney general interpreted the statute which limits the operation to those who have been committed to certain institutions to mean that "the power is so specifically granted and so carefully limited and guarded I do not see how it could be said to grant power excepting in the cases there specified."[45]

So far as civil liability is concerned, consent should be a shield unless the patient is rendered sterile by unauthorized liberties or unless the patient is legally incapable of giving a binding consent because of mental incapacity or minority. Regardless of whether it is the husband or wife who is sterilized, and whether or not the operation is for his or her physical benefit, both should execute the release. If a minor is involved, consent should be obtained from parents or guardian.[46] In the absence of negligence and of a statute forbidding sterilization, it seems likely that the physician is under no civil liability for private therapeutic sterilization with adequate consent.[47] The meaning of "therapeutic," however, is not clear.

STUDIES

Up to January, 1956, the states reported 58,285 sterilizations, 23,368 on males and 34,917 on females. More operations were performed upon the mentally deficient than upon the mentally ill, the ratio being 30,101 to 26,047. California had by far the largest number of operations, 19,962. Of these 10,127 were performed upon males, and 835 upon females; 11,662 upon the mentally ill, and 7,513 upon the mentally deficient.[48] In

---

[44] Personal correspondence with Paul Popenoe (November 3, 1937). The pertinent cases are unpublished. On August 31, 1936, the California Supreme Court denied writs of mandamus and certiorari to the prosecution.

[45] Ops. Atty. Gen., October 10, 1928, p. 524.

[46] Donnelly, "Liability of Physicians for Sterilization in Virginia," *loc. cit.*, pp. 24–27.

[47] "Notes, Human Sterilization," 35 Iowa L. Rev. 251–270 (1950); Frederick Falls and Burke Shartel, "Operations to Produce Sterility: Medicological and Legal Implication," 1 Am. Practitioner, No. 9, 479–488 (May, 1947).

[48] *Sterilizations Reported in the United States to January 1, 1956.*

1951 California modified its statute to tighten procedural requirements, and in 1952 there was a marked drop in the number of operations performed. In 1955 there were only twenty-five reported sterilizations. What will be the ultimate effect of the law in that state remains to be seen.

Early California sterilization activity is largely attributed to E. S. Gosney and Paul Popenoe, who respectively founded and directed the Human Betterment Foundation, replaced by the Human Betterment Association of America, Inc. They made two studies of the effects of the California law. The first, in 1929, gave the results of an analysis of records of over 6,000 sterilizations; the second, in 1939, of about 10,000 records.[49] The investigators found that:

1. The largest number of insane sterilized patients were suffering from dementia praecox.
2. In a large number of cases the insanity of the patient was predictable from family history.
3. Only a small percentage of those sent to institutions were sterilized.
4. Of the feeble-minded on parole only about one half had been sterilized.
5. The work record of the feeble-minded sterilized patients was creditable.
6. Sterilization did not increase promiscuity.
7. Patients and relatives were overwhelmingly in favor of the operation. This attitude was confirmed by the reports of 500 normal intelligent men and women who were sterilized outside of the statutory program.

A more recent study than those of Gosney and Popenoe has been made of the North Carolina program.[50] The statutes of that state provide that the state eugenics board shall have jurisdiction for sterilization purposes only in cases of feeble-mindedness, epilepsy, and mental disease. It cannot authorize a sterilization operation for any normal person on physical or social grounds, and it is precluded from dealing with cases of transmissible physical defect, such as hemophilia, blindness, deaf-mutism. Within these limits the eugenics board is directed to act when it believes that the operation would be for the best interests, mental, physical, or moral, of the individual concerned, or for the public good, or where children who might be born would have the tendency to various physical, mental, or nervous diseases. These provisions apply both to institutional and noninstitutional cases. The law specifically states that nothing contained therein shall be construed so as to prevent the medical or surgical treatment for sound therapeutic reasons of any person whose treatment might require destruction of the reproductive functions.

Moya Woodside, author of the study, found that from 1929 to 1947, 1,901 sterilizations were performed under the laws of the state, placing

---

[49] Paul Popenoe and E. S. Gosney, *Twenty-Eight Years of Sterilization in California,* 3d ed. (Princeton, N.J., Birthright, Inc., 1946), Pub. No. 25.

[50] Moya Woodside, *op. cit.*

it in third place in number of operations performed in the country. Of these, 407 were upon males; 1,494 upon females; and 169 of the males and 770 of the females were less than twenty years old when the operation was performed. The study also showed that 1,141, or more than two thirds of all sterilizations, originated from state institutions; 72 from county institutions, and 688 from local public welfare departments, of which North Carolina has one hundred. Of the total number of operations performed, 1,260 were authorized for feeble-mindedness, 409 for mental disease, and 232 for epilepsy. Although the law has a compulsory character, in practice this power is seldom exercised.

Therapeutic sterilization, or that for benefit of the health of the subject, and the "sterilization of convenience," designed to relieve anxiety concerning the application or reliability of birth control, are popular in North Carolina. Exact figures were obviously impossible to obtain. The study showed that the operation was sought by poor and well-to-do patients. Many doctors favored the operation for social and therapeutic reasons. The practice varied greatly between communities; but in numbers of counties public and private agencies and independent applicants sought and procured co-operation from doctors and hospitals for the operation. Although a state contraceptive service has been available to patients of public health departments since 1937, birth-control methods are unacceptable to a proportion of uneducated groups.

In a sample follow-up study of thirty-three white and fifteen Negro women sterilized under the statute, Woodside found the reactions prevailingly favorable. Sterilization had conferred practical and psychological benefits upon the group as a whole and might have been even more constructive in a number of cases if undertaken earlier. The author of the study concluded her report with the statement that in North Carolina the country is witnessing a most important experiment in the changing of social attitudes. Those sterilized under and outside the provisions of the law and social workers, public health workers, doctors, and taxpayers on the whole favored sterilization generously applied. This means that a state with a rural conservative and religious population, almost a third of whom are Negroes, responded to sterilization education and propaganda in a relatively short time. Given a favorable environment for such education and the opportunity for carrying out the program, she concluded, there is reason to hope that sterilization will have some effects upon the quality of the population and upon the prevalence of certain types of social problems.[51]

---

[51] Moya Woodside, "Sterilization and Social Welfare," *Eugenics Review*, Vol. 11, No. 4 (January, 1949), pp. 205–210.

SUMMARY AND CONCLUSIONS

Sterilization is still subject to many attacks. Legislation on the subject moves slowly; and administration of the statutes is cautious. Opponents complain that it is an invasion of individual liberty, that not enough is known regarding the laws of heredity, and that it is contrary to religious and natural law. Proponents urge that sterilization be used to improve the human race and to reduce the burdens of certain classes of handicapped persons to themselves and to society. Opinion of the biological and social scientists differ as to the probable results of sterilization. Some declare that it is a great tool for race improvement. Some, though opposing compulsory sterilization on the ground that we know too little concerning the heredity of mental diseases and feeble-mindedness, favor voluntary sterilization of persons who have a specific defect or disease known to be inheritable. One author, a professor of sociology, wrote: [52]

> It is all very well to recognize our ignorance of human heredity; but it is becoming increasingly clear that we shall never make a frontal attack on social inadequacy until we recognize that family stocks differ in genetic endowment, and hence in potentialities of their offspring; further, that even if heredity has no influence whatever on social inadequacy, defectives do not make good parents. Therefore, they should not reproduce for social as well as biological reasons.

Regardless of point of view, in 1955, twenty-seven states and Puerto Rico had sterilization statutes. In addition, the United States Supreme Court has placed constitutional approval upon legislation providing for compulsory sterilization of persons with feeble-mindedness of the familial type when due process of law is employed. Conservative laws probably will remain on the statute books and perhaps continue to be passed, but they will remain ineffectual unless an informed public opinion demands their competent execution. To date the small number of operations performed under the laws indicates halfhearted support of sterilization programs.

It seems obvious to this writer that sterilization should be available not only to those who transmit familial defects but to those who cannot decently maintain themselves and their issue. Since the laws of inheritance are uncertain, mandatory sterilization at present should be required only of persons with clear-cut inheritance histories. However, statutes should include provisions for the voluntary sterilization of persons with certain designated disabilities who live outside institutions. Finally, surgeons should not have to fear civil or criminal prosecution because an

---

[52] Norman E. Himes, "Some Inferences from History," *Birth Control Review* (November, 1936), p. 1; C. J. Gamble, "Trends in State Programs for Sterilization of Mentally Deficient," *American Journal of Mental Deficiency*, Vol. 53 (April, 1949), pp. 538–554.

individual with a legitimate reason requests and obtains a private operation. "Legitimate" should include eugenic, social, and therapeutic reasons.

Advocates of sterilization programs favor carefully drawn statutes to include the requirements that adequate procedural and administrative facilities be furnished. If these limiting statutory specifications are carried out, there is little reason to fear that the individual will be deprived of his legitimate freedom, that race "purging" will occur, or that euthanasia will be the inevitable next step. However, there is the possibility of realizing Justice Holmes's sage remark, "Three generations of imbeciles is enough," and the exhortation of his father, Oliver Wendell Holmes, "Choose good grandparents." [53]

Selected References

American Journal of Obstetrics and Gynecology.

BLACKER, Charles Paton, *Voluntary Sterilization* (London, Oxford University Press, 1934).

———, *Eugenics: Galton and After* (London, Duckworth, 1952).

BLANSHARD, Paul, *American Freedom and Catholic Power* (Boston, Beacon Press, 1949).

COBB, Montague W., *Medical Care and Plight of the Negro* (New York, National Association for the Advancement of Colored People, 1947).

COOK, Robert, *Human Fertility* (New York, William Sloane Associates, 1951).

Committee of American Neurological Association, *Eugenical Sterilization* (New York, Macmillan, 1936).

DEUTSCH, Albert, *The Mentally Ill in America,* 2d ed. (New York, Columbia University Press, 1949).

DONNELLY, Richard C., *Legal Bibliography on Sterilization Through September, 1954* (New York, Human Betterment Association of America, 1954).

Eugenics Review, published quarterly by Cassell and Co., Ltd., London.

FLETCHER, Joseph, *Morals and Medicine* (Princeton, N.J., Princeton University Press, 1954).

GODFREY, Thomas, and others, *The Trend of National Intelligence* (London, Eugenics Society, 1947).

GOSNEY, E. S., and POPENOE, Paul, *Sterilization for Human Betterment* (New York, Macmillan, 1929).

GUTTMACHER, Manfred S., and WEIHOFEN, Henry, *Psychiatry and the Law* (New York, Norton, 1952).

HARPER, Fowler V., *Problems of the Family* (Indianapolis, Bobbs-Merrill, 1952).

HENSHAW, Paul S., *Adaptive Human Fertility* (New York, McGraw-Hill, 1955).

[53] Leon F. Whitney, *The Case for Sterilization* (New York, Frederick A. Stokes, 1934), flyleaf.

HINTON, J. P., and CALCUTT, Josephine, *Sterilization: A Christian Approach* (London, Allen and Unwin, 1935).

HUGHES, James E., *Eugenic Sterilization in the United States: A Comparative Summary of Statutes and Review of Court Decisions,* Public Health Reports (Washington, D.C., G.P.O., 1940), Suppl. No. 162.

Human Fertility, periodical.

Journal of American Medical Association.

Journal of Mental Deficiency.

KINSEY, Alfred C., and others, *Sexual Behavior in the Human Male* (Philadelphia, Saunders, 1948).

LANDMAN, J. H., *Human Sterilization* (New York, Macmillan, 1932).

LAUGHLIN, Harry H., *Eugenical Sterilization: 1926* (New Haven, American Eugenics Society, 1926).

LEHANE, Joseph B., "The Morality of American Civil Legislation Concerning Eugenical Sterilization" (Doctoral dissertation, Catholic University of America, 1944).

McKENNEY, Charles R., *Moral Problems in Social Work* (Milwaukee, Wis., Bruce, 1951).

MYRDAL, Alva, *Nation and Family* (New York, Harper, 1941).

PILPEL, Harriet F., and ZAVIN, Theodora, *Your Marriage and the Law* (New York, Rinehart, 1952).

PLOSCOWE, Morris, *Sex and the Law* (Englewood Cliffs, N.J., Prentice-Hall, 1951).

POPENOE, Paul, and GOSNEY, E. S., *Twenty-Eight Years of Sterilization in California,* 3d ed. (Princeton, N.J., Birthright, Inc., 1946), No. 25.

"Symposium on Sterilization," *American Journal of Obstetrics and Gynecology* (September, 1937), pp. 499–525.

VANCE, Rupert B., *All These People: The Nation's Human Resources in the South* (Chapel Hill, N.C., University of North Carolina Press, 1945).

VOGT, William, *Road to Survival* (New York, William Sloane Associates, 1948).

WHITNEY, Leon F., *The Case for Sterilization* (New York, Stokes, 1934).

WOODSIDE, Moya, *Sterilization in North Carolina* (Chapel Hill, N.C., University of North Carolina Press, 1950), contains a good bibliography.

The student should also consult pertinent statutes and judicial decisions, articles in law and medical journals, and the various pamphlets, bulletins, and reviews issued by the Human Betterment Association of America, Inc., 32 West 58th Street, New York, N.Y.

PART II

Parent, Child, and the State

CHAPTER 9

Rights and Duties of Parents

INTRODUCTION

The extent of the responsibilities and duties of parents to their children and the corresponding rights of the parents vary as much from civilization to civilization and from time to time as do marriage and divorce customs. Enforceable parental duties have been few, and frequently the responsibility for care and protection could be evaded by the drastic methods of exposure and slavery. "The ancient Roman law," said Blackstone, "gave the father a power of life and death over his children; upon the principle that he who gave had also power of taking away." [1]

In 1765 when this famous commentator was writing, parents were under a duty to maintain, educate, and defend their legitimate children, and their rights included custody, control, and services. These parental rights and duties were really those of the father, for the mother was entitled only to reverence and respect. If women were virtually slaves to their husbands, or at least subservient to them, as was true in many periods of history and as was the situation in England when Blackstone was writing, it was to be expected that their rights in respect to their children would be few.

We have seen that it was not until the nineteenth century in England that married women had a right to negotiate concerning their property, unless they had a separate estate and could thus reach the equity court. We shall see in this chapter the extent of the parents' rights and duties in relation to their children, the degree of the father's authority as against the mother's, and the extent to which the state has gone in enacting legislation to protect and enforce the rights of the child.

---

[1] Sir William Blackstone, *Commentaries on the Laws of England in Four Books,* (Philadelphia, Rees, Welsh, and Co., 1897), Bk. 1, p. 452.

RIGHTS OF PARENTS: CUSTODY

COMMON-LAW BACKGROUND [2]

The harsh rule that the father had almost unlimited rights to the custody, control, and services of his children, the common-law courts having the function of enforcing his rights but not his duties, and the rule that the mother had a right only to reverence and respect have been changed by legislation both in England and the United States. In fact, the English rule in its severest aspects was never in existence in the United States, although the rule that the father had the primary right as against the mother or third persons did exist. At common law a father was entitled to the custody and control of his heir up to the age of twenty-one, and of his younger sons and daughters up to the age of discretion, which was regarded as fourteen for boys and sixteen for girls. The mother had no legal right to custody; however, through the Court of Chancery the welfare of the child and the rights of the mother as a mother could be protected if there were property upon which the court could act.

In early times, upon the father's death the right to custody and control of the child devolved upon the mother. "This was so even under the feudal law, unless the child were heir to estates held in chivalry, in which case his lord became guardian, with valuable rights over his property and person until he should attain the age of twenty-one." [3] By a 1557 statute, passed in the reign of Philip and Mary, entitled "An act for the punishment of such as shall take away maidens that be inheritors, being within the age of sixteen years, or that marry them without consent of their parents," the right of the mother to the custody of her daughter after the father's death received parliamentary recognition.[4] The mother's position, however, was injured by a later act which empowered the father to appoint a guardian by deed or will. This 1660 act reads in part: [5]

And be it further enacted by the authority aforesaid, that where any person hath or shall have any child or children under the age of one and twenty years,

---

[2] Joseph W. Madden, *Persons and Domestic Relations* (St. Paul, Minn., West Publishing Co., 1931), pp. 369–382, 456–457; see also, W. H. Stuart Garnett, *Children and the Law* (London, John Murray, 1911), pp. 2, 3; James W. Schouler, *Marriage, Divorce, Separation, and Domestic Relations*, 6th ed. (Albany, N.Y., Matthew Bender and Co., 1921), Vol. 1, ch. 6; S. P. Breckinridge, *The Family and the State* (Chicago, University of Chicago Press, 1934), sec. 4; Grace Abbott, *The Child and the State* (Chicago, University of Chicago Press, 1938), Vol. 1, Pt. 1, sec. 1; E. E. Bowerman, *The Law of Child Protection* (London, Pitman, 1923); *Parent and Child*, 39 Am. Jur. 583–800; Fowler V. Harper, *Problems of the Family* (Indianapolis, Bobbs-Merrill, 1952), ch. 5.

[3] Garnett, *op. cit.*, p. 7.

[4] 4 and 5 Philip and Mary, c. 8, s. 4 (1557).

[5] 12 Chas. II, c. 24, s. 8 (1660); see 13 L.R.A. (N.S.) 288 for history and application in the United States.

and not married at the time of his death, That it shall and may be lawful to and for the father of such child or children . . . by his deed executed in his lifetime, or by his last will and testament in writing . . . to dispose of the custody and tuition of such child or children, for and during such time as he or they shall respectively remain under the age of one and twenty years, or any lesser time, to any person or persons in possession or remainder, other than popish recusants.

Before 1557 there was no such legal person as a guardian appointed by a parent. With the passage of the act of 1660, for well over two centuries the power of appointing guardians was denied to mothers. At common law the mother of the illegitimate child was not his legal guardian, since he had none; but her claim upon her child was recognized in equity courts. Because her rights were of an equitable nature the courts did not enforce them if they were not for the welfare of the child. The illegitimate father had a right as against third parties but not as against the mother.

COMMON-LAW AND EQUITY-COURT DECISIONS IN ENGLAND

The inequalities of the common law concerning the respective rights of father and mother to custody of the child are glaring. In the early nineteenth century the English common-law courts seem to have been particularly rigid in their adherence to the theory that the father's right to custody should be exclusively recognized.[6] In *The King* v. *De Manneville*, the mother obtained a writ of habeas corpus to bring up the body of her eight-months-old daughter who had been snatched by the father. The mother had separated from him because of his ill treatment. In restoring the child to the father Lord Ellenborough said: [7]

> We draw no inferences to the disadvantage of the father. But he is the person entitled by law to the custody of his child. If he abuse that right to the detriment of the child, the Court will protect the child. But there is no pretence that the child had been injured for want of nurture, or in any other respect. Then he having a legal right to the custody of his child, and not having abused that right, is entitled to have it restored to him.

In an 1824 case a writ of habeas corpus was applied for to be directed to the father, William Skinner, and to Anne Deverall, to bring up the body of a six-year-old infant in order that it might be placed in the mother's care. Skinner had treated his wife with great cruelty, and a separation had taken place, after which he lived with Deverall. He was confined in Horsemonger-lane Gaol, where he still cohabited with Deverall and where she took the child to him every day. The court of common pleas before which the case came held that it had no authority to take the child out of the custody of the father. If there were enough property to

---

[6] Madden, *op. cit.*, pp. 369–370.
[7] 5 East 221, 102 Eng. Rep. 1054 (1804).

take the case before the chancellor representing the king as *parens patriae,* there might be interference with the father's right; however, as there was no charge here of ill treatment of the child, the common-law court could not interfere with the rights of the father.[8]

In the Greenhill case, where the father obtained a writ of habeas corpus commanding the mother to produce the bodies of their three children whom she had taken with her when she left her husband's home because of mistreatment, Serjeant Wilde, arguing for the mother, said: "The question raised by these proceedings is not whether the father's right over his children is paramount, but whether the rights of the mother are to be wholly disregarded so that she may not claim access even to infants within the age of nurture." [9] In awarding the custody to the father the court held:

> When an infant is brought before the court by *habeas corpus,* if he be of an age to exercise a choice, the Court leaves him to elect where he will go. If he be not of that age, and a want of direction would only expose him to dangers or seductions, the Court must make an order for his being placed in the proper custody. The only question then is, what is to be considered the proper custody; and that undoubtedly is the custody of the father.

Although the courts of law were without power to protect the mother or the infant against the father, in some circumstances the equity courts provided protection. In 1722, in the case of *Eyre* v. *Shaftsbury,* the lord chancellor laid down the principle that: [10]

> the care of all infants is lodged in the King as *pater patriae,* and by the King this care is delegated to his Court of Chancery . . . the King is bound, of common right, and by the laws to defend his subjects . . . and by the law of this realm, every loyal subject is taken to be within the King's protection, for which reason it is, that idiots and lunatics, who are uncapable to take care of themselves, are provided for by the King as *pater patriae,* and there is the same reason to extend this care to infants.

This case is also authority for the rule that one testamentary guardian surviving other testamentary guardians, all having been nominated by the father, had complete authority over the infant, the mother having no legal rights.

Two famous cases where the crown exercised its *parens patriae* or *pater patriae* power and the Chancery Court deprived the fathers of their children are the Shelley and Wellesley cases. In 1816 Lord Eldon acted for what he considered was the welfare of the children of the poet Shelley, an avowed atheist. In 1811 Shelley had married Harriet Westbrooke, whom he later deserted. She returned to her father with their child and

---

[8] *Ex parte Skinner,* 9 Moore 278 (1824).

[9] *King* v. *Henrietta Lavinia Greenhill,* 4 Ad. and E. (K.B.) 624, 111 Eng. Rep. 922 (1836); for convenient access to case see Abbott, *op. cit.,* Vol. 1, pp. 29–38.

[10] 2 P. Wms. 103, 24 Eng. Rep. 659 (1722).

with expectations of another soon to be born. The mother later committed suicide by drowning. Both children were maintained by their grandfather. To protect them from any action of their father which might be brought in the common-law courts on a writ of habeas corpus to obtain their custody, the grandfather placed money at the disposal of the Chancery Court to be utilized for the benefit of the children. The result was that the equity court deprived Shelley of jurisdiction over his children.[11]

Perhaps the best known and most often cited of the equity cases depriving the father of the right to his children is the Wellesley case.[12] In this case a bill was filed in the Chancery Court placing funds and, consequently, the care and custody of the three Wellesley children under the protection of that court. Before the mother's death she had made it clear that she did not wish her children ever again to live with their father, an adulterer and a person who had caused her much grief and suffering. In reviewing the jurisdiction of the court over the persons and estates of the minors, the chancellor said:

> If any one will turn his mind attentively to the subject, he must see that this Court has not the means of acting, except where it has property to act upon. It is not, however, for any want of jurisdiction that it does not act, but from want of means to exercise its jurisdiction; because the Court cannot take on itself the maintenance of all the children in the kingdom.

Here, the court had jurisdiction because property was placed at its disposal; it could therefore decide whether circumstances were such that it was necessary to interpose and select a guardian. The chancellor answered this question in his famous reply:

> If this Court has not the power to interpose, what is the provision of law that is made for the children? You may go to the Court of the King's Bench for a *habeas corpus* to restore the child to its father; but when you have restored the child to the father, can you go to the Court of the King's Bench to compel that father to subscribe even to the amount of five shillings a year for the maintenance of that child? . . . The Courts of law can enforce the rights of the father, but they are not equal to the office of enforcing the duties of the father.

It was not always true, however, that the equity court took so stern and pronounced a position to support the rights of mothers and the welfare of children even when money was available with which to exercise its jurisdiction. In 1827 Mrs. Ball and her fourteen-year-old daughter presented a petition to the Chancery Court, praying that the child be

[11] *Shelley* v. *Westbrooke,* Jac. 266, 37 Eng. Rep. 850; for easy access to case, see Abbott, *op. cit.*, Vol. 1, p. 13.

[12] *Wellesley* v. *Beaufort,* 2 Russ. 1, 38 Eng. Rep. 236 (1827); "The Wellesley Case and the Juvenile Court Movement," *Social Service Review* (March, 1930), pp. 64–81; for easy access to excerpts from case, see Abbott, *op. cit.*, Vol. 1, pp. 5–29; every student will wish to read this, the Greenhill, and other cases in the original.

placed under the mother's care or, at least, that the mother be permitted access to her daughter at all reasonable times. The mother offered to maintain the child. The father was living in habitual adultery and the mother had obtained a divorce in the ecclesiastical courts. The question was whether a father's brutal conduct was to deprive a child of fourteen of the care, protection, and advice of her mother against whom no question could be raised. The court ruled that there must be some conduct on the part of the father with reference to the management and education of the child which would warrant an interference with his legal right and that here there was no sufficient cause to deprive him of his common-law right to care and custody. The vice-chancellor said that if there were a legal way of interfering with the father's common-law right he would take that course and that from a moral standpoint he knew of no act more harsh and cruel than to deprive a mother of proper intercourse with her child.[13]

ENGLISH LEGISLATION OF THE NINETEENTH AND TWENTIETH CENTURIES

In an effort more nearly to equalize the rights of fathers and mothers to the custody of their children and to make it possible for common-law courts to decide custody for the welfare of the child, Serjeant-at-law Talfourd introduced a bill into Parliament which became a law in 1839. Talfourd had been attorney for the husband in the Greenhill case, and he was also familiar with the tragedy of Mrs. Norton, granddaughter of the playwright Sheridan.[14] Mrs. Norton had cruelly been deprived by her husband of access to their three children. Being a woman of letters, she wrote ably on the subject of a mother's rights to her child and did much to influence Talfourd to present a measure correcting the situation. Talfourd was also influenced to do this by the fact that he had been a junior counsel for the defendant in the trial of *Norton* v. *Lord Melbourne,* in which Mrs. Norton's husband attempted unsuccessfully to prove illicit relations between Lord Melbourne and Mrs. Norton as a preliminary to securing a divorce. In arguing for the measure to allow the mother the right of access to infants of tender age Talfourd said:[15]

> I do not seek to alter the law of England as to the father's right—I do not ask you to place the unspotted matron on the level with the frail mother of illegitimate children, who is by law entitled to their custody while of tender age . . . but I do ask . . . some slight control over the operation of that tyranny which one sex has exerted over the helplessness of the other.

---

[13] *Ball* v. *Ball,* 2 Sim. 35, 57 Eng. Rep. 703 (1827).

[14] Jane Gray Perkins, *The Life of the Honorable Mrs. Norton* (New York, Holt, 1909).

[15] Hansard's *Parliamentary Debates* (London, 1837–1838), Vol. 39, cols. 1082–1090; for easy access to Talfourd's arguments before Parliament, see Abbott, *op. cit.,* Vol. 1, pp. 39–46.

In 1839 Parliament passed such an act. It gave the mother the right of access to and the protection of her children under seven through the action of the chancellor.[16] In 1873 Parliament extended the discretion of the court to children under sixteen.[17] It was not until 1886 that the English mother had the right of access to her child of any age, with the equity court paying due regard to the welfare of the infant and the conduct of the parents.[18] Also, by this act, in a decree for judicial separation or for divorce *nisi* or absolute, the court which pronounced the decree might declare the parent whose misconduct caused the divorce to be unfit to have custody of the children. The effect of the law was to withhold from the unfit parent, after the death of the other, the right to the custody or guardianship of such children. Further, the mother could be guardian of her child upon her husband's death or serve jointly with the testamentary guardian and could herself appoint a testamentary guardian for her child to serve jointly with her husband.

Not until 1925 were father and mother equal in their rights to the custody of their children. By the statute which begins, "Whereas Parliament by the Sex Disqualification (Removal) Act, 1919, and various other enactments, has sought to establish equality in law between the sexes, and it is expedient that this principle should obtain with respect to the guardianship of infants and the rights and responsibilities conferred thereby," it was enacted that in any proceeding before any court where the custody or upbringing of an infant was in question, the court should regard the welfare of the infant as of paramount consideration and should not consider the claim of the father or any right at common law possessed by him as superior to that of the mother. Further, if the court awarded custody to the mother, it could also, within its discretion, order the father to furnish support.[19]

AMERICAN LAW

In the United States, courts of law and of equity, aided by legislation, have modified the rule that the rights of the father are paramount as against what we consider to be for the welfare of the child; and furthermore, changes have been made in the rule that the father's rights regarding his children are superior to those of the mother. The American law commentator, Kent, writing in 1832, said: [20]

> The father may obtain the custody of his children by the writ of *habeas corpus,* when they are improperly detained from him . . . but the courts, both of law

---

[16] 2 and 3 Vict., c. 54.
[17] 36 and 37 Vict., c. 12.
[18] 49 and 50 Vict., c. 27.
[19] 15 and 16 Geo. V, c. 45; for excerpts from Parliamentary debates preceding passage of act, see Breckinridge, *op. cit.,* pp. 301–332, and for copy of act, pp. 332–337.
[20] James Kent, *Commentaries on American Law* (Boston, Little, Brown, 1896), Vol. 2, p. 194.

and equity, will investigate the circumstances, and act according to sound discretion, and will not always, and of course, interfere upon *habeas corpus,* and take a child, though under fourteen years of age, from the possession of a third person, and deliver it over to the father against the will of the child. . . . They will consult the inclination of an infant, if it be of sufficient mature age to judge for itself, and even control the right of the father to the possession and education of his child, and when the nature of the case warrants it.

Although early American courts did not usually decide so rigidly in favor of the father as did the English courts, the justices in determining what was improper detention of children from the father often favored him as against the mother, as, for example, in a famous New York case of over a hundred years ago. Here, a husband and wife with two children, a son and a daughter less than two years old, separated. An agreement was entered into in 1838 that the young daughter would remain with the mother and that the son would temporarily stay with her but eventually, be given to his father. This was done. In 1839 the father secured habeas corpus writs for the unlawful detention of his wife and daughter by Mrs. Barry's father, Mr. Mercein. This was the first of five habeas corpus writs that Mr. Barry sought. Several of them were discharged, since the young daughter needed a mother's care and there was, therefore, no unlawful detention. Finally, the state supreme court ordered the daughter, then several years older, to be delivered to her father. The court gave its opinion as follows: [21]

There has been no impeachment of the moral character of the realtor, (the father) nor is there anything to show want of capacity on his part for the proper care and training of the child. He is in all respects as well qualified as the mother for the proper discharge of parental duties. . . . The question then is, which of these parties, the father or the mother, has the best title to the custody of the child? The opinion of the court has been repeatedly expressed, that by the law of the land the claims of the father are superior to those of the mother.

Legislation and judicial opinion have changed since 1840–1842 when the Mercein case was before the New York courts. Today the welfare of the child is the paramount consideration, and the mother is equal to the father in her rights to the custody of their children.

CUSTODY AND THE AMERICAN COURTS

When the problem of custody of children is brought before the court, it is the duty of the court to determine what is wisest for the child and how the interests of the parents, the child, and the community can best be effected. Problems of custody are brought before courts of various jurisdiction under the following conditions:

---

[21] *The People* v. *Mercein,* 3 Hill 399, at 422 (N.Y., 1842). See also *Mercein* v. *The People ex rel. Barry,* 25 Wendell 64 (N.Y., 1840). The cases are long; for convenient access to excerpts, see Abbott, *op. cit.,* Vol. 1, pp. 55–61.

1. When the child is dependent, neglected or delinquent. The court with jurisdiction is the juvenile court which ideally has resources for careful inquiry, which exercises equity jurisdiction, and which acts for the welfare of the child.

2. When one or both parents are deceased and a testamentary guardian has been named. Such actions are brought to the probate courts, which are usually without resources to determine what are the best interests of the child.

3. When both parents are deceased, no testamentary guardian has been named, and property is involved. These cases also come into the probate court.

4. When the parents are legally separated or divorced or are seeking legal separation or divorce. Here, the question of custody is decided by the court having divorce jurisdiction, which is frequently without resources to determine what is for the welfare of the child.

5. When the child is mentally or physically disabled. The court with jurisdiction is sometimes the juvenile court and sometimes the court with authority to commit to institutions.

Although there is some conflict in the cases, the weight of authority establishes several general principles which we shall now discuss: [22]

1. The courts have a discretionary power in contentions over custody of children and will take into consideration the welfare of the child; however, if the parents are fit persons, they will receive the custody. A parent cannot be deprived of his children merely because he is poor. In controversies between the father or mother and third persons as to custody of children, the parent undoubtedly has a strong *prima facie* right. Provided a child's parents can offer him a home that is decent and respectable, the court will not award custody to a third person who is able to offer the child a better home and education. The reason for this is that the beneficent influence of natural affection of parents will outweigh the possible benefit of wealth or culture. In the words of one court: [23]

> It is one of the cardinal principles of nature and of law that as against strangers, the father however poor and humble, if able to support the child in his own style of life, and of good moral character cannot, without the most shocking injustice, be deprived of the privilege by anyone whatever, however brilliant the advantage he may offer. It is not enough to consider the interests of the child alone.

In a Washington case, the mother had died and her two-months-old son was placed in the custody of strangers until such time as the surviving father was able to provide for him properly. The father remarried about three years later and improved his general circumstances, but in the interim, the foster mother had properly reared the child, and a mutual attachment had sprung up between them. In a suit by the father to regain custody of his infant son, the court decided it was best for all concerned to place the child with the father, saying in part: [24]

---

[22] Madden, *op. cit.*, pp. 369 ff.

[23] *Verser* v. *Ford, et al.*, 37 Ark. 27 (1881).

[24] *In re Mead,* 113 Wash. 504, 194 Pac. 807 (1920).

We note a growing disposition of the Court to more and more permit adventitious temporal advantages to interfere with the natural relations of the parents and children, too much emphasizing the assertions that the welfare of the child is the paramount consideration, gauging that welfare by the physical comfort of the child, forgetting the influence of parental association. In spite of all the supervision which modern legislation has imposed on domestic relations, the time has not yet come when the courts are called on to place themselves in *laco parentis*. Some heed must still be paid to the rights and obligations of parents, and the place of father, mother, sisters and brothers, is not taken by the state. We must not lose sight of the fact, too, that the duties which a child owes to its parents are duties which peculiarly form its character and make strong men and women, for, as the parent and child journey through life together, the time comes when the father must be borne upon the shoulders of the erstwhile child, as the "young Eneas did the aged Anchises bear" from the flames of Troy. . . .

A poor home with a father's and mother's love and protection, is still a more fit place for the child than the abode of more prosperous strangers. Upon whomever the custody of the child may be placed by law, it is only a legal obligation, as compared with the fundamental moral obligation of natural parenthood.

It is well-established law that parents have natural rights in their children, of whom the state may not deprive them except for sufficient cause. On the other hand, parents may not treat their children as property, and their natural rights may not be extended to exploitation, cruelty, and neglect.

2. Before the rights of wives and mothers were equal to those of husbands and fathers, the courts gave preference to the father, who was the natural guardian and *prima facie* entitled to the custody of his minor child. Today, if the parents are equally fit, some external condition can usually be found that enables the courts to decide in terms of the welfare of the child. Sometimes the custody is divided, some children going with one parent and some with another, or all of the children going with one or the other parent for certain periods of time. Courts are disposed to award to the mother custody of infants and young children, especially of girls, even where the mother's conduct has been such that if the children were older or of the other sex their custody would be placed elsewhere.[25] The decision of the court is based upon the welfare of the child and not on the superior rights of the father. The various cases cited throughout this chapter show that today the father's earlier *prima facie* rights have yielded to the welfare of the child.

3. Almost all cases where parents have been deprived of custody are those in which they were shown to be unfit or in which they had relinquished their right for a time and then sought the aid of the court to regain custody. In the leading case of *Chapsky* v. *Wood,* where a father entered a petition for the return of his minor daughter, the court held that a child brought up from birth by an aunt should remain with her foster parent

---

[25] *Ross* v. *Ross,* 89 Colo. 536, 5 P 2d 246 (1931).

rather than be returned to her father after five-and-a-half years' absence.[26] The controlling consideration was the welfare of the child, who had received deep, strong, and patient love from her aunt during years of helpless babyhood. If returned to her father, she would be cared for by relatives who had never seen her and who had rejected her mother.

4. In determining what is for the best interests of the child, the court will consider ties of nature and of association, character and feelings of the parties contending for the custody, the age, health, and sex of the child, the benefits of education and development, and the pecuniary prospects. When the child has reached the age of discretion, he will often be allowed to make his own choice; the court is not bound by his wish if the custody would be improper. In a Missouri case, the husband started divorce proceedings, but the wife was granted the decree on countercharges and was awarded alimony. The custody of their fourteen-year-old daughter was awarded to the husband, and the wife appealed. The father, with whom custody was lodged, humored and indulged the child and in several instances tried to alienate the child's affection from the mother. The appellate court reversed the decision of the lower court and awarded the child to the mother. It laid down the principle that although neither parent has an absolute right to the custody of minor children, nevertheless, the respective claim of each of the parents will be considered.[27] It is rare indeed that the mother who prevails in a divorce suit will be deprived of the custody of a daughter of tender years. In a Michigan case the wife was granted the divorce and was awarded the custody of two children under fourteen, but the two older ones were to elect the parent with whom they wished to live.[28] A Kentucky court held that in determining the ultimate custody of children, their preferences, if unsupported by facts showing that their best interests would thus be promoted, could not alter the rights of the parties.[29]

STATUTORY PROVISIONS REGARDING CUSTODY [30]

Like the law of other domestic relations, the law of parent and child is governed by that of the states and not of the national government. All fifty-one American jurisdictions have legislation relating to the general right of custody, and all expressly provide that the child may be removed from parental control under certain circumstances, such as when the parent is unfit or incompetent. Most jurisdictions have legislation relating

---

[26] 26 Kan. 650, 40 Am. Rep. 381 (1881).

[27] *Wells* v. *Wells,* — Mo. —, 117 S.W. 2d 700 (1938).

[28] *Horning* v. *Horning,* 107 Mich. 587, 65 N.W. 555 (1895).

[29] *Edwards* v. *Edwards,* 26 Ky. L. 1051, 64 S.W. 726 (1901).

[30] Chester G. Vernier and others, *American Family Laws* (Stanford, Cal., Stanford University Press, 1931–1938), Vol. 4, pp. 17–18, and table, pp. 24–53; Madden, *op. cit.*, pp. 379–382; *Parent and Child,* 39 Am. Jur. 583–800.

to the right of custody as between the parents. In Kansas equality is guaranteed by the constitution. The mother's equal right to the custody of her minor children is granted in about half the jurisdictions by express provision, and in several jurisdictions, the same result seems to be intended. The common-law preference given to the father seems to be preserved by statute to some extent in very few jurisdictions.

Most jurisdictions have statutes relating to the designation or nomination of testamentary guardians. Statutes vary greatly on the right to nominate a guardian by will; for example, they may provide that mother and father may jointly nominate guardians, with the surving parent having the ultimate right, or they may provide that the surviving parent may, by will, appoint a guardian. The statutory trend is to make it possible for both parents to appoint or nominate testamentary guardians, but not so as to deprive the surviving parent of guardianship during his or her lifetime, unless with the survivor's express consent or unless the survivor is unfit or incompetent.

There are instances where the court does not follow the designation or preference of the testator in nominating a guardian for minor children. In a Michigan case the court held that it would comply with the testator's choice of guardian if it were for the best interest of the ward.[31] In a later case the court held that the judge of probate was warranted in refusing to ratify the appointment of a testamentary guardian in a case in which the widow, who was also named as guardian, could not agree with the executor and the two were mistrustful of each other.[32] Although the common law and equity courts could remove a child from parents under some circumstances, this power was seldom exercised until the nineteenth and twentieth centuries. The power of the state to exercise the authority of *parens patriae* for the benefit of children has been greatly modified and expanded, especially through juvenile court and child welfare legislation.

CUSTODY IN DIVORCE AND SEPARATION ACTIONS [33]

Prior to Parliament's enactment of the Matrimonial Causes Act of 1857 (by which act absolute divorce was permitted for adultery of the wife or for adultery, desertion, and cruelty of the husband), the custody of children in annulment and separation actions was determined by common-law courts and was usually awarded to the father. Following this act, custody was generally awarded to the "innocent" spouse. Today, in both England and the United States the welfare of the child determines

---

[31] *In re Stockman,* 71 Mich. 180, 38 N.W. 876 (1888).

[32] *Ohrns* v. *Woodward,* 134 Mich. 596, 96 N.W. 950 (1903).

[33] Madden, *op. cit.,* pp. 377–378; Judge Clarence H. Gilbert, "Custody of Children Whose Parents Are Divorced or Separated," *Social Service Review* (December, 1933), pp. 655–658; Vernier, *op. cit.,* Vol. 2, pp. 191–213; 19 C.J. 342.

which parent shall be given custody, and it may even be given to the "guilty" party. With divorce granted for causes other than adultery in most American jurisdictions, there is little reason for preservation of the theory that custody belongs with the innocent spouse. Husband and wife, whether plaintiff or defendant, are often equal; and in awarding custody, the welfare of the child, rather than the innocence or guilt of the parties to the divorce action, should be the ultimate determining factor.

In divorce actions, jurisdiction over care, custody, education, and support of children is statutory or inherent in a court of equity. Today, it seems that all jurisdictions, with possibly one or two exceptions, have statutes on these matters. Only a small number have statutes referring to the case where divorce is denied; however, in many others the situation seems to be covered by broad language. In several jurisdictions in which the question has arisen, the court, acting sometimes upon statutory authority and sometimes without, has held that in an action for divorce which fails, the court, although dismissing the action for divorce, may make such provision as it deems necessary for the care of the children.[34]

Without exception, the statutes make the court's power regarding custody a discretionary one. The commonest type of statute provides that the court may make such orders as are "necessary and proper," "just and proper," "reasonable," "expedient," and so forth. Other elements mentioned are safety, well-being of the child, the child's choice if he is of sufficient age to choose, and the child's happiness, comfort, and spiritual welfare. Divorce courts seldom have the social services available to facilitate wise determination of custody. For this reason many child welfare experts recommend that all divorce cases including award of custody shall be in a family court or, at the very least, that contested custody in divorce actions be decided by children's courts.

In most jurisdictions specific provision is made for revising the decree. The general doctrine of United States courts is that in divorce actions the jurisdiction over both custody and support of children is a continuing one and that the courts may modify and change the order when circumstances render such changes proper. The order for custody is usually until "further order of the Court" or "during the child's minority." The courts consider remarriage, increased age of the child, and changed financial conditions sufficient cause for a petition to reconsider the question of custody and support.

In a Wisconsin case a woman who had been divorced only three months, married in another state and returned to Wisconsin to live, in spite of the fact that remarriage is prohibited to divorced persons for one year. The Wisconsin high court held that this did not conclusively

[34] See *Jacobs* v. *Jacobs,* 136 Minn. 190, 161 N.W. 525 (1917), for this point of view, and *Davis* v. *Davis,* 75 N.Y. 221 (1878), for the opposite; see note to 35 L.R.A. (N.S.) 1158 for summary of cases on both sides.

show moral unfitness of the woman to rear her four-year-old daughter and that no change of custody was desirable or necessary.[35] In a New York case the father, an adulterer, remarried in violation of the divorce statute. He later attempted to acquire the custody of the child, who had been given to the mother. The court held that the greater wealth of the father was no reason to remove the custody from the mother; there were no new conditions affecting the welfare of the child which required a change in the order regarding her custody.

In England under the ecclesiastical law, husband and wife could not make a private agreement to separate. Today, in both England and the United States, an understanding of this kind will receive legal sanction within limits. Such agreements, of course, often involve plans for children.[36] The courts apply the same rules regarding custody and maintenance of children in this situation as in situations where there is a divorce; the welfare of the child is the controlling factor.

RIGHTS OF PARENTS: RELIGIOUS EDUCATION [37]

ENGLISH BACKGROUND

The right of parents to determine the religious education of their children is intimately associated with current religious ideas and with prevailing theories concerning custody and education. In the sixteenth century, when there was much conflict between Protestants and Catholics in England, rigid legislation was enacted against Catholics. By 1699 it was a crime punishable by perpetual imprisonment for any Papist to keep school or to assume education of youth. The courts did not hesitate to deprive a widow of the custody of her minor children so that they could be brought up as Protestants, although both parents had always been Catholics. Even in a case where a Catholic mother was bringing up her son as a Protestant in accordance with the wishes of her deceased husband, the court ordered a separation of the mother and her child of seven years.

Toward the middle of the eighteenth century, when Protestants felt more secure, although restrictive statutes were not repealed, courts became more lenient in their rulings and hesitated to interfere with guardianship because of religious considerations. By the early part of the nineteenth century, courts deciding questions of custody seem not to have disfavored any religion. In applying the general rule that the father

---

[35] *Jensen* v. *Jensen*, 168 Wis. 502, 170 N.W. 735 (1919).

[36] R. J. Peaslee, "Separation Agreements under the English Law," 15 Harv. L. Rev. 638–656 (1902); Vernier, *op. cit.*, Vol. 2, p. 486.

[37] For most of the material in this section, see Lee M. Friedman, "The Parental Right to Control the Religious Education of a Child," 29 Harv. L. Rev. 485–500

had the right to the custody of his child and, consequently, the right to choose the child's religion, the English courts divided into two well-defined groups. One line of cases held that the court would enforce the wishes of the father unless he had abandoned his rights thereto and that the mother had no right, even upon the death of the father, to ignore his wishes regarding religious education. Illustrating this rule is the leading Hawksworth case decided in 1870. There the Catholic father had died, leaving a Protestant widow and a six-months-old daughter whom the mother brought up as a Protestant for eight years, for the father had left no directions as to the child's religious education. Upon administrating the father's estate, the court ordered the daughter to be given Catholic instruction. Such a change of religion was not considered prejudicial to her welfare in view of her tender age.[38] The second line of cases regarded the right of the father as a trust and not a power, the best interests of the child being the controlling factor.[39] With the modernization of statutes pertaining to the rights of mothers, there has been a consequent liberalization of court decisions concerning the extent of her rights both during and after her husband's lifetime; this, of course, includes the right to choose the religion of her children.

AMERICAN LAW

Because our federal and state constitutions guarantee religious freedom, there has, until recently, been relatively little litigation, as such, over the religion of children. Although conflict between parents or guardians over the religious education of children may be a matter upon which courts must pass, they have usually considered the problem to be an aspect of the child's welfare. Reports show, however, that conflict over religious education has sometimes been the controlling cause for the change of custody. In a Missouri case, a writ of habeas corpus was sought by a Catholic nun to obtain the custody of an eight-year-old child of an intemperate father, the mother being dead. The child, whose father had placed her in a Catholic institution, was taken by a married couple who agreed to raise her a Catholic; however, the promise was broken. The court gave the custody of the child to the nun in the interests of the child's welfare and out of deference to the wishes of the father that the child be brought up a Catholic.[40]

(1916); see also, Schouler, *op. cit.*, Vol. 1, p. 847; 46 C.J. 1222, under discussion of *Parent and Child*, par. 7, "Religious Education and Affiliation of Child," par. 20, "Religious Convictions"; Garnett, *op. cit.*, p. 9; *Religious Education*, 39 Am. Jur. 684; *Effect of Agreement Between Parents as to Religious Education and Nurture of Child*, 12 A.L.R. 1153; *In re Agar-Ellis*, L.R. 10 Ch. D. 69 (1878); *In re Story*, 2 Ir. R. 328 (1916); *In re Clarke*, L.R. 21 Ch. D. 817 (1882).

[38] *Hawksworth* v. *Hawksworth*, L.R. 6 Ch. App. 538 (1871).

[39] *Austen* v. *Austen*, 34 Beav. 257, 55 Eng. Rep. 634 (1865).

[40] *In re Doyle*, 16 Mo. App. 159 (1884).

In a New York case a similar result was obtained. Here, the facts were that upon the death of the mother, a stepfather was appointed guardian of his wife's children with the consent of the sisters of the deceased father. The stepfather was a zealous Protestant; the children's father, a Catholic. One of the children, who was ten years old, expressed the desire to continue in his father's church. The aunts contested the guardianship of the infant children because of the conflict in religion. The court revoked the guardianship letters of the stepfather and gave them to the paternal aunts. Among other things, it said, "I believe that the welfare of the infants is best promoted by bringing them up in the faith of their father." [41]

Courts differ in the arguments that they use when religious upbringing is either a primary or secondary matter in the determination of the child's welfare. The first line of reasoning favors the father. In a Florida case the parents of two daughters of the ages of seven and five were divorced during the time when the mother and children were living with the grandmother. The father agreed that the mother should retain their custody until they reached the age of fifteen. Before her death the mother attempted to bequeath the children to the maternal grandmother and to a sister. The father remarried and obtained the custody of the two daughters from the grandmother. He agreed to return them if he were unable to support them properly. Because of his new family cares, the father, under court order, placed them in an orphanage to be brought up in the Catholic faith. The grandmother later requested the court to give her the children's custody by reason of the mother's bequest and the father's agreement. The orphanage gave the children the best of care and religious upbringing. The court denied the grandmother's request on the basis that she was not a fit guardian and that she lived in a disreputable neighborhood; it commended the father's action as being for the children's best interests. It further stated that he had the right to educate them in any religion which did not violate the laws of the land. "It is not enough to consider the interests of the child alone. And as between father and mother, or other near relative of the child . . . the father is generally to be preferred." [42]

In a second line of reasoning the Massachusetts court said: "The court will not itself prefer one church to another, but will act without bias for the welfare of the child under the circumstances of each case." Here, the mother, who was an adherent of one form of Christian faith, neglected her nine-year-old daughter, who was committed as a pauper to an orphan home. The foster parents of a different faith, who petitioned the court for adoption of the child, were held fit, and the child's religious educa-

---

[41] *In re McConnon et al.,* 112 N.Y. Supp. 590, 60 Misc. N.Y. 22 (1908); see also, *Commonwealth* v. *McClelland,* 70 Pa. Super. 273 (1918).

[42] *Hernandez* v. *Thomas,* 50 Fla. 522, 39 So. 64 (1905).

tion was considered secondary to her welfare. The mother's wishes carried no weight because of her behavior.[43]

A Wyoming court in a third line of reasoning held that religion would not be given "the slightest consideration." In this case a writ of habeas corpus was sought by a sister of the deceased father for possession of his infant daughter. The sister had been appointed guardian by a Minnesota court. However, the child had been taken to Wyoming relatives by an older brother, who had been told by the father that he did not wish to have the aunt raise his daughter because of religious differences. The Wyoming court disregarded the Minnesota court's action and acceded to the father's dying request, holding that the child's welfare was paramount.[44]

We hazard several generalizations concerning the religious upbringing of children. Parents are expected to choose the religion of their children. Children need not be given any religious training if the parents so elect. This is in contrast to the theory of the English Chancery Court, which something over a century ago deprived Shelley of his children, in part because he was an atheist. If there is conflict between the parents on religious training, the courts will try to decide for the welfare of the child, since the matter of religion is often considered an aspect of the larger problem of welfare. Since father and mother are equally entitled to custody, they will usually be equally entitled to determine the religious education. It is presumed that the surviving spouse, whether father or mother, will have the right to choose the religion of the children. An agreement at or before marriage between husband and wife as to the religion in which their children are to be educated has not the effect of a legal contract, although it may be given weight by the courts unless contrary to the welfare of the child. There are indications that religious upbringing as a main, even controlling, aspect of custody will more frequently come before the courts. This appears to be true as a result of the passage of numbers of "religious-protection" laws applying to foster home and adoption situations. These statutes are similar to that of Massachusetts, to which we shall refer in Chapter 12.

RIGHTS OF PARENTS: PUNISHMENT

EXTENT OF RIGHT [45]

Common-law rules concerning who could correct or punish and to what extent were the logical outgrowths of legal theories regarding parental rights and duties. The father's unquestioned right to the custody of

[43] *Purinton* v. *Jamrock,* 195 Mass. 187, 80 N.E. 802 (1907).

[44] *Jones* v. *Bowman,* 13 Wyo. 79, 77 Pac. 439 (1904).

[45] Blackstone, *Commentaries,* Bk. 1, p. 452; Madden, *op. cit.,* pp. 446–448; 39 Am. Jur. 601.

his minor child gave him the right to correct the child reasonably in the exercise of his judgment, but not so extremely as to constitute cruelty.[46] Today, the ground of the father's right to correct is the welfare of the child and not the father's liberty to act as he wants because he has natural paternal rights. As statutes and court decisions have equalized the rights of the father and mother to the custody of their child, the welfare of the child being paramount, the mother's right to punish has become equal to that of the father. As a matter of everyday occurrence the mother administers a large part of the necessary discipline, with either the express or implied consent of the father and without creating any family dissension.

The courts are not in accord as to what constitutes immoderate and excessive punishment. Some authorities have held that a parent or one standing *in loco parentis* is criminally liable if in correcting the child he acts unreasonably or if the punishment is immoderate, as, for example, where a father was convicted for imprisoning his blind, minor son in midwinter in a cold, unheated cellar,[47] or where he struck his ten-year-old daughter with a saw.[48] Some courts have concluded that the jury should not be permitted to determine without yardstick and rule what punishment is unreasonable. Hence, the court should instruct the jury that unless the parent inflicted permanent injury or acted from malice, it is not justified in finding him criminally liable.[49]

THE RIGHT OF THIRD PERSONS TO PUNISH AND EXTENT OF RIGHT

The parent has the power to delegate the right of correction to another; for instance, to one in whom the parent has confidence, such as an aunt or other close relative. Where the parent is physically incapable of administering the necessary punishment, he may delegate this authority.[50] The courts differ as to whether a school teacher, temporary guardian, nurse or institutional attendant, or other person standing *in loco parentis* may exercise the same degree of punishment as parents. The Wisconsin court, in a well-considered case, stated that the parent ought to be given greater discretion, for he is naturally more restrained in administering correction than one *in loco parentis,* who should be limited to a degree of chastisement that is moderate and reasonable and for the child's welfare.[51] Here, an institutional superintendent, one *in loco parentis,* was held liable for damages to a young boy whom he punished with a horse-

---

[46] *McKelvey* v. *McKelvey, et al.,* 111 Tenn. 388, 77 S.W. 644 (1903).
[47] *Fletcher* v. *People,* 52 Ill. 395 (1869).
[48] *Neal* v. *State,* 54 Ga. 281 (1875).
[49] *State* v. *Jones,* 95 N.C. 588, 59 Am. Rep. 282 (1886).
[50] *Rowe* v. *Rugg,* 117 Iowa 606, 91 N.W. 903 (1902).
[51] *Steber* v. *Norris,* 188 Wis. 366, 206 N.W. 173 (1925).

whip. In a North Carolina case a pupil was awarded damages in a suit against a school teacher for injuring his eyesight by throwing a pencil at him when his attention was distracted by some disturbance in school.[52]

STATUTORY ENACTMENTS [53]

A sizable number of jurisdictions have statutes dealing with the parent's right to correct his child. Some statutes declare it to be murder or manslaughter for a parent to punish his child so immoderately that death ensues, but excusable if the death occurs through accident or misfortune. In all jurisdictions, statutory authority is granted to certain courts to deprive both parents of custody under certain circumstances which, of course, would include abuse and excessive punishment.

During the last half century few criminal actions have been instigated against parents for immoderate punishment of minors, largely because of our juvenile court legislation. In fact, the reports show that at no time have many criminal actions for excessive punishment by parents been brought before the courts. Today, the neglected or abused child can be brought before the juvenile court exercising equity or chancery jurisdiction, and he can be removed from his parents or guardian, or he can be placed under the jurisdiction of the court through the process of probation which often implies supervision of the parents.

MINOR'S RIGHT TO CIVIL ACTION

At common law, a minor could not bring a tortious action against his parent for excessive chastisement, because a parent was not civilly liable for an injury, great or small, willful or negligent, to his minor child.[54] The reason usually offered for this rule was that to allow a child a cause of action against his parent would interfere with parental discipline and would tend to disturb domestic tranquillity. Despite this rule, the courts sometimes impose liability in certain situations, such as when the father is made criminally liable for personal injury to the child. Some states have enacted laws permitting the child to bring an action against his parent for excessive punishment.

RIGHTS OF PARENTS: EARNING AND SERVICES OF MINORS

At common law the father, or the mother upon the father's death, is entitled to a minor child's services and earnings.[55] This means that the

[52] *Drum* v. *Miller,* 135 N.C. 204, 47 S.E. 421 (1904).
[53] Vernier, *op. cit.,* Vol. 4, p. 19, and table, pp. 24–53.
[54] Madden, *op. cit.,* pp. 449–452; Vernier, *op. cit.,* Vol. 4, pp. 480–482.
[55] Blackstone, *Commentaries,* Bk. 1, p. 453; 20 R.C.L. 607; 46 C.J. 1281; 39 Am. Jur. 624; Madden, *op. cit.,* pp. 403–407; Vernier, *op. cit.,* Vol. 4, pp. 20–22.

parent has a right within legal limits to put the child to work in his own family or in business or with others and to collect his wages. The right of the parent to the services and earnings of his minor child being reciprocal to the duty of the parent to support, educate, and protect, his failure to discharge such duties means forfeiture of his rights. These rules are generally followed today in England and the United States, and in some jurisdictions they have been written into the statutes. Many American jurisdictions specifically declare the rights of parents to the earnings of the child, nearly all of which give both parents equal rights thereto. At common law the minor's earnings can be claimed by the parents' creditors. There are statutes in several states exempting the earnings of the child from liability for the parents' debts.

It is well established at common law that the parent, as such, has no control over his child's property other than earnings. He cannot sell or dispose of his child's personal or real property or use the benefits therefrom except for the child's support. This rule has been incorporated into the legislation of a number of states. Although a parent is entitled to his child's earnings, it is possible for this right to be waived or forfeited through emancipation.

EMANCIPATION [56]

In the United States the doctrine of emancipation, both under the common law and statutes, has been liberally applied. Emancipation is the act by which one who was under the power and control of another is freed and made his own master. The term is principally applied to the emancipation of a minor child by its parents. This involves the surrender of the right to care, custody, and earnings and the renunciation of parental duties. The emancipation may be express, such as by voluntary agreement of parent and child, or implied from acts and conduct indicating consent, and it may be complete or partial. Emancipation may take place by consent of the parent, express or implied, or by the operation of law, as in cases where the child becomes twenty-one, or where he contracts a valid marriage, or where the parent abandons or neglects him.

Perfect or absolute emancipation, if it were legally possible, would mean the complete severance of the parent-child relation; but certainly a parent cannot relieve himself of the duty to support the child if the child cannot support himself. Even if the child can support himself and is allowed to collect his wages, the father is still liable for emergencies and unusual expenses. The effect of emancipation is to deprive the parent of control so long as the emancipation continues.

When a parent permits the child to collect his wages over a period of

---

[56] *Black's Law Dictionary*, 3d ed. (1933), p. 652; Madden, *op. cit.*, pp. 407–416; Vernier, *op. cit.*, Vol. 5, p. 240; 39 Am. Jur. 702.

time, the courts will not generally support the sudden reversal of the implied agreement. In a New York case, a father had absented himself from home for several years, had contributed nothing to his minor son's support or education, and had left him to shift for himself and to collect his own wages. The court held that the employer could not claim that the father was entitled to the son's wages, since there had been an implied emancipation.[57] In another case, emancipation took place on an express agreement between parent and children. Two minor daughters were advised by their father that they would have to take care of themselves and could keep their earnings as school teachers. The daughters loaned their earnings to their father on mortgage security, which later the insolvent father's creditors claimed belonged to them on the theory that a minor's earnings are subject to the claims of the parents' creditors. The court held that the daughters were emancipated and that their mortgage was valid.[58]

Emancipation was only partial in the following case. In a suit for medical care rendered to an eighteen-year-old son, it was found that the boy lived at home with his parents and paid his board but had found his own jobs during the three previous years and had collected and had spent his wages as he pleased. He was seriously injured while at work, and the plaintiff, a surgeon, was obliged to perform an urgent operation without consent of the parents. The son was under treatment for nine months with the knowledge and assent of the father. The court decided that there was not such complete emancipation as would relieve the parent of liability for necessaries which could not be met by use of the wages earned.[59]

ENTICEMENT, ABDUCTION, AND SEDUCTION [60]

So firmly entrenched in the common law is the theory that a parent is entitled to the custody and services of his child that this right is extended to an action for loss of services against anyone who wrongfully entices, abducts, or seduces his child. The gist of the action is loss of the child's services, and the relation of master and servant, actual or constructive, must be shown. In an 1885 case a father brought action against the husband of his minor daughter for unlawfully enticing her from him and depriving him of her services. The court held: [61]

> The right of a parent to the earnings of his minor child, upon whatever principle it is founded, is commensurate with the right of custody; and so long as the right to the services of the child remains, the right to control those services

[57] *Conovar* v. *Cooper*, 3 Barb. Ch. 115 (1848).
[58] *Stanley* v. *National Union Bank*, 115 N.Y. 122, 22 N.E. 29 (1889).
[59] *Lufkin* v. *Harvey*, 132 Minn. 238, 154 N.W. 1097 (1915).
[60] Madden, *op. cit.*, pp. 437–439; 20 R.C.L. 614.
[61] *Aldrich* v. *Bennett*, 63 N.H. 415 (1885).

must exist. Whatever, therefore, operates as a release from parental control, necessarily terminates parental right of service; and the emancipation of the minor from legal parental authority, either by the voluntary act of the parent or by operation of law, puts an end to the legal claims of the parent to the minor's earnings.

Here, as the daughter was above the statutory age of consent, she had the legal capacity to form the relation of marriage. "The new relations created by the marriage, being inconsistent with the enforcement of the parental rights, operate as an emancipation from them."

A parent's right to the services of his child also gives him a right to an action for damages for seduction or debauchment of his daughter. This is based, not upon violation of the family honor but upon a legal fiction, the loss of the daughter's services. This means that the relationship of master and servant must be shown. In this connection it is enough to show that the parent has a right to his minor daughter's services. This general rule was enunciated in a Wisconsin case where a father brought an action for loss of the services of his fifteen-year-old daughter.[62] There was no evidence presented which tended to show that Katie was in the service of her father at the time she stopped at the home of her uncle with whom the illicit relations occurred. However, the legal fiction of loss of service was the gist of the action. The same action is usually available for persons standing *in loco parentis* who are entitled to the child's services.

Some states, recognizing that the real reason for the action is not loss of service but the wounded feelings of the parent, have abolished by statute the fiction of loss of service and allow the parent to recover without proof of such loss. In several jurisdictions, in contrast to the common-law rule under which a female cannot bring an action for her own seduction, statutes expressly confer upon the unmarried female a right to maintain an action against her seducer. These statutes do not require that the woman bringing the action shall prove breach of promise to marry.[63]

Vernier is probably right in his disapproval of statutes which permit the female to bring an action for damages in her own behalf. Like breach-of-promise suits, such actions are subject to fraud, oppression, and blackmail. Protection of the young girl, he feels, is offered in the statutory provisions concerning rape and illegitimacy. In a rape action, the state brings a criminal action and punishes the defendant; in an illegitimacy action paternity may be established and support for the child provided. These actions lack the element of damages for personal injury, but it is doubtful if statutory provisions for this omission are a justifiable

---

[62] *Lavery* v. *Crooke*, 52 Wis. 612 (1881).
[63] Vernier, *op. cit.*, Vol. 4, pp. 267–268.

remedy in view of the probable amount of unsavory publicity and of possible fraudulent and malicious actions.

DUTIES OF PARENTS: SUPPORT

COMMON-LAW BACKGROUND

We have seen that at common law a parent had the right to the custody, control, and earnings of his child; this right was founded on the father's duty to maintain, protect, and educate the child. The English chancellor in the Wellesley case made the strong statement that the courts of law could enforce the rights of the father but not his duties, and, hence, the equity court must exercise jurisdiction where it could for the protection of the child. If it is true that the common-law courts were not equal to the office of enforcing the duties of the father, what enforceable rights had the child? To what extent could the parent be required to carry out his three main duties?

In England the extent of the parents' duty to support his child was uncertain. Usually, parents voluntarily and uncomplainingly furnish the standard of living they can afford. At common law if they did not do so and a third person furnished necessaries, there was the question of whether the creditor could collect. Nineteenth-century English cases held that there was only a moral and not a legal obligation and that a parent, even where he neglected to support his child, was not liable for necessaries in the absence of an express promise to pay for them or of conduct from which a promise might be implied as a matter of fact.

In an 1840 English case the court said: "It is a clear principle of law, that a father is not under any legal obligation to pay his son's debts; except, indeed, by proceeding under the 43 Elizabeth by which he may, under certain circumstances, be compelled to support his children according to his ability; but the mere moral obligation to do so cannot impose upon him any legal liability." [64] In an 1867 case the court stated: "It is now well established that, except under the operation of the poor law, there is no legal obligation on the part of the father to maintain his child, unless, indeed, the neglect to do so should bring the case within the criminal law. Civilly, there is no such obligation." [65]

An English lawyer, summarizing this development, wrote: [66]

> Every child has a right to look to his father in the first instance for maintenance, care, education, and control; and that right may be enforced by summary proceedings. But the right is the creature of legislation and has no existence at common law; indeed, so far as the direct interests of the child are con-

---

[64] *Mortimore* v. *Wright*, 6 Meeson and Welsby 482, 151 Eng. Rep. 502 (1840).
[65] *Bazeley* v. *Forder*, L.R. 3 Q.B. 559 (1867).
[66] Garnett, *op. cit.*, p. 29.

cerned, they may be said to have been created within the last few years, for the earlier statutes, which cast upon a parent the duty of maintaining his offspring, or punished him for their abandonment, were devised rather for the relief of the poor rates than for the comfort of the children.

The Elizabethan "poor law" referred to in the above quotations does not really furnish a satisfactory basis for the father's liability to third persons.[67] That statute provided that the father, mother, and grandparents of poor, old, blind, lame, and impotent persons should maintain them if they were of sufficient ability. If a father refused to support his child, the poor-law authorities could compel him to do so to the extent of the relief afforded under the law, an amount which was below a decent subsistence level. A creditor could not collect from any legally responsible person or the town itself unless proper authorization had been given. In other words, a well-to-do, harsh parent could absolve himself of financial responsibility for his child, and kind-hearted friends or merchants had no recourse. It has never been argued, however, that a child should be allowed to pledge his father's credit for anything but necessaries.

Authorities maintaining that a parent had a moral and not a legal duty can back their position by the following propositions: (1) there seems to be no English case where the father was held upon an implied contract to reimburse a stranger who had made provision for a tender child which the father failed to make; (2) the father had the right to disinherit his child and leave him to the parish and also to emancipate him, thus relieving himself of the obligation to support the child; (3) the enactment of Elizabethan poor-relief legislation requiring support of a poor child by a parent seems to have been necessary in order to provide for the omission in common-law remedies. At any rate, admitting a legal duty of maintenance, the sanctions were so slight as to give the child little recourse when his parent did not provide for him.[68]

Those writers who hold that at common law the parent legally had a financial responsibility to his child agree that a creditor could not force a father to pay for debts contracted by his child except under an express contract or under an implied contract with facts indisputably showing responsibility, as, for example, in cases where a father had been paying bills without protest, or where the father had deserted and was not supporting his child, or where he had forced the child out of the home, or where he had allowed the child to stay with the separated or divorced mother.

---

[67] Madden, *op. cit.*, pp. 383–392; 20 R.C.L. 622–627; 46 C.J. 1256–1281, 1337–1341; 39 Am. Jur. 620.

[68] Julian Mack, "Establishment of the Juvenile Court," App. I of S. P. Breckinridge and Edith Abbott, *The Delinquent Child and the Home* (New York, Russell Sage Foundation, 1912), pp. 181–184.

These writers derive their authority from the following principles: (1) the father who neglected to provide for his young child and who thus exposed him to starvation was liable to criminal prosecution; (2) even though the child had independent means for support, the father was still under a primary obligation to provide for the child out of his own means, and a special order had to be obtained from the court to allow the father to draw upon the child's means; (3) in England a wife who had been deserted by her husband might charge him not only for expenses incurred for herself but also for those incurred for her minor children; this presupposed that the father was liable for the support of the child as well as of the wife.

Regardless of authority, it seems inconsistent to hold a parent liable for criminal prosecution if he exposes his child to starvation unless there is a legal duty to supply food. Further, it seems wrong to give the father absolute right to his child's earnings if he is not under obligation for the maintenance of his child. At English common law the facts seem to be that in some circumstances the father was under a legal obligation to support his child, and in other circumstances he was not.

The rule that a father had merely a moral obligation to support his minor child has been maintained in only a minority of American jurisdictions and is generally rejected today. Almost a century ago, in a striking Vermont case, Justice Redfield said: [69]

> And it is obvious, that it (the law) makes no provision for strangers to furnish children with necessaries, against the will of parents, even in extreme cases. For if it can be done in extreme cases, it can in every case, where the necessity exists; and the right of a parent to control his own child will depend altogether upon his furnishing necessaries, suitable to the varying taste of the times. . . . If the parent abandons the child to destitution, the public authorities may interfere, and, in the mode pointed out by statute, compel a proper maintenance.

The weight of authority in the United States has fortunately not been with Justice Redfield. In an earlier New York case the court said: [70]

> A parent is under a natural obligation to furnish necessaries for his infant children; and if the parent neglect that duty, any other person who supplies such necessaries is deemed to have conferred a benefit on the delinquent parent, for which the law raises an implied promise to pay on the part of the parent. But what is actually necessary will depend on the precise situation of the infant, and which the party giving the credit must be acquainted with, at his peril.

Here, the son, living with his father, who comfortably and decently clad him, purchased a coat without his father's consent. The court's judgment was that there was no ground to charge the father with neglect of his duty to provide necessaries.

---

[69] *Gordon* v. *Potter,* 17 Vt. 348 (1845); see also, *Holingsworth* v. *Swendenborg,* 49 Ind. 378 (1875); *Holt* v. *Baldwin,* 46 Mo. 265 (1870).

[70] *Van Valkinburgh* v. *Watson,* 13 Johns 480 (N.Y. 1816).

Kent in his *Commentaries* wrote as follows on the obligation of the parent to support his child: [71]

> During the minority of the child . . . the parent is absolutely bound to provide reasonably for his maintenance and education; and he may be sued for necessaries furnished, and schooling given to a child, under just and reasonable circumstances. The father is bound to support his minor children, if he be of ability, even though they have property of their own; but this obligation in such a case does not extend to the mother, and the rule, as to the father, has become relaxed. . . . The legal obligation of the father to maintain his child ceases as soon as the child is of age, however wealthy the father may be, unless the child becomes chargeable to the public as a pauper.

A leading Iowa case, decided in 1890, reviewed the common-law theories regarding the duty of a father to support his child. Here, the facts showed that the seventeen-year-old daughter, who had been away from her father's house for three years earning and controlling her own wages, contracted typhoid fever, and twenty-one days of professional medical services were rendered at her request and without knowledge and consent of her father. The defendant's contention was that his obligation was moral only, unenforceable in the absence of statute or promise, and that his daughter was emancipated anyway. The court held that a parent was under a legal obligation to supply necessaries to his child and said: [72]

> This obligation to support is not grounded on the duty of the child to serve, but rather upon the inability of the child to care for itself. It is not only a duty to the child, but to the public. The duties extend only to the furnishing of necessaries. What are necessaries must be determined by the facts in each case. The law has fixed the age of majority; and it is until that age is attained that the law presumes the child incapable of taking care of itself, and has conferred upon the parent the right to care, custody, control and services, with the duty to support.

Here, the girl was at best only partially emancipated. The father had not relieved himself from the duty to furnish support for the well-being of his daughter, and from that obligation could be presumed the promise to pay for the services.

The Wisconsin court held that a mother living apart from her husband without a divorce had the legal right to pledge her husband's credit for necessaries for the daughter about to graduate from high school. The court further ruled that a coat, graduation dress, and slip for which the father had refused to furnish cash or credit were so obviously necessaries that judgment should be entered for the creditor, but that as to whether or not the other articles purchased were necessaries was a matter of fact

---

[71] Kent, *Commentaries,* Vol. 2, pp. 191–192.

[72] *Porter* v. *Powell,* 79 Iowa 151, 44 N.W. 295 (1890).

for the jury to determine.[73] The Washington court held that a divorced father, even though he did not have the custody of his daughter, had the duty to supply funds for a college education, which was in this instance considered a necessity.[74]

In American jurisdictions today it is generally held that a third person can recover for necessaries furnished to minor children under proper circumstances. This would doubtless be the rule, even in the absence of statutes imposing such a responsibility. What are necessaries is a mixed question of law and fact, the latter to be determined by the jury. Generally, they include food, clothing, medical attention, and even education, commensurate with the standards to be expected from the family income. In the absence of a statute giving the right, a suit by a child to compel the parent to perform his duty of support continues to be nonenforceable. Such a suit can be brought only by a third person for the reasonable value of necessaries.

STATUTORY DUTY OF PARENTS TO SUPPORT [75]

Under statutes in the United States, parents have both a civil and a criminal liability for nonsupport of their children. Most jurisdictions have statutes affecting civil liability of parents, the majority being public-assistance laws. Provision under these laws is variously made for court action at the instigation of (1) the state, county, or municipality relieving the poor persons; (2) the overseer of the poor; (3) relatives; and (4) the dependent poor person himself. Although a child at common law cannot enforce the duties of his parents, some public assistance statutes today permit such an action. The public-assistance statutes in several jurisdictions specifically mention the duties of parents of illegitimate children. More than half the states have statutes authorizing the courts with jurisdiction to order the parents of dependent, neglected, and delinquent children to support them while the latter are in the care of an agency or institution.

Statutes of a broader nature provide that parents must maintain their children. Juvenile, criminal, and civil courts are given jurisdiction over nonsupporting parents. All American jurisdictions have statutes dealing with the criminal liability of the parent for nonsupport of his child. The most numerous and important type is the family-desertion act. Although often referred to as desertion acts, the gist of the grievance is nonsupport. Some statutes create the two offenses; others, either nonsupport or desertion. Most of the statutes provide for suspension of sentence and permit

---

[73] *Simpson Garment Co.* v. *Schultz,* 182 Wis. 506, 196 N.W. 783 (1924).
[74] *Esteb* v. *Esteb,* 138 Wash. 174, 244 Pac. 264 (1926).
[75] Madden, *op. cit.,* p. 392; Vernier, *op. cit.,* Vol. 4, pp. 56–63.

probation of the defendant. In a good many jurisdictions, desertion or nonsupport laws apply to the parents of illegitimate children also. The ages of children, the desertion or nonsupport of whom constitutes a crime, vary under the statutes up to the age of majority. "Under sixteen" is the age adopted by the uniform act on desertion and nonsupport. The uniform reciprocal enforcement of support act provides a procedure for enforcing responsibilities of support upon any individual who has a legal responsibility for such support, regardless of the jurisdiction in which he is residing. We have already referred to this act in Chapter 6 and shall refer to it again in Chapter 13 and in Chapter 20.

Primarily, the duty to support children, both at common law and by statute, rests upon the father. During the father's lifetime the mother has no obligation to support them in the absence of statutory provision on the subject. The problem of liability between parents seldom becomes important unless they are separated or divorced. With the removal of the common-law disabilities of the wife and her consequent ability to enjoy property and earnings, it has been suggested that there is no longer any reason why she should not be held legally responsible for the support of her minor children equally with her husband.[76] On principle it seems reasonable to assume that if the father does not perform his duty to provide necessary support for his minor child, it should be incumbent upon the mother to perform that parental duty to the best of her ability. The generally prevailing rule is that the father's primary obligation to furnish support is not affected by the mother's ability to perform the duty or her actual performance of the duty.

If parents cannot support children properly, equity, even in the absence of statutes, will order the use of the child's own property. After the father's death, the duty of support falls on the mother. A stepparent has no obligation for the support of the spouse's children unless a statute imposes such a duty or unless he voluntarily assumes the obligation by standing *in loco parentis*. Except under public-assistance statutes, with some exceptions, parents have no obligation to support adult children. The extent to which the responsibilities and rights of the parent-child relationship are destroyed by agreement or by the misconduct of the parent is the question of emancipation and has been discussed earlier.

MAINTENANCE OF CHILDREN IN DIVORCE ACTIONS

In general, the statutes go into little detail in the matter of maintenance of children in divorce actions. A divorce does not relieve parents of liability for the support of their children, and where there is no decree of the court denying either of them custody of the children, the duty of each

[76] 131 A.L.R. 862.

respecting the support is as before the decree.[77] Generally, it is the father's duty.

In the leading case of *State* v. *Langford,* the Oregon court in 1918 pointed out that cases concerning support of children after divorce fall into three classes: [78] (1) where the decree is silent as to both custody and support; (2) where the decree provides for custody but is silent regarding maintenance; (3) where the decree provides for both custody and maintenance. In the first type of case, the general rule is that the obligation of the father after divorce is exactly as it was before dissolution of the marriage. In the second type, there is a difference of opinion. One line of authorities accepts the theory that the duty of the father to support the child and his right to collect the child's wages are reciprocal, and to award the custody of the child to the mother is to deprive the father of the child's actual or potential earnings. However, a majority of the courts denounce this argument, which not only ignores the rights and welfare of the child but enables an unfaithful husband and unnatural father to compel his wife to divorce him on account of grievous wrongs done by him and then to absolve himself of financial responsibility. In the third type of case, since the responsibility for support is fixed, the problems which arise are concerned with increased or decreased responsibility, liability of the estate of the deceased, and so forth.

Today, the courts ordinarily hold that the father remains liable for the support of his minor children when he and his wife are divorced, legally separated, or living apart on an agreement, although there are circumstances when this is not true.[79] With greater equality between husband and wife in regard to property and earnings and the custody of their children, it is reasonable to expect that statutes will be modified to impose greater obligations upon divorced mothers, when financially able, to share in the support of their children.

Even though statutes impose both civil and criminal obligations upon parents, whether living together or separated, to support their children, the courts still have several major problems to solve when action is brought, such as: Did the child or third persons have the right to pledge the parent's credit? Were the goods furnished necessaries? Should one or both parents assume responsibility for support? Was there criminal neglect?

The English common-law anomaly that a father is morally but not legally responsible for his child's maintenance is probably the outgrowth of the theory that a child is *sub potestate parentis.* The theory that the father is supreme has been prevalent with many peoples and for many

---

[77] *Zilley* v. *Dunwiddie,* 98 Wis. 428, 74 N.W. 126 (1898).
[78] 90 Ore. 251, 176 Pac. 197 (1918).
[79] *Pretzinger* v. *Pretzinger,* 45 Ohio St. 452, 15 N.E. 471 (1887).

centuries. So far as England is concerned, it is a direct heir of feudal law, where complete subordination of child to father and of lord to king prevailed. The right of the father to dictate to his child as he saw fit naturally included the right to set the standard of life. The beliefs that the child has the right to be protected by his father and that the state should be absolved of financial responsibility for the child if the parent is financially able have been incorporated into legislation within the last century.

DUTIES OF PARENTS: PROTECTION

The common law sanctions but does not enforce the duty of the parent to protect his child.[80] Blackstone commented that this duty is "rather permitted than enjoined by any municipal laws, nature in this respect, working so strongly as to need rather a check than a spur." It is a generally accepted rule that the use of force, even to the extent of homicide, is justifiable if in necessary defense of the child. An eighteenth-century English case presents a striking example of this rule. Here, the father revenged his son's injury by going almost a mile to punish the assailant, which punishment resulted in death. In his commentaries on this case, Blackstone intimated that the court went out of its way to justify the parent's act.

In a twentieth-century American case where a father found a man attempting to violate his daughter and, in protecting her, caused the assailant's death, the court held the homicide justifiable even though it might afterward appear that the assault could have been prevented by other means.[81] There is every reason to assume that such a rule as that of the common law, now enacted into legislation in some of our states, is as old as the human race. The parent, himself, might have the right to kill his own child under certain circumstances and in some cultures, but no one else could injure or threaten to injure his child without giving him the right to intercede.

Some states have enacted laws which in general provide that parents who willfully neglect to provide necessary food, clothing, shelter, and medical attendance are guilty of a crime. Such laws have been held to apply to parents who refuse necessary medical attention for religious reasons. In an Oklahoma case a father who, because of religious beliefs, refused to provide medical care for his minor child afflicted with typhoid fever was held to be guilty of a misdemeanor.[82]

Today, the state at many points has assumed parental responsibility for the protection of the child. Through the juvenile court the state has

---

[80] Vernier, *op. cit.*, Vol. 4, pp. 64–65; Madden, *op. cit.*, pp. 397–398; Schouler, *op. cit.*, Vol. 1, p. 844; Blackstone, *Commentaries*, Bk. 1, p. 450.

[81] *Litchfield* v. *State*, 8 Okla. Cr. 164, 126 Pac. 707 (1912).

[82] *Owens* v. *State*, 6 Okla. Cr. 110, 116 Pac. 345 (1911).

a right to interfere if the parents neglect, abuse, abandon, do not support, or contribute to the delinquency of their child. Communicable-disease laws, child-labor laws, laws requiring or permitting the licensing of commercial amusement centers, and many other statutes have been enacted in order to protect the child, even if his parent does not want the particular form of protection. Differing from Blackstone's time, it is an enforceable duty today for parents to protect their children, not only from personal abuse and attack but also from injurious social and economic conditions.

DUTIES OF PARENTS: EDUCATION

HISTORICAL BACKGROUND [83]

The parental duty to educate children has often been urged and even at times enforced, but only within the memory of living men has the state made resources available which, in turn, have made possible the enforcement of the responsibility. When children were educated in the home under parental aegis, uneducated or overworked parents obviously could give their children no education in the formal sense and very little training in the everyday conduct of their lives. When education was considered a function of the church, the kind of training provided was limited in scope and, often, in extent. When education took place in private schools, only those to whom these facilities were accessible, who could afford tuition, and who had the leisure to take advantage of the opportunity received the benefits. In other words, at any given point in history, the ability of parents to carry out the duty to educate their children depended upon facilities available and beliefs regarding castes and classes. It is a long step from the practice of those periods, when certain groups gave an education to their children on a purely voluntary basis, to the practice of the present, when there is a general tendency throughout the western world for the state to furnish free elementary education and to require school attendance of all children at least up to fourteen or sixteen years.

The occidental world, under the influence of rapidly changing industrial and commercial conditions, felt the need of a universal system of education sooner than did the oriental world. Earlier than England, the continental countries exerted efforts to make educational facilities gratuitously available; and as early as 1691, Scotland enacted legislation

[83] The material for this discussion has come from I. L. Kandel, "Public Education," *Encyclopaedia of the Social Sciences* (1931), Vol. 5, pp. 414–421; George S. Counts, "History of Education," *Encyclopaedia of the Social Sciences* (1931), Vol. 5, pp. 403–414; E. P. Cubberley, *The History of Education* (New York, Houghton Mifflin, 1920); 39 Am. Jur. 673.

requiring a tax-supported school to be established in each parish.[84] The modern movement for public education started with the French Revolution. A Napoleonic decree of 1808, supplemented by subsequent legislation, is the foundation of France's present system of education: the state alone has the right to provide, maintain, and supervise education, and nonpublic schools may be established only with the permission of the government and with the right of the government to inspect. Not until 1882 was a compulsory school-attendance law enacted requiring attendance from six to thirteen.

As early as the first half of the seventeenth century, some of the Prussian states required the provision of local schools and compulsory attendance. In 1717 the emperor, Frederick William, forced parents under severe penalties to send their children to school to learn religion, reading, writing, and calculation; the tuition fees of poor children were to be paid out of the community poor box. The German Constitution of 1919 provided for compulsory, full-time attendance up to the age of fourteen and compulsory part-time attendance up to the age of eighteen.

At common law the parent had the obligation to educate the child; textbook writers have said that it was to be an education suitable to the station in life. However, this duty, like that of supporting the child, was a moral one, as there seem to be no English common-law cases in which such a duty has been enforced directly or indirectly.[85] With no public schools available, such a duty could have been enforced only for certain groups. Blackstone, writing on this duty, said: [86]

> The last duty of parents to their children is that of giving them an education suitable to their station in life; a duty pointed out by reason and of far the greatest importance of any. . . . Yet the municipal laws of most countries seem to be defective on this point, by not constraining the parent to bestow a proper education upon his children. . . . Our laws, though their defects in this particular cannot be denied, have in one instance made a wise provision for breeding up the rising generation: since the poor and laborious part of the community, when past the age of nurture, are taken out of the hands of their parents, by the statutes for apprenticing poor children. . . . The rich, indeed, are left at their own option, whether they will breed up their children to be ornaments or disgraces to their family.

In England, governmental participation in the provision for and support of education did not occur until 1834, when aid for building elementary school houses was furnished. Education for the poor was provided through apprenticeships and by philanthropic agencies and for others by private elementary and secondary tuition schools. A few writers urged a public system of education, but most of England opposed such

---

[84] Kent, *Commentaries,* Vol. 2, pp. 195–203.
[85] Madden, *op. cit.*, pp. 394–395.
[86] Blackstone, *Commentaries,* Bk. 1, p. 451.

a plan because it would make the lower classes restless or because those who could afford to pay for their own education should do so or because the religious purpose of all instruction was deeply ingrained. Not until 1876 was compulsory education in effect. At that time legislation was enacted which imposed on parents the duty of securing an efficient education for their children, abolished child labor under ten, and restricted child employment between ten and fourteen. By the end of the nineteenth century, elementary education was available to all, and the transition from voluntary education, often provided by religious groups, to free and compulsory education had been made. The Education Act of 1918 raised the upper age of compulsory attendance to the end of the term in which the pupil reached his fourteenth birthday.

The Education Act of 1944 superseded all previous education acts. It is the basis of the present educational system of England and Wales. The modified act requires that there shall be free full-time schooling for every child from the age of five until fifteen and, eventually, free part-time schooling from fifteen until eighteen. At every stage the education children receive must be that which is best suited to their aptitudes and abilities. The central authority for education other than university education in England and Wales is now the Ministry of Education. The authority does not provide, maintain, or control any kind of school; nor does it employ any teachers. It has power to assure the development of a national policy for education. Local education authorities are responsible for seeing that there is a full range of educational opportunities through all three stages of primary, secondary, and further education. The act also provides an opportunity to the voluntary schools—of which Great Britain, following upon centuries of tradition, has a great many—to choose definite lines of action to fit them closely into the tax-supported school system. The act also enlarges ancillary duties, such as medical and dental inspection, the provision of milk and meals, clothing, and so forth. Today, England provides educational facilities for every child up to a specified age and furnishes many social services in and out of the school system to the child and his parents so that maximum value can be derived from the compulsory system.[87]

AMERICAN DEVELOPMENT

From colonial days, the states have required that parents provide some kind of education for their children. This responsibility was imposed

---

[87] British Information Services, Reference Division, *Education in Great Britain*, I.D. 606, revised October, 1952, New York; Garnett, *op. cit.*, pp. 77–78; S. J. Curtis, *History of Education in Great Britain* (London, University Tutorial Press, 1948); C. Birchenough, *History of Elementary Education in England and Wales from 1800 to the Present Day* (London, University Tutorial Press, 1938).

upon them even before there were free educational facilities. One author, in reviewing colonial educational history, wrote: [88]

> Compulsory education in the home, by parents or others, or by masters through the system of apprenticeship, with appropriate penalties for neglect, preceded by two centuries the modern idea of compelling pupils to attend organized schools for free education at public expense. This system, as developed in New England, was of great importance for three classes of children: for apprentices, for those "put out" to service for their maintenance only by selectmen or overseers of the poor, and for the children of illiterate parents or those too poor to pay tuition fees commonly exacted in many town schools in the seventeenth and even in the eighteenth century. In this last case the law virtually forced towns to pay the cost of educating poor children.

The origin of education through facilities other than organized schools came from sixteenth-century England. The English Statute of Apprentices of 1563 provided for industrial or trade education, and the Poor Law of 1601 provided for the maintenance of poor children through apprenticeship or binding out. Although neither of these laws provided that masters must teach the rudiments of education, indenture contracts of the time did occasionally provide for some education. Similar customs and legislation appeared in the colonies; frequently town ordinances required religious training. The responsibility for the enforcement of the various laws providing for education of children through parents or masters of apprentices or those to whom poor children were bound out fell largely on the county courts and the selectmen and overseers of the poor of the towns.

The early New England educational legislation was of two general types. There were laws, like that of Massachusetts passed in 1647, under which each town comprising fifty householders was directed to provide a teacher to instruct children to read and write. These laws did not compel parents or others to send children to school. Along with this type of legislation there were acts requiring parents, masters, or others to see that children should be able to read, a difficult law to enforce if parents or masters could not read and if there were no accessible schools.

Trailing the development of facilities for free, compulsory, elementary education was that of providing facilities for higher education on a public basis. The free high school and college are only about a hundred years old, and there is today no state that requires a college or even a high school education. The state laws do provide, however, that there shall be full-time attendance at school under a certain age, and in some states, compulsory part-time attendance for a higher age. In many localities and

---

[88] Marcus Wilson Jernegan, "Compulsory and Free Education for Apprentices and Poor Children in Colonial New England," *Social Service Review* (September, 1931), pp. 411–425.

in some states the enforcement of compulsory school laws is still inadequate.

The concept that education is a function of the several states and not of the federal government was recognized by those writing our federal charter, and no provision for schools or aid to schools was included in the Constitution.[89] However, members of the early Congresses believed so firmly in universal free education that they developed a method of aiding each new state to establish and maintain a state system of schools. Congress gave to new states a generous grant of national land and, in addition, three townships of land to endow a state university. It remains to be seen what Congress will do with the recommendation of the first White House Conference on Education held in November, 1955, for federal grants-in-aid to the states for education, especially for school buildings. For some time Congress has given grants to the states for vocational and agricultural education. The school lunch program, with federal funds and surplus commodities, is an outgrowth of depression legislation and administration. Early in the history of American education two principles were established: (1) the development of tax-supported, universally available schools, with freedom on the part of private individuals and groups to provide religious and nonsectarian educational facilities; (2) the control of education by the states and not by the federal government. Compulsory school attendance, based on the theories that every child needs an education and that since the taxpayer is required to provide schools the child must attend, came later.

Although a parent has no statutory responsibility to send his child to school beyond the compulsory attendance age, suits have been brought to test whether or not a higher education can be considered a necessary and by whom such a suit can be brought. More than a hundred years ago, in an 1844 Vermont case, the court held that a college education was not a necessary, but that a good common school education was fully recognized as a necessary for an infant.[90] Probably, the prevailing rule today is that a college education may be a necessary, and whether or not it is depends upon the circumstances and the standards of the parents. A Pennsylvania court held that a court order for the support of a deserted child might include such schooling as the father's financial ability and station in life indicated and as the child's ability, progress, and prospects would render useful.[91]

Today, every American jurisdiction has statutes providing for compulsory school attendance of children between certain ages, and for

---

[89] Cubberly, *op. cit.*, pp. 496 ff.

[90] *Middlebury College* v. *Chandler*, 16 Vt. 683 (1844).

[91] *Commonwealth ex rel. Smith* v. *Gilmore*, 95 Pa. Sup. Ct. 557 (1929), 97 Pa. Sup. Ct. 303 (1929).

penalties when parents willfully fail to send their children to school. Mississippi was the last state to enact such a law in 1920. The parent is thus forced to do without the child's services and to maintain him while the state pays for his education. In several jurisdictions the statutes include the duty of education in connection with the broad provision requiring parents to support.[92] Failure to carry out this duty brings many parents before juvenile courts. In some jurisdictions statutes provide that the father, or the father and mother jointly, have control of the education of the minor, except that they must adhere to the compulsory school laws. Some states make it a crime for the parent to neglect to provide proper education for the child.

EDUCATION FOR MINORITY GROUPS

Racial segregation in public schools has long presented problems to the entire country. Inferior facilities and poorly prepared staff are not the only evil results. The superiority and inferiority feelings generated by discrimination in all phases of life, including education, provide sources of anxiety and guilt, hate and resistance for majority and minority groups. The unanimous decision handed down by the United States Supreme Court in 1954 is a milestone in the attempt of the American people to mitigate the evil results of racial discrimination in education.[93] By this decision, delivered by Chief Justice Warren, "separate educational facilities are inherently unequal." Therefore, state legislation providing for racial discrimination in public schools is in violation of individual rights guaranteed by the equal protection clause of the Fourteenth Amendment and the due process clause of the Fifth Amendment (as to the District of Columbia). The crux of the decision was the court's refusal to subscribe to the "separate but equal" doctrine which it had laid down in an earlier decision, *Plessy* v. *Ferguson.*[94] It refused to be satisfied with the provision of equal buildings, books, and budgets and insisted that constitutional protection of the individual must extend to his status, his self-respect, and to community relationships.

This decision imposes a responsibility upon many states to reorganize their public school systems. It did not spell out the details of method by which nonsegregated education must be effectuated. The consideration of appropriate relief was subordinated to the primary question, the constitutionality of segregation in public education.

On the question of relief the court requested further argument. In view of the nationwide importance of the decision, the court invited the attorney general of the United States and the attorney generals of all states

[92] Jernegan, "Compulsory and Free Education . . ." *loc. cit.,* p. 411; Vernier, *op. cit.,* Vol. 4, pp. 63–64.
[93] *Brown et al.* v. *Board of Education of Topeka et al.,* 347 U.S. 483.
[94] 163 U.S. 537 (1896).

requiring or permitting racial discrimination in public education to present their views on the question. In 1955 the United States and the states of Florida, North Carolina, Arkansas, Oklahoma, Maryland, and Texas did so. Chief Justice Warren again delivered the opinion of the Court. School authorities, he wrote, have the primary responsibility for elucidating, assessing, and solving local educational problems. The courts will have to consider whether the action of school authorities constitutes good faith implementation of the governing constitutional principle. Because of their proximity to local conditions and the possible need for further hearings, the courts which originally heard the cases can best perform this judicial appraisal. Accordingly, the United States Supreme Court remanded the cases to those courts. In fashioning and carrying out their decrees, continued Chief Justice Warren, the courts will be guided by equitable principles characterized by a practical flexibility in shaping remedies and by a facility for adjusting and reconciling public and private ends. "But it should go without saying that the vitality of these constitutional principles cannot be allowed to yield simply because of disagreement with them. At stake is the personal interest of the plaintiffs' in admission to public schools as soon as practicable on a nondiscriminatory basis." [95]

These two decisions prick out the essential shape of public policy concerning segregated education and leave the details of implementation to localities and states. Progress in some communities has already been considerable; in many it will be slow. In some places there has already been mob violence and bloodshed. State and district federal courts, however, are charged with a responsibility for reasonable realization of the policy of nonsegregated public schools.[96]

SUMMARY

From this brief review of educational policies in the United States it is clear that parents today must educate their children up to some legally specified age or grade or both. Since free educational facilities are universally available, the duty is no longer primarily a moral but an enforceable one. Enforcement of the obligation of the child to attend and of the parent to see that he attends school is a requirement of compulsory attendance laws, of the parental neglect provisions of juvenile court legislation, and, sometimes, of criminal laws. Beyond the compulsory school attendance age, the courts will exercise their discretion in civil suits to determine whether "higher education" is a necessary. With great variation between states, many additional services are provided

[95] *Brown et al.* v. *Board of Education of Topeka et al.*, 349 U.S. 294 (1955).

[96] For report of conditions in seventeen southern and border states, see "Report on the South: The Integration Issue," *New York Times* (March 13, 1956).

school children from tax money. Separate public educational facilities for minority groups, even though they may be equal to those provided white groups, are on the way out.

PRIVILEGES AND DISABILITIES OF INFANCY [97]

Certain legal conditions are attendant upon the infant by reason of his infancy. Some of these conditions are privileges which, before modern legislation was enacted, somewhat mitigated the disheartening conditions told above. Several of the privileges and disabilities of infancy are briefly stated here merely to introduce the student to the subject.

At common law an infant is any minor under twenty-one, but by statutes in some states, girls attain their majority at eighteen and minors do so by marriage. Legislation may establish a lower age than twenty-one as majority for some purposes and maintain the common-law age for others. In the absence of statutes setting up another age for reaching majority, an infant is legally twenty-one at the first moment of the day preceding the twenty-first anniversary of his birth.

Under certain circumstances an infant can enforce a contract against another party, and he may disaffirm a contract before or after reaching majority, except for necessaries. Infants are responsible for their torts, or some of them, and they may sue for torts committed against them. At common law a parent has the right to maintain an action against one who injures his child, but he is not liable for the torts of his child committed without his knowledge and authority, express or implied. If a parent authorizes his child to act as his servant or agent, he then becomes liable for torts committed by the child in the course of employment; but the liability does not depend upon the parent-child relationship. Present concern for the vandalism of young people has caused many persons to urge legislation imposing financial responsibilities for damages upon parents. Some individuals also favor legislation to permit the requirement of restitution by the child in the discretion of the juvenile judge.

The automobile has created a problem in regard to the torts of children. The extent of a father's liability for his child's negligent driving has caused a split in court decisions. Some hold that the automobile creates a special problem and that financial responsibility for its use by a member of the family should be assumed by the owner. This "family-purpose" doctrine includes minor and adult children if they are members

[97] For material in this section, see Madden, *op. cit.*, pp. 527–614; Blackstone, *Commentaries,* Bk. 1, p. 463; Kent, *Commentaries,* Vol. 2, p. 255. This brief statement of the law of torts and contracts as relating to infants is oversimplified; for a fuller statement on this technical subject, see Madden or any of the legal encyclopedias and texts.

of the owner's household. The opposite view has been held on the theory that the child is competent to handle the machine.

At common law an infant under seven was exempt from criminal responsibility for his acts, and between seven and fourteen it was necessary to prove criminal intent. Beyond fourteen he was treated as an adult. Today, within certain ages named by statute, he is brought before a juvenile court and treated as a child needing protection, not punishment. This subject we shall further discuss in subsequent chapters on juvenile and youthful offenders. A parent is not responsible for his child's crimes to which he is in no way party.

At common law an infant could not sue except through his guardian. By an early English statute infants were authorized to sue by their next friend. This is true today in England and the United States. Every court in which suit is brought against an infant has the power to appoint a person to defend him, called guardian *ad litem.*

By both common-law and public-assistance statutes the infant's domicile is that of his father, if he is legitimate, or of his mother, if he is illegitimate or if she is a widow. There is considerable variation concerning his domicile when he is the child of divorced parents. Very little statutory material exists relating to domicile of minor children except under the financial assistance laws. The emancipation of an infant by act of the parents or by marriage removes some of the disabilities of infancy, but it does not enlarge his capacity to contract or to sue without a next friend or guardian.

SUMMARY AND CONCLUSIONS

This review shows clearly that the common-law courts enforced the English father's rights but not his duties. The equity court afforded recourse for those minors and their mothers who, by reason of wealth, could get into that court. Today legislation in both England and the United States has in large measure corrected the inequalities existing between the rights of father and mother and of parent and child. Through one department or another the state now undertakes to enforce every legal duty of parents.

The modern movement to enact legislation for the special needs and rights of children was not begun until the nineteenth century, and the twentieth century has seen more advance in this field than did the previous hundred years. In England and in the United States the establishment of definite legal rights for the child first appeared in the negative form of the curtailment of the rights of others to govern the child.[98]

---

[98] Elsie Glück, "Child Welfare Legislation," *Encyclopaedia of the Social Sciences* (1930), Vol. 3, pp. 424–428.

This meant primarily that the rights of the father were restricted and those of the mother and child were increased. It was not until the twentieth century that child-welfare legislation showed much interest in causes.

In the last half century legislation has broadened to include not only state protection for children abused by their parents but health, labor, and compulsory school legislation; special provisions for the handicapped or mentally defective and retarded child; greater consideration for the unmarried mother and her child; the establishment of the juvenile court to protect all children in need of care but especially the neglected or delinquent child; and more and better administrative facilities for the inspection and supervision of public and private, state and local agencies concerned with children.

No longer can the father do with his child whatever he wishes. Now, both parents must provide wholesome surroundings for the child whose custody they have. They must support him, send him to school, keep him from working until a specified age, so that he may receive an education and enjoy a wholesome leisure. They must protect him from harmful conditions, such as exposure to communicable disease, and must help him maintain health. Parents, in other words, have both a personal and a social responsibility to their children that the state requires them to perform.

Selected References

ABBOTT, Grace, *The Child and the State* (Chicago, University of Chicago Press, 1938), Vols. 1 and 2.

BLACKSTONE, Sir William, *Commentaries on the Laws of England in Four Books* (Philadelphia, Rees, Welsh, and Co., 1897), Bk. 1.

BRECKINRIDGE, S. P., *The Family and the State* (Chicago, University of Chicago Press, 1934).

BRECKINRIDGE, S. P., and ABBOTT, Edith, *The Delinquent Child and the Home* (New York, Russell Sage Foundation, 1912).

FREDERICKSEN, Hazel, *The Child and His Welfare* (San Francisco; W. H. Freeman and Co., 1948).

GARNETT, W. H. Stuart, *Children and the Law* (London, John Murray, 1911).

HARPER, Fowler V., *Problems of the Family* (Indianapolis, Bobbs-Merrill, 1952).

KENT, James, *Commentaries on American Law* (Boston, Little, Brown, 1896), Vol. 2.

LUNDBERG, Emma O., *Unto the Least of These* (New York, Appleton-Century-Crofts, Inc., 1947).

MADDEN, Joseph W., *Persons and Domestic Relations* (St. Paul, Minn., West Publishing Co., 1931).

Schouler, James W., *Marriage, Divorce, Separation, and Domestic Relations*, 6th ed. (Albany, N.Y., Matthew Bender and Co., 1921), Vol. 1, Pt. 3.

Vernier, Chester G., and others, *American Family Laws* (Stanford, Cal., Stanford University Press, 1931–1938), Vol. 4.

The student should also consult pertinent statutes and judicial decisions and the law encyclopedias.

CHAPTER 10

Guardianship of Children

INTRODUCTION

Legal writers tell us that the necessity of guardians flows from the inability of infants to take care of themselves so far as the law is concerned. The law of infancy invests the child with the legal status of a minor. It confers privileges upon him and imposes disabilities, all for the primary purpose of his protection. The law of guardianship is an old legal method for providing over-all protection of the child while in minority status. At many periods in history the law of guardian and ward has been more concerned with the child's property rights and with the profitable rights of the guardian than with the person of the child. Although this may often be true in practice today, the fact remains that the intent of the modern law of guardian and ward is the welfare of the child. The legal relationship is viewed as one of trust and imposes upon natural or legally appointed guardians the responsibility of acting for the best interests of the child. In this chapter we shall discuss the law of guardian and ward only as it relates to infants, although parenthetically the responsibilities of guardians to "idiots and lunatics" or to "spendthrifts," "alcoholics," or "drug addicts" are, in many respects, similar to those of guardians of minors.

DEFINITIONS

In general, the guardianship of infants is with their parents, who are called "natural guardians." However, there are other kinds of guardians: Testamentary guardians, or those named by the will of parents; guardians appointed by the courts for protection of the person and property of the infant; and temporary, or *ad litem,* guardians appointed by the courts for a particular suit or piece of litigation. Guardians, in other words, may be the parents or some person legally chosen to act in their behalf. For our purposes in this chapter "a guardian is a person to whom the law has entrusted the custody and control of the person or estate, or both, of an infant, whose youth, inexperience, and mental weakness disqualify him for acting for himself in the ordinary affairs of life." [1]

---

[1] James W. Schouler, *Marriage, Divorce, Separation and Domestic Relations,* 6th ed. (Albany, N.Y., Matthew Bender and Co., 1921), Vol. 1, Pt. 4, secs. 810–992;

The relationship of guardian and ward is usually considered to be the legal substitute for that of parent and child. Many of the rights, remedies, and responsibilities of the legally appointed guardian are similar to those of the natural guardian of the child, but there are differences. The parent must himself support his child and, in turn, is entitled to his child's services and earnings. The guardian is not required to supply the needs of his ward, except from the ward's estate, and he is not entitled to the labor of the ward. The parent is guardian of his child's person but not of his estate. The guardian is usually appointed to have management of the estate and is often given custody of the child. Guardianship does not take away the child's right to inherit from his own parents; nor does it give him that right in relation to his guardian.

RESOURCES OF THE COURTS

Inasmuch as the relation of guardian and ward is a substitute for that of parent and child, any court which has the responsibility of appointing or approving a guardian needs facilities for wise selection and effective supervision. American and English laws are deficient in that they do not require that every orphan have a guardian and that the courts be furnished with facilities for the exercise of sound discretion in deciding who shall have custody of the infant and administration of his estate and whether the guardian is wise in the performance of his duties. Guardianship matters concerning infants are brought before courts in several types of situations:

1. Where the child is dependent, neglected, delinquent.
2. In divorce and separation cases.
3. Where the child is defective or diseased.
4. Where there is an altercation between parents and/or relatives, or when one or both parents are disabled.
5. Where a testamentary guardian has been named.

J. G. Woerner, *A Treatise on the American Law of Guardianship of Minors and Persons of Unsound Mind* (Boston, Little, Brown, 1897); see also, 28 C.J. 1058; A. C. Jacobs, "Guardianship," *Encyclopaedia of the Social Sciences* (1932), Vol. 7, pp. 192–195; Frederick Pollock and F. W. Maitland, *The History of English Law Before the Time of Edward I* (Boston, Little, Brown, 1895), Vol. 2, pp. 434–445; Joseph W. Madden, *Persons and Domestic Relations* (St. Paul, Minn., West Publishing Co., 1931), chs. 11–13; James Kent, *Commentaries on American Law* (Boston, Little, Brown, 1896), Vol. 2, pp. 220–232; Edward Jenks, *A Short History of the English Law* (London, Methuen, 1912), p. 26; W. S. Holdsworth, *History of English Law*, 3d ed. (Boston, Little, Brown, 1923), Vol. 3, ch. 4. For the best discussion of this subject from the viewpoint of the social worker and sociologist, read Hasseltine Byrd Taylor, *Law of Guardian and Ward* (Chicago, University of Chicago Press, 1935); S. P. Breckinridge, *The Family and the State* (Chicago, University of Chicago Press, 1934), pp. 282–342; Mary A. Stanton, "The Administration of the Law of Guardian and Ward with Special Reference to Minors: Cook County, Illinois" (Doctoral dissertation, University of Chicago, 1943); Irving Weissman and others, *Guardianship: A Way of Fulfilling Public Responsibility for Children*, U.S. Children's Bureau Publication (Washington, D.C., G.P.O., 1949), No. 330.

6. Upon the death of one or both parents when there is property or when relatives are in dispute.

7. Where the parents are living but where the child is the owner of property.

Juvenile courts are established to deal with the first type of case. The court with divorce jurisdiction acts in the second instance. In the third situation the court with jurisdiction may be the juvenile, probate, or some other court. In the remaining four types of cases the probate court generally exercises jurisdiction. In this chapter we are primarily, although not exclusively, discussing guardianship law as practiced in probate courts. Juvenile courts are presumed to have the resources of the probation officer to enable them to act for the welfare of the child and in the interests of the state. This officer, acting as an arm of the court, helps determine who shall have custody and guardianship of children brought before it. Divorce courts, unless they are a part of a domestic-relations court, generally lack facilities to make wise decisions regarding the custody and guardianship of the children involved. Probate courts are usually without resources to determine who should be guardian.

Statutes require guardians to report to the court on the management of the ward's property, but the courts are not required to follow up the kind of surroundings in which the child lives. Competent supervision of guardians would protect children from unwise influences and would enable the relationship of guardian and ward to be a genuine substitute for that of parent and child. Social service facilities are essential if the courts are intelligently to determine who shall be guardian, whether he is unselfishly interested in his ward's personal welfare, whether he provides a happy, normal home, and whether he administers the estate with conscience and wisdom. Courts with guardianship jurisdiction should act, in other words, not only as judicial but as social agencies. At present, it is well established that the relation of guardian and ward is for the benefit and protection of the ward and the state has the duty to see that the infant's interests are protected; but without means to exercise this authority, only in theory are the child's best interests assured.

CIVIL AND COMMON-LAW GUARDIANS

ROMAN LAW [2]

Under Roman law the relation of guardian and ward was of a simple and uniform nature; every child had a guardian. The head of the family had great authority, *patriae potestas*, which extended to life and death

[2] J. G. Woerner, *op. cit.*, p. 48; see also, W. W. Buckland, *A Text Book of Roman Law* (London, Cambridge University Press, 1921), ch. 4; "Roman Law," *Encyclopaedia Britannica*, 14th ed. (1952), Vol. 19, pp. 447–454; Edward Gibbon, *The Decline and Fall of the Roman Empire*, ed. J. B. Bury (London, Methuen, 1925), Vol. 4,

over infants. Upon the death of the head of the family, the child was required to have a guardian. Both his person and property were trusted to the protection of some discreet friend. If the deceased father had not indicated his choice, then the agnate, or paternal kin of nearest degree, was required to so act.

Guardianship, or *tutela,* had to do with males under fourteen and females under twelve. Puberty *ipso facto* ended the authority of the tutor and the wardship of the pupil. Adults or those who had arrived at the age of puberty, called minors, had curators assigned to them, until they reached twenty-five years, or full majority, in two types of situations: (1) when the minor himself agreed to it, and (2) when the persons who had matters to settle with the minors procured their appointment.

Tutela or guardianship could be given by will, by operation of law, or by appointment of the magistrate. The *tutela* was terminated by emancipation of the pupil, by some supervening incapacity, by legally accepted resignation, and by removal on formal complaint. The tutor's duties related to the care and management of the pupil's property and his custody and education. The tutor always rendered an account of his acts for his pupil, and want of diligence was ground for criminal action for violation of his sacred trust.

The Roman tutor has been described as the person in charge of the maintenance and education of the minor, and the curator as the custodian of his fortune, although sometimes the two were united. Apparently a better way of differentiating the functions of the two is to say that the tutor had authority over younger children, and the curator over older children in certain instances. All children under Roman law had guardians, whether they were their *pater familias,* who were virtually family chiefs, or their father, or another person in case of his death.

ENGLISH LAW

Pollock and Maitland, writing on English guardianship law, point to the fact that no part of the old law was more disjointed and incomplete than that which dealt with the guardianship of infants: [3]

> When it issued from the middle ages it knew some ten kinds of guardians, and yet it had never laid down any such rule as that there is or ought to be a guardian for every infant. It had been thinking almost exclusively of infant heirs, and had left other infants to shift for themselves and to get guardians as best they might from time to time for the purpose of litigation. The law had not even been careful to give the father a right to the custody of his children; on the

pp. 483–484; "The Twelve Tables of Roman Law and the Institutes of Justinian," Bk. I, titles 13–26, in David Nasmith, *Outline of Roman History* (London, Butterworth, 1890); Sir William Blackstone, *Commentaries on the Laws of England in Four Books* (Philadelphia, Rees, Welsh, and Co., 1897), Bk. 1, pp. 459–466.

[3] Pollock and Maitland, *op. cit.,* Vol. 2, pp. 441–443.

other hand, it had given him a right to the custody of his heir apparent, whose marriage he was free to sell. It had looked at guardianship and paternal power merely as profitable rights, and had only sanctioned them when they could be made profitable. . . . The law, at all events, the temporal law, was not at pains to designate any permanent guardian for children who owned no land.

This absence of a comprehensive law of guardianship was the less necessary, said these writers, because the English guardian, different from the civil-law guardian, was not a person "whose consent will enable the infant to do acts which he otherwise could not have done."

The history of English guardianship can be divided into the periods before and after 1660. That before 1660 deals with feudal and borough guardianship; that subsequent to 1660 is largely derived from statutes. The early English theory of guardianship developed out of the feudal system. With the conquest of England by William came the application of the already recognized principle of the right of lordship to the occupation of land.[4] The great nobles held of the king and so with his under vassals down to the lord of the petty manor. The universal formula was *A tenet de B;* and this relationship between lord and tenant was called *tenure.*

The father was the natural guardian of his infant heir and the guardian by nurture of his younger children. If the father died, the question of who was the child's guardian depended upon the nature of the property which he inherited or the kind of tenure which had existed between his father and the next higher noble. For the ordinary orphan who was not an heir, the common law had no general rules regarding guardianship. The ecclesiastical courts helped in some instances, particularly if the infant had personal property, but in general when legal proceedings were necessary, a guardian *ad litem* was appointed. "It may be that here as elsewhere the king was considered to be the guardian of the orphan; but in the middle ages and long after he took no steps to assume the responsibilities of that position unless the infant had property or unless he was involved in litigation." [5]

TYPES OF GUARDIAN [6]

There were ten types of guardianship that emerged from the Middle Ages:

1. In chivalry.
2. In socage.
3. By nature and for nurture.
4. Ecclesiastical.
5. By special custom.

---

[4] Jenks, *op. cit.*, p. 27.
[5] Holdsworth, *op. cit.*, Vol. 3, p. 512.
[6] Schouler, *op. cit.*, Vol. 1, pp. 812 ff.

6. By election of the infant.
7. By prerogative.
8. *Ami prochein* and *ad litem.*
9. Testamentary or statutory.
10. Chancery guardians.

A brief description of these forms of guardianship is included so as to facilitate comparisons between old and new theory and practice.

In Chivalry. This form arose out of the right of the feudal lord to services of his tenant as a soldier or knight. If the tenant died while performing this service, leaving a male heir under twenty-one years of age or a female heir under fourteen years of age, the lord had custody of the child's person and the right to the income from the estate. This was recompense for the loss of the tenant's services as a knight. An oppressive incident of this form of guardianship was the right of the lord to the disposal of such heir in marriage. This originated out of the "reasonable claim of the lord that his (the tenant's) duties of service should not be lost by the inability of an infant to render them, and that an infant heiress should not, by marrying the lord's enemy, introduce a foe into his household."[7] This oppressive form of tenure and guardianship was abolished in 1660 with the whole structure of military tenures.

In Socage. This type arose out of socage tenure instead of tenure by *knight service.* Whenever an infant under fourteen years of age inherited an estate in *socage,*[8] his nearest relative to whom the estate itself could not descend was guardian of the land until the infant arrived at the age of fourteen, when the trust terminated. The service was largely agricultural, as by the payment of rent or by corporal service, such as plowing the lord's land for a specified number of days. It was for the benefit of the ward, the chief object being the protection of the property and the instruction of the young heir in the pursuit of agriculture. The duty of the guardian was to receive the rents and profits until the heir was fourteen, to keep his title clear, and to bring him up well.

By Nature and for Nurture. Guardianship *by nature* applied to the eldest son who, under the English system of primogeniture, was sole heir, and it continued until he was twenty-one years of age; guardianship *for nurture* extended to all the other children and terminated when the ward reached fourteen, if a boy, and sixteen, if a girl. Both these kinds of guardianship conferred control of the person only and gave the father no authority over the child's property.

Ecclesiastical and Others. There has been much dispute as to the ancient right of the *ecclesiastical* courts to appoint guardians, but it seems that such a right existed as to appointment for the personal estate and,

---

[7] Jenks, *op. cit.,* p. 34.

[8] Socage is the holding of lands in consideration of certain inferior services of husbandry to be performed by the tenant to the lord.

sometimes, for the person also. Guardianship by *special custom* was a species peculiar to a particular manor. Guardianship *by election of the infant* arose when he found himself wholly unprovided with a guardian. Today, statutes give infants over fourteen the right to elect their guardians. *Guardianship by prerogative,* since it applied only to the royal family does not concern us, but it apparently resulted from the authority of the king as *parens patriae.* Guardians *ami prochein* and *ad litem* had neither custody nor management of the ward's estate but were appointed by the court when the infant was the plaintiff or defendant in a suit and for the duration of the suit. Testamentary guardians and chancery guardians will be discussed below.

During the Middle Ages not all of England was in feudal territory. These towns and boroughs had their own customs, one of which was borough guardianship. A father could exercise the privilege of naming a testamentary guardian. If the father did not do so, some public authority took jurisdiction over wards and their estates, and it was termed the orphans' court. The court-appointed guardian acted under supervision of the court and was obliged to act for the benefit of the orphan. Borough guardians functioned more like chancery-appointed guardians and like guardians of the present day; they acted for the welfare of the infant, were required to report to a court, and could be held accountable for their actions.

Statutory and Chancery. By the statute of 1660 entitled "An act for taking away the court of wards and liveries, and tenures in capite, and by knights' service, and purveyance, and for settling a revenue upon his Majesty in lieu thereof," military tenures and all other feudal tenures with the incidents connected with them were abolished.[9] In abolishing feudal tenures this act, of course, did away with feudal forms of guardianship. It substituted testamentary guardianship, which gave the father absolute authority to dispose of the custody after his death and of the person and estate of his infant heir until he was twenty-one. No provision was made for guaranteeing the administration of the guardianship as a trust.

After this seventeenth-century legislation and until the nineteenth century most of the changes in English guardianship law occurred by judicial decision. The authority of the chancellor to meet situations where the common law did not provide adequate relief was extended to the management of estates of deceased persons and, later, to the guardianships of infants. The earliest known instance of the appointment by chancery of a guardian for an infant occurred in 1696.[10] By the eighteenth century the authority of the chancellor to act for the king in the appointment of guardians for infants was well established. The *Eyre* v. *Shafts-*

---

[9] 12 Chas. II, c. 24.

[10] Schouler, *op. cit.,* Vol. 2, p. 913.

bury case, as we saw in the preceding chapter, established two principles: (1) that the king was the ultimate guardian of all infants and lunatics, and (2) that when the father devised a joint guardianship, the authority of the remaining guardians upon the death of one was superior to that of the mother.[11] Although the chancery court had the authority to appoint a guardian for any infant, this power was seldom exercised, except for children with property. The *Wellesley* case gave judicial recognition to the king's responsibility for all children, but the court admitted that this power was exercised only when it had funds with which to act.[12] An 1839 act gave the mother the right of access to her child under seven.[13] Not until 1925 were father and mother equal in their right to the custody of their children, the welfare of these being paramount.[14]

GUARDIANSHIP IN THE UNITED STATES

EARLY BACKGROUND

Guardianship history in the United States differs considerably from that of England. Guardians in this country are statutory officers, having no inherent powers but only such as are prescribed by statute. Theoretically, they have always existed for the benefit of the child. Although chancery courts and chancery jurisdiction became a part of our judicial organization, a specially created court rather than the equity court has been prevalently accepted as the one to look after guardianship matters. At the time that America was being colonized, chancery guardianship was unknown in England. Our colonial ancestors were familiar with control of the estates of orphans and their deceased parents by the ecclesiastical courts. These forefathers completely rejected the idea of a spiritual court and so distributed probate and equity powers among the common-law courts. With the growth of population special probate courts were established, and to these courts went business pertaining to estates of the dead, testamentary trusts, and the care of orphans, thus blending ecclesiastical and equity functions. In time, some states gave this jurisdiction to courts of equity as they developed, some to probate courts, and some to both equity and probate courts.[15]

By the nineteenth century most of the states had brought their guardian and ward laws together in one act or chapter which covered the matter comprehensively.[16] Those laws provided (1) that guardianship matters be under the jurisdiction of a special court; (2) for testa-

---

[11] 2 P. Wms. 103, 24 Eng. Rep. 659 (1722).
[12] *Wellesley* v. *Beaufort,* 2 Russ. 21, 38 Eng. Rep. 236 (1827).
[13] 2 and 3 Vict., c. 54.
[14] 15 and 16 Geo. V, c. 45.
[15] Schouler, *op. cit.,* Vol. 1, sec. 818.
[16] Taylor, *op. cit.,* p. 25. As an example, see Wis. Stat., 1957, ch. 319.

mentary guardianship in all states except Iowa; and (3) for administrative details, particularly relating to the protection of the child's estate. In the last century the only important changes in our guardianship law as it pertains to parents have been recognition of the rights of the mother in her children, restriction of the father's power of testamentary appointment, and removal of the disabilities for guardianship of married women. The only fundamental change in the guardianship law pertaining to third parties has come through the juvenile court, which has been given the authority and the means to terminate parental rights and to appoint guardians for dependent, neglected, and delinquent children.

TYPES OF GUARDIAN

By Nature. Since primogeniture never extended to this country, parents are the natural guardians of *all* their children. There never has been a place for the old guardian *by nature* or guardian for the apparent heir. Our guardianship by nature is not confined to the apparent heir but extends to all the children during their minority or until the age of twenty-one. Neither is there any place in our law for guardian *by nurture,* which at common law lasted only until the infant reached the age of fourteen years. Guardianship by nature in the United States has usually meant that the father was recognized as the natural guardian of his legitimate children during their minority. Upon the death of the father, or upon his being adjudged unfit, guardianship passed to the mother. Now numbers of states by statute declare the parents to be joint natural guardians of their minor children, with equal powers, rights, and duties in regard to them.

In England there was conflict of authority as to whether the mother was the natural guardian of her illegitimate children. However, the courts in granting custody of illegitimate children usually considered the wishes of the mother first—providing such wishes were not to the detriment of the welfare of the child.[17] Today, in England and the United States, the unmarried mother is guardian of her child.

The right of the natural guardian to the custody and control of the ward is subject to control by the courts. Unfitness or misconduct can defeat the natural guardian's right of custody and control, since the child's welfare is the supreme consideration and prevails over any legal rights of the guardian. "However, it is not enough to consider the child's welfare alone. The father, no matter how humble and poor, if he be of good moral character and able to support the child in his style of life, cannot be deprived of the privilege." [18] At common law the natural guardian had no right or control over the property of his ward,

---

[17] *Barnardo* v. *McHugh,* Law Rep. App. Cases 388 (1891).
[18] *Hernandez* v. *Thomas,* 50 Fla. 522, 39 So. 641 (1905).

simply over his person.[19] This is followed by statute in most states. Thus, the natural guardian cannot collect and discharge claims due the ward, make contracts regarding the ward's estate, and so forth, unless appointed by the court of appropriate jurisdiction.

Testamentary. The 1660 act abolishing feudal tenures allowed a father in his lifetime to dispose of the custody of his infant children by deed or will. Where this statute was followed in the United States the power to appoint a testamentary guardian was in the father only.[20] The father's right to appoint a testamentary guardian might be lost by abandoning the child or by legally committing its custody and control to others. This form of guardianship statute was enacted in all the states except Iowa, where by judicial decision "the express wishes of the parent, especially when made shortly before death, will have influence with the court and will determine the appointment." [21]

Generally this form of guardianship continues till the age of twenty-one, even though the infant be a female and marry, although the old cases on this latter point are not clear. It has been held that the authority of the testamentary guardian requires no confirmation by the court,[22] but the better view is that although a guardian nominated by will is entitled ordinarily to appointment, his appointment, duties, and powers are governed by the general law regulating guardians.[23] Some statutes expressly require the approval of the court to the appointment of the testamentary guardian and that he be subject to all the restraints of a court-named guardian. Of course, this is desirable.

Greater regard for the rights of women and children has led to the adoption of statutes in both England and the United States equalizing the rights of the father and mother to the custody of their children, and this rule applies also to the testamentary guardianship. In some states the privilege goes only to the surviving parent, whether father or mother. Most states limit the power of appointing testamentary guardians to the surviving parent, or to either, if the other has abandoned the home or is incompetent.[24] With the written consent of the mother, the father may, by will, appoint guardians for the persons or the estate or both in several states. Testamentary guardianships, unless limited by will, extend to the person and estate of the ward.[25] The unmarried mother may appoint a testamentary guardian for her child.

By Judicial Appointment. In the United States, the power to ap-

---

[19] Madden, *op. cit.*, p. 457.

[20] *Ibid.*, pp. 459–461.

[21] *In re O'Connell*, 102 Iowa 355, 71 N.W. 211 (1897); *In re Johnson*, 87 Iowa 130, 52 N.W. 69 (1893); Taylor, *op. cit.*, p. 36.

[22] *Norris* v. *Harris*, 15 Calif. 226 (1860).

[23] *Henicle, Adm'x.* v. *Flack, Guardian*, 3 Ohio App. 444 (1914).

[24] Taylor, *op. cit.*, p. 37.

[25] Madden, *op. cit.*, p. 460; Taylor, *op. cit.*, p. 40.

point permanent guardians when there is no question of the dependency, neglect, or delinquency of the child, in which instances the juvenile court has jurisdiction, is prevalently exercised by special courts variously entitled probate, orphans', or surrogate's courts. These courts perform the function of the English equity courts in regard to guardianship or of the ecclesiastical courts of an earlier period. Practically speaking, the power to appoint guardians for infants, except in divorce actions or when the child is neglected, dependent, or delinquent, is confined to these statutory courts.[26]

Guardians are appointed on the petition of any interested person to the court with jurisdiction. The child's domicile determines jurisdiction.[27] Interested persons, including the person having custody and the minor over fourteen, are given notice to appear at the hearing. At the hearing any person may present facts and may object to the appointment of any particular persons. If there is only one petitioner, frequently he is made guardian. If more than one person seeks the guardianship, the child's welfare controls. Some states list persons who may not be guardians, such as clerks, sheriffs, and probable heirs, except parents.

The selection of a guardian is in the discretion of the court having jurisdiction and is the most important function of the court since much of the relationship of guardian and ward cannot be regulated by statute.[28] The welfare of the infant is the primary consideration and this is often difficult to determine when relatives from both sides seek guardianship.[29] To avoid friction the court will usually appoint one person as guardian for both the person and the property of the ward.[30] Sometimes this tendency creates great confusion, as when the property is in one state and the domicile of the child in another, since in the former situation the law of the state where the property is located controls, and in the latter, the law where the child is domiciled. The United States Supreme Court has held that: "The legislature of the state where the property is situated has power to pass laws for the appointment of guardians of the property of nonresident infants, situate in that state, and to prescribe the manner in which guardians shall perform their duties as regards the care, management, investment, and disposal of such property." [31]

It should be reiterated that our present system of selecting guardians is inadequate. Since there is no rule that minor orphans must be wards, such children without property are generally without guardians unless they have come to the attention of the courts because of dependency, neglect, or delinquency, or are in the custody of some charitable insti-

---

[26] Taylor, *op. cit.*, p. 104.
[27] *Polly A. de Jarnett* v. *Josiah Harper*, 45 Mo. A. 415 (1891).
[28] Madden, *op. cit.*, pp. 464–468.
[29] *Burger, By His Next Friend* v. *Frakes*, 67 Iowa 460 (1885).
[30] *Lawrence* v. *Thomas*, 84 Iowa 362, 51 N.W. 11 (1892).
[31] *Hoyt* v. *Sprague*, 103 U.S. 613, 26 L. Ed. 585 (1881).

tution or agency with whom their guardianship is placed or unless the relatives are in altercation. The indifference of the state and the expense of guardianship procedure result in the failure to select guardians for children without estates. Minors inheriting estates are often placed under the care of anyone who applies for the office of guardian unless more than one person seeks appointment. Once appointed, there is frequently little check on the way the child is cared for. If the ward is mistreated, he has little effectual remedy without costly legal action.

Guardians *ad litem* and *prochein ami* are different from the ordinary guardians because of their temporary nature and specific purpose. Statutory provisions concerning guardianship do not apply to them. Every court in which a suit is brought against an infant, has the power to appoint a person to defend him when he has no guardian, for, since an infant cannot appoint an attorney, he would otherwise be without assistance. Such a guardian's powers are limited to the particular situation for which the appointment is made.[32] The next friend, strictly speaking, is not appointed by the court to bring a suit but is simply one who volunteers for that purpose and is merely permitted to sue in behalf of the infant. The practice of suing by a next friend has been almost entirely superseded by the practice of appointing a guardian *ad litem*.

RELATION OF GUARDIAN AND WARD

RIGHTS AND DUTIES OF GUARDIAN REGARDING PERSON OF WARD

We shall speak here of the rights and duties of guardians by judicial appointment, since in Chapter 9 we reviewed the rights and responsibilities of natural guardians. Custody of the ward will ordinarily be given to his guardian, both as against strangers and as against relatives, but not as against parents unless they are unfit, and then the matter will probably come before the juvenile rather than the probate court.[33] Since statutory provisions regarding guardianship of the person are noticeably brief, it falls upon the courts to interpret the extent of the rights and duties of the guardian.

A guardian cannot by contract bind the ward's person or property unless authorized by statute.[34] He is personally liable on contracts which he makes on behalf of the ward, but in proper cases, as for necessities, he is entitled to reimbursement.[35] A guardian is bound to maintain and educate his ward from the income of the estate, but he is not bound to furnish support, and no promise on his part will be implied, without his consent,

[32] Madden, *op. cit.*, p. 464.
[33] *Coltman* v. *Hall*, 31 Me. 196 (1850); *The People ex rel. Wilcox*, 22 Barb. Ch. 178 (1854); *Bellmore* v. *McLeod*, 189 Wis. 431, 207 N.W. 699 (1926).
[34] *Aborn et al.* v. *Janis et al.*, 62 Misc. N.Y. 95, 113 N.Y.S. 309 (1907).
[35] Madden, *op. cit.*, pp. 471–514.

to pay even for necessaries furnished the ward. When the guardian finds the income of the ward's estate insufficient for his maintenance, it is the guardian's duty to submit the whole matter to the consideration of the court and to act under its directions. By the weight of authority, when the ward lives with the guardian as a member of his family receiving support and rendering the ordinary services of a child, the guardian is not entitled to an allowance for such support, in the absence of agreement, the relative being in such case quasi-parental.[36] When the family relation exists, whether natural or assumed, there is in the absence of an express agreement, or circumstances from which an agreement may be fairly inferred, no implied obligation to pay for board, on the one hand, or for work, on the other.

Generally speaking, an infant must answer for his torts as fully as an adult. The liability of the guardian, like that of the parent, can be worked out if the tort of his infant ward was committed under circumstances in which the guardian knew that the infant might endanger the safety of others and did nothing to prevent it. Naturally this would apply only to cases where guardianship of the person of the ward had been given.

RIGHTS AND DUTIES OF GUARDIAN REGARDING PROPERTY OF WARD

In view of the fact that infants are neither personally nor legally competent to transact business, it is essential that their estates, whether large or small, be competently administered.[37] The responsibilities of guardians in this connection are similar to those of executors and administrators. The statutes are generally very detailed in the restrictions placed upon guardians of estates, but often the courts are not careful in checking upon the activities of guardians.

The guardian necessarily has more freedom in the management of his ward's personal property than of his real property. In the absence of statutes to the contrary, he may sell his ward's personal property without court restraint. He has the duty of cautiously investing the funds of the ward not needed for maintenance and education. There is variation between statutes in the kind of investments that can be made. He may lease the real estate of his ward. Whether or not this requires court approval depends upon the statute.

The most carefully guarded phase of guardianship administration is management and sale of real estate. The guardian has no authority to sell real property without an order from a court of competent jurisdiction. Generally, his powers of mortgaging real property are limited to court authorization under statutes. Real estate may be sold only for the purposes named in the statute. Frequently the grounds upon which the court

---

[36] *Abrams* v. *U.S. Fidelity and Guaranty Co.*, 127 Wis. 579, 106 N.W. 109 (1906).
[37] *Effie Boardman* v. *Orton P. Ward,* 40 Minn. 399, 54 A.L.R. 551 (1889).

may deny the request for sale are specified, as when the title is in doubt, when the proceeds would not justify the sale, when it is not clearly for the benefit of the ward, and so forth.

Guardians must file reports or accounts from time to time as specified by statute, and the final account, when settled and allowed, is by weight of authority *res judicata* or conclusive. Before entering upon his duties, a guardian must swear to do his duties faithfully, and he must give bond if he is to be guardian of property. A large number of states require bond with one or more approved sureties. Sometimes the size of the bond is left to the discretion of the court, and sometimes it is designated.

TERMINATION OF GUARDIANSHIP

Guardianship may be terminated in the following ways: [38]

1. By the ward's reaching his majority. Testamentary guardianships, unless an earlier time is named in the appointment, and statute guardianships all terminate at majority.
2. By death of the ward. The guardianship is necessarily ended by the death of the ward, except, of course, for the adjusting of the accounts, etc.
3. By death of the guardian. The guardian's death terminates the guardianship. The executor of the ward or administrator has no right to act as guardian, but he must settle the accounts of the guardianship.
4. By marriage of a female ward. This terminates the guardianship under the statutes of some states, but in other jurisdictions the husband becomes a joint guardian.
5. By resignation of the guardian. The resignation terminates the relationship if it is allowed, but it does not take effect until a final accounting and a discharge by the courts.
6. By removal of the guardian. A guardian may be removed by the court where he fails to perform his duties or where he is unfit for the position.

All statutes mention specific causes for removal. Power to remove guardians is inherent in chancery courts. The power of removal now generally is vested by statutes in the same court having power to appoint guardians. Whether the statutes list few or many causes for removal, practically, removal is left to the discretion of the court and, unfortunately, the courts have no facilities for detecting situations justifying removal.

IMPACT OF GUARDIANSHIP ON THE SOCIAL SERVICES [39]

FEDERAL STUDY

A U.S. Children's Bureau study of guardianship in the courts of the six states of California, Connecticut, Florida, Louisiana, Michigan, and

---

[38] Madden, *op. cit.*, pp. 515–520; Taylor, *op. cit.*, pp. 149–157.
[39] Much of the material for this section is taken from Weissman, *op. cit.*

Missouri published in 1949, was primarily directed to finding the use made of legal guardianship procedure for protecting the persons and estates of children. It examined and described the philosophy behind guardianship; the historical background of guardianship; the current statutory provisions of the states studied; the relations of guardian and ward in typical situations; the characteristics of guardians and wards; the court of jurisdiction; the court processes of appointing, supervising, and discharging guardians; the court's use of social services; the cost of guardianship. Further, it reviewed the impact of guardianship on social service programs, especially on child-placement programs, on the aid-to-dependent-children programs, on federal benefit programs, including veterans' benefits and old-age and survivors benefits (OASI). We have already made brief reference to several of these items. It is to the matter of the social services and guardianship that we shall now give our attention. Most of our materials will be extracted from this federal study.

GUARDIANSHIP AND SOCIAL AGENCIES

Passage of the federal Social Security Act in 1935 provided the states with momentum for improving their services to children. Numbers of provisions of the act, which we shall discuss in Chapters 22–25, are designed directly or indirectly to benefit children. An important outgrowth of the act has been the increased attention given to problems of custody and guardianship. Public and private social agencies find that questions of legal guardianship are often involved in their work. We discuss these problems again in Chapter 25.

Placement service raises problems of guardianship, since removal of the child from his own home imposes temporary or permanent responsibility for his care upon the agency. If the parents personally request placement without any release of their ultimate guardianship rights, problems of care, custody and guardianship are at a minimum. When, however, children suffering from neglect or improper guardianship are either temporarily or permanently placed with an agency, usually by a juvenile court, many problems arise as to the extent of agency power and responsibility. If the order is for temporary care, the agency has responsibility for a short period of time with uncertain authority over such matters as emergency medical care, removal of the child from the jurisdiction of the court, work with the parents, and supervision of foster homes. If the order is for permanent care, agencies have often falsely assumed that they had complete guardianship responsibility. At times when they have assumed responsibility for such problems as administering the child's estate or for placing him in a permanent foster home, which may or may not lead to adoption, or for giving consent to an adoption, they have encountered objections from the court of commitment or from other courts and often from the parents.

In the absence of clearly stated statutory provisions as to what legal responsibilities are attendant upon temporary and permanent commitments or upon transfer of custody and legal guardianship, the agency may be placed in an ambiguous position. Some states have met this problem by providing for termination of parental rights and transfer of guardianship. After this has been done and permanent commitment or transfer of guardianship made to an agency, it is clear that the agency then has full guardianship responsibilities. Some states, in an effort to avoid uncertainties, are doing away with use of the terms *temporary commitment* and *permanent commitment* and are substituting *transfer of custody* and *transfer of guardianship.* Agencies also encounter difficulties when parents voluntarily release their children to an agency for the purpose of adoption. Some statutes provide, and some courts have held, that parents may transfer their rights and responsibilities to the child only through judicial procedure. The extent of the right of unmarried mothers to transfer guardianship of their children without judicial termination of parental rights or without consent in a judicial hearing for adoption is uncertain in some jurisdictions.

GUARDIANSHIP AND FEDERAL AID TO DEPENDENT CHILDREN (ADC)

All states in the union have programs for financial assistance to needy children who have been deprived of parental support or care by reason of the death, continued absence from the home, or physical or mental incapacity of the parent and who are living with one or both parents or with other specified relatives. Although many states had mother's pensions or aid-to-dependent-children programs before the enactment of the federal Social Security Act, that act has greatly expanded them. Information is unavailable concerning whether children not under parental care are voluntarily transferred into the care of relatives by living parents or through guardianship proceedings.[40] Apparently, most of the children living with relatives other than parents and receiving allowances under the ADC program do not have judicially appointed guardians. The assumption of local, state, and national administrators of the ADC program seemingly is that the majority of these children do not require judicially determined guardians. Although those administering the ADC program have little or no data on the extent of need for judicially determined guardians, the very existence of the program has assured children of the continuous oversight of public servants whose duty is their protection.

---

[40] *Ibid.*, p. 150.

GUARDIANSHIP AND FEDERAL OLD-AGE AND SURVIVORS INSURANCE (OASI)

The Social Security Act entitles children of workers covered by old-age and survivors insurance to money benefits. Ordinarily, payments do not go directly to the children of deceased insured parents but to fiduciaries who act for them. Selection of the payee often raises questions of legal guardianship for the agencies making payments. As of September 30, 1955, 1,246,600 children were receiving OASI benefits at a monthly rate of $45,010,000. An estimated 1,127,200 children were receiving benefits on the records of deceased workers, and 119,400 on the record of old-age beneficiaries. These numbers will increase with the years.

In exercising its authority to designate a payee for benefits to children under eighteen, the Social Security Administration considers that it has the responsibility to make payment to a competent payee whose position and relationship to the child enable him to know the child's needs and to spend the benefits intelligently to meet those needs. The administration describes its assumption of responsibility as follows: [41]

The first consideration in the selection of a payee for a child's benefits is the preservation of the child's family ties. The purpose is to maintain the family unit as an entity wherever possible, and a parent is given priority except in unusual circumstances, as where there is evidence of neglect. Even if the parent is not maintaining a home for the child, he may still be selected as payee if he is continuing to take responsibility for planning for him. The Administration believes that payment to a parent under such circumstances serves as a link between the parent and the child. A relative with whom the child is living, or who maintains a personal interest in his welfare, may also be selected as payee, as may an agency or institution having responsibility for the child. An agency or institution that does not have approved child-placing facilities of its own or available to it is selected only under unusual circumstances, however, since the Administration believes it is best for most children to grow up in a family setting.

Legal guardians are made payee in a relatively small percentages of cases, and seldom if their interest is mainly fiscal. Of all payments made on behalf of children, approximately 8 per cent are today paid to legally appointed guardians. About 70 per cent of these legal guardians are parents.

The administration further requires:

That such payee submit evidence describing his relationship to the individual entitled to benefits and the extent to which he has the care of such individual. In addition, the payee is required to present a statement which is part of his application agreeing to use the benefits for the needs and welfare of the individual on whose behalf he will be paid benefits. Where such a designation of payee is made, the Administration may at any time require evidence that the payments should continue to be made to the payee. If the person to whom pay-

[41] Correspondence from Robert M. Ball, acting director of the Bureau of OASI, U.S. Department of Health, Education, and Welfare (January 27, 1954), and from Alvin M. David of the same bureau (December 13, 1955).

ment is made is not the legal guardian, conservator, or other legal representative, he may also be required by the Administration to account for the funds he has received.

GUARDIANSHIP AND VETERANS' ADMINISTRATION (VA)

Veterans are entitled to numbers of benefits, such as compensation, pensions, insurance, loans. Eligibility requirements are specified by law for each type of benefit. The majority of child beneficiaries under these programs, like those under OASI, receive payment on account of the death of the parent. As of November 30, 1953, 221,427 minors were receiving benefits under acts administered by the Veterans' Administration.[42] Laws governing the Veterans' Administration provide that payment may be made to the guardian or curator or to the person legally vested with the care of the claimant or his estate whom the administration terms "legal custodian."

The Veterans' Administration requires appointment of legal guardians under several types of situation, as when the accrued benefits are in excess of $700, or where the child receives more than $65 a month, or where the benefits are not presently needed. Legal custodians may include the surviving parent unless parental rights have been judicially terminated; then, any other relative who is responsible under state law for the care and support of the child; next, the person standing *in loco parentis;* and, finally, any person who has been vested with custody by judicial decree. It appears that regional offices prefer using legal custodians whenever possible. Further, where official legal guardians are desirable or necessary, Veterans' Administration preference seems to be for the appointment of near relatives, although some regional offices prefer banking organizations, as they are more reliable in reporting and more expert in the investment of funds.[43]

The Veterans' Administration assumes responsibility for the proper expenditure of the funds through the use of investigation, certification, reporting, and supervision. If the applicant's suitability is established, he is designated payee by formal procedure, which involves signing an agreement to apply the payments for the child's benefit and to report any changes in the child's situation affecting his eligibility for benefits. The Bureau of OASI does not require field offices to supervise payees or to obtain accounts from them. Field offices rely on complaints for further follow-up and, under some circumstances, may refer the situation to the

---

[42] Correspondence from C. E. Schuyler, acting assistant deputy administrator for guardianship of the Veterans' Administration (January 20, 1954). For review of various types of programs for veterans, see *Handbook on Federal Benefits for Veterans* (Washington, D.C., Veterans' Administration, 1955), and *Social Legislation Information Service,* 84th Cong. (December 31, 1955), No. 39.

[43] From correspondence with Schuyler cited in n. 42.

state welfare department. The Veterans' Administration requires that for all applications there shall be an investigation, or social survey. This covers the child's physical care, home and neighborhood environment, personal adjustments, and the applicant's ability to handle funds. A regional attorney decides whether the applicant shall be approved as a legal custodian or whether a legal guardian shall be appointed by the local court of jurisdiction. If the latter, the regional office initiates the proceeding and takes an active part in it. In either instance the Veterans' Administration exercises continuous supervision over the activities of legal custodians and guardians. Intermediate social surveys may be made in between accountings by a regional field examiner or by a local social agency upon request.

It is because of the early experience of the Veterans' Administration with misuse and even embezzlement of benefits that two developments occurred. The first, to which we have just referred, resulted in the statutory requirements that the person administering benefits be supervised. The second resulted in the formulation of the Uniform Veterans' Guardianship Act accepted by the National Conference of Commissioners on Uniform Laws in 1928 and subsequently revised. The act provides that whenever, pursuant to any federal law or regulation of the Veterans' Administration, a guardian shall be appointed, the state courts shall make the appointment in the manner prescribed by the act. Under it the Veterans' Administration is a party in interest to guardianship proceedings, with the appointment and initial supervision left to state courts but with ultimate power to make requirements of the guardian retained by the Veterans' Administration. It was the intent of the commissioners that the Veterans' Administration, a federal agency, have ultimate responsibility for the expenditure of federal funds but that, so far as possible, state and local agencies and institutions be used both in the appointment and routine supervision of guardians.[44]

PROPOSALS FOR IMPROVED LEGISLATION

PROBLEMS

Children under twenty-one years of age constitute about one-third of the total population of the United States.[45] In all states the responsibility of guardianship in the first instance belongs to parents. In most states father and mother are equal guardians of children born in wedlock. The mother is the sole guardian of the child born out of wedlock. Natural

---

[44] Veterans' Administration, *The Development and Functioning of the Guardianship Program* (November 7, 1951); "Uniform Veterans' Guardianship Act," *Miscellaneous Acts,* Vol. 9A U.L.A. 361, including commissioners' prefatory note, p. 51.

[45] Weissman, *op. cit.,* p. 166.

guardianship is not an absolute right. Rather, it is a trust which must be exercised for the child's benefit. If the child acquires property, if he loses his parents, if his parents do not exercise their guardianship responsibilities for his welfare, it becomes the duty of the state exercising its *parens patriae* authority to protect the child by providing a substitute guardian. Every state has statutes which provide for the appointment of legal guardians to exercise authority over the child's estate or his person or both. The appointment of guardian of the estate usually rests with courts having probate functions; that of guardian of the person rests with numbers of courts, including the probate, juvenile, family, and divorce courts.

The Children's Bureau study on guardianship referred to above shows that legal guardianship is used infrequently as a resource for the protection of children because the law does not require that every child shall have a guardian. In addition, adequate administrative machinery is not available for making guardianship effective. Many times guardians of small estates are appointed unnecessarily, and, in most instances, guardians of estates are the parent or parents of the children concerned. Often appointments of guardians of persons and estates are made perfunctorily and much court supervision, particularly of guardians of the person, appears to be routine or negligible.

Social agencies encounter troublesome guardianship problems in connection with placements, including foster homes and homes for adoption, and in the handling of benefit funds. Existing legislation is inadequate in its definition of the status and legal relations of children with and without legal guardians. Special confusion arises because of the absence of the requirement that all minors shall have guardians, the lack of clear distinctions between guardianship and custody, and between juvenile and probate court wardship. Additional complications result because juvenile court commitments often do not state whether parental rights have been terminated or what rights are transferred by the court to the agency. Sometimes, this is an omission in the law, but sometimes it is that of the court. Children voluntarily given to agencies for adoption by their parents also present problems with regard to guardianship status. The agency's right to act for these children has been challenged by the courts granting adoption and by health agencies which have been called upon for medical services. To these substantive inadequacies of the laws may be added the absence of a uniform definition of the child subject to guardianship, the absence of accurate terminology for guardian of person and estate and of precise and distinguishing definitions of such terms as *guardianship, wardship, custody, care, control.* Guardianship law, as such, is attached to probate law, which deals principally with estates. This has produced the result that guardianship law is primarily concerned with property and very little with child welfare.

CHILDREN'S BUREAU RECOMMENDATIONS

The federal Children's Bureau, with the advice of a group of lawyers, judges, professors of law and social work, officials of public welfare agencies, and representatives of private child welfare organizations, made a series of recommendations growing out of the above-mentioned study. As to guardians of the child's *person* it recommended that "A special court proceeding should be established to consider a child's need for guardianship of the person separately from his need for guardianship of the estate."

Since guardianship of the person constitutes a substitute for the parent-child relationship, the guardian should be appointed in a court where the principles of child protection and family welfare are controlling. Laws relating to the establishment and transfer of legal responsibility for the child should be correlated. "The special court proceeding for the appointment of the guardian of the person should be available in behalf of the child whose parents are dead or who is otherwise deprived of parental care and protection."

When natural or adoptive parents are dead or questions arise concerning their competence to act as natural guardians, recourse to the courts for clarification and fixing of legal responsibility is indicated but should not be required by law.

The requirement of a legal guardian for every child is impractical in the absence of statutory provisions for adequate administrative facilities. Nevertheless, there is need for a positive statement of legal policy declaring the responsibility of the state for securing the protection and legal representation of the child who lacks parental guardianship. The child has a right to definite legal status in relation to any person or agency assuming his custody. For example, there should be the statutory provision that child custody be assumed on a legally responsible basis; that guardianship proceedings be initiated at the earliest discovery that a child is without the protection and legal status of parental guardianship; that social agencies dealing with children, including public assistance, social insurance, and veterans' agencies be required to assume responsibility for seeing that children without parental protection have judicial consideration given to the appointment of legal guardians when indicated. "The proceeding for the appointment of the guardian of the person should be conducted in a court of general jurisdiction in children's cases."

Jurisdiction should be vested in a local court of broad jurisdiction. In the more populous areas it is desirable to have a special division of the court or a special judge assigned to handle all matters affecting children. In areas where there are different courts handling guardianship and other matters relating to children, jurisdiction over guardianship should be transferred to that court which deals broadly with matters affecting children. It is desirable that the court given jurisdiction be tied into a unified state court system to insure uniformity of procedure. There should be a judge competent to handle children's cases. "The court conducting the proceeding for the appointment of the guardian of the person should have social services available." Local social services should be expanded to provide assistance to the court and may be a part of the court itself or in a local public welfare agency. The state department of public welfare should give leadership in stimulating the development of such services.

CHILDREN'S BUREAU RECOMMENDATIONS REGARDING GUARDIAN OF THE ESTATE

As to guardianship of the child's *estate* the Children's Bureau recommended that "The guardian of the person should be entitled to act for the child when the child's whole estate is valued at $500 or less in lump sums or consists of money payments of $50 or less a month."

Small estates do not lend themselves to effective administration through the regular procedures governing guardianship of estates. When a child has no one legally responsible for his person to whom such a small estate can be entrusted, a proceeding for the appointment of a guardian of the person rather than of the estate should be started. "When a child is entitled to receive assets valued at more than the above-stated amounts this fact should be reported to the local court of jurisdiction for such action as it deems appropriate; in the event that no problem of management of the estate is found, the court should permit the guardian of the person to act for the child without the necessity of an appointment of guardian of the estate."

It should be possible for the court to release to the parent or personal guardian an estate needed for current support, maintenance, and education of a child. The appointment procedure should be reserved for estates for which management functions must be assumed. "The power of appointing the guardian of the estate should be vested in a court of general jurisdiction in estate matters." This court should be a local court of broad jurisdiction. It should be a court of record financed by tax funds rather than by fees and the judges and staff should be paid on a salary rather than a fee basis. Procedure should be simple and informal but should provide adequate protection for the child's benefit, including investigations, bonds, supervision, accounting, and settlement. "The court appointing the guardian of the estate should have social services available to it." This court should have authority to request social services from local public welfare agencies when, in the opinion of the court, they are necessary to carry out such functions as the evaluation of proposed or appointed guardians and the preparation of budgets for the support, maintenance, and education of the child.

CONCLUSIONS

Both common and statutory law tend to lag behind current thought, and some phases lag more and longer than others. Many changes have been made in the law relating to children during the last century, but few adaptations to modern conditions have been made in the law of guardian and minor ward. The Old-Age and Survivors Insurance and the Veterans' Administration programs, the activities of public-assistance agencies, and those of public and private child welfare agencies have brought into bold relief the anachronisms in guardianship law. No matter what court or agency administers guardianship law, it is obvious that that court or agency needs personnel to determine what guardian is best for the welfare of the child. Regardless of whether the child is poor or rich, sought after by no one or by numerous jealous but loving relatives, and regardless of whether the matter of his guardianship is taken into probate, divorce, juvenile, or other courts, he is entitled to the protection of the state, which can be assured him only through wise guardians intelligently selected and supervised.

At the present time considerable attention is given to the child whose situation comes to the attention of the juvenile court, somewhat less to the child in the divorce court, and relatively little to the child before the probate court unless his estate is pretentious. Persons interested in children need to give greater thought to improvements in the law of guardianship and to methods of co-ordinating or consolidating the administrative activities of tribunals hearing guardianship matters. Social service personnel should be available to guardianship courts.

Selected References

BLACKSTONE, Sir William, *Commentaries on the Laws of England in Four Books,* (Philadelphia, Rees, Welsh, and Co., 1897), Bk. 1.

BRECKINRIDGE, S. P., *The Family and the State* (Chicago, University of Chicago Press, 1934).

DONNISON, D. V., *The Neglected Child and the Social Services* (Oxford, Blackwell, 1953).

JENKS, Edward, *A Short History of the English Law* (London, Methuen, 1912).

MADDEN, Joseph W., *Persons and Domestic Relations* (St. Paul, Minn., West Publishing Co., 1931).

POLLOCK, Sir Frederick, and MAITLAND, F. W., *The History of English Law Before the Time of Edward I* (Cambridge, University Press, 1923), Vol. 2.

SCHOULER, James W., *Marriage, Divorce, Separation, and Domestic Relations,* 6th ed. (Albany, N.Y., Matthew Bender and Co., 1921), Vol. 1.

STANTON, Mary A., "The Administration of the Law of Guardian and Ward with Special Reference to Minors: Cook County, Illinois" (Doctoral dissertation, University of Chicago, 1943).

TAYLOR, Hasseltine Byrd, *Law of Guardian and Ward* (Chicago, University of Chicago Press, 1935).

WEISSMAN, Irving, and others, *Guardianship: A Way of Fulfilling Public Responsibility for Children,* U.S. Children's Bureau Publication (Washington, D.C., G.P.O., 1949), No. 330.

WOERNER, J. G., *A Treatise on the American Law of Guardianship* (Boston, Little, Brown, 1897).

The student should also consult pertinent statutes and judicial decisions.

CHAPTER 11

Child Welfare Services

INTRODUCTION

In Chapter 9 we observed that the state has slowly recognized the wisdom of enforcing parental duties as well as rights and of actually, not just theoretically, performing the functions of *parens patriae* when parents are inadequate or unwilling to perform their parental duties. Today the state requires that parents shall furnish decent care for their children and shall support them according to the standards of the family income. Further, the state itself furnishes many services to all children and, if necessary, provides or supervises the provision of a minimum of subsistence and care for special groups. The welfare of the child has become the concern not only of most parents, the church, and private agencies, but actively and affirmatively of the state. One of the significant achievements of the twentieth century has been the amount of legislation enacted on the federal and state levels of government for the well-being of children and young people. "We are," in other words, "witnessing the emergence of the child as a sensitive indicator of the quality of social life. His status is becoming a measure of the value of the whole complex of economic, political and social activities as they affect his health, emotional development, education and maturation."[1] As we pointed out in Chapter 1, so much protective legislation for various groups of people has been passed in the last generation as to cause some fearful persons to claim that we are moving toward an authoritarian state.

DEFINITIONS

The term *child welfare activities or services* has two generally accepted meanings.[2] It is often used to mean almost any effort in behalf of children. Thus it may include all helpful activities carried on by the community for the benefit of all children or any beneficial activity carried on by any individual for a single child. In a more restricted sense it means public and private services for the benefit of dependent, neglected, illegitimate, and delinquent children. The Social Security Act in Title V, Part 3, provides for child welfare services in the following words:

---

[1] Lawrence K. Frank, "Childhood and Youth," in *Recent Social Trends,* 1-vol. ed. (New York, McGraw-Hill, 1933), p. 753.

[2] Spencer H. Crookes, "Child Welfare," *Social Work Year Book: 1954,* pp. 81–94.

> For the purpose of enabling the United States, through the administrator to co-operate with state public welfare agencies in establishing, extending, and strengthening, especially in predominantly rural areas, public welfare services (hereinafter in this section referred to as "child welfare services") for the protection and care of homeless, dependent, and neglected children, and children in danger of becoming delinquent, there is hereby authorized to be appropriated . . .

In this chapter we use the term to mean the provision of public and private services for the benefit of special groups or classes of children. Many children, such as those with physical or mental handicaps, require services and are not necessarily dependent or neglected. It is not always easy to distinguish which children are dependent, neglected, or delinquent. By statutory definition the *dependent* child is usually considered to be one who is homeless or destitute or who lacks proper care through no fault of his parents or guardians. Resources of various kinds exist to serve his needs, such as public and private institutions; child welfare agencies for various purposes, including foster home and adoption placement; and public-assistance and family service agencies.

The *neglected* child is one whose natural parents or guardians willfully and deliberately fail to provide proper care and guardianship. Neglected children are often dependent, and they are frequently delinquent. Before the middle of the nineteenth century, statutes seldom provided that children were to be the subjects of public care except for the poverty of their parents or their own delinquency.[3] Slowly legislation was enacted which gave recognition to the principle that public authorities have the right and duty to interfere in cases of parental cruelty or neglect affecting the health, education, behavior, and well-being of children.

Two organizations were responsible for the enactment of such legislation: the Society for the Prevention of Cruelty to Children and the Society for the Prevention of Cruelty to Animals. The latter was first established in New York City in 1866, and the former in the same city in 1875. In some cities, societies interested in animals added the protection of children to their objectives; and in others, new agencies, often called humane societies, were organized for the double purpose. In their early days, these organizations considered their function in relation to neglected children to be that of punishment of parents. The S.P.C.C., where it exists, now seeks to rehabilitate the child's home. With the expansion of public and private facilities for dealing with children in need of special care, humane societies largely limit their work to the protection of animals.

Where there are independent protective agencies today they often

---

[3] Homer Folks, *The Care of Destitute, Neglected, and Delinquent Children* (New York, Macmillan, 1902), ch. 9, pp. 172–173.

combine protective services with child welfare programs, so that it is difficult to discern much difference between protective and other child welfare functions. In some communities juvenile and family courts carry on protective activities through their social service staffs. The public child welfare agency, with its broad responsibility to help children, should be expected to carry on the narrower service of protecting children neglected by their parents. Although there is considerable hue and cry for the punishment of parents presumed to contribute by their ignorance, indifference, and neglect to the delinquency of their children, the prevailing attitude of public and private agencies is to help family adjustment rather than to punish maladjustment.[4]

The *delinquent* child is one whose behavior is in violation of the law, or who is uncontrollable, or who habitually behaves so as to injure the morals or health of himself and others.[5] He is frequently both dependent and neglected. The development of resources for the care of dependent, neglected, and delinquent children, particularly the juvenile court, is discussed in Chapters 14–16. There, we point out that the Standard Juvenile Court Law eliminates narrow definitions of dependent, neglected, and delinquent children and, instead, describes types of parental and child behavior that confer jurisdiction upon the court.

HISTORICAL BACKGROUND

PRIMITIVE METHODS OF CARING FOR SPECIAL GROUPS OF CHILDREN

Although we occasionally hear of the infanticide of an illegitimate child, civilized society no longer tolerates abortion, infanticide, and slavery as means of ridding itself of unwanted children. Severe punishment is meted out to those who violate prohibitory legislation. In times of great suffering drastic methods of getting rid of dependent children still seem to be used in overpopulated oriental countries. Pearl Buck, in *The Good Earth,* vividly describes a Chinese famine and the resultant slavery and infanticide. Kamala Markandaya, in *Nectar in the Sieve,* describes Indian poverty and its effects upon children. Alan Paton does similarly for African children in *Cry the Beloved Country.* Even though early societies "got rid of" unwanted children, especially in crisis periods, the most common method of dealing with the dependent child, particularly if he were orphaned, was through the family group, the tribe, the clan. The Athenians made legal provisions for orphans provided they were wellborn or were the children of men killed in battle. The primary

---

[4] Crookes, *loc. cit.,* pp. 81–94.

[5] Gist of these definitions taken from *A Standard Juvenile Court Law,* rev. ed. (New York, National Probation and Parole Association, 1949).

motive was to conserve a population diminished by war.[6] Of all the ancient people only the Jews made the care of dependent children a special legal duty.[7] The Old Testament and the Talmud contain numerous references to dependent children. Child placing in Jewish families under legal provisions is nearly 3,500 years old.[8] The first case mentioned in the Bible in which child care was furnished by relatives or kind friends is that of Abraham, who adopted his nephew, Lot; the second, that of Pharaoh's daughter, who adopted Moses. Adoption often conferred the personal and property rights of natural children, but it seems clear that many early adoptions were, in effect, foster home care.

ENGLISH METHODS [9]

The early Christian church carried on much the same methods of child care and assistance as had the primitive Hebrew tribes. With the increase in numbers of orphaned and dependent children under the persecutions of various kings and emperors and because of excessive wars, the methods of child placement and of institutional care developed and expanded. The church parish sometimes made payments to widows to care for their own or other children, the precursor of our modern mothers' pensions or aid to dependent children programs and foster home systems.[10]

Throughout the Middle Ages and up to the sixteenth century, when its properties were extensively confiscated, the church made wide use, perhaps almost exclusive use, of monasteries, orphan asylums, and friendly hospitals for poor children who were not cared for under the manorial organization of the feudal system. With the disintegration of the feudal system after the middle of the fourteenth century, poor persons had little claim for support upon the lord of the manor. Wandering and begging increased. Neither the dispensation of alms by the monasteries and church nor institutional care was adequate to care for those in dire need.

The unsuccessful efforts to restrain migration by punishment culminated in the Elizabethan Statute under which the obligation of caring for poor persons, including children, was imposed upon relatives or the parish, a political and ecclesiastical unit of government. So far as poor children were concerned, the officials of the parish had the right to indenture them for their keep. The law provided "that it shall be lawful

---

[6] W. H. Slingerland, *Child Placing in Families* (New York, Russell Sage Foundation, 1919), p. 28.

[7] *Ibid.*, p. 27; Deut. 14:29, 24:21, 26:12–13.

[8] Max Seligsohn, "Orphan," *Jewish Encyclopedia*, (1905), Vol. 9, p. 438.

[9] For good early historical development in England and the United States, see Henry W. Thurston, *The Dependent Child* (New York, Columbia University Press, 1930).

[10] Henry W. Thurston, "Dependent Children," *Encyclopaedia of the Social Sciences* (1930), Vol. 3, pp. 398–403.

for the said church-wardens and overseers, or the greater part of them, by the assent of any two justices of the peace aforesaid, to bind any such children, as aforesaid, to be apprentices, where they shall be convenient, till such man child shall come to the age of four and twenty years, and such woman child to the age of one and twenty years, or the time of marriage; the same to be as effectual to all purposes, as if such child were of full age, and by indenture of covenant bound him or herself." This section of the statute provided for an early form of foster home care.

Binding out, or the indenture contract, had two main purposes: to exempt the parish from support of impoverished children and to train them for self-support. Blackstone commented that though the English laws were inadequate to provide needed care for poor children, they had "in one instance made a wise provision for breeding up the rising generation: Since the poor and laborious part of the community, when passed the age of nurture, are taken out of the hands of their parents by the statutes for apprenticing poor children; and are placed out by the public in such manner, as may render their abilities, on their several stations, for the greatest advantage to the Commonwealth."[11] However, many children who were placed on indenture contracts received no training in trades and were exploited by their masters for the performance of drudgery.

With the development of textile mills in the eighteenth century, large numbers of poor children were apprenticed long distances from their homes. The conditions under which they lived and worked were so atrocious that agitation for the improvement of the binding out system began. In 1802, under pressure from Sir Robert Owen, himself a cotton mill owner and operator, "An Act for the Preservation of the Health and Morals of Apprentices and Others, Employed in Cotton and Other Mills, and Cotton and Other Factories" was passed.[12] The act was an effort to reduce the miserable conditions of poor and unprotected children whose parents were forced to apprentice them or who were bound out by local officials. It forbade the binding out of children under nine, restricted the hours of labor to twelve and between the hours of 6 A.M. and 9 P.M., and required that for at least the first four years of his indenture every apprentice be instructed in reading, writing, and arithmetic during some part of his daily employment. Although this was an act designed to protect young, helpless apprentices, it was the beginning of the child labor movement in England.[13]

---

[11] Sir William Blackstone, *Commentaries on the Laws of England in Four Books,* (Philadelphia, Rees, Welsh, and Co., 1897), Bk. 1, p. 450.

[12] 42 Geo. III c. 73.

[13] Raymond G. Fuller, "Child Labor," *Encyclopaedia of the Social Sciences* (1930), Vol. 3, pp. 412–424; Grace Abbott, *The Child and the State* (Chicago, University of Chicago Press, 1938), Vol. 1, p. 184.

In 1819 an act, promoted again by Sir Robert Owen and still applying only to cotton mills, extended protection to other than bound children. The coverage of the early factory acts was gradually extended so as to include children in mines, mercantile establishments, ironworks, and so forth. The provision of tax-supported schools, compulsory school attendance laws, the enforcement of child labor laws through such means as the issuance of work permits and factory inspection, the various forms of public assistance and social insurance are responsible for the practical elimination of child labor. If there are any "little Joes" of Dickens' *Bleak House* days, they are rare.

Methods of care other than indenture were, of course, used for children, especially for very young children to whom this method was ill adapted. These included (1) outdoor relief, or relief in the home, and (2) indoor relief, or institutional care, often provided under religious influences. The earliest *public* institutional care for dependents in England was the mixed workhouse, sometimes called the poorhouse or almshouse, where were gathered the young, aged, destitute, sick, diseased, feeble-minded, insane, immoral, and criminal. Many persons, including children, were indentured from the mixed workhouse. As a result of the findings and recommendation of a royal commission in 1834, segregation of children from adults in almshouses was begun.[14] Today, there are few children in these institutions, since other methods of care are available. Another type of institutional care, the scattered home plan, was adopted in 1893 by one poor-law union and soon became widely used. Under this system cottages with a small number of residents are distributed throughout a town. The children generally go to the nearest school and participate in the community life. In addition to these methods, local authorities send children to various private institutions and agencies, including those for the deaf, blind, crippled, and feeble-minded, which are certified by national authority.[15]

In Scotland the poor-law authorities did not use the almshouse extensively for dependent children but paid foster parents to care for them. This method was introduced into England, and, today, foster home programs are carried on extensively by both public and private agencies. Organizations such as The National Incorporated Association for the Reclamation of Destitute Waif Children, otherwise known as Dr. Barnardo's Homes, which started in 1866, developed foster home programs.[16] From 1866 to 1942 this association admitted over 130,000 children to care. At the end of 1942, 8,149 children were in care.[17] Some of the

[14] Thurston, *loc. cit.*, pp. 398–403.

[15] *Ibid.*, p. 400.

[16] Slingerland, *op. cit.*, p. 35; John Herridge Batt, *Dr. Barnardo: The Foster Father of "Nobody's Children"* (London, Partridge, 1904).

[17] Personal correspondence with British Information Services (July 21, 1954).

children are eventually returned to their own families; others are placed in selected families in England and the colonies. Both foster home and institutional methods are used by this organization. Today, England's emphasis on foster home care appears to be largely on boarding care. Except as a preliminary to adoption, free foster home care is negligible.

The most significant twentieth-century developments for the welfare of the citizenry of Great Britain, including children, have come through numerous social insurance measures. Various schemes were introduced between 1908 and 1936. Some were designed to make alternative provisions to the poor law for defined groups of people, and others to cover certain risks for employed persons through compulsory contributory and noncontributory insurance schemes. These programs included noncontributory old-age pensions, unemployment insurance, national health insurance, contributory old-age pensions, contributory pensions for widows and orphans, and pensions for the blind.[18]

Social surveys carried out between World War I and World War II showed that despite these various social insurance and assistance schemes there was a considerable number of families in Great Britain living in primary poverty. According to the precise standards chosen, three quarters to five sixths of all want was due to interruption or loss of earning power. Practically all of the remaining one quarter or one sixth was due to the size of the family. In June, 1941, the Interdepartmental Committee on Social Insurance and Allied Services was appointed, under the chairmanship of Sir William Beveridge, "to undertake, with special reference to the inter-relation of the schemes, a survey of the existing national schemes of social insurance and allied services." The outcome was the famous Beveridge Report, published in 1942, to which we shall give more attention in Chapter 18.[19] Numbers of important acts that related to income services were passed to implement the recommendations, including a family allowances act, a universal medical care scheme, and various insurance and assistance programs. National insurance is now comprehensive and covers the whole population for the main eventualities from birth to burial, including sickness, unemployment, maternity, widows, industrial injuries, death. Although national insurance covers most risks, there remains the need for public-assistance services to residual groups or to those inadequately covered by the insurance programs. The National Assistance Act of 1948 is designed to provide such services. All these various acts are directed to the abolition of want and to the integration of the public social services. By such means all children

[18] British Information Services, Reference Division, *Social Services in Britain,* I.D. 780, revised March, 1953, New York.

[19] Sir William Beveridge, *Social Insurance and Allied Services* (London, His Majesty's Stationery Office, 1942).

of Great Britain who live in their own homes are assured at least a minimum decent standard of living.

Children deprived of their natural homes require special protection. In 1945 this topic received full investigation, after which two important reports dealing with England, Wales, and Scotland were issued. The main recommendation of the reports were embodied in the Children Act, 1948, making provisions for the care of all homeless children under seventeen at the time they are deprived of normal home care. The home secretary, a national official, aided by an advisory council, is given central responsibility for their care, and local authorities (councils of counties and county boroughs and large burghs in Scotland) have the duty of caring for them individually until they are eighteen years old or no longer require it. The act stresses the obligation laid on local authorities to further each child's best interests. In doing this the authority is to use all facilities which would be available for a child in his own home. Some authorities have accordingly set up reception centers for the temporary accommodation of children so that they may be suitably placed on the basis of observation of their physical and mental condition. Boarding out with foster parents is the method given first consideration. If such care is not suitable, the child may be placed in a statutory or voluntary home. All voluntary children's homes are subject to inspection. Generally speaking, the policy of local authorities is to replace large cottage homes by small separate homes, each providing for a group of children from six to twelve years of age of both sexes. One of the provisions of the act empowers local authorities to give financial assistance to young people who have been in care until the age of eighteen and are employed or engaged in training. The assistance may be continued until the training is completed, even if the period required extends beyond the age of twenty-one.

Another measure designed to promote the proper care of children is the Nurseries and Child-Minders Regulation Act, 1948. Many mothers who go out to work place their children in nurseries or in the care of women who mind the child for a fee. These women must register with the local authority and are subject to inspection. These two acts have considerably advanced the quality of child care. In addition, various earlier enactments on the subject of adoption were consolidated and improved in the Adoption Act, 1950. An earlier act, the Children and Young Persons Act, 1933, provides for the prosecution of those who willfully neglect or ill-treat children under sixteen in their charge; it also enables juvenile courts to make arrangements to protect such children and, if necessary, to remove them from parental control. All of these and many other provisions demonstrate the concern of the crown with the welfare of children. In a very real sense the state attempts to exercise its *parens patriae* authority. A similar expansion of interest in the welfare of children by the state is occurring in all countries of the world.

WORLD-WIDE DEVELOPMENTS

The twentieth century, particularly the second half, is witnessing a revolutionary phenomenon. The peoples of the world are demanding a fair share of economic goods so that they may enjoy at least a minimum of health, education, food, shelter, work at respectable wages, and leisure. In many countries where birth and death rates are abnormally high, where most of the population is malnourished, where child labor prevails and the wages for all labor are niggardly, where illiteracy is staggering and educational facilities inadequate, the people are making demands upon their government for political, economic, and social changes.

Reports of the United Nations summarizing legislative enactments around the world on such subjects as health, maternal and infant welfare, birth registration, education, school attendance, employment of children and youth, filiation, guardian and ward, and juvenile delinquency show the great diversity, and in many instances the paucity, of such legislation.[20] New social services are slowly being introduced into countries such as Iraq, Lebanon, India, Pakistan, Thailand, the Union of South Africa. Provisions for expanded, improved, and new services characterize the legislation of Belgium, Norway, Sweden, France, Germany, and the United Kingdom, all with long histories of public and voluntary social services. Countries of the western world, with many variations, provide numbers of forms of public assistance, family allowances, social insurances, preventive medical programs, extended education. These countries seem to be moving from extensive or exclusive institutional care for children to increased use of foster homes with government standard setting, inspection, supervision, and licensing. Apparently only in Russia are all children's institutions under public auspices and publicly financed. In that country, as elsewhere, there is a shift in emphasis from institutional to foster home care for children. All countries everywhere are confronted with the problem of how best to meet the basic needs of their people. The extent of concern can in some measure be gauged by the type and quality of services contemplated for and provided to children by governmental and private agencies.

In an effort to encourage higher standards of child care throughout the world numerous international organizations, both public and private, have been established. The child welfare committee of the League of

[20] United Nations, Department of Social Affairs, *Annual Reports on Child and Youth Welfare* (New York, 1948, 1949, 1951), Sales Nos. 1948, IV, 6; 1949, IV, 9; 1951, IV, 1; United Nations, Department of Social Affairs, *Methods of Social Welfare Administration* (New York, 1950), Sales No. 1950, IV, 10.

Nations has been replaced by numerous agencies organized within or co-operating with the United Nations. The United Nations Children's Fund, formerly the United Nations International Children's Emergency Fund (UNICEF), assists national child health and welfare programs in sixty-nine countries and territories in Africa, Asia, the eastern Mediterranean region, Europe, and Latin America. Financed by voluntary contributions from governments, residual assets of United Nations Relief and Rehabilitation Administration (UNRRA), and private donations, its chief aim is to provide assistance of lasting value, such as maternal and child welfare services and training, mass health programs, child nutrition, milk conservation, and emergency assistance, to large numbers of children. The International Labor Organization (ILO) seeks by international action to improve labor conditions, raise living standards, and promote economic and social stability. Formerly a part of the League of Nations, it is now a specialized agency of the United Nations. It is an association of nations, financed by governments and controlled by representatives of labor, management, and government. The United States became a member in 1934. By 1950 there were sixty member nations. The United Nations World Health Organization (WHO), a specialized agency of the United Nations, promotes attainment by all peoples of the highest possible level of health. The Division of Social Welfare of the United Nations Department of Social Affairs carries on research and gives consultative service to countries desiring assistance in organizing programs. Such voluntary agencies as the League of Red Cross Societies, the International Union for Child Welfare, the World Federation for Mental Health, do a great deal to promote child welfare as an aspect of their broad services. The Pan American Child Congress and the American International Institute for the Protection of Children led in the development of Inter-American child welfare. In 1952 an international conference on child welfare was held in Bombay, India, under the auspices of the International Union for Children.[21]

AMERICAN DEVELOPMENTS

THE ALMSHOUSE

The United States has made many provisions similar to those of Great Britain for the care of dependent and neglected children. The opening of the nineteenth century found the English poor-law system well established in the then sixteen states. At least five methods of care were available for adults and children alike: outdoor relief; farming out, each

[21] Frances K. Kernohan and others, "International Social Work," *Social Work Year Book: 1954*, pp. 266–285.

pauper being awarded to the lowest bidder; contract with some individual who became responsible for the care of all the paupers of a given locality; almshouses; and indenture.[22] At that time most paupers, including children, were cared for by outdoor relief or in mixed almshouses. Outdoor-relief history is discussed elsewhere in this book. The farming-out and contract system had relatively little application to children as such, but the indenture system was extensively applied to this group.

The first almshouses were built in the larger cities where population was concentrated. In 1800 Philadelphia, then the largest city with a population just over 70,000, was making use of its second almshouse, the first having been opened in 1767.[23] New York, the second largest city with a population of about 60,000, had just removed its paupers to its second and larger institution. Both adults and children were housed in these institutions. Baltimore and Boston also had almshouses. In Maryland the county almshouse system was established in 1768, and in Delaware, in 1823. Other states made similar provisions.

In 1823, J. V. N. Yates, then secretary of state of New York, made a report on the conditions of the poor in each county and town in New York and in nearly every other state in the Union.[24] He reached the general conclusion that outdoor relief was harmful in that it increased dependency and that the building of county almshouses was the best method of caring for the needy. In regard to children the report said: "The education and morals of the children of paupers (except in almshouses) are almost wholly neglected. They grow up in filth, idleness, and disease, and many become early candidates for the prison or the grave." [25]

Josiah Quincy's "Report of the Massachusetts Committee on Pauperism" in 1821 came to a similar conclusion.[26] In 1824, New York established the county almshouse system. Almshouses in New York and elsewhere were designed to be houses of employment. Children of the paupers housed within them were to be instructed, and at suitable ages they were to be put out to some useful trade or business.

Throughout the country for at least three fourths of the nineteenth century, the trend in the care of the poor was toward almshouse provisions for both adults and children, with separation of the two groups in the institutions of the larger cities. It was not many years after the general acceptance of almshouses as the most desirable system of caring for the needy that interested persons found much to criticize.

---

[22] Folks, *op. cit.*, p. 3.

[23] *Ibid.*, p. 4.

[24] *Ibid.*, p. 36; see "Thirty-fourth Annual Report of the State Board of Charities of the State of New York," I (1900), in S. P. Breckinridge, *Public Welfare Administration in the United States: Select Documents* (Chicago, University of Chicago Press, 1938), pp. 39–54.

[25] Folks, *op. cit.*, p. 37.

[26] Breckinridge, *op. cit.*, pp. 30–39.

In 1844 Dorothea Dix, in the report of her visitation to the almshouses of New York, said: "They do not guard against the indiscriminate association of the children with the adult poor. The education of these children, with rare exception, is conducted on a very defective plan. The almshouse schools, so far as I have learned from frequent inquiries, are not inspected by official persons who visit and examine the other schools of the county." [27] Not until some twenty years later was there legislation in New York prohibiting the retention of children in almshouses.[28] The conviction gradually spread that almshouses were not appropriate places for children, and, eventually, legislation was enacted in most states forbidding children of any age or below a certain age to be placed in these institutions.

INDENTURE OF APPRENTICESHIP [29]

The system of apprenticing poor children through the indenture contract was brought to this country from England. As in England, the American indenture of apprenticeship was not designed primarily to teach children occupations and trades but to relieve the community of their support, to provide cheap labor for masters, and to inculcate in the very young a habit of work and thrift. In the seventeenth century, hundreds of child apprentices were sent from the almshouses of England to the colonies for the inexpensive labor they could furnish and for relief from the burden of paying for their care. The colonists, too, saved themselves much public money by putting many of their own poor children to work on indenture contracts.[30] As early as 1641 an act was passed in Plymouth Colony providing for apprenticeship of poor children. It reads as follows: "It is ordered by the Court that those that have reliefe from the townes where they live; and have children and doe not Imploy them that then it shalbee lawfull for the Township to take order that those Children bee put to worke in fiting Employment according to theire strength and abillitie or placed out by the townes." [31]

Many states at an early date enacted statutes which contained detailed provisions with regard to the indenture of children. For example, the Massachusetts act of 1793 directed that provision be made in indenture contracts for instructing male children to read, write, and cipher.[32] Since

---

[27] Folks, *op. cit.*, p. 38.

[28] *Ibid.*, p. 39.

[29] For general discussion of apprenticeship and indenture, see Paul H. Douglas, "Apprenticeship," *Encyclopaedia of the Social Sciences* (1930), Vol. 2, pp. 144–147; Carter Goodrich, "Indenture," *Encyclopaedia of the Social Sciences* (1932), Vol. 7, pp. 644–648.

[30] For a discussion of apprenticeship and child labor in England and the United States see Abbott, *op. cit.*, Vol. 1, Pts. 2, 3, and 4.

[31] *Ibid.*, p. 199.

[32] Folks, *op. cit.*, p. 39.

there were few, if any, facilities for inspection and supervision, the obligations of the master to the apprentice frequently were not carried out. Recourse to the courts for broken contracts occasionally occurred, the master being liable for a breach of his contract, and the apprentice receiving punishment for a violation of his.

In the early days, indenture contracts made by parents, public officials, and sometimes by voluntary agencies were usually for domestic and farm work. Many indentured apprentices, however, did learn trades both on farms and in factories. With the growth of the factory system, the then existing type of apprenticeship decreased in importance. A long period of training was not necessary to learn many of the skills, so early in the twentieth century it was generally agreed that the system was archaic and that training for work should be given in trade schools. It was soon learned, however, that trade and vocational schools could not give all the training needed for the skilled trades and that a period of experience in actual employment was desirable and necessary. Wisconsin in 1915 first developed this new type of apprenticeship. The Wisconsin Industrial Commission is authorized to make agreements with employers as to the number of apprentices to be trained, the kind of training to be furnished, and the wage scale to be paid.[33] It also supervises the program. In 1949 apprenticeship for older young people existed in twenty-six states, the District of Columbia, Alaska, Hawaii, and Puerto Rico.[34]

In 1937 Congress passed a national apprenticeship law. It was enacted to promote the furtherance of standards of apprenticeship, to extend the application of standards, to bring together employers and labor for the formulation of standards. It is an enabling act without mandatory provisions. By 1952 over 7,000 local joint apprenticeship committees were formed, and training was going on in 300 skilled occupations under ninety trade classifications. As many as 150,000 employers were taking part in the training of over 238,000 apprentices. The average age of apprentices at the start of training ranged from eighteen to twenty-four years. Minors between the ages of sixteen and eighteen can be employed upon approved indentures.[35]

The indenture contract is an obsolescent means of providing care for children. Contracts, however, are extensively used in the care and placement of children. They provide a legal agreement between individuals, agencies, and institutions for the adequate care and protection of children. For example, the Wisconsin statutes provide that the State Department of Public Welfare may contract for the use of private facilities for

---

[33] Wis. Stat., 1955, c. 106.

[34] United States Department of Labor, Bureau of Apprenticeship, *Apprenticeship, Past and Present* (Washington, D.C., G.P.O., 1952), p. 22.

[35] *Ibid.*, pp. 4, 22, 24.

the care and treatment of children in its legal custody;[36] that certain county welfare agencies performing child welfare services shall have authority to contract with any parent, guardian, or other person for the care and maintenance of any child;[37] that child welfare agencies shall have authority to contract with any parent, guardian, or other person for supervision or care and maintenance of any child.[38]

INSTITUTIONS AND FOSTER HOME CARE

The private institution for child care developed in part as a protest against the use of almshouses and indenture contracts. Prior to 1800, there were only five private institutions for children in the United States. The first one was established in 1729 in the Ursuline convent of New Orleans after a frightful Natchez Indian massacre. Others were soon established in Savannah, Philadelphia, Baltimore, and Boston. In 1797, in New York City, a society for the relief of poor widows with small children was organized. It did not establish an institution but gave relief to widows and children in their homes. The only public institution for children separate from an almshouse at the beginning of the nineteenth century was in Charleston, S.C.[39]

In the first half of the nineteenth century the number of institutions for the care of children grew rapidly. Of the 1,558 institutions caring for children reporting for the *United States Census of Children under Institutional Care: 1923,* only eight were established before 1800; ninety-three were organized in the first half of the nineteenth century.[40] There was a great increase in number of institutions following the Civil War, but many no longer exist.

By 1853 in New York State there were so many children cared for in public or private institutions that the Reverend Charles Loring Brace created the Children's Aid Society, the primary purpose of which was to place children in free rural homes. This was the first private agency to undertake child placing as its primary function, although public officials were well acquainted with indenturing of children into homes as a form of foster home placement. Brace sent dependent children in groups of twenty to forty to the western states, where people received them into their homes. Often, almost nothing was known either about the foster parents or the children. In asking rural people to take into

---

[36] Wis. Stat., 1955, c. 48.52(2).
[37] Wis. Stat., 1955, c. 48.57(1)(h).
[38] Wis. Stat., 1955, c. 48.61(2).
[39] Folks, *op. cit.,* pp. 9–10.
[40] C. C. Carstens, "Dependent and Neglected Children," *Social Work Year Book: 1929,* p. 129; Folks, *op. cit.,* pp. 52–55, lists seventy-seven private institutions created before 1850.

their homes younger children rather than older ones who could probably earn their keep, the appeal was to their humanity rather than to their business interests.[41] This was the beginning of the movement in our country for foster home care for children.

In 1868 the Board of State Charities of Massachusetts initiated the method of taking children from the State Primary School at Monson and boarding them out in private families at public expense.[42] So extensively were both free and boarding homes used by the state of Massachusetts that by 1895 the State Primary School, which was the first state institution for dependent children, was converted into a hospital for epileptics. Today, thousands of dependent children in Massachusetts are placed in boarding homes at public or private expense.

While the state of Massachusetts was developing the method of foster home placement of children at public expense, and while private agencies in several states were stimulating a similar program, some states were building county or state institutions for children. In 1866 Ohio passed a law authorizing the establishment of county children's homes. Connecticut and Indiana adopted the Ohio system of local children's institutions. If we except Massachusetts, which soon abolished its state school, Michigan in 1874 opened the first state public school for dependent children. It was planned that the institution should place children in homes. Twenty states, including Minnesota and Wisconsin, adopted the Michigan method.[43] In 1935 the Michigan legislature abolished the state school and established the Michigan Children's Institute at Ann Arbor, which comprises a foster home service for all public state wards and a shelter for those needing care while their special needs are determined.[44] About one third of the states appear still to maintain congregate institutions for dependent and neglected children.

In many states, private agencies and institutions for child care were developed to supplement the work of public organizations or to furnish services not adequately met. As the work of these private agencies expanded, influential persons backing them asked for partial public support. Two forms of payment were developed: the per capita or per diem payment for services rendered, as in New York and California, and the payment of lump sums to agencies and organizations, as in Maryland and Pennsylvania. Glaring evils have risen out of the subsidy system. Many private agencies are still supported in whole or in part from public

---

[41] Carstens, *loc. cit.*, p. 67; "An Early Adventure in Child Placing, Charles Loring Brace," *Social Service Review* (March, 1929), pp. 75–98.

[42] Slingerland, *op. cit.*, p. 36; Folks, *op. cit.*, pp. 33–35, 150–154.

[43] Folks, *op. cit.*, pp. 73–75.

[44] C. C. Carstens, "Child Welfare Services," *Social Work Year Book: 1937*, pp. 64–72.

funds, but when such is the case, the per capita or per diem method is preferred.[45] This is referred to as "the purchase of care" method. New York in 1874 and Massachusetts in 1913 passed constitutional amendments forbidding the payment of state moneys to private organizations.[46] Other states have done likewise.

By 1900 the systems of public care for dependent children that had been adopted in the various states were as follows: [47]

> 1. The state school and placing-out system, adopted by Michigan and nineteen other states.
> 2. The county children's home system, adopted by Ohio and two other states.
> 3. The plan of supporting public charges in private institutions, which prevailed in three states and the District of Columbia and, to some extent, in several other states.
> 4. The boarding-out and placing-out system, carried on directly by public authorities in Massachusetts; through a private organization, the Children's Aid Society, in Pennsylvania; and by state authority in New Jersey.

In the other states the only public system of caring for children in need was through outdoor relief, almshouses, and occasional placing out in families by local public agencies; this latter work was supplemented by the activities of private agencies.[48] Some states adhere essentially to their earlier public system of care, and others have modified and expanded their public and voluntary methods.

It is inevitable that there should be difference of opinion as to the relative merits of institutional and foster home care of children. The *Proceedings of the National Conference of Charities and Corrections* and, subsequently, *The National Conference of Social Work* reflect this disagreement. William Pryor Letchworth, then New York State commissioner of charities and an early advocate of home care in preference to institutional care, delivered a paper before the National Conference as long ago as 1897, in which he said: [49]

> At one time the orphan asylum and similar institutions were thought to be the only efficient means of saving homeless children; but the difficulty of providing in this manner for the large number of children under the artificial conditions of institutional life have led to the utilization of family homes as a substitute for the orphan asylum, the latter now being regarded more as a temporary refuge and training school for suitably preparing the child for admittance

---

[45] Arlien Johnson, *Public Policy and Private Charities* (Chicago, University of Chicago Press, 1931).
[46] Carstens, "Dependent and Neglected Children," *loc. cit.*, p. 131.
[47] Folks, *op. cit.*, pp. 82–83.
[48] *Ibid.*, p. 166.
[49] "Dependent Children and Family Homes," *Proceedings of National Conference of Charities and Correction: 1897*, p. 94.

into a desirable home. The family home has come to be accepted as the natural provision for all children, the unfortunate as well as the fortunate.

Even though institutions are no longer expected to care for all kinds of children under any and all circumstances, they continue to serve useful purposes. They frequently meet the needs of the following types of children:

1. Those starved for affection and with such personality problems concerning their own parents as to preclude new emotional relationships in foster homes.
2. Those whose parents feel threatened by relationships between their child and foster parents.
3. Those who require only a brief period of care.
4. Large family groups which might otherwise have to be split up among several foster homes.
5. Adolescents, especially those requiring short-time care only.

Different types of foster homes, including free homes, boarding homes, adoption homes, work homes, and day care homes, are used to meet the needs of a great diversity of children. Often it is contemplated that children placed in institutions or foster homes shall be returned to their natural parents. The carefully diagnosed problems of the child should, of course, determine what kind of care he receives. When either institutional or foster home care is contemplated, the services of competent social service staff are essential.

The 1950 United States Census showed that 95,260 children under twenty-one years of age were living in public and private institutions for dependent and neglected children. The Bureau of Census estimated that there were 210 institutions for dependent and neglected children under public auspices and 1,430 under private auspices, a total of 1,640.[50] The Children's Bureau reported on children receiving casework services from public welfare agencies as of March 31, 1953, as follows: [51]

Table 3

Children in homes of parents or relatives	101,310
Children in foster family homes	117,366
Children in institutions and elsewhere (the 35,539 children in institutions represented only those served by workers attached to state or local welfare agencies and not all children receiving institutional care)	44,883
A probable additional number	24,000
Total	287,559

There seems to be no recent national study comparing all child placements in institutions and foster homes. The Children's Bureau did

[50] U.S. Department of Commerce, Bureau of the Census, *Institutional Population* (Washington, D.C., G.P.O., 1950); personal letter from the U.S. Children's Bureau (April 27, 1954).

[51] *The Book of the States: 1954–55* (Chicago, Council of State Governments, 1955), Vol. 10, p. 329.

a special study of children receiving foster care, based on data received from twenty-eight states in 1943. The figures revealed that between 1933 and 1944 there was a reduction from 57 to 46 per cent of child placements in institutions and an increase of foster home placements from 43 to 54 per cent.[52] This phenomenon means that institutions must give serious attention to what their desirable and essential functions are. Some have changed, and others are contemplating change in activities. For example, Wisconsin is considering whether its Child Center, which, in 1934, had a population of dependent and neglected children of around 500 and, in 1956, of less than 100, should convert existing resources to the use of other classes of the population. A large proportion of the children committed to the center are seriously disturbed. Hence, numbers of people conversant with the situation believe that a new type of facility providing extensive psychotherapy services and accessible to the state teaching and research hospital is essential.

INSPECTION, SUPERVISION, AND LICENSING

When for some one of a myriad of reasons the natural home is inadequate and undesirable, arrangements may have to be made for the child in an institution or foster home. In order that the state may fulfill its *parens patriae* responsibility, legislatures have enacted inspection, supervision, and licensing laws. Whether the child is placed on a temporary or permanent basis in an institution or foster home, the state assures him some degree of protection through these provisions. All the states have laws which variously provide for inspection and supervision; not all have specific licensing laws. For example, Massachusetts, New Jersey, New York, and Pennsylvania do not regard their laws authorizing supervision of agencies and institutions as licensing laws.

Most of the states place the responsibility for inspection, supervision, and licensing with a state department. In some states the authority is given to the department of public welfare, in others to the department of health, and in still others, to two or more departments. Legislation differs as to what agencies shall be inspected, supervised, and licensed—for example, child-placing agencies, adoption agencies, maternity homes, institutions, day care centers, and nurseries. States vary in the age of children cared for by agencies over which the departments have some degree of authority. Some states require fees from one or more of the types of agencies. Generally, there is no charge for permits to foster homes. Social workers who carry out these functions attempt to maintain or raise standards by advice and counsel rather than by the exercise of authority. However, workers do have authority to enforce standards

[52] "Changes in Volume of Foster Care: 1933–43," *The Child*, suppl. to Vol. 9, No. 12 (June, 1945), p. 4.

when necessary. This is true since their departments have been given the power to grant and revoke permits and licenses or to refer agencies with persistent bad practices to legal authorities.[53]

INTERSTATE PLACEMENT OF CHILDREN

Legislative interest in regulating the interstate placement of dependent children preceded assumption by the state of responsibility for supervising and licensing child welfare agencies.[54] Regulation of placement of children over state boundaries was the result of the interest of the states in protecting themselves against a financial burden. Michigan passed the first law on this subject in 1895. It required that any person, society, or asylum placing children from another state in Michigan must file a bond with the county probate judge protecting the county from future support of the child. Indiana, Illinois, and Minnesota passed laws in 1899 which, in contrast with the Michigan law, required approval of the bond by the state board of charities rather than by a local court or agency.

Experience demonstrated that the bond method was inadequate, and the laws passed by Michigan in 1915, Minnesota in 1919, and Virginia in 1922 represented a more constructive approach to the problem. These laws, and those subsequently passed by other states, provide for advance approval of a home in which the out-of-state child is to be placed, supervision of the home when the child is placed, and removal of the child if he is not well cared for. Such laws bring the standards of interstate child placement in line with those of agencies operating exclusively within a state. Most states have laws regulating the importation of children. Some are inadequate in their administrative requirements, so that little protection is afforded the child or the state. Relatively little long-distance placement of children by public and private agencies goes on today, although there are numbers of interstate placements in adjoining states.

THE FEDERAL CHILDREN'S BUREAU

As twentieth-century interest in and understanding of the needs of children, particularly of dependent, neglected, and delinquent children, increased, attention was focused on securing a national children's organization to study their needs. Miss Lillian D. Wald, founder of Henry Street Settlement in New York City and of the Visiting Nurse Association, and Mrs. Florence Kelly, general secretary of the National Consumers League, suggested the establishment of a federal Children's Bureau. A bill containing such a proposal was introduced into Congress in 1905, but

---

[53] Gladys Fraser, *The Licensing of Boarding Homes, Maternity Homes, and Child Welfare Agencies* (Chicago, University of Chicago Press, 1937).

[54] Abbott, *op. cit.*, Vol. 2, pp. 133–171; *Laws Relating to Interstate Placement of Dependent Children,* U.S. Children's Bureau Publication (Washington, D.C., G.P.O., 1924), No. 139.

it was not until 1912 that a law creating a bureau was passed. The White House Conference for Dependent Children, called by President Theodore Roosevelt in 1909, had much to do with developing enthusiasm for the Children's Bureau.[55] The section of the original law defining its duties reads: [56]

> The said bureau shall investigate and report to said department upon all matters pertaining to the welfare of children and child life among all classes of our people, and shall especially investigate the question of infant mortality, the birth rate, orphanages, juvenile courts, desertion, dangerous occupations, accidents and diseases of children, employment legislation, affecting children in the various States and Territories. But no official, or agent, or representative of said bureau shall, over the objection of the head of the family, enter any house used exclusively as a family residence. The chief of said bureau may from time to time publish the results of these investigations in such manner and to such extent as may be prescribed by the Secretary of Commerce and Labor.

The bureau was originally established in the Department of Commerce and Labor. When in 1913 an independent Department of Labor was created, the Children's Bureau was placed there. In 1946 it was transferred to the Federal Security Agency. It became a part of the Department of Health, Education, and Welfare when that department was created by executive order and congressional action in 1953. To date there have been four able chiefs of the bureau, the first two of whom are deceased. The first was Julia Lathrop, the second Grace Abbott, the third Katharine Lenroot, and the fourth Martha Eliot. Although the bureau administered the Sheppard Towner or Welfare and Hygiene of Maternity and Infancy Act from 1921 to 1929, it was almost entirely a study and research agency until the passage of the Social Security Act in 1935. It now has the responsibility of administering the child welfare provisions of that act. The Children's Bureau has been and is the greatest single continuous force in the country for drawing attention to the needs of children. Its investigations and publications are reliable, its personnel expert, and its influence for prevention and correction far-flung.

WHITE HOUSE CONFERENCES

In 1909, President Theodore Roosevelt called the first White House Conference to consider the needs of children. He invited about two hundred people, representing every phase of child welfare work, for a

---

[55] Homer Folks, "The National Children's Bureau," *Proceedings of National Conference of Charities and Correction: 1910,* pp. 90–96; Julia Lathrop, "The Children's Bureau," *Proceedings of National Conference of Charities and Correction: 1912,* pp. 30–33; R. L. Duffus, *Lillian Wald* (New York, Macmillan, 1938); Josephine Goldmark, *Impatient Crusader* (Urbana, Ill., University of Illinois Press, 1953). U.S. Department of Health, Education, and Welfare, *Four Decades of Action for Children,* Children's Bureau Publication (Washington, D.C., G.P.O., 1956), No. 358; and U.S. Department of Health, Education, and Welfare, *Your Children's Bureau,* Children's Bureau Publication (Washington, D.C., G.P.O., 1956), No. 357.

[56] U.S. Stat. 79, Pt. 1, c. 73.

two-day session to discuss the needs of *dependent* children. After two days of discussion, the conference unanimously adopted a 3,000-word platform. Among its recommendations was one leading to creation of the Children's Bureau in 1912 and of the Child Welfare League of America in 1919, a permanent voluntary organization, the purpose of which is to give national leadership to the problems of children. The conference did not favor depriving children of their own homes for reasons of poverty. If it were necessary to remove them from their own parents, it preferred foster home to institutional care. In the following words it clearly defined this policy: [57]

> Home life is the highest and finest product of civilization. . . . Children should not be deprived of it except for urgent and compelling reasons . . . Except in unusual circumstances the home should not be broken up for reasons of poverty, but only for considerations of inefficiency or immorality. . . .
>
> As to children who for sufficient reasons must be removed from their own homes, or who have no homes, it is desirable that, if normal in mind and body and not requiring special training, they should be cared for in families whenever practicable. The carefully selected foster home is for the normal child the best substitute for the natural home. Such homes should be selected by a most careful process of investigation, carried on by skilled agents through personal investigation and with due regard to the religious faith of the child. After children are placed in homes, adequate visitation, with careful consideration of the physical, mental, moral and spiritual training and development of each child on the part of the responsible home-finding agency is essential.
>
> The proper training of destitute children being essential to the well-being of the state, it is a sound public policy that the state through its duly authorized representative should inspect the work of all agencies which care for dependent children, whether by institutional or home-finding methods . . .

In 1919 the federal Children's Bureau, at the request of President Woodrow Wilson, called a second conference of child-welfare representatives from throughout the United States. This conference on child health and protection extended its interests to include child labor, the health of mothers and children, the preschool child, the school child, treatment of child dependency, juvenile delinquency, and child welfare laws. It reaffirmed the principles of the 1909 gathering.[58]

In 1930, President Herbert Hoover called the White House Conference on Child Health and Protection. He stated its purpose as follows: "To study the present status of the health and well-being of the children of the United States, and its possessions; to report what is being done; to recommend what ought to be done and how to do it." The emphasis was upon *all* children, including special groups. The conference formulated

---

[57] *Proceedings of the Conference on the Care of Dependent Children,* 60th Cong., 2d sess., S. Doc. 721 (Washington, D.C., G.P.O., 1909).

[58] *Standards of Child Welfare: A Report of the Children's Bureau Conferences, May and June, 1919,* U.S. Children's Bureau Publication (Washington, D.C., G.P.O., 1919), No. 60.

the nineteen-point Children's Charter, which included such provisions as the following: [59]

1. For every child understanding and the guarding of his personality as his most precious right.
2. For every child a home and that love and security which a home provides.
3. For every child from birth through adolescence, promotion of health including health instruction and a health program.
4. For every rural child as satisfactory schooling and health services as for the city child, and an extension to rural families of social, recreational, and cultural facilities.
5. To make everywhere available these minimum protections of the health and welfare of the child, there should be a district, county, or community organization for health, education, and welfare.

In 1940 the Conference on Children in a Democracy was called by President Franklin D. Roosevelt. It dealt with a broad range of topics, especially emphasizing the close relationships of welfare, education, and economics, and their bearing upon *every* child. The entry of the United States into World War II impeded the development and continuation of follow-up programs.[60]

The Midcentury White House Conference on Children and Youth was called by President Harry S. Truman in 1950. The theme of this fifth conference was "A Healthy Personality for Every Child." It emphasized the interrelatedness of all professional groups interested in child development and carried further the concept of the 1940 gathering that services for the best interests of the "whole" child and of "every" child must be co-ordinated. Among the notable features of this conference were (1) the extensive advance preparation and wide citizen participation in its planning and follow-up, and (2) the direct participation of young people in all phases of its activity.[61] Perhaps the greatest values of the five White House conferences have come from a periodic review of conditions affecting children, from a restatement of principles by the country's experts, from the publicity given their statements, and from lay and professional participation in planning for the conferences and in carrying out conference recommendations.[62]

---

[59] "The Children's Charter," in *White House Conference, 1930: Addresses and Abstracts of Committee Reports* (New York, Appleton-Century, 1931), pp. 45–48.

[60] *White House Conference, 1940: Final Report,* U.S. Children's Bureau Publication (Washington, D.C., G.P.O., 1942), No. 272.

[61] Helen Leland Witmer and Ruth Kotinsky, eds., *Personality in the Making: The Fact-finding Report of the Midcentury White House Conference on Children and Youth* (New York, Harper, 1952); Edward A. Richards, ed., *Proceedings of the Midcentury White House Conference on Children and Youth* (Raleigh, N.C., Health Publications Institute, 1951).

[62] Crookes, *loc. cit.,* pp. 81–94.

PUBLIC-ASSISTANCE AND SECURITY PROGRAMS

Readers of this book are cognizant of the fact that the colonies and states early enacted poor relief or outdoor relief legislation, and that the standards of relief-giving under these laws were so inadequate that many children were grossly neglected. The 1909 White House Conference, with its declaration that homes should not be broken up for reasons of poverty and that children should be with their own parents, had an influence in developing the mother's assistance movement.[63] The experiment of granting aid in their own homes to children deprived of the support of the breadwinner was begun on a state-wide basis in 1911 in Illinois. By 1935, when the Social Security Act was passed, all states except Georgia and South Carolina had such laws. The purpose of this type of legislation was to keep children in their own homes, to make it possible for mothers to stay at home, and to raise the standards of assistance. With the passage of the Social Security Act and Title IV, "Grants to States for Aid to Dependent Children," momentum was given to this movement.[64] The Social Security Act further encourages state programs for the benefit of special groups of children. Title V provides for grants to states for maternal and child welfare. These activities we shall describe more fully in subsequent chapters.

REORGANIZATION

State commissions and committees for the study, revision, and codification of child welfare laws have had much to do with securing additional and improved services for children and with obtaining the machinery needed for constructive administration of these services. The Commission to Codify and Revise the Laws of Ohio Relative to Children, created in 1911 by legislative enactment, is credited with being the first official body of its kind. From 1911 to date, most states have had official or unofficial commissions to study children's problems, relief problems, or general public welfare problems, some states having had more than one such body.[65] From the study and experience of these and other groups several principles concerning administration of services for children (as well as for other groups) have emerged: (1) The value of laws, including public welfare laws, lies in the quality of their administration. (2) The smallest

---

[63] Emma O. Lundberg, *Unto the Least of These* (New York, Appleton-Century-Crofts, 1947).

[64] *Compilation of the Social Security Laws, Including the Social Security Act, as Amended, and Related Enactments Through December 31, 1954,* 83d Cong., 2d sess., Doc. 157 (Washington, D.C., G.P.O., 1955).

[65] Emma Lundberg, *State Commissions for the Study and Revision of Child Welfare Laws,* U.S. Children's Bureau Publication (Washington, D.C., G.P.O., 1924), No. 131.

local unit that should have administrative authority for a public social work program is the county. Children's services may be administered by a separate county agency or as a part of an integrated public welfare program, preferably the latter. (3) Provisions for state and federal participation in public welfare administration and financing are desirable and essential. The depression of the 1930's taught us that programs for the relief of distress cannot be met adequately by the local community or even by the state. The federal government must enter the picture if there are to be nation-wide minimum standards of care and service and if these services are to be continuing.

THE CHILD LABOR MOVEMENT

Because the child labor movement has been responsible for such significant accomplishments both for the poor child and for all children, a short summary of developments, particularly on the federal level of government, is included in this discussion of child welfare services.

We pointed out earlier in this chapter that the child labor movement began by restricting the labor of indentured and apprenticed children, and it expanded to include provisions for all children under certain conditions. Grace Abbott, second chief of the Children's Bureau, pointed out that the child labor movement in every country supplied the impetus in the struggle for decent working conditions. The achievements obtained in the early child labor laws prepared the way for general regulation of factory conditions and were a pioneering effort on the part of the state to insure children a minimum standard of life and health which many parents could not afford to give and a few did not wish to give.[66]

Public opinion regarding child labor has changed markedly in the last century. We have rejected the idea that the very young child, especially if he is poor, must be taught thrift and skills through compulsory labor; we believe that every child should attend school for a given number of years. Hence, state legislation has been enacted which largely eliminates the use of the indenture contract for children, which controls the ages and conditions of child labor, and which requires compulsory school attendance for all children. In the United States the greatest argument for the curtailment of child labor has always been general insistence upon universal education. The movements for the regulation of child labor and for compulsory education have inevitably gone hand in hand, sometimes one and sometimes the other being ahead in its achievements.

Despite noticeable changes in attitude toward child labor there are still children who are not covered by either state or federal legislation. This inequality was very great when, beginning in 1916, Congress made two unsuccessful attempts to lay down certain minima. The first federal

[66] Abbott, *op. cit.*, Vol. 1, p. 79.

child labor law, enacted in 1916, provided that no producer, manufacturer, or dealer should ship or deliver in interstate or foreign commerce any article on which children under sixteen had labored. The attorney general, the secretary of commerce, and the secretary of labor constituted a board to make and publish uniform rules and regulations for carrying out the provisions of the act, and its administration was given to the secretary of labor.[67] The Children's Bureau worked out a plan for the issuance of certificates of age on the theory that the successful enforcement of the law depended primarily upon a well-administered certificating system.

In 1917, in *Hammer* v. *Dagenhart*, the United States Supreme Court by a five-to-four decision held the law unconstitutional on the grounds that it was not within the authority of Congress in regulating interstate commerce to forbid the transportation of childmade goods.[68] This grant of power to Congress was to enable it to regulate commerce and not to give it authority to control the states in their exercise of the police power over local trade and manufacture. The Court said:

> In our view the necessary effect of this act is, by means of a prohibition against the movement in interstate commerce of ordinary commercial commodities, to regulate the hours of labor of children in factories and mines within the states, a purely state authority. Thus the act in a twofold sense is repugnant to the Constitution. It not only transcends the authority delegated to Congress over commerce but also exerts a power as to a purely local matter to which the federal authority does not extend. The far reaching result of upholding the act cannot be more plainly indicated than by pointing out that if Congress can thus regulate matters entrusted to local authority by prohibition of the movement of commodities in interstate commerce, all freedom of commerce will be at an end, and the power of the states over local matters may be eliminated, and thus our system of government be practically destroyed.

A strong minority opinion was written by Justice Holmes and was concurred in by Justices McKenna, Brandeis, and Clarke. In part it reads as follows:

> The first step in my argument is to make plain what no one is likely to dispute —that the statute in question is within the power expressly given to Congress if considered only as to its immediate effects and that if invalid it is so only upon some collateral ground. The statute confines itself to prohibiting the carriage of certain goods in interstate or foreign commerce. Congress is given power to regulate such commerce in unqualified terms. It would not be argued today that the power to regulate does not include the power to prohibit. Regulation means the prohibition of something, and when interstate commerce is the matter to be regulated I cannot doubt that the regulation may prohibit any part of such commerce that Congress sees fit to forbid. At all events it is established by the

---

[67] 39 U.S. Stat. 675, Pt. 1, c. 432.

[68] 247 U.S. 251 (1918); for easy access to case, see Abbott, *op. cit.*, Vol. 1, pp. 495–506; see above, Ch. 1, for a short discussion of this case.

Lottery Case and others that have followed it that a law is not beyond the regulative power of Congress merely because it prohibits certain transportation out and out. *Champion* v. *Ames,* 188 U.S. 321, 355, 359, *et seq.* So I repeat that this statute in its immediate operation is clearly within the Congress's constitutional power.

The question then is narrowed to whether the exercise of its otherwise constitutional power by Congress can be pronounced unconstitutional because of its possible reaction upon the conduct of the states in a matter upon which I have admitted that they are free from direct control. I should have thought that that matter had been disposed of so fully as to leave no room for doubt. I should have thought that the most conspicuous decisions of this Court had made it clear that the power to regulate commerce and other constitutional powers could not be cut down or qualified by the fact that it might interfere with the carrying out of the domestic policy of any state.

Following this decision, Congress passed a law in 1919 using the tax power to eliminate child labor. As a part of the Revenue Act of 1918, a tax of 10 per cent was laid on the annual net profits of industries which employed children in violation of the age and hours standards of the bill.[69] In 1922 the United States Supreme Court held that the law did not provide for a valid exercise of Congress' right to levy and collect taxes. Justice Taft in delivering the opinion asked and answered the following questions: [70]

Does this law impose a tax with only that incidental restraint and regulation which a tax must inevitably involve? Or does it regulate by the use of the so-called tax as a penalty? If a tax, it is clearly an excise. If it were an excise on a commodity or other thing of value we might not be permitted under previous decisions of this court to infer solely from its heavy burden that the act intends a prohibition instead of a tax. But this act is more. It provides a heavy exaction for a departure from a detailed and specified course of conduct in business. . . . If an employer departs from this prescribed course of business, he is to pay to the government one-tenth of his entire net income in the business for a full year. . . . Grant the validity of this law, and all that Congress would need to do, hereafter, in seeking to take over to its control any one of the great number of subjects of public interest, jurisdiction of which the states have never parted with, and which are reserved to them by the Tenth Amendment, would be to enact a detailed measure of complete regulation of the subject and enforce it by a so-called tax upon departures from it. To give such magic to the word "tax" would be to break down all constitutional limitation of the powers of Congress and completely wipe out the sovereignty of the states. . . .

In view of the fact that two laws attempting to regulate child labor throughout the country had been declared unconstitutional, many friends of children felt that the Constitution should be amended in order to authorize Congress to enact child labor legislation. Finally in 1924 an amendment was adopted by the necessary two-thirds vote of both houses

---

[69] 49 U.S. Stat. 1138, Pt. 1, c. 18, Title XII.

[70] *Bailey* v. *Drexel Furniture Co.,* 259 U.S. 20 (1922).

and was submitted to the states for ratification. The amendment reads as follows:[71]

Resolved by the Senate and House of Representatives of the United States of America in Congress assembled (two-thirds of each House concurring therein), That the following article is proposed as an amendment to the Constitution of the United States, which, when ratified by the legislatures of three-fourths of the several States, shall be valid to all intents and purposes as a part of the Constitution:

"Article——.

"Section 1. The Congress shall have power to limit, regulate, and prohibit the labor of persons under eighteen years of age.

"Section 2. The power of the several States is unimpaired by this article except that the operation of State laws shall be suspended to the extent necessary to give effect to legislation enacted by the Congress."

By 1954 twenty-eight states had ratified the amendment, the only southern state among them being Kentucky. Eight more states are needed to accomplish ratification. Little effort is being made to secure such acceptance since the same purposes have been achieved through the Fair Labor Standards Act of 1938. In 1941 the United States Supreme Court in *United States* v. *Darby* upheld the act, which included provisions for the regulation of goods made by children and shipped through the channels of interstate commerce.[72] Thus, the 1918 decision of the Court was reversed, and the minority decision of Justice Holmes became law.

Despite more than fifty years of progress in the fight against the evils of child labor, many still exist. The National Child Labor Committee so pointed out in its fiftieth anniversary report. Work continues to substitute for schooling for thousands of migrant and other farm children. Early child labor abuses in coal mines, factories, and cotton mills have been wiped out, but nearly two million children from the ages of fourteen through seventeen still work full or part time in industry and agriculture. Additional thousands under fourteen work on farms, in street trades, and elsewhere.[73] Thousands annually follow their migratory worker parents. The fight against the evils of unregulated child labor requires incessant watchfulness by state and federal officials.

SUMMARY AND CONCLUSIONS

It has been our purpose in this chapter to review some of the historical and present-day programs of care for children whose parents cannot or

---

[71] 43 U.S. Stat. 670, Pt. 1, H. J. Res. No. 184.

[72] 312 U.S. 100; Katharine DuPre Lumpkin, "The Child Labor Provisions of the Fair Labor Standards Act," *Law and Contemporary Problems* (Summer, 1939), Duke University Law School.

[73] Sol Markoff, *The Changing Years: 1904–1954* (New York, National Child Labor Committee, 1954); for brief history, see Gertrude Folks Zimand, "The Changing Picture of Child Labor," *Annals of the American Academy of Political and Social Science*, Vol. 234 (November, 1944), pp. 83–91.

do not provide for them. We have not attempted to describe some of the newer services, such as those for the mentally retarded or for cerebral palsy patients; nor have we discussed the care of the delinquent child, which we shall do in later chapters. Although the nations of the western world have for centuries assumed some degree of responsibility for the welfare of children, it remained for the twentieth century to broaden and extend provisions and to furnish facilities for guarantee of their protection. Legislative bodies define basic public policy concerning child care and protection and administrative agencies carry it out. Public and voluntary agencies co-operate to achieve child welfare.

Many methods are derived from our British forefathers, such as voluntary services, often of an institutional type, by religious and nondenominational groups; local public assistance; almshouse, workhouse, and jail facilities; and indenture of apprenticeship. Twentieth-century provisions do not necessarily exclude these but rather include others, such as expanded schemes of public assistance, with financial and administrative sharing by federal, state, and local governments; the social insurances; inspection, supervision, licensing of child welfare agencies by state departments; and social services rendered by public and private child welfare specialists to help the child in his own home or in foster homes and institutions.

A continuously expanding body of experience and knowledge offer a challenge to all parents, teachers, child welfare workers, and citizens to see that what the best and wisest parent wants for his child, the community assures to all children. It is the responsibility of the state to furnish special facilities for a decent standard of well-being for the specially handicapped child and to provide other services, such as universal education and public health protection, for all children.[74] All child welfare problems touch legislation at some point.[75] However, if the paternal authority of the state is to be efficiently and wisely effectuated, competent administrative services must be available.

For Selected References, see those following Chapter 12.

---

[74] John Dewey, *The School and Society* (Chicago, University of Chicago Press, 1899), p. 3.

[75] Ernst Freund, "The Status of Child Welfare Legislation in Illinois," *Social Service Review* (December, 1928), pp. 541–555.

CHAPTER 12

Adoption

HISTORICAL BACKGROUND

DEFINITION

Adoption was the ancient, as it is the modern, method of creating by law the relationship of parent and child."[1] It "is the act by which relations of paternity and affiliation are recognized as legally existing between persons not so related by nature."[2] The historic motive for adoption has been to strengthen the family; the modern purpose is to confer the privileges of parents upon the childless and the protection of parents upon the parentless or upon those whose parents had not the means or ability to maintain them.[3]

EARLY HISTORY

Adoption was known in Babylonia and is referred to and regulated in the Code of Hammurabi. It has a long history among primitive tribes and in Arabia and India. The biblical book of Esther tells the story of an adopted daughter who became queen of the land from India even unto Ethiopia. In Exodus we find the story of Moses, whose mother hid him in an ark in the bulrushes to protect him from death, and he was found there by Pharaoh's daughter. This kindhearted woman secured his mother for his nurse, "and she called him Moses and said, because I drew him out of the water."[4] It is found today in China and Japan; it was brought to the latter country from China in the thirteenth century.

Early Greek and Roman culture utilized adoption extensively and had

---

[1] Grace Abbott, "Adoption, Modern," *Encyclopaedia of the Social Sciences* (1930), Vol. 1, pp. 460–463; Joseph W. Madden, *Persons and Domestic Relations* (St. Paul, Minn., West Publishing Co., 1931), pp. 354–368; "Adoption," *Encyclopaedia Britannica* (1952), Vol. 1, pp. 177–178; E. Sidney Hartland and others for several articles on "Adoption," *Hastings Encyclopedia of Religion and Ethics* (1908), Vol. 1, pp. 105–116; Emelyn Foster Peck, *Adoption Laws in the United States,* U.S. Children's Bureau Publication (Washington, D.C., G.P.O., 1925), No. 148.

[2] 1 C.J.S. 365–460; 1 R.C.L. 619–77.

[3] W. Clarke Hall and Justin Clarke Hall, *The Law of Adoption and Guardianship of Infants* (London, Butterworth, 1928), p. 5; for history of adoption, see *Appeal of Woodward,* 81 Conn. 152, 70 Atl. 453 (1908), and *Hockaday* v. *Lynn,* 200 Mo. 456, 98 S.W. 585 (1906).

[4] Exod. 2:10.

detailed legal regulations concerning it. The principal reason for its use was the passing on of the religious headship of the family and of the estate. The general idea of adoption and the general effects of the act were the same in Rome as in Athens; but the peculiarly Roman conception of paternal authority, *patria potestas,* and also the Roman distinction between agnatic, or legal, and cognatic, or natural, relationships and rights introduced some modification in details. Adoption in Rome was by two distinct methods: by adrogation, where the head of a family voluntarily submitted himself to the *potestas* of another, and by adoption in the more proper sense, that is, by transference of a *filius familias* from the *potestas* of the natural father by the aid of legal fictions.[5] The rights and duties attendant upon this relationship are defined in the laws of Justinian.[6]

In addition to civil law-adoption, the aim of which was to create a fictitious filiation relationship between individuals, there have been public-law adoptions for political and social reasons. For example, there was the designation of the heir presumptive of the ancient Roman Empire; Napoleon's measures for the adoption of the children of his generals, officers and soldiers killed in the Battle of Austerlitz; and the provision by France for the adoption of French children orphaned in World War I.[7]

RECENT HISTORY IN SELECTED COUNTRIES

The Division of Social Welfare of the United Nations makes worldwide studies of children, including those deprived of a normal life. One such was a study on adoption of children.[8] The countries reviewed included those with different legal systems and diverse social and cultural patterns. In Europe, they were Denmark, France, Greece, Poland, Switzerland, United Kingdom, the Union of Soviet Socialist Republics, and Yugoslavia; in North America, three Canadian provinces and four states of the United States; in Latin America, Argentina, Bolivia, Guatemala, Peru, and Uruguay. This study provides historical material on adoptions generally and summarizes past and current legislation and procedures in the designated countries. It does not include eastern and far eastern countries, since the patterns of family life there give adoption a different function from that in the west. We shall select facts from this study which are relevant to our present discussion.

In a number of countries adoption ceased when its original purpose

---

[5] Hartland and others, *loc. cit.,* Vol. 1, pp. 105–106.

[6] "The Twelve Tables of Roman Law and the Institutes of Justinian," Bk. I, title 11, Bk. II, titles 16, 18, in David Nasmith, *Outline of Roman History* (London, Butterworth, 1890).

[7] United Nations, Department of Social Affairs, *Study on Adoption of Children* (New York, 1953), Sales No. 1953, IV, 19, p. 10.

[8] *Ibid;* most of the material for this section is taken from this study.

lapsed, but it survived in others as an indirect means of acknowledging illegitimate children or of evading succession laws. During the nineteenth century some countries even prohibited it. It was only after World War I that several countries passed their first adoption law or revised old ones as a means of providing permanent homes for war orphans and homeless children. France affords an illustration. The origin of adoption in France can be traced back to Roman law, but the practice disappeared almost completely in the Middle Ages. It was reintroduced in 1792. When the Civil Code was being drafted (1800–1804), adoption was retained, but only adults could be adopted. The only provision for minors was that called "benevolent" guardianship, which allowed adoption by will and as a reward to a person who had saved the adopter's life. France, by modification of its adoption legislation in 1923 and subsequently, made it possible to adopt orphaned or deserted minors. "Ordinary" adoption does not completely sever the links of the adoptee from his natural parents and can be revoked. An ordinance of 1945 introduced "adoptive legitimation" on behalf of children under five who are total orphans, abandoned, or of unknown parentage. It integrates the child completely into the adopter's family. French adoption agencies report that there is preference for adoptive legitimation.

In Greece adoption is still considered mainly a means of satisfying the desires of childless persons for children. Switzerland in 1907 was one of the first European countries to pass twentieth-century type of adoption legislation. Before then only eight out of twenty-two cantons had provisions for adoption. Denmark's first adoption law was passed in 1923. In 1918 the U.S.S.R. prohibited adoption, but in 1926 reintroduced it with a view to protecting abandoned children. Until 1946 there was no uniform adoption law in Polish provinces; a 1950 law limits adoption to minors and stresses their interest as a basic consideration. Adoption law was unknown in Yugoslavia until after World War II. Then, a law was enacted which provided a method of care for some 290,000 war orphans, of whom 30,000 had no near relatives.

Most Canadian laws date from the 1920's. Most Latin American countries have known adoption for some time. Many of them have amended their legislation, which was strongly influenced by Roman law, to bring it into line with modern trends. For instance, Argentina did so in 1948, Guatemala in 1947, and Uruguay in 1945. On the other hand, the 1936 adoption legislation of Peru was more restrictive. So, too, was that of Bolivia, which has the oldest Latin American adoption legislation, first enacted in 1831. It only allows the adoption of minors over fourteen years of age and retains adoption as a reward. In all five of these Latin American countries adoption is rarely used and then usually for family purposes rather than as a means of providing for children.[9]

---

[9] Anna Kalet Smith, *Adoption Laws in Latin America,* U.S. Children's Bureau Publication (Washington, D.C., G.P.O., 1950), No. 335.

There is great variation between the countries in legal provisions, practices, standards, and frequency of adoptions. In countries whose legal system derives from Roman law or the Code Napoléon, the links of the adopted child with his own family are not broken. He is not only entitled to inherit from them and their relatives but may be called upon to support them and they him. In other countries the adopted child's relationships with his natural parents are more sharply severed. Among the variations in legislative provisions and administrative procedures we shall mention three: source of placement, legal institution ordering adoption, and form of surrender or consent.

Plans for adoption may be made by the child's parents or relatives, by a third party, or by an adoption agency. Child welfare experts agree that placements arranged by recognized agencies are likely to prove more favorable for the child and his adoptive parents than are private placements by parents, relatives, or other third parties. Despite the paucity of statistical information on adoptions, it seems that almost everywhere the number of independent adoptions exceeds those arranged by social agencies.[10] Many persons vitally concerned with the welfare of children believe that if agencies are not legally assigned the responsibility of making adoptive placements, at any rate, a careful investigation should be required by the court before adoption is judicially ordered. Preferably, it should be by a public or private agency, the standards of which are approved by a state authority. In countries where adoptions, until recently, were, or still are, mostly of the family type, legislation does not mention adoption agencies. In those countries where adoptions are arranged for homeless children, agencies have a role, although often not one which assures adequate protection of the child.

In all countries adoption legislation requires the participation of a judicial or administrative authority. This authority must be satisfied that adopter and child meet the legal requirements, that the adoption is in the interest of the child, and that the persons whose consent is necessary have duly given it. On the last point there are wide differences as to procedure between countries. If agencies play no part in the adoption process, parents must give their consent at the time of the adoption or must have released the child by some acceptable process before the adoption. If the child is legitimate and both parents enjoy parental rights, they must both give their consent. If the child is illegitimate, the consent of the mother is generally enough, although in some jurisdictions if the father has

---

[10] Richard I. Perlman and Jack Wiener, *Adoption of Children: 1951,* U.S. Children's Bureau Statistical Series (Washington, D.C., G.P.O., 1953), No. 14; Marguerite Bengs, "Study of Independent Adoptions in Connecticut since Passage of Adoption Laws," *Social Service Review,* Vol. 20 (September, 1946), pp. 391–395. The latter study shows that of the 673 adoptions made during a given period, 540 were of children who had been placed independently. See also, Margaret Ward, "The State Welfare Department's Responsibility for Investigation of Adoption Petitions," *Child Welfare,* Vol. 30 (June, 1951), pp. 6–13.

recognized or legitimated the child, he, too, must be consulted. If the unmarried mother is a minor, some jurisdictions require that the consent of her parents or guardian be obtained. Where the child is without parents, the consent of the guardian or of the authorities responsible for the child must be secured. As a rule, parental surrender of the child is interpreted as consent for adoptive placement, but formal consent to the adoption itself must be given in whatever form the law prescribes. In adoptions where agencies play a part the compulsory or voluntary surrender of the child before adoption becomes a matter of importance. In some countries it is a legal requirement, and, in others, agencies on their own initiative ask the natural parent to sign a formal surrender of the child to them. Generally, this surrender does not imply a transfer of parental rights or guardianship to the agency. It merely empowers the agency to select an adoptive home for the child. The parent still has to give formal consent to the adoption. In some jurisdictions there may be transfer of guardianship to the agency. If so, the consent of parents to adoption may not be required.

In Argentina and Peru no public or voluntary agency is concerned with placing children for adoption. In Saskatchewan, Poland, Russia, and Yugoslavia, adoptive placements are made only by statutory agencies. Adoptive placements are made by statutory agencies and voluntary societies in several jurisdictions, including Bolivia, Denmark, France, Greece, Guatemala, Switzerland, the United Kingdom, and several of the United States. In some jurisdictions, such as Quebec, Ontario, and Michigan, only voluntary agencies place children for adoption. Sometimes, as in Switzerland and Quebec, voluntary agencies do not have to be specifically qualified or licensed to make adoptive placements, but in others, such as Denmark, France, and some of the United States, they do.

Adoption laws and practices reflect the experiences of any given state and the prevailing attitudes of its citizenry. Interchange of information and knowledge between countries is increasing the interest of governments and voluntary societies in employing good adoption procedures for child welfare purposes. The great increase in the number of adoptions in many countries will undoubtedly provide incentive for improved practice.

The variations in practice between countries show up clearly when placements are made across state lines. Interest in international adoptions has grown at such a rate since World War II that a large-scale study of the procedures and practices involved is required. This is the opinion of the American branch of the International Social Service, Inc., an agency with a history of more than a quarter of a century. Complex and often mutually defeating regulations and laws face couples who wish to adopt a child of a nationality different from their own. The attempt of agencies to insure sound international adoption practices has been impeded because there is no common pool of information between countries about the social, psychological, cultural, and legal results of child placements for adoption.[11] As a first step in the development of some degree of international similarity, the International Social Service Agency has proposed that member agencies confer, examine the problem, and make efforts to bring the sociological implications of intercountry adoptions before those who make the legislation.

ADOPTION IN ENGLAND

There was no provision for legal adoption in England or Wales until 1926, or in Scotland until 1930, the only English-speaking countries of which this was true. Before that there could be no more than an informal or *de facto* adoption, and the natural parents could recover the child at any time. Parliamentary debates and reports of official committees appointed to study the problem showed resistance to introducing a new method of child care, considered to be another means of disturbing parental rights and, hence, of opening the courts to litigation of unfamiliar problems.[12] The original act, although in line with American developments, contained some exceptions. It did not require a preliminary placement or trial period before consummation of adoption; nor did it require that agencies and persons placing children for adoption comply with regulations; nor did it give inheritance rights to the child from his adopted parents. Between 1926 and 1950 several improvements were made in the legislation, and in the latter year the various acts were consolidated in the Adoption Act, 1950.[13] This act provides that

1. The High Court or, at the option of the applicant, any county court or court of summary jurisdiction within which the applicant or the infant resides shall have authority.
2. The societies which act as intermediaries between those who have children they cannot care for and those who wish to acquire children shall register with a local authority and comply with regulations concerning procedures.
3. There shall be supervision of children placed for adoption by third parties.
4. There shall be restrictions on sending children abroad for adoption.
5. There shall be a probationary period of three months under supervision by the local authority.
6. Adopted children, for the purpose of succession to property, shall be

---

[11] *New York Times* (October 25, 1953); Eugenie Hochfeld and Margaret A. Valk, *Experience in Inter-Country Adoptions* (New York, International Social Service, American Branch, 1953).

[12] Gt. Britain, Parl. Papers, 1921, Vol. 9, Cmd. 1254, p. 161; Gt. Britain, Parl. Papers, 1925, Vol. 9, Cmd. 2401, p. 339, and 1925, Vol. 9, Cmd. 2469, p. 349.

[13] 14 Geo. VI, c. 26; British Information Services, Reference Division, *Social Services in Britain,* I.D. 780, revised March, 1953, New York; Margaret Kornitzer, *Child Adoption in the Modern World* (New York, Philosophical Library, 1952).

treated as children of the adopters. (This provision does not yet apply in Scotland.)

Today Great Britain, like many of the states of the United States, has some of the most advanced legislation in the world for the protection of children. Numbers of acts contribute to the welfare of children who require care in addition to that provided by parents. They include the Children Act, 1948, which made improved provisions for the care of all homeless children under seventeen; the Nurseries and Child-Minders Regulation Act, 1948, which requires that nurseries and child-minders must register with the local authority; the Children Act, 1908, replaced and strengthened by subsequent acts, which provides for the prosecution of those who willfully neglect or ill-treat children under sixteen in their charge and which enables juvenile courts to make arrangements to protect such children and, if necessary, remove them from parental control; and, finally, the Adoption Act, 1950. No law relating to the welfare of children stands alone. Great Britain has made an effort to provide a network of laws and administrative agencies to cover the needs of children. The modernized adoption law of 1950 is one of the important recent enactments. In 1927, one year after the passage of the original adoption law, adoption orders were made for 2,967 children. In 1953 the number was approximately 14,000, the peak year being 1946, with 23,500.[14]

ADOPTION IN THE UNITED STATES: GENERAL

Since England had no law of adoption until 1926–1927, the origin of adoption law in the United States is not the common law of England, as is the case in so many other aspects of American family law. The adoption law of Louisiana and Texas was derived from the Code Napoléon, which followed the provisions of the Roman law; that of California was derived from Spain and also of civil-law origin. Although the early laws of some of the states stem from the civil laws, the present laws have lost practically all resemblance to them and to Roman law.

Adoption, a procedure of the civil law, was a method by which a family without an heir might secure one, and a natural father might permanently divest himself of his child in much the same way as he might give or deed away property. Adoption primarily for the benefit of foster parent and child and not for strengthening the family is essentially an American institution. It could thrive only in a country where worth is attached to the individual and not to inherited position. Although for centuries in England great weight has been placed upon inheritance through blood relatives, preferably through the oldest male, it has nevertheless been

---

[14] British Information Services, *op. cit.*, p. 17.

true that the child has no absolute right to his parent's property and he can be disinherited in favor of relatives or strangers. Thus, regardless of whether or not there was a direct male descendant, the family estates and titles could be continued. This fact undoubtedly had much to do with Great Britain's failure to develop a law of adoption as did Greece and Rome.

The early English common law of master and servant and statutory provisions for indenturing and apprenticing poor children probably also postponed realization of the values of adoption. Although the states had no English legal background to fall back upon as they developed a law of adoption, they did have the English experience in caring for dependent and neglected children, which included the institutional facilities of the church, the poorhouse and almshouse, farming out, out-door relief, and the indenture of apprenticeship. The 1601 Elizabethan statute provided for the last four methods of care, and the American colonists naturally adopted them.[15] Experience with these resources for the care of children showed the necessity for carefully structured and adequately manned agencies dealing with children in any way; it also showed the advantages of permanent home care. This latter form of care came to include supervised care in the child's own home under some circumstances, supervised care temporarily in some other home, supervised care permanently where adoption was not possible or advisable, and adoption with a preliminary period of supervision.

ADOPTION IN THE UNITED STATES: STATUTORY PROVISIONS

Since adoption is unknown to the common law, it follows that a legal adoption can be effected only in accordance with the statute authorizing it. All courts agree that there must be at least substantial compliance with the essential requirements of the statute.[16] The early cases held that there must be strict compliance with every statutory requirement for a valid adoption.[17] The prevailing tendency of the courts is to say that the law must be substantially complied with but not so narrowly interpreted as to defeat an adoption or its essential purposes where intent is clear and there has been compliance on material provisions. The courts are quite uniform in applying the rule of strict construction in favor of a parent's

[15] 43 Eliz. I, c. 2.

[16] I C.J.S. 430; 1 R.C.L. 591; I Am. Jur. 624; Peck, *op. cit.;* Madden, *op. cit.*, pp. 354–369; *In re Thorne's Will, Brantingham* v. *Huff*, 155 N.Y. 140, 49 N.E. 661 (1898).

[17] *Appeal of Woodward*, 81 Conn. 152, 70 Atl. 453 (1908); *Purinton* v. *Jamrock*, 195 Mass. 187, 80 N.E. 802 (1907).

natural rights, especially in those cases where it is claimed that owing to misconduct his consent to the adoption is not required.[18]

Adoption being in derogation of the common law, it is necessary to study carefully the statutes of the various jurisdictions to have an understanding of legal procedures and consequences. It is generally believed that the first statute legalizing adoption in the United States was passed in 1851 in Massachusetts.[19] Actually, Texas and Alabama enacted adoption laws in 1850. However, Massachusetts passed the first law in conformity with our present conception of the purpose of adoption, the welfare of the child rather than heirship. The Massachusetts statute became the model for the laws of six other states. Wisconsin passed such a law in 1853, Maine and New Hampshire in 1855, Oregon in 1864, Rhode Island in 1866, and Minnesota in 1876. Another group of states used the New York Civil Code, drawn up in 1865, as a pattern, although it was never enacted into law in New York State. Still another group of states followed the heirship idea expressed in the early French and Spanish laws. Every American jurisdiction now has adoption legislation.

GENERAL CONTENT OF LEGISLATION

Statutes include variations on the following matters: courts assigned jurisdiction; procedure, including consent of parents or guardians and of the child if over a specified age; social investigation designed to help the judge make a decision; trial period before adoption; court action and adoption decree; effects of adoption, including personal and property rights; annulment and revocation; and records and vital statistics.

JURISDICTION

Adoption by a written statement, filed like a deed and sometimes sanctioned by a judge for consummation, has been common. Today, adoption in every American jurisdiction is carried on by judicial procedure, but some of the older methods may occasionally be used. Prior to the passage of the first adoption legislation in England, the question of the machinery for giving official ratification to adoption was seriously considered. In a debate before Parliament on the Adoption of Children Bill, one of its advocates presented the *obiter dictum* of a New York State appellate judge to the effect that adoption proceedings are really not judicial in their nature but executive and administrative.[20] However, the English act

---

[18] I Am. Jur. 626; *In re Havsgord's Estate*, 34 S.D. 131, 147 N.W. 378 (1914); *Glascott* v. *Bragg*, 111 Wis. 605, 87 N.W. 853 (1901).

[19] Eleanor Nims, *The Illinois Adoption Law and Its Administration* (Chicago, University of Chicago Press, 1928), p. 11.

[20] Gt. Britain, Parl. Debates, House of Commons, ser. 5, Vol. 182, 1924–1925, pp. 1707–1717.

when passed in 1926 made the adoption proceeding judicial and not administrative.

An American authority raised the question as to whether adoption requires judicial procedure, or whether a permanent record of a conclusion reached through careful investigation not unlike the making and filing of a deed, if the registration of the transfer is preceded by sound social inquiry, would be a sounder procedure. "As a matter of fact," wrote Professor Sophonisba Breckinridge, "no adoption should result where there is an issue. The true issue arises with reference to the competence of the natural parents. The question of their unfitness presents a real issue. That question having been determined, the question of adoption becomes chiefly a matter of sound social practice." [21]

It seems settled that adoption procedure will continue to be judicial. There is, however, the problem of which court shall have jurisdiction. Several states give jurisdiction to juvenile courts or to courts of domestic relations, sometimes throughout the state and sometimes in a limited area.[22] In most states the probate court has jurisdiction. Unless this court has special provisions for investigation, adoption may be regarded as one of the many matters of probate and not as one in which protection of the child is the primary obligation. In some states jurisdiction may be exclusively in one court, and in others, concurrent jurisdiction may be given to two or more courts. Many of the states specify that the court before which the petition for adoption is filed shall be the county of residence of the petitioner, but some provide that it shall be that of the child. A few provide that it may be either. It is advisable that jurisdiction be given a single court, which should be a court of record having jurisdiction over children's cases. Unless the statute requires that the petitioners be residents of the judicial district in which the court has jurisdiction it is difficult to make an adequate study of the proposed adoptive home or to provide for the necessary supervision after placement.

PROCEDURE INCLUDING SURRENDER AND CONSENT [23]

The procedural features of adoption legislation include the petition of the adopting parents or their substitutes, notice to the child's parents or their substitutes and their consent, the presence in court of the necessary parties, and the judicial determination. The parties to an adoption are

[21] S. P. Breckinridge, *The Family and the State* (Chicago, University of Chicago Press, 1934), pp. 356–357.

[22] Carl A. Heisterman, "A Summary of Legislation on Adoption," *Social Service Review* (June, 1935), p. 269; Morton L. Leavy, *Law of Adoption Simplified,* Legal Almanac Series (New York, Oceana, 1948), No. 3, pp. 30–32; Federal Security Agency, Social Security Administration, *Essentials of Adoption Law and Procedure,* U.S. Children's Bureau Publication (Washington, D.C., G.P.O., 1949), No. 331.

[23] *Essentials of Adoption Law and Procedure,* pp. 5–26.

the persons seeking to adopt, the child's parents or guardian who must consent, and the child.

The adoption law should require that the petition include identifying information concerning the child and the petitioner. Some authorities, including the Children's Bureau, believe that the petition should be accompanied by the written consents to the adoption. If the natural parents do not consent, the person or agency that does should be required to file documentary evidence of authority to consent at the time that the petition is filed or soon thereafter. This evidence should be filed separately from the petition. Upon the filing of the petition, a date should be set for the hearing, and copies of the petition should be sent to the state welfare department, the agency, if any, designated by the state welfare department to protect the interests of the parties, and the agency, if any, that placed the child in the home for adoption. Reasonable time should be allowed between the date of filing the petition and the hearing so as to permit the state welfare department or an agency it designates to obtain essential information through social study and to report to the court.

Perhaps the aspect of the adoption process which causes most problems at the time of the adoption and subsequently is that of parental consent. Consent is that part of the adoption proceedings by which the parent or legal guardian who has not voluntarily given up parental rights or been deprived of them gives his sanction to the adoption. This may be done in person or, more commonly, in writing before the hearing. Consent is required of both parents or, in the case of an unmarried mother, of her alone except in some jurisdictions where the consent of the acknowledged father also is required. If the parents are dead or their rights terminated by law, consent of the legal guardian, whether a person or an agency, is required. Where parents wish to release their rights prior to and apart from the adoption process they may do so in most states by a written document variously called a surrender, a waiver of consent, relinquishment, or a transfer of parental rights. In a number of states voluntary relinquishment is permitted with no sort of court action. Many child welfare workers believe that statutes separate from adoption laws and requiring court sanction of voluntary relinquishment of parental rights should be enacted. In some states there are provisions for termination of parental rights in the juvenile court. Such termination may be made because of parental neglect or abandonment or by a voluntary release as is often done by unmarried mothers. This process we shall discuss in Chapter 15.

Adoption courts frequently have to determine whether there is such neglect or abandonment as to make parental consent unnecessary, thus terminating parental rights. Such controversial matters do not belong in adoption proceedings. Pennsylvania courts encountered a troublesome situation when the hearing judge found the mother had not abandoned her child in such a way as to make her consent to the adoption unnecessary.[24] The facts here were that the paternal grandparents of a boy about five years of age wished to adopt him. His father had died, and although the mother paid little attention to him, she nevertheless refused to give consent to the adoption. The lower court found that there was not abandonment by the mother and, hence, her consent to the adoption was necessary. The appeal court sustained this position in its finding that there was not the intent to abandon and that there were extenuating circumstances for her behavior. Had the Pennsylvania statutes not permitted a finding of abandonment by the adoption court this distressing situation would not have occurred.

We repeat. Statutes should provide for parental consent to the adoption or for filing with the petition the evidence of judicial termination of parental rights, whether as a result of voluntary relinquishment or of court order on findings. It is unfortunate that in some states individuals, agencies, or departments of welfare may still accept parental surrender directly and with no court intervention. When this is the case it is important for all concerned to be sure of the legality of the surrender and the extent of the authority of the individual or agency receiving the parental release. In some instances of this kind adoption courts have been unwilling to accept as sufficient the consent of the individual or agency to the child's adoption.[25]

On the other hand, some courts have been too ready to accept voluntary parental relinquishment. For example, in a West Virginia case an unmarried mother, less than twenty-four hours after her delivery, signed papers giving her consent to the adoption of her child. Later, she sought the revocation of a decree of adoption on the ground that she had not known what she was doing because of the effects of the anesthetic and because of her fears. The court held that the adoption was legal since she had signed the proper papers, the purport of which had been adequately explained to her. It seems clear in this instance that whether or not the legal provisions of the adoption statute were carried out, inadequate social protection was given the unmarried mother and her child.[26]

Another type of situation coming before the courts involves the question of the validity of adoption when actual parental consent is not secured but notice is given the parents through publication. In a Missouri case an unmarried mother, subsequently married to the father of her child, was suddenly called out of the state to care for her mother who was seriously ill. The parents of the child placed him with a nurse. The mother was away for a year and a half, during which time the father

---

[24] *In re Schwab's Adoption*, 355 Pa. 534, 50 A. 2d 504 (1947).

[25] Henrietta Gordon, *Adoption Practices, Procedures and Problems* (New York, Child Welfare League of America, 1952), pp. 16–18.

[26] *Lane* v. *Pippin*, 110 W. Va. 357, 158 S.E. 673 (1931).

informed her that the child was being adequately cared for. The woman who had charge of the child did not receive support from the father, so she turned the infant over to the Evans Home in Kansas City. That institution arranged for his adoption through a court proceeding. Personal service was not made since the identity and location of the parents were not known; service was by publication only. The adoption in this instance was revoked on the ground that insufficient effort had been made to locate the parents.[27]

The laws of some states make parental consent unnecessary when a parent has been deprived of his civil rights or has lost custody through divorce proceedings. The Children's Bureau believes that the consent of parents should be required in all cases in which the parents are alive and their parental rights have not been terminated. Divorce, imprisonment, or insanity should be given consideration in independent actions for termination of parental rights, but eliminating parental consent for these reasons should not be part of the adoption law. Some states require the appointment of a guardian *ad litem* if the parent or parents are minors. Such a guardian is not a substitute for social services. If a father has legitimized his child, some authorities believe that the statute should protect his rights and require his consent to adoption.[28] This is not the prevailing law in the United States. The consent of the child above a specified age is required in most states. That age is usually twelve or fourteen. Younger children sometimes have preferences which should be considered in the social study and supervisory processes.

If adoptions are to stand up in court, valid consent must be secured. Such consent should be preceded by parental deliberation, often accompanied by counsel from social agencies. If there has been careful consideration by parents and their consent has been legally obtained, or if termination of parental rights has occurred, there should be relatively little litigation on the validity of adoptions. Withdrawal of consent should be permitted only after the court has given full attention to the legalities involved and to the effects upon the child. To help the court make a wise decision, the statutes should require a new social study by the state welfare department or by a social agency it or the court designates.

SOCIAL INVESTIGATION[29]

Next to the consent process in importance is the social study. Without a competent social study there is likelihood that the rights of the parties will be inadequately considered. The adoption law should provide that the state welfare department or a social agency it or the court designates make a study of every petition for adoption, advise whether the child is

---

[27] *Rockford* v. *Bailey*, 322 Mo. 1155, 17 S.W. 2d 941 (1929).
[28] *Essentials of Adoption Law and Procedure*, pp. 13–15.
[29] *Ibid.*, pp. 16–18; Leavy, *op. cit.*, pp. 47–51.

a proper subject for adoption, and whether the adoption proposed will give the child a suitable home. A written statement of the facts should be submitted to the court within a specified period before the hearing, together with a written recommendation as to the desirability of the proposed adoption and a verified transcript of the birth certificate of the child. The law should provide that this report, the verified copy of the birth certificate, the documentary evidence of termination of parental rights, and the acquisition of the legal right to consent to the adoption by the legal guardian of the child be closed to inspection except upon written order of the court. All information and all testimony that discloses or tends to disclose the identity of the natural parents should be presumed immaterial to the court's decision and excluded.

The social study should learn about the child's personality and, if he is old enough, how he feels toward the proposed adoption. It should obtain information about the date and place of his birth, his physical and mental condition, his family background, and his religious heritage. It should inquire about the character of the petitioners, their emotional stability, and their ability to provide for the child. It is common belief that social agencies are unwilling to place any but the "perfect" child with the "perfect" foster parents. Many child welfare agencies today do not rule out adoption of children because the study shows physical or mental pathology or because the child is not an infant. If it seems likely that the child and the foster parent can find satisfaction in family living, the adoption is encouraged.[30]

Most states require a social investigation. There is variation as to who may or shall make it. Several states provide that the agency shall be the state department of welfare. Some permit the court to choose from a number of alternatives, including the state department, local probation officers, local public or child welfare workers, local qualified voluntary agencies, or some other discreet and competent person. It is obvious that unless a competent social worker makes the study there is the possibility that inadequate or inaccurate facts and faulty diagnosis, evaluation, and recommendations will result. States differ on the extent to which the content of the investigation is specified by statute or left to administrative discretion. Statutes generally require a term of residence in the adoptive home before adoption is sanctioned. Statutes do not, however, generally require that this trial period follow the petition, thus necessitating a period of judicial supervision.

RELIGIOUS FACTORS

It is the universal practice of social agencies making adoptive placements to match religion of natural and foster parents, if at all possible.

---

[30] Gordon, *op. cit.*, p. 12; Pearl Buck, "The Children Waiting," *Woman's Home Companion* (September, 1955), pp. 33 ff.

Issues arise both in independent and agency placements when there is difference of opinion on religious faith between the parents or guardians and foster parents or indifference on the part of parents or guardians concerning their beliefs and those of the foster parents. Sometimes these issues reach an impasse requiring judicial settlement.

Commentators and courts have seemed to accept the basic assumption that parents, in the absence of additional disturbing factors, have a right to determine the religious upbringing of their children. Recent enactment by numbers of states of "religious protection" clauses in adoption statutes appears to put this principle in jeopardy. We shall refer to two Massachusetts cases which illustrate the dilemma the courts encounter when the parent has placed the child in a home of religious faith different from his or that of the child.

In the petition of Gally *et al.*, an action for the adoption of a two-year old girl was denied in the lower court because the adoptive parents were not of the mother's religion.[31] The mother had given her consent to the adoption, despite religious differences. On appeal the majority of the court held the adoption valid. The statute involved provides that

> In making orders for adoption the judge, when practicable, must give custody only to persons of the same religious faith as that of the child. In the event that there is a dispute as to the religion of said child, its religion shall be deemed to be that of the mother. If the court, with due regard for the religion of the child, shall, nevertheless, grant the petition for adoption of a child proffered by a person or persons of a religious faith or persuasion other than that of the child, the court shall state the facts which impelled it to make such a disposition and such statement shall be made part of the minutes of the proceeding.

Here, the court had to give meaning to the phrase "when practicable." It held that the legislature did not intend, by enactment of the statute requiring the judge in the adoption proceedings to give custody only to persons of the same religious faith as that of the child "when practicable," that identity of religion should be the sole or necessarily the principal consideration. Nor did the legislature cast aside the criterion of the child's welfare. Practicable, according to the court, meant feasible, capable of being put into useful practice, practical suitability in relation to existing conditions. Here, the child's prospects for a happy, normal, healthy childhood were poor. No persons of the same religious faith as that of the mother had sought to adopt the child. There was the chance that the child might have to be reared at the expense of state or private charity. Under such circumstances it would not be practicable to give custody of the child to persons of the same religion. The decree of the lower court was reversed, and the petitioners therefore, were allowed to

---

[31] 329 Mass. 143, 107 N.E. 2d 21 (1952); General Laws (ter. ed.) C.210, Sec. 6B, inserted by Stat. 1950, c. 737 Sec. 3.

adopt the child. The minority gave a stricter interpretation to the statute. It held that the legislature, by modifying the statutes so as to include a clause regarding religious beliefs, intended that more than incidental consideration be given to religion. Legislative intent, it believed, was not carried out, since no evidence was offered on whether or not other homes were available for the child.

In a 1954 widely publicized case the Massachusetts court denied the petition of Jewish foster parents for the adoption of twins whose mother consented to their adoption but whose faith was different from that of the petitioners. The facts in the petitions of the Goldmans were as follows.[32] Proceedings were brought by husband and wife of the Jewish faith for the adoption of twins whose mother and natural father, the court found, were Catholics. The cases were held upon oral evidence and upon reports filed by the department of public welfare and by a guardian *ad litem.* The petitioners had obtained the children when they were about two weeks old from the hospital where they were born and had cared for them ever since, some two and a half years. The mother gave the twins to the petitioners, knowing that the latter were Jewish. She consented in writing on both petitions to the adoptions prayed for and was satisfied that the children be raised in the Jewish faith. The court held that there was ample evidence that the mother was of the Catholic faith, that although the petitioners had a good home and sufficient means, were fond of the twins, and were giving them adequate care, it would not be for their best interest to decree adoption.

The attorney for the petitioners contended that Section 5B of the Massachusetts statutes was unconstitutional as an invasion of religious freedom. The court made short shrift of this contention saying:

> With this (contention) we cannot agree. All religions are treated alike. There is no "subordination" of one sect to another. No burden is placed upon anyone for maintenance of any religion. No exercise of religion is required, prevented, or hampered. It is argued that there is interference with the mother's right to determine the religion of her offspring, and that in these cases she has determined it shall be Jewish. Passing the point that so far as concerns religion she seems to have consented rather than commanded and seems to have been "interested only that the babies were in a good home," there is clearly no interference with any wish of hers as long as she retains her status as a parent. It is only on the assumption that she is to lose that status that 5B becomes operative. The moment an adoption is completed all control by the mother comes to an end.

Subsequently, the United States Supreme Court denied a writ of certiorari.

In a long analysis of this case published in the Boston University Law Review, the attorney for the Goldmans brought out facts not shown in

[32] 331 Mass. 647, 121 N.E. 2d 843 (1954); Cert. denied 348 U.S. 942 (1955).

the reported case.[33] For example, the twins had never been baptized; it was doubtful whether the mother was in reality a Catholic, although there was probably sufficient evidence to infer that she had at one time been such; the guardian *ad litem,* instead of protecting the temporal interests of the twins, appeared to act as a representative of the Catholic church. The writer of the article suggested that the constitutional implications of the court's interpretation were too serious to be sloughed off. "If," in his words, "the court's interpretation of the statute is correct, then what the law did was to impose upon the twins a particular religion and it did so without regard to the intent or wishes of any person bearing any relevant legal relationship to the twins." This seems to be the first case to come before the courts where the religious protection statutes have been interpreted to bar adoptions outside the faith of the natural parent where the adoption is called for both by the expressed wish of the natural parent and consideration of the child's welfare.

In Chapter 9 we showed that the courts have reacted in several discernible ways when custody and religious matters are involved. We observe here that the courts react to religious objections in custody and adoption matters in four essential and sometimes seemingly inconsistent ways. They have:

1. Given controlling weight to religious differences and have rejected the custodian.[34]
2. Permitted the custodian to have the child on condition that it be reared in a specified religion different from that of the foster parent.[35]
3. Accepted or rejected a potential custodian because of his religious affiliation *and* for other reasons as well.[36]
4. Subordinated religious differences to the welfare of the child.[37]

These decisional patterns result from judicial efforts to balance three standards: [38]

1. A parent has the right to determine his child's religion.
2. An individual has the constitutional right to make decisions regarding his religious beliefs and practices.
3. The child's welfare is paramount in custody and guardianship matters.

Even though in a given case the paramount issue is the "child's welfare," content and meaning must be given to the phrase. Reconciliation

---

[33] Leo Pfeffer, "Religion in the Upbringing of Children," 35 B.U.L.R. 334–393 (1955).

[34] *Palm* v. *Smith,* 183 Ore. 617, 195 P 2d 708 (1948).

[35] *Guardianship of Bynum,* 72 Calif. App. 2d 120, 164 P 2d 25 (1945).

[36] *Hernandez* v. *Thomas,* 50 Fla. 522, 39 So. 641 (1905).

[37] *Guardianship of Walsh,* 100 Calif. App. 2d 194, 223 P 2d 322 (1950).

[38] "Religion as a Factor in Adoption, Guardianship, and Custody," 54 Columbia L. Rev. 376–403 (1954), contains a summary of legislation on this subject throughout the U.S.; "Children's Religion Held Sole Criterion in Proceedings Against Welfare Agency for Change of Custody," 65 Harv. L. Rev. 694–695 (1952).

of these three standards or principles is sometimes difficult or impossible of achievement.

The attorney for the petitioners in the Goldman case pointed out that public and private child welfare agencies, deeply concerned about the "black market" in adoption situations, are eager to obtain legislation restricting private adoptions and requiring all adoptions to be channeled through child welfare agencies. He commented: "The support, or at least neutrality of the church is frequently necessary to obtain enactment of the desired legislation, and the church will demand, probably with increasing frequency, inclusion of a 'religious protection' clause as the price for its support or neutrality." It remains to be seen what the trend in judicial decisions will be when conflicts under "religious protection" statutes are brought before the courts.

TRIAL PERIOD IN PROPOSED HOME [39]

Clearly, a child should live a considerable period of time in the foster home before the adoption is culminated. The majority of states have such a provision. The period most often required is six months or one year. Some statutes provide that in the discretion of the court the trial period may be waived. This may be desirable under such circumstances as when the adoptive parents are relatives or when they are leaving the state.

The trial period affords opportunity for observation, counseling, supervision. If the placement has been made by the state department of welfare or a licensed agency with guardianship authority, it is almost certainly true that this period will be used to help all parties to the adoption make desirable adjustments and decisions. If the placement has been made independently, it is quite likely that the petition is not filed until the waiting period is practically over. Thereupon the court is expected to make a quick investigation so that adoption can occur at once. Such procedure precludes a period of supervision by an agency unless the court, for one reason or another, thinks it desirable and so orders. Regardless of who makes the placement, whether natural parents, guardians, relatives, or agencies, the statutes should require that the probationary or trial period be accompanied by supervision. This result could be accomplished by statutory provision that no placement for adoption be made except by a licensed agency. This is not likely to happen since most people seem to believe that parents should be able to release their children if and how they please. They hold that certainly parents should have this right in relation to relatives. Perhaps statutes could provide that no placement for adoption be made by anyone, other than a parent with relatives, except by a certified or licensed agency. Statutes might also provide that following the petition, a period of observation and supervision by an approved agency be required.

---

[39] *Essentials of Adoption Law and Procedure,* pp. 18–19.

About half the states require a trial period of a designated term before the petition can be approved by the court. As we have indicated, in actual practice the period is often legally completed before a petition is filed. In the other half of the states an interlocutory decree is utilized.[40] The intended effects of interlocutory decrees are:

1. To provide the adoption court with a double opportunity for observation and study of the foster home, the period before the interlocutory decree and that intervening between the temporary and final decrees.
2. To diminish the likelihood of withdrawal of parental or guardian consent by the statutory provision that the entry of the interlocutory decree renders any consent irrevocable.
3. To place the burden of responsibility for the care of the child following the temporary decree upon the court and the foster parents and not upon the parent or guardian.
4. To furnish the adoption court with the incentive and the authority to require competent supervision in the trial period.

There are differences of opinion concerning the merits of interlocutory decrees. Some fear that although the court has jurisdiction over the parties for a considerable period of time before the final decree, the trial period before the interlocutory decree and between it and the final decree will often be perfunctory and the supervision routine and meaningless. One consequence may be hastily secured and thoughtlessly given but irrevocable consent. It is the position of the Children's Bureau that an interlocutory decree is unnecessary because under the statutes which it favors there would be no court hearing until a period of supervised residence was completed, at which time the court would be in a position to enter a final decree. Nor, in the judgment of the bureau, is the interlocutory decree necessary to fix responsibility for the child in the period prior to the final decree. This is because that action should have been taken when parental rights were terminated. Responsibility for the child's welfare should remain during the whole adoption process with whatever individual or agency was appointed guardian.[41] The uniform adoption law of the Commissioners on Uniform Legislation provides for an interlocutory decree. The commissioners believe that all parties involved in an adoption process employing an interlocutory decree will be assured protection of their rights.

COURT ACTION AND ADOPTION DECREE [42]

The adoption laws of many states provide that if, after considering the report of the investigating agency and other evidence, the court is satisfied that the petitioner is qualified to rear the child competently, the

---

[40] Leavy, *op. cit.*, pp. 52–57.
[41] *Essentials of Adoption Law and Procedure*, p. 19.
[42] *Ibid.*, pp. 20–21.

child is suitable for adoption, the residence period has been completed, and the best interests of the child will be promoted by the adopters, a decree of adoption so stating shall be entered. The law should provide that as a result of the decree the child becomes the child and legal heir of the adopting parents, entitled to all rights and privileges and subject to all obligations of one born to them in lawful wedlock; that the child is no longer the child or legal heir of the natural parents and thus is not entitled to any of the rights and privileges or subject to any of the obligations of a child in relation to his natural parents; and that the name of the child is as designated, usually that of the adopting parents. The law should further provide that a child legally adopted in any other jurisdiction be accorded the same rights and benefits in all respects as a child adopted within the state. This provision, designed to forestall problems of conflict of laws, is often not included in the statutes. If for some reason the petition is withdrawn or denied or the interlocutory decree set aside, the law should assure the protection of the state to the child. If the permanent custody and guardianship of the child is legally vested in the state welfare department or in a recognized agency, the child should be returned to the department or agency. In any other case the court should certify the case for appropriate action and disposition to the court having jurisdiction to determine the custody of children, usually the juvenile court.

Occasionally, a situation arises where one of the petitioners dies before the final decree but after the child has become adjusted to the foster home. In such event a petition for adoption should not automatically be dismissed but should be reconsidered.[43] The death of a foster parent before the actual filing of a petition for adoption, and the refusal of the child's guardian, the state department of public welfare, to consent to adoption under the circumstances precipitated a Wisconsin *cause celebre*. Public sympathy was with the bereaved widow and not with the department, which was dubbed "autocratic," "bureaucratic," "hard-boiled," and "uncharitable." Hostility was fanned by the extensive and biased news coverage of the *Madison Capital Times*, a daily newspaper with statewide circulation. Interested citizens from all over the state contributed money to the foster mother, Mrs. Tschudy, so that she was able to employ an able attorney to appeal her case to the supreme court of the state.

The facts in the case were as follows.[44] The child, when less than one year of age, was placed with the foster parents, the Tschudys, with a view to adoption. Slightly over one year later the couple asked the department to arrange final steps for the adoption. About that time Mr. and Mrs. Tschudy sought and obtained permission to take the child on a vaca-

---

[43] *Ibid.*, p. 21.
[44] *In re Tschudy's Adoption*, 267 Wis. 120, 65 N.W. 2d 17 (1954).

tion trip to Florida. En route home the husband suddenly died. Thereafter, the widow indicated her desire to keep and adopt the child. In view of the changed circumstances, a social worker from the department informed Mrs. Tschudy that a continuation of adoption plans would have to await the department's reconsideration. About four months later the department advised Mrs. Tschudy that it had concluded to remove the child from her custody. Mrs. Tschudy refused to give up the child, and the department secured an order for a writ of habeas corpus. Mrs. Tschudy refused for several days to relinquish the child but finally did so. About three months later her petition for adoption was heard before the appropriate county court, which ordered the adoption despite the refusal of the guardian, the state department of public welfare, to consent. The department testified that its general but not rigid rule was to refuse adoption to a single parent. It found numerous instances of behavior on the part of the foster mother indicating instability and, hence, decided to deny consent for the welfare of the child.

The main legal issues involved were: Did the trial court have jurisdiction to decree an order of adoption when the state department of public welfare, the legal guardian, refused consent? Did the adoption court have the right to review the action of the guardian in the absence of a statute permitting such review? Was the action of the department in withholding consent arbitrary and capricious? The appeal court held that the county court was without jurisdiction to decree the adoption since the department, the guardian, had not given its consent; that the adoptive court was without jurisdiction to review the administrative actions of the department, acting as guardian; and that the action of the department in withholding its consent to the adoption was not arbitrary, capricious, and unreasonable.

Numbers of sociolegal problems characteristic of adoption cases were involved in the Tschudy situation. They include: Should an adoptive court be able to obtain jurisdiction when the guardian, whether a third person or agency, refuses consent? Are child welfare agencies and state and local departments of welfare, acting as guardians of children with power to consent to adoption, in any different position regarding that power than the natural parents or other individual guardians? Are there any grounds for an appeal from a refusal to consent by a department or agency? If so, should the grounds be set out in the statutes, as, for example, abitrary, capricious, unreasonable refusal? Should statutes provide that single persons, including widows, widowers, divorced, and unmarried persons be able to adopt? As a result of the Tschudy case, the 1955 Wisconsin legislature modified the adoption statute to provide that: [45]

[45] Wis. Stat., 1955, c. 48.85.

If a guardian whose consent is required by S.48.84(1)(c) refuses to consent, he shall file with the court a summary of his reasons for withholding consent. After a study of this report, the court may dismiss the petition on the ground that the guardian refuses to consent or may set a time and place for a hearing to determine whether the guardian's refusal to consent is contrary to the best interests of the child. At least 10 days notice in writing of the hearing shall be given to both the petitioner and the guardian refusing to consent. If the court, after the hearing, determines that the guardian's refusal to consent is arbitrary, capricious, or not based on substantial evidence, it may waive the requirement of such consent and proceed to determine the petition for adoption in accordance with the best interests of the child.

EFFECTS OF ADOPTION, INCLUDING PERSONAL AND PROPERTY RIGHTS

Adoption creates reciprocal rights and duties between adoptive parents and child. Some states provide that the legal relationship shall be the same as that between natural parents and child. Upon adoption, the natural parents are statutorily deprived of their legal rights regarding the child. However, many cases reach the courts where parents claim subsequent rights. This was the situation in a Wisconsin case where prior to adoption the adopting parents promised to allow the father to see and visit his child after adoption. Following the adoption decree, this promise was repudiated. The court upheld the right of the adopting parents to deny this privilege to the natural father and said: [46]

> The order of adoption changes the status of the child, destroys the parental relationship theretofore existing between it and its natural parents, and creates a new relationship between the child and its adoptive parents, which has all the incidents of a status. The adoptive parents can no more barter away their rights in their adopted child or modify its status by contract than could a natural parent under the same or similar circumstances.

The adoptive parents assume the rights to the child's custody, services, earnings, and control; conversely, the child owes the duties of respect and obedience and receives the right to care, protection, and education.[47] Almost all jurisdictions have statutes which expressly recognize that the court, in ordering adoption, may decree a change of name for the child if it is desired.[48] The domicile of the adopted child becomes that of his parents by adoption.[49]

All of the states have statutes which define to a greater or less extent the rights of inheritance created by the adoption process.[50] Much of the

---

[46] *Stickles* v. *Reichardt,* 203 Wis. 579, 234 N.W. 728 (1931).

[47] Madden, *op. cit.,* pp. 359–361; *Purinton* v. *Jamrock,* 195 Mass. 187, 80 N.E. 802 (1907); *In re Ballou's Estate,* 181 Calif. 61, 183 Pac. 440 (1919).

[48] Chester G. Vernier and others, *American Family Laws* (Stanford, Cal., Stanford University Press, 1931–1938), Vol. 4, p. 453.

[49] *Washburn* v. *White,* 140 Mass. 568, 5 N.E. 813 (1886).

[50] Vernier, *op. cit.,* Vol. 4, pp. 408–410.

litigation on adoption arises out of inheritance difficulties. In order for the courts to determine the rights of the adopted child, it is often necessary to consider together the adoption statutes and the laws on descent and distribution. In the absence of explicit statutory provisions, the courts tend to follow common-law rules. In all jurisdictions, with perhaps one exception, the child inherits from his adoptive parents. In a few jurisdictions the right of the adopted child to inherit is not mentioned, but broad provisions conferring the rights of the parent-child relationship on the child seem sufficient to modify the inheritance statutes so as to permit him to "take" or inherit as the child of the adoptive parents.

A few states have express statutory provisions specifying that the child may inherit from collateral relatives of the adoptive parents by right of representation or permitting the child to inherit from the legal descendants of the adoptive parents. Several jurisdictions deny the child the right to inherit from lineal or collateral adoptive relatives. In the absence of express provisions, it is the tendency of the courts to deny the child the right to inherit from the relatives of the adoptive parents, on the old common-law theory that these rights are limited to heirs of the blood.

This was the decision in a Wisconsin case involving $4,000,000. The facts were that James Bradley, a bachelor, died intestate. At the time of his death the only surviving relatives were the daughter of a brother and the adopted son of another brother. The court had to decide the question of whether or not the adopted son was an heir at law of the deceased. It held that such was not the case. In the absence of statutes covering the situation, there was no reason for the court to depart from the common law on descent of property. The court stated: [51]

> One may have the right to assume the status of a father to a stranger of the blood, but he has no moral right to impose upon his brother the status of an uncle to his adopted son. As was said in *Warren* v. *Prescott,* 84 Me. 483, 487, 24 Atl. 948, 17 L.R.A. 435, 439: "By adoption, the adopters can make for themselves an heir, but they cannot thus make one for their kindred."

Since most statutes specifying the results of adoption are usually enacted at the same time as the other provisions on adoption, "it seems unlikely that the statutes on effect of adoption were meant to create rights in favor of the adopted child as against the parties who are total strangers to the adoption proceedings, as well as strangers in blood to the adopted child," unless the provisions to do so are clear.[52] In 1955 the Wisconsin legislature modified its adoption statute so that adopted children inherit from and through their adoptive parents and vice versa. It further provided that the relationship of natural parents and child are "completely altered."

---

[51] *Bradley* v. *Tweedy,* 185 Wis. 393, 201 N.W. 973 (1925); see also, *Hockaday* v. *Lynn et al.,* 200 Mo. 456, 98 S.W. 585 (1906), which contains a long account of adoption history and practices.

[52] 3 Wis. L. Rev. 238 (1925).

Several jurisdictions have express provisions dealing with the child's right to inherit from his natural parents and kindred. A few jurisdictions prohibit the child from inheriting from his natural parents or relatives. It seems to be true that an adopted child, in the absence of a statute to the contrary, inherits from his natural parents as well as from his adoptive parents.[53]

Provisions regarding the rights of the natural and adoptive parents to inherit from the child are likewise confused.[54] The rights of the adoptive parents and their kindred are expressly referred to in over half the jurisdictions.[55] Of these jurisdictions, several permit the adoptive parents to inherit, and some permit the adoptive parents and their kindred to inherit. Only a very few jurisdictions definitely deny the right of inheritance by the adoptive parent. Several of the states exempt from the inheritance right property which the child received from his natural parents or, in some cases, from his blood relatives. The remainder of the states are silent on the subject; however, the general tendency of the courts is to give the adoptive parents the right to inherit but to limit it to property received from them. The inheritance rights of blood relatives are also confused.[56] In some jurisdictions there are affirmative and in others negative provisions on this subject.

Legislatures have not clearly defined their policies on this subject of inheritance and the courts are left in confusion. It seems that certain policies should be laid down in legislation:

1. An adopted child should inherit from both his adoptive parents and their kin, collateral and lineal.
2. An adopted child should not inherit from his natural parents unless there are no heirs, and it is doubtful whether he should even then.
3. Adoptive parents, their collateral and lineal kin, should inherit from the adopted child unless the property has come from his natural relatives, in which case it should revert to them and their heirs.
4. Natural parents and their kin should inherit from the adopted child only when his property has been received from them.

The wisdom and logic of these principles lies in the fact that upon adoption, contacts and associations with the natural parents cease. In fact, it is often true that the adopted child has no knowledge of, and more often no acquaintance with, his natural parents. Except for the tradition taken from English law that property should descend to heirs of the blood, there seems no fundamental reason why an adopted child should not inherit from the collateral and lineal relatives of his adoptive parents and vice versa. The argument that these relatives had nothing to do with the adopting of the child has no reasonable applicability.

---

[53] *Wagner* v. *Varner*, 50 Iowa 532 (1879).
[54] *Warner* v. *King*, 267 Ill. 82, 107 N.E. 837 (1915).
[55] Vernier, *op. cit.*, Vol. 4, p. 413, and table, pp. 416–451.
[56] *Humphries* v. *Davis*, 100 Ind. 274 (1884).

ANNULMENT AND REVOCATION OF ADOPTION

A considerable number of states have laws allowing a proceeding for the annulment or revocation of a valid adoption. The most common provision is for annulment if the adopted child develops feeble-mindedness, epilepsy, insanity, or venereal infection. A few states permit annulment of the adoption if the adopting parent has violated his agreement for proper care and treatment, or if the child does not show proper respect to his adopting parents.[57] For example, a New York court had to determine whether or not the facts justified an annulment. In this instance, a child was adopted when six years of age. About a year later she showed symptoms of St. Vitus's dance. During the next five or six years her conduct was destructive, disobedient, and incorrigible. The court came to the conclusion that the foster parents had made every honest effort to rear the child properly and that due regard for the interests of the child and foster parents required that the adoption be abrogated.[58] In some states there are provisions requiring the intervention of the state welfare department when annulment proceedings are started. Since many children in annulment proceedings are without guardianship protection, such a provision is sound and reflects the theory that the state is ultimately responsible for the welfare of its children. Some states are interested in doing away with abrogation statutes. Wisconsin, for example, abolished its annulment provision on the theory that once an adoption is culminated, the relationship is like that of natural parent and child.

The laws of some states provide that after a designated date from the issuance of the adoption decree, often two years, any irregularity in the proceedings shall be deemed cured. Thereafter, the validity of the decree is not subject to direct or collateral attack. Attacks upon adoptions on the ground of some technical detail or of fraud are frequently made in property and inheritance cases. All statutes should provide for some period of limitation.[59]

RECORDS AND STATISTICS[60]

Adoption records should be private and confidential. This is true of the court record, including the facts of the social investigation and other evidence. None of this material should be furnished any person except

---

[57] Heistermann, *loc. cit.*, p. 284.

[58] *In re Anonymous*, 157 Misc. N.Y. 95, 285 N.Y. Supp. 827 (1936).

[59] *Essentials of Adoption Law and Procedure*, pp. 22–23.

[60] *Ibid.*, pp. 23–24; Federal Security Agency, Social Security Administration, *The Confidential Nature of Birth Records*, U.S. Children's Bureau Publication (Washington, D.C., G.P.O., 1949), No. 332; Helen C. Huffman, "A First Protection for Children Born out of Wedlock," *The Child*, Vol. 11 (August, 1946), pp. 34–37; Helen C. Huffman, "What a Birth Record Means for a Child," *The Child*, Vol. 11 (June, 1947), pp. 202–204.

upon court order. Most statutes so provide. Likewise, birth records should be protected. This is especially true of the records of adopted and illegitimate children, but it is also true of all children. Birth records do and should contain private information, such as complications of pregnancy, the mother's tests for syphilis, the number of stillbirths, the order of birth, the child's crippling conditions, and illegitimacy. Many statutes require that some of this information shall be conveyed to designated officials, for example, illegitimacy to the state department of welfare, or the crippled condition of the child or the syphilis of the mother to the state department of health. Birth records should contain all this information. Such a requirement makes possible the accumulation of social statistics as well as specialized services to children and their parents. What is *not* necessary is the transmission of this information through photostating the entire record as the certified copy.

Everyone sooner or later needs a birth record for proof of age, citizenship, parentage. In most instances all that is needed is proof of date and place of birth. The other data contained on the original birth record is literally "nobody's business." Numbers of states today provide for the issuance of a birth card or a short birth record. This is all that the armed services, the school, the employer, or the Bureau of Old-Age and Survivors Insurance needs. Much unhappiness could be avoided if the following principles regarding birth registration and records were adhered to by all states: [61]

1. Every child has a right to an accurate and complete birth certificate.
2. Birth records should be confidential documents.
3. Special protection should be given to birth records of individuals born out of wedlock. Every effort should be made to prevent disclosure of illegitimate birth, although the fact of illegitimacy should be recorded for statistical and planning purposes.
4. Provision should be made for a new record when a child is legitimized and the original record issued only on court order.
5. Information concerning every adoption should be reported by the court to the state registrar of vital statistics. When the adoption has been culminated provision should be made for a new birth record. It should contain no reference to the adoption except a citation to the law providing for its creation.
6. A birth card showing only the name, date, and place of birth and some means of identifying the original certificate should be issued as the certified copy for anyone needing proof of date and place of birth. No distinction should be made in color, form, or otherwise for any special group of persons.

Efforts to keep records on adoption private have two primary purposes: to prevent idle and "gossipy" curiosity, and to keep natural relatives from interfering in the relationship of adoptive parent and child. It is

[61] Helen C. Huffman, "The Importance of Birth Records," *Proceedings of the National Conference of Social Work: 1947* (New York, Columbia University Press, 1948), pp. 351–360; see also, *Essentials of Adoption Law and Procedure,* pp. 23–24.

desirable to keep the original birth certificate correct so that figures on illegitimacy and other items may be accurate. However, for the future protection of the child, it is reasonable that the birth record available to the new parents and the child show nothing about illegitimacy or adoption. This does not mean that it is sound social policy to conceal the fact of adoption from the child, but merely that when adoption has occurred, the child's past history is "nobody's business."

UNIFORM ADOPTION ACT [62]

After several years of consideration, the National Conference of Commissioners on Uniform State Laws finally, in 1953, accepted an adoption act. Several aspects of the uniform adoption act warrant comment. The act attempts to eliminate chaos and confusion on the matter of consent. Both parents, if living, must give consent for a legitimate child unless parental rights have been terminated. The mother alone, if the child is illegitimate, is required to give consent. The legal guardian has the power to consent if the parents are dead or if the parental rights have been terminated and if authority to give consent has been ordered by the court appointing the guardian. If custody of the child and authority to consent to an adoption have been given to an agency by a court, the executive head of that agency then has the power to consent. Likewise, any person having legal custody after termination of parental rights has the power to consent but, in addition, the court having jurisdiction over the custody of the child must also consent.

Upon the filing of a petition the court must order an investigation by a state department of welfare or a county department of welfare or an agency or a representative of the court. The report must contain a definite recommendation for or against the proposed adoption and indicate the reasons therefore. Following upon the investigation and hearing, the court, if it so decides, issues an interlocutory decree giving the care and custody of the child to the petitioners pending further order of the court. The entry of the interlocutory decree renders any consent irrevocable. Following upon the interlocutory decree, an investigator for the court must observe the child in the adoptive home and report in writing to the court within six months, after which time the petitioners may apply to the court for a final decree. Notice of the time and place of the hearing must be served on the state department of welfare and the investigator.

The court, if satisfied that the adoption is for the best interests of the child, enters a final decree. This procedure is designed to assure social investigations at the time of the petition and prior to the final hearing.

---

[62] *Handbook of the National Conference of Commissioners on Uniform State Laws. 1953* (Baltimore, The Lord Baltimore Press, 1953), pp. 216–222.

It also is intended to reduce the likelihood of withdrawal of consent by parents or guardians. The effect of the final decree of adoption is to entitle the child to inherit real and personal property from and through the adoptive parents in accordance with the statutes of descent and distribution and the adoptive parents and their kindred from the child. The natural parents, unless one of them is the spouse of an adoptive parent, are relieved of all parental responsibilities for the child and have no rights over such adopted child or to his property by descent and distribution. Records must be confidential. The birth record must be changed, and the original certificate of birth sealed and filed. Annulment for such reasons as physical or mental incapacity is permitted only within a two-year period after adoption. Appeal can be taken from any final order, judgment, or decree.

SUMMARY OF PRINCIPLES

The many variations between states in their child welfare and adoptive laws reflect differences in tradition and public interest, in practice and principle. The following principles, worked out by the Children's Bureau, have been completely absorbed into the legislation and administration of no state. Some have been incorporated into the laws and practice of every state; some may or may not eventually be accepted by legislators and practitioners. They nevertheless furnish a basis for discussion and evaluation of policy and practice. They include: [63]

1. The termination of parental rights is as important as the establishment of new parental ties by adoption and should be safeguarded.

2. Placement for adoption should be made only by an agency authorized to so do by the state department of public welfare, which means an agency licensed, certified, or approved by the state department. This principle implies the abolition of private placements, whether by the parent or a third person. This is, of course, a highly controversial principle.

3. Adoption proceedings should be in a court of record having jurisdiction over children's cases, in the home state of the petitioners for adoption, and preferably in the local community in which they live and are known and where the child is properly before the court.

4. In every proposed adoption the court should have the benefit of a social study and recommendations made by the state department or by a local department of welfare or by an approved child-placement agency. At present many states do not require the court to utilize professional social welfare services for the study. There seems little legitimate reason for not making such a statutory requirement.

5. Consent to adoption should be obtained from the natural parents, or, if their parental rights have been terminated, from the person or agency having legal responsibility for the child and the right to consent to adoption.

---

[63] *Essentials of Adoption Law and Procedure,* pp. 3–4.

6. Court hearings should be private and the records protected.

7. A period of residence in the adoptive home, preferably for one year, should be required before the hearing on the petition.

8. In the event that a final decree is not entered, provision should be made for the removal of the child from a home found to be unsuitable and for his care and guardianship after his removal.

9. Safeguards should be provided in related laws, such as those affecting relinquishment of parental rights, regulation of child-placing services, and determination of guardianship and custody of children, so as to assure the welfare of the child and the rights and obligations of parents.

Some experts would add other principles, including one on the subject of inheritance to guarantee that the adopted child inherit from his adoptive parents and their lineal and collateral relatives and, vice versa, that they inherit from him. Some would abolish inheritance from and by the natural parents.

CONCLUSIONS

The exact number of adoptions taking place each year in the United States is not known since some states have no provision for collecting adoption statistics. On the basis of information from thirty-three states which report data to the Children's Bureau, the number is estimated to have reached 80,000 in 1951 compared to 50,000 in 1944, or an increase of 60 per cent. Large increases occurred in the number of adoptions by stepparents and relatives and also by unrelated persons. Two important factors contributed to this increase: an increase in illegitimate births and a diminution in prejudice toward the illegitimate child. About one half of all adoptions concern children born out of wedlock. Adoption rates vary widely in the states, ranging in 1951 from 5.5 per 10,000 children under twenty-one years of age in Kentucky to 27.6 in Oregon. The average rate of all twenty-five states from which the Children's Bureau took its data was 13.0. Rates were highest in the urban states and for white children.[64]

The number of families desiring children, especially babies, for adoption far exceeds the available number except for children of minority racial backgrounds. This means that many applicants are disappointed and some are antagonistic to social agencies. Child welfare organizations make great effort to interpret their work to the public. They attempt to

---

[64] Midcentury White House Conference on Children and Youth, *Children and Youth at the Midcentury: A Chart Book* (Raleigh, N.C., Health Publications Institute, 1951); Clyde Getz, "Adoption," *Social Work Year Book: 1954,* pp. 26–30; *Adoption of Children: 1951,* U.S. Children's Bureau Statistical Series (Washington, D.C., G.P.O., 1953), No. 14; Citizens' Committee on Adoption of Children in California, *Final Report: A Three Year Study* (Los Angeles, 742 South Hill Street, 1953); Ruth F. Brenner, *A Follow-up Study of Adoptive Families* (New York, Child Adoption Research Committee, 1951).

make at least two facts clear: the importance of maintaining natural family relationships when possible, and the paramount issue of the child's welfare, at the same time preserving the legal rights of natural and adoptive parents.[65] Magazine articles and other publications by child welfare workers, adoptive parents, and adopted children facilitate this education.[66] Professional child welfare literature reveals the dedication of workers in the field to helping children and foster parents achieve satisfying family experiences. The law exists to protect the rights of all parties involved in adoption actions.

Selected References

ABBOTT, Grace, *The Child and the State* (Chicago, University of Chicago Press, 1938), Vols. 1 and 2.

———, "Adoption, Modern," *Encyclopaedia of the Social Sciences* (1930), Vol. 1, pp. 460–463.

Adoption, 40 Iowa L. Rev. No. 2, 1955, a symposium.

BRECKINRIDGE, S. P., *The Family and the State* (Chicago, University of Chicago Press, 1939).

BROOKS, Lee M., and BROOKS, Evelyn C., *Adventuring in Adoption* (Chapel Hill, N.C., University of North Carolina Press, 1939).

BROWN, Florence G., and others. *Adoption Principles and Services* (New York, Family Service Association of America, 1952).

CARSON, Ruth, *So You Want to Adopt a Baby,* Public Affairs Pamphlet (New York, Public Affairs Committee, 1951), No. 137.

The Child, ten issues yearly.

Child Welfare, published monthly (except August and September) by the Child Welfare League of America.

COLBY, Mary Ruth, *Problems and Procedures in Adoption,* U.S. Children's Bureau Publication (Washington, D.C., G.P.O., 1941), No. 262.

DOYLE, Kathleen Cassidy, *Homes for Foster Children,* Public Affairs Pamphlet (New York, Public Affairs Committee, 1955), No. 223.

---

[65] William D. Schmidt, "The Community and the Adoption Problem," *Child Welfare,* Vol. 31 (May, 1952), pp. 3–7; Bernice F. Seltz, "Interpreting Good Adoption Practice," *Child Welfare,* Vol. 29 (October, 1950), pp. 16–17; "Social Workers Look at Adoption," *The Child,* Vol. 10 (January, 1946), pp. 110–112. For a negative attitude toward social work practices and adoption, see two articles by Pearl S. Buck, "The Children Waiting," *loc. cit.,* pp. 33 ff., and "We Can Free the Children," *Woman's Home Companion* (June, 1956), pp. 38 ff.

[66] Valentina Wasson, *The Chosen Baby* (Philadelphia, Lippincott, 1950); Frances Lockridge, *Adopting a Child* (New York, Greenberg, 1947); Lucile Tompkins Lewis, *What about Adoption for Me?* (New York, Child Welfare League of America, 1952); Ernest Cady, *We Adopted Three* (New York, William Sloane Associates, 1952); Lee M. Brooks and Evelyn C. Brooks, *Adventuring in Adoption* (Chapel Hill, N.C., University of North Carolina Press, 1939); Carol C. Prentice, *An Adopted Child Looks at Adoption* (New York, D. Appleton-Century, 1940); Florence Rondell and Ruth Michaels, *The Adopted Family* (New York, Crown, 1951), Vols. 1 and 2.

Federal Security Agency, Social Security Administration, *Essentials of Adoption Law and Procedure,* U.S. Children's Bureau Publication (Washington, D.C., G.P.O., 1949), No. 331.

FOLKS, Homer, *Care of Destitute, Neglected, and Delinquent Children* (New York, Macmillan, 1902).

FRANK, Lawrence K., "Childhood and Youth," in *Recent Social Trends,* 1-vol. ed. (New York, McGraw-Hill, 1933).

FREDERICKSEN, Hazel, *The Child and His Welfare* (San Francisco, Freeman, 1948).

GORDON, Henrietta, *Adoption Practices, Procedures, and Problems* (New York, Child Welfare League of America, 1952).

HEISTERMAN, Carl, "A Summary of Legislation on Adoption," *Social Service Review,* Vol. 9, No. 2 (June, 1935).

HOCHFELD, Eugenie, and VALK, Margaret A., *Experience in Inter-Country Adoptions* (New York, International Social Service, American Branch, 1953).

KORNITZER, Margaret, *Child Adoption in the Modern World* (New York, Philosophical Library, 1952).

LEAVY, Morton L., *Law of Adoption Simplified,* Legal Almanac Series (New York, Oceana, 1948). No. 3.

MADDEN, Joseph W., *Persons and Domestic Relations* (St. Paul, Minn., West Publishing Co., 1931).

PECK, Emelyn Foster, *Laws Relating to Interstate Placement of Dependent Children,* U.S. Children's Bureau Publication (Washington, D.C., G.P.O., 1924), No. 139.

———, *Adoption Laws in the United States,* U.S. Children's Bureau Publication (Washington, D.C., G.P.O., 1925), No. 148.

SLINGERLAND, W. H., *Child Placing in Families* (New York, Russell Sage Foundation, 1919).

TENBROEK, Jacobus, "California's Adoption Law and Programs," *Hastings Law Journal,* Vol. 6, No. 3 (April, 1955).

THURSTON, Henry W., "Dependent Children," *Encyclopaedia of the Social Sciences* (1930), Vol. 3, pp. 398–403.

———, *The Dependent Child* (New York, Columbia University Press, 1930).

U.S. Children's Bureau, *The Meaning of State Supervision in the Social Protection of Children* (Washington, D.C., G.P.O., 1940), No. 252.

U.S. Department of Health, Education, and Welfare, Social Security Administration, Children's Bureau, *Selected References on Adoption: June, 1953* (Washington, D.C., G.P.O., 1953).

VERNIER, Chester G., *American Family Laws* (Stanford, Cal., Stanford University Press, 1931–1938), Vol. 4.

Wisconsin Legislative Council, Child Welfare Committee, *Child Welfare Report: 1955* (Madison, Wis., 1956), Vol. 6, Pt. 1, "Conclusions and Recommendations of the Committee"; Pt. 2, "Research Report"; Pt. 3, "Child Welfare Appendices to Research Report."

The student should also consult pertinent statutes and judicial decisions.

CHAPTER 13

Children of Unmarried Parents

INTRODUCTION

DEFINITION

Blackstone defined an illegitimate child as one born out of wedlock. Today, "while an illegitimate child is ordinarily considered to be one born to an unmarried woman, the term applies also to the child of a widowed or divorced woman when the husband could not have been the father and to the issue of void or voidable marriages in the absence of countervailing legislation." [1] So far as the law is concerned, the child of a married woman whose husband has access to her is infrequently considered an illegitimate child. This subject of "adulterine bastardy" we shall presently discuss.

ATTITUDES

Illegitimacy is a universal social phenomenon, but marital institutions and sex mores "differ so widely and are so differently integrated with economic, moral and religious practices" that its social and legal regulation and control are understandable only in light of the period and its culture.[2] History and literature tell us of many bastards who have become famous or infamous as the case may be. William the Conqueror, Erasmus, Leonardo da Vinci, Alexander Hamilton are among the illustrious names.[3] Shakespeare, in *King Lear,* describes the unhappy life of

---

[1] Frank H. Hankins, "Illegitimacy, Social Aspects," *Encyclopaedia of the Social Sciences* (1932), Vol. 7, pp. 579–582; A. C. Jacobs, "Illegitimacy, Legal Aspects," *Encyclopaedia of the Social Sciences* (1932), Vol. 7, pp. 582–586. For documents on this subject, see S. P. Breckinridge, *The Family and the State* (Chicago, University of Chicago Press, 1934), pp. 415–476, and Grace Abbott, *The Child and the State* (Chicago, University of Chicago Press, 1938), Vol. 2, pp. 493–606. See also, *Bastards,* 10 C.J.S. 3–211; *Bastards,* 7 Am. Jur. 623–733; Sidney B. Schatkin, *Disputed Paternity Proceedings* (Albany, N.Y., Matthew Bender and Co., 1944).

[2] Hankins, *loc. cit.,* pp. 579–582.

[3] See Miriam Allen DeFord, *Love Children: A Book of Illustrious Illegitimates* (New York, Dial, 1931), for short biographies and interpretations of the lives of these persons.

Gloucester's illegitimate son Edmund, who, in the following words, reveals his hates and fears, hopes and plans: [4]

> Thou, Nature, art my goddess; to thy law
> My services are bound. Wherefore should I
> Stand in the plague of custom, and permit
> The curiosity of nations to deprive me,
> For that I am some twelve or fourteen moonshines
> Lag of a brother? Why bastard? Wherefore base?
> When my dimensions are as well compact,
> My mind as generous, and my shape as true,
> As honest madam's issue? Why brand they us
> With base? with baseness? bastardy? base, base?
> Who, in the lusty stealth of nature, take
> More composition and fierce quality
> Than doth, within a dull, stale, tired bed,
> Go to the creating a whole tribe of fops,
> Got 'tween asleep and wake? Well, then,
> Legitimate Edgar, I must have your land.
> Our father's love is to the bastard Edmund
> As to the legitimate. Fine word, "legitimate!"
> Well, my legitimate, if this letter speed
> And my invention thrive, Edmund the base
> Shall top the legitimate, I grow; I prosper.
> Now, gods, stand up for bastards!

Have such men been pushed into morbid behavior and neuroticism in an effort to compensate for their unconventional birth with which society has so severely taunted them?

The illegitimate child, or, more accurately, the child of illegitimate parents, has traditionally been treated with neglect and cruelty. One writer described the fate of these children as follows: [5]

> For centuries while the great "civilized" world . . . developed and held its stupid attitude toward illegitimacy, midwives did a lively business disposing of babies born out of wedlock . . . and this not only in Zagreb, not only in Croatia, in Austria-Hungary, but nearly everywhere else in Christendom . . . They did away with them in several ways—by exposing them to cold air after a hot bath; feeding them something that caused convulsions in their stomachs and intestines; mixing gypsum in their milk, which literally plastered up their insides; suddenly stuffing them with food after not giving them anything to eat for two days . . .

Despite the fact that state and voluntary resources today provide many services to meet the physical, economic, social, and psychological needs of the unmarried mother and her child, the prevailing attitude toward her remains intolerant and punitive. The willingness, even eagerness, of many individuals to adopt the illegitimate child indicates changing attitudes toward him.

---

[4] *King Lear*, Act I, sc. 2.
[5] Louis Adamic, *The Cradle of Life* (New York, Harper, 1936), p. 6.

The unmarried mother has innumerable problems to meet. Many of her adjustments to unmarried parenthood stem from earlier unadjustment in the family situation. Stories of some of these mothers and their disturbances have been told by Sara B. Edlin.[6] Over a 40-year period as superintendent of Lakeview Home, a Jewish home for unmarried mothers in New York, she had contact with hundreds of unhappy unmarried mothers. In her thumbnail sketches she shows that the unmarried mother is often emotionally driven to reckless sexual relations with a man who is not a potential husband. This she may do because of her fears, anxieties, frustrations, and deprivations, which grow out of a family situation characterized by conflict and insecurity. Propelled into irregular sex behavior by her hostilities and by her bid for attention and affection, she, in turn, encounters a hostile society that further aggravates her conflicts. Edlin and her staff attempted to halt this vicious circle by warm, human understanding and sound planning. Often this involved helping the mother release her child for adoption.

The law dealing with the child born out of wedlock has been highly variable with respect to the rights of the child to support, protection, inheritance, and filiation. It has varied also concerning the extent of the offense of the parents, particularly of the mother, and of parental responsibilities for the child.[7] The illegitimate child has always suffered unequal treatment as compared with the legitimate child, while adulterine and incestuous bastards have been even less favored. The word *bastard* has been discarded from the statutes of many American jurisdictions because of morality concepts and legal handicaps associated with it. As the state has become more concerned with the welfare of this group of children, the term *illegitimate child* or *child born out of wedlock* has been substituted.[8] In Soviet Russia the phrase in use seems to be *extramarital child.*

HISTORY OF ILLEGITIMACY

EARLY HISTORY

Among primitive peoples an unmarried woman with a child might be favorably received or severely punished, and, likewise, her child have many or few rights. In early Roman law the illegitimate child had neither father nor mother because of the principle of agnation, or relationship

---

[6] *The Unmarried Mother in Our Society* (New York, Farrar, Straus and Young, 1954); see also, Leontine Young, "Personality Patterns in Unmarried Mothers," *The Family* (December, 1945), and *Out of Wedlock* (New York, McGraw-Hill, 1954); Jacob Kasanin and Sieglinde Handschin, "Psychodynamic Factors in Illegitimacy," *American Journal of Orthopsychiatry,* Vol. 11 (January, 1941), pp. 66–84.

[7] Jacobs, *loc. cit.,* pp. 582–586.

[8] In this discussion we shall interchange the terms. We shall use *bastard* only when it is in appropriate historical or legal perspective.

through the father. With the development of the principle of cognation, or relationship through the mother, the illegitimate child came to have rights of support and succession with regard to her.[9] However, the Christian emperor, Constantine, suppressed all rights of illegitimate children against their mothers except those born of concubines. Illegitimate children came to be classed according to the degree of guilt of the union, and their property rights were dependent on their class. Constantine also introduced the doctrine of legitimation through marriage. Under the legislation of Justinian, the children of concubines had especially favorable rights of inheritance. The Roman theories of marriage and legitimacy were based upon the law of property contract and inheritance.

Under Germanic law bastards were cared for and supported by their mothers. Since the German lord, at least in Christian times, could organize his household as he wanted, he could receive his illegitimate child, and if he did so, the child had rights of inheritance like those of the legitimate child.[10] Legitimation of children by subsequent marriage of their parents was almost unknown. Under the ancient laws of France the illegitimate child had the right to seek out his father at least for support, but the Code Napoléon declared: "*La recherche de la paternité est interdite.*" Both the unmarried mother and the child were without legal rights and remained so until 1912. Since that date, courts can inquire into parentage and establish paternity.

CHRISTIAN HISTORY

As Christianity spread through the Roman and Greek empires to the Germanic tribes and on to England, it greatly influenced attitudes and customs in regard to the illegitimate child. Ecclesiastical notions of marriage, sex, sin, and legitimacy were slow to permeate the new Christian world, but gradually they modified the prevailing customs. "Viewing woman as the chief source of sin Christianity tended to degrade motherhood, to accentuate masculine supremacy and to maintain a double standard of morality."[11] Of course, the consequent attitude toward the unmarried mother and her child was uncharitable and inhumane. In the Middle Ages, and even in recent times, the mother might be required to confess her sin before the church congregation.[12] Plymouth Colony, in 1658, ordained lifelong wearing of the letter "*A*" by the adulteress.

---

[9] Jacobs, *loc. cit.*, pp. 582–586.

[10] "Bastard," *Encyclopaedia Britannica*, Vol. 3 (1952), pp. 191–192; Jacobs, *loc. cit.*, pp. 582–586; Wilfred Hooper, *The Law of Illegitimacy* (London, Sweet and Maxwell, 1911), p. 62.

[11] Hankins, *loc. cit.*, pp. 579–582.

[12] Maud Morlock and Hilary Campbell, *Maternity Homes for Unmarried Mothers*, U.S. Children's Bureau Publication (Washington, D.C., G.P.O., 1946), No. 309.

Hawthorne's *Scarlet Letter* describes the suffering of Hester Prynne, an unmarried mother, who was subject to this penalty. Sir Walter Scott, in *The Heart of Midlothian,* tells the story of Effie Deans, sentenced to death for the supposed murder of her illegitimate baby at birth, who actually had been stolen.

In order to adapt itself to the pagan customs of Europe and to increase morality, the church, as we saw in Chapter 2, was forced to recognize marriages contracted by mere consent of the parties and without the sanction of the church. The ecclesiastical courts were obliged to concede that such marriages were legal, although they could reject them as invalid within the church and could inflict penalties upon the participants. In the early centuries the church did not touch the matter of legitimacy of children or give any rights of succession to children born of irregular unions, as that was a matter of secular law.[13] However, in the eleventh century the church created a situation in which it must decide upon legitimacy. By a canon of the Council of Poitiers (A.D. 1078), birth in a valid marriage was necessary for selection to any ecclesiastical office. In this way, incontinent clergy could not pass on to their sons the benefits of their office. "Parents were to be punished in their children's disabilities more effectively than in themselves."[14] Having a species of legitimacy actions of its own and already possessing jurisdiction in matrimonial causes, it was natural for the church gradually to expand the groups of legitimated children. These groups included those whose parents had entered with good faith into a marriage invalid because of some impediment unknown to them and those born to parents who later married.

The church's usurpation of the power to determine legitimacy brought conflict with the temporal authorities, who based their opposition to legitimation by a subsequent marriage upon the matters of uncertainty and of prudence. It was not that such marriages were invalid, for the ecclesiastical courts passed upon that matter, but proof of such marriages was often difficult. In England this opposition was expressed in the statute of Merton, by which it was provided that "When in the King's Court it is objected to any that he is a bastard because born before the marriage of his parents, the plea is to be sent to the bishops to inquire whether he was born before marriage."[15] The common-law courts were thus, in effect, saying to the church: "We will give you the duty of determining the date of birth in relation to the date of marriage, but you cannot legitimate the child by subsequently solemnizing the marriage." In time the church

---

[13] For erudite discussion of this aspect of the subject, see Joseph Cullen Ayers, Jr., "Historical Background of Legitimacy and Marriage," 16 Harv. L. Rev. 22–42, (1902).

[14] *Ibid.*, p. 37.

[15] 20 Henry III, c. 9.

refused to perform this function for the king's courts if it could not then legitimate the child. This left with the common-law courts the exclusive responsibility of passing on the fact of legitimacy.[16]

ENGLISH HISTORY

COMMON LAW

The illegitimate child was legally isolated from his parents, for the common law from the Middle Ages recognized no legal relationship between him and his mother, much less between him and his father.[17] The child was *filius nullius,* or *filius populi,* or *heres nullius.* He was kin to no one. Since he was not even considered the lawful child of his mother, he could not inherit from her. He could not inherit real property from his own issue. He had no heirs but those of his own body. If he died without lawful issue, any real or personal property he possessed escheated to the crown. He was disqualified from becoming a member of trade guilds. He could not take holy orders without special dispensation. Legally, he was turned adrift. Until the enactment of the poor laws nobody or no unit of government was responsible for him. *Filius nullius* was carried to its logical extreme, for even if the child was born of serf parents, he was free.

Although all this was true, many illegitimate children were born into noble families and were often treated with high regard. William the Conqueror made no disguise of his illegitimate origin, and in the twelfth and succeeding centuries the title "bastard" was borne as a common cognomen by many men of gentle though unlawful birth without suggestion of reproach or shame.[18] Yet legitimacy as the only rightful basis of title to land by inheritance was firmly established in Norman law and custom. Inferiority of legal status was not necessarily accompanied by loss of social status. The Norman *Fitz,* the equivalent of *fils,* is said to have been the prefix given by a father to his bastard son whom he was willing to acknowledge. "Though bastardisme can make no title good, yet know a Bastard may have noble blood; and challenge kindred with the best." [19]

---

[16] Hooper, *op. cit.,* pp. 53–54.

[17] Jacobs, *loc. cit.,* pp. 582–586; Joseph W. Madden, *Persons and Domestic Relations* (St. Paul, Minn., West Publishing Co., 1931), pp. 336–354; Sir William Blackstone, *Commentaries on the Laws of England in Four Books* (Philadelphia, Rees, Welsh, and Co., 1897), Bk. 1, pp. 454–460. Ernst Freund, *Illegitimacy Laws of the United States and Certain Foreign Countries,* U.S. Children's Bureau Publication (Washington, D.C., G.P.O., 1919), No. 42; *Standards of Legal Protection for Children Born Out of Wedlock,* U.S. Children's Bureau Publication (Washington, D.C., G.P.O., 1921), No. 77; Schatkin, *op. cit.,* pp. 7–12.

[18] Hooper, *op. cit.,* p. 6.

[19] Taken from a sixteenth century quotation in Hooper, *op. cit.,* p. 6.

ADULTERINE BASTARDY [20]

Although the problem of illegitimacy is largely concerned with children of unmarried parents, there is an interesting history of adulterine bastardy associated with the theory of presumption of legitimacy. Since the common law was so hard on the bastard, it is not strange that this theory should develop. It was a maxim of the Roman law that a child born in marriage was legitimate. At common law a child whose parents married after its birth was a bastard, but a child born in marriage was presumed to be legitimate.

From the cases reported in the year books of the various kings, it seems that toward the close of the fifteenth century rules respecting the legitimacy of issue born during coverture were well settled. The only possible grounds upon which the child of a married woman, begotten and born during the marriage, could be bastardized was by the "special matter" of the impotency of the husband, a separation by sentence of divorce, or nonaccess because of absence from the king's realm, or the so-called *Quattuor Maria,* or beyond-the-four-seas doctrine. The rule held even if the woman eloped from her husband and lived with her lover. During the reign of Henry VIII, two instances occurred in which women of high social rank had children born in adultery while their husbands were in the realm, and in order to prevent the issue from inheriting, two acts of Parliament were passed bastardizing the children. Without these special acts, the common law would not have declared the children bastards, since the husbands were still in the realm and capable of access.

Up to the eighteenth century, cases in the year books substantiated the same rule. The first deviation from the set rule was to permit the receipt of evidence "of impossibility of access from whatever cause such impossibility might arise" [21] and not merely because of absence from the king's realm. It was necessary, however, to prove impossibility and not improbability of access. A further and later deviation from the general rule was established in the Banbury case, where it was held that circumstantial, in contrast to direct evidence, could be admitted to prove nonaccess. The old rule that the husband was the father of his wife's child if within the realm or unless the most conclusive and irresistible evidence of impossibility of access was given, was shaken by the Banbury case.

Sir Harris Nicolas, who wrote his book on adulterine bastardy in 1836, regretted the overriding of the certain rule that a child could not be bastardized except upon conclusive and irresistible evidence that the husband could not by any possibility have begotten the child. The new rule, which rendered a question of so much delicacy and uncertainty a

---

[20] Sir Harris Nicolas, *A Treatise on the Law of Adulterine Bastardy* (London, William Pickering, 1836), p. 56; 10 C.J.S. 18–24; 7 Am. Jur. 654–660.
[21] Nicolas, *op. cit.*, p. 257.

matter of opinion and not of substantive facts, and which involved in its decision "the pure fame of one of the parties, the inheritance of the other, and probably the happiness of both, which may cause the son to look upon his mother as the author of his shame, and thus break asunder the most beautiful moral tie by which society is united," was in his opinion unsound and unwise.[22]

The English and American rule which finally emerged concerning the legitimacy of children born in wedlock seems to be that in the absence of strong evidence that the husband is not the father, the child is legitimate. If opportunity for access by the husband is shown, there is strong presumption that the child is his. "Sexual intercourse is to be presumed where personal access is not disproved, unless such presumption is rebutted by satisfactory evidence to the contrary; and when sexual intercourse is presumed or proved, the husband must be taken to be the father of the child, unless there was a physical or natural impossibility that such intercourse should have produced such child." [23]

Determining the illegitimacy of children of married women was made more complex by the eighteenth-century rule concerning the competency of husband and wife to testify regarding nonaccess. In 1734 Lord Hardwicke laid down the rule that a wife was a competent witness to prove adultery between herself and her paramour. However, it was improper, because of her interest in relieving her husband of the burden, to charge the defendant with the maintenance of the child upon the mother's *sole* and *uncorroborated* testimony of the nonaccess of the husband.[24] This rule was overridden in 1777 by Lord Mansfield, who announced that as the law of England was founded in decency, morality, and policy, neither husband nor wife would be permitted as a witness to bastardize the issue of the wife by testifying to the nonaccess of the husband.[25]

Wigmore comments on the Mansfield rule as follows: [26]

> In every sort of action whatever, a wife may testify to adultery or a single woman to illicit intercourse; yet the one fact singled out as "indecent" is the fact of non-access on the part of a husband. . . . The truth is that these high sounding "decencies" and "moralities" are mere pharisaical after thoughts, invented to explain an otherwise incomprehensible rule, and having no support in the established facts and policies of our law. There never was any true precedent for the rule; and there is just as little reason of policy to maintain it.

This authority also states that in the United States "the circulation of Lord Mansfield's dogmatic pronouncement, in the treatises of the early 1800's soon brought the new rule to the attention of our courts; and they

[22] *Ibid.*, p. 282.

[23] *Cross* v. *Cross*, 3 Paige 139 (Ch. N.Y. 1832); see also, Freund, *op. cit.*, p. 11.

[24] John Henry Wigmore, *Evidence* (Boston, Little, Brown, 1923), Vol. 4, pars. 2063–2064.

[25] *Goodright* v. *Moss*, 2 Cowper 591 (1777).

[26] Wigmore, *op. cit.*, p. 388.

seem usually to have accepted it with unquestioned faith. It may have become, in some jurisdictions, too deeply planted to be uprooted."[27] For example, in a Wisconsin case the court stated: "No rule of evidence is better settled than that husband and wife are alike incompetent witnesses to prove the fact of nonaccess while they lived together."[28]

Although this rule is still adhered to in numbers of American jurisdictions, it has been modified in some by legislation and court decision. Statutory change was hastened during World War II because of the problem of children born out of wedlock to married women whose husbands were in service. Sometimes the mother wanted to release the child for adoption but could not without her husband's consent. It became necessary for social agencies to ascertain what were the legal rights and responsibilities of husband and wife, of father, mother, and child. If the mother confided in her husband and he was willing to accept the child, no legal question was involved. If she confided in him and they both chose to relinquish their rights and place the child for adoption, the procedure was simple. If, however, the mother did not want her husband to know, social and legal problems arose. There was no uniformity of law and agency practice. In some jurisdictions the mother could illegitimize her child on her own uncorroborated or corroborated evidence. In others, where she was not permitted to testify regarding the nonaccess of her husband, a social agency might obtain evidence from the armed forces of the prolonged absence of the husband. Thereupon the court, often the juvenile court, terminated the mother's parental rights and transferred them to the social agency. Frequently, married women refused to illegitimize their children because of fear of publicity and exposure. The result was that sometimes their children were neglected and even abandoned. Agencies which assumed responsibility for protection of these children with and without court order were uncertain of their legal rights. Sometimes the adoption court, in effect, illegitimized the child and was then in a position to secure the mother's consent to adoption.[29] As a result of this confusion legislatures of several states modified their statutes regarding the competence of husband and wife to testify to nonaccess. For example, Wisconsin in 1945 changed its restrictive law so that it now provides that[30]

---

[27] *Ibid.*, p. 385.

[28] *Koenig* v. *State*, 215 Wis. 658, 255 N.W. 727 (1934).

[29] Frieda Ring Lyman, "Children Born out of Wedlock to Married Women," 3 Brief Case, 56–59 (1945); Maud Morlock, "Adoption of the Child of a Married Woman," *Child Welfare League of America Bulletin* (now *Child Welfare*), Vol. 24 (December, 1945), pp. 10–11; "A Wartime Adoption Problem: The Adoption of Children Born out of Wedlock to Married Women Whose Husbands Are Overseas," *Child Welfare League of America Bulletin*, Vol. 23 (November, 1944), pp. 9, 15.

[30] Wis. Stat., 1955, c. 328.39(1).

Whenever it is established in an action or proceedings that a child was born to a woman while she was the lawful wife of a specified man, any party asserting the illegitimacy of the child in such action or proceeding shall have the burden of proving beyond all reasonable doubt that the husband was not the father of the child. In all such actions or proceedings the husband and wife are competent to testify as witnesses to the facts.

MOTHER'S RIGHTS OF CUSTODY AT COMMON LAW

At common law, since the illegitimate child was regarded as *filius nullius,* no one had the legal right to his custody. The community was eager to shunt responsibility for him, so in the absence of any claims for him, the mother had a moral right which may or may not have carried with it a legal right. As late as the end of the eighteenth century, although the courts granted to a mother a writ of habeas corpus to obtain her child taken from her by force or fraud, they took pains to point out that the issuance of the writ did not mean a legal right to custody.[31]

The legal right of the unmarried mother to the custody of her child was not firmly established in England until 1891 in the case of *Barnardo* v. *McHugh.* The facts here were that an illegitimate boy, born in 1878, baptized a Catholic in 1880 and a Protestant in 1884, was admitted into one of Dr. Barnardo's Homes for Destitute Children in 1888, two years after his mother had married McHugh. The mother signed an agreement to leave the boy there for twelve years. In 1890 the appellant was required to deliver the boy to a person named by the mother, her desire being to have the child brought up a Roman Catholic. When the appellant refused to break the agreement, proceedings were instituted to compel him to do so. The questions before the court were: Under the circumstances, did Dr. Barnardo have the right to retain the child in his home against the will of the mother? Whose was the rightful guardianship? Had the mother of an illegitimate child a legal right to its custody? Lord Herschell said: [32]

I cannot but think that the legislation embodied in the Poor Law Act (4 and 5 William IV, c. 76 sec. 71) renders it impossible in the present day to regard the mother of an illegitimate child as destitute of any rights in relation to its custody. The obligation cast upon the mother of an illegitimate child to maintain it till it attains the age of sixteen appears to me to involve a right to its custody."

ENGLISH STATUTORY PROVISIONS REGARDING ILLEGITIMACY

For several centuries in England the parents of illegitimate children had no legal duties except those under the poor laws. Legislation enacted

[31] *R.* v. *Soper,* 5 Term R 278 (1789); Schatkin, *op. cit.,* p. 10.
[32] L.R. App. Cases 388 (1891).

in 1576 during Elizabeth's reign compelled support by either or both the mother and father, the basic purpose being to relieve the parish of the burden of support. This law provided: [33]

> Concerning bastards begotten and born out of lawful marriage (an offence against God's law and man's law) the said bastards being now left to be kept at the charge of the parish where they be born, to the great burden of the same parish, and in defrauding of the relief of the impotent and aged true poor of the same parish, and to the evil example and encouragement of lewd life: it is ordained and enacted by the authority aforesaid, That two justices of the peace . . . shall and may by their direction take order, as will for the punishment of the mother and reputed father of such bastard child, as also for the better relief of every such parish in part or in all; and shall and may likewise by like discretion take order for the keeping of every such bastard child, by charging such mother or reputed father, with the payment of money weekly or other sustentation for the relief of such child, in such wise as they shall think meet and convenient: and if after the same order . . . any of the said persons, viz. mother or reputed father . . . shall not for their part observe and perform the said order; that then every such party to making default in not performing of the said order, to be committed to work to the common gaol.

Compelling support by the father in order to keep the child from becoming dependent upon the parish and placing the primary obligation for support upon the mother have been the main characteristics of English and American bastardy legislation. Modern English statutes on illegitimacy provide, among other things, that

1. The mother may bring action against the putative father to determine paternity and to secure support.
2. If the illegitimate child is likely to become a public charge or is such, his adjudicated father shall pay the locality for his support.
3. The prime duty to support the child until he is sixteen is that of the mother.
4. A child born out of wedlock becomes legitimate upon the marriage of his parents, with substantially the same rights and duties as a child born legitimate. This was not achieved until 1926.[34]
5. The illegitimate child inherits from his mother if she dies intestate and does not have legitimate children, and she inherits from her illegitimate child.
6. Since 1906 the illegitimate child can receive benefits under the Workmen's Compensation Acts and, more recently, under other insurance acts.[35]

ILLEGITIMACY: CUSTOM AND LEGISLATION AROUND THE WORLD

For centuries no great improvement in the legal position of the illegitimate child occurred. It was not until the twentieth century that new concepts of the rights of illegitimate children were effectuated. Minne-

[33] 18 Eliz. I, c. 3.
[34] 16 and 17 Geo. V, c. 60.
[35] 6 Edw. VII, c. 58, s. 13.

sota passed the first liberal law in this country; Norway the first in Europe.

The Norwegian illegitimacy law of 1915, together with other child welfare laws amended or enacted at the same time, placed the illegitimate child virtually on the same basis with the legitimate child. Organized labor and Johan Castberg were largely responsible for the changes in the Norwegian laws; Castberg's name has become identified with the reform. The Norwegian law had considerable influence on the development of legislation in the United States. The most important provisions of the law were: [36]

1. The burden of establishing paternity and of fixing the obligation of maintenance was placed upon the state instead of upon the mother, and she was required to report to local authorities the information needed. If the identity of the father was not ascertainable, the burden of support of mother and child was placed on the several persons involved.

2. Full rights of inheritance were given to an illegitimate child in the line of the father, and a child of an illegal or void marriage was deemed legitimate.

3. Support according to the means of the better situated of the parents, maintenance to the age of sixteen, and payment of the special expenses of the mother in connection with the birth of the child were required.

We observed in Chapter 9 that great differences exist between the countries of the world with regard to parental rights and duties. This is true of both legitimate and illegitimate parents. Parental authority under most legal systems belongs primarily to the father when both parents live together in the family home. Where the parents are separated or divorced, the child's welfare generally becomes the most important factor in the choice of the parent who is granted parental powers. In most legal systems the legal relationships between the child born out of wedlock and his parents form a pattern different from that of a legitimate child. Most laws recognize more readily the relationship of the illegitimate child to the mother than to the father and, consequently, impose more duties upon her and give her more rights with respect to the child. In several legal systems, as in the Scandinavian countries, where the status of a child born out of wedlock comes closer to that of the legitimate child than of other countries except perhaps Russia, both parents have generally equal rights and duties. In most countries there are provisions for legitimation by subsequent marriage of the parents.

The extent to which legal relations exist between parents and their children born out of wedlock varies between different legal systems.[37] With few exceptions both parents have the same rights voluntarily to

---

[36] Leifur Magnusson, *Norwegian Laws Concerning Illegitimate Children,* U.S. Children's Bureau Publication (Washington, D.C., G.P.O., 1918), No. 31, p. 12.

[37] United Nations, Economic and Social Council, Commission on the Status of Women, *Parental Rights and Duties* (December 8, 1953), Doc. E/CN,6/230.

recognize or acknowledge their illegitimate children. Under several systems the relation of mother to child exists in law as a consequence of birth. In others maternity must be formally acknowledged or judicially established, although proof of birth and identity of the child are sufficient to support a court order. This is true in Argentina, Belgium, Brazil, Chile, and France. In some countries a legal relationship with the father cannot be established. Under most systems some formal act of recognition is a prerequisite to the establishment of parental relations with the father.

Frequently, court actions resulting in the establishment of legal relationships between the alleged father and the child, including inheritance rights, must be distinguished from actions for the purpose of establishing the father's duty to support the child. Some systems which do not encourage establishing general parental relationships between the father and his illegitimate child do adhere to the principle and practice of requiring support. Under Moslem law, as applied to Moslems in Egypt, India, Pakistan, and Saudi Arabia, a child born out of wedlock is in legal relationship only with the mother. There is no provision for voluntary or forced acknowledgment of paternity of a child born out of wedlock for any purpose. Legal relationships exist between father and illegitimate son but not between father and illegitimate daughter under Hindu law. In Belgium the child born out of wedlock has no legal relationships to either parent in the absence of formal recognition voluntarily made or judicially decreed. But with respect to recognition by judicial decree, the law makes a sharp distinction between the father and the mother. Establishment of paternity is permitted as to the father who has neither voluntarily recognized his child nor treated him openly as his own only if he committed rape or seduction against the mother during the period of conception. Under the Greek code a child is always deemed legitimate in relation to his mother, and it permits an action to establish paternity without proof of such criminal acts as rape or seduction. However, proceedings may not be instituted if it is established that the mother was a woman of notoriously loose conduct at the time of conception. Under the Scandinavian systems the establishment of paternity with full legal consequences of the relationship, far from being limited by law, is made compulsory.

Generally, the mother's rights of custody, guardianship, and inheritance and her financial obligations are greater than those of the father. Some systems, by analogy to the father's superior rights with respect to legitimate children, grant him priority over the mother where both seek custody. In some countries where, in the normal family the parents share parental power equally, the mother nevertheless is favored over the father of illegitimate children. Under Moslem law the custody of a child born out of wedlock belongs as a right to the mother and to her relations, who must assume the full burden of maintenance. No inheritance rights exist between the child and his father.

Under Hindu law the mother of the illegitimate child is the lawful guardian and entitled to custody, but if the father admits paternity and seeks custody, he has a preferential right, and the child usually bears his name. Children born out of wedlock may inherit from their mother, but their rights are usually subordinate to those of any legitimate children. Under Belgian law, if the child is acknowledged by both parents, they have equal rights to custody, guardianship, and inheritance, and the child may succeed to the property of either parent subject to the legal portions of legitimate children. Under the Greek code the father who has voluntarily acknowledged his illegitimate child exercises the parental authority, is primarily liable for the child's support, and is entitled to custody. The illegitimate child has the same right as the legitimate child to the estate of his mother and her relatives. He may, if acknowledged, inherit his father's property, but his share is reduced by half if there are legitimate children. In Norway the mother has a prior right to the guardianship and custody of the illegitimate child, regardless of the acknowledgment of the father. There is no difference based on legitimacy between children with respect to inheritance rights, except that the child and his father do not inherit from each other if the child is conceived as a result of rape or other immoral offense. The Swedish law provides that an illegitimate child and his father inherit from each other only if the child was a "bethrothal child" or if the father made a declaration that the child should be entitled to inherit from him on the same footing as a legitimate child. In Denmark, although children born out of wedlock have the same right of inheritance as legitimate children, a father may inherit no more than the child has received from him by gift.

The above data, culled from a United Nations document, bear out the findings and conclusions of earlier reports of the League of Nations. A 1929 study by the Child Welfare Committee of the League of Nations, based on answers from thirty-seven countries to numerous questions on the legal situation of illegitimate children, showed that legislation was hesitating between two tendencies. The first upheld the principles of the inviolability of the family and gave the illegitimate child the position of *filius nullius* while providing for its maintenance on humanitarian grounds. The second granted the illegitimate child all or most of the advantages of legitimacy. The legislation of the countries in the first group stems from the Code Napoléon; that of the second group is more or less directly derived from the Germanic Codes.[38]

In 1932 the Child Welfare Committee of the League of Nations dealt with the position of illegitimate children in respect to social insurance,[39]

---

[38] League of Nations, Child Welfare Committee, *Study of the Position of the Illegitimate Child Based on the Information Communicated by Governments* (C.P.E. 141[1]; Ser. L.o.N.P., 1929.IV.5).

[39] League of Nations, Child Welfare Committee, *Position of the Illegitimate Child under Social Insurance Law* (C.395.M.221, 1932.V; Ser. L.o.N.P., 1932.IV.4).

and in the same year it reported on the values of official guardianship for all illegitimate children.[40] The committee also studied the systems adopted in various countries where the authorities are empowered to issue abridged extracts of birth certificates and other official documents not divulging illegitimacy.[41] In 1939 the League Advisory Committee on Social Questions submitted a report on the legal position of the illegitimate child in twenty-two countries.[42] It showed wide variation between countries in respect to (1) the civil status of the child, (2) the legal protection given him, (3) the legal protection of the mother, (4) the measures of the social insurance laws, and (5) special social welfare measures, including relief and public health. It seems reasonable to believe that various international organizations, especially units of the United Nations, will intensify their concern for children born out of wedlock and their parents. These organizations are in a position to gather and disseminate information and to encourage liberalized attitudes, legislation, and practices.

ILLEGITIMACY LAW IN THE UNITED STATES

The legal sources of most American legislation on illegitimacy are the English common law, the English and American poor laws, and the English law establishing a clear line of descent to the succession of property. Bastardy in England and the colonies was not an offense under the criminal laws, but to have an illegitimate child who was likely to become a public charge was an offense against the poor laws. Bastards did not inherit from either parent, so succession to property was not complicated by the fact of irregular birth. In his discussion of bastards, Blackstone enumerated three problems which the English courts encountered: [43] Who were bastards? What were the legal duties of parents toward bastards? What rights and incapacity attended bastards? The answers were brief: The bastard was any child begotten and born out of wedlock. The legal duties of the parents were limited to those provided for under poor-relief statutes. The child had only those rights which he could acquire, for he was heir to no one and had no heirs except of his own body.

The states early accepted the support type of bastardy legislation enacted in England and have slowly adopted other legislation affecting the status and civil rights of illegitimates.[44] "As early as 1785 Virginia intro-

---

[40] League of Nations, Child Welfare Committee, *Official Guardianship of Illegitimate Children* (C.265.M.153, 1932.V; Ser. L.o.N.P., 1932.IV.1).

[41] League of Nations, Child Welfare Committee, *Disclosures of Illegitimacy in Official Documents* (C.373.M.184, 1933.IV; Ser. L.o.N.P., 1933.IV.2).

[42] League of Nations, *Study of the Legal Position of the Illegitimate Child* (C.70.M.24, 1939.IV; Ser. L.o.N.P., 1939.IV.6).

[43] Blackstone, *Commentaries*, Bk. 1, p. 454.

[44] James Kent, *Commentaries on American Law* (Boston, Little, Brown, 1896), Vol. 1, p. 214.

duced the three reforms most conspicuous in this respect: making the issue of certain annulled marriages legitimate; adopting the civil law principle of legitimation by subsequent matrimony; and creating rights or intestate succession between the illegitimate child and the mother." [45] Since then these reforms have become the law in most states, although only recently has the illegitimate child prevalently had the right of inheritance from his mother. Legislation bearing on the status of the illegitimate child with reference to his father is scanty and uneven.

LEGITIMIZATION [46]

Statutes provide three methods by which a child born out of wedlock may gain the status of a child born in wedlock: (1) by marriage of the parents after the birth of the child, (2) by a petition to a court for legitimization of the child if the parents are not married, (3) by acknowledgment of paternity. There is frequent confusion regarding the distinction between adjudicaton of paternity and legitimization. Whether or not adjudication of paternity, or voluntary acknowledgment, is sufficient to legitimate the child depends upon the statutes and their judicial interpretation. The courts are often required to define acknowledgment, since the statutes do not generally do so. The Illinois court, in a 1905 case, held that the acknowledgment required by statute was a general and public one; that the father must show by his acts, words, and treatment of his children that he regarded and desired the public to regard them as his legitimate offspring; and that all his acts and words taken together must show that he intended to make the children legitimate and capable of inheriting his estate.[47] Many laws provide that the status of the child is changed to that of one born in wedlock upon the marriage of the parents and upon the father's acceptance of the child as his own.

Usually the rights of the father are not an issue, but as against third parties he may have the right to the custody of his child. This was the holding of the court in a Virginia situation. An unmarried, Negro mother died. Before her death she requested that her baby be given to a Negro whom she recognized as the father of the child. A controversy occurred between the maternal and paternal grandparents. The court held that the child belonged with the father and paternal grandparents, since the father of a bastard child should be accorded the same rights as the father

[45] Freund, *op. cit.*, p. 10.

[46] The most recent summaries of legislation on this subject can be found in U.S. Children's Bureau, *Paternity Laws: Analysis and Tabular Summary of State Laws Relating to Paternity and Support of Children Born out of Wedlock in Effect Jan. 1, 1938* (Washington, D.C., G.P.O., 1938), Chart 16; Chester G. Vernier and others, *American Family Laws* (Stanford, Cal., Stanford University Press, 1931–1938), Vol. 4, pp. 148–267; Schatkin, *op. cit.*, pp. 295–366.

[47] *Miller* v. *Pennington,* 218 Ill. 220, 75 N.E. 919 (1905).

of a legitimate child. In this instance, since the welfare of the child was not an issue, the rights of the father should be considered.[48]

Arizona and North Dakota have attempted to provide for equal rights of the legitimate and illegitimate child. The acts in these two states are based on legislation adopted in Norway in 1915. The Norwegian act was the first law which, when paternity was established, imposed upon the father the obligations of legal paternity. The Arizona law provides: [49]

> Every child is the legitimate child of its natural parents and is entitled to support and education as if born in lawful wedlock, except the right to dwelling or a residence with the family of its father, if such father be married. It shall inherit from its natural parents and from their kindred heirs, lineal and collateral, in the same manner as children born in lawful wedlock. This section shall apply to cases where the natural father of any such child is married to one other than the mother of said child, as well as where he is single.

The Arizona court interpreted the act as follows: "This act is intended to legitimize and require the father to support, educate, and give a home to, or otherwise provide for, his children born out of wedlock, who, by reason of their tender years, need much care." [50]

The Arizona and North Dakota laws are similar. About the latter, Freund early commented: "A very simple statute, such as that of North Dakota of 1917, can hardly be accepted as adequate, even if its procedural limitations did not render it rather impracticable." [51] Laws like these do not give consideration to the problems of the relation of the father to his legitimate children. Further, in establishing the right of the child to inherit, legislatures seem to have forgotten that the legitimate father can disinherit his child; it is to be expected that such would frequently be done by the illegitimate father. Other inconsistencies exist; for instance, in both states reports appear to be made to the divisions of vital statistics on births of "illegitimate children," and in both states the uniform illegitimacy act was adopted, which is hardly consistent with the statement that *all* children are the legitimate children of their parents. In the public mind children born to unmarried parents should not have the same rights and privileges as legitimate children, and legislation does not change this attitude. Nor, as a matter of fact, can all conditions be made the same.

Since a marriage declared void at common law was void *ab initio,* the children were illegitimate, just as they would have been had there been no marriage at all. Today, this severe rule has been changed substantially

---

[48] *Hayes* v. *Strauss,* 151 Va. 136, 144 S.E. 432 (1928).

[49] Arizona Code Annotated, Vol. 2, art. 4, secs. 27–401 (1939); Arizona 1921, chap. 114, sec. 1, p. 248.

[50] *In re Silva's Estate,* 32 Ariz. 573, 261 Pac. 40 (1927).

[51] *Standards of Legal Protection for Children Born out of Wedlock,* p. 35; Laws of North Dakota, c. 70 (1917).

by statute. Most jurisdictions have legislation modifying the old common-law rule in certain particulars concerning the illegitimacy of children born of prohibited marriages.[52] The most liberal statutes are those which provide that children of marriages null in law shall be legitimate. Other legislation declares legitimate the issue of marriages declared void for some specific cause, such as idiocy, lunacy, insanity, nonage, want of understanding of the parties, incest, consanguinity, and miscegenation.

The general rule adopted in this country as a result of statutory enactments is that the illegitimate child is the son of his mother, that he takes her domicile and her name, and that he is connected with her by ties of inheritable blood. Nearly all jurisdictions give him the right to inherit from his mother.[53] Most jurisdictions also provide that the mother may inherit from him.[54] In some states illegitimate children may inherit not only from their mother but from her kin.[55] In several states illegitimate children may inherit from each other through their mother. Today, it is fairly well established that the illegitimate child not only has heirs of his own blood but may inherit and transmit through his mother. However, in some jurisdictions he still does not inherit even from his mother like a legitimate child.

JURISDICTION AND NATURE OF PROCEEDINGS [56]

The affiliation proceeding, with its double purpose of determining paternity and securing support for the child, was unknown to the common law. The proceeding is a creature of statute. The requirement of a preliminary hearing by a minor court, which in about half the states is vested in a justice of peace, is a survival from England. This procedure has been eliminated in numbers of jurisdictions. In most instances it imposes a hardship on both mother and father. Variation is found in the statutes as to what court shall try cases; usually it is one having both civil and criminal jurisdiction. There is an encouraging tendency to vest jurisdiction in juvenile or family courts. Most states require that action be initiated in the court of the place in which the mother resides or in which the child was born. A number authorize bringing action in the court of the place where the father resides or is found. The fact that the mother is not a resident of the state should not bar jurisdiction.

With one or two exceptions the begetting of a child out of wedlock seems not to be a crime. The failure of the father to support his child is generally defined as a misdemeanor or a felony. Although the action to establish paternity is not a criminal action, most states initiate the action

---

[52] Vernier, *op. cit.,* Vol. 1, p. 230, and Vol. 2, p. 185.
[53] *Paternity Laws: Analysis and Tabular Summary,* p. 5.
[54] Vernier, *op. cit.,* Vol. 4, p. 192.
[55] Madden, *op. cit.,* pp. 352–353.
[56] Schatkin, *op. cit.,* p. 24.

under criminal or quasi-criminal procedure, even though subsequent procedure is primarily civil. The criminal provisions of the law include arrest of the accused under a warrant; a preliminary hearing in a lower court; detention under bond to appear for trial; and trial by jury. The civil provisions comprise the use of a summons instead of a warrant to bring the accused before the court; rules of evidence as in a civil case; and authority to render judgment in the absence of the defendant. Some states authorize the exclusion of the public from hearings.

Where jurisdiction over paternity cases is in the juvenile or family court, an opportunity is provided in some instances for the use of equity procedures. These include:

1. Initiation of the action by petition rather than by complaint.
2. Social investigation before the hearing.
3. The use of a summons to obtain appearance at the hearing.
4. Informal and private hearings.
5. Decisions based on the needs of the child rather than the guilt of the father.
6. The use of probation to deal with failure to support the child.

Legislation should permit the father to appear before a court without a trial to acknowledge paternity and to agree to provide for the support of his child.

EVIDENCE

There are several rules of evidence so peculiarly applicable to affiliation proceedings as to become identified with them. They may be provided for by legislation or by judicial decision. They are as follows: [57]

1. In the absence of a statute to the contrary an order of filiation may be granted upon the mother's uncorroborated testimony. As a practical matter, if there is no corroboration, her testimony will be carefully scrutinized.
2. If the mother is married, both she and her husband are permitted to testify regarding his nonaccess in numbers of jurisdictions. This is the subject of "adulterine bastardy" discussed earlier in this chapter.
3. In some jurisdictions testimony by the alleged father of access by other men to the mother is inadmissible unless corroborated.
4. Courts generally will not adjudge the defendant to be the father of the child unless the proof is clear, convincing, and satisfying. The standard is not so severe as that of the criminal law, which requires proof of guilt beyond a reasonable doubt, but may be more than that of the civil law, for which a mere preponderance of the evidence is sufficient.
5. Evidence of resemblance of the child to the alleged father is often inadmissible, even without statutory prohibition. When permitted, it may be by testimony or by the actual exhibition of the child to the jury or both.
6. Blood tests which exclude paternity are admissible in numbers of jurisdictions. By this scientific method a man may be proven *not* to be the father of the child. There is some indication of a trend toward admission of

---

[57] *Ibid.*, pp. 65–151.

evidence that he *could* be the father. This provision has been included in the uniform act on blood tests to determine paternity.

Let us examine this last and recent rule sanctioning the use of blood tests in paternity actions.[58] There are three such tests: the Landsteiner-Bernstein, the Landsteiner-Levine, and the Landsteiner-Wiener. In the first the human blood is divided into four groups, *A, B, AB,* and *O.* In the second there are three additional types *M, N, MN.* In the third the rhesus blood factor, divisible into eight *Rh* blood types and at least twelve sub-types, is used. If any one of the three tests indicates an impossible combination of types as between the alleged father and the child, nonparentage is proven, even though the other two tests record an affirmative combination. For example, the alleged father could not be the father if the following combinations were shown:

Table 4

Individual	*Group*	*Type*
Mother	A	M
Child	AB	MN
Alleged father	O	M

According to the laws of heredity of blood groups and types, an *O* parent cannot have an *AB* child, and a child cannot possess the factor *N* absent from both parents. On the other hand, because the child's blood group is like that of the alleged father, it is not necessarily a fact that he is the father or that he is not. Millions of men belong to each group. The following illustrates this principle:

Table 5

Individual	*Group*	*Type*
Mother	A	M
Child	B	MN
Alleged father	B	N

Despite the reliability of the principle of exclusion, blood tests are not used in all jurisdictions. Some states by statute authorize their use. New York was the first state to enact such legislation. In some jurisdictions the courts have made use of the tests without statutory authorization. Not always have the courts denied the paternity charge, even when the blood tests provided conclusive evidence that the alleged father was not the father. The court took this view in the leading California case of *Arais* v. *Kalensnikoff.*[59] Here, despite the fact that the blood-grouping

[58] See excellent discussion on scientific characteristics and the legal aspects of blood tests, in Schatkin, *op. cit.,* pp. 90–151; "Blood Tests as Proof of Non-Parentage," 39 Calif. L.R. 277–285 (1951). There are many articles in medical and law journals on this subject.

[59] 10 Cal. 2d 428, 74 P 2d 1043 (1937).

tests showed that the alleged seventy-year-old father could not have been the father, the supreme court sustained the trial courts' finding of parentage. It reasoned that testimony based on blood-grouping tests is expert testimony; that the law makes no distinction between experts and other testimony; that no evidence is conclusive unless so stated by statute; and, therefore, that when there is a conflict between scientific testimony and other evidence, the jury or trial court must determine the relative weight of the evidence. Hopes that the Arais case would be overruled were practically abandoned when the high court denied a hearing in the sensational *Berry* v. *Chaplin* case.[60] There, the blood tests showed that Chaplin could not be the father of the child involved, but he was nevertheless so held.

Maine seems to have been the first state in which the high court held that blood tests negating paternity cannot be disregarded by a jury where there is no evidence that the tests were inaccurately performed.[61] In this case the complainant, some eight months after sex relations with the respondent, gave birth to twins. Thereupon she brought a bastardy action. Pursuant to court orders, blood tests were made on both parties and the twins. The test disproved the respondent's paternity of one twin. The court recognized the scientific nature of the tests and held that the trial court must give them heed. It ordered a new trial, since the verdict was indivisible, twins being involved. The reliability and accuracy of blood tests seem no longer to be a matter of controversy. Medical and scientific authorities accept them as established fact. The Maine case points the way to acceptance also by lawyers and judges.

In 1952 the Commissioners on Uniform State Laws adopted a uniform act on blood tests to determine paternity.[62] The act provides that in civil actions where paternity is a relevant fact, the court may order blood tests upon its own initiative or upon suggestion. Submission to the test is compulsory on application of any party to the proceedings. If any party refuses to submit to the blood tests, the court may resolve the question against such party or enforce its orders if the rights of others and the interests of justice so require. If the court finds that the conclusions of all the experts are that the alleged father is not the father of the child, the question of paternity is resolved accordingly. If the experts disagree, the question shall be submitted upon all the evidence. If the experts conclude that the blood tests show the possibility of the alleged father's paternity, admission of the evidence is within the discretion of the court, depending upon the infrequency of the blood type. The uniform act establishes several principles:

---

[60] 74 Cal. App. 2d 652, 169 P 2d 442 (1946).

[61] *Gordon* v. *Mace,* 144 Me. 351, 69 A 2d 670 (1949).

[62] *Handbook of the National Conference of Commissioners on Uniform State Laws: 1952* (Baltimore, The Lord Baltimore Press, 1952), pp. 434–446.

1. Tests can be ordered by the court.
2. Failure to consent gives the court power to resolve the question.
3. The infallibility of the tests is recognized in the provision that an order of paternity must be denied when the tests indicate that the alleged father could not be the father.
4. It is scientifically sound to recognize the relevance of the blood tests when they show infrequency of blood type and to admit them as evidence under such circumstances.

In Chapter 7 we discussed the sociolegal problem of legitimacy in cases of artificial insemination, particularly when the husband is not the donor. We reported that in December, 1954, a Chicago judge ruled that artificial insemination from other than the husband, with or without his consent, was contrary to public policy and good morals, constituted adultery on the part of the mother, and illegitimized the child.[63] The ruling was made in a divorce action, where the wife sought sole custody of the five-year-old son.

SUPPORT

Early legislation in the United States concerning the support of illegitimate children was largely concerned with saving the community from the burden of supporting the child. This legislation was closely associated with poor-relief laws. More recently, many states have modified their paternity legislation to make two motives primary: protection of the child and economy for the community. Wisconsin, for example, early enacted a law authorizing local poor-relief officials to apply to the justice of peace for examination of the mother and for apprehension of the father when an illegitimate child was or was likely to become a public charge. It also authorized those officials to make an arrangement with the putative father regarding the child's support. The Wisconsin supreme court in 1865 stated that the clear intent of the law was to indemnify and save the town harmless from all expense for maintenance of the child and the mother's lying-in expenses.[64] The illegitimacy statute has been revised, and its purpose today is "to effectuate the protection and welfare of the child."[65] That the legislation of many states is still designed primarily to protect the community is shown in provisions empowering public-assistance authorities to make the complaint against the father, or requiring a bond, or authorizing a justice of the peace to force the mother to give the father's name or to imprison her if she fails to do this.

Legislative provisions concerning the father's duty to support his child born out of wedlock are extensive and varied. In 1923 a Kansas court

---

[63] *Capital Times,* Madison, Wis. (December 13, 1954).
[64] *State* v. *Jager,* 19 Wis. 251 (1865).
[65] Wis. Stat. 1955, c. 52.45.

held that even in the absence of a statute requiring an unmarried father to support his child, he had that obligation.[66] In most states the court is given discretion to order the amount of payment for the support of the child. In a considerable proportion of the states the laws expressly give the court continuing jurisdiction to change or modify the support order. The length of time during which a child must be supported by his father is defined in a majority of states. In some the provision is during the minority of the child or until he is able to support himself. In others it is until the child has reached a certain age, which varies up to eighteen years. Most laws provide for periodic payments, although there are also provisions for payment of a lump sum. The laws of a number of states provide that all payments shall be paid to the court, a state or local welfare agency, or a trustee appointed by the court. In several states the law gives the court discretion to appoint a trustee.

One of the pronounced weaknesses of paternity laws, according to the Children's Bureau, is that they do not contain effective provisions for collecting support money. The laws of most states authorize the courts to order the adjudged father to give a bond with sureties to secure the payments ordered by the court. In some states the bond is mandatory, and in some the court is given discretion to order the filing of a bond. On failure to pay the bond practically all the laws provide for imprisonment. If the court is given discretion to order a bond filed, imprisonment is a method of punishment for not carrying out the order; but when the filing of a bond is required regardless of financial conditions, imprisonment merely penalizes a man for lack of resources.

It is important for the laws to provide that when the father is released from prison he is still liable for support of the child. In a considerable number of jurisdictions there are such provisions, and in a few others the courts may impose the conditions for his release. It seems obvious that no financial advantage is secured for the child if the father is imprisoned and then absolved of financial responsibility, and yet the statutes of some states make no provision for obtaining support except through ordering a bond and imprisoning the father for failure to comply. The most effective laws are those that require adjudicated fathers to make regular payments under the supervision of the court. Some states have provisions for proceeding against the estate of a deceased father. His obligation should be enforceable against his estate, with due regard to the rights of his widow and legitimate children.

The desertion and nonsupport laws of some states give protection to illegitimate children, either by express inclusion in the nonsupport laws or by provisions in the paternity laws. In the former groups of states some

[66] *Doughty* v. *Engler,* 112 Kan. 583, 211 Pac. 619 (1923).

differences exist as to the applicability of these laws to the father who does not have the child in his custody.[67] The nonsupport laws of a few states specifically state either that the law applies to the father of a child born out of wedlock whether or not the child is in his custody or that it applies to the father of any child born out of wedlock. The attorney general in Minnesota upheld the application of the law to a father of a child born out of wedlock even though he did not have custody.[68] A court in Colorado ruled that the law applied to such a father even when paternity had not been established.[69] A contrary rule was given in Missouri, where the court held that the law applied only to the father having custody.[70]

There is variation in statutory provisions concerning conditions under which a man shall or may make final settlement. Court approval is required in a number of states. Oregon appears to require that all settlements must be approved by the juvenile court, even though paternity cases are handled in other courts. In all states requiring court approval, provisions for support of the child must be made in the settlements and, in some states, for the mother's expenses and court costs also. In a few states such settlement may be made with the *reputed* father, which means that any man financially able can make a settlement without admitting paternity. Little use seems to be made of this provision. It resembles the Norwegian law, which provides that several men may be ordered to support a child when paternity cannot be determined.

OTHER LEGISLATION PERTAINING TO CHILDREN BORN OUT OF WEDLOCK

In Chapter 11 we discussed the authority given to state agencies to license, inspect, and supervise agencies and institutions, public and private, dealing with children in need of special care. Some legislatures have enacted laws giving the state special responsibilities concerning the child of unmarried parents. In 1917 the Minnesota legislature authorized its state board of control to take legal action to establish paternity. The board was given authority to accept from the duly acknowledged father such sum as the court fixed for the care, support, and education of the child. Other states have imposed a responsibility for this group of children upon the state department of welfare. The Wisconsin statute, for example, provides that the department of public welfare shall: [71]

> promote the enforcement of laws for the protection of mentally deficient, illegitimate, dependent, neglected, and delinquent children, and to this end co-

[67] *Paternity Laws: Analysis and Tabular Summary,* p. 19.
[68] Ops. Atty. Gen., May 22, 1932.
[69] *Wamsely* v. *People,* 64 Colo. 521, 173 Pac. 425 (1918).
[70] *State* v. *Porterfield,* 222 Mo. App. 553, 292 S.W. 85 (1927).
[71] Wis. Stat., 1955, c. 46.03 (7)(a)(b).

operate with juvenile courts and licensed child welfare agencies and institutions (public and private) and take the initiative in all matters involving the interests of such children where adequate provision therefore has not already been made.

When notified of the birth or expected birth of an illegitimate child, see to it (through advice and assistance of the mother or independently) that the interests of the child are safeguarded, that steps are taken to attempt to establish its paternity, and that there is secured for the child (as near as possible) the care, support, and education that he would be given if legitimate.

A large percentage of unmarried mothers come from low wage-earning groups. The unmarried father often contributes inadequately to the support of the child; hence, dependency is increased by illegitimacy. Legislation for aid to dependent children, which has been extended throughout the country under the federal Social Security Act, permits providing assistance to mothers of illegitimate as well as legitimate children, although not all states make such an inclusion. If the illegitimate child is to have adequate protection with his mother, very often she must have public assistance; therefore, adequate assistance laws and competent administration of assistance funds are essential.

In Chapter 12 we discussed the importance of vital statistics and court records, which, however, should be held confidential. We know that the extent to which official records are private and unavailable except upon court order varies from state to state. There are many important legal, health, and welfare reasons which make the complete and accurate registration of facts essential. This does not mean that information regarding birth, death, adoption, illegitimacy, and other personal matters should be available to just anyone. In fact, such data may be embarrassing or harmful to many children, especially those born out of wedlock. The confidential nature of birth records and the issuance of an abbreviated form can best be assured by a nation-wide policy implemented by state legislation and procedures. The Children's Bureau and the National Office of Vital Statistics have been actively concerned in promoting such a policy and program. Numbers of states have passed legislation in conformance with this proposal.[72]

No legislation has been passed which subjects all children born out of wedlock to the guardianship of the state because of their status as illegitimates. It is doubtful that such legislation is necessary.[73] Protective legislation is desirable, but fixed rules should not be laid down for this group of children any more than for other groups. What is needed is legislation which assures state protection to all illegitimate children through compulsory reporting of illegitimate births to a state agency,

---

[72] *The Confidential Nature of Birth Records,* U.S. Children's Bureau Publication (Washington, D.C., G.P.O., 1950), No. 332.

[73] Carl A. Heisterman, "State Supervision of Children Born out of Wedlock," *Social Service Review* (June, 1933), pp. 254–263.

which must then make or authorize inquiry into the situation of the child.

UNIFORM ACTS

We have already referred to the uniform act on blood tests to determine paternity. In 1922 the National Conference of Commissioners on Uniform State Laws approved an illegitimacy act, which was essentially a support measure and which was intended to remove some of the stigma of illegitimacy. Few states adopted the proposal. Legislation in many states progressed beyond the provisions of the uniform act, and in 1943 it was withdrawn.

The uniform desertion and nonsupport act first accepted by the Commissioners on Uniform State Laws in 1910 provides that a neglecting or deserting husband and father of children under sixteen, leaving them in destitute and necessitous circumstances, shall be guilty of a crime.[74] The act does not make a distinction between legitimate and illegitimate children. Consequently, states accepting its provisions apply it in accordance with their traditions and related statutes. A majority of jurisdictions have accepted this act. Public sentiment against absconding husbands and fathers has swelled as their numbers have grown and as costs for the aid to dependent children programs have increased. In 1950 the commissioners, responsive to this wave of opinion, approved the uniform reciprocal enforcement of support act, which, again, does not mention a particular class of children but leaves it to the accepting states to make the determination.[75] All jurisdictions but one (the District of Columbia) have adopted the act or some variation of it.

The 1953 reports of the commissioners present a tentative draft of a uniform civil liability for support act. The purpose of the proposed act is to provide a basic code of the duties of support in order to facilitate the operation of the uniform reciprocal enforcement support act. The duties covered already exist under the laws of most states and in some states as a result of court decisions or by inference from statutes. Under the draft, criteria for the amount of support which courts may order include:

1. Standard of living and situation of the parties.
2. Relative wealth and income of the parties.
3. Ability of the obligor to earn.
4. Ability of the obligee to earn.
5. Need of obligee.
6. Age of parties.
7. Responsibility of obligor for support of others.

---

[74] 10 U.L.A. (New York, Edward Thompson Co., 1922). This volume is entirely given over to annotations on the subject in the various jurisdictions.

[75] *Handbook of the National Conference of Commissioners on Uniform State Laws: 1953* (Baltimore, The Lord Baltimore Press, 1953).

Husband and wife are competent witnesses. The obligation to support includes illegitimate and adopted children.

SUMMARY AND CONCLUSIONS

Historically, there are two primary motives for the ruthless treatment of illegitimate children: the desire to protect money and property and the desire to preserve religious and moral precepts. In regard to the first, there was the intent to keep illegitimate children from inheriting property so as not to divert goods and lands from the established line of heirs. The urge to keep property in the family is an understandable, although not necessarily a justifiable, one. The second motive is less understandable. It is a paradox that the Christian religion, built upon the concepts of love and forgiveness, should have taken so harsh and uncharitable a view toward the unmarried mother and her child. This practice seems to have been based upon the belief that if stern disapproval was not heaped upon the child, there would be no adequate method of restraining promiscuity among adults and, hence, immorality would be encouraged. Only recently has the unjust subordination of innocent individuals to these ideas been somewhat replaced by a more nearly Christian spirit.

Modern society to some extent realizes that the common-law, illegitimate "son of nobody" is, in fact, the son of his parents and entitled to the same rights of maintenance, support, and education as the child born in lawful wedlock. Legislation has been passed in every state tending to place the illegitimate child on an approximate legal equality with the legitimate child so far as his mother is concerned. Also, in many states he now has certain rights of maintenance, support, and inheritance from his father. States like Arizona and North Dakota have been liberal in their attempts to equalize the rights of children born in and out of wedlock. Numbers of states have authorized state departments of welfare to see that illegitimate children are protected. The most significant midcentury developments for the protection of children born out of wedlock appear to be the enactment of legislation concerning birth registration, and the admission of evidence from blood tests, especially when exclusion of paternity is proven.[76]

American legislation, in its departure from the common law, is moving toward approximating the status of lawful parent and child so far as mother and child are concerned; giving the child the right to inherit from his mother; giving the child the right to support from his adjudicated father and even the right of inheritance; providing methods of legitimizing the child and of establishing paternity; conferring upon legal agencies the responsibility for establishing paternity and for supervising the welfare of all illegitimate children; enacting legislation, the primary

[76] Letter from Children's Bureau (July 12, 1954).

purpose of which is the welfare of mother and child rather than the financial protection of the community.

Dr. Martha Eliot, then chief of the Children's Bureau, reported in 1955 that approximately 150,000 illegitimate children are born annually in the United States.[77] About 60,000 mothers of these children are under twenty years of age. Half or more adoptions are of children born out of wedlock. It is obvious that laws concerning children born out of wedlock and adoptions should be consistent with each other. Statutes pertaining to records, licensing of agencies, termination of parental rights, judicial process, and so forth should be thought of as aspects of a total child welfare program. Continuous education and planning are necessary to achieve consistent and adequate child welfare legislation; judicial opinions in harmony with modern concepts of child protection; competent administration in public and voluntary agencies; and public understanding of the meaning of child welfare. The humane spirit is making progress in tearing loose the shackles of tradition in the care and treatment of children born out of wedlock. With expanded and improved public and voluntary services for the benefit of this and other groups of children there are better means to exercise the *parens patriae* authority of the state.

Selected References

ABBOTT, Grace, *The Child and the State* (Chicago, University of Chicago Press, 1938), Vol. 2.

Bastards, 7 Am. Jur. 623–733.

Bastards, 10 C.J.S. 3–211.

BRECKINRIDGE, S. P., *The Family and the State* (Chicago, University of Chicago Press, 1934).

EDLIN, Sara B., *The Unmarried Mother in Our Society* (New York, Farrar, Straus and Young, 1954).

Filiation and Related State Legislation (Springfield, Ill., Legislative Council, 1950).

FREUND, Ernst, *Illegitimacy Laws of the United States and Certain Foreign Countries,* U.S. Children's Bureau Publication (Washington, D.C., G.P.O., 1919), No. 42.

HUFFMAN, Helen C., "The Importance of Birth Records," *Proceedings of the National Conference of Social Work: 1947* (New York, Columbia University Press, 1948).

MADDEN, Joseph W., *Persons and Domestic Relations* (St. Paul, West Publishing Co., 1931).

MORLOCK, Maud, *A Community's Responsibility for the Child Born out of Wedlock* (Washington, D.C., U.S. Children's Bureau, 1949).

---

[77] *Social Legislation Information Service,* 84th Cong. (November 15, 1955), No. 36.

NICOLAS, Sir Harris, *A Treatise on the Law of Adulterine Bastardy* (London, William Pickering, 1836).

PLOSCOWE, Morris, *Sex and the Law* (Englewood Cliffs, N.J., Prentice-Hall, 1951).

RICHARDS, Edward A., ed., *Proceedings of the Midcentury White House Conference on Children and Youth* (Raleigh, N.C., Health Publications Institute, 1951).

SCHATKIN, Sidney B., *Disputed Paternity Proceedings* (New York, Mathew Bender and Co., 1944).

TANIGUCHI, Charles Y., "Status of Issue of Void Marriages," 56 Harv. L. Rev. 624–31 (1943).

United Nations, Economic and Social Council, Commission on the Status of Women, *Parental Rights and Duties* (December 8, 1953), Doc. E/CN,6/230.

U.S. Children's Bureau, *Paternity Laws: Analysis and Tabular Summary of State Laws Relating to Paternity and Support of Children Born out of Wedlock in the United States* (Washington, D.C., G.P.O., 1938), Chart 16.

U.S. Children's Bureau, *Services for Unmarried Mothers and Their Children* (Washington, D.C., G.P.O., 1945).

U.S. Department of Health, Education, and Welfare, Children's Bureau, *Selected References on Social Services for Unmarried Parents: 1940 Through 1953* (Washington, D.C., G.P.O., 1953).

U.S. Department of Health, Education, and Welfare, Children's Bureau and National Office of Vital Statistics, *The Confidential Nature of Birth Records,* Children's Bureau Publication (Washington, D.C., G.P.O., 1949), No. 332.

U.S. Department of Health, Education, and Welfare, Public Health Service, National Office of Vital Statistics, *Illegitimate Births 1938–1947: Vital Statistics—Special Reports—Selected Studies,* Vol. 33, No. 5 (February 15, 1950).

VERNIER, Chester G., and others, *American Family Laws* (Stanford, Cal., Stanford University Press, 1931–1938), Vols. 1, 2, and 4.

YOUNG, Leontine, *Out of Wedlock* (New York, McGraw-Hill, 1954).

CHAPTER 14

Youthful Offenders and the Juvenile Court I

INTRODUCTION

Are there justifications for present-day alarmist reactions to the volume and often serious nature of juvenile delinquency? What is its extent, and what is its nature? Are court and community resources adequate to deal with the problem? What causes juvenile delinquency? What can be done about its prevention and treatment? Let us look at answers to these questions before we describe the juvenile court system.

What are some of the facts about juvenile delinquency? Dr. Martha Eliot, then chief of the Children's Bureau, in her 1953 testimony before the Senate Subcommittee to Investigate Juvenile Delinquency, gave significant information on the problem of juvenile misbehavior.[1] In 1940 an estimated 235,000 children were brought to the attention of the juvenile courts of the country because of alleged delinquent behavior. After 1940 the number of juvenile delinquents taken to juvenile courts began to rise. In the years 1943 and 1945, there were roughly 400,000 of these children. Following World War II the number decreased until, in 1948, there were less than 300,000 juvenile delinquents brought before the courts. In 1949, with the stresses of the cold war and the Korean hostilities, juvenile delinquency began to rise again. In 1952 about 385,000 children were brought before the juvenile courts for delinquent behavior. Between 1948 and 1952, then, there was a 29 per cent increase in this phenomenon. In the same period, 1948–1952, the number of boys and girls in the age group

[1] U.S. Senate, *Hearings Before the Subcommittee to Investigate Juvenile Delinquency of the Committee of the Judiciary,* 83d Cong., pursuant to S. Res. 89, Pt. 1, Nov. 19, 20, 23, 24, 1953 (Washington, D.C., G.P.O., 1954), pp. 11–14; U.S. Children's Bureau, *Some Facts about Juvenile Delinquency,* U.S. Children's Bureau Publication (Washington, D.C., G.P.O., 1953), No. 340. See also, U.S. Senate, *Hearings Before the Subcommittee to Investigate Juvenile Delinquency of the Committee of the Judiciary,* 84th Cong., pursuant to S. Res. 62, *Indians,* March 11, April 28, 29, 30, 1955 (Washington, D.C., G.P.O., 1955); U.S. Senate, *Hearings Before the Special Subcommittee on Juvenile Delinquency of the Committee on Labor and Public Welfare,* 84th Cong., 1st sess., on S. 728, S. 894, S. 1088, S. 1832, July 6, 7, 8, 9, 1955 (Washington, D.C., G.P.O., 1955).

from ten to seventeen increased only 6 per cent. The percentage increase in juvenile delinquents brought before the juvenile courts was therefore almost five times as great as the percentage increase in the child population. In 1953 about 435,000 delinquent children were brought before the special courts, an increase of 13 per cent over the previous year. It is predicted that between 1953 and 1963 there will be a 40 per cent increase in the number of children of juvenile court age. It is logical to conclude that there may be a corresponding increase in the number, and even the percentage, of children taken to juvenile courts. Juvenile delinquency is not just a "big city" problem. Less densely populated areas of the country seemed to experience sharper increases even than 29 per cent. The courts serving jurisdictions of less than 100,000 persons showed a combined increase of 41 per cent.

Juvenile court statistics are not the only measure of juvenile delinquency. A much greater number of children are dealt with by the police than are referred to the courts. Of the approximately 1,000,000 boys and girls who came to the attention of the police for misbehavior in 1952, about 725,000 were dealt with directly by the police. In these cases the police took whatever steps they thought might alter delinquent behavior. About 275,000 children were taken to the juvenile court by the police. An additional 110,000 were taken by parents, teachers, social agencies, and others. At least 125,000 of the 385,000 were held overnight or longer in detention homes, police stations, jails, or other facilities while awaiting action on their situation. An estimated 100,000 children were held in jail in 1952, although many of these were never brought to the attention of the courts for delinquent behavior. The cases of about half of the 385,000 children were dismissed, adjusted, or held open without further action. Of the remaining, approximately 100,000 were placed on probation, and 40,000 were committed to the training schools for delinquent youth. The rest were referred to other agencies or handled in a number of other ways.

How accurate are these figures? It is difficult, if not impossible, at present to obtain precise figures on juvenile delinquency. Definitions and practices lack uniformity between jurisdictions. Strictly speaking, only those cases adjudicated as delinquent should be included. Even if this were done, there remain difficulties due to statutory age differences. Communities vary greatly also in the types and numbers of cases referred to the courts. In many localities the police deal informally with the greatest proportion of delinquents. Besides these problems there is the additional fact that a uniform reporting system for the country as a whole is not yet in effect. The Children's Bureau collects juvenile court figures; the FBI provides police-arrest data based on fingerprint records; the Bureau of Prisons accumulates materials on federal offenders; and the Bureau of the Census records the population of institutions for delinquent children. All these data furnish a crude index of national trends in the number of children getting into trouble with the law.[2]

What brings children before the courts? Reports show that boys are most frequently referred for stealing, including petty theft, auto theft, burglary, and robbery, and for acts of carelessness and malicious mischief. Some boys are referred for such serious offenses as homicide, rape, and assault. Most of the girls are referred for being ungovernable, for running away, or for sexual offenses. The majority of boys and girls brought before the juvenile courts for delinquent behavior are between fifteen and seventeen years of age. During the first half of 1952 more serious crimes were committed by eighteen-year-old boys and girls than by persons of any other age group. About 83 per cent of young offenders are boys, and 17 per cent girls.

How adequate are the services for handling juvenile delinquents? It has been estimated that about 5 per cent of a community's total police force should be assigned to work with children. At the present time only about one out of six communities has a sufficient number of police officers assigned to juvenile work. The majority of cities fail to require any special qualifications for juvenile police work. There are somewhat over 170 detention homes in the country, but there are about 2,500 juvenile courts to be served. The lack of adequate facilities for shelter care and for detention is the primary reason that children are so often detained in jail. Juvenile court judges should be law-trained and possess an understanding of child behavior and a good knowledge of social problems. Yet many of the judges who preside over juvenile courts perform this task as an incident to their main function of handling criminal and civil matters. More than one half of the counties in the United States fail to provide probation services to their juvenile delinquents. Many training schools are too large. More than one third of them are designed for more than 200 children. Experts think 150 children is a better work group. Only slightly over one half of the counties have full-time public child welfare workers who may perform an important role in delinquency prevention.

What causes juvenile delinquency? Of course, there is no single cause, and in the case of any particular delinquent multiple causes are usually at work. Poverty, overcrowding, lack of opportunities for recreation, unwholesome associations, neighborhood condition, discrimination, have long been known as environmental factors contributing to delinquency. More recently we have come to recognize that a child's experiences and relations with his own family play a significant part in his behavior. The development of healthy personalities requires love, guidance, discipline from parents. In the absence of these controls anxieties, frustrations, fears,

---

[2] I. Richard Perlman "The Meaning of Juvenile Delinquency Statistics," *Federal Probation,* Vol. 13, No. 3 (September, 1949), pp. 63–67.

hates may occur, which, in turn, may be factors in delinquent behavior.

The Senate subcommittee studying juvenile delinquency in the Eighty-third Congress wrote of the causes of delinquency as follows: [3]

> The causes of juvenile delinquency are not unknown, although much remains to be learned about how they operate in relation to a particular individual. Neither is the causation of delinquency so complex that an intelligent attack upon the problem cannot be launched.
>
> No child is born delinquent, but he is subject to a wide variety of influences and conditions which tend to either lessen or increase his chances of becoming delinquent. He is subjected, first of all, to the profound influence exerted by his parents and immediate family . . . But influences bearing upon a child's development are not limited to those within the family, and many delinquent boys and girls do not come from homes marked by internal conflict and abnormal relationships.
>
> Through both acts of commission and omission larger society may and does contribute to the development of delinquency. The child who is denied acceptance and opportunity because of his race, religion, or nationality, for example, may learn to hate and rebel . . . The child exposed to adult example of vice and crime, reared in neighborhoods whose most influential and opulent residents are racketeers, may group up into a life of crime, despite the devoted efforts of law-abiding parents. . . . The materialism of our age, with its emphasis upon getting ahead and financial success, subjects children to great strain and often times frustration. Modern advertising coupled with easy pay-as-you-go plans . . . may throw added strains upon family life.
>
> Through TV, radio, movies, and comics, children are fed a heavy diet of violence and crime . . .

What can we do about all this? Must we be hysterical or punitive in our suggestions for prevention and treatment? Must we rush to trite explanations and easy solutions? Are communities, including juvenile courts, coddling these boys and girls? Ought juvenile delinquents to be punished? Should parents be fined or sent to jail or prison for the delinquent acts of their children? Does every delinquent child need the juvenile court or psychiatric treatment or a social agency? Can local communities alone handle the problem of juvenile delinquency?

There is no single remedy for juvenile delinquency any more than there is a single cause. Parent understanding of children, community interest in the provision of multiple public and voluntary resources, religious education, experts qualified to work with parents and children, juvenile courts equipped to deal constructively with children brought before them—all are necessary for prevention and treatment of juvenile misbehavior. "Just as juvenile delinquency is caused by unsatisfactory conditions

---

[3] U.S. Senate, *Juvenile Delinquency: Interim Report of the Committee on the Judiciary,* 83d Cong., 2d sess., S. Rept. 1064, pursuant to S. Res. 89, 83d Cong., 1st sess., March 15, 1954 (Washington, D.C., G.P.O., 1954), pp. 9–10. See also, *Understanding Juvenile Delinquency,* U.S. Children's Bureau Publication, rev. ed. (Washington, D.C., G.P.O., 1949).

within family and community, so is delinquency prevented by all measures which improve family and community life for children." [4]

ORIGIN AND DEVELOPMENT OF JUVENILE COURTS

THEORY OF INDIVIDUALIZED JUSTICE

Let us turn our attention now to a consideration of special courts dealing with children, particularly the juvenile court. Roscoe Pound, former dean of the Harvard Law School, termed the juvenile court the greatest advance in judicial history since the Magna Charta.[5] It was he who characterized the essential philosophy of the juvenile court and other specialized courts dealing with children's cases as that of "individualized justice," a phrase he preferred to that of "socialized justice," since all justice is social in purpose.[6] Another student described it as follows: [7]

> The Juvenile Court is conspicuously a response to the modern spirit of social justice. It is perhaps the first legal tribunal where law and science, especially the science of medicine and those sciences which deal with human behavior, such as biology, sociology, and psychology work side by side. It recognizes the fact that the law, unaided, is incompetent to decide what is adequate treatment of delinquency and crime. It undertakes to define and readjust social situations without the sentiment of prejudice. Its approach to the problem which the child presents is scientific, objective, and dispassionate. The methods which it uses are those of social case work, in which every child is studied and treated as an individual.

Juvenile courts are of recent origin, but the principles underlying them are not. These courts represent a development out of common-law and equity doctrines.[8] They have incorporated the ideas of chancery or equity

---

[4] *Juvenile Delinquency: Interim Report of the Committee on the Judiciary,* p. 10. See also, Bertram Beck, "What We Can Do about Juvenile Delinquency," *Child Welfare,* Vol. 33, No. 1 (January, 1954), pp. 3–7; Donald A. Block, "Some Concepts in the Treatment of Delinquency," *Children,* Vol. 1, No. 5 (March–April, 1954), pp. 49–55; "The Secretary's Conference on Juvenile Delinquency," *Children,* Vol. 1, No. 5 (September–October, 1954), pp. 177–184.

[5] Quoted from Roscoe Pound, "The Juvenile Court and the Law," in *National Probation and Parole Association Yearbook: 1944* (New York, 1944), p. 13.

[6] "The Future of Socialized Justice," *National Probation Association Yearbook: 1946* (New York, 1947), pp. 6–18; Gustav L. Schramm, "Philosophy of the Juvenile Court," *Annals of the American Academy of Political and Social Science,* Vol. 261 (January, 1949), pp. 101–108.

[7] H. H. Lou, *Juvenile Courts in the United States* (Chapel Hill, N.C., University of North Carolina Press, 1927), p. 2.

[8] Bernard Flexner and Roger N. Baldwin, *Juvenile Courts and Probation* (New York, Century, 1914), p. 3; Julian W. Mack, "The Chancery Procedure in the Juvenile Court," in Jane Addams and others, *The Child, the Clinic, and the Court* (New York, New Republic, 1925), pp. 310–319; 14 R.C.L. 277; *Infants, Custody and Protection,* 43 C.J.S. 50–99; *Crimes and Commitment of Juvenile Delinquents and Dependents,* 43 C.J.S. 210–265; 31 Am. Jur. 783–809; Bernard Flexner and Reuben N. Oppenheimer, *The Legal Aspects of the Juvenile Court,* U.S. Children's Bureau

courts in relation to the dependent and neglected child; and, in relation to the delinquent child, they have extended the theory of an absence of criminal intent under a certain age.

We know that through the English chancery court the crown exercised the authority of *parens patriae* over the persons and estates of minors. The king owed a duty to protect his wards. This theory was enunciated in the case of *Eyre* v. *Shaftsbury* in 1722 [9] and in the Wellesley case in 1827.[10] The Shaftsbury case, as we have seen, laid down the theory that idiots, lunatics, and infants were entitled to the protection of the crown. The Wellesley case made it clear that although the court had jurisdiction, it could act for the welfare of the child only when it had the means to exercise its authority by applying property for the maintenance of the infant; it was not from lack of authority but from want of means that the court failed to exercise its protective jurisdiction over children needing protection. This doctrine was extended some years later when the chancellor said: "I have no doubt about the jurisdiction. The cases in which the crown interferes on behalf of infants are not confined to those in which there is property. This court interferes for the protection of infants, *qua* infants by virtue of the prerogative which belongs to the crown as *parens patriae,* and the exercise of which is delegated to the great seal." [11]

The delinquency jurisdiction of the juvenile court is founded on the

---

Publication (Washington, D.C., G.P.O., 1922), No. 99, p. 7; Grace Abbott, *The Child and the State* (Chicago, University of Chicago Press, 1938), Vol. 2, Pt. 2, pp. 323–485; Thorsten Sellin, ed., *Annals of the American Academy of Political and Social Science: Juvenile Delinquency,* Vol. 261 (January, 1949); Paul Tappan, *Juvenile Delinquency* (New York, McGraw-Hill, 1949); *Federal Probation,* Vol. 13, No. 3 (September, 1949), entire issue; Charles L. Chute, "The Juvenile Court in Retrospect," *Federal Probation,* Vol. 13, No. 3 (September, 1949), pp. 3–8; Donald R. Taft, *Criminology: A Cultural Interpretation* (New York, Macmillan, 1950); Sheldon Glueck and Eleanor Glueck, *Unravelling Juvenile Delinquency* (New York, The Commonwealth Fund, 1950); Negley K. Teeters and John Otto Reinemann, *The Challenge of Delinquency* (Englewood Cliffs, N.J., Prentice-Hall, 1950); Lowell Juilliard Carr, *Delinquency Control,* rev. ed. (New York, Harper, 1950); Nochem S. Winnet, "Fifty Years of the Juvenile Court: An Evaluation," 36 A.B.A.J. 363–366 (1950); *Unravelling Juvenile Delinquency: A Symposium of Reviews,* 41 J. Crim. L. 732–759 (1951); Edward A. Richards, ed., *Proceedings of the Midcentury White House Conference on Children and Youth* (Raleigh, N.C., Health Publications Institute, 1951); *The Child,* Vol. 17 (December, 1952), delinquency issue; Pauline Young, *Social Treatment in Probation and Delinquency* (New York, McGraw-Hill, 1952); U.S. Children's Bureau, *A Selected Bibliography on Juvenile Delinquency* (Washington, D.C., G.P.O., 1953); Alfred J. Kahn, *A Court for Children* (New York, Columbia University Press, 1953); Clyde B. Vedder, ed., *The Juvenile Offender* (New York, Doubleday, 1954); Martin H. Neumeyer, *Juvenile Delinquency in Modern Society* (New York, Van Nostrand, 1955).

[9] 2 P. Wms. 102, 24 Eng. Rep. 659 (1722).

[10] 2 Russel 1 (1827).

[11] *In re Spence,* 2 Phillips 247 (1847); see the article by Julian W. Mack in S. P. Breckinridge and Edith Abbott, *The Delinquent Child and the Home* (New York, Russell Sage Foundation, 1912), pp. 181–201.

theory of the common-law age of criminal responsibility.[12] At common law children under seven could not be found guilty of a felony because the law presumed them incapable of having a felonious intent or discretion to commit a crime. A guilty intent, or a *mens rea,* is a necessary element of a crime. Between the ages of seven and fourteen, no presumption of guilty intent from the mere commission of the act was assumed, but the *doli capax,* or guilty intent, had to be proved from the evidence. After the age of fourteen, children, like adults, were presumed to be responsible for their actions.[13]

Notwithstanding early recognition by the common law that minors occupied a peculiar position, the father had almost complete rights to do with his child as he saw fit, and the duties of parents to their children were enforced by the common law to a limited extent only. The parental power of the crown, was exercised very seldom, since few children were rich and influential enough to get into the crown's special courts. The brutal fact is that most children had no protection from the excesses of their parents. Today, juvenile courts afford a method by which the state can, in reality, act for the welfare of any child. In the juvenile court we have the means by which a child in need of protection, whether he has property or not (and usually the child before the juvenile court is without property), can be protected; when necessary, parental relationships can be severed. The probation service, an outgrowth of the common-law method of conditionally suspending sentence, affords a method by which the real needs of the child can be ascertained.[14] Whereas the chancery court had no means with which to operate and could not take upon itself the burden of investigation for the welfare of the child, the juvenile court, through its probation officers, makes social inquiries and is thus enabled to exercise its discretion for the welfare of the child.

PRECURSORS OF THE JUVENILE COURT

All through the Middle Ages offending children were treated with severity, and extreme vindictiveness was shown in the seventeenth and eighteenth centuries. Blackstone tells of children eight, nine, and ten years of age being sentenced to death. The colonists also applied harsh theories of punishment; for example, Plymouth Colony, in 1671, enacted a law providing death for sixteen offenses, among which were stubbornness and rebelliousness of any child over sixteen toward his parents.[15] In the nineteenth century, considerable legislation was enacted in the United States and other countries which recognized the desirability of treating

---

[12] Flexner and Oppenheimer, *op. cit.,* p. 8; Lou, *op. cit.,* p. 6.

[13] *Regina* v. *Smith,* 1 Cox C.C. 260 (1845); Blackstone, *Commentaries* (Philadelphia, Rees, Welsh, and Co., 1897), Bk. 4, pp. 22–24.

[14] Flexner and Oppenheimer, *op. cit.,* p. 8.

[15] Abbott, *op. cit.,* Vol. 2, p. 324.

juvenile delinquents in a different manner from adult criminals. Because some reformers and judges recognized that children, even though guilty of a crime, should not be treated as adults after conviction, there was a movement to develop reformatories. The first reformatory, called the House of Refuge, was established in 1825 in New York and was supported by public and private funds. The first state reform school in the United States was opened in Massachusetts in 1848.[16]

The early reformers were more concerned with treatment of offenders *after* conviction than before. Gradually interest shifted, and reformers advocated a change in the procedure preceding punishment. In 1869 Massachusetts provided that a visiting agent or officer of the State Board of Charities should attend the trial of juvenile cases to protect the child's interests and to make recommendations to the judge.[17] The same state, by an 1870 law, required separate hearings for the trial of juveniles in the county of Suffolk, in which Boston is located. New York passed a similar law in 1877. Although probation for boys in a limited form started in Chicago in 1861, Massachusetts took the lead in establishing a system by which the juvenile offender was placed under supervision instead of in confinement.[18] In 1892 New York added a new section to the penal code allowing separate trial, docket, and records for children under sixteen. Rhode Island, following the general line of Massachusetts experience, provided by law in 1898 for separate hearings of juvenile offenders, the presence of state agency representatives at the trial, and detention apart from adults before trial.

HISTORICAL BACKGROUND IN THE UNITED STATES

Although much of the theory of the juvenile court derives from English common and equity law, its development is of distinctly American origin and genius. There is some dispute as to whether Colorado or Illinois had the first real juvenile court. The Colorado act was originally passed and approved on April 12, 1899. It was essentially a part of the school law, and provided for probation officers in the person of truant officers or teachers. According to Judge Lindsey, it "foreshadowed what some twenty years afterwards a group of child welfare advocates have fostered; namely, a plan to make the juvenile court a part of the school system." [19]

However, it is to Illinois that the credit for passing the first juvenile

---

[16] *Ibid.*, pp. 325–328, 343–365, for some of the early laws regarding delinquent children and their care, and reports of operation of early institutions; Lou, *op. cit.*, p. 16.

[17] Abbott, *op. cit.*, Vol. 2, pp. 366–368; Lou, *op. cit.*, pp. 16–17; for convenient access to act, see Sheldon Glueck and Eleanor T. Glueck, *One Thousand Juvenile Delinquents* (Cambridge, Harvard University Press, 1934), ch. 2.

[18] Lou, *op. cit.*, pp. 17–18.

[19] Ben Lindsey, "Colorado's Contribution to the Juvenile Court," in Addams, *op. cit.*, p. 275.

court law is usually given. "Illinois has the distinction of being the first state in the United States, and I may venture to say in the world to draft a specific law for the welfare of juvenile offenders, later known as the Illinois Juvenile Court law, which was enacted July 1, 1899." [20] For a good many years before the passage of the Illinois act, leaders concerned with child welfare studied the problem and introduced bills into the legislature. As early as 1892 the Chicago Woman's Club became interested in a juvenile court, and, in 1895, a bill was drafted at the instance of this club providing for a separate court and a probation staff; but the project was abandoned because the club's legal advisers doubted the constitutionality of the proposed measure. Several groups joined together, and a committee emerged which drafted the Illinois Juvenile Court Act. The Chicago Bar Association was influential in helping to secure its passage.

The title of the original act was "An Act to Regulate the Treatment and Control of Dependent, Neglected, and Delinquent Children." "The law," according to Miss Julia Lathrop, first chief of the Children's Bureau, "was secured because of a great though slowly developed popular interest in the protection of helpless children." [21] It created no new or special court; in all parts of the state, except Cook County, it conferred jurisdiction upon circuit and county courts; in counties with a population over 500,000 the circuit court judges were to designate one or more of their number to hear all juvenile cases. A juvenile courtroom was to be separately provided and a separate record kept. So far as Cook County was concerned the law brought under one jurisdiction the care of all delinquent, neglected, and dependent children. Its only innovation was the principle that a child who broke the law was not to be treated as a criminal. This first statute, as a result of the compromise process, omitted any provision for paid probation offices. In 1905 the Illinois legislature amended the law to make this possible.

In the next five years juvenile court laws were passed in California, Indiana, Iowa, Maryland, Missouri, New Jersey, New York, Ohio, Pennsylvania, Rhode Island, and Wisconsin.[22] Every state in the Union today has express juvenile court and probation laws for children. Comparatively few states have provisions for separate juvenile courts. In most jurisdictions, with the exception of some of the largest cities, where separate

---

[20] Timothy D. Hurley, "Origin of the Illinois Juvenile Court Law," in Addams, *op. cit.*, p. 320; see also, Helen Rankin Jeter, *The Chicago Juvenile Court,* U.S. Children's Bureau Publication (Washington, D.C., G.P.O., 1922), No. 104. For convenient access to the first juvenile court act, see Abbott, *op. cit.*, Vol. 2, pp. 392–401; and for access to case upholding law by Illinois Supreme Court, see *ibid.*, pp. 404–412

[21] Julia Lathrop, "The Background of the Juvenile Court in Illinois," in Addams, *op. cit.*, pp. 290–297.

[22] Francis H. Hiller, *Juvenile Court Laws of the United States* (New York, National Probation and Parole Association, 1933)

courts are set up, juvenile court authority is assigned to some court of record. Articles regarding courts and their jurisdiction in state constitutions have been responsible, in part, for this phenomenon; it is also true, however, that many counties are too small in population to justify the establishment of a separate court.

FOREIGN JUVENILE COURTS

COMMON PRINCIPLES [23]

The juvenile court movement, which originated in the United States and which was adopted in England in 1908, has slowly spread throughout the world. Despite the many differences in legislation and practice between countries, they have several principles in common:

1. Protection and treatment for the young offender rather than punishment.
2. Juvenile court judges who have an understanding of children and their problems.
3. Imposition of an age limit, most often sixteen and, sometimes, as high as eighteen.
4. Informal and private hearings.
5. Investigations or social studies to help determine how best to help the offender and protect the community.
6. Less severe penalties for children than those prescribed for adults guilty of like offenses when penalties are considered necessary.
7. Separation of young offenders from adults during detention prior to the hearing and afterward.
8. Separate institutions for minors.

We shall briefly examine the legislation of several countries.

ENGLAND

The Children's Act of 1908 was the great charter of children's safety and included the first English provisions for juvenile courts or, more

---

[23] The materials for this discussion of foreign courts are taken largely from Anna Kalet Smith, *Juvenile Court Laws in Foreign Countries,* U.S. Children's Bureau Publication (Washington, D.C., G.P.O., 1949), No. 328. Smith summarizes the laws of twenty-six European, six Asiatic, four African, ten South American, three North American (other than U.S.), four Central American states, and those of Australia and New Zealand. See also, Albert Kiralfy, *The Juvenile Law-Breaker in the U.S.S.R.,* 15 Mod. L. Rev. 472–478 (1952); Benedict S. Alper, "Prevention and Control of Delinquency at the International Level," *Proceedings of the National Conference of Social Work: 1948* (New York, Columbia University Press, 1948), pp. 366–372; Wiley B. Sanders, "Children's Court Movement in England," *National Probation Association Yearbook: 1945* (New York, 1946), pp. 58–70; Glenn R. Winters, *Modern Court Services for Youth and Juveniles,* 33 Marq. L. Rev. 99–111 (1949–50); Thorsten Sellin, "Sweden's Substitute for the Juvenile Court," *Annals of the American Academy of Political and Social Science,* Vol. 261 (January, 1949), p. 137; Adolphe Delierneux, "The United Nations in the Field of Prevention of Crime and Treatment of Offenders," *National Probation and Parole Association Yearbook: 1949* (New York, 1950), p. 248.

accurately, for courts hearing children's cases.[24] By that act a court of summary jurisdiction was given authority over certain cases pertaining to children and young persons, and when hearing such cases the court was to sit either in a different building or room or at a different time from other hearings. Although much of that act has been repealed and amended by subsequent enactments, nothing has altered the fact that today the English juvenile court is a court of summary jurisdiction and is still a criminal court, despite simplification of procedure and modification of punishment.[25] It deals with all offenders between the ages of eight and seventeen except those accused of homicide, and with all children and young persons in need of care and protection up to the age of seventeen. A child is a person under the age of fourteen, and a young person is one who has attained the age of fourteen but not seventeen. The common-law rule that a child under seven cannot be guilty of a felony has been extended so that no child under the age of eight can be guilty of an offense.

There are nearly 1,000 juvenile courts in England and Wales. Each is normally composed of three unpaid lay magistrates selected from special panels of persons experienced or interested in the problems of children. At least one must be a woman. None need be a lawyer. The responsible government department in England and Wales is the Home Office. Hearings must be separate from those otherwise brought into the same court, and they must be private. The lord chancellor may make rules for regulating procedure. No conviction of a child or young person can be regarded as a conviction of felony for the purposes of any disqualification attaching to felony. Several restrictions on the type of punishment have been made. For example, no person under twenty-one can be sentenced to imprisonment unless the court finds no other appropriate manner of treatment; and a child under fourteen cannot be imprisoned at all. No sentence of death can be pronounced on any person under eighteen, but he may be detained under sentence and, like other persons in need of care, sent to a remand home or an approved school, committed to the care of a fit person, or put on probation. Offenders over fourteen and under twenty-one can be detained for short periods under discipline suitable to their age and description. The regime is designed as a "short, sharp shock."

---

[24] Edw. VII, c. 67, Pt. 5 (1908).

[25] J. A. F. Watson, *British Juvenile Courts* (London, Longmans, Green, 1948); G. L. Reaks, *The Juvenile Offender* (London, Christopher Johnson, 1953); British Information Services, Reference Division, *Social Services in Britain*, I.D. 789, revised March, 1953, New York; Sir Cyril L. Burt, *The Young Delinquent* (London, University of London Press, 1948); F. T. Giles, *The Juvenile Courts: Their Work and Problems* (London, Allen and Unwin, 1946); Winifred A. Elkin, *English Juvenile Courts* (London, Kegan Paul, Trench, Truebner, 1938), ch. 2; E. E. Bowerman, *The Law of Child Protection* (London, Pitman, 1933), chs. 8, 9, 10.

The Borstal system for offenders over sixteen and under twenty-one years of age provide suitable training for adolescents in conditions other than those of a prison. The general framework of training includes a full day of work in a workshop or on the land, regular physical training, and a reasonable period for recreation, reading, and writing. The period of supervision after release is an integral part of the training.

The court likewise has wide powers of discretion in providing treatment for children and young persons in need of special care or those who are particularly designated as refractory. Approved schools are extensively used for residential education and training. A court or the secretary of state, in determining the approved school to which a child or young person may be sent, must select, whenever possible, a school of the committed child's religious persuasion. With some exceptions, when children are sent to approved schools, they are under supervision for at least three years. They can be kept longer under care within the discretion of the managers of the school with the approval of the secretary of state. The Home Office issues rules for the management of the approved schools. Among these rules are those concerning discipline and punishment, including the type and extent of physical punishment permissible. Boys and girls detained in approved schools are subject to discipline but not to physical restraint. The managers of the schools have the right to place the child or young person out on license when he has made sufficient progress, but if such is done within the first twelve months of his detention, the consent of the secretary of state is necessary.

In the United States the juvenile court is not a tribunal for the trial of children who have committed offenses but an equity or chancery court where the state assumes parental responsibilities. So far as delinquents are concerned, the juvenile court in England remains a criminal court, although considerably modified. As in other countries, there is not complete agreement among British jurists, legislators, and students of social problems on juvenile court theories and methods. Although the reasons are not clear, the fact is that a marked decrease of delinquency in England and Wales has been taking place at a time when the trend in the United States has been decidedly upward. The British Information Services reports that the chief factor in the reduction of juvenile crime undoubtedly has been the return to comparative normalcy in British family life. Part of the credit, they believe, should be given to English methods of dealing with juvenile delinquency.[26]

EUROPE

In Europe the laws of the various countries have undergone many modifications since their original enactment. In Germany juvenile courts

[26] *Milwaukee Journal* (October 23, 1955).

were established by municipal regulation in several cities between 1908 and 1922. In 1923 a federal law prescribed a uniform system for the entire country. After the Nazi party gained control in 1933 the methods of dealing with juvenile delinquents became more rigorous and more closely approached those used in dealing with adults, although the 1923 law remained on the books. In 1934 special criminal courts were set up for hearing political cases, including those of persons under eighteen. In 1936 probation work formerly done by trained employees of the children's bureaus was transferred to political groups, such as the Hitler Youth. In 1943 the government issued an order on the treatment of young offenders, prescribing severe measures and lowering from fourteen to twelve the age at which a child could be punished under the criminal law. At the end of World War II in 1945 the control council for Germany ordered the repeal of the laws on Hitler Youth and other Nazi organizations, and the statute of 1923 on juvenile courts was reinstated. In the American zone the military government ordered that children under fourteen who violated German laws be referred to the local children's bureaus and those between fourteen and eighteen to the German courts.

Juvenile courts were established in some czarist Russian cities in 1908. They were abolished in 1918, a year after the establishment of the Soviet government, and were replaced by "commissions on minors." These commissions, given authority to deal with children under seventeen and later under eighteen who violated a law, were abolished in 1935, and most of their functions were transferred to the regular courts. In 1943 a definite step toward special jurisdiction in children's cases was taken. The order provided for setting up special divisions in the people's courts to hear cases of offenders under sixteen. The children's divisions hear cases of children under this age who are accused of serious or minor offenses against the law, who present serious or mild behavior problems, who repeatedly break the rules of discipline in the compulsory residential schools for vocational training, and who run away from such schools. All cases must be investigated by well-qualified persons. Hearings must be attended by parents, guardians, or school principals. The court may take any of a number of measures to deal with the child. If he is between fourteen and sixteen and guilty of a serious offense or presenting a serious behavior problem, he may be punished according to the criminal law with consideration for his age and other circumstances. If he is under sixteen and the offense is minor, the court may dismiss the case and decide whether to leave the child with his parents or place him in an institution. A new type of institution set up under a 1943 order is the "educational work colony" for offenders between eleven and sixteen. Correctional training and vocational education are given here, and the child may be kept until he is sixteen or seventeen.

The first law on juvenile courts in France was enacted in 1912. It has been modified numbers of times. Legislation provides for a separate juvenile court in each court of first instance. The court is presided over by a judge selected from among the judges of the court. He is assisted in his consideration of the case by nonprofessional men and women. The courts hear cases of persons under eighteen who are accused of major or minor offenses or who present serious behavior problems. During the investigation of his case the child is placed in an observation center instead of a police detention station. Preferably, the investigation is made by trained social workers. Hearings are closed to the general public. The court may dismiss the case, admonish the child, return him to his parents, or place him with a suitable family or public or private welfare agency or in an institution. Probation may be ordered and continued until the young person is twenty-one. Every person, agency, or institution offering to care for children or young persons must meet specified requirements, whereupon a permit is issued by the prefect of the department (administrative division of government).

In the Scandinavian countries there are no juvenile courts proper. The cases of young offenders are handled by local child welfare committees or agencies. In Denmark, for example, these committees in addition to watching over care given to children under fourteen in foster family homes, to children under seven born out of wedlock but living with their mothers, and to children under eighteen whose parents receive public aid, also deal with children who are physically or morally neglected, who present behavior problems, or who are accused of offenses against the law. Children under fifteen are not subject to penalties under the law and, if accused, are referred to the child welfare committees. Children between the ages of fifteen and eighteen are detained for questioning by the police, who are required to notify the local child welfare committee immediately. From then until the final disposition of the case the child may not be left in police custody. The police may question the child only in the presence of the committee's agent. The case is then referred to the district attorney, who decides whether to turn the child over to the committee for certain measures or to take court action. The latter is seldom done. The work of the local child welfare committee is supervised by the National Child Welfare Board of the Ministry of Social Welfare.

SOUTH AMERICA

The first juvenile court law in South America was enacted in Argentina in 1919. By this law judges of designated courts in the federal capital, Buenos Aires, and in the national territories (not included in its states) receive sole jurisdiction in all cases of children under eighteen who are accused of felonies or misdemeanors or who are victims of such offenses.

Juvenile courts have been introduced in at least four of the fourteen provinces under separate provincial laws. The law of the province of Buenos Aires, enacted in 1938, gives the juvenile court jurisdiction over children under eighteen who are accused of offenses against the law or who are mistreated by their parents or who present behavior problems. The judge of the court is assisted by a physician and two probation officers, one a woman. The law requires a physical and mental examination of each child brought before the court and an investigation by a probation officer. Parents may be deprived of parental authority. The children's bureau of the province is directed to help in the work of the juvenile courts.

In Brazil the movement for juvenile courts originated in 1921, when a law was passed affecting Rio de Janeiro. Legislation on juvenile courts is now in effect in Rio de Janeiro, capital of the federal district and of the country, and in at least eight of the twenty-one states and territories. The juvenile court of Rio de Janeiro consists of one judge assisted by a lawyer, a psychiatrist, an official acting as public prosecutor, clerks, and probation officers. This court has jurisdiction over neglected, wayward, and delinquent children, over the issuance of "work books" or work permits, and over nonsupport actions. The court is authorized to take various kinds of welfare measures for children under fourteen and for those between fourteen and eighteen.

The 1924 penal code of Peru provided for the establishment of a juvenile court in the capital, Lima. The court consists of a specially appointed judge, a physician, and a secretary. Outside the capital a suitable judge of the lower court may be appointed to hear children's cases or any other suitable person if such a judge is not available. To be appointed to the juvenile court as judge or physician the candidate must be married, have a family, and be a man of irreproachable conduct. The court has jurisdiction over persons less than eighteen years of age accused of offenses against the law and over those who are physically or morally neglected, morally endangered or perverted. A child under thirteen is not responsible under the law and is not subject to penalties. A young person thirteen to eighteen, guilty of an act punishable by imprisonment in the case of an adult, may be committed to an industrial, agricultural, or correctional institution. Suspended sentences and probation are permitted.

The first step toward the creation of juvenile courts in Bolivia was a decree of 1947 which called for the appointment of a children's judge in La Paz, the capital. The judge is to hear cases of children under eighteen accused of numbers of offenses, including truancy, the use of habit-forming drugs and alcoholic beverages, traffic in tobacco and obscene literature, prostitution, habitual begging and vagrancy, and irregularities of behavior, such as serious disobedience of parents.

ASIA

On the continent of Asia several countries have juvenile court legislation. In India legislation on this subject is in force in some of the provinces, among them Madras (1920), Bengal (1922), and Bombay (1924). In the province of Bombay, for example, the courts have jurisdiction over children under sixteen who are accused of offenses punishable with banishment or imprisonment; they also deal with children who are homeless or lack visible means of support or who have no parent or guardian or whose parent or guardian is unfit. If a separate court has not been established, the court before which the child is brought must, whenever practicable (unless the child is tried jointly with an adult), sit apart from regular trials. An investigation must be made. Publication of names of children is prohibited. Numbers of measures can be taken, including discharge, probation, commitment to an institution, whipping in the case of a boy, imposition of a fine on the child or his parents, and imprisonment.

Juvenile courts were established in Japan in 1922. They deal with persons between fourteen and eighteen who have violated provisions of the penal code or have shown tendencies to so do; cases of serious crime, however, are referred to the ordinary courts. At the request of the governor of a province the juvenile courts may also deal with young offenders under fourteen years of age. The measures that can be taken by the court can be divided into two categories: (1) protective measures, including the use of temples, agencies, private individuals, reformatories, houses of correction, hospitals, probation; and (2) imprisonment in a juvenile prison especially constructed for that purpose or in a place set apart in an ordinary prison.

This brief review of juvenile court legislation in several countries around the world shows how recent enactments on this subject are; how few juvenile courts exist, even though considerable legislation permits their establishment; and how diverse their practices are.

For Selected References, see those at the end of Chapter 16.

CHAPTER 15

Youthful Offenders and the Juvenile Court II

JUVENILE COURTS IN THE UNITED STATES: VENUE AND JURISDICTION

GENERAL

Juvenile courts do not deal with situations in which large sums of money are involved, but they do handle delicate human relationships. It is important, then, that the special court have status so that first-class personnel will be available.[1] It should be a court of record and of comparable status to courts having general civil jurisdiction. Responsibility for children's cases ought not to be left to justices of the peace or to municipal judges having inferior jurisdiction, although this is the case in many jurisdictions. Only some eighty of the more than 3,000 counties in the United States have special judges, and only half of these serve full-time in the juvenile court. The rest of the jurisdictions have judges elected or appointed to other courts. The result is that many judges are primarily interested in the criminal or civil functions of the court and only incidentally in children.

VENUE

The venue, or geographical area, of juvenile courts is usually the county. Jurisdiction of the court means the inherent power to decide a case, whereas venue designates the particular county or city or locality in which a court with jurisdiction may hear and determine the case. Aside from metropolitan communities, there often is not a large enough volume of work to justify special local juvenile courts. This explains, in part, the considerable interest in either replacing the juvenile court prevalently operating on a county-wide basis to a state-wide system or expanding the jurisdiction of the juvenile court. Suggestions for a state-wide system take one of two lines of thought: (1) the creation of a special juvenile court, with staff and facilities operating on either a district or state-wide basis;

[1] Sol Rubin, "State Juvenile Courts: A New Standard," in Clyde B. Vedder, ed., *The Juvenile Offender* (New York, Doubleday, 1954), pp. 310–315.

or (2) the creation of a special division within a unified state-wide system of courts, with staff and facilities operating on either a district or a state-wide basis. Utah in 1908, Connecticut in 1941, and Rhode Island in 1944 enacted legislation establishing state-wide systems. Utah before 1908 had twenty-nine ex-officio juvenile court judges who were replaced by one part-time and four special full-time judges. In Connecticut instead of 169 town and city judges who heard children's cases, only two of whom were juvenile judges, there are three special and no ex-officio judges. In Rhode Island there were formerly twelve district court judges functioning in an ex-officio capacity. With the establishment of a state-wide court the work was taken over by two special juvenile judges.

The 1949 Standard Juvenile Court Act contains alternative sections for establishing local or state juvenile courts.[2] If a state chooses a state-wide system, the act leaves number and size of districts to individual state legislatures to determine. Under the act, when a legislature accepts a state system the territory is divided into several districts, according to population, area, and other factors, and one judge is appointed for each district, which he covers on a circuit basis. The act calls for appointment by the governor from an approved list of candidates nominated by a panel of representatives of the courts, the bar, and the departments of education, mental hygiene, and public welfare.

A state-wide system offers the advantages of uniform practice, better qualified judges, the planned distribution of probation services throughout the state, and greater specialization in children's problems. Since in most states this plan necessitates major reorganization of the judicial system, it is not likely to develop rapidly. An alternative, perhaps requiring less modification of the existing court system, is the enlargement of the local area by the combining of judicial districts or counties. This plan also faces the opposition of those who are strong advocates of local institutions. Another way of obtaining adequate courts is to add cases over which the juvenile court has jurisdiction or to add cases over juveniles to some court already having jurisdiction over numbers of types of family situations. We shall discuss family and domestic relations courts in the next chapter. The juvenile court is likely to remain a local institution, although there is some interest in a state or district system in a few states. Because the juvenile court is generally a local service, a heavy responsibility rests with local communities to select competent judges, and, with these judges, to achieve greater uniformity of administration, to abolish the political aspects of their activities, and to improve their services generally.

---

[2] *A Standard Juvenile Court Act,* rev. ed. (New York, National Probation and Parole Association, 1949); another revision is expected to be published in 1957.

JURISDICTION OVER CLASSES AND AGES OF CHILDREN

In most states the statutes define who are neglected, dependent, delinquent children. The laws enumerate and describe numbers of types of behavior which are included under these classifications.[3] Several jurisdictions have eliminated the terms and substituted descriptions of the type of problem or behavior over which the court has jurisdiction. The standard acts of 1943 and 1949 did away with classifications. The 1949 act on this subject reads as follows: [4]

ARTICLE II JURISDICTION: CHILDREN, MINORS

7. JURISDICTION: Children, Minors. Except as otherwise provided herein and subject to the prior jurisdiction of a United States court, the court shall have exclusive jurisdiction in proceedings;

1. Concerning any child living or found within the county: [(a)]
   a. who is neglected as to proper or necessary support or education as required by law, or as to medical, psychiatric, psychological, or other care necessary for his well-being; or who is abandoned by his parent or other custodian;
   b. whose occupation, behavior, condition, environment, or associations are such as to injure or endanger his welfare or that of others;
   c. who is beyond the control of his parent or other custodian;
   d. who is alleged to have violated or attempted to violate any federal, state, or local law or municipal ordinance, regardless of where the violation occurred.
2. Concerning any minor eighteen years of age or older living or found within the county alleged to have violated or attempted to violate any federal, state, or local law or municipal ordinance prior to having become eighteen years of age. Such a minor shall be dealt with under the provisions of this act relating to children.
3. To determine the custody or guardianship of the person of any child living within the county; for the adoption of a minor; and to terminate parental rights in connection with such proceedings.
4. For judicial consent to the marriage of a child, when such consent is required by law.
5. For the treatment or commitment of a mentally defective or mentally disordered or emotionally disturbed child.

Nothing contained in this act shall deprive other courts of the right to determine the custody of children upon writs of habeas corpus, or to determine the custody or guardianship of children when such custody or guardianship is incidental to the determination of causes pending in such other courts. Such other courts, however, may certify said questions to the juvenile court for hearing and determination or recommendation.

(a) Or other jurisdictional areas

---

[3] Frederick B. Sussmann, *Law of Juvenile Delinquency* (New York, Oceana, 1950), pp. 18–19. In Chapter 11 we referred to definitions of dependent, neglected, and delinquent children.

[4] *A Standard Juvenile Court Act,* pp. 16–17.

Some authorities are fearful that descriptions rather than definitions and classifications will make jurisdiction ambiguous and uncertain. This anxiety appears unwarranted, especially if adequate procedural protections are afforded. Those who favor descriptions rather than narrow definitions hope that the result will be less derogatory labeling of children and more extensive use of a wide range of treatment resources.

Numbers of statutes do not provide for exclusive original jurisdiction of all children under a given age. Rather, they stipulate that juvenile and criminal courts shall have concurrent jurisdiction over children of certain ages who have committed certain offenses, or they exclude certain offenses from juvenile courts. Unfortunately, these may be the very children most needing the methods and resources of the special court. Original jurisdiction should remain with the juvenile court, but statutes should provide that the juvenile court be permitted to waive its authority when it finds that there are no adequate facilities for the protection of certain older children and the community. This matter we shall discuss in the next chapter when we consider the constitutionality of juvenile court legislation. A considerable number of states carry on the practice of transferring difficult youths from training institutions to reformatories or prisons. This often is done on administrative order of the state department of welfare or of corrections and without further judicial inquiry. Since the cases of children in juvenile court are not conducted as criminal procedures, some authorities believe that such administrative action is unconstitutional. They argue that if transfer is considered necessary and desirable, the child should be returned to the juvenile court for a new determination of facts. If the court finds that he needs more restrictive and rigorous care than can be provided in training schools, it should wave jurisdiction and transfer the case to the criminal courts.

The age jurisdiction for the largest number of states is eighteen, with a range of from sixteen to twenty-one in the others. In most states the age jurisdiction is the same for boys and girls.[5] A few states make the court's jurisdiction concurrent with criminal courts for children between eighteen and twenty-one. The disadvantage of this plan is that it allows a relatively short time for treatment, with the result that only minor offenses tend to be brought to the specialized court. Cases involving young people between eighteen and twenty-one should have special attention. If they are brought before the juvenile court, these youths should be dealt with under special provisions rather than under the law governing the handling of juveniles; or they should be given attention in special

[5] National Probation and Parole Association, *Probation and Parole Directory, United States and Canada: 1952* (New York, 1952); *A Standard Juvenile Court Act,* p. 8.

branches of other courts or in youth offender courts. The procedure should be individualized and noncriminal in nature. Treatment for them may require more security than that offered in training schools and less than that offered in reformatories and prisons. We shall discuss youth courts in the next chapter.

There seems to be considerable agreement among experts that it is undesirable for the juvenile court to exercise jurisdiction over children committing minor traffic violations. These can be handled by police or traffic courts, with such safeguards as the requirement that the parent or guardian be present at the hearing. Jurisdiction with respect to major traffic violations, such as unauthorized use of a vehicle, manslaughter, driving under the influence of liquor or drugs, should be with the juvenile court.

JURISDICTION OVER ADULTS

Authorities differ as to the classes of adults over whom the juvenile court should exercise jurisdiction. For example, they are not in agreement that the juvenile court should have jurisdiction over all adults charged with a crime against a child. Some believe that criminal jurisdiction over adults is foreign to the nature of the juvenile or family court. Others think it is reasonable to grant the court jurisdiction over adults charged with actions against children, especially where there is a continuing relationship between the adult so charged and the child. It appears that there is little reason for bringing action in the specialized court against an unrelated adult or one who has no continuing relationship with the child. In the opinion of the Children's Bureau, the specialized children's court should have jurisdiction only over the following cases involving criminal adults: (1) parents who are alleged to have willfully abandoned or failed to support their child; and (2) parents or other adults who are alleged to have committed an act forbidden by law or ordinance or failed to perform an act required by law with respect to such child, whether or not such action or failure to act contributes to a situation bringing the child under the jurisdiction of the court.[6]

Jurisdiction over adults in family matters ought to be in a special court with special facilities for social study. This court can be a juvenile court with broad jurisdiction or a family or domestic relations court with jurisdiction over many family matters. Numbers of states have enacted legislation extending the jurisdiction of the juvenile court over classes of situations involving adults. There is a difference between the states as to what classes of adults are brought under this broadened jurisdiction. Divorce

---

[6] U.S. Children's Bureau, *Standards for Specialized Courts Dealing with Children* (Washington, D.C., G.P.O., 1954), No. 346, p. 34.

cases and the resultant problems of custody of children are seldom handled by the court dealing with children.

DURATION OF JURISDICTION

Most statutes provide that once jurisdiction has been obtained it shall continue until the child reaches the age of twenty-one unless the court orders a shorter period or sooner discharges him. After the court has made an order it should have the power to modify or rescind it on the application of the child, his parent or legal guardian, or the agency vested with legal custody. The court should also have the power to change orders on its own initiative. This is true where an order of probation or an order appointing a guardian requires change. However, orders vesting legal custody in an agency, institution, or individual should not be modified by the court on its own initiative. In such instances, the parent or legal guardian should initiate the action for change. Orders once made should not be modified without notice to all parties concerned, a hearing, and an opportunity for the parties to appear in court.

JUVENILE COURTS IN THE UNITED STATES: PROCEDURES

THE POLICE [7]

Intake for the juvenile court, particularly of children involved in delinquency, generally begins with the local police department. Referrals in neglect cases are likely to come from a variety of sources. Some police departments, recognizing the importance of their role in the prevention and control of delinquency, have established special bureaus or departments to work with children and youth.[8] Police officers who find a child in a situation dangerous to himself or to others, or who find one who has committed a "delinquent" act, must decide whether the situation or act is serious enough to take the child into court. The decision should be based upon the gravity of the situation as determined by investigation of the officer. If the officer does not believe court action is necessary, he has several alternatives: (1) referral to a social agency; (2) advice to the child or parents, particularly as to the existence of resources; (3) warning; (4) temporary arrangements for the child's safety, such as taking him to his home, finding lodging, or referring the child to an emergency shelter.

The police should not employ methods of penalties or restraint, such

[7] *Standards for Specialized Courts Dealing with Children,* pp. 36–40.

[8] U.S. Children's Bureau, *Police Services for Juveniles* (Washington, D.C., G.P.O., 1954), No. 344.

as placing the child on "informal probation," ordering restitution, or revoking a driving permit. If the parents cannot be found, or if, after consulting with them, the officer is of the opinion that a petition should be filed with the court, he should either take the child to the court or to the place of detention or shelter designated by the court. In these situations the officer should give written reasons for his actions and make contact with the intake worker of the court as soon as possible within twenty-four hours to consider filing a petition with respect to the child.

If the police officer needs to make further investigation after the child is placed in detention, he should have access to the child for interviews. The interview should be conducted with numbers of safeguards. For example, where a child has been questioned alone by a police officer without the presence of parents, guardian, or counsel, it should be presumed that his statements during the interview are excluded from admission as evidence before a criminal court. Both child and parents should be told before an interview that they are entitled to legal counsel and that they can refuse to answer questions if counsel should so decide. Fingerprinting should be allowed only on an individual basis and by court order. If the court authorizes the use of fingerprints, these should subsequently either be returned to the court for destruction or kept on a civil identification card. The police should not take pictures of the child except on authorization of the court and, then, only for purposes of identification. The police may give evidence in court necessary to the establishment of the court's jurisdiction and a finding of the facts alleged in the petition.

INTAKE SERVICE [9]

Experts generally agree that a central intake service of the special court is essential, especially in metropolitan areas. In children's cases involving delinquency or neglect the basic function of the intake unit is to make a preliminary inquiry to determine whether the interests of the public or of the child require that further action be taken. The preliminary inquiry should not be confused with the social study made by a probation officer for the purpose of helping the court arrive at a disposition; nor with the investigation for determining facts which might sustain the petition. Typical matters surveyed at intake are: Does the complaint or the action appear to be a matter over which the court has jurisdiction? Can the interests of the child and the public be best served by court action or by referral to another agency? If court action is indicated, what type of proceeding should be initiated? If the child is in detention, should he be released or kept longer? Such facts as age of the child, number of times the child and other members of the family have been known to the court, time the act took place, attitudes of child and parents should be

[9] *Standards for Specialized Courts Dealing with Children,* pp. 36–43.

obtained. Most of this information can be secured from the complainant or through office procedures. The intake worker should have access to legal advice.

Where the complainant has insufficient evidence to file a petition or is unwilling to do so, the intake worker should refer the complainant to an agency, usually the police, having statutory powers to investigate such complaints and to file petitions. Generally, the court should not accept complaints for investigation by its own staff. In the minds of the child and his parents this puts the probation officer in the position of an adversary for the state. However, the court staff will often conduct its own investigation under such circumstances as when the child is already on probation to the court or when one parent complains against the other in nonsupport situations. In some courts the intake worker has responsibility for authorizing the initiation of criminal proceedings against adults. In others this responsibility rests with some such person as the prosecuting attorney.

INFORMAL ADJUSTMENT [10]

Difference of opinion exists among experts on the handling of cases in an unofficial manner, that is, without petition and with unofficial supervision or probation. In the early days of the juvenile court, when there were few social services for children, numbers of courts provided informal services. They did so in their eagerness to forestall more serious difficulties and to provide protection which no other resources were available to give. Today, some juvenile courts refuse to handle cases on an informal basis, although others extensively use the practice. Some judges justify the practice on the grounds that it permits more flexible handling than can be done in the courtroom and that it does not require the filing of a legal record on the child. This is a logical position for those who think of the court as the core agency of the community, unique in its objectives and treatment resources. On the other hand, it is argued that unofficial and informal handling does not necessarily mean adequate service; that it can be arbitrary and incompetent; that whether the record is official or unofficial it exists and may be used to injure the child. One of the great objections to informal adjustment is that it attempts to do, sometimes well and sometimes not, what other agencies in the community may be set up to do, often with better facilities and personnel. This position is rational for those who firmly believe that the juvenile court should be used as a treatment resource only when there appears to be need for authoritative action with respect to the child or to the adults responsible for his care and protection.

The Children's Bureau takes the position that there is a place for the

---

[10] *Ibid.*, pp. 43–45.

use of unofficial handling or informal adjustment in disposing of complaints but that this action should generally be limited to referral of the child or family to a social agency, such referral to be considered as advice and not compulsion; and a conference between the complainant and the child or his family or, in the case of nonsupport, between the parents. No action which denies or abridges the rights of the child or parent, as, for example, the continued detention of a child beyond the time limitation imposed or probation, should occur unless a petition is filed and a hearing held. Public and private social agencies in the community should be used to provide the counsel and supervision required. It remains a fact that there are many communities where such services are unavailable and, hence, it is understandable that courts continue informal practices to compensate for gaps in the local situation. If the court gives casework services to a child and family on an informal basis, court rules should provide safeguards against possible abuse. "Casework services should be clearly differentiated from probation status. Unlike probation status, the worker providing this service has no authoritative control in the situation." [11]

DETENTION AND SHELTER CARE [12]

Most communities in the country encounter the problem of where to keep children, pending final disposition of their case, when they cannot be returned to the home of their parents or guardian. Over half the states forbid detaining the child in jail or require, when the jail is used, that separate facilities from those for adults shall be furnished. Despite such prohibitions, and in the absence of other and better facilities, jails and other inadequate detention quarters are and will continue to be used. Each year about 100,000 children from seven to seventeen are held in county jails and police lockups, most of which are substandard for adults. Thousands of additional children are held in basement cells or behind bars in detention homes which offer "nothing more than the cold storage of physical care and custody." Still more thousands of children are removed from unfit homes and placed in secure custody. These children are often held in detention for the convenience of officials or for lack of shelter facilities, such as emergency foster homes.

Detention care improperly given can arouse hostilities in children

---

[11] *Ibid.*, p. 45.

[12] *Ibid.*, pp. 45–47; Sherwood Norman, "Detention of Children in the United States," paper presented at the Children's Bureau Juvenile Delinquency Conference (June 28, 1954); Sherwood Norman and Helen Norman, *Detention for the Juvenile Court: A Discussion of Principles and Practices* (New York, National Probation and Parole Association, 1946); Sherwood Norman, *The Detention of Children in Michigan* (New York, National Probation and Parole Association, 1952); Austin H. MacCormick, "Children in Our Jails," in Vedder, *op. cit.*, pp. 204–211, and "Keeping Children out of Jails: It Can Be Done," *ibid.*, pp. 219–228.

which may "backfire against society." The detention period can do much to aggravate the feelings of already antagonistic children, or it can be a positive resource in the treatment process. Most communities do not have a large enough volume of cases going through the specialized court to justify construction of modern detention facilities. Over 2,500 counties have from one to a few dozen children a year to detain. District detention homes have been suggested as a method for meeting this situation. The use of foster home care for children not requiring security resources is increasing. Authorities seem to believe that state departments of welfare should have the responsibility of setting standards for detention care, of providing consultant services to detention homes, and of inspecting detention facilities. Perhaps the state should provide subsidies to local detention homes meeting recommended standards and encourage the development of joint detention homes owned by one county but serving others with a state subsidy for construction. Perhaps, also, the state should encourage the growth of shelter care in subsidized foster family homes by making grants to the locality for this purpose.

Authority to place a child in detention or shelter care without the consent of parents or guardian should be vested only in the court, its probation staff, the police, or an administrative agency having statutory powers to do so. A child should not be detained for a period longer than twenty-four hours without the filing of a petition to bring him to court. After a petition is filed the decision as to whether the child is to continue in detention or is to be released should be made by the judge or a member of the probation staff. Since most communities have inadequate facilities for the detention of children, the courts are left on their own to work out arrangements for temporary care of children coming under their jurisdiction. If there is insufficient staff available to the court for finding and supervising foster homes, if there are no facilities except the jail for security detention, many children, while awaiting disposition of their cases, will continue to have experiences potentially or actually harmful.

PETITION, SUMMONS, NOTICE, SOCIAL STUDY [13]

The procedure of the juvenile court involves numbers of steps, some of which are defined by statute, and some by administrative regulation. The petition starts the formal legal procedure. It should include:

1. The facts alleged to bring the child within the jurisdiction of the court.
2. The name, age, and residence of the child.
3. The names and residence of his parents or guardian.
4. The names and residence of any other persons having legal custody.
5. The child's spouse in case of marriage.
6. The name and residence of the nearest known relative when parents or guardian cannot be located.

---

[13] *Standards for Specialized Courts Dealing with Children,* pp. 47–53.

Immediately upon the filing of the petition, which should be under oath, a tentative date for the hearing should be set.

Authorities differ as to whether initiation of the social study should await a finding that a delinquent or other specific act has been committed or should come after the filing of the petition and before the hearing. Advocates of the first procedure are in agreement with Paul Tappen, who argues that the prehearing investigation is unsound because of the following reasons: [14]

1. The social and psychological sciences have not yet achieved such infallibility as to determine from the problems of the individual either the fact of his delinquency or the potential character of his behavior.
2. A court is not the proper place for the performance of general child welfare activities but is a resource for authoritative action.
3. The facilities of the court are inadequate in quantity and quality to carry out such an extensive function.
4. The social history or evidence secured is apt to be composed of hearsay statements that no other court would heed.

The Children's Bureau, on the other hand, takes the position that the social study should begin with the filing of the petition. Exceptions include situations where the child denies delinquent behavior or where court staff has doubts of delinquent acts. In these cases a court hearing is necessary to determine the facts and whether the court should exercise jurisdiction. Until this is done there should not be a social study. The social study should not be confused with the investigation to secure evidence necessary to substantiate the facts alleged in the petition; nor should it be identified with the preliminary inquiry at the intake desk to determine whether the interests of the child and of the public require further action. The social study is for the purpose of helping the court determine what disposition is best for all concerned. The court's determination should be based on all relevant facts derived from the social study and from other testimony. The study may be made by the probation staff of the court or by the staff of other agencies upon the request of the court. If the latter, the worker should be administratively responsible to the court.

The content of the study depends on the type of case and the issue involved, as, for example, adoption, legal custody, temporary or permanent guardianship, paternity, neglect, and delinquency. The study requires more than the aggregation of facts, important as these are. It requires evaluation and interpretation. The attitudes of the child and of others involved in the situation are significant in determining disposition. Information may be secured from many sources, including school, church, medical and psychiatric agencies, neighbors, family, and the child. The

---

[14] Paul Tappen, *Juvenile Delinquency* (New York, McGraw-Hill, 1949), pp. 212–215.

probation officer or agency conducting the study should make recommendations to the court for disposition, which may include discharge, probation to the parents or others, foster home placement, commitment to an agency or institution, termination of parental rights, or appointment of a guardian. Such an inquiry clearly requires competent personnel.

Following the filing of the petition the parents, guardians, and others named in the petition should be notified of the content of the petition and the date of the hearing. The persons having the care and control of the child should be required to bring him to court at the time indicated. The court may summon the appearance of any person, including those whom the child and family wish to be present, whose presence seems necessary and desirable. Service of summons should be made personally by the delivery of a copy to the person summoned. If after diligent search the parents cannot be found, service of summons should be by registered mail to the last known address or by publication or by both. The court should have the power to pay or to authorize reimbursement for travel expenses. The family and child should be duly notified of their right to legal counsel if they wish. If they do not have the money to employ counsel, the court should make this service available through legal aid or other resources.

Most states have statutes which assure the noncriminal nature of juvenile court proceedings by providing that an adjudication of delinquency shall not be deemed to be a conviction of crime; nor shall it operate to impose the civil disabilities of criminal conviction, such as disqualification for public office or civil service employment. Statutes provide, too, that evidence in, or disposition of, a juvenile court proceeding shall not be admissible against the child in any other proceeding. Even in the absence of specific statutory provision on the matter, adjudication of a child as delinquent in the juvenile court generally does not operate as a criminal conviction, since the juvenile court proceeding is not criminal.[15]

THE HEARING [16]

Statutes provide that juvenile court hearings be informal. This does not mean that the hearing is without rules of evidence and regularized procedures. Rather, it means that the hearing should proceed without the employment of technicalities confusing to the child or unnecessary to the exercise of justice. Hearings may be in a small or large room, but the space should be reserved for court activities. It need not have bench and witness stand. Nor do the judges need to wear robes. Nor is it necessary

---

[15] Sussmann, *op. cit.*, pp. 31–34.

[16] *Standards for Specialized Courts Dealing with Children*, pp. 53–60; Walter H. Beckham, "Helpful Practices in Juvenile Court Hearings," in Vedder, *op. cit.*, pp. 250–256.

that formal charges be read by the clerk. The child should not be required to sit on a witness stand. It is important, however, that court proceedings be dignified and conducted in an orderly manner. There are two parts of any judicial process which may or may not be continuous: the hearing of evidence necessary for a determination as to the court's jurisdiction and application of the remedy. In the juvenile court this means determination of the facts alleged in the petition and use of social evidence for disposition of the case. In many situations the facts in the petition are admitted, as when a child concedes he has participated in the alleged actions, so the two judicial processes fuse. Nevertheless, the judge should make the dual purposes of the hearing clear to all concerned.

Before a court hearing starts the probation officer should help the child and his family understand what is about to occur. The child should be attended by his parents or guardian. If they cannot be located, a guardian *ad litem* should be appointed. After the facts of the petition have been established through admission or by sworn testimony of witnesses, the social history is presented by the probation officer. The information which he presents should be open to rebuttal by the child, his family, and counsel when there is such. The social history, which often contains circumstantial evidence, is not in lieu of other evidence. It is part of the total hearing which requires examination, weighing, and judging of its validity and significance. A fair hearing does not require a jury trial; in fact, as we have observed, some statutes have no provisions for jury trials. Statutes which do so provide specify that they shall be conducted only upon request of one of the parties involved. This seldom occurs. It is not necessary that the child or his parents be present at all times. The judge may exclude the child from the hearing when he thinks it proper, as when the evidence is not fit for the child to hear or, in neglect cases, when testimony concerning his parents might be damaging. So, too, parents may be excluded when their presence might inhibit the child in telling his story. Often the court conducts a completely private interview with the child in order to obtain his confidence and to help him make adjustments.

A verbatim recording of the hearing is desirable, although it is not a prevalent practice. Such records are valuable when there is an appeal and when legal custody is given to agencies and institutions which seek to help the child in the treatment process. The findings of the court should be made on the rules of "preponderance of the evidence," as in civil cases, and not upon the rules of "beyond a reasonable doubt," as in criminal cases. The judge should have discretion under the law for deciding who may be admitted to the courtroom. When the judge makes his disposition of the case, he should carefully explain the reasons for his judgment and the rights of the parties to appeal. Appeals should be allowed to the proper court on matters of both law and fact. On appeal of children's cases the appellate court should be authorized to dismiss the petition originally filed or to send the case back to the juvenile court for disposition consistent with the higher court's findings. The higher court should not order a particular type of treatment or care for the child. So far as adults are concerned, appeals from decisions of the specialized court should be on the same basis as appeals from decisions by other courts of record in civil or criminal cases.

Numbers of states allow for hearings before referees. When this method is employed the persons involved should know that they have a right to a hearing before the judge. The authority of the referee should be limited to hearing the evidence and making findings and recommendations. When these are confirmed by the judge they become the decree of the court.

JUVENILE COURTS IN THE UNITED STATES: DISPOSITION

GENERAL

Disposition of the child should be for his and society's best interests.[17] It is an assumption today that a child's welfare generally requires him to be with his parents, who are expected to provide him with economic and emotional security. When they cannot or will not, and the child needs the protection of the state as substitute parent, a clear finding of facts supporting that need should be made by the special court. After it has been established that the child requires services in addition to, or instead of, those for which parents are responsible, the court must decide what they shall be. It has numbers of alternatives. When the child is a violator of a law or ordinance or is beyond the control of his parents, the court may dismiss the case, place him on probation, or vest his legal custody on a temporary or permanent basis with an authorized individual, agency, or institution. If the parents have failed to provide the child with care, education, and protection necessary for his well-being, the court may order protective supervision or vest custody or guardianship with an authorized individual, agency, or institution.

PROBATION AND PROTECTIVE SUPERVISION [18]

Probation for children is a legal status in which a child, following adjudication of delinquency, is permitted to remain in the community subject to supervision by the court either through the court's probation department or through an agency designated by the court. It does not involve transfer of legal custody or change of guardianship. It does in-

[17] *Standards for Specialized Courts Dealing with Children,* pp. 63–82.
[18] *Ibid.,* pp. 69–73.

volve a limitation of some of the powers of the parent or person vested with legal custody or guardianship. Protective supervision is a service for neglected children or those beyond the control of their parents analagous to that of probation for delinquent children. It is rendered by the probation department of the court or by an agency designated by the court.

Probation did not originate in the juvenile court; various experiments with probation had been carried on in the criminal courts.[19] As early as 1849 a Boston shoemaker, John Augustus, prevailed upon the courts to place certain persons under his supervision instead of sentencing them to prison. An experiment in provision for children, somewhat resembling probation, was started in 1869 under the Massachusetts Board of State Charities. Following these innovations and several other experiments by children's aid societies and similar organizations, a law was passed in 1878 authorizing the mayor of Boston to appoint a probation officer for Suffolk County. Not until 1891 did Massachusetts pass an act requiring criminal courts to appoint probation officers and defining their duties. Outside of Massachusetts little progress was made in the development of probation for twenty years. The next significant movement in the recognition of the value of probation came with the establishment of juvenile courts. Probation is a vital part of the machinery of the juvenile court system, since without it the court is in much the same position as the English equity court, which could not operate for the protection of children because it did not have the means to exercise its jurisdiction. Some authorities would like to change the term *probation,* especially for children, to some such term as *counseling* and to designate the workers as *social workers* rather than *probation officers.*

The Gluecks, in *One Thousand Juvenile Delinquents,* state that the success of the juvenile court does not depend exclusively, or even primarily, on the understanding hearing that a wise and humanitarian judge conducts but on the day-to-day treatment carried out by various officers and agencies after the judge has had his contacts. Rehabilitation does not take place in the courtroom but, if it occurs, in the home, the school, the playground, the club, or the place of work. As juvenile courts are now organized, probation officers are the keystone, since it is they who are required to understand the child and his situation before he is brought into court, and it is they who must utilize themselves and the

---

[19] Charles H. Z. Meyer, "A Half Century of Federal Probation and Parole," *Journal of Criminal Law and Criminology,* Vol. 42 (March–April, 1952); Frank W. Grinnel, "The Common Law Background of Probation," *National Probation Association Yearbook: 1941* (New York, 1941), pp. 23–29; John Rumney and Joseph P. Murphy, *Probation and Social Adjustment* (New Brunswick, N.J., Rutgers University Press, 1952); *National Probation and Parole Association Yearbook: Reappraising Crime Treatment* (New York, 1953), contains several articles on the process and administration of probation and parole.

community's resources for treatment. Every state has a juvenile probation law, and most of the statutes authorize the use of paid probation officers. This is not to say that there is complete coverage of probation service in all parts of the country. More than half of the counties in the United States fail to offer probation service for juvenile delinquents. In 1952 there were about 1,700 local probation officers giving service exclusively to juveniles, and another 2,000 giving service to both juveniles and adults.[20]

One way of encouraging the establishment and improvement of probation systems is through the participation of state agencies. State action may take various forms. We observed earlier that there are only a few state-administered courts, but where there are such, they have their own probation services. In several states examinations are given by state departments for the purpose of establishing eligibility lists for local officers. In others probation officers are directly appointed by state agencies. In a number of states county welfare agents appointed by, and operating under, a state department of welfare are called upon by local juvenile court judges to render probation services. In Virginia, state aid is provided by paying half the salary of probation officers in juvenile courts in cities of over 10,000. In New York the Division of Probation of the State Department of Correction has general supervision of probation officers for adults and juveniles throughout the state. There are several states where the law authorizes the state agency to co-operate with the courts, to collect reports from probation officers on their case loads, or to give advisory service.

When a child is placed on probation, or when his parents and he are under protective supervision, it is important that all concerned know what the relationships and responsibilities are. The official has authority to require the keeping of appointments and certain hours, the performance of certain work and activities, attendance at school, and so forth. On the other hand, he has no authority to remove a child from his home without court order, or to administer punishment or require others to do so. Nor should the court or probation officer order the parent to administer particular kinds of punishment or prescribe in detail methods of disciplining the child. A New York court in this connection held that [21]

> The vast majority of matters concerning the upbringing of children must be left to the conscience, patience, and self-restraint of father and mother. No end of difficulty would arise should judges try to tell parents how to bring up their children. Only when moral, mental, and physical conditions are so bad as to

---

[20] See chart on "Number of Probation and Parole Officers in the United States," in *Probation and Parole Directory, United States and Canada: 1952*, p. xii; John Otto Reinemann, "Probation and the Juvenile Delinquent," in Vedder, *op. cit.*, pp. 342–351.

[21] *People ex rel. Sission* v. *Sission,* 271 N.Y. 285, 2 N.E. 2d, 660 (1936).

seriously affect the health or morals of children should the court be called upon to act.

LEGAL CUSTODY, LEGAL GUARDIANSHIP, TERMINATION OF PARENTAL RIGHTS AND GUARDIANSHIP [22]

Custody and *guardianship* are terms used with widely different meanings. Some statutes use the terms interchangeably. As a result courts, agencies, institutions, and parents are uncertain as to what their powers and responsibilities are with respect to the child. The Children's Bureau attempts to clarify the distinctions between legal custody, guardianship with and without termination of parental rights, and residual parental rights and duties. For any number of reasons the court may find it necessary to change some or all parent-child relationships. We recall from an earlier discussion in Chapter 9 that parental rights include care, custody, control, and collection of earnings. Parents have a right to administer reasonable disciplinary measures and the power to make major decisions affecting their child's life, such as consenting to medical care, adoption, marriage, and enlistment in the armed forces. They have the power to decide where the child shall live, to represent him in legal actions, and to determine his religious affiliation. As a corollary to these rights and powers they have the responsibility of protecting and supporting the child and the duty to provide food, clothing, training, shelter, medical care, and education.

In the absence of precise statutory definitions the courts often do not make clear whether the transfer of custody is for a temporary or permanent period, what rights of the individual or agency accompany the commitment or transfer, and what parental rights and duties remain. The Children's Bureau favors dropping the terms *temporary and permanent commitment* and substituting *transfer of custody* and *appointment of guardian of the person.* Partial or complete transfer of authority over the child occurs through one of three judicial processes: change of legal custody, appointment of a guardian of the person without termination of parental rights, or transfer of guardianship with termination of parental rights. Different rights and duties accrue to each of the parties under these three circumstances.

Legal custody as used by the Children's Bureau denotes those rights and responsibilities associated with the day-to-day care of the child. It includes the right to the care, custody, and control of the child and the duty to provide food, clothing, shelter, education, ordinary medical care, and to train and discipline. It is legal custody which is normally transferred to an agency when a child is found neglected or delinquent and the court determines that the child must live away from his home. Sometimes the agency cares for the child in a facility under its own direction, and

---

[22] *Standards for Specialized Courts Dealing with Children,* pp. 14–18, 73–82.

sometimes it contracts with a foster home or school. Under the latter circumstances the child remains within the control of the agency. When legal custody is vested in an agency it should be permitted to make certain treatment decisions without a return to the court for approval. These rights should include:

1. Provision of the type of foster care needed.
2. Removal of the child from one foster care facility to another.
3. Trial placement of the child in his own home.
4. Provision of routine medical, dental, and psychiatric treatment and academic and vocational training.
5. Utilization of ordinary reasonable discipline.

On the other hand, there are certain things the agency should not be permitted to do, since guardianship rights of the parents remain. It should not be able:

1. To place the child outside the state, since then the child is beyond the jurisdiction of the court.
2. To authorize major surgery unless specific consent is obtained from the parents or guardian of the child.
3. To subject the child to medical care contrary to the religion of the child without written consent of parents or guardian.
4. To deny rights of visitation.
5. To consent to adoption.
6. To consent to marriage and to enlistment in the armed services.

Neither the right of parents to the legal custody of their child nor the right of a child to his own home should be taken away for a time longer than is reasonably necessary. The agency vested with legal custody should be statutorily required to make a periodic review of the situation and to submit a report to the court.

Guardianship of the person as contrasted with *legal custody* is a phrase used to describe certain legally conferred parental powers and duties in addition to those incident to the day-to-day care of a child. These powers and duties are broad, including most of the duties and responsibilities of the parent but with some differences, as we indicated in Chapter 10. We repeat some of these dissimilarities.

Guardianship of the person is established through legal process, whereas the powers of the natural guardian are inherent in parenthood. Guardianship of the person is effective during the minority of the child while certain aspects of the legal relationship between parent and child continue, for example, the right of the child to inherit from his parent but not from the guardian. Different from those of the parent, the duties and responsibilities of the guardian of the person do not include financial responsibility for the support and education of the child or the right to the child's earnings or services. The appointed guardian of the person is subject to supervision of the court but a parent is not.

Ordinarily, guardianship of the person includes the right to the care, custody, and control of the child, which means that the powers and duties involved in legal custody are included in guardianship of the person. Sometimes, however, this is not true. In cases where legal custody is vested in another individual or agency, the powers and duties incident to the day-to-day care of the child are vested in the individual or agency given legal custody rather than in the guardian of the person. The guardian of the person has the power to make major decisions affecting the long-time planning for the child, including such matters as the right to consent to marriage, to enlistment in the armed forces, to major surgery, and to represent the child in some legal actions before the court. The guardian of the person has the right to reasonable visitation of the child unless this right is limited by the court. There are certain rights and responsibilities of the parent as natural guardian which may be retained by him, even though guardianship of the person has been judicially vested in some other person or agency. These include the right to reasonable visitation of the child, to consent to adoption, to determine the child's religious affiliation, and the responsibility for support. If, however, the parent's rights are judicially terminated, the right to consent to adoption and to determine religious affiliation are vested in the person or agency appointed guardian.

Guardianship of the person as distinct from legal custody should not be removed from the parents without their consent except in clear cases of abandonment, desertion, inability. *Termination of parental rights with appointment of a guardian* may occur in these situations or when an unmarried mother seeks the release of her child. Ordinarily, parental rights need not be terminated unless adoption is anticipated or unless the child requires long-time institutional care. When termination of parental rights occurs the court must necessarily appoint a guardian of the person of the child. Until there has been a termination of parental rights the action of the court in the transfer of legal custody or of guardianship of the person is revocable. With termination of parental rights and transfer of guardianship the action is irrevocable, and all rights and duties between natural parent and child cease.

Wisconsin affords an illustration of a state which has attempted to reduce the statutory ambiguities of the phrases *legal custody, guardianship,* and *termination of parental rights with appointment of a guardian.* When the 1955 legislature revised the Children's Code it included new definitions of these three terms and carefully outlined the juvenile court processes for achieving each result. The definitions of guardian and legal custody read as follows: [23]

"Guardian" means guardian of the person and refers to the person having the right to make major decisions affecting a child, including the right to consent

[23] Wis. Stat., 1955, c. 48.02 (9, 10).

to marriage, to enlistment in the armed forces, to major surgery, and to adoption. The guardian has legal custody of the child unless legal custody is given by the court to another person. A person may be appointed legal guardian of a child only by court action.

"Legal custody" means the right to the care, custody, and control of a child and the duty to provide food, clothing, shelter, ordinary medical care, education, and discipline for a child. Legal custody may be taken from a parent only by court action. If legal custody is taken from a parent without termination of parental rights, the parents' duties to provide support continue, even though the person having legal custody may provide the necessities of daily living.

Under the 1955 Wisconsin law the rights of parents may be terminated by the juvenile court with the written consent of the parents to that termination or if it finds that the parents have abandoned the minor; that they have substantially and continuously or repeatedly refused to give the child necessary parental care and protection; that they have substantially and continuously neglected, when able, to provide subsistence, education, or other care necessary for his health, morals, or well-being; that they are unfit for reasons of debauchery, habitual use of intoxicating liquor, narcotic drugs, and so forth; or that they have been legally determined mentally deficient and because of this condition are and will continue to be incapable of giving the minimum proper parental care and protection. Parental rights may also be terminated if a parent has been legally found mentally ill and when grounds for termination existed prior to the time of the finding of mental illness. If the juvenile court terminates parental rights, it must transfer guardianship and legal custody of the minor to certain specified individuals, agencies, or departments.[24]

INSTITUTIONS

For centuries, children were huddled indiscriminately into institutions for adults. The movement to separate children from adults and, later, to provide adequate training has had a long uphill pull. The first separate institutions for the treatment of juvenile offenders in the United States were called houses of refuge. Training institutions for boys and girls found delinquent by the courts are maintained by all the states and the District of Columbia. These schools, both publicly and privately financed and variously called agricultural, industrial, or vocational schools, should not be confused with reformatories, which accept delinquents beyond sixteen or seventeen years of age. Children are admitted to training institutions by commitment from juvenile courts. Standards vary tremendously from one institution to another, depending, in part, on the kind of supervision given by state departments of welfare, the caliber of the members of the boards of managers when there are such, and the qualifications of the superintendent and staff.

---

[24] Wis. Stat., 1955, c. 48.40–48.44.

The objectives of institutions for delinquent boys (and the same principles apply to girls) have been summarized in a study of *Institutional Treatment for Delinquent Boys* as follows: [25]

An institution for delinquent boys exists for the purpose of re-educating the individual child committed to its care by the court. Re-education here means something much broader and deeper than any amount of improvement or increase in the academic instruction or vocational training which the individual child is to receive. It means reshaping his behavior patterns. It means giving thoughtful attention to his personality difficulties to the end that he may achieve healthy emotional development as well as growth in mental equipment or manual skill. It means giving the child an opportunity to meet and experience life under controlled conditions, in order that he may be more readily redirected and guided into behavior channels that will gratify him and be acceptable to others. It also implies making quite sure before he is released that he has acquired sufficient re-education or redirection, to enable him to make those personal and social adjustments that will be necessary if he is to lead a fuller, happier, more productive life and if he is to avoid those conflicts which had previously brought him, and would again bring him, into conflict with society and its laws. To imply that all these things can be done for all boys would be to sidestep reality flagrantly. Realistically the institution's task is to discover each boy's assets and liabilities in relation to the social scheme, and then to go as far as possible in each case toward building up a personality capable of satisfactory self-direction.

A study by Albert Deutsch describes many of the training schools in the country and shows how far this ideal is from realization.[26]

In a survey conducted by the Children's Bureau it was found that for some part of the year from October 1, 1952, to September 30, 1953, a total of 39,382 children were residing in 104 state training schools.[27] The age range was as follows:

Table 6

Age	*Per cent of children*
under 13	6
13–14	21
15–16	48
17–18	23
19 and over	2

The median length of stay for children in 103 schools was 11.5 months, or ten months for boys and fifteen months for girls.

Most children do not require institutional care. But if for some reason, including neglect and delinquency, they must have that type of service, the state should assure them that it will be adequate. This means that all agencies and institutions, public and private, dealing with children should

[25] Alida Bowler and Ruth Bloodgood, *Institutional Treatment of Delinquent Boys*, U.S. Children's Bureau Publication (Washington, D.C., G.P.O., 1935), No. 228, Pt. 1, p. 3.

[26] Albert Deutsch, *Our Rejected Children* (Boston, Little, Brown, 1950).

[27] U.S. Children's Bureau, *Facts about State Training Schools for Juvenile Delinquents: A Preliminary Report* (Washington, D.C., G.P.O., 1954).

be subject to inspection, supervision, and perhaps licensing by a state agency.[28] Parole should be a part of the function of the services of institutions. Adequate study of the child within the institution is a prerequisite for parole. After the formulation of a parole plan, exceedingly careful supervision by well-qualified persons should be provided.

COURT VERSUS COMMUNITY SERVICES [29]

Currently, there is discussion among those involved in juvenile court administration as to whether the court itself or the larger community should provide services for individuals under the jurisdiction of the court. Maxine Boord Virtue, in a discussion on the proliferation of services for Michigan children, identified three approaches.[30] First, there are those who think the court should provide most or all of the services itself. Advocates of this position say that the court, which has authority to take children from their homes, should directly control all facilities leading up to the court order and necessary to its enforcement. The famous Family Court of Toledo, which has developed its own specialized services, including a system of institutions, foster homes, and supervision, illustrates this position. Second, there are those who argue that the community should furnish the facilities, since few judges are equipped with the personality, training, or experience to administer wisely a full program of specialized services. Third, there are those who take a middle position and argue for availability of services regardless of whether they are managed by the court or by other agencies. The third position is the most practical and most likely to prevail.

The author of these observations emphasized that it is not so much what agency furnishes the service as that all agencies develop channels of intercommunication. The Children's Bureau takes the position that the juvenile court, an institution designed to help and not to punish children, is a judicial and not an administrative agency. According to one of the bureau's experts: [31]

> It (the court) has authority and power to make far-reaching decisions in regard to the legal status of a child. It can terminate or suspend parental rights when the interests of the child or the community require it. It can enforce obligations to and from individuals . . . We see the juvenile court exercising

[28] Harrison Allen Dobbs, "Are Correctional Schools Evil or Are We?" in Vedder, *op. cit.*, pp. 432–440.

[29] Tappen, *op. cit.*, pp. 195–223; Harleigh B. Trecker, "The Use of Community Agencies in Probation Work," in Vedder, *op. cit.*, pp. 377–382.

[30] Maxine Boord Virtue, "Public Services to Children—A Study in Confusion," 26 J. Am. Jud. Soc., No. 2, 46–49; see also, Maxine Boord Virtue, *Study of the Basic Structure for Children's Services in Michigan* (Ann Arbor, Mich., American Judicature Society for the James Foster Foundation, 1953).

[31] Alice Scott Nutt, "The Juvenile Court and the Public Welfare Agency in the Child Welfare Program," *Child Welfare at the Crossroads,* U.S. Children's Bureau Publication (Washington, D.C., G.P.O., 1949), No. 327; Katharine F. Lenroot, "The Juvenile Court Today," in Vedder, *op. cit.*, pp. 327–336.

functions primarily judicial and law enforcement in nature . . . We see the public welfare agency exercising functions primarily administrative in nature. This means providing social services for children who, by reason of personality problems or circumstances under which they live, need help in order to develop into well-adjusted adults. Specifically it includes making social studies, planning for the care of children, and carrying on treatment; placing children in foster-family care and for adoption; developing resources for care and treatment; administering group-care facilities; and furnishing leadership in community organization for child welfare."

JUVENILE COURTS IN THE UNITED STATES: PERSONNEL, RECORDS, ADMINISTRATION

PERSONNEL [32]

Most statutes contain few qualifications for juvenile court judges. In electing or appointing the judge who has juvenile court functions numbers of qualifications should be considered. He should be a lawyer with experience in the practice of law. In addition, he should have numbers of personal characteristics conducive to carrying out the treatment function of the specialized children's court. These have been listed as follows:

1. A deep concern about the rights of people.
2. A keen interest in the problems of children and families.
3. An awareness of the findings and processes of psychology, psychiatry, and social work so that he can give due weight to the findings of these sciences and professions.
4. An ability to evaluate evidence and situations objectively.
5. An eagerness to learn.
6. Administrative ability.
7. Ability to conduct hearings in a kind, warm, and sympathetic manner.

If judges are to possess desirable characteristics and qualifications, the court must have status and the remuneration must be commensurate with the responsibilities assumed. Unfortunately, it is often true that the position of juvenile court judge is given to, or assumed by, weaker members of the bar and bench. Until the community expects a high caliber of service from juvenile judges and gives them prestige equivalent to that of judges of other courts, it is unlikely that the best legal minds and most adjusted personalities will seek juvenile court judgeships.

Referees, if used, should be selected by the judge after they have been certified by some type of merit system. To be qualified a referee should probably be a member of the bar, and he should certainly be familiar with the philosophy and practice of the court. The office of the referee should be clearly distinct from that of the probation staff. The functions are not the same.

---

[32] *Standards for Specialized Courts Dealing with Children,* pp. 83–88; Charles H. Boswell, "If I Were Judge," in Vedder, *op. cit.,* pp. 257–262.

Training in social work as preparation for probation work is gaining acceptance. Most probation officers are not graduates from accredited graduate schools of social work, which require two years of study and practice. This, however, is the goal of the Children's Bureau and the National Probation and Parole Association. Pending the achievement of this standard, minimum educational requirements should be college graduation, preferably with specialization in the social sciences and one year of casework experience under competent supervision. The staff should have civil service or merit system rights to tenure, salary, promotions, vacations, and leave. Probation work of a professional quality is indispensable to a specialized children's court that expects to realize its sociolegal objectives.

The court should have available, either as part of its own organization or through community resources, the services of physicians, psychologists, psychiatrists, and other specialists. Small communities that lack the specialists needed for adequate diagnosis and treatment will have to make use of traveling clinics and state resources, including hospitals, clinics, and diagnostic centers.

RECORDS [33]

An adequate clerical staff is essential if the records of the court are to be complete and up to date. Legal records generally include the petition, notices and summons, motions, orders, summary or transcript of the hearing, and findings and disposition. These should be in the possession of a clerk of court. Records should be available to the concerned parties but to no one else except upon court order. The information contained in juvenile court records should not be available for use against the child in any suit before any other court. The social history compiled by the probation staff requires even greater protection because intimate family details are often included. If the various records of the court are carefully maintained, fact-gathering by the court will be facilitated. Quantitive data is necessary in order to provide information to the taxpayer, to improve administrative organization, and to furnish the basis for special studies and research. Some states, through the state department of welfare, act as the collecting agency for juvenile court statistics. Such states are in a position to participate in the juvenile court statistical reporting system of the Children's Bureau.

ADMINISTRATION [34]

The administrative structure of the court and the size and characteristics of its staff and plant facilities will differ greatly between large and

[33] *Standards for Specialized Courts Dealing with Children,* pp. 90–93.
[34] *Ibid.,* pp. 94–96.

small courts. Whatever they may be, the principles of privacy, informality, dignity, and comfort should be present. We need not labor the point that if the court is to work effectively, it must have good relationships with schools, churches, civic groups, professional organizations, recreational agencies, social agencies, and law-enforcement agencies, especially the police.

For Selected References, see those at the end of Chapter 16.

CHAPTER 16

Youthful Offenders and the Juvenile Court III

CONSTITUTIONALITY OF JUVENILE COURT LEGISLATION

GENERAL

A juvenile court deals with violations of the criminal and civil law, but it is neither a criminal nor a civil court.[1] Nor is it, strictly speaking, an equity court, although it bases some of its functions and procedures upon equity principles. An equity court, like a court of law, is bound by many rules of evidence. A juvenile court is informal in procedure and bound by few rules of evidence, some say too few. An equity court is primarily concerned with money and property; the juvenile court with the behavior and problems of people. The equity court, like civil and criminal courts, is concerned with altercations between person and person or person and state. These courts must resolve conflicts and impose remedies, fines, sentences, and punishment. The juvenile court is not primarily interested in the settlement of contests, although it often has to decide between the rights and responsibilities of individuals. Nor is its major remedy the imposition of penalties. Rather, it hunts for modes of treatment, sometimes lasting for long periods, which will improve a personal or a family condition.

All of this means that the juvenile court has more or less abandoned warrants, arrests, indictments, formal prosecution, public trials, rules of evidence requiring proof beyond a reasonable doubt, jury trials, sentences involving fines, jail detention, definite terms of incarceration, and the labels of misdemeanant, felon, criminal, and convict. But it does not mean doing away with legal protections. Every individual brought into the juvenile court is entitled to protection of his constitutional rights. He has a right to a definite charge, counsel, a fair though informal hearing, reasonably relevant evidence, and appeal. Sometimes he has been deprived of these protections by individual courts, despite the fact that the statute under which the court operated was adequately drafted. Some-

---

[1] Sol Rubin, "State Juvenile Court: A New Standard," in Clyde B. Vedder, ed., *The Juvenile Offender* (New York, Doubleday, 1954), pp. 310–315; Katharine F. Lenroot, "The Juvenile Court Today," in Vedder, *op. cit.*, pp. 327–336.

times the statutes have not been well drafted and are minus protective provisions. Dean Pound once commented that the powers of the Star Chamber were a trifle in comparison with those exercised by some juvenile and domestic relations courts. Mr. Justice Frankfurter wrote that "the history of liberty is to a large extent the history of procedural observances." [2]

CONSTITUTIONAL QUESTIONS

Juvenile court legislation has been tested many times in the courts, and today a well-drawn law generally will be held constitutional. For the most part, the constitutional questions raised have been in connection with the following subjects: deprivation of liberty without due process of law, violation of the right to trial by jury, denial of right of appeal, imposition of unequal penalties, deprivation of the equal protection of the law.

Juvenile court laws were first attacked on the ground that children and their parents were deprived of due process of law since the statutes provided no safeguards designed to protect the offender in a criminal prosecution. The courts generally held that juvenile court proceedings are not criminal in nature inasmuch as the purpose of the laws is not to punish but to save the child by giving him aid, encouragement, and guidance. In 1905 the Pennsylvania court held constitutional the law "defining the powers of the several courts of quarter sessions of the peace, within this commonwealth with references to the care, treatment, and control of dependent, neglected, incorrigible, and delinquent children under the age of sixteen years, and providing for the means in which such power may be exercised." The court said: [3]

> The objection that "the act offends against a constitutional provision in creating, by its terms, different punishments for the same offense by a classification of individuals," overlooks the fact, hereafter to be noticed, that it is not for the punishment of offenders, but for the salvation of children, and points out the way by which the state undertakes to save, not particular children of a special class, but all children under a certain age, whose salvation may become the duty of the state in the absence of proper parental care or disregard of it by wayward children. No child under the age of sixteen years is excluded from its beneficent provisions. Its protecting arm is for all who have not attained that age and who may need its protection. It is for all children of the same class . . .
>
> To save a child from becoming a criminal, or from continuing in a career of crime, to end in maturer years in public punishment and disgrace, the legislature surely may provide for the salvation of such a child, if its parents or guardian be unable or unwilling to do so, by bringing it into one of the courts of the state without any process at all, for the purpose of subjecting it to the state's guardianship and protection . . .
>
> The last reason to be noticed why the act should be declared unconstitutional is that it denies the appellant a trial by jury. Here again is the fallacy, that he

[2] *The Public and Its Government* (New Haven, Yale University Press, 1930), p. 60.

[3] *Commonwealth* v. *Fisher,* 213 Penn. 48, 62 Atl. 198 (1905).

was tried by the court for any offense. "The right of trial by jury shall remain inviolate," are the words of the bill of rights, and no act of the legislature can deny this right to any citizen, young or old, minor or adult, if he is to be tried for a crime against the commonwealth. But there was no trial for any crime here, and the act is operative only when there is to be no trial. The very purpose of the act is to prevent a trial . . .

This same view was expressed by the federal courts in a 1911 case as follows: [4]

the purpose of the statute is to save minors under the age of seventeen from prosecution and conviction on charges of misdemeanors and crimes, and to relieve them from the consequent stigma attaching thereto; to guard and protect them against themselves and evil-minded persons surrounding them; to protect and train them physically, mentally, and morally. It seeks to benefit not only the child, but the community also, by surrounding the child with better and more elevating influences and training it in all that counts for good citizenship and usefulness as a member of society. Under it, the state, which through its appropriate organs, is the guardian of the children within its borders . . . assumes the custody of the child, imposes wholesome restraints, and performs parental duties and at a time when the child is not entitled, either by the laws of nature or of the state, to absolute freedom, but is subjected to the restraint and custody of a natural or legally constituted guardian to whom it owes obedience and subjection . . . The statute is neither criminal nor penal in its nature, but an administrative police regulation.

In 1923 the Connecticut Supreme Court, in the leading case of *Cinque* v. *Boyd,* reviewed the history and purpose of juvenile courts and upheld the constitutionality of its 1921 act.[5] It was contended that the act denied the right of bail; that it did not permit the accused to be confronted by the witnesses against him; that it denied the protection of the same rules of evidence that are allowed in criminal cases; that it denied the right of trial by jury; that it provided for the detention of a person committed to a penal institution, although there might be no conviction of a crime; that it discriminated unjustly between communities in the same state, because juvenile courts were established in some and not all jurisdictions; and that its definition of delinquent was too inclusive. The court disposed of these objections when it said: "In holding the act now before us for construction is not of a criminal nature we dispose of all claims founded upon its want of conformity to the constitutional guarantees in that regard." The court cited many cases from other states where the rulings were identical, and in only a few states had it found contrary holdings. A 1924 California decision and a 1930 Iowa case contain excellent summaries of the history and philosophy of juvenile court laws.[6]

---

[4] *Ex Parte Januszewski,* 196 Fed. 123 (1911).

[5] 99 Conn. 70, 121 Atl. 678 (1923).

[6] *In the Matter of the Application of Paul Daedler, a Minor, for Writ of Habeas Corpus,* 194 Calif. 320, 228 Pac. 467 (1924); *Wissenberg* v. *Bradley,* 209 Iowa 813, 229 N.W. 205, 67 A.L.R. 1075 (1930).

In 1946 the New Mexico court reviewed a number of constitutional questions in detail. Here a writ of habeas corpus was issued upon the petition of a minor acting by and through his father. The minor had theretofore been found and adjudged to be a juvenile delinquent and had been sentenced to confinement in the county detention home for thirty days. The court held that the writ should be discharged and the petitioner remanded to the proper authorities. It ruled on several matters, including the following: [7]

1. The act creating the juvenile court was not unconstitutional on grounds that it deprived district courts of exclusive original jurisdiction.
2. A proceeding in juvenile court against an alleged delinquent was a special statutory proceeding and not a criminal proceeding. So the fact that the act creating the juvenile court failed to protect against double jeopardy and self-incrimination did not deprive the petitioner of due process.
3. The act did not impose "involuntary servitude" upon the minor since, historically, a child may be subjected to restraints necessary for his welfare.
4. Although penalties imposed on adults and juveniles were unequal, this was not a violation of constitutional provisions concerning equal rights.
5. Although the statute creating the juvenile court did not prescribe a method for conduct of hearing and did not require that a record be made of the evidence, these omissions were not deprivation of due process of law.
6. Although the statute did not provide for the right of trial by jury or for appeal, and although the requirements as to notice to the child and its parents or guardian were somewhat informally set out, there was not deprivation of due process of law.
7. The statute relating to juvenile delinquency should be construed so far as the law and the constitution permitted so as not to compel a public trial and a prosecution by the district attorney.
8. When a statute is before the court for construction and its language is susceptible of two constructions, one of which would render it inoperative and the other of which would uphold it, the duty of the court is to adopt the latter construction.

Courts have not universally upheld the constitutionality of all aspects of juvenile court acts. Some courts have held that juvenile offenders who commit offenses punishable by fine, imprisonment, and death must be tried in criminal courts. For example, New Jersey, in 1935, passed a law providing that a person under sixteen was incapable of committing a crime. This legislation was reviewed by the court of chancery in *Ex parte Mei*, where a boy under sixteen committed murder. The court said: [8]

We think that a charge which is in effect that of murder cuts so deeply into human emotions, collides so violently with life's experiences and fair expectations, and is so horrible in fact and in the contemplation of society, that it remains a crime within the purview of the constitution, whatever name and whatever treatment may be appended to it by the legislature. . . .

---

[7] *In re Santillanes,* 47 N.M. 140, 138 P 2d 503 (1946).

[8] 122 N.J. Eq. 125, 186 Atl. 577 (1936); see also, *Ex parte Daniecki,* 117 N.J. Eq. 527, 177 Atl. 91 (1935).

It is plain, therefore, that if a lad be charged with being a delinquent in that he has done that which, in a person of age, would be murder, the charge will carry upon its face that which entitles the accused to the constitutional procedure, just as completely as if such a reservation had been set out in terms in the juvenile court statute.

Following this case there was legislative change, but the courts thereafter held that the juvenile court law still did not have exclusive jurisdiction to include murder cases. A recent decision of the New Jersey Supreme Court has altered this.[9]

In an Illinois case the court had to decide whether the defendant, a ward of the juvenile court who had been indicted for murder, could, on such indictment, be tried in the criminal court without the consent of the juvenile court. Here, a fifteen-year-old girl had been found guilty of an atrocious murder and sentenced to imprisonment for twenty-five years in the Illinois State Reformatory for women at Dwight. Some four months before the murder she had been made a ward of the Cook County Juvenile Court for behavior having nothing to do with the murder. The court held that the criminal court had jurisdiction of the defendant and of the cause. It said: [10]

The juvenile court is a court of limited jurisdiction. The legislature is without authority to confer upon an inferior court the power to stay a court created by the constitution from proceeding with the trial of a cause, jurisdiction of which is expressly granted to it by the constitution; nor, in our opinion, was it the legislative intent to attempt to confer such power upon the juvenile court.

Apparently only a constitutional amendment can change this rule in Illinois. Illinois statutes specify the age jurisdiction of boys as seventeen, and of girls as eighteen; but jurisdiction over children who are ten years of age or more and are accused of a crime is concurrent with the criminal courts.

Numbers of other states provide for concurrent jurisdiction with criminal courts under some circumstances or exclude certain offenses from the jurisdiction of the juvenile court. Several illustrations follow.[11] In Colorado all juvenile courts have jurisdiction over dependent, neglected, and delinquent children under eighteen, except for the following instances: juvenile courts do not have jurisdiction when the delinquency involves a crime of violence punishable by death or life imprisonment and the accused is over sixteen; any district court in the state may try any child of ten years or over for any crime if the district attorney elects to file a criminal infor-

---

[9] Personal correspondence with Sol Rubin of the National Probation and Parole Association (December 20, 1955).

[10] *People* v. *Lattimore,* 362 Ill. 206, 199 N.E. 275 (1935); "Homicide by Juveniles as Within Jurisdiction of Juvenile Court," 110 A.L.R. 1084–1090.

[11] National Probation and Parole Association, *Probation and Parole Directory, United States and Canada: 1952* (New York, 1952).

mation in that court. In Delaware capital offenses are excepted from juvenile court jurisdiction, and children between sixteen and eighteen may be prosecuted criminally at the discretion of the attorney general and with the consent of the criminal court. In Florida the juvenile courts have exclusive original jurisdiction over delinquent, neglected, and dependent children under seventeen, except children sixteen or over charged with a capital offense. In Iowa the juvenile court has exclusive jurisdiction over dependent, neglected, and delinquent children under eighteen and concurrent jurisdiction over young people eighteen to twenty-one and children charged with felonies. In Louisiana the juvenile courts have jurisdiction over neglected and delinquent children under seventeen; excluded from delinquency jurisdiction are capital crimes and attempted aggravated rape by a child fifteen years of age or over. In Massachusetts the juvenile courts have jurisdiction over neglected children under sixteen and wayward and delinquent children under seventeen. Offenses punishable by death are excluded from the jurisdiction of the juvenile court. In Pennsylvania the juvenile courts have exclusive jurisdiction over delinquent, neglected, and dependent children under eighteen. Murder cases are excepted from the delinquency jurisdiction of the juvenile court. In Utah, where the state is divided into five juvenile court districts, each one embracing several counties, and where the judges are appointed by the Public Welfare Commission, the court has exclusive original jurisdiction over delinquent, neglected, and dependent children under eighteen, except in felonies involving children fourteen years or over, in which cases juvenile courts have concurrent jurisdiction with the district courts.

There have been contests concerning the validity of juvenile court legislation on other matters than that involving jurisdiction over crimes. For example, provisions giving the juvenile court power to appoint probation officers have been challenged and upheld. In a California case the court held that appointment of probation officers in the city and county of San Francisco was lawfully designated to the judge of the superior court and that the salary provided by the act was lawfully payable out of the treasury of the city and county.[12] In an Illinois case the court held that a statute giving the Cook County Board of County Commissioners the power to appoint probation officers was unconstitutional because it interfered with judicial functions which, by constitutional law, are separate from executive and legislative functions.[13] A New Jersey court upheld the constitutionality of an act providing that the conviction of juveniles was not admissible as evidence in other proceedings, except within the limiting provisions of the law.[14]

Most juvenile court cases carried to higher courts today involve ques-

---

[12] *Nicholl* v. *Koster*, 157 Calif. 416, 108 Pac. 302 (1910).
[13] *Witter* v. *Cook County Commissioners et al.*, 256 Ill. 616, 100 N.E. 148 (1912).
[14] *Kolzer* v. *New York Telephone Co.*, 93 N.J.L. 279, 108 Atl. 375 (1919).

tions pertaining to the application of statutes to specific situations, with constitutional questions sometimes raised. In an Illinois case the court held that the juvenile court had not sufficient evidence to render the child subject to dependency guardianship. The statute was valid, but the child did not come under its provisions. The court said: [15]

> The purpose of this statute is to extend a protecting hand to unfortunate boys and girls who, by reason of their own conduct, evil tendencies, or improper environment, have proven that the best interests of society, the welfare of the state, and their own good demand that the guardianship of the state be substituted for that of natural parents. To accomplish this purpose the statute should be given a broad and liberal construction; but it should not be held to extend to cases where there is merely a difference of opinion as to the best course to pursue in rearing a child. There should be evidence of neglect, abandonment, incapacity, or cruelty on the part of the parent or that the child is being exposed to immorality and vice. The right of parents to the society of their offspring is inherent, and courts should not violate that right upon slight pretext or unless it is clearly for the best interests of the child to do so.

CRITICISMS OF JUVENILE COURT LEGISLATION

The fiftieth anniversary of the establishment of juvenile courts was celebrated in 1949. At that time Charles L. Chute, for many years executive director of the National Probation and Parole Association, commented that perhaps the greatest defect of the juvenile court movement has been the failure to provide complete and exclusive jurisdiction over children. By 1949 twenty-one states still excluded some offenses. This failure, he emphasized, is inconsistent with the original purpose of the juvenile court.[16] In 1955 Sol Rubin, legal counsel of the same organization, stated that although constitutional questions surrounding the establishment of juvenile courts should have been settled long ago, problems relating to the basic character of the court continue to arise.[17]

Most legal and other commentators praise the actions of courts in upholding the validity of juvenile court laws. There are a few, however, who are highly critical of juvenile court statutes and even argue that the special court should be abolished. Some take the position that juvenile courts are usurping the prerogatives of other courts and that they are developing a system of authoritarianism, with youths bailed, jailed, granted or denied rights on the mere whim of probation officers, county attorneys, sheriffs, and other administrative officials. Others say that juvenile courts are socialistic, that they block law enforcement, that operating through hireling sob-sisters they mollycoddle and overprotect vicious

---

[15] *Lindsay et al.* v. *Lindsay et al.*, 257 Ill. 328, 100 N.E. 892 (1913).

[16] Charles L. Chute, "Fifty Years of the Juvenile Court," *National Probation and Parole Association Yearbook: 1949* (New York, 1950), pp. 1–20.

[17] Personal correspondence (October 27, 1955, and December 20, 1955); for digests of cases see Sol Rubin, "Legislation and Court Decisions, 1954," *National Probation and Parole Journal*, Vol. 1, No. 1 (July, 1955), pp. 63–74.

and dangerous youths.[18] Fortunately, few responsible people take these positions. Far more individuals seek ways of improving the operation of courts and other social and legal institutions dealing with the problems of children.

STANDARD JUVENILE COURT ACTS

The original standards for juvenile courts were adopted jointly by the National Probation Association and the U.S. Children's Bureau in 1923. They became the basis for the first Standard Juvenile Court Act, adopted in 1925. This act has been revised numbers of times—in 1927, 1933, 1943, 1949—in order to keep step with experience in the field. Another standard act is due shortly as a result of the standards published in 1954, from which we have taken so much of the material of this and the last two chapters. Many of the principles of the original Standard Juvenile Court Act are still good. We have already discussed them in Chapter 14.

Six major points are made in the 1954 standards which emphasize the legal as contrasted with the social nature of the court. Essentially, they summarize what we have been attempting to say concerning the legal and constitutional aspects of the juvenile court and we enumerate them here: [19]

1. Due process of law is just as applicable to the procedures of a juvenile court as of any other court. The right of a child to live with his own family and the right of parents to the care, custody, and control of their children are paramount, and these rights should be limited only through due process of law under clearly defined conditions. In observing due process of law, a specialized court dealing with children must keep its procedures flexible and maintain the basic philosophy of the court, which is to treat and not punish the child.
2. The powers of the court should not be drastically limited or removed.
3. Unlimited discretion should not be placed on any judicial officer to do as he sees fit with any child.
4. All parties coming before the court have a right to know the facts on which the court makes its decision. The public has a right to know about the general operation of the court but not at the expense of the privacy of the individual child and his family.
5. The parent and child have a right to legal counsel, and, under certain conditions, counsel for the child or the parents should be appointed by the court.
6. An administrative agency should be able to take some kinds of action with respect to a child placed in its custody without recourse to further court order.

---

[18] Jesse Olney, "The Juvenile Courts—Abolish Them," 13 California State Bar Journal 4–5 (1938); Joseph Brenner, "The Juvenile Courts Are Defended—A Reply to Judge Olney," 13 California State Bar Journal 6–7 (1938); Isabelle R. Cappello, "Due Process in Juvenile Courts," 2 Catholic University of America Law Rev. 90–97 (1952).

[19] "Standards for Specialized Courts Dealing with Children, a Legal View and a Social Work View," *Children,* Vol. 1, No. 3 (May–June, 1954), pp. 102–106.

THE FEDERAL JUVENILE OFFENDER

Under several statutory enactments the federal system of justice attempts to treat federal juvenile offenders as children needing treatment and not as adult criminals. In 1932 Congress enacted a law authorizing the transfer of federal juvenile offenders to state authorities. Under Title XVIII, section 5001, U.S. Code, federal district attorneys may surrender any child under twenty-one years of age who has committed a federal offense to state jurisdiction when the local authorities can and will assume responsibility and when it is to the best interest of the juvenile and of the United States.[20]

The Juvenile Delinquency Act of 1938 applies to federal juvenile offenders under eighteen. Up until 1938 children who violated such laws as the antinarcotic act, the postal laws, and the white slave or Mann Act, were treated as adult criminals. Under Title XVIII, sections 5031–5037, U.S. Code, a juvenile who has violated a law of the United States not punishable by death or life imprisonment shall be proceeded against as a juvenile delinquent and not as a criminal if he consents to such procedure and unless the attorney general directs otherwise.[21] Under this act he can be prosecuted on information rather than indictment; he can be heard in a private hearing and without a jury trial; he can be placed on probation, committed to a public or private agency or to the custody of the attorney general until he is twenty-one. The key person in administration of the act is the probation officer. Immediately upon arrest of a young offender the probation officer interviews him, investigates his family situation, and consults the United States attorney about the possibility of diverting the case to a local juvenile court. The officer's findings are made available to the attorney and to the United States commissioner, to the federal court, to the Bureau of Prisons, and to the Board of Parole. He notifies the United States marshal of suitable places of detention for the particular offender and arranges an early court hearing. He does not permit the youth to be fingerprinted. Finally, he makes sure the juvenile is supervised during the period from arrest to the end of his sentence.

In 1946 an official attempt was made to circumvent the necessity of a court record for juvenile offenders. The Attorney General authorized all United States attorneys to make use of the "deferred prosecution" procedure whenever juveniles are involved in court proceedings. The United States attorney, on the basis of a report made by the probation officer, may defer prosecution for a definite period and request the probation

---

[20] 47 U.S. Stat. 301, c. 243 (1932); U.S. National Commission of Law Observance and Enforcement, *Report on the Child Offender in the Federal System of Justice* (Washington, D.C., G.P.O., 1931), pp. 3–4.

[21] 52 U.S. Stat. 764, c. 486 (1938).

officer to exercise supervision over the youth. Thus, the young person is treated as if he were on probation. The officer must submit progress reports to the United States attorney as well as make a recommendation at the termination of the supervision. If the report is favorable, the original complaint against the offender is dropped and so the youth is protected against the stigma of an official criminal record.[22]

In 1950 Congress passed a Youth Corrections Act, which did not become really effective until 1954.[23] Under Title XVIII, sections 5005–5024, U.S. Code, there is created within the Board of Parole of the Department of Justice the Federal Youth Correction Division. Its duties are to administer the Federal Youth Corrections Act. A youth offender is a person under the age of twenty-two at the time of conviction. The court may suspend the imposition or execution of sentence and place the youthful offender on probation, or it may sentence him to the Attorney General for supervision and treatment, or it may commit him to the Attorney General for a period of observation, study and classification with the requirement that the division report its findings to the court. Committed youth offenders not conditionally released undergo treatment in institutions of maximum, medium, or minimum security, including training schools, hospitals, farms, and forestry camps. The act thus invokes the idea of the indeterminate sentence and gives the quasi-judicial youth board great latitude in determining the type of treatment provided.

Administration of these several statutes is carried on by three separate units of the Department of Justice: (1) the United States attorneys in the various judicial districts throughout the country; (2) the Youth Correction Authority Division of the Board of Parole; (3) the Bureau of Prisons, which administers federal penal institutions. If a juvenile is placed on probation in a United States district court, he is supervised by an officer appointed by the judge. If he is placed under the jurisdiction of state agencies, still another set of influences may be brought to bear upon him, since the work of the federal probation officer ends with the investigation. Heavy responsibility is thus placed upon federal officials, including judges, probation officers, and other officials in the Department of Justice, to co-ordinate their activities for the benefit of the individual, to develop uniform rules and standards, and to employ personnel qualified to provide competent service.

Table 7 shows the disposition of young offenders brought before the federal courts in 1953.[24]

---

[22] Clyde B. Vedder, "Comments on Probation," *op. cit.*, pp. 337–341.

[23] 64 U.S. Stat. 1085, c. 1115 (1950); George J. Reed, "The Federal Youth Corrections Act in Operation," *Federal Probation*, Vol. 18, No. 3 (September, 1954), pp. 10–15.

[24] U.S. Senate, *Hearings Before the Subcommittee to Investigate Juvenile Delinquency of the Committee on the Judiciary*, 83d Cong., pursuant to S. Res. 89, Pt. 2, January 14, 15, 16, 1954 (Washington, D.C., G.P.O., 1954), p. 375.

Table 7

	All juvenile offenders	*Committed to custody*	*Placed on probation*	*Case dismissed or not convicted*	*Diverted to state authorities*
Male	2,391	857	803	316	415
Female	152	24	67	24	37
Total	2,543	881	870	340	452

In that year the cost for federal probation services was $96.41 per person, and for imprisonment, $1,295.75 per person.

DOMESTIC RELATIONS AND FAMILY COURTS

We have stated that problems coming before juvenile courts are those of the family and community and that courts other than juvenile courts deal with domestic situations involving children. Because of the belief that the family should be treated as a legal as well as a social unit, there has been some interest in the creation of family courts with broad jurisdiction over family problems. Family and domestic relations courts embody two ideas: the extension of new methods of legal treatment to certain classes of cases and the prevention of duplication of jurisdiction by different courts. These courts with broad jurisdiction have developed partly as a result of the use of probation in criminal cases and partly through the extension of ideas underlying juvenile courts.

The earliest development of the family court idea was extension of the jurisdiction of the juvenile court. In 1903 Colorado enacted special legislation making contribution to delinquency or dependency of children an offense within the jurisdiction of the juvenile court. Nearly all juvenile courts now have jurisdiction over certain types of adult cases, although the nature of the jurisdiction varies from state to state. This broad jurisdiction may include nonsupport or desertion, determination of paternity and support of children born out of wedlock, adoption cases, and custody of children with mental defect or disorder.

The second line of development started in Buffalo, which, in 1910, established a domestic relations division in the city court under the provision of the law creating the city court and authorizing the chief judge of the court to determine the parts into which it should be divided. The domestic relations division exercised jurisdiction over all criminal business relating to domestic affairs, including illegitimacy cases and cases of wayward minors between the ages of sixteen and twenty inclusive. A 1924 law authorized the establishment of a domestic relations court as part of the city court, and equity as well as criminal jurisdiction was conferred upon it. Several cities, including Chicago, have followed the example of Buffalo in setting apart by rule or law a division of the municipal court to deal with domestic relations, chiefly nonsupport and desertion.

These two developments started by Colorado and Buffalo have tended to converge into family courts of the broadest jurisdiction. In 1914 the first family court, as distinguished from a domestic relations court with jurisdiction over adults only, was created in Hamilton County (Cincinnati), Ohio, as a division of the court of common pleas. For the first time divorce and alimony cases and all those arising under the juvenile court act, including cases of failure to provide and of contributing to the dependency or delinquency of children and the administration of mothers' pensions, were brought under one jurisdiction. If such a court was to be effective, it had to have administrative facilities, so a central record system, a clinic, and staff were added to the court organization.

Judge Charles W. Hoffman of the Hamilton County Court of Domestic Relations, a leader in the movement for the establishment of such courts, has stated that the aim of family courts is provision for the consideration of all matters relating to the family in one court of exclusive jurisdiction, where the same methods of procedure shall prevail as in the juvenile court and in which it is possible to consider social evidence as distinguished from legal evidence. In fact, he believes that providing for a family court is no more than increasing the jurisdiction of the juvenile court and designating it by the more comprehensive term of family court.

Judge Paul W. Alexander of the Division of Domestic Relations and Juvenile Court of the Lucas County Court of Common Pleas in Toledo, Ohio, has listed fourteen advantages of the integrated family court as follows: [25]

1. It provides for integration in one court, in one place, with one staff under one head, one responsibility, with one set of records and one philosophy.
2. It avoids conflict of jurisdiction.
3. It encourages resolution of several kinds of conflict in one proceeding.
4. It is more economical for the family.
5. It saves lawyers' time and effort.
6. It saves courts' time and effort.
7. It provides a common repository for all family records.
8. It encourages social agency co-operation.
9. It develops specialist judges.
10. It develops more effective staff work.
11. It is the cheapest way to render service.
12. It makes for greater certainty.
13. It helps judges avoid mistakes.
14. It seems to reduce the number of dissolved homes.

Judge Alexander, in an article entitled "The Family Court of the Future," presents a diagram showing that throughout the country there are

[25] Paul W. Alexander, "The Integrated Family Court," 21 Journal of the Bar Ass'n. of the D. of C. 5–15 (1954).

some seven types of courts which hear cases on twenty-six family problems. To illustrate: nonsupport and neglect cases may come before domestic relations, juvenile, felony, or police courts; divorce cases, before a trial court of general jurisdiction, equity court, or juvenile court; custody cases, before a trial court of general jurisdiction, equity court, domestic relations court, juvenile court, or probate court. It is impossible to know what court has jurisdiction over the various types of cases not only from one jurisdiction to another but also in a single jurisdiction.[26] Every social worker knows how frequently it is possible for the problems of a single family to be brought before several courts simultaneously and how distraught are the persons who have to endure this "run-around."

The main kinds of organization found among family courts include:

1. A family court of juvenile and broad adult jurisdiction, including children's cases, cases of divorce, desertion and nonsupport, and contributing to delinquency and dependency.
2. A family court of juvenile and limited adult jurisdiction, including some but not all of the types of cases listed in item one.
3. A juvenile court of broad jurisdiction, not including jurisdiction over divorce.
4. A domestic relations court, without juvenile jurisdiction and with adult jurisdiction over cases of desertion and nonsupport and, sometimes, illegitimacy and certain offenses against children (divorce not being included).
5. A municipal or district court, with juvenile and domestic relations jurisdiction and special organization by law or rule of court for domestic relations work.

Court procedure is customarily based on contests between parties. The adversary or litigious method of procedure has little place in courts dealing with family problems where the purpose of the proceeding is or should be readjustment rather than change of parent-child relationships, family dissolution, or punishment. If such courts are to be established, it is necessary that a specific court be given jurisdiction over these problems; that the court be given authority to utilize investigations made out of court and that extradition procedure be available when necessary; that investigational and treatment staff and resources be placed at the disposal of the court; and that the court be given the right to use both equity and criminal procedures, the use of equity methods obviating the need for arguments and contests, and the use of criminal methods giving individuals their constitutional protections. Clearly, a family court should be a court of record, with superior jurisdiction over both civil and criminal cases.

There is some difference of opinion among lawyers and judges as to whether or not it is advisable to establish a family or domestic relations court with very broad jurisdiction. It is not constitutional obstacles that

---

[26] 36 J. Am. Jud. Soc. 38–46 (1952).

disturb them but whether unified family courts are based upon a correct analysis of social conditions.[27] Courts have traditionally proceeded on the theory of individual rather than family justice. Some who disfavor family courts believe that rights of the *person* will be subordinated to rights of the *family*. They fear this particularly in divorce actions. Extreme individualists see the absorption of divorce jurisdiction by family courts as a step toward treating adults as children. They resent the idea that agents of the court may supply social evidence and that the court may insist upon delay and mediation. Less tradition-minded persons recognize the limitations of existing machinery and desire to push forward to newer and improved methods. Such organizations and groups as the National Probation and Parole Association, the Children's Bureau, the American Bar Association, and the National Conferences on Family Life promote public interest in family courts. From a practical point of view there are, at present, few communities ready to provide the facilities and personnel needed to carry on courts with such broad responsibilities.

FACILITIES FOR YOUTH OFFENDERS

The theories and practices of the juvenile court have influenced several areas of sociolegal activities. These influences include the idea and practice of the family court; the introduction to the criminal courts of such juvenile court methods as presentence investigation and probation; the establishment of special courts for adolescents; and the creation of youth correction authorities.[28] We have discussed the first of these points. We shall omit discussion of the second, since it is concerned with adult offenders. Here, we shall review the last two of these developments.

YOUTH COURTS

Chicago pioneered not only the juvenile court but special facilities for the handling of adolescents apart from older offenders. It has had a boys' court since 1914. The court is designated as one of the specialized branches of the municipal court of Chicago and is established without any special legislation.[29] It deals with cases involving boys from the ages of seventeen to twenty-one. It has no power to deal with such offenses as waywardness, incorrigibility, or association with undesirable persons. In order to bring a case into Boys' Court a definite criminal or quasi-criminal

[27] Wm. Seagle, "Domestic Relations Courts," *Encyclopaedia of the Social Sciences* (1931), Vol. 5, pp. 194–198.

[28] John Otto Reinemann, "The Expansion of the Juvenile Court Idea," in Vedder, *op. cit.*, pp. 280–288.

[29] Jacob M. Braude, "Boys' Court: Individualized Justice for the Youthful Offender," in Vedder, *op. cit.*, pp. 315–322.

charge must be brought. The court conducts preliminary examinations in cases of felony, holding the boys for action by the grand jury and possible trial by the criminal court of Cook County. In this court boys' cases are segregated from others. A degree of specialization of judicial function is therefore possible, although it is reported that there is still too much shuffling in the assignment of judges. Available to the judges in Boys' Court are the facilities of the Social Service Department and Psychiatric Institute. Although the facility of probation is available, it is used to a minimum degree because of the necessity of first finding the boy "guilty." Instead, many boys are placed on informal probation with four voluntary agencies. If, after the period of supervision, the agency reports apparent adjustment and the boy ready for discharge, he is officially discharged, and to all intents there is no criminal record against him.

In 1915 the Municipal Court of Philadelphia, vested with broad jurisdiction in civil, criminal, domestic relations, and juvenile matters, was given exclusive jurisdiction over minors above juvenile court age, which, at that time, was sixteen. The new branches were called Boys' and Men's Misdemeanant's Division and Girls' and Women's Misdemeanant's Division. The law applies to those who disobey their parents' command, who are found in the streets, or who are deemed disorderly, meaning those deserting their home without good or sufficient cause or keeping company with dissolute or vicious persons against their parents' command. Social investigation precedes and largely guides the disposition of cases.[30]

The 1923 Wayward Minors' Act of New York State provided that a person between the ages of sixteen and twenty-one who was habitually addicted to liquor or drugs, who habitually associated with undesirable persons, who was found in a house of prostitution, who was willfully disobedient to the reasonable and lawful demands of his parent or guardian, or who was morally depraved could be deemed a wayward minor. Jurisdiction was given to the children's courts and all criminal courts. In 1956 the New York legislature passed a youth court law. As of February, 1957, all cases affecting youth between the ages of sixteen and twenty-one will come into the new youth courts under the jurisdiction of the county courts and, in New York County, the Court of General Session. Implicit in the law is the requirement that judges with special human aptitudes, who are experts in the law but also dedicated to the rehabilitation of youth and free of personal bias, will sit on these courts. It is expected that they will be humane, calm, firm, well grounded in criminal law, and have special knowledge and experience in dealing with adolescents and families.[31]

---

[30] Reinemann, *loc. cit.*, pp. 280–288.

[31] *Ibid.; New York Times* (June 19, 1956).

YOUTH CORRECTION AUTHORITY

Youth or adolescent courts have not had an extensive development. They have been called hybrid institutions, embodying some, but not all, juvenile court aspects; eliminating some, but not all, criminal procedures; and, in so doing, possibly depriving the offender of the protections afforded adult offenders.[32] Some experts favor extending juvenile court age to twenty-one as a method of helping the older young offender, an unlikely development as it has little public support. Some favor separation of judicial and treatment functions for older youth, regardless of whether he is brought before a special court for adolescents, a criminal court, or a juvenile court with extended jurisdiction.

In 1940 the American Law Institute, a research body devoted to the clarification and systematization of American law, published a model act for the treatment of adolescent offenders, entitled "Youth Correction Authority Act." [33] In its introductory explanation, the institute pointed out that youthful offenders are an especially serious factor in the crime problem of the country.[34] For example, boys of from seventeen to twenty-one were arrested for major crimes in greater numbers than persons of any other four-year group. They came into the court not for petty offenses but for serious crime twice as often as adults of from thirty-five to thirty-nine; three times as often as those of from forty-five to forty-nine; and five times as often as men of from fifty to fifty-nine. Nineteen-year-olds offended more frequently than persons of any other age, with eighteen-year-olds next. The organization emphasized that a tremendous proportion of adult criminality has its inception in conviction of crime before the age of twenty-one. If the known criminals between sixteen and twenty-one could somehow be prevented by that conviction from continuing a course of crime the country's burden of offenses would be greatly reduced. Youth is the focal source of the country's crime burden and, therefore, should be the focus of crime prevention.

The act formulated by the American Law Institute does not attack crime prevention by the improvement of community conditions. Rather, it is directed toward treatment of persons after conviction. Its companion act, "The Youth Court Act," deals with the treatment of young persons during the processes leading up to conviction or acquittal. The youth correction authority act is designed to protect the public from repeated crime, first, by safe segregation of dangerous persons so long as segregation is necessary, and, second, by such treatment of the individual of-

[32] Negley K. Teeters and John Otto Reinemann, *The Challenge of Delinquency* (Englewood Cliffs, N.J., Prentice-Hall. 1950), p. 354.

[33] *Youth Correction Authority Act* (Philadelphia, American Law Institute, 1940).

[34] John W. Waite, "Introductory Explanation," in *Youth Correction Authority Act*, pp. 7–17; Thorsten Sellin, *The Criminality of Youth* (Philadelphia, American Law Institute, 1940).

fender as is calculated to increase the probability that he will refrain from crime in the future. The purpose of the act is rehabilitation as opposed to punishment. It creates a youth correction authority, a central state agency invested with power to set up appropriate agencies and to determine the proper treatment for each youth committed to it by the courts. Judges are left with wide discretion as to whether they will sentence convicted youths to the custody and control of this commission or not. But no youth can merely be committed to prison.

The judge of any court, except a juvenile court, before whom a youth is convicted, unless he discharges the youth or sentences him to payment of a fine only, must commit him to the authority. The authority is given power to decide to what treatment the youth shall be subjected and is authorized to use all the facilities of the state. The act does not affect the jurisdiction or authority of existing juvenile courts. It does not extend the juvenile court age but leaves the handling of older young people (that is, those beyond juvenile court age and up to twenty-one) to the criminal courts. By the act the use of probation by order of the youth court or criminal court is terminated; probation remains, of course, for juvenile courts and to courts dealing with those over twenty-one. This does not mean that probation will not be used for youths. The difference is that orders for probation will be made by the correction authority instead of by the trial judge. Proponents of the act point out that it is neither a radical departure from existing law nor even basically novel. Rather, it is a synthesis of theories and practices already widely accepted and is designed to improve public protection against crime by effective utilization of scientific knowledge and modern methods.

The youth court act, which is different from the youth correction authority act, was not thought of as a model act but as a declaration of principles. Conditions in the states, and even in different districts of a single state, differ so much in the nature of preconviction proceedings that the institute decided against proposal of a model act. The two primary objectives of the youth court plan are a shortening of the time which elapses between the arrest of a youth and final disposition of his case, and improvement of the conditions to which he is subjected during that period. The court act proposes that responsibility for performance of all functions, from the time of arrest until final disposition, shall be centered in one official, the judge or chief judge of a court which deals particularly with youthful offenders. It adopts the practice of placing investigation and preparation of accusations in the hands of an official appointed by, and responsible to, the court. It invests the judge or judges of the youth court with power to act as examining magistrates as well as triers of cases and with jurisdiction over all sorts of criminal cases when a youth is the defendant. It adopts the principle of public defender so that youth may be properly protected.

The late Judge Joseph N. Ulman of the Supreme Bench of Baltimore, who helped draft the youth correction authority act, summarized its main features as follows: [35]

> In briefest possible outline this act provides that convicted offenders within the age group over the juvenile court age and under twenty-one shall be committed to a Correction Authority for correctional treatment in all cases except those in which the trial court imposes the death penalty or life imprisonment at one end of the scale, or imposes a fine or a short term of imprisonment for minor offenses at the other end. The act provides an extended period of control by the Authority which may in exceptional cases, and subject to judicial review, continue for the life of the offender.
>
> The Authority is given wide discretion and the greatest measure of elasticity in dealing with the offender. It may release him under supervision before any period of incarceration whatever; it may limit his freedom slightly in a work camp or a supervised boarding home, or severely in a prison cell; and it may change its method of treatment from time to time and from less to more, and again to less severe forms as the exigencies of the individual case require. This plan differs from all existing practice in that it subjects the offender to continuous planned control by a single responsible administrative body instead of shifting him from one control to another. Finally, the Authority is given the right to terminate its control over the offender conditionally or unconditionally as soon as it appears that the protection of society and the welfare of the individual will be served by such termination.

California, Wisconsin, Minnesota, Massachusetts, Texas, Kentucky, Illinois, and the federal government have enacted youth authority acts. We shall not attempt a discussion of all of the acts but shall refer to several of the California provisions. That state enacted its first statute in 1941. It was the first of the youth authority acts. The California courts have sustained the constitutionality of the act at least twice.[36] The statute has undergone numbers of revisions. As first enacted it differed in several ways from the model act of the institute. It empowered the court to grant probation; allowed the authority to accept boys and girls from the juvenile court; set the upper age limit at twenty-three but subsequently lowered it to twenty-one; gave uncontemplated administrative powers to the authority; imposed upon the authority the responsibility for the development of local delinquency prevention committees and councils. Since the initiation of the program several institutions have been transferred to the authority. Large appropriations have been made for new facilities, such as a diagnostic center, camps, schools, a special facility for older boys, small institutional quarters, consultation services.

Among the contributions of the California Youth Authority and of those in other jurisdictions as well have been public discussion of delinquency, its prevention and treatment; growth in facilities and improvement in

---

[35] "The Youth Correction Authority Act," *National Probation Association Yearbook: 1941* (New York, 1941), p. 234.

[36] *In re Herrera*, 23 Cal. 2d 206, 143 P 2d 345 (1943), and in *Ex Parte Ralph*, 27 Cal. 2d 866, 168 P 2d 1 (1944).

quality of service; emphasis upon expert diagnostic services with treatment based upon the findings of multiple disciplines. The strongest criticisms of the California act and the statutes of other states incorporating several of the provisions of the California law are the following:

1. Removal of the sentencing or treatment function from the courts, a method inherent in the whole scheme of youth authorities.
2. Transferral of the administration of numbers of state institutions from the over-all department of welfare.
3. Expansion of state powers at the expense of the local community.
4. Concentration of attention by the authorities on *juvenile* delinquents rather than on *youthful* offenders, for whom the model act was drawn.

This last point has aroused the concern of numbers of experts who believe that certain principles of the original juvenile court movement have been destroyed by separating treatment functions from court processes. The juvenile court is not a criminal court, as is the youth court. The youth authority act, they believe, deprives the juvenile court of the opportunity to act for the best interests of the whole child and his total situation.[37]

The independent nature of youth authorities has been abolished in Wisconsin and Massachusetts. In Wisconsin parts of the program have been incorporated into the Division of Children and Youth of the State Department of Public Welfare and parts into the Division of Corrections. In Massachusetts the independent agency has been lodged in the State Department of Education.

ADDITIONAL SERVICES AND PROPOSALS

The adolescent court and the youth corrections authority are not the only recent responses to the treatment needs of juvenile and youth offenders. Numbers of states have provided reception and diagnostic centers for persons committed to the facility or to the state department of welfare or for the use of governmental agencies. New Jersey, Pennsylvania, California, Wisconsin, and New York are among the states having such facilities.[38]

---

[37] Bertram M. Beck, *Five States: A Study of the Youth Authority Program as Promulgated by the American Law Institute* (Philadelphia, American Law Institute, 1951); Paul Tappan, *Juvenile Delinquency* (New York, McGraw-Hill, 1949), pp. 274–281; Teeters and Reinemann, *op. cit.*, pp. 354–371; John R. Ellingston, *Protecting Our Children From Criminal Careers* (Englewood Cliffs, N.J., Prentice-Hall, 1948); John T. Perkins, "Defects in the Youth Correction Authority Act," in Vedder, *op. cit.*, pp. 288–294; Karl Holton, "California Youth Authority: Eight Years of Action," 41 Journal of Criminal Law and Criminology 1–23 (1950); "Youth Correction—The Model Act in Operation," 17 U. Chi. L. Rev. 683–697 (1950); Paul W. Tappan, "The Young Adult Offender under the American Law Institute's Model Penal Code," *Federal Probation*, Vol. 19, No. 4 (December, 1955), pp. 20–24; Luther W. Youngdahl, "Give the Youth Corrections Program a Chance," *Federal Probation*, Vol. 20, No. 1 (March, 1956), pp. 3–8.

[38] New York State Department of Correction, "The New York State Reception Center," in Vedder, *op. cit.*, pp. 403–416

Two significant programs of New York State should be mentioned. The New York State Youth Commission, a delinquency prevention agency, was established in 1945. The commission is composed of a chairman and the heads of seven state agencies, the commissioners of the departments of Correction, Education, Health, Labor, Mental Hygiene, Social Welfare, and the chairman of the Parole Board. It has concentrated its efforts on stimulating the development of municipal programs. State financial assistance is given to municipalities for the operation of new and expanded services, including recreation projects, youth bureaus, and youth service projects.[39]

The New York City Youth Board has developed an extensive program specifically adapted to the needs of young offenders. In high delinquency areas it has set up a network of referral units which are charged with the responsibility of locating children with problems and finding appropriate sources of help. Casework, groupwork, and mass recreation services are purchased from established agencies by the Youth Board and made available to the referral units. The board has also established an extensive "detached-worker" program. These workers recognize that young offenders resist conventional recreation, so they seek out gangs in their natural locations.[40]

Numbers of legislative proposals, some of which have become law, have been introduced into Congress as a result of the activities of the Senate Subcommittee to Investigate Juvenile Delinquency of the Eighty-third and the Eighty-fourth Congress. One of the results was the establishment, in 1954, of the Division of Juvenile Delinquency Service in the Children's Bureau. It was set up for the purpose of providing technical advice and guidance to states and communities that want to improve their services and facilities for juvenile delinquents. The division will help states and communities move toward such long-range goals as the following: [41]

1. At least one specially trained juvenile police officer in every community of over 20,000 population.
2. Improved detention facilities.
3. Expert physical and psychological examination available to every juvenile court in the country.
4. At least one special institution in every state for emotionally disturbed children, separate and apart from adults.
5. All juvenile courts staffed with probation officers trained in social services and appointed from civil service registers.
6. Comprehensive and uniform reporting on juvenile delinquency.

---

[39] Robert C. Capes, "New York State's Blueprint for Delinquency Prevention," *Federal Probation,* Vol. 13, No. 2 (June, 1949), pp. 45–50; see also, *Youth Service News,* published five times a year by the New York State Youth Commission.

[40] See the *Youth Board News,* published monthly by the New York City Youth Board.

[41] Sylvan S. Furman, ed., *Reaching the Unreached* (New York, New York City Youth Board, 1952).

Another committee of the Eighty-fourth Congress concerned with the problem of juvenile delinquency was the Senate Special Subcommittee on Juvenile Delinquency of the Senate Committee on Labor and Public Welfare, headed by Senator Herbert Lehman of New York. It was unsuccessfully engaged in an effort to achieve legislation designed to provide federal aid to states and communities in dealing with juvenile delinquency and to elevate the Children's Bureau to the status of the Office of Children's Affairs, with direct access to the secretary of health, education, and welfare.[42] All persons genuinely interested in child welfare and juvenile delinquency hope that Congress will soon make possible the development of a federal grant-in-aid program for the study and treatment of juvenile delinquency. There is disagreement, however, among experts as to the desirability of making the bureau an independent unit of the federal Department of Health, Education, and Welfare.

SUMMARY AND CONCLUSIONS

The large number of written and spoken words on various aspects of juvenile delinquency indicates the extent of current interest in the problem. Some of the statements are inaccurate, punitive, anachronistic; fortunately, many are factual, restrained, and constructive. In this and the two preceding chapters we have attempted to show the size and seriousness of the problem, the multiple factors in causation, the kinds of agencies serving the delinquent and predelinquent child, especially the courts, aspects of legislation and administration affecting such children, and types of legal issues confronting the special and appeal courts. In conclusion we attempt several summary observations:

1. There is world-wide interest in juvenile delinquency and in the provision of special courts and other services to deal with the problem. Throughout the world there appears to be general acceptance of the basic juvenile court philosophy of treatment and prevention, even though application of the principles is uneven.
2. Despite the inadequacy and inaccuracy of statistics, the size and seriousness of the problem is obvious. It is not entirely clear whether the percentage of juvenile delinquency is actually increasing in the United States or whether reporting is more complete and accurate. It appears, however, that the number of delinquency cases is increasing more rapidly than the age group of delinquents.
3. There is a great amount of the two opposites of apathy and alarmism about the problem. This means that there is need for industry and intelligence in attacking it. Community deliberation and education are needed. Parent education for improved family relationships is implicit.
4. Even though there is much greater understanding of personality structure and of individual motivation and behavior than when juvenile courts were

---

[42] *Social Legislation Information Service,* 84th Cong. (April 18, 1955), No. 15.

established, there is great need for more research in the field and for more treatment facilities for personality problems.

5. Juvenile courts have not fulfilled the expectations of their originators. Perhaps they have attempted too much. Undoubtedly personnel has been inadequate in quantity and quality. State-wide standards for personnel, including judges and probation officers, have been slow in developing and in most states do not exist. The development of state-wide procedures has been negligible and reporting tardy.

6. There has been extensive discussion by specialists concerning several issues upon which unanimity of opinion does not exist. Should juvenile court functions include informal probation? Should the juvenile court restrict its activities to cases requiring adjudication? Should evidence comply with strict rules, or should circumstantial and "social" evidence be admissible? Does the use of individualization processes, including social investigation, preclude protection of legal rights? Should the court itself carry on many treatment services, or should it limit itself to judicial activities and turn over treatment services to local or state resources? Should juvenile court jurisdiction be extended in the direction of family courts?

7. Workers dealing with potential or actual juvenile delinquents require high professional qualifications. This is true of clergymen, teachers, recreation workers, judges, probation officers, guidance and clinic workers. In the field of delinquency treatment there is special need for better equipped judges and probation staffs; more and better trained police officers; proper detention facilities; improved training schools; extension of mental health services; expansion and co-ordination of federal, state, and local services; and parent and community education.

8. There has been considerable interest in what judicial and administrative services can best meet the problems of youthful offenders. Several states are experimenting with special courts and youth authorities.

9. Numbers of professional organizations have been established, including councils or commissions of juvenile judges, district attorneys, probation officers, institutional workers, and police officers. These organizations, with their conferences, training institutes, and studies, are valuable not only in education of their members but of a wider public.

10. The creation of the Division of Juvenile Delinquency Service of the Children's Bureau, if adequately financed, can do much to encourage state and local programs for delinquency prevention and treatment. If and when federal grants-in-aid are made available to the states, these programs can develop more rapidly and soundly.

Despite the extent of rowdyism, vandalism, illegal liquor drinking, "hot rodding," gang wars, rape, brutality, and even murder among juveniles and youth, and despite the tendency of the public to strike back, to meet aggression with aggression, to retaliate, and to punish severely, there is much serious discussion of what to do to prevent delinquency and of how better to treat it when it occurs. Inquiries by Congress, state legislatures, and local commissions, the formation of neighborhood and community councils, the discussion of parent and other adult groups, the conferences of experts are methods for gathering accurate information and for steering public concern into considered channels. American resourcefulness and ingenuity are needed to cope with today's problems of juvenile and youth delinquency.

Selected References

ABBOTT, Grace, *The Child and the State* (Chicago, University of Chicago Press, 1938), Vol. 2.

ADDAMS, Jane, and others, *The Child, the Clinic, and the Court* (New York, New Republic, 1925).

Annals of the American Academy of Political and Social Science: Juvenile Delinquency, Vol. 261 (January, 1949).

BARRON, Milton, *The Juvenile in Deliquent Society* (New York, Knopf, 1954).

BECK, Bertram M., *Five States: A Study of the Youth Authority Program as Promulgated by the American Law Institute* (Philadelphia, American Law Institute, 1951).

BLACK, Herbert A., and FLYNN, Frank T., *The Juvenile Offender in America Today* (New York, Random House, 1956).

BLACKSTONE, Sir William, *Commentaries on the English Law in Four Books* (Philadelphia, Rees, Welsh, and Co., 1897), Bk. 4.

BRECKINRIDGE, S. P., and ABBOTT, Edith, *The Delinquent Child and the Home* (New York, Russell Sage Foundation, 1912).

CARR, Lowell Juilliard, *Delinquency Control,* rev. ed. (New York, Harper, 1950).

The Child (December, 1952), juvenile delinquency issue.

Child Welfare, published monthly (except August and September) by the Child Welfare League of America.

Children, published six times annually by the U.S. Department of Health, Education, and Welfare.

COHEN, Albert K., *Delinquent Boys* (Glencoe, Ill., The Free Press, 1955).

DEUTSCH, Albert, *The Trouble with Cops* (New York, Crown, 1954).

———, *Our Rejected Children* (Boston, Little, Brown, 1950).

ELLINGSTON, John R., *Protecting Our Children From Criminal Careers* (Englewood Cliffs, N.J., Prentice-Hall, 1948).

Federal Probation (September, 1949), special issue commemorating the fiftieth anniversary of the Juvenile Court.

Federal Security Agency, Social Security Administration, Children's Bureau, *A Selected Bibliography on Juvenile Delinquency* (Washington, D.C., G.P.O., 1953).

Federal Security Agency, Social Security Administration, Children's Bureau, *Child Welfare at the Crossroads* (Washington, D.C., G.P.O., 1949), No. 327.

Federal Security Agency, Social Security Administration, Children's Bureau, *Juvenile Court Laws in Foreign Countries* (Washington, D.C., G.P.O., 1949), No. 328.

FLEXNER, Bernard, and OPPENHEIMER, Reuben N., *The Legal Aspects of the Juvenile Court,* U.S. Children's Bureau Publication (Washington, D.C., G.P.O., 1922), No. 99.

———, OPPENHEIMER, Reuben, and LENROOT, Katharine F., *The Child, the Family, and the Court,* U.S., Children's Bureau Publication, rev. ed. (Washington, D.C., G.P.O., 1933), No. 193.

Focus, published bimonthly by the National Probation and Parole Association, New York.

FURMAN, Sylvan S., ed., *Reaching the Unreached* (New York, New York City Youth Board, 1952).

GLUECK, Sheldon, and GLUECK, Eleanor, *Unravelling Juvenile Delinquency* (New York, The Commonwealth Fund, 1950).

Hearings Before the Special Subcommittee on Juvenile Delinquency of the Committee on Labor and Public Welfare, 84th Cong., 1st sess., on S. 728, S. 894, S. 1088, S. 1832, July 6, 7, 8, 9, 1955 (Washington, D.C., G.P.O., 1955).

KAHN, Alfred J., *A Court for Children: A Study of the New York City Children's Court* (New York, Columbia University Press, 1953).

LOU, H. H., *Juvenile Courts in the United States* (Chapel Hill, N.C., University of North Carolina Press, 1927).

LUDWIG, Frederick J., *Youth and the Law: Handbook on Laws Affecting Youth* (Brooklyn, N.Y., The Foundation Press, 1955).

National Commission on Law Observance and Enforcement, *Report on the Child Offender in the Federal System of Justice* (Washington, D.C., G.P.O., 1931), No. 6.

National Probation and Parole Association, *A Standard Juvenile Court Act,* rev. ed. (New York, 1949).

National Probation and Parole Association, *Probation and Parole Directory: United States and Canada, 1952* (New York, 1952).

National Probation and Parole Association, *A Selected Reading List* (New York, 1954).

National Probation and Parole Association Yearbook.

PIGEON, Helen D., *Probation and Parole in Theory and Practice* (New York, National Probation and Parole Association, 1942).

POUND, Roscoe, *Criminal Justice in America* (Cambridge, Mass., Harvard University Press, 1945).

PUNER, Helen W., *Children in Court,* Public Affairs Pamphlet (New York, Public Affairs Committee, 1954), No. 207.

REAKS, G. L., *The Juvenile Offender* (London, Christopher Johnson, 1953).

SUSSMANN, Frederick B., *Law of Juvenile Delinquency* (New York, Oceana, 1950).

TAPPAN, Paul W., *Juvenile Delinquency* (New York, McGraw-Hill, 1949).

TEETERS, Negley K., and REINEMANN, John, *The Challenge of Delinquency* (Englewood Cliffs, N.J., Prentice-Hall, 1950).

U.S. Department of Health, Education, and Welfare, Children's Bureau, *Juvenile Court Statistics,* Statistical Series (Washington, D.C., G.P.O., 1955), No. 28.

U.S. Department of Health, Education, and Welfare, Children's Bureau, *Police Services for Juveniles* (Washington, D.C., G.P.O., 1954), No. 344.

U.S. Department of Health, Education, and Welfare, Children's Bureau, *Standards for Specialized Courts Dealing with Children* (Washington, D.C., G.P.O., 1954), No. 346.

U.S. Senate, *Juvenile Delinquency: Interim Report of the Committee on the Judiciary*, 83d Cong., 2d Sess., S. Rept. 1064 (Washington, D.C., G.P.O., 1954).

VEDDER, Clyde B., ed., *The Juvenile Offender* (New York, Doubleday, 1954).

YOUNG, Pauline V., *Social Treatment in Probation and Delinquency* (New York, McGraw-Hill, 1952).

The student should also consult pertinent statutes and judicial decisions.

PART III

The Dependent and the State

CHAPTER 17

The Secularization of Relief

HISTORY

ANCIENT HISTORY

Mutual aid, the church, organized private benevolence, and the state have been and still are the fundamental resources for the care of the poor. Today, the order of importance is in reverse. In primitive societies the poor and helpless were cared for by family or clan. Poverty, as a social problem, was unknown among the earliest primitive groups. This was true of the early Hebrews who, as nomads, shared the land and had few personal needs. When there were unusual requirements they were met by the tribe. With settlement in cities and the development of the institution of private property, there arose social distinctions and the need of organized methods for the care of the weak and poor.

Hebrew prophets, like Hosea, Amos, and Isaiah, complained against and denounced the rich. The book of Deuteronomy contains much social legislation which urges humane treatment of the weak and consideration for widows, orphans, and strangers. These exhortations fostered the knowledge that poverty and riches are of no account in God's eyes but are worldly distinctions which afford a field of action for the highest ethical forces. The declaration of Jesus that the poor in spirit are blessed had its roots in this early legislation.[1] The present Catholic and non-Catholic emphasis upon the blessedness of the poor and of those who give to the poor derives from these early Hebrew ideas.

The Romans and Greeks had more than one method of relieving or removing distress. Neighborly impulse, concubinage, which has been termed a form of mother's pension, slavery, elimination by death, and various means of care by the state were all practiced at the time of Jesus Christ. During the period of the Roman republic, plans for the care of the poor mainly involved placement on the land. Free grain seems sometimes to have been distributed, but it was in the imperial period that this

[1] "Poor Laws, Hebrew," *New Schaff Herzog Encyclopedia of Religious Knowledge* (1953), Vol. 9, p. 125.

method was so extensively and extravagantly used.[2] Lecky, treating of the Roman methods of care for the unfortunate, said: [3]

> Every rich man was surrounded by a train of dependents, who lived in a great measure at his expense, and spent their lives in ministering to his passions and flattering his vanity. And, above all, the public distribution of corn, and occasionally of money, was carried on to such an extent that, so far as the first necessaries of life were concerned, the whole poor free population of Rome was supported gratuitously by the Government. To effect this distribution promptly and lavishly was the main object of the Imperial policy, and its consequences were worse than could have resulted from the most extravagant poor-laws or the most excessive charity. The mass of the people were supported in absolute idleness by corn, which was given without any reference to desert, and was received, not as a favor, but as a right, while gratuitous public amusements still further diverted them from labour.

In addition to public distribution of grain, free public baths were established; special public and private provisions were made for poor children; hospitals were built through private benevolence. The Romans even went so far as to provide the circus for the amusement of both poor and rich.

Among the Greeks almsgiving was not a part of their early religious principles, owing partly to the close relationship between the individual and his family or clan. Hospitality and loyalty to family were so strong that among the gravest offenses were injury to a guest, seduction of a brother's wife, defrauding an orphan, and unfilial conduct. The wandering beggar was an inevitable adjunct of the great house; but as itineracy increased, the traveler became more dependent upon individual impulse and generosity, and his lot grew harder. The duty of private almsgiving was less imperative in Athens, where there was a state system of outdoor relief for infirm paupers, originally developed for those invalided from military service. Perhaps this is the origin of the theory of "veteran's preference"! In Crete and Sparta, poor citizens were publicly supported. In Attica, citizens were aided by legal enactments for release from debts, for emigration, and for public relief to the infirm and children of fathers fallen in war.

Despite the fact that neither Greek nor Roman religion did much to emphasize benevolence as a virtue, the practice was never entirely severed from religious sanctions. Human sympathy was active, of course, even among pagan groups; widespread public care of the poor, however, existed nowhere in antiquity.[4]

---

[2] Tenney Frank, "The Roman World," *Encyclopaedia of the Social Sciences* (1930), Vol. 1, pp. 42–60.

[3] William Lecky, *History of European Morals from Augustus to Charlemagne* (New York, D. Appleton, 1883), Vol. 1, pp. 262–263.

[4] Numbers of articles on "Charity and Almsgiving," *Hastings Encyclopedia of Religion and Ethics* (1911), Vol. 3, pp. 376–392; O. F. Lewis, "Social Service and the Church," *New Schaff Herzog Encyclopedia of Religious Knowledge* (1953), Vol.

EMPHASIS OF THE CATHOLIC CHURCH

Christianity, with its emphasis upon good deeds, love of one's enemies, and entry into heaven through mercy and charity, modified and perhaps even revolutionized religious and social concepts in the ancient world. In the early centuries after Christ, in those areas influenced by Christianity the needy were dependent upon private benevolence and the more or less organized efforts of church officials.[5] As the economic decline of the Roman Empire progressed in the fourth century, institutions appeared for the care of the sick and poor. They were founded and supported by the church and supplemented neighborly care. Added to these two forms of assistance were the provisions by monasteries for the relief of transients, beggars, and the sick.

After the barbarian invasions and from the time that parishes originated in western Europe, it was customary to set aside a part of the church revenue for the care of the poor. Charlemagne (A.D. 802) decreed that tithes collected by the priest must be divided into three equal parts, one for the use of the poor, one for the support of the edifice, and one for the support of the priests. By the twelfth century, parish poor relief, although found everywhere, was the least important of all forms of church relief. Hospitals designed for the care of the sick, the aged, and the destitute, which were in reality almshouses as well as hospitals, were scattered by the hundreds all over Europe and England. They were the most characteristic form of medieval charity and formed the link between monasteries and private charity.[6] In time they degenerated into sources of income for the clergy and efforts by the church to improve its methods of caring for the poor met only partial success.

The golden age of Catholic charity began during the time of Innocent III (1198–1216) who, among other notable works, established a model city hospital in Rome. From then to the Black Death, "ecclesiastical poor relief adapted itself to the need for centralization, owing to the growth of the towns and cities; it enlisted municipal aid in the work of relief and encouraged the erection of town and city hospitals."[7] The Black Death crushed institutional poor and sick relief, and never again did the church's system of relief attain "the universal effectiveness that it had enjoyed during the 13th century."

Very early in the history of Christianity, almsgiving for the welfare of

---

10, pp. 466–483; "Charity," *Encyclopaedia Britannica* (1952), Vol. 5, pp. 248–253; T. J. Beck, "Poor, Care of, by the Church," *Catholic Encyclopedia* (1911), Vol. 12, pp. 236–249.

[5] W. J. Ashley, *An Introduction to English Economic History and Theory* (New York, Putnam, 1910), Vol. 1, p. 306.

[6] Carl R. Steinbicker, *Poor Relief in the Sixteenth Century* (Washington, D.C., Catholic University of America, 1937), p. xix.

[7] *Ibid.*, p. xxiv.

the soul of the giver became prominent. "Medieval charity is a certain indication that the popular desire for salvation and sanctification was one of the strongest popular feelings of that age."[8] Charity has always been a Christian virtue and extolled by all faiths. However, the Catholic church, more than any other, has resisted the secularization of relief giving.

According to Mary Elizabeth Walsh, writing in the midst of the widespread depression of the 1930's, the church holds that caring for the poor[9]

> has been—and now is—largely the responsibility of religious communities. . . . The Church has traditionally regarded the care of the poor as a very sacred responsibility, as something calling for love and generosity and self-sacrifice, and there is no reason why the attitude should be altered today. If the lay worker is to take over some of the work of the religious, she must not do so in a narrow professional spirit. She must do so in the spirit of self-sacrificing love which has characterized the saints.

She compared the methods of twenty-five modern Catholic saints with those of the professional social worker in caring for the poor. The saints emphasized personal responsibility for the poor and were willing to give continuous service over long hours and to answer every need; they emphasized the spiritual works of mercy more than the corporal and spent much time and effort in prayer for the unfortunate.[10] "What the poor need is more Christian charity, not a new form of social work set-up. . . . Fraternal charity with a supernatural motive must be the basis for all our Christian social work."[11] She continued:[12]

> charity implies love of one's neighbor for the sake of God, because the neighbor is a part of the Mystical Body of Christ. The saints, because of their vivid faith, saw Christ in the poor, and hence, they treated the poor with respect and reverence and loved them intensely. This is an attitude entirely different from that which follows the naturalistic approach used in modern social work.

Another Catholic author expressed a like point of view:[13]

> The impulse to associate personal love of the poor with abiding faith in Christ is so thoroughly organized into the historical conscience of the Church that she meets with deep regret all tendencies that will secularize the service of the poor or make it merely a natural phase of social progress. . . . In all relief work of whatsoever kind, the presumption is against action by the state

---

[8] *Ibid.*, p. 7.

[9] Mary Elizabeth Walsh, *The Saints and Social Work* (Washington, D.C., Catholic University of America, 1936), p. 49.

[10] *Ibid.*, p. 145.

[11] *Ibid.*, p. 149.

[12] *Ibid.*, p. 15.

[13] Wm. J. Kerby, *The Social Mission of Charity* (New York, Macmillan, 1921), pp. 117, 120; John O'Grady, "Catholic Charities in the United States," *National Conference of Catholic Charities: 1930* (Washington, D.C., 1930); Thomas Gill, "Catholic Social Work," *Social Work Year Book: 1954,* pp. 74–81; Cecil C. North, *The Community and Social Welfare* (New York, McGraw-Hill, 1931), ch. 4.

and in favor of private initiative. . . . The presumption does not forbid state action. It yields when the facts warrant yielding.

The usurpation of the church's function by the state in the sixteenth century is denounced by Carl Steinbicker, a Catholic author whom we have quoted previously, as follows: [14]

Secularization of poor relief in the sixteenth century was an evil thing. In those places where it became established, the Church and all that the Church stood for, was reduced ultimately to a function of the State. . . . The legalism, respectability and a strong desire for material comfort which came along with the purely patriotic attitude of the Church toward the poor, soon repressed religious enthusiasm, self-sacrifice and personal holiness which had always been characteristic of Catholic charity. Religion sank into good citizenship, or cold morality, or stiff orthodoxy or latitudinarian indifference.

Today, the Catholic church continues to maintain an extensive organization of private charities. It recognizes, however, that the great burden of caring for the poor cannot be borne exclusively, or even largely, by private benevolence but must be assumed by the state. It frequently seeks public funds for the partial maintenance of charities controlled by the church. In general, public funds, when made available to voluntary associations, are on a fee or purchase-of-service basis. The church realizes that both private and public social welfare responsibilities must be carried on by competent, objective, and preventive-minded personnel. However, its major emphasis is still on the superior value of individual charity and the spiritual benefits in this world and the next for giver and recipient. The *primary* focus in Catholic philosophy continues to be the individual rather than the group, the spiritual and religious value of charity to individuals rather than social responsibility for those in distress, although many of the clergy and prominent laymen are outspoken in their concern about social and political problems.

EMPHASIS OF PROTESTANT AND JEWISH GROUPS

Numerous students have been critical of a motive primarily personal for dispensation of goods to the needy. About medieval Christian charity, one authority wrote: [15]

It has been substituted for the love of mankind and the love of Christ which were the original motives of Christian philanthropy. It has broken down the safeguards thrown around early charitable relief. It curses both the giver and the recipient.

This evil tendency in medieval charity certainly was not checked when poverty of the most abject type was made a Christian virtue and those who practised it were canonized. Then, with the rise of the Mendicant Friars, the last touch was given to the religious process of pauperization in Europe.

---

[14] Steinbicker, *op. cit.*, p. xxxi.

[15] J. L. Gillin, *Poverty and Dependency*, 3rd ed. (New York, D. Appleton–Century, 1937), p. 144.

The prevailing attitude of Protestant churches toward the function of the church in the field of poverty and charity is different from that of the Catholic church. The break was made during the Reformation and has continued to the present, making it possible for one author to write: "The Protestant Church, following the general tendency of modern social institutions, has moved in the direction of a more specialized agency, confining its activities to worship and religious education, and leaving academic education and social work to secular organizations."[16] Although this is perhaps the prevailing emphasis of Protestant organizations, a tremendous number of activities for the unfortunate nevertheless are carried on. These vary from the local, often unorganized and spontaneous relief-giving of the Ladies Aid, Christmas basket, and handmade quilt variety, to the maintenance of institutional churches, homes, and hospitals for special groups, and to prevention, which includes the promotion of interest in civil liberties, co-operatives, and the child labor and planned parenthood movements. Since individual denominations locally and nationally carry on special education, missions, charity, and social work activities, the National Council of the Churches of Christ in the United States of America, formed in 1950 by the merger of twelve interdenominational organizations, attempts to correlate these many services.[17]

The Jewish synagogue today appears to have much the same point of view toward charity and good works as many Protestant churches. In the United States numbers of nineteenth-century activities, including relief and institutional care for Jews and preservation of the Jewish culture, revolved around the synagogue. These activities now are largely secularized and organizationally quite separate from the synagogue. Twentieth-century Jews, like the Old Testament prophets, are vitally concerned with conditions affecting their own and all peoples wherever they may be.[18] It seems clear that the main emphases of present-day Jewish and Protestant charity are upon secularization of charitable activities, upon professional competency, and upon prevention rather than upon personal salvation and religious duty.

Churches of all denominations will continue to give occasional, individual services. The depression of the 1930's taught us, since we had not learned it from European experience, that long-time and widespread needs must be met by the state because (1) it has an obligation to see that every individual in need is furnished a decent minimum of care,

---

[16] North, *op. cit.*, p. 77.

[17] F. Ernest Johnson, "Protestant Social Work," *Social Work Year Book: 1954*, pp. 377–387; Reinhold Niebuhr, *The Contribution of Religion to Social Work* (New York, Columbia University Press, 1932).

[18] Boris D. Bogen, *Jewish Philanthropy* (New York, Macmillan, 1917); Martin M. Cohn, "Jewish Social Work," *Social Work Year Book: 1954*, pp. 285–295; Harry L. Lurie, "The Approach and Philosophy of Jewish Social Welfare," *Jewish Social Service Quarterly* (Spring, 1953).

(2) it has the duty to attempt the prevention of extensive destitution, and (3) only the state can provide sufficient continuous funds to meet extensive individual needs. The day for private agencies, including the church, to assume responsibility for widespread poverty is gone and, with it, a large part of the subsidizing of private agencies by public funds.[19] In 1933 Harry Hopkins, then head of the Federal Emergency Relief Administration, adopted this policy when he required that all federal relief funds be publicly administered and not, as was frequently the case, handed over to private agencies for administration. His rule was based on two theories: administrative responsibility should go along with the source of funds, and only as the taxpayer recognizes the extent of a problem and the costs involved in dealing with it will he be vitally interested in judicious administration. Sectarian and nonsectarian welfare agencies will continue to furnish valuable services on a limited basis. The bulk of the social services, however, will be rendered by tax-supported organizations.

DEVELOPMENTS IN EUROPE AND ELSEWHERE

It would be entirely inaccurate to say that maladministration of relief by the European churches was responsible for the assumption of responsibility by the state for the care of the poor. Economic and social factors, such as famine and pestilences, changes in agrarian customs, enclosure of the land, the growth of cities and the increase in their importance industrially, and the rapid development of commerce, were primarily responsible for the great increase in vagrancy, poverty, and begging. However, the frequently indiscriminate methods of the church, the glorification of extreme self-imposed poverty and begging, the emphasis upon the salvation of the giver rather than the needs of the recipient were factors in the resistance to church-dominated charity and had much to do with the introduction of other systems of care for the unfortunate.

In the balance of this chapter we shall look at several developments moving away from ecclesiastically and privately controlled charity to state-assured economic security.

DEFINITIONS

Because numbers of terms will be used throughout the next several chapters, we shall stop long enough to identify and to define them. These terms include: *social services, social security, pensions, allowance, social insurance, social or special assistance,* and *general assistance,* often still referred to as *poor relief.* Innumerable definitions for each term have

---

[19] Arlien Johnson, *Public Policy and Private Charities* (Chicago, University of Chicago Press, 1931).

been given, but we shall expect to use them in approximately the following senses.[20] The reader should keep in mind that the content of meaning varies considerably between countries and even between states in the United States.

Social services is the broadest term. The social services include the activities and resources involved in furthering personal welfare. More specifically, they include public health services; health services to individuals from hospitals and institutions; maternal and infant health services; mental health services; correctional and penal services; economic security measures of the assistance, pension, and insurance type; and counseling services to individuals with many kinds of personal and family problems. Some, although not all commentators, also include labor protection activities, such as minimum wage and factory inspection laws, and provisions for education. English writers include the labor and educational classifications. Often writers in the United States do not. The funds to provide these resources may come from public or private sources.

Social security generally is used to include income maintenance or economic security measures provided by the state. These services embrace public assistance, pensions, social insurances, child welfare services, health services to individuals, retraining resources, and, in a broader sense, the opportunity to work based on a "full employment" policy. Sir William Beveridge defined the term as follows: [21]

> the securing of an income to take the place of earnings when they are interrupted by unemployment, sickness, or accident, to provide for retirement through age, to provide against loss of support by death of another person, and to meet exceptional expenditures such as those connected with birth, death, and marriage. Primarily social security means security of income up to a minimum, but the provision of an income should be associated with treatment designed to bring the interruption of earnings to an end as soon as possible.

The objectives of social security may include: (1) prevention of want by anyone; (2) the guarantee to each person or family of a reasonable standard of living; (3) the maintenance of the functioning of the economic system by redistributing purchasing power; (4) the use of a social security system as a device for equalizing the distribution of income.[22]

When the term *pensions* is strictly defined it means the right of an individual to monetary benefits because some specified condition, such as

---

[20] Ronald Mendelsohn, *Social Security in the British Commonwealth* (London, Athlone Press, 1954), pp. 2–8, for a discussion of definitions; see also, International Labor Office, *Post-War Trends in Social Security, Income Security, and Medical Care* (Geneva, 1949); International Labor Office, *Objectives and Advanced Standards of Social Security,* International Labor Conference, 35th sess. (Geneva, 1952), Report V(b).

[21] *Report on Social Insurance and Allied Services* (New York, Macmillan, 1942), p. 120, par. 300.

[22] Lewis Meriam, *Relief and Social Security* (Washington, D.C., Brookings Institution, 1946), p. 558.

age, widowhood, or military service, exists and often irrespective of destitution. As a matter of fact, many statutes impose conditions of eligibility, such as morality, citizenship, and degree of need, so that the programs lose the characteristic of automatic service or reward. Many schemes are in reality programs of social assistance. The benefits may or may not be based on fixed formulas. In general, pension programs impose no loss of status and require no contribution from the beneficiary.

Allowance is a term used in the administration of pension and assistance schemes. The sum granted may be derived from a table of universal practice or from budgetarily estimated requirements. It may be based on need or, as in the case of family allowances in some countries, granted to all who have a stipulated number of children.

Social insurance is, by analogy with private insurance, a system which requires certain defined groups to contribute to a common fund, out of which are paid benefits of fixed or calculable amounts, the benefits depending upon proof of eligibility and having no reference to the beneficiary's financial circumstances.

Social or special assistance, as distinguished from *general assistance* and often administered apart from it, includes noncontributory "pensions" for the aged and for invalids, mothers' "pensions," assistance to special groups as the blind or crippled, family allowances, unemployment assistance, medical assistance, and rehabilitation of the disabled. Social assistance may cover much the same income group as social insurance, but its origins lie in charity and the old poor or general assistance laws. Generally social assistance depends upon need, although in such programs as family allowance schemes, this is not necessarily true.

General assistance, or *poor relief,* is the term applied to programs for the relief of those groups of individuals for whom no other legal provision is available or who do not fall within the provisions of special assistance or insurance laws. The laws of the United States derive from centuries of British experience with public responsibility for the destitute.

Social insurance lays stress upon contributions for, or on behalf of, the applicant as the main condition of benefit, and social assistance stresses lack of means. Social insurance is a routine service, and social assistance is a needs service, except in the case of universal family allowances, where this is not always true. Social insurance is based on the theory of presumptive need, and social assistance on that of a gratuity. Social insurance beneficiaries can qualify without regard to resources and benefits are provided on the assumption that most people will need cash income under certain risks, although some of those covered will not. The insured person knows that given certain conditions, stipulated benefits will be available to him. Only objective factors determine his eligibility for insurance. Social assistance has taken on some of the characteristics of social insurance. For example, exemptions of real and personal property up to certain amounts are allowed under many statutes. Investigations have been standardized, and assistance grants are frequently issued under formulas or scales. Often, there are provisions for appeal procedure. In effect, there is a legal right to assistance. Much evidence exists for the assertion that "social assistance is a progression from poor relief in the direction of social insurance, while social insurance is a progression from private insurance in the direction of social assistance.[23]

Let us look now at several social security developments outside the United States.

YPRES AND BRUGES PLANS

From what is today Belgium came two of the important sixteenth-century movements for the improvement of relief methods. They both developed civic responsibility rather than improvements in the administration of Catholic institutions. These reforms came chiefly from the systems of relief instituted at Ypres in 1525 and at Bruges in 1526. The Ypres scheme bestowed upon four of the city fathers of good name and fame the duty of caring for the poor. They were to choose others of great zeal to make the inquiries. There was to be no tax imposed, but collections were to be made from house to house, and there was to be an almsbox in the church "after the olde manner." Begging was forbidden, but it was believed that it would not be necessary to beg if appropriate assistance were afforded.[24] In 1531, the Ypres plan went to the Sorbonne for review and criticism. In general, this Catholic faculty threw its influence on the side of poor-relief reform. However, it made very clear the point that "the secular magistrates are to take care that they do not presume . . . to embark on sacrilege and take to themselves the goods and revenues of churches and priests . . . for this would be the part of impious heretics." [25]

The Bruges plan, largely devised by Vives (1492–1540) and described in his *De Subventione Pauperum,* was also built on the theory of civil supervision of all poor relief. "While very careful to weave both religious and civic virtue into his plan of poor relief so that it must be acceptable to both the religious and the civic ideals of people, Vives certainly minces no words in proclaiming the failure of the Church and churchmen in the field of poor-relief, nor in indicating the reasons for this failure." [26] He believed that the community had the duty to provide for the

---

[23] Quoted from a statement by Oswald Stein in Arthur Altmeyer, "Persistent Problems in Social Security," *Public Welfare,* Vol. 2, No. 11 (November, 1944), pp. 258–263.

[24] F. R. Salter, ed., "The Ypres Forma Subventione," *Some Early Tracts on Poor Relief* (London, Methuen, 1926), pp. 32–80.

[25] George Ratzinger, *Geschichte der kirchlichen Armenpflege* (Freiburg, Herder [im. Br.], 1884), quoted in Steinbicker, *op. cit.,* p. 124.

[26] Steinbicker, *op. cit.,* p. 117.

poor but ruled out a compulsory poor rate. There was to be diligent inquiry into the conditions of the poor, for classification and facts regarding them were necessary before remedies could be tried. The mentally and physically defective, particularly, were to have attention. The able-bodied were to work, and the feeble and helpless were to receive assistance. The Vives or Bruges plan achieved more influence in the long run than did the Ypres plan, although they were similar in many respects.

Over the centuries Belgium, like most European countries, has moved from reliance on individual charity and ecclesiastical benevolence for destitute persons in the direction of a guaranteed minimum economic level for several classifications of persons. Social insurances, pensions, and allowances afford the main resources to assure respectable minimum standards of living for those without employment or with limited financial means. Today, Belgium has schemes for old age, invalidity, and survivors stemming from a 1924 law; a compulsory health and maternity insurance scheme, begun in 1944 and preceded by an extensive voluntary system dating to 1894; workman's compensation, begun in 1903; unemployment insurance, begun as a voluntary system with government subsidy in 1933 and replaced in 1944 by a compulsory system; and a family allowance scheme, governed by a 1944 law as amended. This latter plan reaches families with one or more dependent children of stipulated ages if in school. Residual assistance appears to be handled by local authorities, with private charities rendering numbers of social services and, undoubtedly, also furnishing some financial assistance.[27]

GERMANY [28]

Prior to the Reformation, poor relief all over Europe was the responsibility of the church. The Reformation had much to do with divesting the church of its authority and functions, both in England and in some continental countries. Germany and the Scandinavian countries, under the influence of Luther, early moved far in the secularization of their relief administration. In connection with this movement Steinbicker wrote: [29]

> The one group of men in Germany at that time, namely the German Bishops, who could have effectively reformed the crippled conditions of the ecclesiastical system of relief, were not interested in the poor; the great clerical cry was for

---

[27] Carl H. Farman and Veronica Marren Hale, *Social Security Legislation Throughout the World,* U.S. Social Security Administration, Division of Research and Statistics, Bureau Report (Washington, D.C., G.P.O., 1949), No. 16; U.S. Department of Health, Education, and Welfare, *Major Changes in Social Security Legislation: 1952* (Washington, D.C., G.P.O., 1953), 3d Suppl. to Farman and Hale, *op. cit.*

[28] Some of this historical material was gathered by Hilde Waletzky, a former German student at the University of Wisconsin, and was checked in 1939 by Hertha Kraus, associate professor of social economy at Bryn Mawr College.

[29] *Op. cit.*, p. 52.

more and more benefices and greater income: and the greed of the higher ecclesiastics, rather than relieving the condition of the poor, often made it more oppressive.

German poor relief during the Middle Ages was characterized by the same lack of organization as the English system, with which we are more familiar.[30] The various institutions of the church, which gave alms, contributed to the great increase in begging by giving too much and, at the same time, too little. In Luther's 1523 Ordinance for a Common Chest, which was drawn up in conjunction with the leading citizens of Leisnig, we find a mixture of ecclesiastical reform and civil measures for poor relief. He demanded that every community take care of its own poor. After rigorous examination, the really needy were to be provided with the absolute essentials. Foreign poor and able-bodied vagrants were to be expelled. Funds for the common chest were to come from free-will offerings in church, from money previously devoted to church purposes and legacies, and from a compulsory rate to be levied on all parishioners. This last was in contrast with most other schemes of the period, which emphasized the voluntary nature of almsgiving. Administration was to be in the hands of overseers democratically elected.

Luther's efforts resulted in the establishment in a good many German cities of chest ordinances (*Kastenordnungen*), a mixed secular-clerical institution. That the common chests finally degenerated was due to lack of funds and to an inadequate supply of competent personnel. After the Thirty Years' War several cities attempted to establish municipal systems of poor relief, but many of these measures consisted primarily of police regulations and the prohibition and control of begging. Protection of the community rather than the individual was the primary motive. However, the Humanitarianism of the eighteenth century contributed to the growth of quasi-public and private philanthropic organizations.

The *Hamburger Armenanstalt* is the best example of the semiprivate institutions of this period. Individualized treatment of the poor was accomplished by a large personnel. A strong central administration insured uniformity of treatment. Attempts were made to find work for every able-bodied person, either in institutions maintained by the organization or by subsidizing privately employed, underpaid men and women. Extensive educational facilities likewise were provided. The relief population in Hamburg dropped to one third of its previous size during the first decade of the *Armenanstalt's* functioning. The systems of Hamburg and Munich attracted attention throughout Germany and elsewhere, and the names of Baron Kaspar von Voght and Benjamin Thompson, an Ameri-

---

[30] For historical background, see Ludwig Elsber, *Handwörterbuch der Staatswissenschaften,* 4th ed. (Jena, Gustav-Fischer, 1923), Vol. 1, pp. 927 ff.

can who became Count Rumford, were identified respectively with the achievements of the two cities. Hamburg's program was started in 1788, and Munich's in 1790.[31]

Of great importance in the history of public poor-relief administration was the establishment of the Elberfeld plan in 1852. The main characteristics of this program can be described as follows:

1. Individualization of treatment was accomplished by dividing the city into small sections where a small number of poor were under the supervision of one volunteer. Visits took place every two weeks, and careful records were kept of the client's financial and social situation.

2. The districts were comprised of fourteen sections; the district volunteers assembled in biweekly conferences under a district superintendent. Collective decisions were reached about the necessary type of care for each relief case in the district sections.

3. The relations of the poor district to the central poor authority, comprising the mayor, four city officials, and four interested citizens, guaranteed a unified policy with a decentralized administration. The duty of the central authority was to issue a general administrative policy, approve the district decisions, fix the budget, and audit expenditures. Standard regulations were issued for the care of the able-bodied unemployed, children, and aged and sick persons.

A further development of the Elberfeld plan was the Strassburg system (1900), under which trained, paid social workers replaced many of the volunteers, and the division of the city into small sections was abolished. The poor were classified according to their need not their domicile. Most of the larger German cities adopted modifications of these two systems of municipal poor-relief administration.

There has been widespread local public relief based on taxes ever since the Reformation. This came rapidly with the confiscation of church property in the Protestant parts of Germany, more slowly in the Catholic sections. The political struggle between local autonomy and national dominance carried over into the field of public relief. The communities set up more restrictions to free themselves from the burden of poor relief by prohibiting newcomers to settle, restricting the right to marry, and so forth. The expanding state authority fought against these local restrictions, and, in 1842, in the Prussian *Landrecht,* the freedom to settle in any community was established and every community had the duty to care for all of its poor. Although formerly the basis of eligibility for relief was the *Heimatsrecht,* based on residence gained by birth, marriage, or formal initiation into the citizenry, later *Unterstützungswohnsitz,* based on one to three years of settlement, gave the right to relief. In 1870 this provision of *Unterstützungswohnsitz* (UWG) became obligatory for

[31] Karl de Schweinitz, *England's Road to Social Security* (Philadelphia, University of Pennsylvania Press, 1947); see especially, ch. 10 for discussion of the contributions of these two cities to relief of the poor.

all German states but Bavaria and Alsace-Lorraine. The right to relief was thereby uniformly established, but the type of care was to be determined by state, district, and local authorities.

The Prussian *Landrecht* further provided for the establishment of local poor organizations (*Ortsarmenverbände*); intercommunal organizations, comprised of several smaller localities (*Gesamtarmenverbände*); and district poor organizations, comprised of a county, a province, or a state (*Landarmenverbände*). The district organizations maintained their own institutions for vagrants and delinquents. The care of the sick, except the mentally sick, has been considered a local function. The locality had to give relief to all persons in need. If an assisted person had his legal settlement in another community, that community was held for reimbursement. The district organization had to reimburse the locality for aid given to a person without any legal settlement. Dr. Hertha Kraus described this development in these words: [32]

> After the founding of the Reich in 1870, the widely scattered public relief legislation was made uniform through the introduction of a Federal law which, although establishing administrative uniformity, did not introduce any regulations on standards. The establishment of standards remained the function of the states, which had to provide for State legislation in supplementation of the Federal law. In an indirect way, unity of standards was promoted by the jurisdiction of a special Federal Court dealing exclusively with relief matters, particularly in regard to inter-state settlements. The decisions of this court, which still exists have had decisive influence on the development of public relief policies. This court, located in Berlin, is the *Bundesamt für Heimatwesen.*

Until the Public Assistance Law (RFV) of 1924, public relief was primarily pauper assistance.[33] Dr. Kraus's statement of development in the decade prior to the passage of this act is as follows: [34]

> Poor relief administration had developed quite progressively in some communities, adding volunteer public services beyond the minimum required by the law. There was wide discussion of a modernized public welfare law on the Federal basis shortly before 1914, this Bill being already drafted and presented in many public meetings. The outbreak of the Great War stopped these efforts, but the general plans for a more progressive approach to public welfare were carried over into the local basis, and into the administration of a considerable number of the categorical relief laws introduced during the War period and directly following it. It is widely recognized that the experience of this legislation and social practice in caring for War victims, including widows and orphans and the aged who had lost their income, were the bases for the modernized Federal legislation of a more comprehensive character, and including both general and categorical relief, introduced in 1922 and 1924.

---

[32] Personal correspondence with Hertha Kraus (April 12, 1939).

[33] E. Schmidt, *Sozialversicherung und Öffentliche Fürsorge* (Stuttgart, W. Kohlhammer, 1932).

[34] Personal correspondence with Hertha Kraus (April 12, 1939).

In 1918 a national relief system was established to meet extensive unemployment; it was intended as a temporary emergency measure and was financed by local, state, and federal funds. This system remained until 1923, when the first steps were taken to transform it into an unemployment insurance system by requiring employers and employees to contribute four fifths of the cost. In 1924 a Public Assistance Order (RFV) was issued which provided for a unified system of public assistance by setting certain basic requirements for the entire system, including both general and categorical relief; it represented a complete break with the administration and spirit of poor relief.[35]

This law partially removed the stigma which was formerly attached to the receipt of relief. Among the most important features of this act was the provision for work relief. The former relief methods primarily aided the old, the sick, the disabled, and the dependent and neglected child, but this new system started to provide for the large class of able-bodied unemployed by attempting to preserve their ability to work.[36] Paragraph 19 of the RFV stated: "In selected cases, aid for persons capable of work may be given by assigning them to suitable employment of benefit to the community; or relief may be granted, dependent on the client's performing such work; the latter may only be required if it does not create obvious hardship or if no law is opposed to it."

Two main types of work relief were developed under the RFV: (1) the "work-for-wages" scheme, in which employment was to be paid at a fixed wage rate adjusted to the normal wage scale and sufficient work was to be provided for the client to enable him to meet his and his family's needs; and (2) the "work-for-relief" plan, in which the client was to perform a certain amount of work in return for direct relief supplied to his family. The second type was not so satisfactory in its rehabilitation aspect as was the first. Out of the second plan developed the Voluntary Work Service, corresponding somewhat to the Civilian Conservation Corps, initiated in the 1930's in the United States.

The federal law on unemployment insurance and employment service passed in 1927, primarily an insurance law, provided for extended benefits to unemployed no longer eligible for insurance benefits. The law was administered by the Employment Service of the Federal Institute for Unemployment Insurance. The coverage of the extensive benefits was often changed, so that a considerable group of long-time unemployed fluctuated between the Federal Institute and the municipal public wel-

---

[35] Personal correspondence with Hertha Kraus (April 12, 1939); International Labor Office, *International Survey of Social Services: 1933* (Geneva, 1936), Vol. 1, pp. 305 ff.

[36] Hertha Kraus, *Work Relief in Germany* (New York, Russell Sage Foundation, 1934), pp. 10 ff.

fare departments administering public assistance to those not eligible for insurance or extension benefits.[37]

Nazi attitudes toward relief and methods of care for needy persons were considerably different from those of the preceding period, with much more emphasis placed upon personal responsibility.[38] Because of the large military program there was no problem of unemployment. The party attitude toward tax-supported national relief was expressed in Hitler's words: "The social responsibility of every person may not be weakened by taxation." The individual's duty to help himself was stressed, and emphasis was put on "the destined and decisive solidarity" of the whole nation.[39] Most private charity organizations were abolished. The work of the National Sozialistische Volkswohlfahrt (N.S.V.), a party organization, was confined to the congenitally sound, and care for the diseased and permanently infirm was left to denominational institutions and to the state.[40] State subsidies for the maintenance of lunatics, cripples, incurables, and prisoners were reduced to a minimum. The main functions of the welfare work of the N.S.V. were a continuation of early activities under the republic. They comprised the "winter relief work" and the "mother and child" activities.[41] The first of these was essentially mass distribution carried on by 1,500,000 workers, most of whom were volunteers. The second included economic help for large families, housing aid, and "mother vacations."

One of the most important phases of Nazi welfare policy was emphasis on large families. Rigorous enforcement of abortion and birth-control prohibitions was of great importance in reaching this goal.[42] The grant of marriage loans was undoubtedly a factor in the increased number of marriages. Under the republic special favors had been granted to large families, and this policy was much extended under the Nazis. The father of a large family was favored by income tax reduction, inheritance tax favors, rent allowances, gifts and extension of public services, medical and traveling aid, special safeguards against discharge, and preference in public employment.

Although the Public Assistance Act was still in force, its cost decreased 52.2 per cent in the first three years of the Hitler regime. This was caused partly by lowering of standards and partly by the absorption of unemployed in the expanded armament industry, in large public work

---

[37] Personal correspondence with Hertha Kraus (April 12, 1939).

[38] Walter A. Friedlander, "Social Work under the Nazi Regime," *Social Work Today* (November, 1939), pp. 9–11.

[39] Hermann Althans, *Nationalsozialistische Volkswohlfahrt* (Berlin, Junker und Dünnhaupt, 1936).

[40] Werner Reher, *Social Welfare in Germany* (Berlin, Terramare Office, 1938).

[41] Reher, *op. cit.*

[42] Hans Staudinger, "Germany's Population Miracle," *Social Research* (May, 1938), pp. 125–148.

programs, and in the military service. By the 1933 Act to Reduce Unemployment a more extensive public works program was planned. It included the construction of public buildings and utilities, the erection of small-scale suburban and rural settlements, and subsidies for private small dwellings and farm repairs. This work was promoted through federal loans to state and communal organizations and to private house owners. Other factors contributing to the decrease of the relief population were the agricultural aid, the year-on-the-land scheme, compulsory work, and military services and employment regulations.

In Western Germany, following the Nazi regime, public social services reverted to pre-Nazi days. The federal law, *Reichsgrundsätze über Voraussetzung, Art und Mass der Öffentlichen Fürsorge vom Dec. 4, 1921,* with some postwar modifications, provides that the states shall furnish money, goods, and services to people in need. The means test is used, and relatives are responsible. Need includes the basic physical necessities, and several designated conditions for which such additional services as scholarships and special educational facilities are furnished. Local administration is through county (*kreis*) welfare departments under the supervisory authority of the state minister of social welfare. All the public-assistance programs of Germany except the refugee program are administered through county welfare departments. Funds for "native" needy come from county tax moneys, with reimbursements from the federal, state, and municipal governments for various designated classes of persons.

The federal law, *Gesetz über den Lastenausgleich vom Aug. 14, 1952,* sets up extensive and complicated programs for refugees and certain classified groups of native Germans, such as those who lost their homes and businesses in World War II. This program is locally administered but is separate from other county assistance services. Local expenditures for refugees and others under the statute are reimbursed 85 per cent by the federal government, and the balance is evenly distributed between the county and the municipality. The administration of these two laws is fairly uniform throughout the states, with adjustments in amount of help granted to fit local conditions.[43]

No review of Germany's history in regard to developments in the care and treatment of the poor and unemployed is complete without reference to its insurance schemes, of which only the unemployment insurance law of 1927 has been previously mentioned.[44] Germany was a pioneer in

---

[43] This information is taken from *Textsammlung fürsorgerechtlicher Bestimmungen, nach dem Stande vom 1, 1, 54* (Hanover, Buchdruckerei Aug. Eberlein, 1954), transl. by Karl-Heinz Briesenick, from Luchow, Germany, a student at the Graduate School of Social Work, University of Wisconsin in 1954.

[44] Maxwell Stewart, *Social Security* (New York, W. W. Norton and Co., 1937), pp. 107–108; U.S. Committee on Economic Security, *Social Security in America: The Factual Background of the Social Security Act As Summarized from Staff Re-*

nation-wide compulsory social insurance. This means that Germany was the first country to take large groups out from under private charity and the poor laws and to give them benefits as a "right." In 1881 Bismarck introduced the first comprehensive plan of social insurance protection. At the time he was engaged in a battle to stem the tide of social democracy, and he needed some scheme to check the growing discontent of the working classes. He also wanted to extend the power of the central government. He believed that the creation of a national insurance scheme which would afford protection against accidents, sickness, and age would do what he desired.

Bismarck was responsible for a national plan for accident compensation in 1884; for compulsory insurance against sickness in 1883; and for compulsory insurance for the aged in 1889. Germany's first old-age benefit law as passed in 1889 was changed in 1891 to include the entire working population in a scheme for contributory invalidity and old-age insurance. In 1911 an amendment was adopted adding survivor's insurance.

The Nazis made modifications in the various forms of social insurance which we shall not attempt to follow. Following World War II and the creation of zones of occupation, there were minor changes in German social insurance laws. For the United States, British, and French zones of occupation the workman's compensation program was governed by the National Insurance Code of 1911 as amended by German laws and by measures of occupation authority. For the Russian zone of occupation this form of insurance was governed by law promulgated by order of U.S.S.R. military government in 1947. This same pattern of adjustment and modification prevailed for health and maternity insurance, for old age, invalidity, and survivors insurance, and for unemployment insurance. Germany does not have a family allowance scheme.[45] Upon withdrawal from Germany by the countries of occupation, the federal and state lawmaking bodies will be free again to modify social legislation as the people of the country see fit.

FRANCE [46]

In France, as in other European countries, poverty, vagrancy, and begging were so extensive by the fifteenth and sixteenth centuries that it

---

ports to the Committee on Economic Security by the Social Security Board, Social Security Board Publication (Washington, D.C., G.P.O., 1937), No. 20, pp. 469–497.

[45] Farman and Hale, *op. cit.*

[46] The material for this discussion is taken from Barbara Rodgers, "Social Security in France," *Public Administration* (London), Pt. 1 (Winter, 1953), pp. 377–398, and Pt. 2 (Spring, 1954), pp. 99–117; Gertrude Willoughby, "Social Security in France and Britain," *Political Quarterly,* Vol. 19, No. 1 (January–March, 1948), pp. 49–59, and "Population Problems and Family Policy in France," *Eugenics Review,* Vol. 45, No. 2 (July, 1953), pp. 93–100; Emile Graille, *Services publics d'assistance* (Paris, Libraire du Recueil Sirey, 1947); Apolline de Gourlet, *Cinquante Ans de*

became necessary for the state to come to the rescue of the church, the primary institution for alleviating the ills of the poor. At an early date, in fact shortly after the first Frankish king in A.D. 496 had been converted to Christianity, the church and royalty seem to have co-operated in furnishing provisions for the poor. At the time of the Crusades (1096–1204), due to the aggravation of need, parochial institutions, such as hospitals and leprosaries, were increased. Dating from approximately this period, the earlier tendency of the crown to work with the church and to order the church to furnish facilities for the care of the needy expanded.

By 1453, Louis XI, without denying authority to the church over the charitable institutions, placed their administration in the hands of civil officials. The secularization of the hospitals proceeded slowly; a decree of Parliament (May 2, 1505), entrusted the temporal government of the *Hôtel-Dieu de Paris,* an institution for the care of a diverse group (founded about A.D. 695), to certain commoners chosen by the prevost of the merchants and aldermen. By the edict of 1543, Francis I transferred the surveillance of the asylums for the sick to the bailiffs, the seneschals, and prevosts, but the resistance of the clergy necessitated the issuance of more edicts to confirm the change. In 1544, Francis I also established the charity bureaus (*bureaux de charité*) to satisfy the strong municipal spirit of the time; the charity bureaus are the predecessors of the welfare bureaus (*bureaux de bienfaisance*). By the edict of Moulins in 1566, the principle of settlement was established and provision made for a tax for the support of the poor.

Intermittently, the church and its leaders introduced reforms in the methods of caring for persons in need. For example, St. Vincent de Paul (1581–1660), not satisfied with existing provisions for certain classes of the needy and with the secular management of many institutions, initiated numerous reforms. These included the modification of the *bureaux de charité,* which were really organizations of lay people to help the poor in a systematic manner; the founding of the order *Les Filles de Charité,* which ran a huge establishment for illegitimate foundlings; and the alleviation of the lot of convicts and galley slaves.

---

service social (Paris, Les Editions Sociales Françaises, 1947); "France, Social Conditions," *Encyclopaedia Britannica* (1952), Vol. 9, pp. 608–611; E. H. Lewinski-Corwin, "Hospitals and Sanatoria," *Encyclopaedia of the Social Sciences* (1932), Vol. 7, pp. 464–471; S. P. Breckinridge, "Institutions, Public," *Encyclopaedia of the Social Sciences* (1932), Vol. 8, pp. 90–94; Charles W. Pipkin, "Poor Laws," *Encyclopaedia of the Social Sciences* (1934), Vol. 12, pp. 230–234; I. M. Rubinow, "Poverty," *Encyclopaedia of the Social Sciences* (1934), Vol. 12, pp. 284–292; Jean Hourticq, "L'Assistance," *L'Encyclopédie française* (1935), Vol. 10, pp. 42–2 to 42–8; Pierre Laroque, "La Prévoyance," *L'Encyclopédie française* (1935), Vol. 10, pp. 42–8 to 42–14; E. Garnier, "Bienfaisance," *La Grande Encyclopédie* (1895), Vol. 6, pp. 755–768; Leon Lallemand, *Histoire de la charité* (Paris, Librairie Alphonse Picard et fils, 1902–1912), 4 vols.; H. Derouin, A. Gory, F. Worms, *Traité théorique et pratique d'assistance publique* (Paris, L. Larose, 1900), 2 vols.

In 1662, Louis XIV (1643–1715) issued an edict for the establishment of a general hospital by every important city, thus embedding in French culture the practice of indoor municipal care for certain classes. Both church and state were obliged to extend their services greatly during the Great Plague in southeastern France in 1720–1722. The national government spent large sums of money for various kinds of relief, including food, drugs, and clothing.[47] This was temporary national assistance for those provinces in dire need; apparently with the abatement of the plague, they returned to local public and private care, the latter being largely ecclesiastical. France, like England as we shall see later, had a short interval of experience with a national program. It was many years before France again adopted a national public-assistance program.

During the Revolution, with its drive toward national control of many activities, the state confiscated hospitals and almshouses owned and administered by the church. Later, under Napoleon, the property was returned to the church but with stronger municipal and civil control. There was also set up during the revolutionary period a central commission with local branches, known as welfare bureaus, to replace the charity bureaus. The central organization was more or less ineffectual until 1886 when a new division of assistance was created in the Ministry of the Interior. A 1930 law created the Ministry of Public Health, within which were placed the divisions of assistance, public hygiene, low-cost public housing, and the medical inspection of schools.

Within the communes, which are the smallest geographical units of government, there are: *hospitals and hospices, bureaux de bienfaisance,* and *bureaux d'assistance*. Every commune has a *bureau d'assistance* but not necessarily a hospital, hospice, or *bureau de bienfaisance.* The *bureau d'assistance,* except in a commune where there is no *bureau de bienfaisance,* is a local organization for carrying out the obligatory services for which the prefect, the head of the governmental unit called the *département,* is responsible. He is charged with the administration of certain obligatory services of public assistance such as those to dependent children; persons in need of free medical care; the mentally afflicted; the aged, the infirm, and the incurable; maternity cases; and large families.[48] The cost for these services is divided among the state, the departments, and the communes. The role of the state seems to be supervisory rather than administrative.

Relief to persons with local settlement, and to the aged and others not entitled to the obligatory services, is lodged with the *bureaux de bienfaisance,* which are created in many but not all of the communes. They are

[47] Shelby T. McCloy, "Government Assistance During the Plague of 1720–22 in Southeastern France," *Social Service Review* (June, 1938), pp. 298–318.

[48] G. Montagu Harris, *Local Governments in Many Lands* (London, P. S. King, 1933), pp. 23–24.

concerned with indoor relief, with relief to indigents who do not fall in another category, and with the repression of vagrancy and begging.

France has enacted numbers of categorical assistance statutes, the administration of which is by local assistance offices under the supervision of a division within the Ministry of Health and Population or some other agency. Mention will be made of several of these laws: [49]

1. The plan of assistance to children was first regulated by an act passed in 1904. It is designed so that poor mothers can keep their children with them, although it also covers foundlings, deserted children, orphans, and children placed with institutions or private persons. The costs of this plan are borne jointly by the commune, department, and state.

2. By an 1893 act, a scheme of free medical assistance was established. Every destitute French person who is suffering from an illness is cared for free of charge at home or in a hospital at the expense of the commune, department, or state, depending upon the settlement of the sick person.

3. Assistance to the insane is regulated by two fundamental laws, the act of 1838 and the royal order of 1839. The cost of assistance for care provided in departmental asylums, independent public asylums, special wards, or private asylums, with permission of the prefect, is defrayed by the commune, the department, or the state in proportions varying with the insane person's domicile for assistance purposes.

4. A law providing for assistance to the aged, infirm, and incurable was first passed in 1905, the cost being borne by the commune, department, or state according to the domicile of the assisted person. All French citizens who are destitute and over sixty-five years of age or unable to earn a living because of infirmity or incurable disease are eligible.

5. Maternity or pregnancy assistance was instituted in 1913, the costs being met jointly from state, department, and commune budgets.

6. Because of France's low birth rate, several plans have been initiated to encourage large families. In 1913 an act was passed providing for local assistance to every French citizen supporting more than three children and having insufficient means for their upbringing. A national scheme was provided in the law of 1923. Under it, any family of French nationality residing in France and including three living children under thirteen, legitimate or legitimized, could receive from the state a monthly allowance for each child beyond the second under thirteen. Since that time numbers of liberalizations have been made in the family allowance program. The Ministry of Labor and Social Security is responsible for general policy and supervision.

The state also participates in an unemployment relief scheme. Its object is to facilitate the working of an unemployment fund of the communes and departments by refunding them a part of their expenditures. The municipal and departmental unemployment funds are set up in the communes or departments only when authorities consider it necessary. Under a 1905 act, relief is granted to persons dependent on their work for a livelihood, thus excluding persons under the Social Insurance Act or in receipt of relief for the aged, infirm, or incurable. Flanking the public assistance schemes

---

[49] International Labor Office, *International Survey of Social Services: 1933*, Vol. 1, pp. 220–301; Barbara Rodgers, "Social Security in France," *loc. cit.*, Pt. 2, p. 99.

are the social insurance plans. The principle of workmen's compensation first was established in 1898. The obligation to insure against sickness and maternity was provided for by 1928 legislation, and for old age, invalidity, and survivors in 1910. Special classes of workers have been insured for various disabilities under several different laws. Voluntary unemployment insurance was instituted in 1905. France is still without a compulsory unemployment insurance plan.

Many charitable activities are still carried on by the church. The principle on which these services rests is that "charity should be voluntary, unconnected with government or laws, the outpouring of the spirit inspired by religious zeal." [50] The government, despite the fact that church and state are separate, subsidizes many activities of the church and other private agencies. The struggle between church and state for control of eleemosynary activities continues in greater or lesser degree. Today, social security measures in France include the social insurances, family allowances, special forms of assistance, and local assistance for residual groups. Many additional health and welfare services are rendered by the hierarchy of governmental agencies. The major expenditures on these programs in France, like other countries, now come from the taxpayer and not from the almsgiver or philanthropist. A comparatively small amount of costs is borne exclusively by local units of administration for a relatively small number of persons.

SOVIET RUSSIA [51]

Poverty under the Russian czars was infamous. Songs like "The Volga Boatman" and such paintings as Repin's on the same subject describe the barbarous neglect and cruelty of the old days. The Soviet Union today appears to have extensive insurance schemes for workers and elaborate social assistance provisions for nonworkers.

In the first days of the October, Revolution in 1917 the Soviet government published the news that it was setting about the passing of a social insurance decree. From November, 1917, to January, 1918, four such decrees or principles based on Lenin's earlier insurance program were issued. In essence they said that the best form of social insurance is state insurance constructed on the following principles:

---

[50] Carlotta Welles, "Social Work in France," *Social Service Review* (December, 1927), pp. 537–557.

[51] This discussion on Russia came largely from Farman and Hale, *op. cit.;* International Security Association, *Proceedings, Reports and Resolutions, Constitution, and Standing Orders,* 8th General Meeting (Montreal, 1948); the unpublished translation by Hildegarde Pilger of A. Godunov and M. Fridev, *Soviet Social Insurance: The Conquest of the Great October Socialist Revolution* (Moscow, Trade Union Publishing House, 1938); Susan M. Kingsbury and Mildred Fairchild, *Factory, Family, and Woman in the Soviet Union* (New York, Putnam, 1935); Fannina W. Halle, *Women in Soviet Russia* (London, Routledge, 1934). These materials provide little current information.

1. It must guarantee protection to workers in all cases of loss of ability to work.
2. Insurance must extend to all hired labor and their families.
3. The amount of remuneration under the insurance plan should be the full wage, all expenses of insurance to fall on the entrepreneurs and the state.
4. All forms of insurance must be administered by a single insurance organization on the principle of self-administration of the insured.

The Russian insurance system is built on the Labor Code of 1922, with many revisions. The unions execute the program under the surveillance of the All-Union Central Council of Trade Unions (VTsSPS). They provide medical care for all and pay benefits to the ill, to pregnant and lying-in women, to old people, to the permanently disabled, to those injured in their occupations, and to members of families which have lost their breadwinner. In 1944 Russia inaugurated a family allowance program for families with four or more dependent children. Rest homes, parks of culture and rest, and sanatoria are provided for working mothers and their children and for vacations of whole families. There is no unemployment insurance scheme, since all who can work are expected and presumably enabled to do so. None of the insurance expenses is borne by the laborer but entirely by commerce, industry, collective farm enterprises, and the state. Various formulas determine the benefits, which are commensurate with Russian standards of living.

In May, 1938, an historic document published by the Council of People's Commissars reviewed past developments and outlined a further extensive program of social insurance. This report pointed out that the administration, in 1937, transferred the costs of medical aid, nurseries, kindergartens, housing construction, and payment of pensions to nonworking pensioners from the social insurance budget to state and local budgets, making possible increased benefits for aid in pregnancy and childbirth, rest homes, sanatoria, camps, and so forth. This document also makes criticisms and recommendations for the future. It states, for instance, that some trade union organizations underestimate the importance of preventing illness and such inadequacies call for a more effective mobilization of their forces.

Social assistance in the Soviet Union is based on the citizen's *right* to employment or assistance from the state and not on *charity*. Public assistance or relief, in contrast with insurance measures, appears to be available for disabled unemployed persons, including those crippled by war and other causes, the blind, the deaf and mute, children and young persons in need of medical care, members of collective farms incapable of working, and so forth. Social assistance is granted under a single scheme covering every case of need and every class of the population. The funds come from national and local budgets.

In order to secure active co-operation by the mass of workers in improving the work of assistance, "special assistance" sections have been attached to the soviets of each town. The functions of these sections or committees include explanation of the assistance laws, supervision and enforcement of legislation, and sharing in the work of administering the assistance. The various assistance schemes for different classes of unemployed provide for work and cash; they have the character of pensions, for cash payments seem to be made in amounts fixed and standardized by the Commissariat of Social Assistance. The exercise of discretion in the determination of budgetary needs is omitted from the Russian plan, smacking apparently too much of charity and the dole. The Russian insurance and assistance plans are based (1) on the constitutional right of workers to complete security, and (2) on the constitutional right to assistance of those who cannot work because of personal disabilities, such assistance to be given on what amounts to a "schedule" basis, thus avoiding the exercise of administrative discretion which the Russians think is demoralizing.

ELSEWHERE IN THE WORLD

Over a period of several centuries parts of the world have been in the process of developing legislation and methods of administration to relieve acute economic need. For great parts of the globe this effort to alleviate human distress through governmental sanctions is almost exclusively a twentieth-century phenomenon. What such countries as Great Britain, Australia, New Zealand, Canada, Germany, France, and the United States have achieved in varying degrees much of the rest of the world is struggling to attain. Various United Nations and other governmental publications give some indication of progress and of similarities and differences between countries. Article 22 of the Universal Declaration of Human Rights lays down the principle that "everyone, as a member of society, has the right to social security and is entitled to realization, through national effort and international co-operation and in accordance with the organization and resources of each state of the economic, social, and cultural rights indispensable for his dignity and the free development of his personality." Article 23 provides that everyone has the right to a just and favorable remuneration, supplemented, if necessary, by other means of social protection. Other articles provide for the right to work, to equal pay for equal work, to rest and leisure, to adequate food, clothing, housing, and medical care.[52]

Numbers of United Nations agencies are working to achieve these goals. For example, the International Labor Organization (ILO) advocates that each country build up an income security organization com-

[52] United Nations, Commission on Human Rights, *Activities of the United Nations and of the Specialized Agencies in the Field of Economic, Social, and Cultural Rights* (New York, 1952), Sales No. 1952, IV, 4; E/CN, 4/364/Rev.1; see also, United Nations, Department of Social Affairs, *Methods of Social Welfare Administration: France* (New York, 1950), Sales No. 1950, IV, 10; E/CN, 5/224.

prising a unified social insurance system, or several schemes co-ordinated under a single authority, working closely with medical and employment services, and supplemented by a social assistance system. It believes that economic security should be afforded normally through the social insurance system and that the social assistance system, except for services to children, should have only a transitional or subsidiary part to play.[53] The ILO has made many studies on social insurance and related schemes of social assistance. In 1950 it surveyed the social security systems in the territories of forty-five state members.[54] The study comprised two parts: the first briefly reviewed and compared the main features of national systems; the second summarized the legislation of each country. In an earlier study, *Approaches to Social Security,* the organization pointed out how social assistance measures have liberalized the old poor law of many countries and, in turn, have been supplemented or replaced by social insurance laws.[55]

A United Nations study, *Methods of Administering Assistance to the Needy,* reviewed similarities and differences in the programs of Egypt, the United Kingdom, Australia, Denmark, France, Japan, and the United States. Numbers of countries, according to the report, now rely more heavily on public assistance than they will in a generation, when various insurance schemes have become firmly established and large percentages of the population are covered. Distinctions between countries on such matters as eligibility, methods of determining need, level of assistance, methods of financing and administering assistance, and related services were summarized.[56]

A voluminous survey prepared by the United Nations Secretariat for the tenth session of the Social Commission in 1955 showed that forty-five nations have adopted new constitutions or made major changes in their basic laws, many of which are designed to place responsibility for social welfare on the state. The trend was accelerated by the impact of a prewar depression, World War II, and a postwar determination to produce a better world. Resources for public health, education, labor relations, social security, and the organization of co-operatives with government support are some of the new developments. As a result, functions formerly carried out on the basis of charitable or other motivations are

---

[53] For this explanation, see *Activities of the United Nations and of the Specialized Agencies in the Field of Economic, Social, and Cultural Rights,* p. 34. The text is set out in the "First Report of the International Labor Organization to the United Nations," Vol. 2, attached to Doc. E/586/add. 1.

[54] International Labor Office, *International Survey of Social Security: Comparative Analysis and Summary of National Laws,* Studies and Reports New Series (Geneva, 1950), No. 23.

[55] International Labor Office, *Approaches to Social Security, an International Survey,* Studies and Reports Series (Montreal, 1942), No. 18.

[56] United Nations, Department of Social Affairs, *Methods of Social Welfare Ad ministration: France* (New York, 1950), Sales No. 1950, IV, 10; E/CN, 5/224.

incorporated into law and exercised on the impersonal basis of the law. Throughout the world social thought is moving away from traditional conceptions of poverty and is regarding needy persons as victims of circumstances over which modern society can and should exercise control.[57] The trend in the development of legislation to assure economic security is shown in the following table: [58]

Table 8

Type of program	*Number of countries having laws in operation* *January, 1939*	*January, 1949*
Old-age, invalidity, survivors insurance and pension (or assistance) programs	33	44
Health and maternity insurance	24	36
Workmen's compensation	Not available	57
Unemployment insurance	21	22
Family allowance programs	7	27

SUMMARY AND CONCLUSIONS

By the beginning of the fifteenth century in Europe there were five distinct methods of caring for the poor:

1. Parish distribution of alms.
2. Monastery distribution of alms at the gate.
3. Hospitals usually run by the monasteries for the aged, sick, and children.
4. Guild distribution of alms and administration of almshouses.
5. Benevolence by the rich.

In the sixteenth century the movement to impose responsibility upon the community and to restrict the influence of the church got well under way. All European countries were enacting restrictive legislation, and the large cities were passing ordinances under which they set up civilly administered poor relief. Conditions made it necessary for towns to assume much responsibility for the poor. Begging was either to be punished by town officials or licensed by them. The able-bodied were to be set to work; the impotent were to be cared for in institutions which were often under Catholic control, with varying amounts of civil inspection, financing, and administration. In those European countries which remained Catholic, a more or less satisfactory division of labor and responsibilities was worked out by civil and ecclesiastical authorities. In those countries which came under Protestant influence and where state and church were completely separated, the influence of the church in the care of the poor diminished as more responsibility was assumed by the state. For several centuries this responsibility took the form of poor relief, of both an outdoor and indoor nature; only recently has it taken the form of social insurance.

---

[57] *New York Times* (May 2, 1955).

[58] Farman and Hale, *op. cit.*, p. 2.

An English poor-relief historian wrote: [59]

> It would appear, then, that the natural impulse of charity, aided by the higher influences of religion, and organized into a system through the agency of institutions richly endowed, and governed by the most powerful priesthood the world has ever known, failed in effectually relieving poverty; whilst such institutions and miscalled charities directly operated to the encouragement of idleness and vice, by leading the people to rely upon alms and casual contributions for support, instead of depending on their own exertions.

Economic and social conditions and the inability of the church to cope adequately with those conditions are responsible for secularization of relief in Europe beginning with the sixteenth century. From the sixteenth to the twentieth century assistance was provided under statutory enactment in England and upon the Continent. Minor modifications in the statutes and in the methods of administration were effected occasionally, but there were no fundamental changes in theory.

Although for centuries many countries of the western world recognized the responsibility of the state for the survival of the poverty-stricken, it was not until the twentieth century that they came to a full realization of the primary causes of poverty. When this awareness became widespread, governments began to take action to assure every individual a decent minimum standard of living through nonpunitive social assistance and social insurance measures. Assurance of a job at fair wages is not yet an actuality in any country except perhaps Russia, although laws which guarantee minimum wages have been passed. Russia seems to be the only western country which accepts the principle that man has a right to work, in fact he *must* work. In the second half of the twentieth century many underdeveloped countries will take strides in the direction of assuring their citizenry a right to a decent life, to education, to employment, and to protection against the exigencies of life. This represents a modern revolution perhaps as important as the discovery and utilization of atomic energy.

Selected References

ASHLEY, W. J., *An Introduction to English Economic History and Theory* (New York, Putnam, 1910).

FARMAN, Carl H., and HALE, Veronica Marren, *Social Security Legislation Throughout the World,* U.S. Social Security Administration, Division of Research and Statistics, Bureau Report (Washington, D.C., G.P.O., 1949), No. 16.

GILLIN, J. L., *Poverty and Dependency,* 3d ed. (New York, D. Appleton-Century, 1937).

[59] Sir George Nicholls, *A History of the English Poor Law* (London, John Murray, 1854), Vol. 1, p. 5

Haber, William, and Cohen, Wilbur J., eds., *Readings in Social Security* (Englewood Cliffs, N.J., Prentice-Hall, 1948).

International Labor Office, *Minimum Standards of Social Security,* International Labor Conference, 35th sess. (Geneva, 1951–1952), Report V (a) (1 and 2).

International Labor Office, *Objectives and Advanced Standards of Social Security.* International Labor Conference, 35th sess. (Geneva, 1952), Report V (b).

Lecky, William, *History of European Morals from Augustus to Charlemagne* (New York, D. Appleton, 1883).

Niebuhr, Reinhold, *The Contributions of Religion to Social Work* (New York, Columbia University Press, 1932).

Salter, F. R., ed., *Some Early Tracts on Poor Relief* (London, Methuen, 1926).

Steinbicker, Carl R., *Poor Relief in the Sixteenth Century* (Washington, D.C., Catholic University of America Press, 1937).

United Nations, Department of Social Affairs, *Children Deprived of a Normal Home Life* (New York, 1952), Sales No. 1952, IV, 3; E/CN, 5/271.

United Nations, Department of Social Affairs, *Methods of Administering Assistance to the Needy: Study by the Secretary-General of the Programmes in Seven Countries* (New York, 1952), Sales No. 1952, IV, 10; E/CN, 5/273.

United Nations, Department of Social Affairs, *Methods of Social Welfare Administration: France* (New York, 1950), Sales No. 1950, IV, 10; E/CN, 5/224.

United Nations, Department of Social Affairs, *Preliminary Report on the World Social Situation, with Special Reference to Standards of Living* (New York, 1952), Sales No. 1952, IV, 11; E/CN, 5/267/Rev. 1.

United Nations, Department of Social Affairs, *Study on Assistance to Indigent Aliens* (New York, 1951), Sales No. 1952, IV, 1; ST/SOA/7, 1951.

United Nations, *Child, Youth, and Family Welfare,* Legislative and Administrative Series (New York, 1951), ST/SOA/Ser. E/2/add. 4.

U.S. Department of Health, Education, and Welfare, *Major Changes in Social Security Legislation: 1952* (Washington, D.C., G.P.O., 1953), 3d suppl. to U.S. Social Security Administration, Division of Research and Statistics, Bureau Report No. 16.

Walsh, Mary Elizabeth, *The Saints and Social Work* (Washington, D.C., Catholic University of America Press, 1936).

The student also should consult articles in the various encyclopedias and volumes of the *Social Work Year Book.*

CHAPTER 18

English Social Security Policies

INTRODUCTION

Since England's poor law is the ancestor of the public relief policies of the American colonies, and since numbers of the poor-law policies and practices of the colonies prevail today, this chapter will be devoted to tracing the English development. In reviewing English poor-law history, it is fitting that we pause to acknowledge the contributions of the Webbs, who for years studied that problem in England. An American poor-law authority said of them that they were the most distinguished poor-law critics and students of any time and that they were the great pioneers in making the abolition of the English poor law seem a practicable national policy.[1] Beatrice Webb, who died in 1943, lived to see the publication of the report by Sir William Beveridge, *Social Insurance and Allied Services,* which set out many of the principles and recommendations for Great Britain's present social security system. Sidney Webb, who was made first Baron Passfield in 1929 and who died in 1947, saw the passage of four comprehensive acts which provided for new or improved social insurance, social assistance, and social service schemes.

Although England since the sixteenth, and the colonies since the seventeenth, century have had legislation providing for the local support of the poor through taxation, the community has frequently favored private and voluntary care as a more acceptable method of giving and receiving relief. Persons receiving public assistance have often been legally labeled "paupers" and, as a consequence, have sometimes lost their right to vote. The general implication on the part of those who used the term was that anyone receiving public relief was an unworthy and inferior person. With the depression of the 1930's the United States accepted the principles that the central or national government must assume primary financial responsibility for persons with certain types of need,

[1] Edith Abbott, "The Webbs on the English Poor Law," *Social Service Review* (June, 1929), pp. 252–270.

particularly those affected by involuntary unemployment, and that those who receive such assistance must not be stigmatized. England somewhat earlier accepted these principles. The care of those with economic need in England and the United States today is recognized as a public duty. Under the common law of England it was a moral and not a legal duty. The church early assumed the major responsibility for carrying out the obligation. It was not until the break-up of the feudal system, under which the serf had the obligation to work and the master the duty of maintaining him, that poor-relief legislation, or in more modern terms, public-assistance legislation, developed.[2]

EARLY HISTORY

In opposition to the almsgiving practices of the medieval church, which encouraged begging and vagrancy, the kings and nobles were intent upon maintaining the existing order "based on a social hierarchy of rulers and ruled, of landowners and those who belonged to the land."[3] For more than six hundred years, from the beginning of Athelstan's reign (A.D. 924–940) and Canute's (1016–1035) down to the reign of Henry VIII (1509–1547), the English statutes were directed toward restraint of vagrancy, whether sturdy beggars and criminals or laborers seeking work. "It is hard to say which was the most detrimental to the common weal, the hindrance to the migration of the enterprising labourer, the hardships and suffering that the occasional compulsory removal caused

---

[2] Charles W. Pipkin, "Poor Laws," *Encyclopaedia of the Social Sciences* (1934), Vol. 12, pp. 230–234. See John L. Gillin, *Poverty and Dependency*, 3d ed. (New York, D. Appleton-Century, 1937), chs. 12, 13, 14, for a good short history on the development of poor relief.

[3] Much of this history has been taken from the following books by Sidney and Beatrice Webb: *English Local Government: English Poor Law History* (London, Longmans, Green, 1927–1929), Pt. 1: *The Old Poor Law* (1 vol., 1927), p. 23, and Pt. 2: *The Last Hundred Years* (2 vols., 1929); *The Break up of the Poor Law, Being Part One of the Minority Report of the Poor Law Commission* (London, Longmans, Green, 1909); *The Prevention of Destitution* (London, Longmans, Green, 1911); *English Poor Law Policy* (London, Longmans, Green, 1910). But see also, Sir Frederick Morton Eden, *The State of the Poor* (New York, Dutton, 1929); Helen Bosanquet, *The Poor Law Report of 1909* (London, Macmillan, 1909); Sir George Nicholls, *A History of the English Poor Law* (London, John Murray, 1854); P. E. Aschrott, *The English Poor Law System: Past and Present*, trans. Preston-Thomas (London, Knight, 1888); Sir William Ashley, *An Introduction to Economic History and Theory* (London, Longmans, Green, 1925); William Lecky, *History of European Morals from Augustus to Charlemagne* (New York, D. Appleton, 1883); B. Kirkman Gray, *A History of English Philanthropy* (London, King, 1905); E. M. Leonard, *The Early History of English Poor Relief* (Cambridge, The University Press, 1900); John J. Clarke, *Social Administration Including the Poor Laws* (London, Pitman, 1922); Karl de Schweinitz, *England's Road to Social Security* (Philadelphia, University of Pennsylvania Press, 1943); Hilary M. Leyendecker, *Problems and Policy in Public Assistance* (New York, Harper, 1955); Walter A. Friedlander, *Introduction to Social Welfare* (Englewood Cliffs, N.J., Prentice-Hall, 1955).

to the poor, or the demoralization that the inter-parochial litigation effected in the whole administration of the Poor Law."[4]

The Statute of Labourers, enacted in 1350, following immediately upon the Black Death and accompanying the break-up of the feudal system and the emergence of free labor, required all persons able to labor and without means of support to serve any master at rates existing prior to the pestilence.[5] Laborers were forbidden to wander, and no one was to give alms to able-bodied beggars. A statute enacted in 1360 dealt with any man who had run away from his place of work, who was claimed and recovered by his employer, and who, at the discretion of the justices, could be branded on the forehead with the letter "*F*" in token of his falsity.[6]

FIVE HUNDRED YEARS OF HISTORY

The Act of 1388, commonly called the 12th Richard II, is generally considered the parent of the English poor law. It, too, was designed to prevent vagabondage and provided:

> That no servant or labourer, be he man or woman, shall depart at the end of his term out of the hundred, rape, or wapentake, where he is dwelling, to serve or dwell elsewhere, or by colour to go in pilgrimage, unless he bring a letter patent containing the cause of his going, under the King's seal, which for this intent shall be assigned to the keeping of some good man, at the discretion of the Justice of the Peace. That every person that goeth begging, and is able to serve or labour, it shall be done of him as of him that departeth out of the hundred, or other place, with letter testimonial, as afore is said. Beggars impotent to serve shall abide in the cities and towns where they be dwelling at the time of the proclamation of this statute; and, if the people of the cities and towns will not, or may not, suffice to find them, that then the said beggars shall draw them to other towns within the hundred, rape, or wapentake, or to the towns where they were born, within forty days after the proclamation made, and there shall continually abide during their lives.

The section separating those impotent to serve from those able to serve is significant for poor-law history. Subsequent statutes with their "severe and persistent oppression" enforced by cruel punishment led to evasion and did little or nothing to lessen destitution or maintain order.

From time immemorial in England every person legally belonged to some parish; every person as a serf or a freeman was a member of some community. Restraints on mobility, with rigid punishment for violation, were imposed from time to time by statute; but with the beginnings of a general system of relief, at first out of voluntary funds and later out

---

[4] Webb and Webb, *English Local Government: English Poor Law History,* Pt. 1, p. 330.

[5] 25 Edw. III, c. 5.

[6] 34 Edw. III, c. 10.

of taxes, local authorities became concerned that they should not have to support those who did not belong.

We have just observed that in 1388 during the reign of Richard II an act prohibiting vagrancy and wandering about the country was passed. It provided that beggars impotent to serve were to remain in the place where they were staying at the time of the proclamation of the act; if they could not be maintained there, they were to be sent back to their birthplaces. Heavy penalties were imposed on "sturdy vagabonds" and "valiant beggars." From these restrictions on vagrancy, strengthened by the severe statutes of 1547 and 1549,[7] came the later law of settlement. These statutes required the expulsion of the itinerant and provided that "'The officers were directed to convey' them 'on horseback, cart, chariot or otherwise to the next constable, and so from constable to constable, till they be brought to the place where they were born or most conversant for the space of three years, there to be nourished of alms.'" [8] Thus, we have the beginning of our still persistent "settlement and removal" theories.

We saw in the preceding chapter that in the first quarter of the sixteenth century a new philosophy and policy toward the poor began to emerge in the Netherlands, Germany, France, and other countries. Both church and state reformed and modified the treatment of the poor. The earliest English law aimed at relief of the poor, as well as at repression of vagrancy, was the 1531 statute of Henry VIII, entitled "How Aged Poor and Impotent Persons Compelled to live by Alms shall be ordered." [9] By this act the justices gave licenses to the poor to beg, each being assigned to a district. Legislation of 1536 ordered parish officials to obtain the resources by voluntary contributions to care for the poor, so that none should go begging to ask alms.[10]

The city of London, in 1547, enacted legislation providing for the first compulsory poor rate in England, and, in 1553, furnished a comprehensive scheme which recognized three degrees of the poor: the impotent, those affected by casualties, and the thriftless. For the first two, hospitals were provided; and for the thriftless, the first Bridewell was created between 1555 and 1557. The licensing of beggars appears to have been usual. Other towns adopted measures similar to those of London.[11] The action of municipal authorities in particular towns was the main feature in the development of the English system of poor relief in the first half of the sixteenth century but became of relatively less importance as national legislation was enacted.[12]

---

[7] 1 and 2 Edw. VI, c. 3; 3 and 4 Edw. VI, c. 16.

[8] George Coods on the "Law of Settlement and Removal of the Poor," quoted in Webb and Webb, *English Local Government: English Poor Law History*, Pt. 1, p. 318.

[9] 22 Henry VIII, c. 12.

[10] 27 Henry VIII, c. 25.

[11] Leonard, *op. cit.*, ch. 3.

[12] *Ibid.*, p. 67.

Elizabeth's Act of Apprenticeship was passed in 1562.[13] The intent was to banish idleness by enacting that all persons between twelve and sixty without property or a fixed income were to be compelled by two magistrates to serve in husbandry in the country or to work at a trade. In 1572 and 1576, the first comprehensive poor laws were enacted which aimed at complete systematic maintenance in parishes for all indigents needing relief, including for the first time apart from mere penal repression, a definite provision for the able-bodied unemployed, and another for the appointment of collectors and overseers with power to tax and assess the inhabitants.[14]

In the famous Act of 1601 (43 Elizabeth I, c. 3) there was re-enacted in simpler form the legislation of 1572–1576. It made the civil power more important than the ecclesiastical by requiring appointment of overseers of the poor by justices of the peace in every parish. For three centuries the parish remained the most important unit for poor-relief administration. The act further provided for a compulsory tax assessment; set up methods of caring for certain categories of the needy, such as the able-bodied, the impotent, and children; imposed obligations upon certain enumerated relatives; provided for commitment to the house of correction of those who would not work and for apprenticeship of minors. It contained no provisions regarding settlement and removal. In 1662 Charles II enacted the law of settlement, empowering the justices of peace to return to his former home any newcomer who might, in the opinion of the overseers, become a public charge.

Somewhere between 1586–1597 the Privy Council, made up of the principal officers of the crown, decided to attempt centralized administrative control, which would ensure uniform execution of the law in all the thousands of parishes. It assumed the duty of seeing that measures of relief for the poor, impotent, and able-bodied were put in operation; hence, it issued many orders to local officials. It also insisted upon reports from local agents, who were largely justices of the peace, although in some parishes, overseers of the poor were being appointed. With civil war around 1640, national direction and supervision of the administration of poor relief ended. This short period of national authority was succeeded by two centuries of completely local autonomy.[15]

Relatively little is known of what was done locally in the next half century. In 1696 Parliament passed an act allowing one city, Bristol, to establish a union of its nineteen parishes, to create a large joint workhouse, and to take away from parish officials the administration of poor

[13] 5 Eliz. I, c. 4.

[14] 14 Eliz. I, c. 5; 18 Eliz. I, c. 3; Webb and Webb, *English Local Government: English Poor Law History,* Pt. 1, pp. 52–53.

[15] Webb and Webb, *English Local Government: English Poor Law History,* Pt. 1, pp. 65–79, 99.

relief and give it to the Corporation of the Poor.[16] This city-wide corporation comprised the mayor, the aldermen, the church-wardens of the parishes, and four persons elected from their wards. Except for London and a few other municipalities, this was the first local governing body directed by Parliament to be based upon popular election, and it was the second board of guardians, London having the first established in 1647.

The application by towns for local acts of Parliament to permit the creation of unions of parishes, primarily so that the poor might be employed in workhouses, continued for over a century and, with it, the creation of the Incorporations of Guardians of the Poor. The guardians comprised the clergy, gentry, and leading tenants of the union; they delegated their authority to smaller bodies of directors and acting guardians who in turn often turned over the administration to paid officers.[17] Thus, the guardians, where they existed, took over the responsibility for the administration of poor-law relief from the parish overseers, although the parishioners continued their statutory obligation to serve as overseers. This merely meant that the overseers were responsible to new masters, the guardians rather than the justices, for, actually, the overseers carried out many of their old functions under the orders and direction of the guardians.

The interest of the guardians was largely concerned with the workhouse, for that institution was intended to organize profitable labor by paupers. Gradually, it became clear that the workhouse was a general dumping ground for all kinds of incompetents as well as for the able-bodied, that the unemployed were not making money for the guardians, that relief was being too freely given in the community, and that the guardians themselves were not interested in the administration of relief. However, on the favorable side it can be said:

> that many of these statutory Poor Law authorities had the undoubted advantage of combining a number of small or thinly populated parishes into a union large enough to effect a substantial equalization of rates and to escape the greater part of the difficulties presented by the Law of Settlement, as well as to admit of some sort of classification of paupers, and the employment of permanent salaried officials. On the other hand it was a grave drawback that these statutory Poor Law authorities escaped all outside control.[18]

Although there were many minor revisions of legislation between 1601 and 1723, it was not until this later date that the act of Sir Edward Knatchbull set up a system of mixed workhouses by single parishes or a union of parishes for the able-bodied, who were there to be employed, and for the sick, aged, and children.[19] In 1782 the act of Thomas Gilbert increased the powers of parishes to combine for the provision of institu-

---

[16] *Ibid.*, pp. 118–119.

[17] For discussion of boards of guardians, see *ibid.*, ch. 3, pp. 101–148.

[18] *Ibid.*, p. 147.

[19] 9 Geo. I, c. 7; Webb and Webb, *English Local Government: Poor Law History*, Pt. 1, pp. 150–151.

tions for the maintenance of all in need except the ablebodied.[20] For this group, if they could not find employment through the ordinary channels, parish officials were to give relief in homes. This attempt to care for the able-bodied in the community was accompanied by indiscriminate and widespread outdoor relief. The worst effects came not when relief was given to those totally unemployed, but when it took the form of small regular sums insufficient for maintenance and intended to be supplemented by earnings from casual or underpaid labor.

"Rate in aid of wages" became a prevailing method of caring for the underemployed during the latter part of the eighteenth century. Low wages of agricultural and industrial workers and high prices caused much distress. Attempts at minimum wages were unsuccessful, and in 1795 the district of Speenhamland adopted a system by which all laborers with wages below a certain level were granted allowances.[21] It was resolved that when the rate of bread was a certain amount, "then every poor and industrious man" and his family was to have a certain weekly income produced by his own or his family's labor or an allowance from the poor rates. The system spread and brought with it many difficulties, including the encouragement of low wages.

Poor-relief officials utilized another method of providing care for the poor: they urged and encouraged employers to give employment to the destitute. As early as 1528 the Privy Council urged the cloth manufacturers, even in depression times, to provide employment as a duty.[22] Throughout the eighteenth century, parish officers billeted the agricultural unemployed in rotation upon parishioners, each employer providing maintenance and exacting service. It was economically analogous to the parish apprenticeship system. The new capitalist entrepreneurs of the Industrial Revolution were anxious to obtain the services of the unemployed, from both the cities and the rural communities, and the overseers literally poured the poor into the cities.

The principle of apprenticeship was firmly fixed by the Elizabethan Act of 1601. This system of caring for poor children was extensively used, the three main plans for their apprenticeship being (1) the binding of an individual child to a master, who, being paid, undertook the child's maintenance and education; (2) the ceding of children in batches to manufacturers requiring child labor in the new factories; (3) the allotment of parish children among rate payers of the parish, who were compelled either to accept them as employees or pay a fine.[23] In numbers of ways the parish sought to transfer to some employer, if necessary by compulsory assignment, the duty of enforcing labor and discipline on the

[20] 22 Geo. III, c. 83; Webb and Webb, *English Local Government: English Poor Law History,* Pt. 1, pp. 151, 272–276.

[21] 22 Geo. III, c. 83; Webb and Webb, *English Local Government: English Poor Law History,* Pt. 1, pp. 172–189.

[22] *Ibid.,* pp. 189–196.

[23] *Ibid.,* pp. 196–211.

poor. The rapid capitalist developments of the seventeenth and eighteenth centuries, in both agriculture and industry, promoted these measures except, of course, for the impotent, that is, the helpless.

By the beginning of the nineteenth century, nearly all urban parishes and many rural ones had, either separately or in combination, superseded the village poor house by an organized workhouse. It is impossible to say when the first workhouse as distinguished from the poor house, on one hand, and the Bridewell, or house of correction, on the other, was established in England. By 1815, there were over 4,000 workhouses containing something like 100,000 paupers.[24]

SUMMARY OF EARLY ENGLISH HISTORY

From the Dark Ages to the Poor Law Amendment Act of 1834, the laws relating to the poor included two distinct functions: maintaining the destitute and punishing the idle. Hence, wrote the Webbs, these laws may be epitomized as the "Relief of the Poor Within a Framework of Repression" or "Charity in the Grip of Serfdom." This brief history of old English poor law reveals six stages or periods: [25]

1. Repression of vagrancy and leaving to the church any provisions for the destitute from 1350 and earlier to the sixteenth century.
2. Public provision for those in need from 1536 on.
3. A premature attempt at a nationalized poor law from about 1590 to 1640.
4. Complete local autonomy with strengthened settlement and vagrancy laws, haphazard relief, and the flourishing of workhouses and houses of correction from the Restoration into the last quarter of the eighteenth century.
5. Transfer of the obligation for providing for the unemployed from public officials to employers in the last part of the eighteenth century.
6. Subsidizing the low wages of employers by relief from the parish from 1796–1824.

LEGISLATION SINCE 1832

By 1832 the inadequacies of English legislation were so obvious and the costs so great that a royal commission was created to study the problem. Probably what was most influential in driving the government to appoint the commission was the unmistakable evidence that the task of dealing with the poor had far outgrown parochial machinery. Some 15,000 separate parishes and townships, each having to maintain its own poor, were in existence; unions absorbed only about one eighth of the parishes. The division of authority and the horrible conditions in the workhouses contributed to the creation of the commission.[26]

The report dealt almost entirely with treatment for adult, able-bodied

[24] *Ibid.*, p. 215.
[25] *Ibid.*, pp. 396–401.
[26] *Ibid.*, pp. 426–428.

laborers with dependent families. The commission, reporting in 1834, recommended: [27]

1. Outdoor relief to the able-bodied and to families was to be discontinued, except for the apprenticeship of children and for the provision of medical relief.
2. Substitution of relief in kind rather than in money.
3. All able-bodied who needed relief were to work for the parish for less wages than independent laborers.
4. The able-bodied, even of good character, were to be offered a mere subsistence.
5. Workhouses were to be continued; but the mixed workhouse was to be abolished, and there were to be indoor provisions by classification for such groups as the able-bodied, children, and the aged.
6. Vagrants were to be treated like able-bodied paupers and provided work when they were able-bodied; when disabled they were to be cared for in workhouses.

The result of the inquiry was the Act of 1834, which repealed most of the existing legislation. The basic provisions of the act expressed in terms of principles were as follows: (1) the theory of national uniformity in the care of the various classes of the destitute so that there would be identity of treatment over the kingdom for each class; (2) the theory of less eligibility, which required that the condition of the pauper be less desirable economically than that of the humblest independent laborer; (3) the theory of the workhouse, or the substitution of indoor over outdoor relief for the able-bodied.[28]

A central national authority compromising three poor-law commissioners had control of the entire administration and regulated the work of local officials, which was to be accomplished by the abolition of the parish system and its replacement by poor-law unions or groups of parishes, each of which elected a board of guardians. The act, itself, did not abolish any existing local authority. It established "for the first time in Great Britain, a new form of government which was destined to spread to other services, namely, the combination of a specialized central Department exercising executive control but not itself administering, with a network of elected Local Authorities covering the whole kingdom, each carrying out, at its own discretion, within the limits of that control, the very large powers entrusted to it by Parliamentary statutes." [29]

The legislation of 1834 and its subsequent modifications did not pro-

---

[27] Webb and Webb, *English Local Government: English Poor Law History*, Pt. 2, Vol. 1, pp. 57–61; for report see Great Britain, Parl. Papers, 1906, Vol. 102, Cmd. 2728, pp. 227–362.

[28] 4 and 5 Will. IV, c. 76; Webb and Webb, *English Local Government: English Poor Law History*, Pt. 2, Vol. 1, pp. 90–103; Ronald C. Davison, "The Evolution of British Social Services," *Social Service Review* (December, 1935), pp. 651–663.

[29] Webb and Webb, *English Local Government: English Poor Law History*, Pt. 2, Vol. 1, p. 57.

duce extensive reform. During the rest of the century, neither the mixed workhouse nor outdoor relief was abandoned; administration by the boards of guardians was inexpert and extravagant; the amount of sickness among the poor was appalling; the national authority did not bring about uniformity; the ratio of pauperism to the total population increased; in fact, the "principles of 1834" had to be greatly relaxed.

One of the results of the inadequacies of the 1834 law and its administration was the creation, in 1869, of the London Charity Organization Society. The Reverend Thomas Chalmers was the society's immediate source of inspiration, although it benefited also from the experiences of such communities as the German cities of Hamburg, Munich, and Elberfeld. Chalmer's experiments in the Glasgow parish of St. John furnished numbers of the principles and methods upon which the new organization was based. Beginning in 1819, and continuing for several years, Dr. Chalmers supervised the administration of relief in his parish. Public relief was abolished; investigation of applicants for assistance from church funds was made by volunteers of larger means who were given careful instructions; district organization was established; and the poor were expected to provide their own resources whenever possible. In contrast with the work of Chalmers and some German cities the London organization early made use of paid agents. This factor of permanent employment furnished the opportunity for the development of what was to become the new profession of social work.

The Charity Organization Society movement, with which such prominent English names as those of John Ruskin, the Earl of Shaftesbury, Cardinal Newman, William E. Gladstone were associated, spread rapidly throughout Great Britain and also the United States, beginning in Buffalo in 1877. In both countries it was an influence *against* indiscriminate public relief and the extension of governmental activity in the field of relief giving, and *for* careful administration including social investigations. Its practices were based on the assumption that most persons asking for assistance were in need of reform and so must be dealt with firmly though kindly.[30] For more than half a century the Charity Organization Society movement was resistant to the slowly growing realization that poverty was more a social than a personal matter. Many forces contributed to the undermining of the premise that unemployment resulted chiefly from personal deficiency.[31] We shall refer to three influences: the Fabian Society, the Booth and Rowntree studies, and the 1905-1909 findings of the Royal Commission on the Poor Laws and Relief of Distress.

The Fabian Society, founded in 1883, was intended to achieve social

---

[30] De Schweinitz, *op. cit.*, ch. 14.

[31] A. C. C. Hill, Jr., and Isador Lubin, *The British Attack on Unemployment* (Washington, D.C., Brookings Institution, 1934), p. 23; Abraham Epstein, *Insecurity: A Challenge to America* (New York, Random House, 1938), ch. 20, pp. 349–396.

reform. Over the years its members, comprising such prominent persons as Sidney and Beatrice Webb, Graham Wallas, and George Bernard Shaw, interested themselves in many practical reforms. These included suffrage for women, the eight-hour day, municipal water, public housing, public education, minimum wages, and abolition of the poor law. The program of the society on this last measure appears in the minority report of the 1905 Royal Commission on the Poor Laws and Relief of Distress.

Three years after the founding of the Fabian Society, Charles Booth, one of England's successful industrialists, undertook a study of great significance. In 1885 he began an inquiry into the life and labor of the people of London. His wife, describing the influences that impelled him to his studies, included the works of Ruskin, the labors of Octavia Hill, and the principles and practices of the Charity Organization Society.[32] Booth's first report appeared in 1889, and the last, the seventeenth, in 1903. He studied people by trades and by the districts in which they lived. His objective was twofold: (1) to show the numerical relation of poverty, misery, and depravity to earnings and (2) to describe the general conditions under which each class lived. Taking twenty-one or twenty-two shillings weekly for a small family as the poverty line, he estimated that 32 per cent of the population of the wealthiest city in the world were living "in the perpetual grip of poverty." He reported that perhaps another third had ten shillings more a week.[33]

In 1901 Booth's findings for London were confirmed for a small city by Rowntree's study of York. He reported that 27.84 per cent of that city were living in poverty.[34] Of this group, 9.91 per cent were living in conditions of what he called "primary poverty," and 17.93 per cent in "secondary poverty." He defined the former as a condition in which the total earnings of a family were insufficient to obtain the minimum necessary for the maintenance of physical efficiency, and the latter as that in which the total earnings of a family were sufficient for the maintenance of mere physical efficiency if some portion of the wages were not absorbed by other expenditures, either useful or wasteful.[35]

In 1905 the Royal Commission on the Poor Laws and Relief of Distress was appointed. It submitted a majority and minority report; the latter was largely the work of the Webbs, Mrs. Webb having served on the commission. Both reports agreed that drastic changes were needed in the poor law and its administration; that the board of guardians must be replaced; that the unions of parishes must be replaced by the county and

---

[32] De Schweinitz, *op. cit.*, p. 177

[33] Charles Booth, ed., *Life and Labour of the People of London* (London and Edinburgh, Williams and Norgate, 1891), Vol. 1.

[34] B. Seebohm Rowntree, *Poverty: A Study of Town Life* (London, Macmillan, 1903); de Schweinitz, *op. cit.*, ch. 16.

[35] David C. Marsh, *National Insurance and Assistance in Great Britain* (London, Pitman, 1950), pp. 4–5.

county borough councils, which must add to their other functions those of the boards of guardians; that the general mixed workhouse must be abolished; and that the treatment of children, the sick, and the aged must be improved.[36] Both reports further agreed that existing methods for handling the unemployed should be changed, that a national system of labor exchanges should be established, and that state-subsidized unemployment insurance should be instituted.

The *majority* report favored relief of the various classes in specialized institutions, more adequate provisions for outdoor relief, a single authority to handle all matters pertaining to public assistance, and the abandonment of the deterrent philosophy of the principles of 1834.[37] The *minority* report recommended the complete abolition of the poor law, the substitution of various social insurance measures, and the transfer of the duties of the board of guardians to the four already existing assistance committees of the county council: the educational, health, asylum, and pension committees.[38] "The individual was not to be dealt with because of his destitution, but because of his special needs." [39] Destitute children were to be cared for by the education authority, sick persons by the public health authority, the aged and widowed by asylum and pension authorities, and the residual able-bodied destitute by special committees of the local authorities. The battle for the prevention of destitution and the break-up of the poor law was waged around the principles of the minority report.

World War I interrupted consideration and application of the principles of the 1909 report, but in 1917 the whole question was re-examined by a committee appointed by the Ministry of Reconstruction.[40] This committee, which included representatives of the majority and the minority of the 1905 royal commission, recommended the abolition of the boards of guardians and the transfer of all their functions to county and county borough councils, provision for special classes of persons by special authorities, and assumption of the cost of all transferred functions by county and county borough councils. Nothing was done, however, until Neville Chamberlain, then minister of health, took action. In 1925 he carried a measure through Parliament which was an important preliminary step to abolition of the guardians. Under the Rating and Valuation Act the parish was abandoned as the valuation area and all the rating functions of the overseers of the poor were transferred to the town and district councils. Various plans for the break-up of the poor law followed,

---

[36] Webb and Webb, *English Local Government: English Poor Law History*, Pt. 2, Vol. 2, pp. 529–531; Webb and Webb, *The Break up of the Poor Law*, Pt. 1, Introd.

[37] Webb and Webb, *English Local Government: English Poor Law History*, Pt. 2, Vol. 2, pp. 532–539.

[38] *Ibid.*, pp. 539–546.

[39] Marion Phillips, "Labor and Poor Law Reform in England," *Social Service Review* (December, 1927), pp. 581–597.

[40] "Poor Law," *Encyclopaedia Britannica* (1952), Vol. 18, pp. 213–222.

and in 1929 the machinery of poor-law administration was changed under the Local Government Act. Boards of guardians were replaced by public-assistance committees, appointed by the county or county borough councils and acting under the Ministry of Health. The break-up of the poor law was not achieved by this legislation, but it did represent an important step in that direction. The advance was accomplished, first, by the merging of public-assistance administration in the general system of local government, and, second, by the power conferred on local authorities to declare that services which could be provided either under the poor law or under public health acts or similar legislation be provided under the applicable social service act and not under the poor law.[41]

In the forty years between 1909, when the royal commission made its recommendations, and 1948, when the National Assistance Act eliminated local poor relief, numbers of significant developments occurred which changed "the balance of importance of poor-law duties." In 1909 the Labour Exchange Act was passed, and in 1911 the Unemployment Insurance Act, the world's first national compulsory unemployment insurance law. The latter act had great significance in the eventual abolition of the poor law.[42] Under it eligibility for benefits depended upon contributions from employer, worker, and Parliament. A minimum number of contributions was required and, after the statutory amount of benefit had been received, no more was obtainable until a credit of contributions was again built up. The workman had to show that he was capable of work but unable to find it. He was not entitled to a benefit if he had lost his job through misconduct or left it voluntarily or without just cause. Due largely to the low rate of unemployment between 1911 and 1919 the law proved successful, so much so that in 1920 it was modified in order to extend benefits to a large proportion of wage earners. Some twelve million workers were brought under the scheme, which was about eight million more than were previously covered. A postwar depression broke out soon thereafter, and the actuarial principles upon which the scheme was founded were abandoned.

Parliament, over a period of several years, extended the provisions of the unemployment insurance acts and provided for new kinds of benefits. In 1921 an "uncovenanted benefit" was provided for. With some modifications it became "extended benefit" in 1924, "transitional benefit" in 1928, and "transitional payment" in 1931. These new benefits crystal-

---

[41] William A. Robson, ed., "Introduction: Present Principles," *Social Security*, 3d ed. (London, Allen and Unwin, 1948), p. 27.

[42] Ronald Mendelsohn, *Social Security in the British Commonwealth* (London, Athlone Press, 1954); Sir William H. Beveridge, *Social Insurance and Allied Services* (New York, Macmillan, 1942), *Power and Influence* (London, Hodder and Stoughton, 1953), and *The Pillars of Security* (London, Allen and Unwin, 1942); David C. Marsh, *National Insurance and Assistance in Great Britain* (London, Pitman, 1951); Janet Beveridge, *Beveridge and His Plan* (London, Hodder and Stoughton, 1954).

lized the policy of distributing money to those who were not entitled to benefits under the original purpose because they had lost their jobs before they had made the statutory number of contributions or because they had not made the statutory number of contributions or because they had exhausted their rights to benefits. Except for a short period in 1924 these benefits were not given as a right but on the basis of need. The minister of labour was given the discretion to determine need, and actual administration was carried on by local employment exchanges and committees.

Of course, the unemployment scheme set up to handle short-term unemployment could not stand the burden of the costs of long-term unemployment. By 1931 the unemployment fund had an indebtedness of £110,000,000. In an effort to correct this condition of rapidly mounting indebtedness Parliament, in 1934, passed the Unemployment Act. This law set up a second-line income maintenance service centrally administered by the Unemployment Assistance Board. It was a major move in (1) the achievement of sounder financial policies for the unemployment insurance scheme, and (2) the transfer of the relief function from its traditional place with the local community to the central government. This transfer was completed fourteen years later as an integral part of the Beveridge plan for social security. When created the board was an agency specializing in the assistance of the unemployed, but gradually it was given other categories of needs to administer. For example, the Unemployment Assistance Act of 1939 empowered the board to help citizens over sixteen who could prove distress on account of the war.

The final abolition of the ancient poor law was accomplished by the 1948 National Assistance Act. In the words of the act "the existing poor law shall cease to have effect." The law retains the responsibility of the community to support those who are in need but completes the transfer of responsibility from locality to center. It takes away the last vestiges of the workhouse principle and removes most of the objectionable features of the means test.

In the first place the act provides for financial assistance to persons with economic need under the administrative direction of the National Assistance Board with its twelve regional and some 350 local offices. The National Assistance Board is given wide powers and considerable discretion in the exercise of these powers. The board, subject to regulations approved by Parliament, determines whether the person is in need, the nature and extent of his need, and how his need can be relieved, not why he came to be in need or his moral responsibility for his situation.

The principal clients of the board are the aged who find their pensions inadequate or who do not qualify for national insurance and pensions; the unemployed who have exhausted their benefits or who do not qualify; and the unemployables and others who need to be helped for short periods of time. A mild means test which permits the applicant to obtain benefits while owning considerable property is imposed. Benefits are given according to a system of scales or formulas. Assistance is not given except in emergencies without a routine visit from a board's officer who is not a social worker. The law provides for a right of appeal against decisions of the board's officers. The minister of national insurance has general responsibility for the work of the board.

In the second place the act provides for institutional and individual services to be administered by county councils. The county councils provide welfare services, such as old people's homes and institutions for the infirm, blind, deaf, crippled, and mentally deficient. If the condition of residents requires that they have all or part of their way paid, it is furnished by the National Assistance Board. The county is empowered to provide numbers of other social services, including workshops, vocational training, and recreation. The care of orphaned, neglected, and deserted children remains the responsibility of the county council. The Children's Act of 1948 provides that each county council shall appoint a children's committee as the authority for child care.

SOCIAL INSURANCES AND ALLIED SERVICES

The abolition of the poor law could not have occurred without a change in British attitudes toward the causes of widespread poverty and toward the responsibility of the state for its prevention and treatment. A slow but steady change in understanding and attitudes is evidenced in the growth of social legislation for the benefit of those affected by economic crises. Twentieth-century liberalization of public-assistance measures is paralleled by the development of the social insurances, public health, and allied measures.

Let us backtrack now and look at the evolution of the British social insurances, which were greatly expanded and unified as the result of the Beveridge report, *Social Insurance and Allied Services.* This famous report grew out of the work of an interdepartmental committee established by the Rt. Hon. Arthur Greenwood, M.P., minister without portfolio, of which Sir William Beveridge was chairman. Beveridge wrote the report, thus relieving committee members from involvement in issues of high policy which might ultimately have affected their departments.

The report pointed out that the British schemes of social insurances and allied services grew piecemeal. Apart from the poor law, the schemes were the product of less than half a century of effort, beginning with the Workmen's Compensation Act of 1897. That act applied, at first, to a small number of occupations but was made general in 1906. Compulsory health insurance began in 1912. Unemployment insurance, which started for a few industries in 1912, was extended generally in 1920. The first Pensions Act, providing for noncontributory pensions subject to a means test at the age of seventy, was enacted in 1908. In 1925 Parliament passed an act initiating contributory pensions for widows, orphans, and the aged. Unemployment insurance and assistance provisions, as we showed above, were greatly modified in 1934 when a new national service of unemployment assistance was begun.

Along with these measures had gone developments of medical care, particularly in hospitals and other institutions, child welfare services in and before school, and a vast growth of voluntary provisions for death and other contingencies. In this evolution each problem was dealt with separately; hence, the report included a survey of the whole field to show what provisions existed for many different forms of need and then proceeded to make specific proposals for modifications, additions, and integration.

Beveridge adopted three guiding principles for his recommendations:

> 1. Proposals for the future should use the experiences of the past but should not be bound by them. At a time when war is abolishing landmarks of every kind is the opportunity for using experiences in a clear field. A revolutionary moment in the world's history is a time for revolution not for patching.
>
> 2. Social insurance should be treated as one part only of a comprehensive policy of social progress. Social insurance may provide income security and is an attack upon want. But want is only one of five giants on the road to reconstruction and, in some ways, easiest to attack. The others are disease, ignorance, squalor, and idleness.
>
> 3. Social security must be achieved by co-operation between the state and the individual. The state should not stifle incentive, opportunity, responsibility. In establishing a national minimum it should leave room and encouragement for voluntary action by each individual to provide more than that minimum for himself and family.

Abolition of want, according to the report, required improvement of the social insurances against interruption and loss of earning power and, hence, improvement of existing schemes by extension of purposes to cover risks not yet covered, by extension of scope to cover persons then excluded, and by raising the rates of benefit. But abolition of want required other measures too. Beveridge believed (1) that benefits should be adequate to cover a minimum standard of subsistence, hence reducing the need for residual public assistance, but Parliament disagreed; (2) that adjustment of incomes in periods of earning could be accomplished by initiation of a plan for family allowances; (3) that establishment of a comprehensive health and rehabilitation service was basic; and (4) that maintenance of employment, especially avoidance of mass unemployment, was indispensable to a plan for economic security.

The scheme itself embodied six fundamental principles:

> 1. Flat rate of subsistence benefit irrespective of the amount of earnings interrupted by unemployment, disability, or retirement, with exceptions for prolonged disability. The flat rate was the same for all the principal forms of cessation of earning, unemployment, disability, and retirement, with a slightly

higher benefit rate for maternity and widowhood. This differed from the schemes of Germany, the Soviet Union, the United States, and most other countries.

2. Flat rate of contributions irrespective of means. All insured persons, rich or poor, were to pay the same contributions for security. Those with larger means would pay more only to the extent that as taxpayers they paid more to the national treasury and so to the state's share of the social insurance fund.

3. Unification of administrative responsibility. For each insured person there would be a single weekly contribution in respect to all benefits. All contributions would be paid into a single social insurance fund.

4. Adequacy of benefit. The flat rate of benefit proposed was intended to be adequate in amount and in time span.

5. Comprehensiveness. The social insurances were to be comprehensive in respect to both persons covered and their needs. The scheme was not to leave to national assistance or voluntary insurance any risk so general or so uniform that social insurance could be justified.

6. Classification. Social insurance, although unified and comprehensive, was to take account of the different ways of life of different sections of the community, of those dependent on earnings by employment under contract of service, of those earning in other ways, of those rendering unpaid services as housewives, of those not yet earning, and of those past earning.

The Beveridge report and its proposals, although not totally subscribed to by Parliament, formed the basis for the passage of several comprehensive acts: the Family Allowance Act of June 15, 1945; the National Insurance (Industrial Injuries) Act of July 26, 1946; the general National Insurance Act of August 1, 1946; and the National Health Service Act of November 6, 1946. Family allowances have been in effect since August, 1946, and the other aspects of the program since July, 1948.[43] These laws achieved a family allowance plan; the extension of various insurance schemes over the whole community; the widening of unemployment insurance to cover all employed persons, regardless of income or type of work; changes in the character of health protection; provision of a centrally organized subsistence service for all persons whose needs were not covered by one of the specific services and as a method of bringing benefits up to subsistence levels; inclusion of a death benefit as a new form of social insurance; conversion of the existing scheme of workmen's compensation into a social insurance against industrial injuries and disease; introduction of the new principle of universal retirement pensions. A Ministry of National Insurance was established in 1944 to prepare for and administer the anticipated scheme. This minister administers national insurance, industrial injuries insurance, and family allowances and is ministerially responsible for national assistance. The minister of health is responsible for the National Health Service. The minister of labour and national service administers employment exchanges and unemployment benefits as agent for the Ministry of National Insurance.[44]

---

[43] See Mendelsohn, *op. cit.*, for digest of various acts.

[44] *Ibid.*, pp. 45–46.

Family allowances apply to all school-age children except the first, if one parent, at least, lives in Great Britain. Allowances are payable to the mother but may be encashed by either parent and are for a fixed weekly amount of eight shillings. The allowance, which is small, is not intended to cover the full cost of maintenance but, in conjunction with the daily allowance of free milk and free or cheap meals at school, is intended to insure that children shall not be raised in want. In September, 1952, the allowance was raised from five to eight shillings a week. At the beginning of 1952 some 4,800,000 family allowances were being paid to more than three million families at an estimated cost of almost £65,000,000 a year.[45]

The National Industrial Injuries Act of 1946 replaced outmoded workmen's compensation legislation by a scheme of compulsory insurance against personal injury from accidents arising out of and in the course of employment and against prescribed occupational diseases and injuries. Benefits are higher than in the general scheme. There is no link with capacity to earn, but compensation is awarded as a percentage of the maximum pension payable according to the degree of loss of faculty. The three benefits are for injury, disablement, and death.

The provisions of the National Assistance Act of 1948 were discussed above.

The National Insurance Act, providing for a unified and comprehensive scheme, the technical details of which we shall not touch upon, will eventually cover practically everyone in Great Britain for the following: sickness benefit, guardians allowance, death grant, maternity benefits, widows benefits, unemployment benefits, and retirement pensions. Contributions and benefits are linked. Persons in Class I (employed persons) are covered for all benefits; those in Class II (self-employed persons) for all contingencies except unemployment and industrial injury; and those in Class III (persons not gainfully employed) for benefits other than sickness, unemployment, industrial injury, and maternity allowance. Practically everyone is insured or protected as a result of the contributions of himself or another. Contributions have been unified and are payable by one weekly stamp on a single contribution card serving for all purposes.

The British health scheme is unique in its coverage and comprehensiveness. It is not a social insurance. Social insurance under the National Insurance Act is provided for unemployment due to disability. The health scheme is a service available to all who are in the country, without distinction of age, sex, means, employment, place of residence, or nationality. The law permits physicians to stay outside or become a part of the system and, if they wish, to retain private practice also. Further, it allows individuals to choose their doctors. Many problems have been encountered,

[45] "The Cost of Social Services, 1938–1952," *Planning* (London), Vol. 20, No. 354 (June 15, 1953); see also, *Social Security Bulletin*, Vol. 17, No. 2 (February, 1954), pp. 11–13 ff.

some of which have required modifications in legislation and administration. Among them are size and methods of payment to physicians and the correlation of the supply of practitioners with the needs of local areas.

SUMMARY AND CONCLUSIONS

Social or income security measures are now established phenomena in England. They are supported by both conservative and liberal parties. Arguments are over details of procedure and rate of change and not over the responsibility of the state for the services. In the six centuries of English poor-law history, which we have just traced, we see a gradual acceptance of several principles: (1) that most persons are in need because of economic conditions and through no fault of their own; (2) that they have a *right* to a minimum decent standard of living and the state the *obligation* to guarantee it; and (3) that various methods for the prevention of destitution must be encouraged. A framework of repression has been superseded by a structure of pensions, social insurance, social assistance, and such allied services as family allowances, child welfare services, and health services.

Modern British social security developments have done away with the theory of expendables or sacrifices to capitalism and industrialism. It took many centuries for the people to learn that fear of starvation was not an essential means for achieving industrial efficiency. Lord Beveridge took pains to point out that without a high level of production and the full co-operation of every citizen in producing the greatest amount of wealth no country can have genuine social security. Freedom from want must be won. This is the way he said it in the final paragraph of his epochal report: [46]

> Freedom from want cannot be forced on a democracy or given to a democracy. It must be won by them. Winning it needs courage and faith and a sense of national unity; courage to face facts and difficulties and overcome them; faith in our future and in the ideals of fair-play and freedom for which century after century our forefathers were prepared to die; a sense of national unity overriding the interests of any class or section. The plan for Social Security in this Report is submitted by one who believes that in this supreme crisis the British people will not be found wanting, of courage and faith and national unity, of material and spiritual power to play their part in achieving both social security and the victory of justice among nations upon which security depends.

Selected References

ASCHROTT, P. E., *The English Poor Law System: Past and Present,* trans. Preston-Thomas (London, Knight, 1888).

---

[46] Beveridge, *Social Insurance and Allied Services,* p. 172.

ASHLEY, Sir William, *An Introduction to Economic History and Theory* (London, Longmans, Green, 1925).

BEVERIDGE, Sir William H., *Social Insurance and Allied Services* (New York, Macmillan, 1942).

———, *Full Employment in a Free Society* (London, Allen and Unwin, 1944).

———, *Voluntary Action* (London, Allen and Unwin, 1948).

BOOTH, Charles, ed., *Life and Labour of the People of London* (London, Macmillan, 1892–1897), 10 vols.

British Information Services, Reference Division, *Social Services in Britain,* rev. ed. (March, 1953), I.D. 780.

BURNS, Eveline M., *British Unemployment Programs: 1920–1938* (Washington, D.C., Social Research Council, 1941).

CHALMERS, Thomas, *Select Works of Thomas Chalmers* (London, 1856).

COHEN, Emmeline W., *English Social Services, Method, and Growth* (London, Allen and Unwin, 1949).

COLE, Margaret, *Beatrice Webb* (New York, Harcourt, Brace, 1946).

DAVIDSON, Ronald, *British Unemployment Policy* (New York, Longmans, Green, 1938).

DE SCHWEINITZ, Karl, *England's Road to Social Security* (Philadelphia, University of Pennsylvana Press, 1947).

DONNISON, D. V., *The Neglected Child and the Social Services* (Oxford, Blackwell, 1953).

HABER, William, and COHEN, Wilbur J., eds., *Readings in Social Security* (Englewood Cliffs, N.J., Prentice-Hall, 1948).

HALL, M. Penelope, *The Social Services of Modern England* (London, Routledge and Kegan Paul, 1952).

HILL, A. C. C., Jr., and LUBIN, Isador, *The British Attack on Unemployment* (Washington, D.C., Brookings Institution, 1934).

HOBMAN, D. L., *The Welfare State* (Oxford, John Murray, 1953).

LAFITTE, François, *Britain's Way to Social Security* (London, Pilot Press, 1945).

LECKY, William, *History of European Morals from Augustus to Charlemagne* (New York, D. Appleton, 1906).

LEONARD, E. M., *The Early History of English Poor Relief* (Cambridge, The University Press, 1900).

LEYENDECKER, Hilary M., *Problems and Policy in Public Assistance* (New York, Harper, 1955).

MARSH, David C., *National Insurance and Assistance in Great Britain* (London, Pitman, 1951).

MENDELSOHN, Ronald, *Social Security in the British Commonwealth* (London, Athlone Press, 1954).

MILLETT, John D., *The Unemployment Assistance Board* (London, Allen and Unwin, 1940).

MOSS, John, ed., *The Duties of Local Authorities under the National Assistance Act, 1948* (London, Hadden, Best, 1948).

NICHOLLS, Sir George, *A History of the English Poor Law* (London, John Murray, 1854).

ROBSON, William A., ed., *Social Security*, 3d ed. (London, Allen and Unwin, 1948).

ROWNTREE, B. Seebohm, *Poverty: A Study of Town Life* (London, Macmillan, 1903).

WEBB, Sidney, and WEBB, Beatrice, *The Break up of the Poor Law, Being Part One of the Minority Report of the Poor Law Commission* (London, Longmans, Green, 1909).

———, *English Poor Law Policy* (London, Longmans, Green, 1910).

———, *The Prevention of Destitution* (London, Longmans, Green, 1911).

———, *English Local Government: English Poor Law History.* (London, Longmans, Green, 1927–1929), Pt. I (1927) and Pt. II (1929), 3 vols.

White Paper on Social Insurance. Pt. I, Cmd. 6550; Pt. II, Cmd. 6551 (H.M.S.O., 1944).

WICKWAR, H., and WICKWAR, M., *The Social Services: A Historical Survey*, rev. ed. (London, John Lane, 1949).

The student should also consult pertinent English statutes.

CHAPTER 19

General Assistance Legislation I

(IN THE UNITED STATES)

INTRODUCTION

There are five prevailing forms of public assistance in the United States—four types of special assistance and general assistance. The special programs include old-age assistance, aid to dependent children, aid to the blind, and aid to the permanently and totally disabled. These programs are administered by the states, with extensive grants-in-aid from the federal government and under rules and regulations established by the federal Department of Health, Education, and Welfare and by state departments of welfare. Of these four programs all except aid to the permanently and totally disabled, which was not provided for by Congress until 1950, are found in all states. These forms of assistance we shall discuss in later chapters. Numbers of states have added another classification of special assistance, that for indigent service men and their dependents. Federal and state benefits of various kinds for veterans are extensive and generous, although special local veterans' relief programs are small in size and importance. There seems little justification for separating a veterans' relief program from that of general assistance, and in many states there is no such special program. We shall not attempt to describe it as a fifth categorical assistance program.

General assistance is available in all states. As commonly used, general assistance means home relief as contrasted with institutional help. Strictly speaking, it includes both kinds of care, but unless we indicate contrariwise we shall mean noninstitutional care in the form of cash and/or commodity assistance. General assistance laws are largely derived from and are frequently little changed from the old poor law. The early poor laws were intended to provide both outdoor and indoor help for the desperately destitute. General assistance laws today are intended to furnish financial and other kinds of aid for persons for whom no other help or inadequate help from other programs is provided. The past and present policies and practices of general assistance, especially outdoor relief, we shall discuss in this and the following chapter.

UNITS OF ADMINISTRATION

Since the general assistance laws of all of the United States except Louisiana derive from sixteenth- and seventeenth-century England, it is not strange that the American unit of administration traditionally has been the smallest local unit of government. The parish, a political as well as an ecclesiastical unit, was used in England. In the early days of our country, especially in New England, the town, township, or village was the unit of administration. This political unit is still extensively used in several New England and midwestern states. Some states, including those in the far west, require county administration. Some jurisdictions give the county governing body the power to set up a county system of administration, which means that in such states there may be several forms of local administration. Some states provide a state-wide system, with standards set by a state department. In those states where most or all of the responsibility for the administration of general assistance rests with town or county, there is no uniform pattern. Very often, an elected township officer is the administrator of the program, and in innumerable units the case load is too small to warrant employment of staff. Applicants eligible for assistance in one locality may not be in another. The amount of assistance may vary as much among recipients with similar needs and within the same local unit as among different units or states. These disparities are due in large part to absence of state leadership.

General assistance is administered in nearly 10,000 local units throughout the country. In some states it is integrated with all or some other assistance programs at the local level. In others it is administered separately. The amount of financial aid and supervision furnished by state welfare departments to local agencies varies greatly from state to state. In 1954 ten states paid the entire bill for general assistance. In seventeen others it paid one half or more of the costs of assistance. On the other hand, in eleven states the localities paid the entire bill with no help from the state treasury.[1] For the fifty-three jurisdictions, 48.7 per cent of expenditures came from state funds and 51.3 per cent from local funds. State financial assistance may be restricted to particular groups or geographical areas, such as the "unsettled" or "state" poor, or to an "area of special need," or it may be furnished to all persons for whom financial help is necessary.

In December, 1954, about 351,000 persons were receiving general assistance.[2] The average payment per case for June, 1955, was $53.78 com-

---

[1] *Social Security Bulletin,* Vol. 18, No. 9 (September, 1955), p. 76, table 65.
[2] *Ibid.,* p. 74, table 63.

pared with $51.62 for June, 1954. Expenditures for general assistance in 1954 were $198,106,000. The highest state average monthly payment in June, 1955, $78.06 in New York, was over six times the average in Mississippi where it was $12.69, lowest in the country.[3] The disparity between states in their standards of administration of general assistance is even greater than for the special assistances, which we shall subsequently describe. The best standards of administration are found in those states where general assistance and the special assistances are integrated at the local level of government and to which units the state provides supervisory service. Under these circumstances federal and state standards for the special assistances are reflected to a greater or less extent in general assistance. It should be noted that the mere fact of state participation in the financing and administration of general assistance does not necessarily assure an adequate local program.[4]

WHAT IS NEED AND WHO IS A PAUPER?

DESTITUTION

We have seen that under the common law the church and other private institutions and agencies provided for those in need and that the duty to care for the poor was moral and not legal. With the enactment of statutes, both in England and the colonies, some degree of responsibility for needy persons was assumed by the state. For centuries English laws and their American derivatives required that local assistance be given to "the lame, impotent, old, blind, and such others among them, being poor and not able to work," as were in need of assistance. The able-bodied poor in need of help were forced to work.[5] The statutes did not define what need or destitution was; nor did they provide adequate methods of forcing public officials to come to the aid of needy persons.

An English authority, William A. Robson, in a 1932 appearance before a British Royal Commission on Unemployment Insurance, observed that it was a remarkable fact that during the many years of British poor-law legislation and administration, no authoritative definition of destitution had been issued. He cited one offered to the Royal Commission on the Poor Laws (1905–1909): [6]

---

[3] *Ibid.*, p. 26, table 17.

[4] Felix M. Gentile and Donald S. Howard, *General Assistance: With Special Reference to Practice in 47 Localities of the United States, 1946–1947* (New York, American Association of Social Workers, 1949), p. 33; Eveline M. Burns, *The American Social Security System* (Boston, Houghton Mifflin, 1949), p. 393; Hilary M. Leyendecker, *Problems and Policy in Public Assistance* (New York, Harper, 1955), pp. 293–295.

[5] 43 Eliz. I, c. 2 (1601).

[6] "Unemployment Insurance and Poor Relief: Further Testimony Before the Royal Commission on Unemployment Insurance," *Social Service Review* (March, 1934), p. 110, contains testimony given by William A. Robson.

Destitution, when used to describe the condition of a person as subject for relief, implies that he is for the time being without material resources (1) directly available and (2) appropriate for satisfying his physical needs (a) whether actually existing or (b) likely to arise immediately. By physical needs in this definition are meant such needs as must be satisfied (1) in order to maintain life or (2) in order to obviate, mitigate or remove causes endangering life or likely to endanger life or impair health or bodily fitness for self-support.

This definition implies a more liberal relief policy than public officials in either England or the United States have generally applied or than the courts have approved. Ordinarily, relief has been given for present and not for future or anticipated needs and, then, on a low subsistence or less eligibility level and not for the protection and preservation of health, morals, and morale. For example, the Wisconsin Supreme Court in 1910 held that it was a question for the jury to decide whether a family of three was poor and indigent enough to be entitled to relief when it owned an equity of $275.00 in a homestead, the wife had $7.00 cash, the husband had some credit at the grocery, and all were sick with typhoid.[7] The court pointed out that a distinction exists between that degree of poverty and indigence which entitles one to support and that which qualifies one for temporary relief in an emergency. In an earlier Wisconsin case the court held that if a person has property not absolutely indispensable for daily use he must apply it to his support by sale or security.[8]

Until the depression of the 1930's, with its emergency legislation, many jurisdictions considered the word *poor* under the poor law to be synonymous with *destitute,* which denotes extreme want or helplessness. The courts rejected the idea that any effort should be made by officials to prevent destitution by present planning. A considerable number of states have liberalized their general assistance laws to permit the holding of insurance policies with cash surrender value of a maximum amount, the ownership of a homestead, equity in a home, and cash assets.

Although there is less strictness today in the definition of poverty in some states and by some administrators than before the depression, relaxation is by no means universal. It is not difficult even now to find local officials who know as little concerning the applicants for general assistance and the extent of their needs as did the officials in the Leslie County Court of Kentucky in 1925. At that time the Kentucky statutes provided that it was the duty of the county court to furnish funds for the support of paupers. The court was composed of the county judge *ex officio* and the magistrates or squires, one from each magisterial district, usually seven or eight in number. The court met three or four times a year and decided routine matters of the county's business, including poor claims.

---

[7] *Coffeen v. Town of Preble,* 142 Wis. 183, 125 N.W. 954 (1910). A considerable number of Wisconsin cases are referred to in this chapter and the next, since they are familiar to the author and are undoubtedly typical of those found in most states.

[8] *Rhine v. Sheboygan,* 82 Wis. 352, 52 N.W. 444 (1892).

The following illustrations from the records of this Kentucky county reveal what have been and still are typical methods of determining the needs of poor persons for centuries and the limited extent to which relief has been granted, regardless of the extent of distress: [9]

Woman, about 50: asked pay for caring for sick neighbor. No help granted.

Man, aged 55: able-bodied, owned 68 acres of land; asked money for caring for mother. Allowed $10.

Woman, about 45: 2 sons, aged 14, crippled; 2 daughters; no support. No relief granted.

Man, about 70: claimed he had nothing to live on nor anyone to help him—"just me and the old woman." (Known as a moonshiner and about 30 years previous had served time in penitentiary for stealing.) Allowed $20.

Single woman, about 30: lived below the county seat with her father; epileptic; granted $10 last term of court. Allowed $15.

Gentile and Howard in their study of the administration of general assistance, with special reference to practices in forty-seven localities in twelve states, cited numerous instances of inadequate and niggardly general assistance administration. They reported local agencies granting entire families as little as $2.50 for a whole month. Under these circumstances persons suffering from tuberculosis or cardiac diseases were forced to disregard medical advice in order to eke out an existence for their families. Eventually, they might land in a hospital, where the cost to the localities was many times that of an adequate grant. In a county where general assistance grants averaged $2.75 per person per month, the administration reported that there were no other organized facilities for help. One administrator boasted to the investigators that whenever he saw a recipient of general assistance driving a car or visiting a tavern, he wrote himself a letter about such a person and signed it "The Citizens' Committee." The letter was alleged to represent citizens' objections to the expenditure of tax funds for assistance to such a person. When the individual again asked for help the letter was presented as evidence that the community would not tolerate further help. If, after repeated refusals, the applicant still persisted in requests for help, the officer informed him that the "citizens' committee" would meet again in two weeks. If the applicant was willing to sign a statement promising, in the event that he was given relief, not to visit a tavern or drive his car, the officer promised to see what could be done. This officer expressed no concern as to what happened to the man's family in the interval.[10]

THE POOR AND THE PAUPER

The early poor relief laws designated recipients of assistance as *paupers* and often deprived them of basic civil rights. Generally, the newer

---

[9] Arthur Estabrook, "Poor Relief in Kentucky," *Social Service Review* (June, 1929), pp. 226–227.

[10] Gentile and Howard, *op. cit.*,

special assistance statutes do not refer to paupers, and some states have deleted the word from their general assistance laws. Unless there is a penalty imposed upon the individual receiving relief because he is a pauper, there is no *legal* reason for removing the word from the statutes. However, because of associations with the condition the word should be eliminated from the statutes. Just as many states have removed the word *bastard* and replaced it with the term *child of unmarried parents,* so the word *pauper* should be erased and replaced by some phrase with no context of opprobrium, such as *person receiving public assistance,* or *public charge.*

Since the statutes of several states still refer to paupers and the courts frequently talk about them, we shall look into the confusion caused by loose usage of the words *pauper* and *poor.* The American law encyclopedias recognize that a distinction is sometimes made between the *poor,* or *indigent,* and the *pauper,* but admit that for legal purposes the terms are often interchangeable. The poor person may be one who is not rich, or he may be one who is so destitute or helpless as to be dependent on public or private assistance. Likewise, the pauper may be one who is destitute, or one who is actually receiving public aid. Many persons, when speaking of the pauper, still use the term as one of censure. They mean that in their judgment a particular person has a helpless or "sponging" attitude. In legal language the term generally means someone dependent upon public aid. It is usually held by the courts that a poor person who is cared for by the voluntary action of friends, relatives, or private agencies is not a pauper. This was not the definition, however, used in an 1887 Wisconsin case which quoted Webster as follows: "A pauper means a poor person, especially one so indigent as to depend on charity for maintenance; or one supported by some public provision." In this situation the man concerned was held to be a pauper under both clauses of the definition, since from 1872 to 1881 he was a public charge, from 1881 to 1885 he was cared for by a private individual, and after 1885 he was again a public charge.[11]

Not all who are wholly or partially dependent upon public assistance for livelihood are considered to be paupers. Some statutes, exclusive of the poor laws, are not clear as to whether persons receiving public care and assistance are paupers, with the disabilities sometimes attendant upon that condition, or whether they are "favored" and "privileged" poor. For example, is a prisoner a pauper? Is a person who, because of sudden illness or calamity, lacks means to secure medical attention a pauper? Are families of veterans which require help in times of war or afterward paupers? Are persons who need assistance because of quarantine paupers? Because the statutes are not clear on these matters, recourse must be had to the courts. The newer special assistance statutes intend a more

[11] *Town of Saukville* v. *Town of Grafton,* 68 Wis. 192, 31 N.W. 719 (1887).

liberal interpretation of what constitutes need than the old poor laws and do not set out to penalize persons who, for one reason or another, must have public assistance.

There is no legal definition of "paupers" or "poor persons" that is uniform for all states. The following law encyclopedia definition, which seems to include both the able-bodied and the incapacitated, does not differentiate between those who receive relief under the poor law and those who obtain it under other public-assistance statutes: [12]

> it may be said that a person is chargeable as a pauper, when he is without means, and unable, on account of some bodily or mental infirmity, or other unavoidable cause, to earn a livelihood, and has no kindred in the state liable under the statute for his support, or whose kindred within the state are of insufficient ability or fail or refuse to maintain him.

The only way that an interested person can determine who is a pauper and what the consequences are of being so labeled is to consult the statutes, reported cases, opinions of the attorney general, and administrative rulings of each jurisdiction.

DUTIES AND LIABILITIES OF GENERAL ASSISTANCE UNITS AND OFFICIALS

THE RIGHT TO RELIEF

The dispensation of some form of relief is mandatory in most states. In a few the law is optional. In some states, outdoor care is mandatory but indoor care is not; in others, the reverse is true.[13] Wisconsin, which in some respects has as liberal a relief law as any in the country, provides that assistance *shall* be given to any poor and indigent person lawfully settled in any town, village, or city. The county, if it so decides, may provide for a county system of public-assistance administration. The statute further provides that the county may (not shall) have the care of all poor persons in said county who have no legal settlement in the town, city, or village where they may be, and if it elects to do so shall designate or establish an agency to administer the same.[14] Such an enactment does not mean, of course, that local officials always perform the duty imposed upon them under the statutes, but it does mean that the legislature has recognized the principle of responsibility for needy persons, whether settled or unsettled.

If the statute requires that assistance be dispensed, does that mean

---

[12] 21 R.C.L. 706; see also, 48 C.J. 428.

[13] Work Projects Administration, *Digest of Poor Relief Laws of the Several States and Territories as of May 1, 1936* (Washington, D.C., G.P.O., 1936); Robert C. Lowe, *State Public Welfare Legislation*, WPA Research Monograph (Washington, D.C., G.P.O., 1939), No. 20.

[14] Wis. Stat., 1955, c. 49.02(1,2,3).

that poor and needy persons have a legal right to relief? According to Edith Abbott, an authority on the subject, the answer must be "yes and no."[15] Although the poor laws may give a right to relief to persons in need and the duty to dispense relief may be mandatory, it remains a fact that very often the right and duty are not enforced or enforceable. This may be the case because the administering official determines that the extent of need does not justify aid, or because the poor person has not the income to employ efficient legal service, or because there are not funds to supply the need. Public assistance, in other words, is prevalently furnished as a duty rather than an obligation, and the ministerial duty of determining the extent of relief and its character has been given to officials who may have little regard for twentieth-century standards of living.

LEGAL REMEDIES

There are difficulties in the way of establishing a legal right to relief or of enforcing the duty of dispensing relief. It is well established that some designated official must determine who is eligible for assistance and what degree of need there must be before assistance can be granted. Any legal action by an individual against a poor-law official to compel him to grant relief or for damages because of denial of relief has little chance of success, although cases can be found in which a poor person who has been neglected by officials has maintained a successful action under proper circumstances; particularly is this true where the officer has assumed care in a public institution.[16]

In a striking Iowa case, neither the county nor the overseer of the poor was liable for the loss of a transient pauper's legs, even though the statute required temporary relief and proper attention had not been given. In this instance an itinerant woodsman named Wood, whose legs had been frozen, was denied anything but emergency care by the poor-law officials where he was found. He was then passed on to a second town, which, in time, passed him on to a third community, which found it necessary to amputate his neglected legs. He sued the county for damages; but the supreme court held that the unfortunate man could not recover because the county and its agent, the overseer, were not liable for negligent performance of the statutory duty requiring that temporary relief be given.[17] The court could not close, however, without the suggestion that the practice of shifting foreign paupers from one county to another was a disgrace to our civilization and should be remedied by new legislation. This case bears out the following theory:[18]

[15] Edith Abbott, "Is There a Legal Right to Relief?" *Social Service Review* (June, 1938), pp. 266–276.
[16] *Flower* v. *Allen*, 5 Cowper 654 (N.Y. 1825); *Meier* v. *Paulus*, 70 Wis. 165, 35 N.W. 301 (1887); *Tozeland* v. *West Ham Union*, 1 K.B. 538 (1906).
[17] *Wood* v. *Boone Co*, 153 Iowa 92, 133 N.W. 377 (1911).
[18] 21 R.C.L. 713.

A poor district is an instrumentality of government, and the furnishing of aid to the poor is a governmental function. It is a general rule that where a governmental duty rests on a state or any of its instrumentalities, there is absolute immunity in respect to all acts or agencies, and consequently there can be no liability of a district to a pauper for failure to furnish relief, no matter how grievous the consequences or for the negligence of its officers in furnishing relief.

It is an equally well-settled rule of law that neglect, failure to perform, or omission of the performance of a duty by a public official is a crime for which he may be indicted, convicted, and punished. Thus, administrators of assistance programs are criminally liable for *willful* neglect or refusal to discharge their official duties to paupers under their charge; but it is obvious that cases of this kind seldom reach the courts, as district attorneys are reluctant to initiate such actions.

Even though the poor person himself may have little legal recourse for remedying his situation, another person or district may have cause of action against the district or officials; but reimbursement, no matter how just the claim, cannot be secured without compliance with the statutes.[19] In another Iowa case involving the same man, Wood, the county which provided humane care attempted to collect over $700.00 and costs from the negligent county. The Iowa Supreme Court upheld the lower court and denied recovery. It held that there was no obligation, since whatever obligation existed was statutory and there was no statute authorizing reimbursement of one county by another for aid given the unsettled poor. The only way, therefore, that Cerro Gordo County could collect from Boone County was on an implied promise to repay, which promise could not be inferred since relief dispensation was entirely statutory. That the Boone County officers avoided a manifest duty in neglecting to care for the dire needs of Wood did not charge it with the expense incurred by another county in giving him decent care. There was no recovery.[20]

The question of the district's liability also arises frequently when services are rendered by third persons, such as physicians. It has been held that a doctor cannot recover for his services if he was not employed by the proper officers; but the general rule is that in case of emergency, a doctor may hold the district liable, although he acted without the request or consent of the statutorily designated official.[21] The courts frequently have to determine whether the situation was an emergency and how long the emergency lasted. The important question in such cases

[19] *Patrick* v. *Baldwin,* 109 Wis. 342, 85 N.W. 274 (1901).

[20] *Cerro Gordo County* v. *Boone County,* 152 Iowa 692, 133 N.W. 132 (1911).

[21] *Patrick* v. *Town of Preble,* 142 Wis. 183, 125 N.W. 954 (1910); *Newcomer* v. *Jefferson Township,* 181 Ind. 1, 103 N.E. 843 (1914); *Sheridan Co.* v. *Denebrink,* 15 Wyo. 342 (1907), for opposite position; but in earlier cases, see *Hull* v. *Oneida Co.,* 19 Johns 259 (N.Y. 1821), and *Morgan Co.* v. *Seaton,* 122 Ind. 521, 24 N.E. 213 (1890).

is the nature of the obligation. If it is merely moral, no action can be maintained. If, however, it is an absolute legal obligation, then the law implies a promise and an action can be sustained.[22] Some states have enacted legislation to protect hospitals and physicians in emergency situations.

Sometimes persons other than physicians give emergency care. Have they a right to collect from the district for care given persons in desperate need? In an early Wisconsin case, to which further reference will be made, an old woman had been removed from her almshouse home and sent to her children, who refused to care for her. When a third person took her in and cared for her, the court held that the county was liable to him for her maintenance.[23] When the courts give approval to this type of situation, it is again on the theory of an express or implied contract. Creditors who have been authorized by the proper officials to furnish goods to the poor person can bring an action to collect, and the county board must pay. In an Illinois case, it was held that even though the local government was without funds, the overseer could pledge the credit of the town and the creditor could collect.[24]

Where suffering is widespread, there remains the possible remedy of mandamus against recalcitrant officials who refuse to carry out the provisions of the statute.[25] In 1937 the Nebraska court upheld the district court in its ruling that the commissioners of Douglas County (Omaha) could not be mandamused to feed the hungry, for there were no available funds and credit was exhausted.[26] The Washington court took the opposite position in a similar case. The commissioners in Seattle appropriated funds in excess of the statutory debt limit to care for the hordes of needy, and the court upheld the commissioners' action on the ground that there was a duty to care for the poor and that when thousands of families were in need, an emergency existed sufficient to justify obtaining funds in excess of the statutory limit.[27]

Innumerable cases have reached the courts on the right of the poor person to relief and the duty of the district to supply it. Inconsistency of opinion in the same jurisdiction is frequent, and some jurisdictions have been more liberal than others in their interpretation of the statutes. Generally, in the past the statutes have been strictly construed and in the absence of explicit statutory provisions the district and its officials

---

[22] *Trustees of Cincinnati Township* v. *Ogden,* 5 Hammond (Ohio) 23 (1831).

[23] *Mappes* v. *Iowa Co.,* 47 Wis. 31, 1 N.W. 359 (1879).

[24] *Town of Kankakee* v. *McGraw,* 178 Ill. 74, 52 N.E. 1128 (1899).

[25] Abbott, *loc. cit.,* p. 271.

[26] *St. ex. rel. Boxberger* v. *Burns et al.,* 132 Neb. 31, 270 N.W. 656 (1937).

[27] *Rummens* v. *Evans et al.,* 168 Wash. 527, 13 P 2d 26 (1932); see a decision reached by the Vermont court in *St.* v. *Dwyer,* 108 Vt. 303, 187 Atl. 522 (1936), where it ruled that if relief were necessary, the duty to render it was compulsory, regardless of whether those who needed it were on strike.

have been protected, often to the disadvantage of the poor person. With the depression of the 1930's and a new group of poor persons there was some change in the practice of relief officials concerning the duty of the public to provide decent relief and the right of the needy person to receive it. Under the special public-assistance provisions of the Social Security Act a needy person denied assistance can take his case to an appeal body. The general assistance laws do not provide this recourse. However, in those states where the administration of general assistance is integrated with that of the special assistances some effects of the right to appeal are undoubtedly felt.

OBLIGATIONS OF RELATIVES

Most American jurisdictions have statutory provisions regarding support of the dependent by relatives.[28] This is true for both special and general assistance programs. The majority of states with provisions for relative responsibility derive their authority from general support laws, a sizeable number from the general assistance statutes, and a few from administrative regulations. The extent to which litigation is employed to enforce the obligation of relatives to support varies greatly between programs and agencies in the same state and between states. Public assistance agencies make limited use of courts to compel relatives to support applicants and recipients, since it is an expensive process and a grueling one for the dependent person. However, judicial action is involved in many cases under all public-assistance programs.

Some states make the obligation of relatives to support primary, and only if the relatives cannot support is the administrative unit to come in and assume responsibility. In some states the reverse is true.[29] In Wisconsin the community has the obligation to furnish assistance if needed, whether or not there are financially able relatives; subsequently authorities can take action to force the relatives to support. In *Mappes* v. *Iowa Co.* the court held: "The primary obligation remains—in this case upon the county—notwithstanding a remedy is afforded to enforce contribution on the part of relatives." [30] In this instance a woman about one hundred years old was forcibly removed from an almshouse by the officials of that institution and returned to her children, who left her on a public street. She was eventually harbored by a stranger, who charged the county with her support. The court, in taking leave of the case, was

[28] Lowe, *op. cit.*, pp. 63–67; Edith Abbott, "Abolish the Poor Laws," *Social Service Review* (March, 1934), p. 15; Minnesota Legislative Research Committee, *Public Assistance Policies among the States: 1951* (August, 1952), No. 47.

[29] *Della Hendrickson* v. *Town of Queen*, 149 Minn. 79, 182 N.W. 952 (1921); *Board of Commissioners of Tipton County* v. *Brown*, 4 Ind. App. 288, 30 N.E. 925 (1892).

[30] 47 Wis. 31, 1 N.W. 359 (1879).

"constrained to say, that the ingratitude of the children of this aged pauper, and the neglect of the public authorities in discharging their duties in respect to her, are complimentary neither to the affection and filial duty of the former, nor to the humanity and public duty of the latter. 'Man's inhumanity to man' is not a mere figment of poetic genius." [31]

Which relatives must assist are not always designated; nor are they always the same from state to state. The relatives usually required to assist when able are husband, wife, father, mother, children, sometimes grandparents and grandchildren, and brothers and sisters.[32] Only a few states have provisions regarding the responsibility of stepparents for the support of minor stepchildren. A few jurisdictions have provisions that relatives, or certain designated ones, are not liable if indigency is caused by bad conduct or intemperance or if the dependent person has deserted and neglected his financial responsibilities.

Persons charged with support of their relatives may be ordered to do so only when they are of sufficient ability, and what that is depends on the circumstances.[33] The matters to be considered are present state of the property, present indebtedness, present income and reasonable expenses, present number in the family, their health, and ability to labor.[34] A statutory liability imposed upon kindred to support their indigent relatives can be enforced only by means of the remedy provided by statute.[35] The right to prosecute is usually determined by the statute, and only the persons designated by the statute can bring action.[36] The order or decree of support must be complete, and unless the statute limits the amount of support, the court may specify in its order a fair and reasonable sum, according to the financial ability of the relative. Opinion differs as to what is fair and reasonable.

The Federal Social Security Act does not require the states to insist that relatives, when able, contribute to the recipients of the special assistances. A large proportion of the states, however, have such a provision. It is logical, since the standards of assistance are higher for these programs than for general assistance, that the standards of exemptions for relatives should also be higher. The high costs of the special assistances, especially for the aged and for dependent children, have caused legislators to examine policies and administrative practices concerning relative responsibility for all classifications of dependents. Numbers of

---

[31] *Mappes* v. *Iowa Co., ibid.*

[32] *Asa Howard* v. *The Trustees of Whetstone Township,* 10 Ohio 365 (1841); *Guardians of the Poor* v. *William P. Smith,* 6 Pa. L.J. 433 (1847); *John Clinton* v. *Benjamin H. Laning and Isaiah C. Laning,* 61 Mich. 355 (1886).

[33] *Matter of Conklin,* 78 Misc. 269, 139 N.Y. Supp. 449 (1912).

[34] *Colebrook* v. *Stewartstown,* 30 N.H. 9 (1854)

[35] *Saxville* v. *Bartlett,* 126 Wis. 655, 105 N.W. 1052 (1906).

[36] *Gray* v. *Spalding,* 58 N.H. 345 (1878).

legislatures tightened their laws on this subject in the 1950's. For example, in 1953 the Wisconsin legislature provided that upon failure of relatives to support any class of dependent person, the administering authority shall submit to the district attorney a report of its findings, and upon receipt thereof, the district attorney shall, within sixty days, apply to the county court where the dependent person resides for an order to compel maintenance. The county court has the ultimate responsibility for determining ability to pay, as it has had for years, but the district attorney is now expected to carry through on the enforcement procedure when public-assistance administrators make a complaint.[37] If local agencies are to decide fairly concerning whether relatives shall help, and, if so, how much, they must have access to standards. State agencies are developing criteria and formulas to be applied to the relatives of applicants for the security aids. Unless general assistance is administered under a local integrated system or a state-wide system there are many local agencies which will not employ objective standards for determining financial ability of relatives.

ELIGIBILITY REQUIREMENTS AND CONSEQUENCES OF RECEIPT OF RELIEF

ELIGIBILITY

All applicants for all types of public assistance must establish eligibility. The requirements of eligibility differ for each type of public assistance. Eligibility for general assistance may be denied because of (1) limiting settlement or residence requirements; (2) receipt of other forms of public assistance; (3) employable persons in the family; (4) possession of assets; (5) unacceptable behavior; (6) lack of citizenship.[38] The law of settlement is a difficult one, and we shall discuss it in some detail in the next chapter.

Statutory provisions on these matters vary greatly in their explicitness. Often there is no statutory requirement, but one is imposed by administering officials. Many statutes forbid the receipt of more than one kind of public assistance except, perhaps for medical care. Local units without legislative authority sometimes deny help to the able-bodied. This denial reflects the old position that the well and healthy poor are eager to avoid work. Standards of employability and methods of determining it vary. In general, the localities which deny general assistance as a matter of principle to employable persons provide aid in case of temporary illness or accident. Sometimes help is given to the wife and children of the employable man, but often not. Some communities deny

---

[37] Wis. Stat., 1955, c. 52.01.

[38] Burns, *op. cit.*, p. 341.

general assistance if there are any resources whatsoever of income and property. Others make grants to persons in supplementation of full-time earnings. Some place limitations upon the granting of help to stipulated groups of individuals, such as drunkards, vagrants, and the immoral. Citizenship requirements during the nineteenth-century period of heavy immigration inflicted hardship upon many persons. Today, general assistance, and not the old-fashioned workhouse or almshouse, is intended to meet the financial needs of persons not otherwise provided for. Many eligibility requirements are therefore completely anachronistic.

The ultimate test of eligibility is need. After all other statutory eligibility requirements have been complied with, there is still the necessity of determining whether there is need and, if so, how much. In a large percentage of the units administering general assistance, determination of need is made without the use of accurate and scientific budget devices. In most instances, decision undoubtedly is based on a combination of factors, including availability of funds, acuteness of need, public opinion, and the likes and dislikes of the administrative official. In some larger municipalities and in some states, examination of need for general assistance is as carefully and scientifically determined as that for the special assistance programs. This implies the employment of competent personnel. Such personnel proceeds on the assumption that the needs of the residual group are as real as those of any other group, that all applicants have feelings of one kind or another about applying for and receiving help, that financial aid should be given as needed and as determined by a scientifically established minimum budget, and that social services should be available and used.

CONSEQUENCES OF APPLICATION FOR AND RECEIPT OF RELIEF

The legislation of some states makes easy the continuation of the old poor-law position that the applicant shall be denied help if at all possible. For example, some states require an affidavit confirming financial conditions, and others the taking of a "pauper's oath." The constitutions or statutes of several states deprive the pauper of his right to vote or hold office. In some states the provision applies only to those receiving institutional care of a specified kind. Conversely, some states through their constitutions or by statute provide, for example, that no person shall be deemed to have lost his legal residence by reason of absence because of living in an almshouse, or other kind of institution, or that he shall not lose his civil rights because he receives assistance.

The states generally have statutory provisions concerning penalties for fraudulent receipt and use of public assistance. Penalties should be imposed upon any who misuse public funds, but statutes should not impose unreasonable restrictions upon those seeking and obtaining public assistance. Ultimately, what happens to those who falsely obtain or misuse public-assistance funds depends upon the attitudes of the public officials administering the program and the citizens whom they serve. Such provisions of public-assistance laws as removal orders and publication of names of recipients are outmoded and should be repealed. Provisions regarding the sale, assignment, and disposition of real and personal property can be unreasonably enforced, as can also the provisions concerning enforcement of relative responsibility and legal settlement. It appears that there can be no assurance of fair and reasonable administration of general assistance in the absence of a state-wide system of advice and supervision given by a competent professional staff and with at least partial state payment of costs.

For Selected References, see those following Chapter 20.

CHAPTER 20

General Assistance Legislation II

(IN THE UNITED STATES)

INTRODUCTION

Our primary concern in this chapter is with the outmoded settlement provisions of general assistance legislation.[1] Most unsettled persons who need public aid are without the required period of residence because they are hunting work or satisfying or healthful communities in which to live and not, as many still believe, because they are vagrants, or hoboes, or bums. These people who are searching for something and some place to better their circumstances may encounter financial difficulties before they achieve their objectives. Then they must ask for help, frequently to be told they do not belong. Free population movement characterizes our American culture. It is partially responsible for our fabulous growth in agriculture, industry, commerce. The wealth of our country today, as in the past, is dependent upon mobility. Despite this acknowledged fact, our relief laws continue to punish energetic persons who move for commendable reasons.

Population movement reaches unprecedented proportions in the crisis periods of depressions and wars. In the depression decade of the 1930's

---

[1] Myron Falk, *Settlement Laws* (New York, American Association of Social Workers, 1948), "Settlement Laws: A Welfare Anachronism," *Public Welfare,* Vol. 3, No. 6 (May, 1945), pp. 125–128, and "Social Action on Settlement Laws," *Social Service Review,* Vol. 18, No. 3 (September, 1944), pp. 288–294; Margaret Creech, "Migrants, Transients, and Travelers," *Social Work Year Book: 1954,* pp. 355–360; Eleanor J. Davis, "This Question of Length of Residence," *Public Welfare,* Vol. 7, Nos. 8 and 9 (August–September, 1949); U.S. National Resources Planning Board, Committee on Long-Range Work and Relief Policies, *Security, Work, and Relief Policies,* Report for 1942, 78th Cong., H. Doc. 128 (Washington, D.C., G.P.O., 1943), Pt. 3; Louis P. Kurtis, "A Local Director Looks at Settlement," *Public Welfare,* Vol 3, No. 7 (July, 1945), pp. 149–152; Federal Interagency Committee on Migrant Labor, *Migrant Labor —A Human Problem: Report and Recommendations* (Washington, D.C., G.P.O., 1947); John N. Webb and Malcolm Brown, *Migrant Families,* WPA Research Monograph (Washington, D.C., G.P.O., 1938), No. 18, p. xxv; Dorothea Lange and Paul S. Taylor, *An American Exodus: A Record of Human Erosion* (New York, Reynal and Hitchcock, 1939); Carey McWilliams, *Factories in the Field: The Story of Migratory Farm Labor in California* (Boston, Little, Brown, 1939).

hordes of people migrated in unsuccessful search for work. When they could not find it, an appreciable proportion required public assistance. When they sought help, they were often rebuffed and insulted. They might be removed to their place of legal settlement or threatened with jailing for vagrancy unless they moved. Occasionally, they might be given help, with or without any strings attached. States like California, overburdened with the dimensions of the migrant worker group, stationed police patrols at the borders to warn away those obviously without resources. John Steinbeck, in his eloquent novel, *Grapes of Wrath,* concentrated all the tragedies of the migrant unemployed family in the Joads. Federal agencies relieved some of the direst distress of these people.

In a war period population movement is accelerated by the gravitation of millions to war industry and military activities. The Bureau of the Census estimated that between December, 1941, and March, 1945, civilian migrants reached a total of more than 15,000,000.[2] (A migrant was considered a person who in March, 1945, was living in a county different from that in which he lived in December, 1941.) From April 1, 1950, to April 1, 1951, more than 31,000,000 people moved from their home towns. About one sixth of these moved between states, and about one fifth within the same county. About 4,000,000 more people moved during the year ending April, 1951, than in either of the two preceding years. California's growth from migration into the state was two and a half times that from the natural increase of excess of births over deaths. On the other hand, several states, such as Mississippi, Oklahoma, North Dakota, and Arkansas, suffered a migration away from the state which was not offset by natural increase.[3]

Communities which require a large amount of migratory agricultural or other short-time labor, or which undergo rapid expansion because of industrial or military installations, face the necessity of supplying new and expensive services. They include education, sanitary and medical resources, housing, recreation, police protection, relief. Resistance is strong to meeting these costs from local taxes. In the absence of special help from state and/or federal funds such services may be woefully inadequate. Hostility to the unsettled poor is especially acute, and the restrictive provisions of general assistance laws encourage niggardly programs. The Tolan Congressional Committee, investigating national defense migration during World War II, heard testimony on the multiple welfare problems aggravated by military conditions. One welfare director appearing before the committee emphasized that the problems arising out of the wartime situation were intensifications of the normal problems that welfare departments have to face. When there is unem-

[2] Arthur J. Altmeyer, "People on the Move: Effect of Residence Requirements for Public Assistance," *Social Security Bulletin,* Vol. 9, No. 1 (January, 1946), pp. 3–7.

[3] Margaret Creech, *loc. cit.,* pp. 355–360.

ployment or inability to work and no family resources, the social agency is called upon to provide assistance.[4] State and municipal welfare directors were in agreement that if wartime dependency was to be adequately met, there should be federal help with general assistance and a uniform settlement law. These goals have not yet been realized.

President Truman's Commission on Migratory Labor, in 1951, pointed out that there were many problems associated with the phenomenon of population movement. It indicated that solutions revolved around such matters as the use made of alien contract labor; restrictions on "wetbacks," or Mexican labor; recruitment of farm labor; employment management and labor relations; employment, wages, incomes; housing; child labor; education; health, safety, and welfare.[5] It is not our intent to analyze the multiple problems and solutions associated with moving populations, so we shall content ourselves with this brief statement that they exist. Our purpose for the inclusion is to show the inconsistencies in our governmental policies—at the same time that we encourage the free movement of labor we simultaneously penalize some parts of it. We turn our attention now to settlement and residence laws, a contributor to the miseries of a proportion of the moving population.

SETTLEMENT LAW IN PLYMOUTH COLONY AND MASSACHUSETTS

The settlement provisions of the general assistance laws determine financial responsibility for the poor. They are an outgrowth of the old belief that everyone belongs somewhere and that no locality is under obligation to provide for those who do not belong. No two states have identical general assistance legislation or precisely the same settlement and residence provisions. Massachusetts has a long history and a reasonably representative one, so we shall refer to the principles regarding settlement early established in that state.[6]

In 1620 the first village community of white persons in New England was established at Plymouth. The "pinch of poverty" and the difficulties of existence were reflected in the early legislation of the group. In 1636 Plymouth Colony enacted "that no pson coming from other ptes bee allowed an inhabitant of this jurisdiction but by the approbacon of the

[4] U.S. House of Representatives, *National Defense Migration: Hearing Before the Select Committee Investigating National Defense Migration,* 77th Cong., 2d sess., pursuant to H. Res. 113 (Washington, D.C., G.P.O., 1942), Pt. 25, pp. 9807, 9812.

[5] President's Commission on Migratory Labor, *Migratory Labor in American Agriculture* (Washington, D.C., G.P.O., 1951); see also, Howard E. Thomas and Florence Taylor, *Migrant Farm Labor in Colorado: A Study of Migratory Families* (New York, National Child Labor Committee, 1951).

[6] This history is taken from Robert W. Kelso, *The History of Public Poor Relief in Massachusetts: 1620–1720* (Boston, Houghton, Mifflin, 1922), pp. 39–40.

gou and two of the magistrates att least." This regulation was quickly followed by Boston town authorities, who, in 1636, "ordered that no townsmen shall entertain any strangers in their houses for above 14 dayes without leave from those that are appointed to order the townes businesses." Another safeguard against the influx of poor persons was that no owners of property should sell to a stranger without approval of the authorities.

Poverty and incompatibility of religions were two causes for strict regulations concerning the stranger, but even more important was the custom of English poor-law officials of dumping their undesirables upon the colonies. This method began to be used by English authorities about 1617, the earliest cases being sent to Virginia; to this colony between 1617 and 1619 some one hundred dependent children were shipped from London. Paupers, able-bodied as well as sick and disabled, criminals, and undesirables of all kinds were sent from England to the new America.

To meet the situation, Plymouth Colony sought to deal with the problem of "inhabitancy" or residence. By an act of 1642 each town had the obligation to support its own poor, and the status of "inhabitant" was attached to any person who remained quietly settled in the locality without exception being taken by the town within three months after his coming. This law furnished the standard for many years. When the Massachusetts, Plymouth, and Connecticut colonies were consolidated under the Articles of Confederation of 1672, there was an express provision retaining the three-month rule of inhabitancy, warning out, and town responsibility.

These various practices regarding inhabitancy or settlement were incorporated in the 1794 legislation. The basic features of this codification were:

1. A married woman has the settlement of her husband if he has any; if not, she retains her own at the time of her marriage.
2. If the unsettled husband of a settled wife requires aid from the state, he shall receive it in the place of her settlement, the state reimbursing.
3. Legitimate children follow and have the settlement of their father, if he has any, until they gain one for themselves; if he has none, then they follow the mother in like manner.
4. Illegitimate children follow the mother's settlement at the time of their birth if she had any: but no child gains settlement by birth if neither parent had a settlement in the place of birth.
5. Any citizen twenty-one years of age or over who has an estate of inheritance of £3 yearly net income, taking the rents and profits three years in succession, is settled in the town where he has such estate and so dwells.
6. Any citizen, as above, who has an estate or freehold of £60 value and pays taxes on the same for five years in succession, is settled where he has such an estate.
7. Any town officer is settled *ipso facto.*

8. An ordained minister is settled in the place of his pastorate.

9. Any minor who serves four years apprenticeship and actually sets up in business in the town where he has served within one year after his term, being then twenty-one years old and who continues such trade for five years, is settled in that place.

10. Any citizen twenty-one years or over who resides in any town for ten years and pays all taxes duly assessed for any five years within that time is settled in that town.

11. Every settlement when gained continues till lost or defeated by the gaining of another elsewhere.

The principles underlying this early legislation include: (1) persons of independent citizenship gain settlement by their own acts; (2) certain persons, such as wives and children, do not independently gain settlement but derive it from their husbands and fathers; (3) ownership of property and payment of taxes entitle persons to settlement, a principle generally discarded today; and (4) settlement continues until lost or defeated by gaining another. The Massachusetts settlement law has undergone numerous revisions, but the essential principles, with some exceptions, are those of generations and even centuries ago. Today, as yesterday, legal settlement is an arbitrary rule based on two theories: that everybody should belong somewhere, and that if any person has a need for public assistance, he should receive it from the place where he belongs. In other words, the Massachusetts settlement law, like that of every state, fixes financial responsibility.

DEFINITIONS OF RESIDENCE, DOMICILE, SETTLEMENT

There is confusion among lawyers and public welfare workers in definitions of the terms *domicile, residence,* and *settlement.* By domicile the lawyer may mean a place where a person has a true and fixed abode, the place where he intends to stay permanently. By residence he may mean the place where a person is or the place which he intends to leave when the purpose for which he took up residence no longer exists.[7] A person domiciled in one spot for temporary reasons, such as health or business, may reside for a considerable period of time in some other place deemed more favorable. Temporary absence does not destroy domicile; intent is the essence. Actually, the courts often use the words *domicile* and *residence* interchangeably. They do likewise for *residence* and *settlement.* Settlement may mean "a right acquired by a person, by continued residence for a given length of time in a town or district, to claim aid or relief under the poor laws in case of his becoming a pauper."[8] The courts generally say that settlement requires a combina-

[7] *Black's Law Dictionary,* 3d ed. (1933), pp. 607, 1543; 48 C.J. 448.

[8] *Black's Law Dictionary,* p. 1613.

tion of physical presence with intent to remain.[9] Thus, criminals detained against their will in prisons maintain their settlement at the place of usual abode; the same is true of patients in hospitals and institutions for the mentally ill and defective.

Confusion concerning the legal meaning of these terms prevails in the administration of both the general and special assistance programs. In our subsequent discussion of residence in relation to the special assistances we shall again refer to this subject. We point out here that settlement is a term used in the administration of general assistance; that it has a long history; and that traditionally it imposes legal restrictions and particular penalties upon the recipient. Residence requirements in the administration of the special assistances generally carry no legal penalties and inflict little or no ignominy upon the recipient. Administrators of the special assistance programs are careful to point out that settlement for general relief purposes and residence for the special assistances are not the same thing.

ACQUISITION AND LOSS OF SETTLEMENT

ACQUISITION OF SETTLEMENT

The time required to gain residence for general assistance in the fifty-three American jurisdictions ranges from no designated time period to five years. As of January 1, 1955, eight jurisdictions appeared to have no specific time provisions; two had six months; four had two years; eight had three years; one had four years; five had five years. The largest number, twenty-five, required one year. Similarly, the provisions concerning duration of absence to lose settlement vary. About one third of the jurisdictions had no designated period. Slightly over one half had one year. The balance had six-month, three-year, four-year, or five-year provisions.[10]

The table published by the American Public Welfare Association, from which the above information is derived, shows how difficult it is to generalize regarding settlement (or any other) provisions of general assistance legislation. For example, Alabama had no general assistance program as such. It provided limited temporary aid. Emergency assistance required six months' residence. Eligibility for temporary aid was lost by six months' absence. Aid might be given for thirty days to sick and disabled persons, regardless of residence. Colorado required three years to establish residence and one year to lose residence; emergency assistance might be

[9] *Whately* v. *Hatfield,* 196 Mass. 39, 82 N.E. 48 (1907).

[10] *The Public Welfare Directory: 1955,* pp. 368–375, and *Compilation of Settlement Laws of All States in the United States: Revised as of September, 1939,* both published by the American Public Welfare Association, Chicago, Ill.

granted to nonresidents if county departments so desired. Idaho required one year to gain or to lose settlement. Reciprocal agreements between Idaho, Washington, and Oregon fixed two years as the required period of residence for care in a mental hospital. Illinois required one year to gain or lose residence, but the program of assistance to the medically indigent (limited to medical or burial expenses for persons not otherwise eligible for public assistance) had no residence requirement. Texas required one year of residence to be eligible for general assistance, which was administered on the local basis only. In most counties the applicant was required to have one year of residence in the state and six months in the county. This varied from county to county. Intent to abandon residence was the criterion for loss of settlement. Six months' residence was required for care in a mental hospital unless the patient was dangerously ill when admission was requested.

Important questions arise in determining whether or not legal settlement has been acquired. We indicated above that what constitutes a residence is one of them. In Wisconsin the court has defined it to mean "the place where a person has voluntarily fixed his abode, not for a mere special or temporary purpose, but with the present intention of making it his home." [11] Thus, a temporary absence, coupled with intention to return, does not interrupt the period of residence required to establish a legal settlement if the intention is carried out. It has been held that absence for the purpose of working in another municipality, coupled with an intention to return when the work is finished and an actual return, especially when clothing and personal property are left at the place of residence, does not cause a loss of residence.[12] Ordinarily, the place where the wife and children reside is the husband's residence when he is away only temporarily.

Another problem which confronts officials is whether the assistance granted was such relief as to defeat acquisition of legal settlement. In a given case, aid may have been properly granted, but that does not mean that it was *ipso facto* the kind of assistance which defeats gaining a settlement for general relief. In Wisconsin there have been judicial decisions and attorney general's rulings holding that the following types of aid are *not* support to a pauper and, hence, do not defeat gaining a legal settlement for general relief purposes:

1. Red Cross aid.
2. Receipt of a loan from the Resettlement Administration or Farm Security Administration.

---

[11] *St. ex rel. Wood Co.* v. *Dodge Co.,* 56 Wis. 79, 13 N.W. 680 (1882). This definition appears to be the same as that given above for domicile. It illustrates the confusion in definitions between domicile, residence, and settlement.

[12] *Salem* v. *Lyme,* 29 Conn. 74 (1860); *Gouldsborough* v. *Sullivan,* 132 Me. 342, 170 Atl. 900 (1934).

3. Care at the State General Hospital or at institutions for the feeble-minded.
4. CCC and CWA wages.
5. Eating at the same table with *but* working for a family receiving aid.
6. Receipt of money from the Soldier's and Sailor's Relief Commission for transportation to a prospective job.

In general, the statutes and decisions must be consulted as to whether or not living in homes, asylums, institutions, and obtaining medical care in and out of hospitals conditions the residence period for settlement.

Still another question frequently arises: Does *any* aid, no matter how small, make the recipient a pauper and unable to establish legal settlement? Once more, it is necessary to consult the opinions and rulings of attorney generals and courts. In Wisconsin, although no definite criteria can be laid down, it is probably safe to say that the receipt of $15.00 worth of necessities within a twelve-month period does not constitute pauper relief. However, if $10.00 worth of supplies were issued toward the end of the first year of residence and were followed by continuous grants thereafter, the aid thus given would constitute pauper relief from the first. A small grant, standing alone in a twelve-month period, is a strong indication that the recipient was not a pauper, although he might have had need of temporary aid.[13]

LOSS OF SETTLEMENT

Loss of settlement is of equal importance with acquisition of settlement. The general, although by no means universal, rule is that a person moving about within a single state does not lose his old settlement until he has acquired a new one in that state or has resided elsewhere for some indicated period of time. Courts tend to hold to this rule in the absence of a statute to the contrary. The time period for loss of settlement may be the same as that required for gaining settlement, but this is not always true.

Loss of settlement causes many problems for those working with both intrastate and interstate transients. If the applicant for assistance is an intrastate transient with a legal settlement somewhere in the state, the charges for his care can eventually be allocated and collected. If he is an intrastate transient with no legal settlement in the state but clearly a resident of the state, he may receive care at state expense if there is legislation on the subject. If he has no legal residence in the state and there is no assignment of responsibility for his care, he may or may not receive either temporary or permanent help. If he is an interstate transient, he may have lost settlement in one state and not yet acquired it in another.

---

[13] *Holland* v. *Belgium,* 66 Wis. 557, 29 N.W. 558 (1886); 25 Ops. Atty. Gen. (Wis.) 718 (1936); *Town of Rolling* v. *Town of Antigo,* 211 Wis. 220, 248 N.W. 119 (1933); *City of Two Rivers* v. *Town of Wabeno,* 221 Wis. 158, 266 N.W. 274 (1936).

It is impossible to estimate the amount of time taken by officials to verify settlement and the amount of ignominy endured by those whose residence is in question. Likewise, no one knows how many thousands of cases have been taken to lower and higher courts and to attorney generals for decisions on moot settlement questions. It is all highly undesirable and unnecessary.

REMOVAL AND EXCLUSION OF UNSETTLED PERSONS

REMOVAL

The practice of removing the indigent to the place where he "belongs" is as old as the concept of local residence. In the famous 1388 English statute, the 12th Richard II, we find that servants or laborers and able-bodied beggars were not to leave their dwellings without a letter under the king's seal and that impotent beggars were to remain where they were at the passage of the act. If the inhabitants of those places were unwilling or unable to maintain such people they were to be taken to other towns or to the place of their birth within forty days of the proclamation and live there the rest of their days. We also recall that in early English law the wandering poor person often was whipped and ordered to return home. An English act of 1530 assisted the vagrant to return home, with the provision that on producing a testimonial of having been whipped, he be given board and lodging every ten miles. If he loitered and again became vagabond, the upper part of the gristle of his ear was to be cut off; on again offending, he was to suffer death as a felon.

The colonies acquired their concept of removal along with the rest of English settlement law.[14] Early practice was to pass the unsettled individual from one community to another until he finally reached home. There was much passing back and forth because of disputed responsibility. Some early attempts were made to render the system less objectionable. For example, New York in 1817 enacted a statute decreeing that a person be removed directly to the community in which he had settlement instead of to an adjoining community. The practice of dumping paupers by stealth on other communities was frequently used. In fact, it became so prevalent that many states enacted legislation imposing fines on any who brought or caused to be brought any pauper into the state with the object of leaving him there for care. Private individuals and officials could be

[14] Carl A. Heisterman, "Removal of Nonresident State Poor by State and Local Authorities," *Social Service Review* (June, 1934), pp. 289–301; Robert C. Lowe, *State Public Welfare Legislation*, WPA Research Monograph (Washington, D.C., G.P.O., 1939), No. 20, pp. 54–62, table; U.S. House of Representatives, *Interstate Migration: Report of the Select Committee to Investigate the Interstate Migration of Destitute Citizens*, 77th Cong., 1st sess., H. Report No. 369 (Washington, D.C., G.P.O., 1941), pp. 607–667.

prosecuted under these laws. Not until 1942, when the United States Supreme Court ruled on such a California statute in the Edwards case, did this particular practice disappear. Warning out was permissible too. This meant that an individual thought likely to become a public charge was warned to leave. Having received such a warning, he could not acquire settlement if he chose or was permitted to remain.

About three quarters of the states have enacted legislation authorizing the removal of an indigent to his place of settlement. About half the states have statutes authorizing removal to the state of legal settlement, and somewhat more than half have laws authorizing removal to the place of settlement within the state. Thus, removal laws are of two types: those providing for removal from one state to another, and those providing for removal from one locality to another within the state. The courts have generally supported this legislation, although not always have they found that the individual to be removed came under the provisions of the law.[15] A New York case, *In re Chirillo,* pertaining to interstate removal, evoked comment and concern from social workers and others when, in 1940, it was before the courts.[16] It involved the validity of a removal order for a family from New York to Ohio, the state of legal settlement. The majority of the court held that the removal order was valid. A minority chose to consider the constitutional question involved and found that it was not "a privilege or immunity of a citizen of the United States to impose upon any state of his choice the burden of supporting himself and his family before he has satisfied reasonable settlement qualifications." Nor was "a statute designed to safeguard the welfare of the individual and the welfare of the state and to protect a citizen of the United States from starvation and return him to his former place of settlement where he will receive succor a violation of the constitution of the United States." The Federal district court refused to look into the constitutionality of the statute on technical grounds. Welfare workers had hoped the New York and federal courts would find the law unconstitutional and thus stop the practice of coercive interstate removals and perhaps in some measure halt intrastate removals.

Intrastate removals between districts are more common than between states. The official or agency given the responsibility of removal varies from state to state. It may be given to the overseer of the poor, the justice of the peace, the judge of a designated court, the local board of public welfare, and so forth. Situations like that revealed in an 1892 Illinois

---

[15] *Lowell* v. *Seeback,* 45 Minn. 465, 48 N.W. 23 (1891); *Town of Bristol* v. *Town of Fox,* 159 Ill. 500, 42 N.E. 887 (1896); *Harrison* v. *Gilbert,* 71 Conn. 724, 43 Atl. 190 (1899); *Hilborn* v. *Briggs,* 58 N. Dak. 612, 226 N.W. 737 (1929); *In re Barnes,* 119 Pa. (Sup. Ct.) 553, 180 Atl. 718 (1935); *Anderson* v. *Miller,* 120 Pa. (Sup. Ct.) 463, 182 Atl. 742 (1936). For digest of these cases, see *Interstate Migration,* pp. 10074–10075.

[16] 283 N.Y. 417, 28 N.E. 2d 895 (1940).

case are not atypical. Here, a mother and her five minor children were ordered by the town of settlement to move back to that town. The mother refused to heed the order. The court held that under these circumstances neither the town of settlement nor the town where the woman was residing had any obligation to supply support. It stated: [17]

By refusing to go to the town which was supporting her, after suitable provision for her support there had been made, this woman terminated any claim for support as a public pauper, and any other town or person afterward furnishing her necessaries, thereby obtained no right of action against the town of Fox. Under the contention of counsel for appellee, the town of Fox would be liable for this woman's support, if she insisted upon living in Chicago, preferring the whirl and excitement of that busy metropolis to the rural ways and simple manners of the denizens of Fox. We see nothing in the Pauper Act indicating a legislative intention to depart from the old proverb, "Beggars should not be choosers."

The old removal statutes and those still in existence are similar, and so, too, are the removal orders. One of these old removal orders and a modernized statute are cited to show the anachronisms of present administration and legislation. The old law states: [18]

Whereas the Town Council of Exeter in the County of Washington and State of Rhodeisland Province Plantations hath Cradible Information and Complaint By one of the overseers of the Poor of sd town that one Stephen Draper and Ann Draper abideth in this Town Not Being Inhabitants and is Likely Soon to Become Chargeable to this Town unless they Be Speedily Removed, and upon the best information this Council can git they the aforesaid Town Council do adjudge that the Town of South Kingston in the abovesd County to Be the Proper place of settlement and Residence of them the sd Stephen and Anna and their Bad Conduct and Ill Behaviour is Likely soon to Become Chargeable to Sd Town unless they be speedily Removed and therefore Voted that the Clarke of this Council should Grant a Warrant of Removal to Remove the sd Stephen and Anna to the town of South Kingston.

On the other hand, if intrastate and interstate removal statutes are to exist at all, the provisions of the current Wisconsin law are probably as lenient and fair as any. The law of that state on this subject reads in part as follows: [19]

49.09(1) Removal of Dependents. (1) When a dependent person other than a recipient of old-age assistance, aid to blind, aid to dependent children, or aid to totally and permanently disabled persons is receiving relief elsewhere than at his place of settlement and refuses to return thereto, the office or agency of the place administering relief or of the place of settlement may petition the judge of the county court . . . for an order directing such person to return to his place of settlement . . .

---

[17] *Town of Fox* v. *Town of Bristol*, 45 Ill. App. 330 (1892).

[18] Margaret Creech, *Three Centuries of Poor Law Administration: A Study of Legislation in Rhode Island* (Chicago, University of Chicago Press, 1936), p. 276.

[19] Wis. Stat., 1955.

(2) If the judge finds that return to the place of legal settlement does not substantially reduce the employment and earning opportunities of the dependent person, does not materially disrupt family ties, and does not work any material injustice to him, he may order the dependent person to return to his place of settlement . . .

(3) When a dependent person who does not have legal settlement in a county or municipality within this state applies for relief other than temporary medical care, if such person is found in need, the relief agency shall furnish temporary assistance and immediately investigate as to the legal settlement of such person. If it is found that such person has a legal settlement in another state and the municipality of legal settlement in such other state admits its responsibility for such person's relief and authorizes the return of such person to such municipality, then the relief agency in this state shall offer to the person requesting releief, transportation for such person, and for his dependents if necessary, to such municipality of legal settlement. After making such order such relief agency shall not be required to furnish further relief to such person or his dependents.

According to Wisconsin officials, the courts of the state order very few removals. However, such statutes give officials the power to restrict the free movement of a segment of our population.

EXCLUSION

Until 1941, when the United States Supreme Court rendered its decision in *Fred S. Edwards* v. *The People of the State of California,* exclusion of paupers or indigents was legal in twenty-eight states. The California law was typical and read: "Every person, firm or corporation, or officer or agent, that brings or assists in bringing into the state any indigent person who is not a resident of the state, knowing him to be an indigent person, is guilty of a misdemeanor." The decision of the United States Supreme Court, however, rendered such statutory provisions invalid.

The facts here were that Edwards, a resident of California, was convicted of violation of the aforementioned statute, having brought his wife's brother-in-law, Duncan, from Texas to California. Duncan had been employed in Texas by the Works Progress Administration. When he left Texas he had about $20.00, which was spent by the time Edwards and Duncan reached California. Duncan lived with Edwards for some ten days until he obtained financial assistance from the Farm Security Administration. Justice Byrnes, who delivered the *majority* opinion of the court, held that the California law imposed an unconstitutional burden upon interstate commerce. Justice Douglas, in a *concurring* opinion, held that the statute imposed a limit on the right of free movement as an aspect of national citizenship. To allow a statute imposing such restrictions of free movement as were here imposed [20]

---

[20] 34 U.S. 160, 62 Sup. Ct. 164 (1941). For a full discussion of this case and its implications for the national welfare, see "Constitutional Rights of Destitute Citizens of the U.S. to Move from State to State—The Edwards Case," *National Defense*

would permit those who were stigmatized by a state as indigents, paupers, or vagabonds to be relegated to an inferior class of citizenship. It would prevent a citizen, because he was poor, from seeking new horizons in other states. It might thus withhold from large segments of our people that mobility which is basic to any guarantee of freedom of opportunity. The result would be a dilution of the rights of *national* citizenship, a serious impairment of the principles of equality. Since the state statute here challenged involves such consequences, it runs afoul of the privileges and immunities clause of the fourteenth Amendment.

Of the two lines of reasoning, that of Justice Douglas is more favored by many lawyers and welfare workers. One commentator on the Constitution and the right of free movement does not rely on either of the arguments employed in the Edwards case, namely, that imposition of residence requirements is in effect a limitation of the right of liberty guaranteed by the Fourteenth Amendment or that such a restriction is in violation of the interstate commerce authority of Congress. He prefers to use the equal protection clause of the Fourteenth Amendment, which provides that "no state shall deny to any person the equal protection of the laws." TenBrock says on the subject:[21]

Length-of-residence requirements in public welfare violate the equal protection command of the Fourteenth Amendment. Public welfare aids and services are granted for the purpose of meeting needs. Newcomers have these needs as well as long-time residents. They therefore stand in the same relationship to the purpose of the law as do long-time residents. Under the Equal Protection clause they must be treated alike.

In view of the Edwards decision, which makes illegal the exclusion of indigent unsettled persons from any state, it may be that the federal courts, when the occasion is presented, will invalidate interstate removals. As long as settlement laws remain on the statute books there will be charge-backs. When there are charge-backs from more generous administrative units to less generous ones or vice versa, there are bound to be demands for returns if they are statutorily allowed. It seems, however, that forcible removal is an unreasonable and arbitrary procedure which should not be tolerated. Removal is unjust, whether it be between communities in the same state or between states. Some states forbid removal of recipients of the special assistances. Almost two centuries ago Adam Smith, in his *Wealth of Nations,* wrote that to remove a man who com-

---

Migration, Pt. 26. See also, "Notes and Comments by the Editor: The United States Supreme Court and the Pauper Laws," *Social Service Review,* Vol. 16, No. 1 (March, 1942), pp. 103–109; Leonard W. Mayo, "Fred F. Edwards v. The People of the State of California," *Proceedings of the National Conference of Social Work: 1942* (New York, Columbia University Press, 1942), pp. 139–147.

[21] Jacobus tenBrock, *The Constitution and the Right of Free Movement* (New York, National Traveler's Aid Association, 1955); for comment on this pamphlet see "Notes and Comments," *Social Service Review,* Vol. 29, No. 4 (December, 1955), pp. 395–396.

mitted no misdemeanor from the parish where he chose to reside was an evident violation of natural liberty and justice.

REMEDIES

Private and official groups disturbed by these primitive methods of *passing on, removal, warning out, exclusion* of the unsettled poor have sought measures for alleviation of the problem. In 1902 the National Conference of Charities and Corrections drew up a set of rules called the "Transportation Agreement." This agreement applied to such social agencies as chose to sign it. The regulations provided that individuals were not to be passed on but sent directly to their place of residence after inquiry indicated the wisdom of such a plan. This was true whether the removal was within the state or between states. Transportation was to be furnished by the locality where the unsettled person was. By 1931 there were more than 850 signatory agencies, mostly private. By 1934 the committee which administered the program, believing that the principles of the agreement had been accepted by a large proportion of casework agencies, decided to disband. Some years later, in 1948, with the realization that the evil still existed, the same principles were set down in more up-to-date language by the Social Case Work Council of the National Social Welfare Assembly in a pamphlet entitled *Service to Migrants.*[22]

The American Public Welfare Association in 1930 took the initiative in appointing a committee on uniform settlement laws and the transfer of dependents. In co-operation with the Commissioners on Uniform State Laws, this committee drafted the uniform transfer of dependents act. In 1935 the commissioners accepted the act, which reads as follows: [23]

> SECTION 1 (Reciprocal Agreements.) The (Department of Public Welfare), subject to the approval of the Attorney General, is hereby authorized to enter into reciprocal agreements with corresponding state agencies of other states regarding the interstate transportation of poor and indigent persons, and to arrange with the proper officials in this state for the acceptance, transfer, and support of persons receiving public aid in other states in accordance with the terms of such reciprocal agreements; provided that this state shall not nor shall any county or other political subdivision of this state be committed to the support of persons who are not in the opinion of said (Department of Public Welfare) entitled to public support by the laws of this state.

The obvious purpose of the act is to encourage reciprocal agreements between state departments of welfare that will facilitate the support of poor persons where they are or will permit their transfer to their home

---

[22] Margaret Creech, "Migrants, Transients, and Travelers," *loc. cit.*, p. 357; National Social Welfare Assembly, Social Case Work Council, *Service to Migrants: A Statement of Principles and Procedures* (New York, 1948).

[23] *Miscellaneous Acts,* 9A U.L.A. 270.

states if that is desirable. In 1954 there were few states which had adopted this act.[24] Numbers of factors seem to be responsible for the small number of jurisdictions enacting the uniform transfer of dependents act, such as upward revision of settlement requirements by several states, heavy relief claims, slim resources, and local administration of general assistance. In contrast, the uniform reciprocal enforcement of support act, adopted in 1950 and since amended, or some adaptation of it, has been enacted by all jurisdictions.[25] The purposes of this act are to improve and extend by reciprocal legislation the enforcement of the duties of support and to make uniform the law with respect thereto. No type of interstate agreement at the state level is necessary for the local courts of two states to carry on negotiations and judicial processes.

Two other kinds of statutes have been passed by numbers of states in their efforts to deal effectively with needy persons of certain categories and to fix financial responsibility. One has a combination of reciprocal and retaliatory features. To illustrate (although from special assistance rather than from general assistance legislation), the Wisconsin law on persons eligible for old-age assistance reads: [26]

> 49.22(1) Any needy person who complies with the provisions of ss 49.20 to 49.38 shall be entitled to financial assistance in old age . . . only if . . .
> (c) He has resided in the state continuously during the year immediately preceding the date of application. An applicant who has resided less than one year in Wisconsin may be granted old-age assistance if the state from which he removed his residence to Wisconsin grants assistance to any resident of Wisconsin who has moved to such state and lived there less than one year; provided that an applicant who has removed his residence to Wisconsin from a state which requires that an applicant who has removed his residence from Wisconsin to such state, reside in such state more than one year before he is eligible for old-age assistance be required to reside in this state for a like period before becoming eligible for old-age assistance in this state; and provided that old-age assistance may be continued when a recipient removes his residence to another state until he satisfies the residence requirements for eligibility for old-age assistance in such state.

In a jurisdiction having a state supervisory, as contrasted with a state-administered program of the special assistances, this kind of law opens up the opportunity for innumerable local irritations, although it may sometimes benefit an applicant for assistance.

Another type of law designed to deal with the problem of the out-of-state poor receiving assistance, in this instance institutional care, is like-

---

[24] *Miscellaneous Acts,* 9A U.L.A. 160 (Cumulative Annual Pocket Part, 1954).

[25] Brevard E. Crihfield, "Recent Developments in Reciprocal Support Legislation," *Social Casework,* Vol. 36, No. 3 (March, 1955), pp. 113–118; Council of State Governments, *Reciprocal State Legislation to Enforce Support of Dependents: 1955–56,* (Chicago, 1955).

[26] Wis. Stat., 1955.

wise illustrated by a Wisconsin law. In substance it provides that the state's Department of Public Welfare may determine whether any institutionalized patients are subject to deportation. On behalf of the state the Department of Welfare may enter into reciprocal agreements with other states for deportation and importation of persons who are public charges upon such terms as will protect the state's interests and promote mutual amicable relations with other states.[27]

No laws have been passed providing for interstate compacts on the problem of public assistance. Perhaps we should pause here to explain briefly several distinctions between interstate compacts and interstate agreements or reciprocal legislation.[28] A compact is a contract, is of superior status in the legal hierarchy, and supersedes any statutory law in conflict. A compact must be entered into without any substantial variation in language. It cannot be tinkered with or changed after it has been entered into unless the other parties are agreeable to the same. Parties can withdraw only in the manner prescribed. The uniform transfer of dependents act and the reciprocal enforcement of support act are simply additional statutes on the books and are to be construed as such. They contain none of the elements of a contract. They may be amended unilaterally at the wish of any state which has enacted them.

Congressional consent is *necessary* (1) if the compact affects the balance of the federal system; (2) if the compact affects a power delegated to the national government; (3) if the compact is to be participated in by a territory or possession of the United States or by a foreign power; (4) if the United States government itself is to be a party to the compact. For many reasons consent by Congress to a compact may be *desirable,* even if not *necessary.* For example, the Interstate Compact on Juveniles, making possible the return of run-away and absconding juveniles, is a case in point. Between the states this compact could be operated without the consent of Congress, but the Council of State Governments and other groups interested in the measure wanted to make the territories, possessions, and the District of Columbia eligible to participate. Also, these groups felt that congressional consent and approval would serve as a desirable nudge to securing ratification by the largest number of states. There appear to be few, if any, signs on the horizon that Congress will be urged to pass legislation authorizing or sanctioning interstate compacts on aspects of special or general assistance programs.

---

[27] Wis. Stat., 1955, c. 46.10(8)(b).

[28] The information contained in this paragraph is derived from a most helpful personal letter from B. E. Crihfield, eastern representative of The Council of State Governments, New York (December 27, 1955). See Art. I, sec. 10 of the Constitution of the United States of America for authority for congressional approval of interstate contracts.

DERIVATIVE SETTLEMENT: WIVES AND CHILDREN

In the absence of statutory provisions as to how settlement is gained, the courts generally hold that every person who is by law incapable of gaining a settlement in his own right shall have the settlement of the person on whom he depends for support and who, at the same time, has the control of his person and the right to his services. The statutes have many provisions regarding derivative settlement. Settlement laws regard the family as a unit, with the settlement of husband and father ordinarily determining that of wife and children.[29] Over half the states have provisions that a minor takes the settlement of his father, sometimes adding if he has one within the state, and, if not, then the settlement of his mother if she has one.

Marriage generally emancipates minors so that they acquire settlement in their own right. Since the statutes do not usually specify what the settlement of minors is upon the divorce of their parents, this situation often presents problems to the court. For example, the Ohio court had to decide this question in a situation where a divorced mother was given the custody of eight children. Nineteen months after the divorce the mother remarried and joined her new husband in a town in another county where he had his legal settlement. Something over a year later he abandoned his wife and her children. The court ruled here that the children had the legal settlement of their mother, which was that of her second husband.[30]

The migratory child laborer, with or without his family, and the child in the migratory family cause anxiety to relief and school officials. Since the family often has no legal settlement, the child has no derivative settlement. What agency, then, is to see to it that the child attends school and does not labor in violation of state laws or to his detriment? There seems to be no legislation dealing directly with the subject of emancipation of children by their parents in relation to settlement. There are numerous court decisions which have dealt with the subject, although there is no agreement among the decisions.[31] It has been held that even a sane child is not necessarily emancipated on reaching the age of twenty-one. As long as he continues single, acquires no settlement for himself, makes his father's home his own, and enters into no contract inconsistent

---

[29] 48 C.J. 448–456, 480–486; 21 R.C.L. 718; *Fayette* v. *Chesterville,* 77 Me. 28 (1885).

[30] *Board of Commrs. of Summit County* v. *Board of Commrs. of Trumbull County,* 116 Ohio 663, 158 N.E. 172 (1927).

[31] For the point of view that an emancipated minor loses the settlement of his parent, see *Portland* v. *New Gloucester,* 16 Me. 427 (1840); for opposite view that emancipation does not mean independent settlement, see *City of Bangor* v. *Inhabitants of Veazie,* 111 Me. 371, 89 Atl. 193 (1914).

with his being in a subordinate position in his father's family, he follows the newly acquired settlement of his father.[32] Where a child's mind is so deranged as to render it impossible for him to acquire a settlement of his own, he keeps his father's settlement, even after reaching his majority.[33] An insane person or idiot cannot acquire a settlement by his own volition.[34]

Provisions regarding settlement of the wife and of the divorced, separated, or deserted wife differ from state to state. In general, the settlement of a married woman is that of her husband, and that of a widow or separated wife is that of her husband at his death or at the time of divorce, separation, or desertion.[35] From then on, she gains or loses her settlement by her own movements.

PROPOSED MODIFICATION OF SETTLEMENT AND RESIDENCE LAWS

Neither federal nor state legislators paid much attention to problems growing out of archaic settlement laws until the depression period of 1930–1940. Then, the size of the unsettled dependent population caused Congress to include in the Federal Emergency Relief Act of 1933 a provision designating special funds for the care of homeless and transient needy persons. With the dropping of this program in 1935 the states reverted to their old methods of dealing with the unsettled poor. Except for the camps, commodities, and medical care provided by the Farm Security Administration to migratory agricultural unemployed workers, there was no nation-wide program for migrants.

When the special assistance provisions of the federal Social Security Act were written, Congress had to determine what policy to pursue on the residence question. It rejected the idea of legal settlement in a locality and the restrictive connotations associated with settlement and adopted that of residence in a state. It decided that no state "which excludes any resident of the state who has resided therein five years during the nine years immediately preceding the application for old-age assistance and has resided therein continuously for one year immediately preceding the application" could receive federal grants-in-aid.

Today, many states require only one year of residence in the state for all forms of special assistance. Although the states have now had extensive experience with liberalized residence laws for the special assistances, many have done little to modernize settlement laws for the residual group of needy persons. In fact, some states, since the depression, have extended

[32] *Alexandria Twnsp.* v. *Bethlehem Twnsp.,* N.J.L. 119 (1837).
[33] *Fayette* v. *Chesterville,* 77 Me. 28 (1885).
[34] *Payne* v. *Dunham,* 29 Ill. 125 (1862).
[35] *Bradford* v. *Worcester,* 184 Mass. 557, 69 N.E. 310 (1904).

the required period. The revision of settlement laws is obviously bound up with the source of funds. State legislatures are reluctant to liberalize or abolish settlement laws unless federal funds are available. Certainly, localities are not going to urge legislatures to liberalize settlement provisions until and unless state funds are available.

As we have already indicated, official and nonofficial groups have turned their attention in and out of crisis periods to the residence provisions of public-assistance laws. It is possible from the deliberations of these diverse groups to summarize arguments for and against settlement and residence laws.[36] The main arguments for the maintenance of strict residence requirements are:

1. They establish a legal basis for placing responsibility for the cost of care given to needy persons.
2. They protect the community against undesirables. This argument is founded largely on the belief that the migrant is a vagabond, hobo, or beggar.
3. They safeguard local resources for local persons.
4. They prevent an influx of indigent persons into localities which have high assistance grants, a temperate and desirable climate, good opportunities for employment, and so forth.

The case against strict residence laws is much stronger and includes the following points:

1. They have no place in our democratic country, in which mobility of population is encouraged and essential.
2. They are unfair and discriminatory, since they prevent the granting of assistance on the basis of need.
3. They are costly in administration, especially in the amount of staff time needed to verify residence.
4. They cause undue hardship and deprivation for persons who lack any legal settlement.

Numbers of proposals for modifying settlement and residence laws have been made, including the following:

1. The elimination of all residence and settlement laws for all classifications of needy persons. This is not likely to occur unless and until federal grants-in-aid are available for all forms of public assistance and Congress requires that settlement provisions be eliminated as a prerequisite for the receipt of federal funds. Students of public assistance have long and unsuccessfully advocated doing away with residence requirements.[37] In 1944 Rhode Island, which at one time had a ten-year residence provision, abolished residence requirements for all forms of public assistance. It did not find, as many people argued it would, that high standards of relief administration and abolition of residence requirements induced migration into the state for relief purposes.

---

[36] Falk, *Settlement Laws.*

[37] John L. Gillin, "The Need for a Uniform Settlement Law," *Proceedings of the National Conference of Social Work: 1926* (New York, Columbia University Press, 1926), pp. 539–545; Arthur P. Hasking, "The Need for a Uniform Settlement Law," *ibid.*, pp. 536–539; Edith Abbott, "Abolish the Poor Laws," *Social Service Review* (March, 1934), pp. 1–17.

2. The modification of the Social Security Act to provide for a uniform residence law for the special assistances. The period of time most frequently mentioned is one year of state residence, as contrasted with that or some other period in a municipality. In time this measure might affect settlement provisions for general assistance.

3. The provision of a new category, *general assistance,* in the Social Security Act to include the unsettled poor. Congress would have to decide whether to eliminate all residence requirements, to establish a uniform requirement of one year or some other period, or to do as it does now with the special assistances, define a maximum requirement.

4. The amendment of the Social Security Act to permit states, if they *chose,* to eliminate all classifications of needy persons so as to furnish help to anyone in need. Federal grants-in-aid could then be furnished to states for designated categories, including general assistance, or for uncategorized persons. Congress would still have to establish a policy on residence provisions. Opposition to abolishing categories is strong from representatives of special groups and from those who believe greater public interest is aroused for specially designated groups.

Congressman John H. Tolan, acting as *amicus curiae* for Edwards in the Edwards-California case, presented his position on outdated residence and settlement laws as follows: [38]

> It is our belief that the welfare of the nation is seriously jeopardized by penal statutes which have the effect—whatever be their intent—of confining or blocking the free flow of human migration in the United States . . .
>
> We have come a long way from the days of a crumbling feudalism, when the manor lords of rural England sought by repressive measures to bind their restless serfs to the land. We do not today have the flogging, branding, mutilation, and death penalty provided by early "vagrancy statutes" for the wandering poor. We do not now, as we did in our earlier history, auction the poor like chattels to willing bidders, apprentice and indenture them, house them with the criminal and the insane, subject them to the degrading test of the workhouse.
>
> We have not outlived, however, the legacy of the English poor laws, which chained men to their native places and kept strangers on the move. Our statutes of settlement, removal, and exclusion, and our administrative practices bear a startling likeness to their antecedents 400 years ago.

SUMMARY AND CONCLUSIONS

From our review of general assistance legislation in this and the preceding chapter it is apparent that most provisions are derived from Elizabethan legislation. In the last fifty to one hundred years, both in England and the United States, there has been a gradual emergence of special provisions for the relief and treatment of persons with particularly designated needs. These services have been divorced from poor-law administration and carry little or no stigma of pauperism. We shall discuss these special assistance programs of the United States in subsequent

[38] *National Defense Migration,* pp. 10118, 10143.

chapters. In other words, there has been a slow breaking up of the poor law, a policy urged by the Webbs at the beginning of the twentieth century. A British report comments on this development in England as follows: [39]

> The break-up of the comprehensive poor-relief service has been partly due to changes in public opinion concerning the responsibilities of the State and partly to the spirit in which the nineteenth-century Poor Law was administered. It is conceivable that most of the new social services of the last thirty years might have evolved within the comprehensive framework of the Poor Law if the spirit of the "workhouse test" and a narrow interpretation of "less eligibility" had not created an atmosphere which was wholly prejudicial to such a development.

In removing many classes of the poor from under the poor law, legislation has moved in two directions: (1) supplying assistance without stigma to certain designated groups of persons, such as the blind, the aged, dependent children, the disabled, and the veteran, and (2) setting up insurance schemes, such as workmen's compensation, old-age insurance, unemployment insurance, and, in some countries, disability and health insurances. The effect of the insurances given as a right, upon the administration of the various categories of relief, is to emphasize the right to assistance of the individual demonstrated to be needy. These conditions reflect an increasing tendency "to obliterate the distinction between certain classes of paupers and nonpaupers." [40]

In the future, because of the social insurances, there will be a reduction in the percentage of persons receiving public assistance. Probably categorical assistance measures will continue to favor particular groups. What will happen to those who, for some reason or another, do not receive social insurance protection or who do not fall into a category eligible for special public assistance? For these persons a general assistance program administered under revised and modernized public-assistance statutes is necessary. Such a law is "the last and ultimate dragnet for all sorts and conditions of men, women, and children who become destitute . . . It is the residuary legatee of the social services." [41] Either such a provision or the dropping of categories altogether is essential.

To assure needy unclassified persons the assistance they require, pending the abolition of categories, the states should drop the following old poor-law provisions: (1) exclusive parochial or local responsibility for administration and costs, and (2) obligatory support from relatives. General assistance statutes should be rewritten to include a new and

---

[39] Political and Economic Planning, *Report on the British Social Services* (London, PEP, 1937), p. 11.

[40] "Unemployment Insurance and Poor Relief: Further Testimony Before the Royal Commission on Unemployment Insurance," *Social Service Review* (March, 1934), p. 111.

[41] *Ibid.*, p. 114.

liberalized definition of assistance; requirements for a co-ordinated public-assistance program on the local and state levels; shared state and local financial responsibility; and qualified administrative staff selected under a merit system. Preferably this should be the same staff as that which administers the special assistance programs.

Selected References

ABBOTT, Edith, "Abolish the Poor Laws," *Social Service Review,* Vol. 8, No. 1 (March, 1934), pp. 3–7.

———, *Public Assistance* (Chicago, University of Chicago Press, 1940).

———, "Is There a Legal Right to Relief," *Social Service Review,* Vol. 12, No. 2 (June, 1938), pp. 260–275.

ALTMEYER, Arthur J., "People on the Move: Effect of Residence Requirements for Public Assistance," *Social Security Bulletin,* Vol. 9, No. 1 (January, 1946), pp. 3–7.

BRECKINRIDGE, S. P., *Poor Law Administration in Illinois* (Chicago, University of Chicago Press, 1939).

———, *Public Welfare Administration in the United States: Select Documents* (Chicago, University of Chicago Press, 1938).

BROWN, Josephine, *Public Relief: 1929–1939* (New York, Holt, 1940).

BURNS, Eveline M., *The American Social Security System* (Boston, Houghton Mifflin, 1949).

CREECH, Margaret C., *Three Centuries of Poor Law Administration: A Study of Legislation in Rhode Island* (Chicago, University of Chicago Press, 1936).

DE SCHWEINITZ, Karl, *People and Process in Social Security* (Washington, D.C., American Council on Education, 1948).

FREDERICKSEN, Hazel, *The Child and His Welfare* (San Francisco, Freeman, 1948).

FRIEDLANDER, Walter A., *Introduction to Social Welfare* (Englewood Cliffs, N.J., Prentice-Hall, 1955).

GEDDES, Anne E., and HAWKINS, Charles E., "Public Assistance," *Social Work Year Book: 1954,* pp. 394–405.

GENTILE, Felix, and HOWARD, Donald S., *General Assistance: With Special Reference to Practice in 47 Localities of the United States, 1946–1947* (New York, American Association of Social Workers, 1949).

GILLIN, John Lewis, *Poverty and Dependency.* 3d ed. (New York, D. Appleton-Century, 1937).

HABER, William, and COHEN, Wilbur J., eds., *Readings in Social Security* (Englewood Cliffs., N.J., Prentice-Hall, 1948).

KELSO, Robert, *History of Public Poor Relief in Massachusetts: 1620–1720* (Boston, Houghton Mifflin, 1922).

LEYENDECKER, Hilary M., *Problems and Policy in Public Assistance* (New York, Harper, 1955).

LOWE, Robert C., *State Public Welfare Legislation,* W.P.A. Research Monograph (Washington, D.C., G.P.O., 1939), No. 20.

LOWE, Robert C., and HOLCOMBE, John L., *Legislative Trends in Public Relief and Assistance: December 31, 1929 to July 1, 1936,* WPA Special Reports (Washington, D.C., G.P.O., 1936).

LUNDBERG, Emma O., *Unto the Least of These* (New York, Appleton-Century-Crofts, Inc., 1947).

McWILLIAMS, Carey, *Factories in the Field: The Story of Migratory Farm Labor in California* (Boston, Little, Brown, 1939).

MERIAM, Lewis, *Relief and Social Security* (Washington, D.C., Brookings Institution, 1946).

Minnesota Legislative Research Committee, *Public Assistance Policies among the States: 1951* (August, 1952), No. 47.

Public Welfare, quarterly.

RYAN, Philip, *Migration and Social Welfare* (New York, Russell Sage Foundation, 1940).

SMITH, A. Delafield, "Public Assistance as a Social Obligation," 63 Harv. L. Rev. 266–288 (December, 1949).

U.S. Department of Health, Education, and Welfare, Social Security Administration, Bureau of Public Assistance, *Characteristics of State Public Assistance Plans,* Public Assistance Report (Washington, D.C., G.P.O., 1953), No. 21.

U.S. Department of Health, Education, and Welfare, Social Security Administration, Bureau of Public Assistance, *Public Assistance: Graphic Presentation of Selected Data* (April, 1954).

U.S. Department of Health, Education, and Welfare, Social Security Administration, Bureau of Public Assistance, *Public Assistance: Selected Charts on Program Characteristics and Administrative Costs* (December, 1954).

U.S. National Resources Planning Board, Committee on Long-Range Work and Relief Policies, *Security, Work, and Relief Policies,* Report for 1942, 78th Cong., H. Doc. 128 (Washington, D.C., G.P.O., 1943).

WEBB, John N., and BROWN, Malcolm, *Migrant Families,* WPA Research Monograph (Washington, D.C., G.P.O., 1938), No. 18.

WINSTON, Ellen, "Public Welfare," *Social Work Year Book: 1954,* pp. 429–439.

WISNER, Elizabeth, *Public Welfare Administration in Louisiana* (Chicago, University of Chicago Press, 1934).

The student should also consult statutes, judicial decisions, and opinions of state attorneys general; the law encyclopedias; and the monographs, reports, and studies of the FERA, WPA, NYA, and CCC.

CHAPTER 21

Emergency Legislation for Unemployment Relief

(IN THE UNITED STATES)

INTRODUCTION

A review of the development of public-assistance legislation in the United States is incomplete without inclusion of the income maintenance legislation of the 1930–1940 depression period. At the time of its enactment it was often labeled radical, socialistic, and a departure from the "American way." But it was also hailed as a fulfillment of that governmental purpose covered under the welfare clauses of the Constitution. The administration of numbers of depression agencies was frequently flexible, creative, bold, but hardly radical or un-American. The emergency relief programs as such have died, but many of their values have not. Numbers of other programs which developed during this period continue in modified form. New Deal legislation and administration have left indelible marks on public welfare administration and broad public policy.[1]

Many people began to be aware of increasing unemployment in 1928 and 1929. By April, 1930, it was estimated that there were 3,800,000 idle persons, including the ill and disabled; excluding these two groups, the unemployed totaled 3,400,000.[2] In 1932 it was generally accepted that there were between 13,000,000 and 14,000,000 unemployed persons, and in 1933, between 14,500,000 and 15,500,000. Testimony given in 1933 before a congressional committee concerned with the passage of a relief bill showed that in 1932, 65 per cent of men in the building trades were unemployed, 46 per cent in the metal trades, 42 per cent in manufacturing, 50 per cent among musicians and other professional groups, and that unemployment had increased more than 124 per cent in two years.[3]

---

[1] For an excellent abbreviated statement of relief prior to and after WPA, see *Final Report on the WPA Program: 1935–1943* (Washington, D.C., G.P.O., 1947), pp. 1–7.

[2] Paul H. Douglas and Aaron Director, *The Problem of Unemployment* (New York, Macmillan, 1931), p. 17.

[3] Testimony of Dr. Billikopf in U.S. Senate, *Hearings Before a Senate Subcommittee of the Committee of Manufacturers,* 72d Cong., 2d sess. on S. 5125, Pt. I (January 3–17, 1933), p. 6.

After the stock market crash in the latter part of 1929, when unemployment rapidly mounted, the country was completely unprepared to meet the problem of destitution. The United States lagged far behind European countries in social insurance provisions for unemployment, old age, disability, and medical care. We continued to depend upon the established methods of local care for those in need and were reluctant to modernize our assistance legislation and to establish social insurances. In the winter of 1929–1930, the increased load of unemployment was borne by local public and private agencies. In the summer of 1930, citizens' emergency committees were widely organized to raise larger amounts of private funds. The governors of several states appointed committees to study the problem. The President's Emergency Committee for the Unemployed was organized in November, 1930, and functioned as national advisor. The winter of 1930–1931 was characterized by a rapid increase in local government relief funds, by the administration of large amounts of public funds by private agencies, and by a wide development of work relief programs. During 1931 and 1932, state aid for relief appeared.[4] In the first half of 1931 a few states made relatively small sums of money available for unemployment relief. Starting in September, 1931, many states began to pass legislation providing for financial help from the state.

FEDERAL EMERGENCY RELIEF LEGISLATION

Beginning in 1932, when the first federal relief law was enacted, there were three periods of federal emergency relief legislation. The first covered the short period of 1932–1933, when the Reconstruction Finance Corporation lent $300,000,000 to the states for relief; the second covered a little over two years from 1933, when the first grant-in-aid relief law was passed, to the beginning of the Works Progress Administration (WPA) in 1935; and the third extended from the beginning of the WPA to its liquidation in December, 1942.

THE FEDERAL RELIEF LAW OF 1932

President Herbert Hoover's policy concerning the unemployment problem was to encourage expansion of normal work opportunities and use of state and local public and private relief resources.[5] During 1931 and 1932 numerous unsuccessful attempts were made in Congress to pass

---

[4] Rowland Haynes, *State Legislation for Unemployment Relief from January 1, 1931 to May 31, 1932* (Washington, D.C., G.P.O., 1933), p. 4.

[5] Harry Hopkins, *Spending to Save* (New York, Norton, 1936), pp. 13–96; Edward Ainsworth Williams, *Federal Aid for Relief* (New York, Columbia University Press, 1939), ch. 1; Marietta Stevenson, *Public Welfare Administration* (New York, Macmillan, 1938), ch. 2.

unemployment relief bills. Finally, in spite of administration opposition, the Emergency Relief and Construction Act of 1932 was passed.[6] Under it the Reconstruction Finance Corporation, an agency receiving administrative favor and designed to lend funds to distressed corporations, was authorized to set aside $300,000,000 for relief loans to states as advances on future federal highway allotments. Not more than 15 per cent of the amount was to be available for any one state. Aside from this restriction, no strings were attached to the manner of allocating loans to the states. No serious attempt was made by the Reconstruction Finance Corporation to supervise relief administration as it considered itself a banking and not a social agency.[7] Disappointing as were its provisions, this law did make small but much needed funds available to the states. Further, it departed from the unyielding attitude that the federal government did not belong in the relief picture and that the problems of unemployment, both as to relief and as to re-employment, were local.

THE 1933 AND OTHER RELIEF ACTS

The provisions of the 1932 act were entirely inadequate. Two months after his inauguration President Roosevelt approved the Federal Emergency Relief Act of 1933, which appropriated $500,000,000 for aid to the states for unemployment relief.[8] The pressures placed upon Congress convinced that body that unemployment was a national problem, that the states needed federal grants rather than loans, and that the moneys expended for relief programs should be obtained by federal borrowing rather than taxation. By this act the federal relief program was not left with the Reconstruction Finance Corporation but was given to an especially created organization, the Federal Emergency Relief Administration (FERA). Immediately, Harry L. Hopkins, director of the emergency relief program of New York State, was appointed administrator by President Roosevelt. All of the half-billion dollars, except $350,000, which were earmarked for administration, were to go to the states on a nonreimbursable basis. By special provision the administration was enabled to certify funds to the states for aid of needy persons without legal settlement and also for co-operative and self-help associations for the barter of goods and services.

From May, 1933, through February, 1936, the federal government spent more than $3,000,000,000 for the relief program jointly undertaken by the Federal Emergency Relief Administration and the states. The administration received its funds under the provisions of several acts of Congress. Each act was based on the theory that the need was temporary;

---

[6] 47 Stat. L. 709.

[7] See Arthur E. Burns, "Federal Financing of Emergency Relief," *Monthly Report of FERA* (February 1–29, 1936), pp. 1–17, for review of methods.

[8] 48 U.S. Stat. 55; for discussion, see Arthur E. Burns, *loc. cit.*

as a consequence, the funds provided were often sufficient to last only a few months. The Federal Relief Administration was able to carry on its program because of the authority given to the President by the various acts to make interagency fund transfers.

THE CREATION OF THE WPA

By executive order of President Roosevelt on May 6, 1935, under authority of the Emergency Relief Appropriation Act of 1935, the Works Progress Administration, which, in 1939, became the Work Projects Administration, was established, and the FERA was gradually liquidated. The WPA, the CCC, the NYA were all manifestations of the president's policy that "work must be found for able-bodied but destitute workers" and that "the federal government must and shall quit this business of relief." [9] The rest of this chapter will be given over primarily to a discussion of the policies and programs of the FERA and WPA. Before doing so, however, we shall introduce a statement concerning state relief legislation, methods of financing state programs, and constitutionality of state legislation.

STATE EMERGENCY RELIEF LEGISLATION

From the meager beginnings of 1931, the states continued to enact legislation for the relief of the poor largely as emergency measures. In the decade 1931–1940 there were three periods of state emergency relief legislation corresponding to those on the federal level. The first enactments prior to 1933 provided small sums, often for work projects, and set up loose state organizations. The second period was inaugurated with the passage of the 1933 Federal Emergency Relief Act with its provisions for grants-in-aid to the states and with the setting up of state emergency relief administrations. The third period was one characterized by reorganization of the welfare structure and the incorporation of state emergency relief agencies into the permanent welfare agencies. During the period from January 1, 1931, through June, 1935, forty-two states enacted a total of approximately 350 relief statutes. In this interval twenty-five states utilized both state and local funds for unemployment relief, and seventeen states dispersed state funds alone, the localities not contributing to the emergency program. During the days of the FERA there were no state programs for unemployment relief in Georgia, Mississippi, North Carolina, South Carolina, Utah, and West Virginia.[10]

---

[9] Doris Carothers, *Chronology of the FERA: May 12, 1933 to December 31, 1935*, WPA Research Monograph (Washington, D.C., G.P.O., 1937), No. 6, p. 70.

[10] "Digest of State Legislation for the Financing of Emergency Relief," *Monthly Report of FERA* (May 1–31, 1935), pp. 38–89; Public Administration Service, *Poor Relief Laws: A Digest of Existing State Legislation* (Chicago, 1934); Marietta Steven-

The laws gave the responsibility of state unemployment relief administration to special boards, commissioners or officers, or existing departments. Some states amalgamated the emergency relief and general welfare agencies. In some states the central organization had full power to allot funds as it saw fit; in others, it had supervisory powers in regard to a part of the funds; and in still others, it was a channel for distributing funds by formula. Some states set up new and additional machinery for local administration; others used existing machinery. Various methods of distributing funds made their appearance, including matching, percentage, loan, and free fund schemes. The money was spent on both direct and work relief. Legislatures varied greatly in the amount of supervision and control they gave to the state departments.

FUNDS FOR EMERGENCY RELIEF PROGRAMS

Funds for financing the unemployment relief program came from all three levels of government. From January, 1933, through December, 1935, the FERA supplied over $2,900,000,000, or 70.9 per cent, of the expenditures; the states, over $523,000,000, or 12.8 per cent; and the localities, over $669,000,000, or 16.3 per cent.[11] There was great variation between the states in the amount of federal funds received. The FERA and WPA never made clear many of the factors that went into the determination of why one state received almost 100 per cent of its unemployment relief funds from the federal government and another less than 50 per cent, but the ostensible reason for making some differentiation was the variation between states in the extent of need and financial resources.

There were great differences in the amounts of money raised by the states and localities. In some states the larger percentage of the funds came from state revenues, and in some, the reverse was true. State legislatures and agencies distributed federal and state funds to the localities on the basis of their need and their ability to raise money and worked out various methods of determining the amounts to be granted in order that there should be reasonable equity between localities. As the federal government prescribed rules of eligibility by the states, so the states did for the localities.

Federal relief funds came primarily from bond issues or through deficit financing. Revenue sources of *state* emergency relief funds in order of importance were: bonds, general revenues, sales taxes, automotive rev-

---

son and Lucy Brown, *Unemployment Relief Legislation, Federal and State: 1933* (Chicago, American Public Welfare Association, 1933); Marietta Stevenson and Susan Posanski, *Welfare, Relief, and Recovery Legislation, Federal and State: 1933–34* (Chicago, American Public Welfare Association, 1935).

[11] Anita Wells, "The Allocation of Relief Funds by the States among Their Political Subdivisions," *Monthly Report of FERA* (June, 1936), p. 57.

enues, beer and liquor revenues, income tax, and miscellaneous.[12] Only Montana and Wisconsin obtained funds from the income tax, the former raising a very small sum by this method. Local ability to raise funds was tremendously unequal. In allocating federal and state funds to the localities, the states considered such factors as the total number of relief cases, the population, the extent of unemployment, past expenditures, current expenditures, and some combination of these methods.[13] Since the property tax is the major source of local revenue, the availability of *local* relief funds largely depended upon tax levies, assessed valuations, and revenue collection.

CONSTITUTIONAL PROVISIONS AFFECTING STATES

Many of the states were cramped by constitutional restrictions which prohibited the appropriation of public money in aid of any individual and incurring indebtedness for such aid.[14] The constitutions of thirteen states, Arizona, California, Colorado, Georgia, Louisiana, Mississippi, Missouri, Montana, New Mexico, North Dakota, Pennslyvania, Texas, and Wyoming, contained definite limitations on *state* aid to individuals. Four of these states, California, New Mexico, North Dakota, and Wyoming, however, exempted therefrom aid to the poor or to certain classes of the poor, and Pennsylvania exempted pensions or gratuities for military service.[15] Although the constitutions of several states prohibited state appropriations to individuals or in aid of individuals, these same states by statute made funds available for aid to certain classes of persons. It was necessary for the courts to interpret whether under this type of constitutional provision special legislative enactments for assistance to such groups as aged persons and dependent children were constitutional.

The experience of Pennsylvania illustrates the problem the courts encountered with new types of assistance legislation. Pennsylvania had long recognized its duty to care for the needy under its poor laws. In 1931 the Pennsylvania legislature passed an emergency relief law appropriating $10,000,000 to the state's Department of Welfare for unemployment relief and assigning the distribution of funds to local poor-law authorities.

[12] R. L. Lászlóecker-R, "Sources of State Emergency Relief Funds, July 1, 1930 through June 30, 1935," *Monthly Report of FERA* (July 1–31, 1935), pp. 61–73; see also, "State Relief Borrowing," *Monthly Report of FERA* (August 1–31, 1935), pp. 1–14.

[13] Wells, *loc. cit.*, p. 57.

[14] Carl A. Heisterman, "Constitutional Limitations Affecting State and Local Relief Funds," *Social Service Review* (March, 1932), pp. 1–20; see also, Lászlóecker-R, "Sources of State Emergency Relief Funds," *Monthly Report of FERA* (August 1–31, 1935), pp. 61–73; Earle K. Shaw, "An Analysis of the Legal Limitations on the Borrowing Power of the State Governments," *Monthly Report of FERA* (June 1–30, 1936), pp. 121–123.

[15] Heisterman, *loc. cit.*, p. 5.

A friendly suit was initiated in 1932 to test the constitutionality of this law.[16] The state constitution provided that "no appropriations, except for pensions or gratuities for military services, shall be made for charitable, education, or benevolent purposes, to any person or community, nor to any denominational or sectarian institution, corporation, or association." This type of constitutional provision was originally intended by Pennsylvania (and other states) to safeguard the state and municipalities from exploitation by individuals and corporations for purposes of private business or enterprise; it was not intended to keep the poor, as such, from receiving relief. The court, in deciding upon the constitutionality of the emergency legislation, reviewed its earlier decision concerning the unconstitutionality of its old-age assistance law of 1923.[17] There the court held that persons entitled to old-age pensions were not poor persons within the meaning of the poor laws, that the money proposed to be given was a benevolence, and, hence, the individuals who were to receive it were "persons" or a "community" within the meaning of the Pennsylvania constitution. The result of the earlier decision was the amendment of the constitution in 1933 to allow payment of assistance to aged persons without means of support. In the unemployment relief case the court held that the unemployed could not be classed with the aged under the earlier law. Further, appropriations to perform obligatory public functions, among which was providing relief for the destitute poor, including the unemployed, were not charities or benevolence.

The second of the constitutional limitations prohibited the borrowing of funds by the state or local units of government. The constitutions of almost half the states prohibited the extension of state credit to, or in aid of, the various local units and/or the assuming of any liability of these units.[18] Most state constitutions expressly prohibited the state from extending credit to, or in aid of, any individual association or corporation, and some states prohibited the legislature from authorizing local units to extend such credit. Also, most of the states had constitutional limitations on the amount of indebtedness which the state could incur, with certain authorized exemptions.[19] The states found methods of circumventing constitutional limitations on borrowing by diverting moneys from one fund to another. Some set up private corporations which borrowed funds for state purposes. Despite constitutional provisions directly or indirectly affecting the giving of assistance to the unemployed and special classes of needy, legislatures enacted much legislation for their

---

[16] *Commonwealth of Pennsylvania ex. rel. William A. Schnader, Attorney General* v. *Alice F. Liveright, Secretary of Welfare of the Commonwealth of Pennsylvania et al.*, 308 Penn. 35, 161 Atl. 697 (1932).

[17] *Busser* v. *Snyder*, 282 Pa. 440, 128 Atl. 80 (1925).

[18] Heisterman, *loc. cit.*, p. 12.

[19] *Ibid.*, p. 15; for a good summary on the ability of states to borrow see Shaw, *loc. cit.*, pp. 121–123.

benefit. The courts were inclined to consider relief-giving to special classes of poor persons as a public duty within the police power. In effect, they gave new meaning to such phrases as *the poor* and *the needy.* They acknowledged the justification of new standards of eligibility for help.

FERA AND WPA: RELIEF AND WORK POLICIES

THE POLICY OF WORK

From the beginning of the federal relief programs the administration recognized that the mass of unemployed on the relief rolls constituted a cross section of the population. Most of these people before the depression had never been dependent upon public or private assistance. In appreciation of these facts the FERA defined several major objectives, which included adequate relief, work programs, and a diversification of programs to fit the needs of different skills.[20]

Until the program of the Civil Works Administration (CWA) was inaugurated in November, 1933, nearly all public assistance given to persons in need was extended under general relief programs as either direct or work relief. The CWA, with Harry L. Hopkins as its director, lasted from November, 1933, to March, 1934, and provided employment for over 4,000,000 persons, half from the relief rolls. It was a federally administered and financed work program and only in part a relief program. After the demobilization of the civil works program, which was a remarkable although expensive achievement, the Emergency Work Relief Program was organized as a part of the FERA. It was financed by the federal government in part only. When the federal government abolished the FERA, discontinued grants to the states for relief, and started the Works Progress Administration, which provided employment to employables at federal expense, the state and local authorities became responsible for the care of "unemployable" persons in need of assistance and for those employables who could not be given a place on the WPA program.

From the small beginnings of 1931, unemployment work relief programs grew tremendously. Opposition to the federal government's work programs accompanied the increase in costs. This was not because the public generally was opposed to the idea of relief work but because of the heavy financial burden and confusion as to what administrative units should operate and control the program, what amounts of money should be appropriated for its operation, how the money should be apportioned, what wages should be paid, and what projects should be undertaken.

---

[20] Arthur E. Burns and Edward A. Williams, *A Survey of Relief and Security Programs* (Washington, D.C., G.P.O., 1938), pp. 16–17.

ALLOCATION OF FUNDS AND WORK QUOTAS [21]

Determination of the size of grants-in-aid to the states by the FERA and of work quotas by the WPA presented difficulties to the agencies administering the programs. FERA grants were administered on the discretion of the administrator. Except in the original 1933 act, which provided that the first $250,000,000 were to be given to the states on the basis of one federal dollar to every three of state funds and the balance on a discretionary basis, there was not even the requirement that the states match federal grants in some ratio. Critics of Hopkins' methods of distributing relief funds under the loose policies established by Congress maintained that he became an omnipotent dispenser of public largess and political favor. They felt there was never any adequate explanation of why, in 1934, Illinois was getting 68 per cent of its relief bill paid by the FERA when it had 13 per cent of its families on relief; Wisconsin, 79 per cent with 11 per cent on relief; Missouri, 80 per cent with 11 per cent on relief; Nebraska 78 per cent with 9 per cent on relief; Kansas, 73 per cent with 11 per cent on relief; North Carolina, 99 per cent with 10 per cent on relief; Louisiana, 98 per cent with 13 per cent on relief; Virginia, 88 per cent, with 7 per cent on relief, and so forth.

In November, 1933, the percentage of all families receiving relief in the states varied from less than 5 per cent to 29 per cent. In order to distribute funds with reasonable fairness to the states, the administration gave consideration to per capita income and taxpaying ability.[22] Through the sworn applications of governors, supporting statements and briefs, and visits of field representatives, the administration attempted to find the need of each state and its ability to meet that need. Federal funds were withdrawn from Colorado and Missouri because reasonable amounts of state funds were not furnished.

The vague methods of estimating the ability of each state to pay were replaced to some degree in 1934 by more certain methods. The aim was to range the states in order of ability to raise funds. Data were gathered on the following:

1. Those economic factors, such as manufacturing, mining, agricultural output, retail and net wholesale sales, which were available on a comparable basis.
2. Various kinds of population statistics, such as number of gainfully unemployed workers, percentage of urban dwellers, percentage receiving relief.
3. Federal tax collections.
4. The relative financial status of the states, including size of public debt and assessed value of property.
5. Modifying factors, such as drought and flood.

---

[21] Most of this discussion is derived from Williams, *op. cit.*, chs. 5 and 6; see also, Wells, *loc. cit.*, pp. 56–87.

[22] J. Roy Blough, "Equalization Methods for the Distribution of Federal Relief Funds," *Social Service Review* (September, 1935), pp. 423–444.

After the information was gathered and analyzed, the states were divided into groups, each of which was presumed to have the ability to raise the quota assigned to it. In other words, amounts which the states themselves were to raise were allocated to them.

As the FERA developed, objections of all kinds were raised against it. It was too autocratic and too erratic; it demanded too high standards of state and local personnel; it raised standards of living unreasonably; it favored Negroes and strikers and "chiselers"; it gave too much or too little to certain states. Undoubtedly, due to growing opposition to the FERA and the consequent jeopardy of New Deal policies and to the belief that unemployment was a national and not a local problem, that work and not relief should be given to the able-bodied unemployed, the FERA was abandoned by presidential order, and the WPA was initiated. The WPA was essentially a federal agency, the locality being required to sponsor projects and to furnish a portion of the costs. How many projects and how many workers to approve for any state were baffling problems, since Congress provided no certain guide as to how the WPA should distribute the millions of dollars made available for a work relief program.

FERA AND WPA: STANDARDS OF ASSISTANCE

ELIGIBILITY FOR RELIEF

An essential service in the relief program of the FERA was the determination of eligibility for relief. The criterion was need, which, theoretically at least, was based on budgetary deficiency. The determination of need was made by the local social service division.[23] Under the WPA the determination of eligibility for the federal works program was made by the local relief organization, if the WPA designated it to perform this function, or by an especially created certification bureau. In either case, it was planned that the investigation of family need should be made by a social service staff.

The duties of the local social service divisions under the FERA were to receive applications, investigate and establish the eligibility of the applicant for relief, determine the amount of the need, certify to the local work divisions for work relief, administer the direct relief, and supervise the families to see that their needs were being met. Under the WPA, the certification staff had no obligation to supervise expenditures. If supervision was needed, the family was taken off of WPA or referred to another agency for that purpose. Not until 1938 was periodic checking of need required; such a stipulation was included in the 1939–1940 Relief Appropriations Act.

[23] Josephine Brown, "Social Service Division," *Monthly Report of FERA* (March 1–31, 1936), p. 1.

PERSONNEL ADMINISTERING RELIEF

The size of the FERA and WPA created a demand for qualified social workers which could not be met. The great bulk of home visitors were local people sometimes unemployed themselves. Often, they were blessed with good intentions but handicapped by lack of experience in meeting personal problems brought on by widespread unemployment. Trained supervisory staff was employed as much as possible. Training courses were organized to fill in the gaps in the knowledge of staff members.

RULES

To encourage the furnishing of minimum services and reasonable relief all over the country the FERA early issued several fundamental rules governing relief dispensation and administration. Grants of federal emergency relief funds were to be administered by public agencies after August 1, 1933.[24] To carry out the purpose of the Federal Emergency Relief Act of 1933 investigations of all applications for direct and/or work relief were required. Each local relief administration was to have at least one trained and experienced investigator on its staff. Any or all of the following types of relief could be granted:

1. Food, in the form of food order, determined by the number, ages, and needs of the individual members of the family in general accordance with standard food schedules.
2. Orders for the payment of current rent, or its equivalent, where necessary.
3. Orders for light, gas, fuel, and water for current needs.
4. Necessary household supplies.
5. Clothing, or orders for clothing, sufficient for emergency needs.
6. Orders for medicine, medical supplies, and/or medical attendance to be furnished in the home.

The FERA urged that cash relief be given to meet basic needs.[25] This was favored because it preserved the normal purchasing function of the family and maintained existing channels of retail trade. Although the FERA approved the cash method of relief dispensation, it was months before it was used to any extent. At the beginning of the depression there were breadlines, soup kitchens, commissaries, and disbursement orders. It took a long time for the public and many social workers and relief administrators, accustomed to dealing with the chronic poor of predepression days, to realize that most persons coming under the federal government's relief programs were able to manage their own relief money,

---

[24] Federal Emergency Relief Administration, *Rules and Regulations* (Washington, D.C., G.P.O., 1933).

[25] See Joanna Colcord, *Cash Relief* (New York, Russell Sage Foundation, 1936), Pt. 1.

little as that might be. About the time the federal government withdrew from the direct relief picture, an increasing number of communities were favoring cash relief instead of requisitions.

The fact that relief was intended to be administered on a budgetary and not on either a desultory or scale basis meant that standards of living were actually raised in parts of the country and that a new concept of need was recognized, including treatment and preventive health services. The withdrawal of federal funds from the relief picture jeopardized these methods and threw relief administration back onto the doorsteps of local poor-law officials, with all the attendant flaws of inadequacy, inequality, repression, arbitrary selection, and sporadic administration. Those employable unemployed who, after being certified, were placed on the WPA rolls were in a favored class.

FERA AND WPA: WAGES, HOURS, WORKMEN'S COMPENSATION

Work relief refers to those activities undertaken primarily to afford employment to the destitute unemployed, the economic and social values of the work being secondary. Because this is true, the work programs of the depression period encountered problems in the evolution of wage and hour policies. Both the FERA and WPA showed ingenuity and flexibility in their proposals and rulings.[26] A valiant effort was made to keep work relief wages high enough to provide a living income but not so high as to offer undue competition with private industry. Work relief wage practices ranged from regulations requiring the payment of a minimum wage or the local prevailing wage for the type of work performed to the requirement of "work for relief." This latter practice was local and was not condoned by federal agencies.

When federal funds and policies superseded local financing and administration, there was more effort to make cash payments as much like wages as feasible. At one time the FERA policy was that of a fair rate of pay. At another time relief wages were required to be thirty cents an hour or more, with the local prevailing rate of pay for type of work performed to be paid if in excess of thirty cents an hour. Usually, total wages paid per individual were not in excess of the budget deficiency. With the establishment of the Works Progress Administration there was a change in federal policies. The new program repudiated the prevailing wage and budgetary deficiency principles and adopted the "security wage." This meant a predetermined monthly salary or security payment. It varied in accordance with broad occupational groups, regions, and

[26] Arthur E. Burns, "Work Relief Wage Policies: 1930–1936," *Monthly Report of FERA* (June 1–30, 1936), pp. 22–55.

urban-rural areas within regions. Limitations were placed on the length of the working day, week, and month.

The problem of determining reasonable hours of labor was likewise difficult. When work programs were local the most frequent policy was employment by two-, three-, or four-day shifts, with everybody working the same amount of time. When the locality paid unequally for different occupations, hours of labor were adjusted accordingly. The number of hours of work varied, too, with federal wage policy, whether it was a fair or prevailing or security wage or some other plan. Hours were sometimes enough to furnish the budgetary deficiency or sometimes a maximum number per week or month. These few illustrations of wage and hour policy are cited to show that policies on such matters changed with public reactions, experience, and costs.

Policies and practices regarding workmen's compensation varied between jurisdictions and at different times. Legislators, judges, and administrators had to decide whether a person earning his support by work relief was an employee or an object of charity. When local and state governments first launched work programs in 1931 and 1932, no special legislative or administrative consideration was given to the problem of compensation for relief workers.[27] At that time there were workmen's compensation acts in force in all but four states, Arkansas, Florida, Mississippi, and South Carolina. Most states starting work relief programs did not recognize relief workers as coming within the meaning of "public employees." The Michigan Supreme Court in 1933 handed down a decision under its workmen's compensation law, in which it held that the plan of work used in Grand Rapids, which had been heralded throughout the country as a city with a plan where every man had a job and any kind of work was better than charity, was only charity and that such work did not constitute employment. The court said: "Citizens needing public aid are, in a sense, wards of the municipality required to support them, and if the able among them are set to work at common and unremunerative tasks, there does not arise the contract of hire or the relation of employer and employee, but only a helping hand in behalf of public charity." [28] This case brought the judicial view of public poor relief into sharp contrast with the purposes of work relief.

Similar decisions were rendered in the states of Washington,[29] Indiana,[30] and West Virginia.[31] In Wisconsin, where the supreme court

---

[27] William M. Aicher, "Workmen's Compensation on Work Relief Programs," *Monthly Report of FERA* (July 1–31, 1935), pp. 1–16.

[28] *Vaivida* v. *City of Grand Rapids,* 264 Mich. 204, 249 N.W. 826 (1933); Glenn E. Callen, "Some Workmen's Compensation Problems of Persons on Work Relief," *Social Service Review* (June, 1934), pp. 211–225.

[29] *Thurston Co. Chapter, American National Red Cross* v. *Department of Labor and Industries of Washington,* 116 Wash. 488, 7 P 2d 577 (1932).

[30] *In re Moore,* 97 Ind. A. 492, 187 N.E. 219 (1933).

[31] *Basham* v. *Co. Court, Kanawah Co.,* 114 W. Va. 376, 171 S.E. 893 (1933).

held that relief workers were not employees and not entitled to the benefits of the state compensation act,[32] special funds were set aside under the provisions of a special enactment in 1933, to make payments to emergency relief administration workers who sustained injuries arising out of and in the course of employment, such benefits to be paid only for permanent injury and death. In contrast to the above decisions were those of the courts of Nebraska,[33] New York,[34] Louisiana,[35] Georgia,[36] and, again, Michigan, which reversed, in part, its earlier decision.[37] Gradually, relief workers in a number of states secured protection under existing workmen's compensation laws or under those laws amended or under specially enacted laws.

With the creation of the Civil Works Administration in 1933, the federal government gave impetus to the movement to care for persons injured on work relief projects. In the early stages of the CWA, those injured or killed in performance of their work received benefits based upon a modification of the Federal Compensation Act of 1916. In February, 1934, an act of Congress restricted benefits.[38] Under this act, the maximum monthly benefits that could accrue to an injured work relief employee were fixed. With the passage of the Emergency Relief Appropriations Act of 1935, under which the WPA was established, the federal government assumed compensation responsibility for workers injured on relief projects. Congress, in several ensuing acts, laid down numbers of restrictions on compensation to work relief recipients, but federal policy was clear. The injured person was a workman and entitled to certain benefits as a matter of legal right.

FERA AND WPA: PROGRAMS FOR THE UNSETTLED POOR

Federal legislation creating various relief agencies left much latitude with the administrations for establishing policies and programs.[39] As programs evolved policies emerged, and vice versa. We have referred to several of the fundamental policies of the FERA and WPA and have commented on some of the numerous changes through which they went. It is impossible, in a short review, to present all the depression relief

---

[32] *West Milwaukee* v. *Industrial Commission,* 216 Wis. 29, 255 N.W. 728 (1934).

[33] *Senator* v. *City of Lincoln,* 124 Neb. 403, 245 N.W. 924 (1933).

[34] *Barlog* v. *Board of Water Commissioners, City of Dunkirk,* 267 N.Y. Supp. 822 (1933).

[35] *Durrett* v. *Unemployment Relief Committee et al.,* 152 S (La.) 138 (1934).

[36] *City of Waycross* v. *Hayes,* 48 Ga. 317, 172 S.E. 756 (1934).

[37] *McLaughlin* v. *Antrim Road Commission,* 266 Mich. 73, 253 N.W. 221 (1934).

[38] 48 Stat. L. 351.

[39] For good brief summary on this subject, see Emmett H. Welch, "Various Government Provisions for the Unemployed," *Annals of the American Academy of Political and Social Science* (March, 1938), pp. 36–44.

and works programs of the federal government, but some of the most important will be described. Some may have been misconceived and some may have been unjustifiably dropped or modified, but the fact remains that deep concern for human welfare went into their conception and execution.

Among the major programs was that set up to meet the critical problem of the nation's transient population. Because the transient group was generally ineligible for local general assistance, special provision was made for it in the Federal Emergency Relief Act of 1933.[40] The administration defined transients as unattached persons or family groups that had not resided one continuous year or longer within any state at the time of application for relief. A distinction thus was made between transients for whom the federal and state governments were expected to assume responsibility.

The first transient relief grant was made by the FERA to Alabama in September, 1933. Between that date and September, 1935, when intake at transient bureaus was closed, forty-seven states and the District of Columbia operated transient relief programs. Great divergencies existed between the states in their transient programs and administrative structure. The FERA, in its definition of policies, attempted to apply principles tested by agencies working with this group. It rejected certain local traditional practices and laid down others. Food, clothing, laundry, medical care, education, and recreation were to be furnished as required. There was to be no "passing on." Families were dealt with on a casework basis. Special attention was given to physical needs.

Prior to the relief act of 1933, the number of transients was variously estimated at between 1,500,000 and 5,000,000 persons. With the experience of a federal program more accurate and realistic figures became available. At its peak the transient relief population reached approximately 400,000 unattached persons and 16,000 family groups. Most transients were young, healthy, and willing to work. Consequently, the FERA developed a plan for operating camps from which men worked at fish hatcheries, game preserves, pest-control projects, river and stream clearance projects, and so forth. They received board and room and from $1.00 to $3.00 a week in cash. The initial belief that transients as a group needed casework techniques and therapeutic treatment was discarded. With the

---

[40] John N. Webb, *The Transient Unemployed,* WPA Research Monograph (Washington, D.C., G.P.O. 1935), No. 3, p. 7; *Relief for Unemployed Transients: Hearings Before the Senate Subcommittee of the Committee on Manufactures,* 72d Cong., 2d sess. on S. 5121 (January 13–25, 1933); Carothers, *op. cit.;* M. Starr Northrop, Malcolm J. Brown, Katherine Gordon, *A Survey of the Transient and Homeless Population in Twelve Cities: September, 1935 and September, 1936,* WPA Special Report (Washington, D.C., G.P.O., 1937); Ellery F. Reed, *Federal Transient Program: An Evaluative Survey* (New York, Committee on Care of Transients and Homeless, 1934), pp. 34–35; W. J. Plunkert, "Public Responsibility and Transiency," *Social Service Review* (September, 1935), pp. 484–491.

initiation of the WPA the federal transient program was abolished.[41] It was Hopkins' conviction, confirmed by facts and figures, that transients were no different, except for the accident of residence, from the rest of the unemployed. Hence, they should be included in work programs. Many transients were placed on WPA work programs, but in view of the fact that these programs could not absorb all able-bodied residents, local officials were reluctant to certify the eligible unsettled. Since there had been little or no change in the basic poor laws of the states, doing away with the federal transient program in many instances meant a reversion to archaic methods of treating members of this group.

YOUTH PROGRAMS

Census figures for 1930 showed there were approximately 20,000,000 persons falling within the sixteen- to twenty-five-year age group.[42] Reasonably accurate estimates indicated that about 5,000,000 of this number were out of school and unemployed as late as the spring of 1935 and that nearly 3,000,000 were on relief. As of the end of 1935, it was estimated that 20 per cent of the total unemployment consisted of young people between the ages of eighteen and twenty-five. Such data challenged the interest and ingenuity of federal agencies and the public generally.

THE CIVILIAN CONSERVATION CORPS

The CCC, the first specific youth program launched by the New Deal, was created an independent agency by Congress in 1937.[43] It succeeded an agency known as Emergency Conservation Work, established by executive order in 1933. Its purpose was to remove single, unemployed men from the glutted labor market, to give them healthful constructive work, and to provide for the restoration of the country's natural resources.[44] The age period at first was eighteen to twenty-five years; later,

---

[41] 49 U.S. Stat. 115.

[42] W. Thatcher Winslow, *Youth, A World Problem: A Study in World Perspective of Youth Conditions, Movements, and Programs* (Washington, D.C., G.P.O., 1937), pp. xi ff.; Bruce L. Melvin, *Rural Youth on Relief*, WPA Research Monograph (Washington D.C., G.P.O., 1937), No. 11; National Youth Administration, *Facing the Problems of Youth: The Work and Objectives of the NYA* (Washington, D.C., G.P.O., 1937); National Youth Administration, *Administrative and Program Operation of the NYA: June 26, 1935–January 1, 1937* (Washington, D.C., G.P.O., 1937); circulars and bulletins of NYA for rules and regulations; Howard M. Bell, *Youth Tell Their Story* (Washington, D.C., American Council on Education, 1938).

[43] 50 U.S. Stat. 319.

[44] U.S. Senate *Hearings Before the Committee on Education and Labor,* 75th Cong., 1st sess. on S. 2102, "A Bill to Establish a Civilian Conservation Corps and for Other Purposes" (April 9 and 13, 1937); U.S. House of Representatives, *Hearings Before the Committee on Labor,* 75th Cong., 1st sess. on H.R. 6180, "To Make the CCC a Permanent Agency"; U.S. House of Representatives, *Hearings Before the*

for junior enrollees, it was seventeen to twenty-three years. In July, 1939, the CCC ceased to be an independent agency with various aspects of its activities administered by several departments of government. By presidential order it and the NYA were moved to the Federal Security Agency. By additional legislation its life was extended to 1943.

No major emergency undertaking of the Roosevelt administration met with more general approval than the CCC. It had little difficulty in gaining and keeping congressional interest and support. There were several apparent reasons for this: Some aspects of the program provided genuine training opportunities; recruitment was for definite periods of time not related to continuing eligibility for relief; administrative responsibility, though split between the Veterans' Administration, and the departments of Labor, Agriculture, and Interior, was well co-ordinated under the CCC director; War Department facilities were used for the efficient management of the camps, with the exception of Indians on Indian reservations. During the quarter beginning July 1, 1935, CCC enrollment reached its peak of over 500,000 young men. The majority of them received a monthly wage which did not exceed $30.00. Over $2,000,000,000 were spent on the program.

THE NATIONAL YOUTH ADMINISTRATION

Since the CCC at any given time could take care of only a small percentage of unemployed young men, additional methods of assisting young people were devised. The NYA was launched in June, 1935, by executive order under the authority of the Emergency Relief Appropriation Act of 1935. Its enthusiastic and zealous director was Aubrey Williams. It was transferred to the Federal Security Agency in 1939 and, in 1942, to the War Manpower Commission, where it remained until it was liquidated in 1943.[45] The purposes of the NYA were fourfold: (1) to provide funds for part-time employment of needy secondary school, college, and graduate students between sixteen and twenty-four inclusive, so they might continue their education; (2) to provide funds for the part-time employment of out-of-school youths between eighteen and twenty-four inclusive, and chiefly from relief families, on projects designed to afford valuable work experience and to benefit youth and the community generally; (3) to encourage the establishment of job-training, counseling, and placement services for youth; and (4) to encourage the development and extension of constructive leisure-time activities.

The NYA reached its peak registration of 443,986 in April, 1937. In

---

Committee on Labor, 76th Cong., 1st sess. on H.R. 2990 (February 9, 23, 24, 1939); Henry Lanpher, "The CCC: Some Aspects of Its Social Program for Unemployed Youth," *Social Service Review* (December, 1936), pp. 623–636; *U.S. Government Organization Manual: 1954–55* (Washington, D.C., G.P.O., 1955), p. 606; Beulah Amidon, "Civilian Conservation Corps," *Social Work Year Book: 1939, pp.* 79–83.

[45] *U.S. Government Organization Manual: 1954–55,* p. 630.

April, 1938, 333,320 young people were enrolled in 25,606 schools and colleges. In that month average hourly earnings were 28.5 cents and average monthly earnings $6.75 per student.[46] This program, like the CCC, was expensive. It cared for only a small percentage of the youthful unemployed. Authorities in the field of public-assistance administration, as well as the general public, queried whether a relatively small group of young people should be selected out from the mass of those needing assistance and favored with special work, education, and training before all families and persons needing assistance received it.[47]

FERA AND WPA PROJECTS

CONSTRUCTION PROJECTS

Except for the short-lived Civil Works Administration (CWA) the most extensive work relief experience of the federal government was the WPA. As a result of statistics gathered by the FERA the WPA knew the kinds of projects best suited to the qualifications of the unemployed needy. An appreciable percentage of people could be used, with benefit to themselves and the community, on nonconstruction projects, but the greatest percentage could best be employed on multiple types of construction activities. Among the major construction projects of WPA were new and repaired state and local public buildings, construction and repair of thousands of miles of highway, new dams for conservation purposes, new water mains and sewers, new and expanded parks, playgrounds and athletic fields, new and improved ditches for mosquito control, and construction and improvement of many airport facilities. As public opinion became more critical of work relief projects Congress responded by curtailing the program. Under the 1939 relief act the WPA was prohibited from undertaking any new building project costing more than $52,000 in federal funds. This prohibition particularly penalized urban communities.

NONCONSTRUCTION PROJECTS [48]

Col. F. C. Harrington, successor to Harry Hopkins, testifying before a congressional committee in March, 1939, showed that there were more than 2,750,000 persons on WPA for the week ending January 28.

---

[46] M. M. Chambers, "Youth Programs," *Social Work Year Book: 1939*, pp. 484–492; testimony of Aubrey Williams, administrator of NYA, in U.S. House of Representatives, *Hearings Before the Subcommittee of the Committee of Appropriations*, 76th Cong., 1st sess. on "Bill Making Appropriations for Work Relief and Relief, Fiscal Year, 1940."

[47] Marie Dresden Lane and Francis Steegmuller, *America on Relief* (New York, Harcourt, Brace, 1938), ch. 7; Betty Lindley and Ernest K. Lindley, *A New Deal for Youth* (New York, Viking, 1938), from Foreword.

[48] Work Projects Administration, *Government Aid During the Depression to Professional, Technical, and Other Service Workers* (Washington, D.C., G.P.O., 1936).

Somewhat less than $500,000, or 18.8 per cent, were on nonconstruction projects. A minority of these workers were on projects which required professional skill, such as educational, recreational, and library activities; engineering, legal, and archaeological studies; and the arts. Some of the projects were of minor importance if numbers were of paramount significance, for example, transcribing literature into Braille, providing school lunches, bookbinding, and so forth. Each of these activities, however, absorbed persons in need of work and also provided essential community services. The largest percentage of the nonconstruction projects were sewing activities which employed about 200,000 women.[49]

The first group of service workers to receive federal aid from FERA funds were teachers. Beginning in 1933, federal grants were made to thirty-three states to keep open rural schools that were closed or about to close, thus giving employment to some 33,000 teachers and affording school facilities to more than 1,000,000 children. The educational program came to include nursery schools, vocational instruction for unemployed and other adults, vocational rehabilitation, and parent education. An important phase of the educational program was workers' education, with a curriculum dealing largely with current industrial and social problems.

The most criticized of the WPA nonconstruction projects, the ones most often labeled "boondoggling" and frequently believed to benefit the radical or the agitator, were those, which, until 1939 congressional action, were sponsored by the WPA itself. They were the art, music, theater, writing, and historical records activities, all of which were eliminated under the Emergency Relief Appropriations Act of 1939. This law provided that after August 31, 1939, none of the funds made available under the act were to be used for the operation of any project sponsored solely by the WPA, and, after June 30, 1939, no federal moneys were to be used for the operation of any theater project. The amounts spent on the federal projects were relatively small.

Of the arts projects, the one concerned with music was the most quickly, widely, and easily organized. Its purpose was to establish high standards of musicianship, to educate the public to an appreciation of musical opportunities, and to rehabilitate and retrain musicians so as to enable them to become self-supporting. It provided employment for instrumentalists, vocalists, composers, teachers, librarians, copyists and arrangers, tuners, and music binders. The art project, not so sizable as the music and theater projects, gave employment to persons interested not only in pure art, such as sculpturing and painting, but also in commercial art.

Probably the most criticized of the federal arts projects were those

---

[49] Lane and Steegmuller, *op. cit.*, ch. 4.

of the theater. Brooks Atkinson, writing in the theatrical section of the *New York Times* a month before Congress completely abolished the theater project, commented as follows on this program: [50]

> Many things about the Federal Theatre are hard to defend. Being the most conspicuous of the WPA arts projects, it is the one Congress enjoys worrying most. Art seems like boondoggling to a Congressman who is looking for a club with which to belabor the Administration, and there is always something in the Federal Theatre that can be blown up into a scandal. But for socially useful achievement it would be hard among the relief projects to beat the Federal Theatre, which has brought art and ideas within the range of millions of people all over the country and proved that the potential theatre audience is inexhaustible. . . .
>
> Although the Federal Theatre is far from perfect, it has kept an average of 10,000 people employed on work that has helped to lift the dead weight from the lives of millions of Americans. It has been the best friend the theatre as an institution has ever had in this country. It has brought the theatre and people together realistically. In short, it deserves to be rescued from partisan politics which, on the one hand, are creeping into its administration, and, on the other, are threatening to put it out of business.

The largest of the federal writers projects involved the preparation of guide books of the various states. This idea was first tried out in 1934–1935 in Connecticut under the FERA. Another writing project was copying valuable historical documents. Still another experiment was to send members of the North Carolina, Tennessee, and Georgia staffs to interview ordinary people. The first volume published as a consequence of these interviews contained thirty-five life histories, including the biographies of a country doctor, a Negro dentist, a housemaid, a CCC boy, and a small-town merchant.[51]

Although the nonconstruction projects of the WPA represented a relatively small proportion of its total activities, we have chosen to emphasize them. We have done this in order to point out three principles upon which the WPA operated in respect to these projects and the people who worked on them: (1) in a period of heavy unemployment there are large numbers of white-collar unemployed who need to have their skills and self-respect preserved; (2) the community needs the skills of this group, including the professions and the arts; (3) from an economic point of view nonconstruction projects are relatively noncompetitive with private industry.

RESEARCH PROJECTS

The Division of Research of the FERA, later of the WPA, gathered great volumes of information concerning the unemployed in the coun-

[50] *New York Times* (May 28, 1939).

[51] *These Are Our Lives* (Chapel Hill, N.C., University of North Carolina Press, 1939).

try.[52] Figures on unemployment were grossly inadequate since there had been no comprehensive federal employment office system. The data gathered by this division of the FERA and WPA formed the basis for subsequent federal legislation and programs. A part of the work of this division was to analyze the characteristics and status of the unemployed on relief in order to predict whether they could and would leave relief rolls and to plan work projects wisely.

The Research Division learned that the typical unemployed city worker on relief was a white man, thirty-eight years of age, the head of a family, more often unskilled than skilled; that he had not finished elementary school; and that he had not been working at his usual occupation for over two and a half years. It further learned that three fourths of the workers were men, and one fourth women; that the men on the average were five years older than the women and that both men and women were two years older than those workers still employed in their various fields.[53] In March, 1935, a total of 3,250,000 relief families were certified as eligible for the works program. These families included 4,885,000 workers or about one tenth of all gainful workers in the country.

In addition to the 3,250,000 families eligible for the works program, two other important groups were represented on the relief rolls. The first comprised 900,000 cases in which there was no employable person. These were largely aged persons, women with dependent children, and physically incapacitated persons. The second group included some 400,000 families in which the breadwinners were privately employed but, because of part-time or inadequate wages, could not maintain themselves without supplementary public assistance. Responsibility for these two groups was turned back to the states, partial responsibility for the former group being assumed by the federal government under the Social Security Act of 1935. Since the studies showed that the majority of persons on relief were employable, Congress replaced the FERA program of providing funds for relief to the states by a federal works program.

SUMMARY OF WPA ACTIVITIES

The WPA was liquidated on December 4, 1942. *The Final Report on the W.P.A. Program: 1935–43* summarizes the colossal activities of that organization. During the eight years in which the program was in oper-

---

[52] Emerson Ross, "Research Statistical Program of FERA," *Journal of the American Statistical Association* (September, 1934), pp. 288–295.

[53] Hopkins, *op. cit.*, p. 161; Work Projects Administration, *Workers on Relief in the United States, March, 1935: A Census of Usual Occupations,* WPA Special Report (Washington, D.C., G.P.O., 1937); Work Projects Administration, Division of Research, *Statistical Summary of Emergency Relief Activities: January, 1933 through December, 1935* (Washington, D.C., G.P.O., 1936); Work Projects Administration, Division of Research, *Local Wage Rates for Selected Occupations in Public and Private Construction: 1936* (Washington, D.C., G.P.O., 1936).

ation it provided employment at one time or another for about 8,500,000 individuals. This means that nearly one fourth of all families in the United States were dependent on WPA at some time. Peak WPA employment was reached in the fiscal year 1939 when it averaged well over 3,000,000 persons. Sponsors' contribution provided $2,837,713,000, or more than one fifth of the total cost of WPA operated projects; the federal share was $10,136,743,000. Although the earnings of WPA workers varied according to skill and location, they averaged only $54.33 a month over the eight-year period. The report concluded that the WPA had made valuable advances over traditional poor-law methods of providing relief; nevertheless, public work and relief should not be combined. In the language of the report:

> (1) Eligibility for relief should not be the test for public employment. Workers on public projects should be paid the wages customary for such work. The unemployed who are able and willing to work should not be compelled to suffer the humiliation of "going on relief" in order to secure jobs. Direct relief should be reserved for the needy unemployables. (2) Federal, state, and local governments . . . should plan their needed public works amply and well in advance of the construction date; they should be prepared with plans and financing to launch useful public works promptly to cushion large-scale employment fluctuations in the construction industry.

FEDERAL FARM PROGRAMS

Between 1929 and 1935, one rural family in four received some form of public assistance.[54] The agency most responsible for dealing with farm poverty was the Farm Security Administration. It was created in September, 1937, successor to the Resettlement Administration established in 1935 by a merger of the rural rehabilitation work of the FERA and the subsistence homestead program of the Public Works Administration (PWA). The Farm Security Administration aided about 1,000,000 destitute farm families in the following ways:

1. It made rehabilitation loans for such items as farm animals, machinery, seed.
2. It carried out a debt-adjustment program.
3. It made subsistence grants to farm families in drought areas.
4. It administered a resettlement program which provided assistance to farmers in finding new locations.
5. It carried out a large land-utilization program directed toward the pur-

---

[54] Benson Y. Landis, "Rural Social Programs," *Social Work Year Book: 1939,* pp. 384–391; *U.S. Government Organization Manual: 1954–55,* p. 616; Berta Asch and A. P. Mangus, *Farmers on Relief and Rehabilitation,* WPA Research Monograph (Washington, D.C., G.P.O., 1936), No. 8; Rebecca Farnham and Irene Link, *Effects of the Works Program on Rural Relief,* WPA Research Monograph (Washington, D.C., G.P.O., 1938), No. 13; Walter Wynne, Jr., *Five Years of Rural Relief,* W.P.A. Special Report (Washington, D.C., G.P.O., 1938).

chasing of land unsuited for farming and encouraging its use for forestry and recreation.

Other federal work and relief programs benefited farmers and rural sections of the country. The CCC reached rural communities, since more than half the enrolled men were from such areas and all the activities were in rural territories. Rural families also benefited from NYA. The WPA helped rural communities through such means as employment of workers on road and other projects, improvements in school buildings, and better facilities for recreation and adult education. The depression brought to rural areas many agencies and services which prior to 1930 had not been available to them.

A special activity of the FERA benefiting farmers and many other groups was the Federal Surplus Relief Corporation, chartered in October, 1933, under the laws of Delaware. This agency was transferred to the United States Department of Agriculture and became known as the Federal Surplus Commodity Corporation. Eventually, in 1942, it was merged into the Agricultural Marketing Administration. Surplus goods, such as pork, cotton, vegetables, fruit, butter, and seed, were bought and distributed to state relief agencies for supplies for needy persons. The supplies were in addition to those received in the relief budget.[55]

RELATED GOVERNMENTAL ACTIVITIES

Starting in 1933, Congress enacted much legislation setting up programs and services designed to assist low-income groups, both the employed and the unemployed, and to stimulate economic recovery. These programs clearly were not relief activities, but they were part of a recovery program and were designed to gear into a comprehensive program to include prevention of unemployment. Brief reference is made to several of these programs because they were aspects of the federal government's efforts to relieve the depression and to protect our democratic form of government. They represented an attempt on the part of the government to furnish some of the economic and social advantages of our country to millions of persons with low incomes. Numbers of them are very much alive today.

EMPLOYMENT OFFICE SYSTEM

The depression made it clear that there was great need of an adequate employment office system. Prior to the passage of the Wagner-Peyser Act of 1933,[56] the federal employment office program was limited to the operation of 129 offices of which thirty served veterans alone; and only

---

[55] *U.S. Government Organization Manual: 1954–55,* pp. 238, 621.
[56] 48 U.S. Stat. 113.

twenty-four states maintained local public services.[57] The act abolished the existing federal employment service and established within the Department of Labor the United States Employment Service, based on the principle of federal-state co-operation. By June 30, 1938, the employment services of fifty-one American jurisdictions had become affiliated with the United States Employment Service. Approximately 3,000 employment offices operated under the act. The passage of the Social Security Act quickly affected the expansion and efficiency of public employment offices, since all states had to make unemployment compensation payments through public employment offices or through other agencies approved by the Federal Security Board. Between 1933, when the Wagner-Peyser Act was passed, and 1950 the federal employment office system led an unsettled life. At one time or another it was lodged with the Social Security Board and the Manpower Commission. It is now a permanent part of the Department of Labor. Today, in addition to general services for all unemployed persons, it also furnishes special services for several categories of workers, such as professional workers, farm workers, and veterans.

CONSTRUCTION ACTIVITIES

In numerous ways the federal government stimulated and carried on construction activities other than those administered by the WPA. One of the most important agencies in this field was the Federal Emergency Administration of Public Works, which was established in June, 1933, pursuant to Title II of the National Industrial Recovery Act [58] and which had its life extended by successive acts. Eventually, it was turned over to the office of the Federal Works Administration; but this agency was abolished in 1949, and its functions were transferred to the General Services Administration. The chief aim of the Federal Emergency Administration of Public Works was the reduction of unemployment and the restoration of purchasing power through the construction of useful public works and the encouragement of long-range planning in public works. Loans and grants were made to public bodies for the construction of useful projects under contracts entered into by private contractors and the public body receiving the allotment. Employment on these projects was obtained through the offices of the United States Employment Service and recognized union locals. From the time of its creation to February 1, 1939, the PWA spent more than $4,000,000,000.[59]

---

[57] Arthur W. Motley, "Employment Services," *Social Work Year Book: 1954,* pp. 185–192.

[58] 48 U.S. Stat. 195.

[59] Public Works Administration, *The Story of PWA Building for Recovery* (Washington, D.C., G.P.O., 1939); *U.S. Government Organization Manual: 1954–55,* pp. 392, 621.

HOUSING PROGRAMS [60]

A federal housing policy began to develop during the depression period. Numbers of services were initiated. For example, government credit was furnished to lending institutions and to home owners. From 1933 to 1936 the Home Owners Loan Corporation (HOLC) refinanced over 1,000,000 home owners in danger of foreclosure. Of these, more than eighty per cent were able to save their homes. When liquidated in 1951 the corporation had paid its way and netted a profit of $14,000,000. The United States Housing Act, passed in 1937, provided the basic procedures of public low-rent housing which have been followed with only minor changes to the present day. The Housing and Home Finance Agency today carries on this and many other housing activities.

THE NATIONAL LABOR RELATIONS ACT [61]

The National Labor Relations Board is an independent federal organization established in 1935. It is an agency designed to prevent industrial strife and to assure certain rights to organized labor, including that to bargain collectively. The act was amended by the Labor Management Relations Act, the so-called Taft-Hartley Law, which prescribes certain limits on the conduct of employers and labor unions and forbids conduct going beyond these limits as "unfair labor practices." Methods are established for prosecution of such practices. The act also provides for polls of employees covered by a union shop agreement to determine whether or not they wish to revoke the union's authority to make such an agreement.

THE FAIR LABOR STANDARDS ACT OF 1938 [62]

The purposes of this act are outlined in its declaration of policy:

Section 2 (a) The Congress hereby finds that the existence, in industries engaged in commerce or in the production of goods for commerce, of labor conditions detrimental to the maintenance of the minimum standard of living necessary for health, efficiency and general well-being of workers (1) causes commerce and the channels and instrumentalities of commerce to be used to spread and perpetuate such labor conditions among the workers of the several states; (2) burdens commerce and the free flow of goods in commerce; (3) constitutes an unfair method of competition in commerce; (4) leads to labor disputes burdening and obstructing commerce and the free flow of goods in commerce; and (5) interferes with the orderly and fair marketing of goods in commerce.

---

[60] Bryn J. Hoode, "Housing and City Planning," *Social Work Year Book: 1954*, pp. 257–266; *U.S. Government Organization Manual: 1954–55*, pp. 403–414.

[61] *U.S. Government Organization Manual: 1954–55*, pp. 431–435; Clara M. Beyer, "Labor Standards," *Social Work Year Book: 1954*, pp. 308–320.

[62] *U.S. Government Organization Manual: 1954–55*, pp. 299–301; Beyer, *loc. cit.*, pp. 308–320.

(b) It is hereby declared to be the policy of this act, through the exercise by Congress of its power to regulate commerce among the several states, to correct and as rapidly as practicable to eliminate the conditions above referred to in such industries without substantially curtailing employment of earning power.

By the act there was established a Wage and Hour Division in the Department of Labor, headed by an administrator appointed by the President and confirmed by the Senate. Every employer engaged in interstate commerce was required to pay his employees not less than 25 cents an hour during the first year from the effective date of the act, during the next six years not less than 30 cents, and not less than 40 cents thereafter. The work week was forty-four hours during the first year, forty-two during the second year, and forty hours thereafter. Maximum hours for certain work periods also were set. Oppressive child labor was prohibited. Subsequent legislative changes have raised the minimum wage until, in 1956, it reached $1.00 an hour.

SUMMARY AND CONCLUSIONS

Thus far in the third section of this book we have attempted to review the British movement away from an old poor law to a modern system of social security; to sample the experiences of other parts of the world with such a growth; to review the American experience with general assistance; and to summarize the income security legislation of the depression decade of 1930 to 1940.

Our particular objectives in this chapter have been:

1. To review the legislation, particularly federal legislation, which undertook to help the needy unemployed in the depression decade.
2. To describe some of the policies, practices, and programs of federal agencies operating under legislative mandate.
3. To point up the contributions of that decade to temporary and permanent modifications in principles and standards of public assistance.
4. To show that policies and programs were effected by multiple factors, including the past of public-assistance administration, the experience and resourcefulness of the then administrators, the positive and negative attitudes of the public, and the feelings of the beneficiaries.
5. To emphasize the departure from the historic constitutional principle that public assistance is exclusively a state function.
6. To make evident that large portions of the American people came to realize that the need for public assistance is primarily the result of social and economic factors rather than individual sloth and "cussedness."
7. To indicate the extent to which special groups, such as migrants, youth, farmers, and workers with special skills, were singled out for special programs.
8. To direct attention to the fact that good public administration requires a combination of opposites, flexibility and stability.
9. To call attention to the importance of data for adapting and planning and the extent to which such data were used for the development of emergency and permanent programs.

10. To stress the importance of work as a means of alleviating unemployment and helping the unemployed and to raise the question of whether work should or should not be a relief measure.

In the balance of this section of the book we shall describe the principles and programs of the Social Security Act. In so doing, we shall attempt to show similarities to, and departures from, predepression and depression legislation and administration.

Selected References

ABBOTT, Edith, *Public Assistance* (Chicago, University of Chicago Press, 1940).

ABBOTT, Grace, *From Relief to Social Security* (Chicago, University of Chicago Press, 1941).

BELL, Howard M., *Youth Tell Their Story* (Washington, D.C., American Council on Education, 1938).

BREMNER, Robert H., *From the Depths* (New York, New York University Press, 1956).

BROWN, Josephine, *Public Relief: 1929–1939* (New York, Holt, 1940).

BURNS, Eveline M., *The American Social Security System* (Boston, Houghton Mifflin, 1949).

CAROTHERS, Doris, *Chronology of the FERA: May 12, 1933 to December 31, 1935*, WPA Research Monograph (Washington, D.C., G.P.O., 1937), No. 6.

COLCORD, Joanna, *Cash Relief* (New York, Russell Sage Foundation, 1936).

DOUGLAS, Paul H., and DIRECTOR, Aaron, *The Problem of Unemployment* (New York, Macmillan, 1931).

DUNN, Catherine M., *What Price Local Poor Relief?* (Chicago, American Public Welfare Association, 1936).

Final Report on the WPA Program: 1935–43 (Washington, D.C., G.P.O., 1947).

GILL, Corrington, *Wasted Man Power* (New York, Norton, 1939).

HEISTERMAN, Carl A., "Constitutional Limitations Affecting State and Local Relief Funds," *Social Service Review* (March, 1932), pp. 1–20.

HOPKINS, Harry, *Spending to Save* (New York, Norton, 1936).

KURTZ, Russell, ed., *The Public Assistance Worker* (New York, Russell Sage Foundation, 1938).

LANE, Marie Dresden, and STEEGMULLER, Francis, *America on Relief* (New York, Harcourt, Brace, 1938).

LEYENDECKER, Hilary M., *Problems and Policy in Public Assistance* (New York, Harper, 1955).

LINDLEY, Betty, and LINDLEY, Ernest K., *New Deal for Youth* (New York, Viking Press, 1938).

MERIAM, Lewis, *Relief and Social Security* (Washington, D.C., Brookings Institution, 1946).

MITCHELL, Broadus, *The Depression Decade* (New York, Rinehart, 1947).

SHERWOOD, Robert E., *Roosevelt and Hopkins* (New York, Harper, 1948).

U.S. Department of Health, Education, and Welfare, Social Security Administration, *Social Security in the United States* (Washington, D.C., G.P.O., 1953).

United States Government Organization Manual: 1954–55 (Washington, D.C., G.P.O., 1955).

U.S. National Resources Planning Board, Committee on Long-Range Work and Relief Policies, *Security, Work, and Relief Policies,* Report for 1942, 78th Cong., H. Doc. 128 (Washington, D.C., G.P.O., 1943).

WILLIAMS, Edward Ainsworth, *Federal Aid for Relief* (New York, Columbia University Press, 1939).

The student should also consult presidential executive orders, federal and state statutes, and judicial decisions; the monographs, reports, studies, and other publications of the FERA, WPA, CCC, and NYA; hearings and reports of congressional committees; and the various volumes of the *Social Work Year Book.*

CHAPTER 22

Old-age Assistance

(SOCIAL SECURITY ACT)

INTRODUCTION

In a special message to Congress on June 8, 1934, President Franklin D. Roosevelt announced his intention of presenting a program for social security to Congress for action and said: [1]

> Next winter we may well undertake the great task of furthering the security of the citizen and his family through social insurance.
>
> This is not an untried experiment. Lessons of experience are available from states, from industries and from many nations of the civilized world. The various types of social insurance are interrelated; and I think it is difficult to attempt to solve them piecemeal. Hence, I am looking for a sound means which I can recommend to provide at once security against several of the great disturbing factors in life—especially those which relate to unemployment and old age. I believe there should be a maximum of co-operation between states and the federal government. I believe that the funds necessary to provide this insurance should be raised by contribution rather than by an increase in general taxation. Above all, I am convinced that social insurance should be national in scope, although the several states should meet at least a large portion of the cost of management, leaving to the federal government the responsibility of investing, maintaining, and safeguarding the funds constituting the necessary insurance reserves.

By Executive Order No. 6757 on June 29, 1934, the Committee on Economic Security, consisting of the secretary of labor as chairman, the secretary of the treasury, the secretary of agriculture, the attorney general, and the administrator of the Federal Emergency Relief Program, was created.[2] Its function was to study the problems relating to economic security and to make recommendations for a long-term and an immediate program of legislation. By the same order, three subordinate agencies were created to assist the committee in the discharge of its duties: the

[1] H. Doc. 397, 73d Cong., 2d sess. (1934).

[2] U.S. Committee on Economic Security, *Social Security in America: The Factual Background of the Social Security Act as Summarized from Staff Reports to the Committee on Economic Security by the Social Security Board*, Social Security Board Publication (Washington, D.C., G.P.O., 1937), No. 20; U.S. Committee on Economic Security, *Report to the President of the Committee on Economic Security* (Washington, D.C., G.P.O., 1935).

Advisory Council on Economic Security, comprised of persons outside the government; the Technical Board on Economic Security, comprised of individuals within government service; and, finally, the position of executive director. Edwin E. Witte, then and until his retirement in 1957, professor of economics at the University of Wisconsin, was appointed to this office to conduct studies and to serve as secretary of the committee, the board, and the council. The committee rapidly completed the major part of its task and filed its report with the president, who transmitted it to Congress in a special message on January 17, 1935. Congress held public and executive hearings on the committee's proposals, made extensive policy and technical changes in these proposals, strenuously debated the controversial issues, and reported out a complex piece of legislation consisting of ten separate programs.[3]

On August 14, 1935, President Roosevelt attached his signature to the most ambitious and comprehensive public welfare act ever passed up to then in this and perhaps in any country. The filibuster of Senator Huey Long from Louisiana prevented Congress from making appropriations for carrying out the provisions of the act, and not until February 11, 1936, when it did so, were grants-in-aid made to the states. However, the Social Security Board, set up to administer aspects of the act, was organized in October, 1935. In 1939, shortly before Congress made significant changes in the Social Security Act, a congressional committee made the following summary statement of the purposes of the original act: [4]

> The enactment of the Social Security Act marked a new era, the federal government accepting, for the first time, responsibility for providing a systematic program of protection against economic and social hazards . . . The Social Security Act aimed to attack the problem of insecurity upon two fronts: first, by providing safeguards designed to reduce future dependency, and, second, by improving the method of relieving existing needs. The first objective was promoted by providing a federal system of old-age insurance and by granting federal aid to state-administered programs of unemployment compensation; the second objective was promoted by providing federal grants to state programs for aid to the needy aged, aid to dependent children, aid to the needy blind. Funds were also provided to stimulate development and extension of various health and welfare services.

[3] Wilbur J. Cohen, "Factors Influencing the Content of Federal Public Welfare Legislation," *Proceedings of the National Conference of Social Work: 1954* (New York, Columbia University Press, 1954), pp. 199–215.

[4] Report to accompany H.R. 6635, No. 728, 76th Cong., 1st sess. (June 2, 1939), p. 3.

PROVISIONS FOR THE AGED BEFORE 1935

CLASSIFICATION OF THE AGED

The President's Committee on Economic Security classified the aged into ten groups: [5]

1. Those who are employed until seventy and afterward.
2. Those who have independent wealth or savings.
3. Those who have earned a pension from their former employer.
4. Those who are in receipt of a war pension.
5. Those who are supported by relatives.
6. Those who are in receipt of relief from private agencies.
7. Those who are residents of private homes for the aged.
8. Those who are inmates of almshouses.
9. Those who are patients in hospitals or asylums for the incurable.
10. Those who are recipients of old-age assistance.

What proportion of this population of aged persons needed economic protection the committee did not know. It did know that there was a large segment already receiving public and private help in one form or another.

THE DESTITUTE AGED

Prior to the twentieth century the only extensive provisions for needy old persons were those afforded by the almshouse or poor farm and under the local poor laws. Concerted agitation for special assistance or insurance provisions for the aged did not occur until the second decade of this century. The American Association of Labor Legislation, founded in 1911, was the first organization in this country advocating social insurance measures, including those for the aged. The American Association of Old Age Security was organized in the middle twenties. From about 1920 the Fraternal Order of the Eagles was the principal private advocate of old-age pension laws. Arizona passed the first old-age pension or assistance law in 1914, but it was promptly declared unconstitutional because of its vagueness. In 1923 Montana enacted the first constitutional old-age pension or assistance law. By 1934 thirty-four states had such laws. The acts generally applied only to citizens of long residence, of good character, with no financially competent relatives, and with few assets, the maximum income allowed frequently being specified. The act was entirely inoperative in three states because of lack of funds, and in only ten was the system state-wide. California, Massachusetts, and New York were the leaders in old-age assistance legislation and administration.

---

[5] *Social Security in America,* ch. 8.

PENSION AND INSURANCE SCHEMES

In addition to the state programs for old-age assistance several hundred companies had voluntarily created pension systems for their own employees when they became aged or disabled. The first important federal legislative measure for the provision of old-age security was the United States Employees Retirement Act of 1920. A majority of all federal employees now enjoy old-age protection under retirement systems financed by contributions from employee and employer, the government. The largest of the retirement systems is that under the 1920 act and its amendments. The United States Civil Service Commission administers the program. The Railroad Retirement Act passed by Congress in 1934 was another important measure for the benefit of the aged. It established contributory old-age annuities for employees of steam railroads, sleeping car companies, and express companies. In 1935 it was declared unconstitutional by the United States Supreme Court on the theory that it attempted to regulate intrastate commerce. A second act, remedying the unconstitutional features of the earlier act, was shortly passed. It provides annuities for the same groups of employees. A number of states and municipalities had one or more types of pension schemes for their employees.

In 1935 the American program for providing economic security through social insurance measures was far behind those of European countries. In that year seven continental countries, England, Australia, and Canada had nation-wide compulsory unemployment compensation schemes. Eight states and the District of Columbia enacted compulsory unemployment insurance laws in 1935, Wisconsin having enacted the first in 1932. Eleven European countries had unemployment insurance schemes under which government subsidies were paid to voluntary plans. Only one country which had enacted a nation-wide compulsory unemployment insurance plan has ever revoked it. Soviet Russia reported that it had done so because widespread unemployment no longer existed.[6] Estimates for 1935 showed that about 43,500,000 persons in these various countries were insured under compulsory systems, and about 4,250,000 under voluntary schemes. Of the thirty-nine foreign nations providing some form of old-age security in 1933, thirteen had noncontributory old-age assistance laws; twenty had compulsory contributory old-age insurance laws of general coverage; and six, including several cantons of Switzerland and five nations in Central and South America, had compulsory contributory old-age insurance laws of limited coverage.[7] China, India, and, until

[6] *Social Security in America,* pp. 5–8.
[7] *Ibid.,* pp. 182–184.

1935, the United States were the only large countries of the world without any national system of old-age security.[8]

The slow development of the social insurance movement, except for workmen's compensation, in the United States can be attributed to several factors. First, until 1929 only a few individuals realized the dimensions of the unemployment problem, the increasing number of aged in the population, and the disabling effects of sickness. Second, many people believed that the number needing security against unemployment was sufficiently small to permit localities to care for those whose situations became serious. They were further convinced that enterprise and ambition would be quashed if life were made too easy for some persons at the expense of the benefactor or taxpayer. Third, voluntary social insurance plans were favored on the premise that autocratic and bureaucratic methods would quickly develop under governmental management. As late as 1931 organized labor fought proposals for unemployment insurance. Fourth, so far as unemployment insurance was concerned, legislation was blocked by the fear of progressive states that employers within their boundaries would be placed at a competitive disadvantage. Fifth, there were doubts concerning the constitutionality of federal social insurance legislation. Sixth, there were many differences of opinion as to the kind of protection which should be offered and the methods for providing it.

It is obvious that the majority of the aged in the United States had little assurance of economic security prior to the enactment of the Social Security Act. It was evident to those who formulated the recommendations for the act that neither a noncontributory old-age assistance plan nor an insurance plan was sufficient by itself. An assistance program would meet present and future economic contingencies on a needs basis, and an insurance program would meet future needs on a "rights," or "contract," basis. Hence, the President's Committee on Economic Security recommended a federal program of grants-in-aid to the states for old-age assistance; a federal system of old-age annuities; and a system of voluntary old-age annuities for persons of low incomes not covered by the old-age insurance law. Congress accepted the first two suggestions but rejected the third. The Social Security Act thus included an old-age assistance and an old-age insurance scheme.

In May, 1937, the Supreme Court rendered opinions in four cases which sustained the constitutionality of the controversial sections of the Social Security Act.[9] In the Helvering case, the Court upheld the validity

---

[8] Abraham Epstein, *Insecurity: A Challenge to America* (New York, Random House, 1938), ch. 29, pp. 551–565; Paul H. Douglas, *Social Security in the United States* (New York, McGraw-Hill, 1939), ch. 1.

[9] *Helvering and the Edison Electric Illuminating Co. of Boston* v. *Davis,* 301 U.S. 619; *Chas. C. Steward Machine Co.* v. *Davis,* 301 U.S. 548; *Carmichael* v. *Southern*

of the system of old-age benefits created by Title II and the validity of the tax imposed on employers by Title VIII. In a seven-to-two decision, the Court said that the scheme of old-age benefits was within the power of Congress to spend money in aid of the general welfare. In the Steward Machine Company case, the constitutionality of the payroll tax imposed by Title IX on employers of eight or more for unemployment compensation—challenged on the grounds that it was not an excise, that it was not uniform, and that there was an unlawful invasion of the reserved powers of the states—was upheld. In a five-to-four decision Justice Cardozo, writing the opinion, held these contentions to be without merit. In the two Carmichael cases Justice Stone, in delivering the opinion of a five-to-four majority, upheld the validity of state unemployment compensation laws. The Court held that there was no coercion by the federal government to make the states pass such laws, for each state was free to pass and repeal them at any time. Thus, the principle was firmly established that the federal government legitimately belonged in the permanent, as contrasted with the emergency, welfare picture.

FACTS CONCERNING THE AGED

Before proceeding with an analysis of the Social Security Act, let us look at some population data particularly as they relate to the problems of the aging. Although many such facts soon lose their current characteristics and become history, we submit them as indicative of demographic history and trends. It is data of this type that supported the need for the Social Security Act in 1935, although statistical materials then were neither so plentiful nor so accurate as today. Figures such as these furnish Congress with information for continued revision of the act. We take our materials from an article by Edwin E. Witte, drafter of the first Social Security Act.[10]

Between 1955 and 1960 the country's population will probably increase from about 165,000,000 to around 177,000,000 people. We shall have many more older persons and children to serve and the likelihood of many

---

Coal & Coke Co. and *Carmichael* v. *Gulf States Paper Corp.*, 301 U.S. 495 (1937). See above, Ch. 1 for additional discussion of these cases; see also, Reuben Resnick, "Some Social Work and Legal Notes on the Constitutionality of the Social Security Act," *The Compass* (August, 1937), pp. 3–7; U.S. Social Security Board, *Second Annual Report* (Washington, D.C., G.P.O., 1937), pp. 8–9.

[10] All of the material for this section is taken from Edwin E. Witte, "Basic Data on the Old-age Problem" (September, 1954), an unpublished article for classroom use at the University of Wisconsin. Professor Witte derived his figures from such sources as the U.S. Census, U.S. Bureau of Labor Standards, and Robert J. Myers and E. A. Rasor, *Illustrative United States Population Projections: 1952*, Actuarial Study of the Division of the Actuary, Social Security Administration, (November, 1952), No. 33. The reader will recall that Professor Witte served as executive director of the Committee on Economic Security and drafted the original Social Security Act.

more individuals with chronic disabilities or costly periods of illness. From 1860 to 1950 a great increase in the number and percentage of old people took place as the following table indicates:

Table 9

Year	*Total population (in thousands)*	*No. 65 and over (in thousands)*	*Per cent 65 and over*	*Increase over preceding date*	
				Total population	*No. 65 and over*
1860	31,443	849	2.7		
1870	38,558	1,154	3.0	22.6	35.9
1880	50,156	1,723	3.4	30.1	49.4
1890	62,622	2,424	3.9	24.5	40.3
1900	75,995	3,089	4.1	21.3	27.4
1910	91,972	3,958	4.3	21.1	28.2
1920	105,711	4,940	4.7	15.0	24.9
1930	122,775	6,634	5.4	16.2	34.5
1940	131,410	8,956	6.8	7.2	35.0
1950	150,697	12,271	8.1	14.5	36.1

In the last half century the number of people sixty-five years of age and over increased almost four times, although the total population merely doubled. In the last twenty-year period the number of people over sixty-five increased more than 75 per cent, but the total population increased less than 25 per cent. The number of people sixty-five and over is increasing at about 11,000 per day or 2.5 per cent per year. As of January 1, 1953, there were 13,400,000 people sixty-five years of age and over in the United States, or 8.4 per cent of the total population of continental United States.

Population students agree that both the number and percentage of older people will continue to increase for several decades. There are differences in the estimates, depending on what assumptions are made as to birth and death rates. As a result, estimated totals of the number of individuals sixty-five years of age and over range from 25,800,000 to 28,000,000 in the year 2000 and from 34,000,000 to 47,000,000 in 2050. Table 10 below indicates the anticipated increase in the number and percentage of people sixty-five years and over in future years in the entire (as distinguished from the continental) United States. These figures are based on the assumption of high fertility and low mortality.

Men exceeded women among the people over sixty-five years of age until 1940. In 1950 there were 6,473,774 women and 5,797,404 men over sixty-five in the population—a ratio of 89 men to every 100 women. It is expected that by 2000, 60 per cent of all the people sixty-five years and over will be women—about 150 old women to 100 old men.

Two out of three men over sixty-five are married. Only slightly more than one in three women in this age group are wives, and nearly one half are widowed. The number of single persons (widows, widowers, divorcees, persons who never married) exceeds that of couples. Widows increased by 25 per cent between 1940 and 1950, widowers by only 3 per cent. The average age at which women are now widowed is fifty-one.

Table 10

Year	*No. of people 65 and over (in millions)*	*Aged as percentage of total population*
1950	12.4	8.0
1960	15.5	8.9
1970	18.7	9.8
1980	22.8	10.8
1990	26.7	11.5
2000	28.0	11.0
2050	47.9	12.2

The aged population is not evenly distributed throughout the United States. In 1950, 35.3 per cent of the people sixty-five years of age and over lived in rural areas, and 64.7 per cent in urban areas. These percentages were not very different from the distribution of the entire population between rural and urban areas. There is, however, a heavy concentration of older people in small towns and villages and a less than average number of older people in large cities. There is a wide variation between states in the percentage of their total population of sixty-five years of age and over. The extremes are shown by New Mexico and New Hampshire. In the former state less than 5 per cent of the total population was sixty-five and over in 1950; in the latter nearly 11 per cent. The most acute problems regarding old-age support are in the older states, where the over-all population increase is less than the average of the country, and in the smaller towns and villages with an excessively large percentage of older people.

The financial situation of many older people is precarious. In 1950 the United States Bureau of Labor Statistics figured that the costs of living for older people in urban centers ranged from $1,537 in New Orleans to $1,831 in Milwaukee. These were minimum costs of an adequate budget for an elderly couple. Some costs, particularly medical and hospital costs, tend to be higher in old age than in early life. Although the situation is improving, a smaller percentage of people over sixty-five years of age have hospital and medical care insurance than the total population. Many people in old age have dependents for whom they must provide. This includes husbands, wives, and children. Of all married men over sixty-five years of age, 10 to 15 per cent have children or foster children under eighteen who are dependent on them. More than two thirds of the men who are sixty-five years of age or over have others dependent on them in comparison with a smaller percentage for women of the same age group.

Employment among older people decreases with age. Of all men between the ages of sixty-five and sixty-nine, 58 per cent were still in the labor market and 55 per cent actually employed in June, 1952; but only

40 per cent of those between the ages of seventy and seventy-four, and less than 20 per cent of those seventy-five years of age and over were actually employed. While the life expectancy of older people has been increasing, work life expectancy has been decreasing.

People who live from savings have been adversely affected by a reduction in interest rates and the decreased purchasing power of their savings. On the average, Americans who are sixty-five years of age and older have much smaller incomes than other adults. The United States Census Bureau reported that in 1950 the median income of all American families was $3,319, while that of families headed by a person over sixty-five years of age was $1,903. Forty per cent of all aged persons not living with relatives had incomes in that year of less than $500.00.

Approximately one third of all people of sixty-five and over receive their incomes from employment, another one third from social insurance and related programs, one fifth from old-age assistance, and less than one fifth from savings, assistance of children, and retirement income from private sources. There is some but not much overlapping of income from these sources.

The average life expectancy of all who attain the age of sixty-five is 13.5 years, or 12.6 for men and 14.9 for women. This means that at present mortality rates, half of all men of sixty-five will live to beyond the age of seventy-seven and half of all women of that age to eighty and above. Witte emphasizes that old age is a long period of time and is probably increasing. It presents numbers of problems to the aged and to society. They include health, housing, recreation, psychological, and economic needs. The economic problem is one that has received extensive consideration by governmental and industrial institutions. Experts in other fields of endeavor are giving more and more consideration to the problems of the aging. Geriatrics is a branch of medical knowledge and gerontology is the scientific study of old age, its phenomena, diseases, and so forth. Data like those just cited clearly demonstrate the size of our aging population and point up some of the problems associated with the process of growing old. The Social Security Act attempts to assure some measure of economic security to our present and future older citizens.

TITLES AND ADMINISTRATION OF THE ACT

TITLES [11]

The Social Security Act is a multipurpose measure frequently referred to as an omnibus statute. As we have indicated, it covers a variety of in-

[11] *Compilation of the Social Security Laws, Including the Social Security Act, as Amended, and Related Enactments Through December 31, 1954,* 83d Cong., 2d sess., S. Doc. 157 (Washington, D.C., G.P.O., 1955).

come maintenance and social service programs. As of 1956 the titles of the Social Security Act as amended are:

Title I—Grants to States for Old-age Assistance
Title II—Federal Old-age and Survivors Insurance Benefits and Disability Insurance Benefits
Title III—Grants to States for Unemployment Compensation Administration
Title IV—Grants to States for Aid to Dependent Children
Title V—Grants to States for Maternal and Child Welfare
Title VI—Public Health Work (repealed)
Title VII—Administration
Title VIII—Taxes with Respect to Employment (now contained in Internal Revenue Code)
Title IX—Miscellaneous Provisions Relating to Employment Security
Title X—Grants to States for Aid to the Blind
Title XI—General Provisions
Title XII—Advances to State Unemployment Funds
Title XIII—Reconversion Unemployment Benefits for Seamen
Title XIV—Grants to States for Aid to the Permanently and Totally Disabled
Title XV—Unemployment Compensation for Federal Employees

The act provides for two forms of social insurance—unemployment and old-age and survivors; four forms of public assistance—to the aged, blind, dependent children, and permanently and totally disabled; three forms of social services under the general heading of maternal and child welfare, including maternal and child health, crippled children, and child welfare. The original act has been amended on numbers of occasions. Some of the laws have made extensive and significant changes, particularly those of 1939,[12] 1946,[13] 1950,[14] 1954,[15] and 1956.[16]

ADMINISTRATION

Administration of the original Social Security Act was largely the responsibility of the Social Security Board. Exceptions were the three children's programs under Title V, which were carried on by the Children's Bureau, then a part of the Department of Labor; the vocational rehabilitation programs of Title V, carried on then and now by the Office of Vocational Rehabilitation;[17] and public health work under Title VI, carried on by the United States Public Health Service.[18] The last two

[12] 53 U.S. Stat. 1360.
[13] 60 U.S. Stat. 978.
[14] 64 U.S. Stat. 477.
[15] 68 U.S. Stat. 1052.
[16] Public Law 880, 84th Cong., 2d sess., ch. 836, H.R. 7225 (Washington, D.C., G.P.O., 1956).
[17] This part of the original act has been replaced by the Vocational Rehabilitation Act, 29 U.S.C., c. 4.
[18] This title has been repealed by the Public Health Service Act, approved July 1, 1944, 42 U.S.C., c. 6a.

of these programs are no longer a part of the Social Security Act but are administered under the Department of Health, Education, and Welfare. The Social Security Board was transferred to the Federal Security Agency by Presidential Reorganization Plan 1 of 1939. Its functions were then carried on under the direction and supervision of the federal security administrator. By Reorganization Plan 2 of 1946 the functions of the Social Security Board, as well as those of the Children's Bureau (and the Secretary of Labor) under Title V of the Social Security Act, were transferred to the federal security administrator, and the board was abolished. The Department of Health, Education, and Welfare was created by Reorganization Plan 1 of 1953. To it were transferred all functions of the Federal Security Agency, which, in turn, was abolished. The functions of the federal security administrator were transferred to the secretary of health, education, and welfare. The Bureau of Employment Security, with its unemployment compensation and employment service functions, was transferred from the Federal Security Agency to the Department of Labor by Reorganization Plan 2 of 1949.

FEDERAL PROVISIONS FOR OLD-AGE ASSISTANCE

REQUIREMENTS FOR STATES

Except for the old-age and survivors insurance provisions of the Social Security Act, which is a 100 per cent federally administered program, all others are federal-state in nature. They are built upon the principle that the federal government will assist the states with designated programs but will not command the states to set them up. If states wish to receive federal grants, they must comply with certain conditions. This means that every state must enact compliance legislation and submit an acceptable plan to the federal administrative agency before federal resources become available. In order to be approved for federal reimbursements under the Social Security Act, a state plan for the four public assistances must provide for: [19]

1. Statewide operation.
2. State financial participation.
3. A single state agency to administer the plan or supervise its administration by local agencies upon which state rules, regulations, and standards are mandatory.
4. Methods of administration necessary for proper and efficient operation of the plan, including the establishment and maintenance of personnel standards on a merit basis.
5. Restriction of information about applicants for and recipients of assist-

[19] U.S. Department of Health, Education, and Welfare, Social Security Administration, *Characteristics of State Public Assistance Plans under the Social Security Act*, Public Assistance Report (Washington, D.C., G.P.O., 1956), No. 27.

ance to purposes directly connected with the administration of the program. A provision enacted as a part of the Revenue Act of 1951 permits exceptions to this prohibition under appropriate state legislation. The names and addresses of recipients and the amounts of their assistance payments may be a matter of public record and open to interested persons if the state legislation prescribes the conditions of access and prohibits the commercial or political use of information so obtained.

6. Opportunity for anyone wishing to do so to apply for old-age assistance (OAA), aid to dependent children (ADC), aid to the blind (AB), or aid to the permanently and totally disabled (APTD) and to have his application acted upon with reasonable promptness.

7. Opportunity for a fair hearing before the state agency for any claimant for assistance whose claim is denied or is not acted upon with reasonable promptness.

8. Submission to the Social Security Administration of such reports as it requires.

9. Consideration, in determination of the need of a claimant for assistance, of any income and resources that he may have (with exemption of up to $50 a month of earned income in aid to the blind).

10. Designation of a state authority or authorities responsible for establishing and maintaining standards for all the types of public and private institutions in the state in which, under the state plan, a needy person may receive assistance (applicable to all programs except aid to dependent children).

11. Prompt notice to law-enforcement officials of the furnishing of aid to dependent children with respect to a child deserted or abandoned by a parent.

12. The prohibition of the concurrent receipt of more than one form of public assistance under the state plan.

13. An examination by a physician skilled in diseases of the eye or by an optometrist, whichever the individual may select, in determining blindness.

14. A description of the services (if any) which the state agency makes available to applicants for and recipients of OAA to help them attain self-care, of AB and APTD to help them attain self-support or self-care, and of ADC to help the relatives with whom the dependent children are living attain self-support or self-care or to maintain and strengthen family life.

The Social Security Act does not require that a state plan impose any residence or citizenship requirement as a condition of eligibility, but it does provide that a state may not impose: [20]

1. Any residence requirement more restrictive than the maximum in the acts; namely, five years in the last nine and one year immediately preceding application in old-age assistance, aid to the blind, and aid to the permanently and totally disabled; and one year in the case of aid to dependent children.

2. Any age requirement of more than sixty-five years in the old-age assistance program.

3. Any citizenship requirement barring a citizen of the United States who is otherwise eligible for aid.

In case there is any substantial violation by any state of its accepted plan, the secretary of the Department of Health, Education, and Welfare, after giving the state agency administering or supervising the plan

---

[20] *Characteristics of State Public Assistance Plans under the Social Security Act.*

Table 11

LEGISLATIVE CHRONOLOGY OF PROVISIONS FOR FEDERAL PARTICIPATION IN PAYMENTS OF PUBLIC ASSISTANCE

Legislation *	*Maximum amounts of individual monthly payments subject to federal participation*			*Federal share of expenditures within specified maximums*	
	Aged, blind, and disabled †	*Aid to dependent children*		*Aged, blind, and disabled* †	*Aid to dependent children*
		First child	*Each additional child*		
Assistance Subject to Federal Participation Defined to Include Only Money Payments to Recipients					
1935 original act	$30	$18	$12	½	⅓
1939 amendments	$40	$18	$12	½	½
1946 amendments	$45	$24	$15	⅔ of first $15 (average) plus ½ the balance	⅔ of first $9 (average per child) plus ½ the balance
1948 amendments	$50	$27	$18	¾ of first $20 (average) plus ½ the balance	¾ of first $12 (average per child) plus ½ the balance
Assistance Subject to Federal Participation Defined to Include Money Payments to Recipients and Payments to Vendors for Medical and Remedial Care					
1950 amendments	$50	$27 plus $27 for 1 needy relative with whom child lives	$18	¾ of first $20 (average) plus ½ the balance	¾ of first $12 (average per person) plus ½ the balance
Puerto Rico ‡ Virgin Islands §	$30	$18	$12	½	½
1952 and 1954 amendments **	$55	$30 plus $30 for 1 needy relative with whom child lives	$21	⅘ of first $25 (average) plus ½ the balance	⅘ of first $15 (average per person) plus ½ the balance

Puerto Rico ‡ Virgin Islands §	No change from 1950 provisions				
1956 amendments (Oct. 1, 1956 through June 30, 1957)	$60	$32 plus $32 for 1 needy relative with whom child lives	$23	4/5 of first $30 (average) plus 1/2 the balance	14/17 of first $17 (average per person) plus 1/2 the balance
Puerto Rico ‖ Virgin Islands ¶	$30	$18 plus $18 for 1 needy relative with whom child lives	$12	1/2	1/2

Separate Provision for Federal Participation in Money Payments to Recipients

1956 amendments (July 1, 1957 through June 30, 1959)	$60	$32 plus $32 for 1 needy relative with whom child lives	$23	4/5 of first $30 (average) plus 1/2 the balance	14/17 of first $17 (average per person) plus 1/2 the balance
Puerto Rico ‖ Virgin Islands ¶	$30	$18 plus $18 for 1 needy relative with whom child lives	$12	1/2	1/2

Separate Provision for Federal Participation in Vendor Payments for Medical and Remedial Care

Legislation *	*Maximum average monthly amount per recipient subject to federal participation*			*Federal share of expenditures within specified maximums (all programs)*
	Aged, blind, and disabled †	*Aid to dependent children*		
		Per adult	*Per child*	
1956 amendments (Effective July 1, 1957 for all jurisdictions)	$6	$6	$3	1/2

* Effective date of legislation: The 1935 original act was effective February, 1936; the 1939 amendments in January, 1940; and the 1946, 1948, 1950, 1952, and 1954 amendments in October of the year in which enacted. The changes in basic formula made by the 1956 amendments become effective October 1, 1956; the separate provision for federal participation in payments to vendors for medical and remedial care, July 1, 1957.

† Program for aid to the permanently and totally disabled became effective in October, 1950.

‡ Maximum federal payment in a fiscal year, $4,250,000.

§ Maximum federal payment in a fiscal year, $160,000.

** 1952 amendments carried an expiration date of September 30, 1954; 1954 amendments extended expiration date to September 30, 1956.

‖ Maximum federal payment in a fiscal year, $5,312,500.

¶ Maximum federal payment in a fiscal year, $200,000.

reasonable notice and opportunity for hearing, shall notify such state that further payments will not be made to the state until compliance occurs.

The federal act defines old-age assistance as money payments or medical or remedial care of needy individuals sixty-five years of age or older; but such payments shall not be made to inmates of public institutions, except a patient in a medical institution; to any patient in an institution for tuberculosis or mental diseases; or to an individual who has been diagnosed as having tuberculosis or psychosis and is a patient in a medical institution as a result thereof.

PAYMENTS TO STATES

Federal payments to the states with approved plans are made on the basis of a stipulated proportion of expenditures for each person or family receiving public-assistance grants and for administration. The past and present formulas for reimbursement for the four assistance programs are shown in Table 11 (pp. 564–565).[21]

This table clearly shows that effective July 1, 1957, federal reimbursement to the states includes an amount equal to one half of the total sums spent in the form of medical or any other type of remedial care (including expenditures for insurance premiums for such care or the cost thereof), not counting so much of such expenditure for any month as exceeds the product of $6.00 times the total number of individuals receiving OAA, AB, and APTD. For ADC recipients the formula provides for a reimbursement not to exceed one half of the product of $3.00 multiplied by the total number of dependent children plus one half of the product of $6.00 multiplied by the total number of other individuals receiving ADC grants.

Reimbursements to the states for administrative costs of public-assistance programs are for an amount equal to one half of the total sums expended during a quarter as found necessary by the secretary of health, education, and welfare for the proper and efficient administration of the state plan. Such reimbursements, beginning in 1957, include services provided for self-care (OAA), self-support or self-care (AB, APTD), and self-support, self-care, or maintenance of family life (ADC).

For the fiscal year starting June 30, 1957, and for an unspecified period thereafter, sums are authorized to be appropriated for grants to the states and public and other nonprofit organizations and agencies for paying part of the cost of research or demonstration projects relating to the prevention and reduction of dependency or which will aid in effecting co-ordination of planning between private and public agencies or which

[21] Table prepared by U.S. Department of Health, Education, and Welfare, Social Security Administration, Division of Public Assistance, 1956.

will improve the administration of the programs carried on under the Social Security Act. For the fiscal year ending June 30, 1958, and for four succeeding years, sums are authorized to be appropriated for grants to the states in order to increase the effectiveness and efficiency of administration of public assistance. These funds can be expended (1) as grants to public or other nonprofit institutions of higher learning for training personnel employed or preparing for employment in public-assistance programs, (2) for special courses or seminars of short duration conducted by experts hired on a temporary basis for the purpose, (3) for establishing and maintaining directly or through grants to such institutions, fellowships or trainee-ships for such personnel at such institutions.

The general method of computing and paying the amounts due the states is defined. If the secretary finds the reports accurate and within the provisions of the plan, then the amount estimated to be needed shall be certified to the secretary of the treasury. This amount must be adjusted to the extent that state estimates for prior months were greater or less than anticipated and to the pro rata United States share of amounts recovered during any prior quarter by the state or any political subdivision. The secretary of treasury shall thereupon pay to the state the amount so certified.

STATE PROVISIONS FOR OLD-AGE ASSISTANCE

In 1956 the Social Security Administration published a tabular summary of the characteristics of state public-assistance plans under the Social Security Act. It made its analysis of all four special assistance programs under the following fifteen headings: [22]

1. Age.
2. Citizenship.
3. Residence.
4. Blindness, dependent child, permanent and total disability.
5. Institutional status.
6. Need.
7. Property and income limitations.
8. Other.
9. Maximum payments.
10. Recoveries, liens, and assignments.
11. State agency.
12. Local agency.
13. Place of application.
14. Responsibility for decision.
15. State-local financing of assistance costs.

[22] *Characteristics of State Public Assistance Plans under the Social Security Act.* The fifty-three jurisdictions referred to throughout our discussion of the Social Security Act include Alaska, the District of Columbia, Hawaii, Puerto Rico, and the Virgin Islands.

We shall make our summary statement of the similarities and dissimilarities between states for these special assistance programs in accordance with this outline and shall take our information largely from this study. Let us seriatim examine the provisions pertaining to old-age assistance. We shall not go into so much detail in describing the characteristics of the other three public-assistance programs, since numbers of provisions are similar or identical.

AGE, CITIZENSHIP, RESIDENCE (1, 2, 3)

By 1939 all jurisdictions were participating in the old-age assistance program. Since no state may exclude any needy person sixty-five years of age or over, all state legislation conformed. Colorado appeared to be the only state which provided for grants to persons sixty to sixty-five years of age under some highly restrictive circumstances. State funds bore this expense. Thirty-eight jurisdictions had no citizenship requirements. Of the remaining fifteen, some imposed citizenship requirements, and others required either citizenship or long periods of residence (ten, fifteen, or twenty-five years) in the United States. The trend has been toward legislative elimination of citizenship requirements. When the Social Security Act was passed, two thirds of the states making old-age assistance grants required fifteen or more years of state residence, and many also required a specified period of county residence.[23] In 1956 twenty-three jurisdictions seemed to have a one-year requirement; twenty-five more than one year.[24] Five jurisdictions—Hawaii, New York, Puerto Rico, Rhode Island, and the Virgin Islands—appeared to have no stipulated period of time required for the establishment of legal residence. Some states reduced residence requirements on a reciprocal basis.

Statutes do not clearly spell out definitions of residence; hence, administrative and judicial agencies must do so. The administrative interpretation of the required one year of state residence for old-age assistance by the Wisconsin Department of Public Welfare, for example, reads as follows:

> The following interpretation should be applied to the question of residence. Every individual should be held to live or reside somewhere; that is, he should not be adjudged to be without a residence. He shall be considered to have his residence at the place where he is living, if he is found to be living there voluntarily and not for a temporary purpose, that is, with no intention of presently

[23] Eveline M. Burns, *The American Social Security System* (Boston, Houghton Mifflin, 1949), p. 298.

[24] *Characteristics of the State Public Assistance Plans under the Social Security Act.* Data from the Division of Public Assistance, Wisconsin Department of Public Welfare, Madison, Wis., as of May 23, 1955, are somewhat different. Because so many statutes provide for alternative residence requirements for different situations, it is difficult to determine the exact number of states in any category. In addition, legislative changes occur frequently.

removing therefrom. An intent to return to a place of former residence at some indefinite time in the future cannot be construed as meaning that he does not have residence at the place where he is currently living.

To be eligible a person must have resided in the state continuously during the year immediately preceding the date of application. An applicant who has resided less than one year in Wisconsin may be granted OAA if the state from which he removed his residence to Wisconsin grants assistance to any resident of Wisconsin who has moved to such state and lived there less than one year. However, if an applicant who has removed his residence to Wisconsin from a state which requires that an applicant who has removed his residence from Wisconsin to such state reside in such state more than one year before he is eligible for OAA, he shall be required to reside in this state for a like period before becoming eligible.

Continuous residence in the state for one year preceding the date of application should not be interpreted to mean that the person must have remained there physically throughout the year or even for a substantial part of the year, so long as the individual was a resident of the state at the beginning of the year and has not abondoned such residence and acquired residence elsewhere during the twelve-month period.

This definition attempts to distinguish between residence for old-age assistance and legal settlement for general relief.

INSTITUTIONAL CARE (4, 5)

Point 4 does not apply to the old-age assistance program.

The original Social Security Act forbade federal reimbursement for payments to the aged and the blind if they were residents of public institutions. The 1950 amendments permit federal matching for assistance granted to institutional beneficiaries of the old-age assistance (OAA), aid to the blind (AB), aid to the permanently and totally disabled (APTD) programs under certain conditions. Money payments cannot be made to residents of public institutions except as patients in a medical institution. Nor can they be made to patients in any private or public institution for tuberculosis or mental diseases or to individuals who have been diagnosed as having these diseases and who are patients in a medical institution as a result thereof. The amendments most significantly required that if a state plan includes payments to individuals in private or public institutions, there shall be the designation of a state authority, effective July 1, 1953, which shall be responsible for establishing and maintaining standards for such institutions. It was congressional intention in 1935 to keep individuals out of badly run poor farms and almshouses, to encourage the abandonment or change in function of such institutions, and to facilitate normal home and family living. The result was the closing of many public homes and a great growth in the number of proprietary nursing homes.[25]

Most states now provide for OAA, AB, and APTD payments to quali-

[25] Lester Breslow. "Chronic Illness," *Social Work Year Book: 1957*, pp. 157–164.

fied individuals in private and some public institutions. Sometimes statutes enumerate the types of institutions in which recipients may live. For example, New York provided that payments could be made to qualified individuals in any of the following institutions if operated in compliance with established rules and regulations: a private proprietary or nonprofit nursing or convalescent home; a private incorporated nonprofit home for the aged; a private proprietary or nonprofit institution for adults; a public home, infirmary, or similar medical facility for adults operated by a public welfare district; or, in case of persons already in receipt of assistance, in a public incorporated or proprietary hospital. Some states provided that payments be made to persons in private institutions if life care had not been purchased. Most states provided for payments to persons in public medical institutions and often limited care to a temporary period, sometimes defined as two or three months. Exclusions were generally identical with those in the federal act for both public and private institutions. Since the Social Security Act provides for the establishment of standards by a state agency for any institution used under the program, much effort has gone into the development of rules and regulations. This requirement is doing much directly and indirectly to raise the general standards of institutional care for the aged.

STANDARDS OF NEED (6)

The Social Security Act limits federal grants to the states for all four assistance programs to *needy* persons. Money payments are required except when medical or remedial care is provided. The principle of "unrestricted cash payments" characterizes the assistance programs. This means that each recipient spends his allowance as he sees fit. Discretion is left with the states to determine what need is, except that the law effective as of July 1, 1941, requires that in determining need, all other income and resources of an applicant shall be considered. Beginning August, 1943, the Social Security Board required at least an annual review of eligibility and as much oftener as was indicated.

Most state laws provide a loose definition of need. The most common provision is "insufficient income or other resources to provide subsistence compatible with decency and health." Wisconsin defines need more explicitly to mean insufficient income or other resources to provide any or all of the necessities of life, such as food, housing, clothing, fuel, light, water, medicine, medical, dental, and surgical care. A few states, according to the study from which we are taking our materials, provided a standard of need by specifying a minimum maintenance income. California statutorily specified $85.00 for "basic maintenance," with special needs as related to circumstances included above the statutory amount. Colorado provided for $45.00 as a statutory minimum payment, plus such additional amount as might accrue from constitutionally earmarked funds.

Louisiana stipulated that the applicant's income from all sources should be compatible with decency and health and set $50.00 as a statutory minimum for assistance for one recipient and $45 for each of two or more recipients in the same household. Massachusetts required that assistance be computed by budgetary standards, but the income should not be less than $75.00 a month for persons who lived outside a family group and $55.00 for those in a family group, with additional allowance for leisure-time activities. Nevada provided for a statutory minimum of $40.00 for assistance plus other income, with need beyond the minimum to be determined on a budgetary basis. New Mexico specified that income plus assistance must not be less than $50.00 a month for one recipient and $30.00 for the spouse.

Burns has pointed out that the extent to which the definition of need limits eligibility will, in practice, be affected by three factors: the minimum standard of living against which the resources of the applicant are measured; the evaluation of the applicant's resources of income and property; the extent to which resources of relatives are treated as being available.[26] We add a fourth, the extent to which federal, state, and local legislatures make funds available for assistance payments.

PROPERTY AND OTHER INCOME (7)

Most states imposed limits on the value of homesteads and other real property and also on insurance and other personal property which an applicant might own. California provided that real property of recipient or recipient and spouse be limited to $3,500 assessed value less encumbrances; personal property to $1,200 less encumbrances; personal property of any married person living with spouse who was also an applicant or recipient to $2,000 less encumbrances. Connecticut provided that equity in real property other than homes must be liquidated. Delaware permitted ownership of a homestead if the value was in reasonable relation to the value of other homes owned by low-income families. It required that if reasonable income was not produced from nonresident property, the property must be sold. The District of Columbia provided that all property be considered in determination of eligibility in each case. This left standards of need entirely to administrative discretion and available funds. The standard of indigency for a resident of the District of Columbia was income insufficient to provide for needs according to the budgetary standards of the agency. Most states provided that property should not have been assigned or transferred, usually within some designated time period, in order to qualify for assistance.

[26] Burns, *op. cit.*, p. 299.

OTHER ELIGIBILITY REQUIREMENTS (8)

Some states imposed employment, morality, and other requirements. Arizona, for example, provided that if employable, the applicant must not refuse available work; if conditions involved in such employment were not satisfactory to him, the county was to determine whether the acceptance of employment was a condition of eligibility. Connecticut required that the applicant not be serving a jail or prison sentence. Iowa demanded that the applicant should not have been convicted of a charge of desertion or nonsupport by a criminal court during the preceding ten years and permitted the receipt of no other assistance from the state or its subdivisions, except for fuel and dental, nursing, osteopathic, chiropractic, medical, and surgical care and hospitalization. Ohio insisted that the individual must be able to care properly for himself, not be convicted of drunkenness or offense punishable by imprisonment, and not waste or misspend assistance funds. Pennsylvania required that the applicant must not advocate or participate by overt act in movements proposing change in the form of the United States government by means not provided in the Constitution of the United States. A good number of states did not have such restrictive legislation. Of those that so limit eligibility a majority provided that no other public assistance, perhaps with some exemptions, could be received.

MAXIMUM PAYMENTS (9)

The majority of states chose to limit their assistance payments by setting a maximum amount for which reimbursement was allowed. This was usually done by legislative determination but occasionally by administrative action. A large proportion of states provided that maximum payments should not be in excess of the maximum for which federal reimbursement was allowed. A very few specified a smaller amount; Mississippi, for example, appeared to limit the legal maximum to $30.00 per month. Some states allowed a maximum larger than the federal reimbursable amount, in which instance the state and/or local governments made up the difference. Illinois is an illustration of such a state. It provided for a legal maximum of $65.00 per month adjusted up or down $1.00 for each three full points of change in the "Consumers Price Index for Moderate Income Families in Chicago—all items" issued by the Federal Bureau of Labor Statistics; but this maximum could be exceeded for medical care.

Social Security figures for average grants by states show how greatly the standards of assistance vary between states. It remains congressional intent for each state to set its own standards of need in recognition of its own problems, citizen attitudes, and available funds. The Social Security Administration, through its advisory and supervisory relationships with the states, attempts to help them raise their standards if grants are budgetarily deficient.

RECOVERIES, LIENS, AND ASSIGNMENTS (10)

The Social Security Act has no provisions on this subject. It does require, however, that the federal government shall benefit in its pro rata share from whatever amounts the states collect from recipients. The Social Security Administration does not favor these devices, believing that they are administratively expensive, may impose hardships on survivors, and often humiliate the applicant. It insists that elimination of these provisions would not prevent the states from entering claims and making recoveries from the estates of deceased recipients. However, states are reluctant to abolish these provisions, since they are directly responsible for bringing in sizable amounts of money.

About one third of the states appeared to have no provisions on this subject. The balance set definite limits on the value of various kinds of property which the applicant might own. The amounts of cash or liquid assets varied from as little as $100.00 to as much as $1,500. In some states cash surrender value of insurance in excess of some amount, say $1,000, had to be assigned. In Minnesota a lien had priority over all other debts after such items as expenses of adminstration, last illness, funeral, and debts having preference under laws of the United States were settled. In New Hampshire assistance paid constituted a lien on the estate of the recipient. Bank accounts, insurance policies, stocks, and bonds had to be assigned to the Department of Public Welfare. Withdrawals from bank accounts could only be made with signed permission from the public welfare commissioner.

ADMINISTRATION AND FINANCING (11, 12, 13, 14, 15)

We observed earlier in this chapter that the Social Security Act requires that the assistance programs be in effect in all political subdivisions of the state, that there be financial participation by the state, and that there be a state-administered or state-supervised plan. Students of public welfare are acquainted with the diversity in administrative structure and program responsibilities of state and local welfare agencies. Great variation is found, likewise, in the degree of responsibility assumed by state and local departments in the administration of the special public assistances. Two patterns emerge with variations. One, is a state department actually administering the special public-assistance programs. Additional public welfare programs are usually administered by the agency also. The department may have a single administrator to interpret and carry out legislative policy or a board to make policies and an administrator to carry them out. District and local offices receive the applications, which means that the state agency has the final determination of who may be recipients. General assistance may or may not be a responsibility of the state agency. The program is, with very few exceptions, state financed, the money coming from various sources, including general funds and special earmarked funds.

The other pattern is a state-supervised program. The state agency may be structured with or without a policy-making board and is usually a multiservice department. The department may or may not supervise general assistance. It operates through local offices usually on the county level of government; applications and decisions are made there. It sets standards, gives counsel, and hears appeals. Nonfederal funds for the programs come from state or state-local sources. Thirty jurisdictions carried on their special assistance activities through a state-administered program, and twenty-three on a state-supervised basis.

RESPONSIBILITY OF RELATIVES

The Social Security Act contains no provisions regarding the responsibility of relatives for dependents. State legislatures and assistance agencies have provided many different methods of handling this problem, especially the responsibility of adult sons and daughters for support of their aging parents. Since under the common law children had no responsibility for the support of their parents, legal responsibility is established by statute or not at all.

A 1954 study by the Social Security Administration showed that twelve states had no legislation of any kind (public assistance, general support, or criminal legislation) establishing the duty of children to support their parents.[27] In one of these states the law specifically stated that children should not be held legally responsible for the support of their parents. Six states had some type of general support legislation in the tradition of the old poor laws that established the duty of support of indigent parents but that had not been specifically applied in any way in the administration of old-age assistance. In these six states the old-age assistance laws made no reference to responsibility of relatives. The only legal remedy specifically authorized in these states was for the "poor" person to bring suit for support against his legally responsible relatives (in two states) or for local units of government to recover the amounts spent for relief of needy persons from the legally responsible relatives (in four states). In these four states no local funds were provided for old-age assistance, so the laws seemed to have no possible applicability to the administration of old-age assistance. Thirty-three jurisdictions (including Alaska, Hawaii, and the District of Columbia) had either public-

---

[27] The information in this section comes from an article by Elizabeth Epler, "Old-Age Assistance: Plan Provisions on Children's Responsibility for Parents," *Social Security Bulletin,* Vol. 17, No. 4 (April, 1954), pp. 3–12.

assistance legislation establishing responsibility of children for support of old-age assistance applicants and recipients or some other type of legislation establishing the responsibility of children for parents that was applicable to the administration of old-age assistance.

Provisions for enforcement of children's responsibility—court action by the assistance agency or other government unit or by the parent—might be included in old-age assistance laws (or public-assistance laws applicable to old-age assistance and other assistance programs), general support laws, or criminal laws. Enforcement provisions appearing only in general support or criminal statutes were not ordinarily the basis for old-age assistance provisions, unless the public-assistance laws included some reference to children's responsibility for parents.

Almost all provisions for old-age assistance concerning the responsibility of children outside the household for supporting or contributing to the support of applicants for old-age assistance may be classified in three broad and oversimplified categories:

1. Provisions that may encourage contributions from children able to contribute but that do not include any means of seeking to require support from children who do not voluntarily contribute. These provisions take into account in determining eligibility and the amount of assistance payments only such contributions as are clearly and voluntarily made.

2. Provisions that seek to require support by some type of court action, initiated by the agency or the recipient, from children determined by the agency to be able to support but that take into account, in determining eligibility and payments, only such contributions as are clearly available.

3. Provisions that take into account in determining eligibility and payments contributions that the agency determines the children are able to make, whether or not the contributions are actually available at the time of agency determination. The wording of some of these plans indicates they intend to require support by denying assistance.

The old-age assistance plan in any given state may include two or even three of these general types of provisions, each relating to a different group of persons, as, for example, children out of the state. Sixteen states had only the first type of plan provision, that is, children were not required to contribute. In these states any plan provision seeking to encourage or to coerce children to support rested on agency policies only. In twenty-one states the plans included the second type of provision—for court action against children able to support who failed to do so—but did not include any provision for denying assistance merely on the basis of a determination of children's ability to support. Plans in the other fourteen jurisdictions included the third general type of provision, basing eligibility and payments, under specified circumstances, on the ability of children to contribute, whether or not they did. In most of these states and in those in the second type of provision the plans rested on both laws and agency policies.

All of these types of plan provisions involve problems of administration and questions of equitable treatment of recipients, their children, and taxpayers who support these programs. We give two illustrations. In Alabama, which falls in the third classification, applicants and recipients were advised of their rights to bring civil suit under the reciprocal enforcement-of-support legislation as well as under the Alabama support law. There was, however, no practical remedy when legally responsible children lived in a state with no applicable reciprocal support legislation. In *Atkins* v. *Curtis* [28] the Alabama court upheld the constitutionality of its support law and the validity of deducting from the assistance payment the expected contribution from a child living in another state but held to be legally responsible because he had been in Alabama after the support law was passed.

In Wisconsin, which belongs in the second grouping, the law was tightened in 1953 to provide: [29]

> 52.01—The parent, spouse, and child of any dependent person . . . who is unable to maintain himself shall maintain such dependent person, so far as able, in a manner approved by the authorities having charge of the dependent, or by the board in charge of the institution where such dependent person is; but no child of school age shall be compelled to labor contrary to the child labor laws. Upon failure of relatives so to do said authorities or board shall submit to the district attorney a report of its findings, and upon receipt thereof the district attorney shall, within sixty days, apply to the county court of the county in which such dependent person resides for an order to compel such maintenance. Upon such application said district attorney shall make a written report thereof to the county welfare department, with a copy to the chairman of the county board and to the department.

As a consequence of this statute the Division of Public Assistance of the State Department of Public Welfare drew up an income-exemption schedule and a formula for the county departments to apply to all legally responsible relatives of recipients under the four special assistance programs. After the income-exemption schedule is applied the legally responsible relative is expected to provide a fraction of the balance between this amount and his income. Liberal exceptions are allowed. Some, but not many, cases of recalcitrant relatives have been taken to the courts. This recently initiated scheme involves a great amount of administrative time and effort and client and relative resistance. It has, however, brought thousands of dollars into the public-assistance coffers, an item of interest to legislators and taxpayers! Occasional sensational news stories of well-to-do but nonsupporting relatives stimulate public insistence upon this type of legislation and administration.

---

[28] 66 S. 2d 455 (1953).

[29] Wis. Stat., 1953, c. 52.

ADDITIONAL FEDERAL-STATE RELATIONSHIPS

FAIR HEARINGS

The Social Security Act requires, as one of the conditions for federal participation in state public-assistance programs, that the state laws provide an opportunity for a fair hearing to any person whose claim for assistance is denied or is not acted upon with reasonable promptness.[30] When the act was passed, the right to a fair hearing was a new concept in public-assistance administration, although it had been extensively used in such states as Wisconsin in the administration of workmen's compensation and other labor-management laws. The political philosophy underlying this requirement is that due process must be observed in the administration of this, as of any law, and that all individuals coming under it are entitled to equal protection. An opportunity for the citizen to be heard on decisions affecting his welfare is a fundamental democratic safeguard to achieve this objective. The provisions of the Social Security Act on fair hearings are based on the belief that the claimant who meets the requirements established by law has a right to benefits and to a fair hearing when he is denied these benefits.

Hearings on public assistance are not an appeals process in which the state agency merely reviews the record of the action taken by the local unit and then either confirms that action or sends the case back for further consideration. Rather, the state agency proceeds as if there had been no previous local action and looks at all the facts, reviews all the evidence, and listens to witnesses with the sole objective of settling the issue raised by the claimant. The issue may involve eligibility factors, such as age, residence, relationship. It may concern decisions affecting the amount of the assistance payment. It may relate to agency procedure.

Since all public assistance had previously been administered on a discretionary and arbitrary basis there was no experience with problems of, and procedures in, hearings. Many questions soon arose, such as: What constitutes an "opportunity" for a fair hearing? What is a "claim?" Has a claimant had an opportunity for a fair hearing if he cannot be present at the hearing or if months elapse between his request for a hearing and the hearing? Has the agency met the provisions of the act if it fails to advise applicants and recipients of their right to a fair hearing or if it reserves the right to accept or dismiss a request for a hearing? With experience, the Social Security Administration has issued materials and standards on the fair hearing process.

Experiences of the states with fair hearings have varied. Some have had

[30] Bernard W. Scholz, "Hearings in Public Assistance," *Social Security Bulletin,* Vol. 11, No. 7 (July, 1948), pp. 14–18.

hundreds of hearings; others have had few. Some states appear anxious to prevent hearings whenever possible; others welcome them. In general, the states which accept the principle that needy people have a legal right to public assistance are likely to accept the implementation of this right. Jurisdictions that still think of the state's function in granting assistance as primarily discretionary and the grant as a gratuity are likely to question the purpose and usefulness of the hearing process.

PERSONNEL

When Congress amended the Social Security Act in 1939 to require that the federal and state governments select all personnel administering any aspect of the act through a merit system, it applied two principles: (1) that political appointments have no place in administration of public welfare activities, and (2) that the administration of these programs requires competent personnel, many of whom will look upon their work as a career. By far the largest number of individuals who work directly with the clients of the special assistance agencies are people of good will who develop skill in their work. A very small percentage, and those mostly in supervisory or administrative positions, are professionally educated social workers.

In 1950 there were 75,000 persons in the United States employed in positions defined as social work. Of these, 30,000 were employed in public-assistance agencies and 4,000 in public child welfare agencies. The balance were employed in other public and private agencies. Of the 30,000 in public assistance, slightly more than two out of ten had some graduate social work education; among child welfare workers the ratio was six out of ten.[31] The statutory provision enacted in 1956, authorizing funds to be appropriated for increasing the number of adequately trained public welfare personnel available for work in public-assistance programs, will facilitate improved services.

PUNITIVE PROVISIONS

Fear that the taxpayer was being unnecessarily bled by fakes, frauds, and malingerers resulted in two restrictive measures being added to the Social Security Act in the early 1950's. The first removed provision for compulsory confidentiality of all assistance records, and the second added the requirement of prompt notice to law-enforcement officials of the desertion and abandonment by a parent of children needing funds from the program for aid to dependent children. We shall refer to the latter provision when we discuss the ADC program in Chapter 23. Social work

[31] U.S. Department of Health, Education, and Welfare, Bureau of Public Assistance and Children's Bureau, *Public Socal Welfare Personnel* (Washington, D.C., G.P.O., 1953); Eleanor T. Hadley, *Report from Washington* (Washington, D.C., National Association of Social Workers, March 9, 1956).

groups manifested great concern for what they feared might occur in the states which chose to modify their laws to permit access to certain kinds of information regarding beneficiaries of the special assistances.[32] Although many, perhaps most, persons concerned with the administration of these programs regretted and resented the enactment of this provision by the federal government and by numbers of states, there have been few, if any, apparent ill results. A very small number of people have inquired regarding recipients. What has been the intangible effect upon the feelings of recipients is not statistically known.

STATISTICS ON OLD-AGE ASSISTANCE

In June, 1955, 2,549,000 persons were receiving old-age assistance, in comparison with 2,582,000 in June, 1954. Average monthly payments for the country were $52.30 in June, 1955, and $51.45 in June, 1954. These figures conceal the variation in number and size of grants between states. For example, Delaware had 1,627 recipients of old-age assistance in June, 1955, and California 269,190. At one extreme Puerto Rico had an average monthly grant of $7.86, West Virginia of $27.69, and Mississippi of $27.90, and, at the other, Colorado had an average monthly grant of $85.10, Connecticut of $85.01, and New York of $79.07. The average for the country was $52.30. The total amount spent on old-age assistance in June, 1955, was $133,297,014.[33] Social Security Administration figures show that as more and more aged persons have received larger OASI benefits the size of OAA case loads has fallen.[34] This phenomenon has caused some people, including members of Congress, to inquire whether or not the federal government should reduce or terminate its grant-in-aid program for the public assistances, especially for OAA. Many persons administering the program believe that if the federal government were to withdraw its extensive support, large numbers of aged persons would suffer great hardships.

For Selected References, see those following Chapter 20.

---

[32] Many articles appeared on this subject. For a good summary, see Margaret Greenfield, *Confidentiality of Public Assistance Records,* Legislative Problems (Berkeley, University of California Bureau of Public Administration, 1953), No. 2.

[33] *Social Security Bulletin,* Vol. 18, No. 9 (September, 1955), p. 1 and p. 24, table 12. September issues of the *Social Security Bulletin* include an "Annual Statistical Supplement." Figures such as those used here change from month to month and from year to year, but they afford the reader a starting point for comparisons.

[34] Sue Ossman, "Concurrent Receipt of Public Assistance and Old Age and Survivors Insurance," *Social Security Bulletin,* Vol. 18, No. 9 (September, 1955), pp. 3–12.

CHAPTER 23

Other Assistance and Service Programs

(SOCIAL SECURITY ACT)

AID TO THE BLIND

GENERAL INFORMATION [1]

Title X of the Social Security Act provides for grants to states for aid to the blind. At the time of the passage of the act figures on the extent of blindness were incomplete and inaccurate. The 1930 census listed over 63,000 blind persons. This was an understatement. With the initiation of the federal program for aid to the blind the number appeared to be nearer 200,000. In 1955 there were about 300,000 blind in the United States. With special training the majority can lead normal, productive lives; but almost 100,000 blind people cannot support themselves, have no relatives who can sufficiently help, and have no other adequate source of income.

Analysis of the blind population shows a far greater proportion of old persons and a much smaller proportion of young people than are found among the general population. It appears that not more than 10 per cent of the blind are under twenty years of age, and at least 50 per cent are over sixty-five. This is explained, in part, by the increasing longevity of the general population, so that the problem of blindness is added to that of old age. At least two thirds of the blind lose their sight after reaching twenty years of age.

The prevalence of blindness in the United States varies in different geographical areas. The high and above-high areas are in the south and southwest portions of the country. Blindness has numbers of causes, of which a large proportion, perhaps 50 to 75 per cent, is thought to be

---

[1] U.S. Committee on Economic Security, *Social Security in America: The Factual Background of the Social Security Act as Summarized from Staff Reports to the Committee on Economic Security by the Social Security Board,* Social Security Board Publication (Washington, D.C., G.P.O., 1937), No. 20, ch. 17; see also, M. Robert Barnett and Helga Lende, "The Blind," *Social Work Year Book: 1954,* pp. 55–60, and pertinent articles in earlier volumes of the same publication.

preventable. In the school-age group about 64 per cent is of prenatal origin, and almost 14 per cent is due to infectious diseases. Data gathered in one study of about 50,000 blind persons showed cataract as the most frequently reported type of eye defect causing blindness (18.8 per cent). Next in order of frequency were diseases of the optic nerve (17.7 per cent), the cornea (14.2 per cent), the choroid and retina (13.6 per cent), and glaucoma (11.6 per cent).

Federal legislation has brought about important developments in the care, treatment, and training of the blind. In 1943 Congress passed an amendment to the Vocational Rehabilitation Act of 1920, called the Barden-LaFollette Act. According to its provisions, the Office of Vocational Rehabilitation (within the Department of Health, Education, and Welfare) assumes the necessary state administrative costs and the costs of vocational counseling and placement, but the costs of medical treatment and vocational training are shared by the federal and state governments. Responsibility for administration of rehabilitation of the blind is lodged in the state agency for the blind if it meets certain federal requirements and if it is authorized by state law to render such services.

The Randolph-Sheppard Act of 1936, administered by the Office of Vocational Rehabilitation since 1946, authorizes the operation of vending stands by blind persons in federal and other buildings. The federal government co-operates in providing a market for articles made by the blind under the Wagner-O'Day Act of 1938. This law requires that federal departments under stipulated conditions purchase certain articles from workshops for the blind at fair market prices. Since 1879 federal funds have been available to the American Printing House for the Blind to provide books for schools for the blind. In 1931 an act was passed which authorized an annual appropriation to the Library of Congress for books for the blind. The Revenue Act of 1943, subsequently modified, permits a personal income-tax exemption of $600.00 each for the blind taxpayer and his spouse. The federal government, through the Veterans' Administration, assumes full responsibility for the rehabilitation of war blinded and provides a disability compensation according to the degree of disability.

In 1935 twenty-seven states had laws providing pensions or cash grants to the blind.[2] The first state law for the relief of the needy blind was enacted by Indiana in 1840. The laws, like all public-assistance laws, differed between states on such details as age, residence, size of maximum grant, allocation of costs, and administrative agency. The courts encountered relatively little difficulty with the legality of blind relief legislation. However, in 1906 an Ohio law enacted in 1904 was declared unconstitutional on the ground that it was appropriating public funds for the pri-

[2] *Social Security in America,* p. 302.

vate use of a special class. In 1913 the constitutionality of another Ohio blind relief law enacted in 1908 was contested; it was upheld upon the grounds that it is a function of the state to care for its poor and that this law provided for a special group of poor persons.[3] In Missouri, in order to prevent an issue of constitutionality, an amendment was secured especially authorizing the enactment of a blind pension law. Generally speaking, blind assistance laws are constitutional, since it is now assumed that it is within the police power of the state not only to care for poor persons as such but for special classes of poor persons.[4] The cases which reach the courts are on procedural questions and on the same type of problems encountered in other relief legislation.

FEDERAL PROVISIONS

Opinion differs as to whether or not grants to the blind should be made on the basis of need or as pensions to all blind persons in partial compensation for their conditions. Although the pressure group comprising the blind is much smaller and less influential than that of the aged, similar arguments are presented by this group for a pension system for all blind persons. In the enactment of provisions for the blind in the Social Security Act, Congress accepted the principle of grants for *needy* blind instead of universal pensions. The act authorizes an open-end appropriation, a sum sufficient to make grants to the states which have submitted plans approved by the United States Department of Health, Education, and Welfare. These plans are required to contain the same provisions as those for the aged, for dependent children, and for the totally and permanently disabled, except that the state agency shall disregard the first $50.00 of earned income in determining need and shall, in determining whether an individual is blind, require an examination by a physician skilled in diseases of the eye or by an optometrist at the applicant's choice.

Federal administration of this program, as for the other three assistance programs, lies with the United States Department of Health, Education, and Welfare, the Social Security Administration, Bureau of Public Assistance. Grants-in-aid are made to the states by the department according to formulas (see Ch. 22, pp. 564–565). When the Social Security Act was passed, some fears were expressed that the provisions for aid to the blind might hinder the development of specialized programs which had prevention and rehabilitation as their primary objectives. Some of the blind feared that the administration of the grants would be done with the old poor-law psychology. Because of the stabilization of all the special assist-

---

[3] *Auditor of Lucas Co.* v. *The State,* 75 Ohio 114, 78 N.E. 955 (1906); *St. ex rel. Walton* v. *Edmonson,* 89 Ohio 351, 106 N.E. 41 (1913).

[4] Robert Benjamin Irwin and Evelyn C. McKay, *Blind Relief Laws* (New York, American Foundation for the Blind, 1929), p. 38.

ance programs under the Social Security Administration neither of these things has occurred to the degree feared.

STATE PROVISIONS

In our analysis of old-age assistance in the preceding chapter we used the Social Security Administration's study of the *Characteristics of State Public Assistance Plans* as a framework for the discussion of the various provisions of state legislation and administration. We do the same in less detail in this chapter for the other three public assistance programs of the Social Security Act. There is a possibility, if not a likelihood, that each state provides the same or similar requirements, when applicable, for the four assistance programs. For example, if there is no citizenship requirement for one program, there may be none for the others. The residence requirement for one program may be the same for the others. Definitions of need and standards of care are frequently the same. If the legal maximum payment is the same as the corresponding federal maximum for one program, the federal maximum is likely to prevail for the other programs as well. It is unsound, however, to generalize much further on this subject, since each of the special assistance programs developed as an independent entity.

The Social Security Act imposes no age limitations upon those eligible for aid to the blind. In the early days of the federal-state program a majority of the states specified a minimum age, ranging from sixteen to twenty-one, under which a person was ineligible for blind assistance. As of February 1, 1956, the date of the study from which we are taking our materials, twenty-nine jurisdictions had no age requirements. In the same year forty-seven jurisdictions had no citizenship or long-time residence requirements for aid to the blind, whereas thirty-six jurisdictions had no such requirements for old-age assistance. Residence requirements within a given state, at least for the three programs of old-age assistance, aid to the blind, and aid to the permanently and totally disabled, were essentially the same in the majority of states. Numbers of states permitted grants to the needy blind, despite inability to meet residence requirements if the blindness occurred while the applicants were residents of the state.

The Social Security Act contains no definition of blindness. It only requires that in determining whether an individual is blind there shall be an examination by a physician skilled in diseases of the eye or by an optometrist, whichever the individual may select. The definition usually accepted by the states, and generally under administrative regulation rather than by legislative fiat, was absence of visual acuity of 20/200 or less in better eye with correcting glasses or field defect in which peripheral field has contracted to such extent that widest diameter of visual field subtends at an angular distance no greater than 20 degrees. Property and income limitations within a particular state were often the same, or essentially the same, as those for old-age assistance. Statutory provisions regarding recoveries, liens, and assignments were less exacting than for old-age assistance, with twenty-nine jurisdictions appearing to have no provisions on the subject. In most states all four of the assistance programs were carried on by the same state and local agencies. In several states a state agency for the blind carried on the blind assistance program.

FACTS AND FIGURES

In 1934, in twenty-four of the twenty-seven states then having blind pension laws and for which figures were available, there was a total of almost 32,000 recipients, with a total expenditure at the end of the year of $6,880,015 and an average grant of $19.96 per month ranging from 83 cents in Arkansas to $33.12 in California. All jurisdictions now participate in programs for aid to the blind. In June, 1955, almost 104,000 blind persons were receiving aid at a total expenditure for that month of $5,965,151. The size of the average grant for all jurisdictions was $57.41. The average monthly grant at one extreme was $7.80 in Puerto Rico and $32.13 in West Virginia, and at the other was $93.81 in Massachusetts and $128.12 in Minnesota.[5]

AID TO THE PERMANENTLY AND TOTALLY DISABLED

FEDERAL PROVISIONS

Title XIV of the Social Security Act provides for this group of persons. Amendments in 1950 added this to the other three public-assistance programs. A similar program was already in operation in Wisconsin and in a few counties and cities elsewhere. The Wisconsin statute is more limiting than the federal act in that it requires that the disability be such as to require constant and continuous care.[6] Under the Title XIV program the federal government participates in payments by the states to needy persons who are at least eighteen years of age and who are permanently and totally disabled. For a state plan to be approved it must include and may not impose the same requirements as for the other assistance programs (see Ch. 22).

Prior to the 1950 amendments, proposals that the federal government take some responsibility for financial help to disabled persons were discussed at length and in detail by congressional committees.[7] Some of

[5] *Social Security Bulletin,* Vol. 18. No. 9 (September, 1955), p. 24, table 13.
[6] Wis. Stat., 1955, c. 49.61 (1).
[7] Most of the materials in this section on aid to the permanently and totally disabled came from Phyllis Hill, "Aid to the Permanently and Totally Disabled," *Social Security Bulletin,* Vol. 13, No. 12 (December, 1950), pp. 11–15; *Social Security*

the proposals would have expanded the old-age and survivors insurance program so that insurance benefits would be paid to disabled workers. In fact, the House of Representatives in 1949 approved a bill (H.R. 6000) which contained provisions for both disability insurance and disability assistance. This proposal would have established in the field of disability a complementary relationship similar to that of old-age and suvivors insurance and old-age assistance. During that legislative session proposals were also made that any new grant-in-aid program cover general assistance or, alternatively, embody a broader concept of disability than the term *permanent and total disability* permitted. Congress rejected these various proposals and, in 1950, accepted the compromise measure we are now discussing. As of February, 1956, the program was in effect in forty-five jurisdictions.

If it is logical to provide through social insurance some measure of financial security to the American people against the hazards of old age, death, and unemployment, then it appears equally sound to provide through social insurance for the risk of disability. The program of public assistance for the permanently and totally disabled is not a substitute for either an insurance scheme or a general assistance program. Pressure upon Congress to provide for universal temporary and permanent disability insurance has not yet been sufficiently strong to overcome the opposition of such powerful groups as the American Medical Association. However, Congress has partially relaxed its attitude and made some beginnings in providing protection of disabled persons against wage losses.

STATE PROVISIONS

By 1950, when this new form of assistance was initiated, most of the states had had fifteen or more years of experience with eligibility requirements, including age, residence, and standards of care for the other special assistances. The eligibility requirement of permanent and total disability was a new factor in assistance administration and involved complex problems of medical definitions and co-operative relationships between medical and social work staffs. Congress did not require that the program be restricted to the completely helpless, so the Social Security Administration developed interpretations of the federal law that do not require a state program to be so limited.

Permanently and totally disabled, according to the administration, defines any individual who has some physical or mental impairment, dis-

---

Bulletin, Vol. 18, No. 8 (August, 1955), anniversary issue; Lester Breslow, "Chronic Illness," *Social Work Year Book: 1957,* pp. 157–164; Anne E. Geddes and Charles E. Hawkins, "Public Assistance," *Social Work Year Book: 1954,* pp. 394–405; "Social Security Protection, 1935–55," *Social Security Bulletin,* Vol. 18, No. 8 (August, 1955), pp. 10–11; Jay L. Roney, "Twenty Years of Public Assistance," *Social Security Bulletin,* Vol. 18, No. 8 (August, 1955), pp. 17–22.

ease, or loss that substantially precludes him from engaging in useful occupations within his competence. It suggests that the disability factor be considered as consisting of two parts: the medical findings and the social study of the individual's ability to carry out his responsibilities as, for example, homemaker or wage earner. Permanently has been interpreted to refer to the nature of the physiological or anatomical impairment that is present and verifiable by medical findings. To be permanent the impairment must be a condition likely to continue throughout the remaining lifetime of the individual and not likely to improve or disappear spontaneously. This definition does not preclude recovery from the impairment or physical and vocational rehabilitation.

Within the limits of the provisions of the Social Security Act and the interpretation of the Social Security Administration, each state makes its own definitions. The Social Security Administration recommends that state laws do not spell out details concerning the scope of the eligibility factor of permanent and total disability but leave definitions to the state administrative agency. As regards acceptance of medical treatment, the Social Security Administration believes that no individual should be required to take treatment unless that treatment can be demonstrated to be such that a "reasonably prudent man" would accept it. Under this principle certain factors can be considered, such as whether the individual is unreasonable, and, if so, how much; whether his refusal endangers the life of others; whether religious scruples enter the picture; whether he would risk the loss of what remaining physical ability he has by treatment; and what degree of fear exists. The Social Security Administration believes that if the states do impose acceptance of medical treatment as an eligibility factor, the responsibility for deciding about any individual case should rest with medical staff. Such a decision would, like others, be subject to the fair hearing process. State and local agencies are expected to utilize the best treatment and retraining facilities available. This means co-operation and planning with numbers of kinds of resources.

FACTS AND FIGURES

On an average day in 1954, probably more than 9,000,000 persons of all ages were disabled—unable to work, attend school, keep house, and so forth, because of temporary or permanent physical or mental incapacity. It is estimated that in 1935 the long-term disabled comprised about half of the 6,000,000 persons then incapacitated on an average day, and by 1954 they were estimated at over 5,000,000, or about 60 per cent of all disabled persons.

In 1935 public protection to the disabled for wage loss was limited to work-connected disabilities under state and federal workmen's compensation laws; to service-connected and non-service-connected disabilities under Veterans' and Armed Forces' programs; to sickness and disability under several programs for employees of federal, state, and local governments; and to special programs for the blind in about half the states. By 1955 there were, in addition, both permanent and temporary disability benefits under the railroad retirement system, temporary disability insurance programs for industrial and commercial workers in four states, and federal-state public-assistance programs for the blind and permanently and totally disabled. In 1954 federal legislation provided for the expansion of the federal-state vocational rehabilitation program and for preservation of old-age and survivors insurance benefit rights for individuals with extended total disability. In 1956 Congress provided for additional insurance protection against loss of income due to disability. As more social insurance protection becomes available to greater numbers of disabled persons, enlarged opportunities for vocational rehabilitation will also be supplied to and required of the recipients. Conspicuous results in the number of disabled persons returned to employment followed the 1954 sharply increased financial support of the federal-state vocational rehabilitation program.

The number of persons between the ages of fourteen and sixty-four with long-term total disabilities who are receiving some support from public programs designed to maintain income in case of disability has increased, it is estimated, from something less than 200,000 in 1934 to about 1,000,000 in 1954, or from one in ten in 1934 to about one in three in 1954.[8] In December, 1954, there were 224,000 persons receiving assistance under the aid to the permanently and totally disabled program, 102,000 receiving aid to the blind, 266,000 receiving insurance benefits under the railroad retirement and public-employee retirement systems, and about 470,000 totally disabled veterans under sixty-five years of age receiving veterans' benefits.

In June, 1955, 236,840 persons were receiving aid to the permanently and totally disabled.[9] The total amount spent for this program in that month was $12,010,252. The average grant for the country was $54.93. The grants in the forty-two jurisdictions then having the program ranged from $8.61 for Puerto Rico, $19.27 for the Virgin Islands, and $24.60 for Mississippi to $100.35 for Massachusetts and $107.13 for Connecticut.

A study of the social and medical characteristics of recipients of this program was made by the Social Security Administration in the middle of 1951, when the number was approaching 100,000. The study showed that the recipients were about equally divided between the two sexes. The median age was fifty-six, with half the recipients between the ages of fifty-five and sixty-four. Younger recipients, those under thirty-five, comprised 10 per cent of the total and were more severely disabled than older

[8] "Social Security Protection, 1935–55," *loc. cit.*, pp. 5–11.
[9] *Social Security Bulletin*, Vol. 18, No. 9 (September, 1955), p. 26, table 16.

recipients. Some 70 per cent of the recipients had a history of paid employment at some time. Four groups of diseases accounted for the major impairments of about 65 per cent of the recipients. Diseases of the heart and circulatory system accounted for over three out of ten cases. Arthritis, paralyzing conditions, and congenital conditions each accounted for the impairment of at least one out of ten cases.[10]

AID TO DEPENDENT CHILDREN

The child welfare proposals of the President's Committee on Economic Security were prepared in consultation with the child welfare, medical, and public health advisory committees. These groups believed that three forms of public service for children needed expanding and strengthening: (1) care of dependent children in their own homes; (2) welfare services for children needing special care, such as homeless and neglected children; and (3) services for maternal and child health and for crippled children. The Social Security Act provides for all these services.

EXTENT OF PROGRAMS PRIOR TO 1935

Title IV of the Social Security Act provides for grants to states for aid to dependent children. In Chapter 11 we referred to the fact that the White House Conference of 1909 advocated legislation to provide aid to dependent children in their own homes, popularly called "mothers' pensions" or "widows' pensions," and that the first law of the kind was passed in Missouri in 1911, applying only to Jackson County (Kansas City), and that the first state-wide law was enacted in Illinois in the same year. Within the first ten years, laws were passed in forty-one states; and by the time of the passage of the Social Security Act, all jurisdictions but Georgia and South Carolina had passed some kind of mothers' aid law.[11] Some outstanding social workers objected to the early laws because they feared that *public* relief for mothers and their children would be badly administered, that there would be political interference, and that pauperism would be encouraged. Today, there is no opposition to the program as such from social workers but rather a desire to expand and improve it and perhaps to integrate it with child welfare activities. Such resistance as there is comes largely from citizens who feel that aid is too easily available to the families of deserting fathers, to divorced parents, and to unmarried mothers.

The early mothers' assistance laws placed both administrative and financial responsibility upon the county. By 1934 seventeen states were paying a part of the costs and exercising varying degrees of administra-

[10] Geddes and Hawkins, *loc. cit.*, p. 403.
[11] Grace Abbott, *The Child and the State* (Chicago, University of Chicago Press, 1938), Vol. 2, sec. 4.

tive responsibility for the programs. Most of the state laws before the passage of the Social Security Act were permissive rather than mandatory, which meant that even in those states with legislation, many counties never had a mothers' assistance program. With the prolongation of the depression of the 1930's many counties which had been granting mothers' assistance discontinued the practice and passed the responsibility for the care of this group back to the poor-law officials. When federal funds became available for unemployment relief, persons eligible for mothers' assistance as well as for other forms of categorical aid were often placed on these rolls. Even where grants were made to mothers, the amounts were often so small as to defeat the purpose of the law. In order to remedy this situation, Congress provided for dependent children in their own or relatives' homes through the Social Security Act.

FEDERAL PROVISIONS

Title IV of the act provides that under the same conditions as are specified for the other three special assistances the federal government will assist in the care of children who come within the definitions. A special restriction applies to this program. It requires that effective July 1, 1952, the state plan shall provide for prompt notice to appropriate law-enforcement officials of the furnishing of aid to dependent children with respect to a child who has been deserted or abandoned by a parent. This is informally referred to as NOLEO, meaning "notification of law-enforcement officials." The residence requirements differ somewhat from those of the other three assistance programs. The state plan may not impose

> as a condition of eligibility . . . a residence requirement which denies aid with respect to any child residing in the State (1) who has resided in the State for one year immediately preceding the application for such aid, or (2) who was born within one year immediately preceding the application; if the parent or other relative with whom the child is living has resided in the State for one year immediately preceding the birth.

A dependent child is defined as a needy child under eighteen who has been deprived of parental support or care because of the death, continued absence from the home, or physical or mental incapacity of a parent, and who is living with his father, mother, grandfather, grandmother, brother, sister, stepfather, stepmother, stepbrother, stepsister, uncle, aunt, first cousin, nephew, or niece in a place of residence maintained by one or more such relatives as his or their own home. Aid to dependent children means money payments or medical or remedial care not only for the child but for the relative with whom the dependent child is living. Inclusion of the relative who maintains the family home in the budgetary calculations for federal reimbursement purposes did not occur until the 1950 amendments to the Social Security Act.

Responsibility for the administration of this program, as for the other three assistances, is lodged with the Department of Health, Education, and Welfare. Prior to the establishment of this department, the Social Security Act provided for the administration of all four assistance programs by the social security administrator. This practice continues, with the Bureau of Public Assistance of the Social Security Administration within the department carrying on the program. There has always been some difference of opinion among administrators and social workers as to whether the aid to dependent children program is primarily an assistance or a child welfare program. Some of those who insist that it is a child welfare program argue that it should be administered by the Children's Bureau. On state and local levels of administration it is operated as an aspect of the special assistance programs. Particularly on the local level of government, more and more departments of welfare are administering both public-assistance and child welfare programs. Consequently, at the point of contact with the individual needing services there is a desirable trend toward co-ordination of public-assistance and child welfare objectives and approaches.

STATE PROVISIONS [12]

The ADC program, like those for OAA and AB, is in effect in all fifty-three American jurisdictions. Although the pattern of ADC programs is set by the Social Security Act, the act affords states wide latitude for determining eligibility, as it does for the other three assistance programs. It does not define such terms as *need, incapacity,* and *continued absence from the home* but leaves them as elastic concepts to be interpreted by state legislatures and administrations. Although the act permits a state to impose a state residence of one year and a requirement of United States citizenship, ten states, in 1956, had no durational residence requirements. Texas, a border state, was the only one to require United States citizenship. Among state-imposed conditions of eligibility are those relating to employability or employment status of the parents or children, "suitability of the home," "fitness of the parent," and, in the case of desertion or abandon-

---

[12] Materials for this section came largely from the following: U.S. Department of Health, Education, and Welfare, Social Security Administration, *Characteristics of State Public Assistance Plans under the Social Security Act,* Public Assistance Report (Washington, D.C., G.P.O., 1956), No. 27; Anne E. Geddes, "Children and the Assistance and Insurance Programs," *Children,* Vol. 2, No. 4 (July–August, 1955), pp. 154–159; Phyllis R. Osborn, "Aid to Dependent Children—Realities and Possibilities," *Social Service Review,* Vol. 28, No. 2 (June, 1954), pp. 153–172; U.S. Department of Health, Education, and Welfare, Social Security Administration, *Aid to Dependent Children in a Postwar Year: Characteristics of Families Receiving ADC, June, 1948,* Public Assistance Report (Washington, D.C., G.P.O., 1950), No. 17; Charles Schottland, "Toward Greater Security in Childhood," *Social Security Bulletin,* Vol. 18, No. 4 (April, 1955), pp. 3–7; Lucy Freeman, *Children Who Never Had a Chance,* Public Affairs Pamphlet (New York, Public Affairs Committee, 1953), No. 183.

ment of a child by a parent, the filing of a complaint by the remaining parent to compel support.

Like the other forms of public assistance, states may make ADC payments larger or smaller than the amounts up to which the federal government will reimburse, but it will not share in that part of any payment which goes beyond $64.00 for a family comprising one adult relative and a child, plus $23.00 for each additional child beyond the first. (See Ch. 22, pp. 564–565 for the formula). Within these maximums the federal share is fourteen seventeenths of the first $17.00 (average per person), plus one half the balance. The size of the payment is presumed to be based on budgetarily determined needs, but the principle is by no means universally applied. Federal payments for ADC have always been more limited by inadequate appropriations than have payments for the other three assistances.[13]

FACTS AND FIGURES

Prior to the enactment of the Social Security Act, state reports on mothers' aid were not currently available and were by no means complete. In 1931, out of 2,723 administrative units authorized to grant mothers' aid, 1,578 reported to the United States Children's Bureau that such help was being given. From reports assembled by the bureau it was learned that 45,825 families were receiving aid in 1921 and 93,620 in 1931, the increase being due largely to the growth in the number of counties carrying on the program. In the more than 93,000 families, there were 253,298 dependent children. The grants varied from an average per family of $4.33 in Arkansas to $69.31 in Massachusetts.[14] In June, 1955, almost 1,700,000 children in over 600,000 families were receiving ADC. With the caretakers, almost 2,240,000 individuals received ADC. The average family grant for the country was $86.78, with a range from $10.38 in Puerto Rico and $22.99 in Mississippi to $136.58 in New York. The average per individual for the country as a whole was $24.04, with a range of $3.03 in Puerto Rico and $6.10 in Mississippi to $38.01 in New York.[15]

If the 1955 proportion of children on ADC remains constant—approximately 30 per 1,000 in the child population under eighteen—we shall add about 150,000 more children to the case load by 1960 and another 150,000 by 1965.[16] If this happens, it will result in an ADC case load of

---

[13] Geddes, "Children and the Assistance and Insurance Programs," *loc. cit.*, pp. 154–159.

[14] *Social Security in America*, pp. 235–236; Grace Abbott, "Mothers' Aid," *Social Work Year Book: 1937*, pp. 284–289.

[15] *Social Security Bulletin*, Vol. 18, No. 9 (September, 1955), p. 25, table 14.

[16] Wilbur Cohen, "Trends in Public Welfare," speech (mimeographed) given at meeting of American Public Welfare Association in Milwaukee, Wis., on June 29, 1955. Mr. Cohen at that time was director of the Division of Research and Statistics, Social Security Administration.

2,000,000 children in 1965. This means that there will be as many or more children receiving assistance as there are likely to be aged persons receiving OAA. If we take into account the adult caretakers on the ADC program, it is possible that the total ADC case load (children and one caretaker per family) may exceed the OAA case load in the nation within the next few years.

The character of the ADC program has been changing over the years.[17] This is largely because the responsibility for providing income to families whose chief breadwinner has died or retired has been increasingly assumed by OASI. In 1942 there were only 18 child OASI beneficiaries for every 100 ADC children. By 1954 it was 71. With similar economic conditions in the next decade the number of child beneficiaries in relation to the number of ADC children may be expected to rise substantially. The result is that to an increasing extent the ADC program is becoming one for children whose deprivation of parental support is the result of inability or failure of a living parent—usually the father—to provide support. Whereas in 1931 about 82 in every 100 ADC families were those of widows, in 1953 the father was dead in only 17 families out of 100. Proportionately, the number of families with an incapacitated father has remained fairly constant, representing about one fifth of all ADC families. As the proportion of families with the father dead has declined, the proportion of families with a living father absent from the home has increased. Such families comprised 39 per cent of the total in 1942 and 59 per cent in 1953.

Changes in the composition of the families receiving ADC appear to be largely responsible for public reaction against the program and for enactment of the NOLEO provisions of the Social Security Act. It is too early to know what are and will be the results of the amendment, but a study conducted co-operatively by state public-assistance agencies and the Bureau of Public Assistance of the Social Security Administration in 1955 was designed to find answers to such questions as: What efforts do law-enforcement officials and public-assistance agencies make to locate fathers whose whereabouts are unknown? To what extent have support orders been issued? What are the reasons complaints are not filed or further action taken? What use is made of reciprocal enforcement-of-support laws?

With changes in the character of the composition of ADC families, state and local administering agencies have been intensifying their social work services and trying to improve the quality of their personnel. Among the welcome 1956 amendments to the Social Security Act was the authorization for appropriations to enable the states and localities to render services to relatives with whom the dependent children are living. These

[17] Geddes, "Children and the Assistance and Insurance Programs," *loc. cit.*, pp. 154–159.

moneys and those for training workers will encourage state and local administrations to employ personnel which has had professional social work education. The children in these families deserve the best. Such studies as *Future Citizens All* point out the potentials of this large group of children.[18]

LEGAL ASPECTS

The constitutionality of mothers' aid laws has been established generally for a long time.[19] In a 1917 Utah case it was contended that the tax for this purpose was void because it took private property for other than a public purpose and was discriminatory because it favored a special class.[20] The court said:

> It will be conceded, we take it, that the proper rearing and bringing up of children, their education, their moral welfare, can all be subserved better by giving to such children the companionship, control, and management of their mothers than by any other system devised by human ingenuity. The object of the act is to provide means whereby mothers who are otherwise unable may be enabled to give such attention and care to their children of tender years as their health, education, and comfort require.

In other words, the Utah tax was a child welfare measure and was valid because it was for a public purpose.

In a 1916 Washington case a mother who had been receiving mothers' aid challenged the constitutionality of a 1915 law repealing the mothers' assistance law of 1913 and replacing it with another law setting up different eligibility requirements.[21] She claimed that the law was class legislation and that it denied equal protection of the law to all citizens. The court answered that any rule of law which declared the 1915 law unconstitutional would equally hold the earlier law unconstitutional; that it was not the intent of either law to provide pensions for all classes of indigent mothers but only for certain designated classes, and anyway the state might care for its poor in any manner it pleased. "No individual or class of individuals can acquire a vested right to be cared for in any particular manner."

The courts have been called upon to decide questions pertaining to programs for aid to dependent children, which are like those coming before the courts under other forms of public assistance. For example, in

---

[18] Gordon W. Blackwell and Raymond F. Gould, *Future Citizens All* (Chicago, American Public Welfare Association, 1952); Kermit T. Wiltse, "Social Casework Services in the Aid to Dependent Children Program," *Social Service Review*, Vol. 18, No. 2 (June, 1954), pp. 173–185.

[19] Abbott, *Child and State*, Vol. 2, sec. 4, particularly the cases, pp. 276–302.

[20] *Denver & Rio Grande Railroad Co.* v. *Grand County*, 51 Utah 294, 170 Pac. 74 (1917).

[21] *In the matter of the Petition of Mrs. Rose Snyder*, 93 Wash. 59, 160 Pac. 12 (1916).

1933 the Minnesota court had to decide whether mothers' aid was poor relief.[22] In that case it was claimed that since the settlement of the family for poor-relief purposes was in another county, and since the family upon the death of the husband and father received relief from the county of settlement, it could not establish settlement for the purpose of obtaining a mothers' aid grant. The court held that the mothers' assistance law was no part of the poor law, that the beneficiaries were the children and not the mother, and that settlement as distinguished from residence for the latter group was of no moment. A year's residence was required, but not a year of residence without the receipt of relief, which was the settlement provision of the poor-relief laws.

The question of procedure in revoking a grant came before the West Virginia court in 1928.[23] The court held that although the statute did not prescribe the procedure by which a grant should be terminated, nevertheless the same kind of procedure should be provided for termination of an award as for granting it. Upon the findings of a probation officer, without notice to the mother and without a hearing, her grant was terminated. The lower court was therefore directed to give her a hearing. These and other cases clearly show that courts are liberally interpreting the intent of legislatures in enacting ADC legislation. They are saying that the statutes should not be strictly construed in the tradition of the poor laws and that for the benefit of the future citizens of America every consideration possible should be given them.

COSTS OF THE FOUR PUBLIC-ASSISTANCE PROGRAMS

GRANTS TO STATES

The amount of federal funds required for the four federally aided assistance programs is determined by the amounts spent by the states in support of these programs. For the fiscal year ending June 30, 1957, the total amount of federal, state, and local expenditures for assistance and administration was estimated at $2,641,000,000, of which 51 per cent represented the federal share. Table 12 compares anticipated state expenditures by programs and for administration for the years 1956 and 1957.[24]

---

[22] *St.* v. *Juvenile Court of Wadena County,* 188 Minn. 125, 246 N.W. 544 (1933).

[23] *Densmore et al.* v. *County Court of Mercer County,* 106 W. Va. 317, 145 S.E. 641 (1928).

[24] *Social Legislation Information Service,* 84th Cong. (January 23, 1956), No. 42.

Table 12

	1956 estimate	1957 estimate
Program by activities:		
State expenditures:		
1. Payments to recipients:		
a. Old-age assistance	$ 865,500,000	$ 802,500,000
b. Aid to dependent children	345,000,000	332,000,000
c. Aid to the blind	34,500,000	33,500,000
d. Aid to the permanently and totally disabled	82,500,000	82,500,000
Total	1,327,500,000	1,250,500,000
2. State and local administration:		
a. Old-age assistance	46,000,000	48,600,000
b. Aid to dependent children	29,600,000	33,300,000
c. Aid to the blind	2,500,000	2,700,000
d. Aid to the permanently and totally disabled	9,900,000	9,400,000
Total	88,000,000	94,000,000
Total for all programs	1,415,500,000	1,344,500,000

Table 13 shows the estimated average number of recipients per month in 1956 and 1957 for each of the four programs.

Table 13

	Current fiscal year (1956)	Next fiscal year (1957)
Program by activities:		
Old-age assistance	2,545,000	2,516,000
Aid to dependent children *	2,265,000	2,265,000
Aid to the blind	105,000	108,000
Aid to the permanently and totally disabled	248,000	268,000

* Children, parents, and adult relatives.

These two tables show that among the significant anticipated changes were reduction in the size of the OAA case load and in the amount of payments to recipients of that program. This is the result of the expanding and maturing OASI system.

PROPOSED CHANGES IN PUBLIC-ASSISTANCE PROVISIONS

Proposals for amendments to the public-assistance provisions of the Social Security Act continue to be made. We referred to some of them in Chapter 20. Recommendations before the Eighty-fourth Congress included: [25]

1. Provide separate matching of state and local expenditures for medical care for recipients of old-age assistance, aid to dependent children, aid to the blind, and aid to the permanently and totally disabled.
2. Provide that for persons added to the old-age assistance rolls after July 1, 1957, who also receive OASI benefits, federal matching in assistance payments

[25] *Social Legislation Information Service*, 84th Cong. (February 13, 1956), No. 45.

be limited to 50 per cent instead of the higher federal participation now applicable to all recipients.

3. Make explicit that one purpose of federal grants is to assist the states to provide appropriate public welfare services to enable applicants for or recipients of public assistance to achieve more fully their potentials for self-support or self-care and to strengthen the family life of homes with dependent children.

4. Amend the aid to dependent children program by extending the list of relatives with whom the child may live and receive aid, and by raising the school attendance requirement for children from sixteen to eighteen years of age.

5. Provide for part payment to states or other nonprofit organizations for research or demonstration projects in social welfare.

6. Authorize federal grants for training of personnel for employment in public-assistance programs, and for establishing fellowships or traineeships and special short-term courses of study.

7. Increase the annual dollar limitation on federal grants to Puerto Rico and the Virgin Islands.

In 1956 Congress substantially accepted these recommendations except the second to which there was extensive opposition. It is unfortunate that there continues to be little congressional inclination to provide either for a federal grant-in-aid program for recipients of general assistance or for the more comprehensive measure, complete abolition of all classifications of persons needing public assistance.

MATERNAL AND CHILD WELFARE SERVICES [26]

The Social Security Act has done much to give momentum to state programs for the health and welfare of mothers and children. Although the appropriations for these services are relatively small, Congress has given evidence of its realization of the need for, and value of, such services. Title V of the Social Security Act provides for grants to states for maternal and child welfare services. This title is in three parts: "Maternal and Child Health Services," "Services for Crippled Children," and "Child Welfare Services," each of which we shall discuss separately in the following pages. These three services are administered by the Department of Health, Education, and Welfare. The Children's Bureau carries on the programs. In its report to President Roosevelt the Committee on Economic Security advised as follows:

> It must not for a moment be forgotten that the core of any social plan must be the child . . . old-age pensions are in a real sense measures in behalf of children. They shift the retroactive burdens to shoulders which can bear them with less human cost, and young parents thus released can put at the disposal of the new member of society those family resources he must be permitted to enjoy if he is to become a strong person, unburdensome to the state. Health

[26] *Compilation of the Social Security Laws, Including the Social Security Act, as Amended, and Related Enactments Through December 31, 1954,* 83d Cong., 2d sess., S. Doc. 157 (Washington, D.C., G.P.O., 1955); and Public Law 880, 84th Cong., 2d sess., ch. 836, H.R. 7225 (Washington, D.C., G.P.O., 1956).

measures that protect his family from sickness and remove the menacing apprehension of debt, always present in the mind of the breadwinner, are child welfare measures. Likewise, unemployment compensation is a measure in behalf of children in that it protects the home. Most important of all, public job assurance which can hold the family together over long or repetitive periods of private unemployment is a measure for children in that it assures them a childhood rather than the premature strains of the would-be child breadwinner.

Title V puts into effect two principles: that the state has a responsibility for providing social services as well as income maintenance services, and that all levels of government can legally and legitimately participate in the provision of these social services.

MATERNAL AND CHILD HEALTH SERVICES [27]

FEDERAL PROVISIONS

Until the Social Security Act was passed the only experience of the federal government with grants for maternal and child health purposes was with the Maternity and Infancy Act of 1921, commonly referred to as the Sheppard-Towner Act.[28] The act expired in 1929. Services under that statute had been confined to those relating to the maternity cycle and early childhood. Under the Social Security Act (by administrative practice) the service age of children is raised to twenty-one years. Of greatest significance is the fact that the grants under the Social Security Act are not conceived as temporary measures. The size of the "closed-end" appropriations for this and the other two programs of this title have been increased on several occasions since 1935.

Title V, Part 1, of the Social Security Act makes sums available for payments to states which submit plans approved by the secretary of the Department of Health, Education, and Welfare for extending and improving services for promoting the health of mothers and children, especially in rural areas and in areas suffering from severe economic

---

[27] The material for this section comes from Edward R. Schlesinger, "Child Health Services since 1935," *Children,* Vol. 2, No. 4 (July–August, 1955), pp. 127–132; Samuel B. Kirkwood, "Twenty Years of Maternal Care," *Children,* Vol. 2, No. 4 (July–August, 1955), pp. 133–138; Martha M. Eliot, "Twenty Years of Progress for Children," *Social Security Bulletin,* Vol. 18, No. 8 (August, 1955), pp. 23–28. See also, U.S. Committee on Economic Security, *Report to the President of the Committee on Economic Security* (Washington, D.C., G.P.O., 1935); Katharine F. Lenroot, "Health Security for Mothers and Children," *Annals of the American Academy of Political and Social Science* (March, 1939), pp. 105–115; U.S. Children's Bureau, *Federal and State Cooperation in Maternal and Child Welfare Services under the Social Security Act,* Maternal and Child Welfare Bulletin (Washington, D.C., G.P.O., 1938), No. 2.

[28] 21 U.S. Stat. 224; *The Promotion of the Welfare and Hygiene of Maternity and Infancy: The Administration of the Act of Congress of November 23, 1921, for Year Ended June 30, 1929,* U.S. Children's Bureau Publication (Washington, D.C., G.P.O., 1931), No. 203; for excerpts from Children's Bureau reports regarding administration of this act. see Abbott. *Child and State,* Vol. 2, pp. 1068–1071.

distress. These requirements are similar to several of those for the four forms of public assistance. The state health agency is required to administer the program. Each state must provide for financial participation. The department is responsible for the following services:

1. Formulation of federal policies and procedures.
2. Advisory and consultative service through a medical and public health nursing staff and other professional consultants.
3. Review and approval of state plans, budgets, reports, etc.
4. Auditing of state accounts.
5. Compilation of statistical and descriptive materials relating to activities carried on and publication of reports.
6. Research.

STATE PROGRAMS

In 1934, thirty-nine states had funds for some kind of health work for mothers and children. Prior to the Social Security Act only thirty-one states had a division of child health in the state department of health, and in only twenty-two of these was the director a physician employed full time. Within a short time after the passage of the act all the states had doctors employed as full-time directors; in a few instances these directors also had charge of the crippled children's program. The majority of the directors are obstetricians or pediatricians and many have had public health training.

State programs are concerned with health education, demonstration, supervision, and direct services. Each year literally millions of mothers and children are served by clinics and by medical, hospital, nursing, and other services provided by the states with the aid of federal grants. These services go to expectant mothers, well babies, preschool and school-age children, and many specially designated groups. In 1954 federal grants helped pay for more than 4,000,000 immunizations of school children against diphtheria and smallpox and for more than 2,500,000 inspections for dental defects. Many babies and children are better off because of research conducted or stimulated by the Children's Bureau and because of publications it has made available to health and welfare practitioners, parents, writers, and researchers.

The availability of federal funds to the states for maternal and child health services coincided with a period of rapid increase in the child population and in scientific and medical knowledge. Expanded federal funds have been a factor in making new knowledge available to a growing population. In 1935, 1 out of every 172 mothers died in childbirth; in 1955, 1 out of every 1900. If 1935 rates prevailed in 1955, 24,000 expectant mothers would die. Instead, it was predicted that about 2,000 would lose their lives. The same major causes of maternal death continue in the lead, but all have been drastically reduced. The major causes are sepsis, toxemia, hemmorrhage, trauma, and shock. Much has been scientifically learned concerning methods of prevention and treatment of these characteristic diseases of maternity, and consequently morbidity and mortality rates have both fallen. There has been a vast improvement in the condition in which the postpartum mother now is returned to a nonpregnant condition. An increasing realization of the impact of disability of the mother upon the whole family has brought about an appreciation of the close relation between the physical and social elements in maternal care. Changes have taken place in anaesthesia and analgesia, in natural childbirth methods, in number of hospital deliveries, in rooming-in of baby and mother in the hospital, in academic obstetrics, in understanding of emotional factors of expectant and new mothers, in teamwork between specializations, including doctors, nurses, nutritionists, and social workers.

In 1954 the population of the United States included 12,000,000 more children than in 1935, and a considerably greater proportion of children under five years and between the ages of five and nine. In 1935 there were 48,000,000 children under 21, and in 1954, 60,000,000. In 1935 the death rate of children between the ages of one and four from all causes was 440.9 per 100,000 population; in 1952 it was 141.2. For those from five to fourteen years of age it was 152.9 in 1935 and 59.2 in 1952; and for the group from fifteen to nineteen years of age it was 222.3 in 1935 and 112.8 in 1952. Despite great improvements in medical knowledge and practice, and even though federal grants-in-aid to the states have made more services available to more people, there are still many program gaps. Most noticeable are the failures of many individuals and communities to take advantage of knowledge available and the absence of assured medical care for all regardless of income.

State and local funds for maternal and child health services have increased steadily. In 1940 total anticipated expenditures were $11,-700,000. Of this amount $6,100,000 were from state and local funds, and $5,600,000 were from federal funds. By 1954 the total amount of such planned expenditures had increased to $52,500,000, of which $40,-500,000 were derived from state and local funds, and $12,000,000 from federal funds.

SERVICES FOR CRIPPLED CHILDREN

FEDERAL PROVISIONS

By 1934 some provision had been made in thirty-seven states for a state department or commission or a state hospital to undertake special services for crippled children, and thirty-five of those states had made appropriations for the purpose. Except in a few states where funds were available for hospital care only, services included location and registration of crippled children by surveys or a school census; development and extension of diagnostic and follow-up clinics; and the provision of medical and nursing care and aftercare in the child's home, in a hospital, in a convalescent home, or in a foster home. Title V, Part 2, of the Social Security Act authorizes appropriations to states having approved plans for extending and improving services for crippled children or children who are suffering from conditions which lead to crippling conditions, particularly in rural areas and areas suffering from severe economic distress. The services include locating crippled children and providing medical, surgical, corrective, and other services and care, and facilities for diagnosis, hospitalization, and aftercare. The act requires the states to contribute to the costs of the program.

STATE PROGRAMS

In 1955, all fifty-three jurisdictions, with the exception of Arizona, participated in the programs of services for crippled children. These programs are administered by the state health department in most states, by the state welfare department in a small number of states, and by a combined state welfare and health department, by a crippled children's commission, by the state department of education, and by the state medical school in the balance of the states.[29]

The directors of the state programs for crippled children in 1955 reported numbers of significant developments and trends in the twenty years since the passage of the Social Security Act. These included: [30]

1. The most significant and enduring contribution of state programs has been the way they, encouraged by the Children's Bureau, have carried the torch for high standards of medical care. These high standards of state public agencies have greatly influenced those of private agencies.
2. Since the major portion of specialized medical services are available only in urban communities, federal funds have helped rural children with transportation and with follow-up facilities.
3. The team approach has been extensively employed.
4. Great emphasis has been placed on prevention. State programs have been responsive to the many new discoveries in medical diagnosis and treatment.
5. Physical and mental rehabilitation has received extensive emphasis largely because of many remarkable new ideas and procedures learned during World War II.
6. The most consistent trend nationally has been the broadening of the definition of a crippling condition.

In respect to this last point, several facts are pertinent. Federal figures show that the expansion of federally aided services to crippled children

---

[29] Eliot, "Twenty Years of Progress for Children," *loc. cit.*, pp. 23–28.

[30] Edward Davens, "Services to Crippled Children, 1935–55," *Children*, Vol. 2, No. 4 (July–August, 1955), pp. 139–144.

has been primarily for children with other than orthopedic diagnoses. From 1937 to 1953 the total number of crippled children served more than doubled. In the earlier year, about 110,000 children were served, and in 1953, 250,000. In 1955 the numbers of children under this program receiving orthopedic and nonorthopedic services were approximately equal. During the early years of the program most states concentrated on providing services for orthopedic handicaps in conformity with the then current definition of "crippled." Disabilities amenable to plastic surgery, such as cleft lips and palate, were soon added.

About 1941 several states, stimulated by federal funds for "special projects," began to set up demonstration programs for children with rheumatic fever, rheumatic heart disease, and hearing impairments. Then cerebral palsy, considered an orthopedic condition, began to receive special attention in several states. These projects were designed to integrate medical and educational services by providing physical, occupational, and speech therapy and medical, psychological, and social supervision simultaneously with the education of the child. Recently, the integrating trend has been extended to a host of new handicapping conditions, such as eye disorders, including even the clinical aspects of reading disability, and epilepsy, diabetes, asthma, severe orthodontic defects, and nephritis. These trends have been accompanied by concern with the attendant emotional factors. Because programs have been so broadly conceived and medical costs per individual unit have increased so rapidly, directors of programs eagerly search for more funds and for a greater supply of competent personnel. No state has achieved an ideal crippled children's program, but all struggle toward it. The ideal program has been described as one which has available the broadest possible range of high quality medical care and related services to meet the needs of children who have a broad spectrum of medical diagnoses.

In 1954 unduplicated counts of children under care showed that 265,000 were provided physicians' services. They received care for congenital malformations, conditions of bone and organs of movement, poliomyelitis, cerebral palsy, ear conditions, burns and accidents, rheumatic fever, eye conditions, epilepsy and other diseases of the nervous system, tuberculosis of the bones and joints, and birth injuries. By 1955 more than half the states had rheumatic fever programs for which they receive some federal funds. State and local funds for services for crippled children have steadily increased. At the beginning of the fiscal year 1939–1940 the states reported that their anticipated expenditures for the year were $9,300,000. Of this amount $5,600,000 were from state and local funds, and $3,700,000 from federal funds. By 1954 total anticipated expenditures had increased to $40,500,000 of which $29,800,000 were from state and local funds, and $10,700,000 from federal funds.

CHILD WELFARE SERVICES

FEDERAL PROVISIONS

The need of federal aid for services to socially handicapped children was emphasized by the 1930 White House Conference on Child Health and Protection. When the Social Security Act was under consideration, only one fourth of the states had provisions for county organizations for child welfare work under state leadership, and in only one state was the program in effect in practically all counties. Only twenty-six states and the District of Columbia had divisions within their welfare departments the duties of which included supervising child welfare activities on a state-wide basis. Eleven states had no legal basis for the establishment of a child welfare division within the state department, although in a number of these states there were laws giving the state some responsibility for the care and protection of children and for some form of institutional care for dependent or delinquent children.

Title V, Part 3, of the Social Security Act authorizes an annual appropriation for federal grants to state public welfare agencies to enable them to develop a program, especially in predominantly rural areas, for the protection and care of homeless, dependent, and neglected children, and children in danger of becoming delinquent. The state agency to administer the program is not designated, undoubtedly because of the diversity in public welfare structures between states. Plans must be developed jointly by the state agency and the United States Department of Health, Education, and Welfare. Federal funds can be used for payment or part payment of the costs of district, county, or other local child welfare services; for developing state services for the encouragement and assistance of adequate methods of community child welfare organization; and, since 1950, for paying the cost of returning any runaway child not yet sixteen to his own community in another state when in the interest of the child. The act requires that in developing these services, as well as the other maternal and child health services, the facilities and experience of voluntary agencies shall be utilized.

STATE PROGRAMS [31]

The states promptly took advantage of the act. In 1955 all jurisdictions had child welfare programs. Federal grants in the original act were $1,500,000 annually. By amendments to the Social Security Act in 1956,

---

[31] Most of the material in this section comes from Leonard W. Mayo, "Directions in Child Welfare Programs," *Children,* Vol. 2, No. 4 (July–August, 1955), pp. 149–153; Martha M. Eliot, "A Twenty-Year Perspective on Services to Children," *Children,* Vol. 2, No. 4 (July–August, 1955), pp. 123–126, and "Twenty Years of Progress for Children," *loc. cit.,* pp. 23–28.

the amount was raised to $12,000,000 annually, beginning June 30, 1958. Over the years states and communities have assumed an increasing proportion of program costs. In the fiscal year 1954 state and local agencies spent a total of $126,000,000 from their own and federal funds. Of this, 28 per cent went for professional and facilitating services, and 72 per cent for direct foster care payments. One fifth of the former and less than 1 per cent of the latter stemmed from federal sources. Because federal grants were small at the start of the program they were used in the main to employ trained child welfare workers and not to finance the support of children in foster care or in other types of direct care. Since 1946, and especially since 1950, with increased annual grants available, this restriction has been lifted and states are using a small part of their federal money to pay for support of children in foster care.

Child welfare work in the first twenty years of the Social Security Act took certain directions. In the early years of the program children served by the child welfare grants were mainly those taken from their own homes and for whom foster care in homes or institutions had to be found, children born out of wedlock, and children referred by courts because of delinquency or parental neglect or abuse. These problems still absorb much of the time of child welfare workers, but more and more they are called into situations at an earlier point. Also, they work extensively with seriously disturbed children.

No adequate figures have yet been assembled for measuring the total number of children helped by public and private agencies or the financial contributions to their care and treatment. Partial figures only are available. In 1933, for example, there were 249,000 children in foster homes and institutions, 29 per cent of whom were in the care of public agencies. In 1953 public agencies were caring for 50 per cent of the 265,000 children in both kinds of foster care. At the start of 1955, of the 277,000 children reported to the Children's Bureau as receiving casework services from public child welfare agencies, 41 per cent were living in the homes of parents or relatives. By far the largest proportion of work with delinquent children outside their own homes is borne by public agencies. In contrast a large share of the costs for dependent children in institutions is carried by voluntary agencies. It seems entirely likely that public child welfare programs will continue to expand more rapidly than those of private agencies.

Behind the progress made in child welfare activities has been the insistence of the Children's Bureau on professional competence. Since 1950 from 7 to 10 per cent of federal child welfare funds have been used for training workers. About 45 per cent of all child welfare workers employed by the states have one year or more of graduate training. Most of the remaining are at least college graduates.

There is still a big child welfare job ahead. It includes:

1. Bringing the most backward child welfare programs up to the level of the most advanced and extending help to many thousands of families and children in cities as well as in rural areas.

2. Eliminating outmoded statutory provisions and bringing legislation up to date.

3. Improving detection, diagnostic, and treatment facilities for seriously disturbed children.

4. Increasing the co-operation between agencies in different fields and developing the team approach.

5. Continuously helping to shape public attitudes.

6. Securing more federal and state funds for providing more and better services.

The original Social Security Act contained provisions for two programs which have been dropped from the act and picked up in other legislation. Title V, Part 4, entitled "Vocational Rehabilitation," has been withdrawn and supplanted by the Vocational Rehabilitation Act. In 1955 Congress approved an appropriation of $30,000,000, as compared with the $24,-500,000 of the preceding year, for expansion of vocational rehabilitation. Title VI of the original act, entitled "Public Health Work," has been replaced by the Public Health Service Act. These two programs render many important services for the welfare of the American people. Since these programs are no longer a part of the Social Security Act, we shall not attempt a digest of their content.

MEDICAL CARE PROGRAMS

Medical care programs in the United States include:

1. Public medical care facilities of diverse types financed by tax funds and administered by public agencies.

2. Private community health programs, including hospitals and clinics.

3. Voluntary medical care insurance financed through earmarked regular prepayments and administered by voluntary organizations.

4. Social insurances, such as workman's compensation, some public employee plans, and those for railroad employees.

Public medical care programs with which we are here concerned include services designed to serve individuals belonging to certain socioeconomic groups, and services for the prevention and control of such diseases as tuberculosis, venereal and other communicable diseases, psychiatric disorders, physical handicaps, cancer, and so forth. Civilians eligible for public medical care include all persons for some programs; specific classes, such as veterans, merchant seamen, Indians, Eskimos, and certain employees of civilian federal agencies, for other programs; and recipients of public assistance under the Social Security Act or under general assistance statutes. Numerically and proportionately, the veterans constitute the largest single group of persons eligible for public medical care—more than 20,000,000 in 1953. Next in order are the needy and medically needy—more than 5,000,000 in 1953. In 1951 the tax funds spent for medical care of civilians exceeded $3,000,000,000, representing about one fourth of the total expenditures for medical care of civilians and 1.3 per cent of the national income. State and local agencies contributed more than two thirds, and federal agencies less than one third of the total.[32]

Well-planned and organized medical programs for recipients of public assistance and for the medically needy, that is, persons able to maintain themselves except for medical care, are of recent origin, although their forerunners date back centuries. Modern interpretation of need, federal grants-in-aid to the states for public assistance, and greatly increased costs of medical care to the individual account, in large part, for increased public expenditures for medical care programs. Amendments to the Social Security Act in 1950 permitted federal financial participation in payments made by the states to suppliers of medical services for recipients of the four assistances. Federal participation was available only to the extent that the total money payment, including medical care, did not exceed the maximum designated in the federal act. Numbers of states modified their statutes to permit grants above the federal maximum for medical services. Amendments to the act in 1956 advanced medical care programs for public-assistance recipients when Congress provided for separate matching of expenditures for medical care. (See Ch. 22 for formula.)

It was estimated in 1955 that public-assistance programs were aiding nearly 1,300,000 persons whose need was attributed primarily to disability, chronic illness, or severe infirmities of old age. This number included some 460,000 recipients of old-age assistance who were bedridden or who required a substantial amount of care because of some physical or mental impairment; 230,000 receiving aid for permanent and total disability; about 103,000 receiving aid for blindness; and about 450,000 in 125,000 families receiving aid for dependent children because of the incapacity of a parent. In addition, a high proportion of the 2,000,000 recipients of old-age assistance who were able to care for their own daily needs had health problems.

Wilbur Cohen, then a staff member of the United States Department of Health, Education, and Welfare, in a speech given to public welfare officials in 1955, made the following statement concerning medical care for public-assistance recipients: [33]

> The medical care needs of assistance recipients are going to require much more consideration. Old-age assistance recipients are, on the average, about 75 years old. Their age, income level, physical status, and their previous environ-

[32] Franz Goldman, "Medical Care," *Social Work Year Book: 1954,* pp. 327–339; Wilbur J. Cohen, "Social Insurance," *ibid.*, pp. 486–495.

[33] Cohen, "Trends in Public Welfare"; see *Social Security Bulletin,* Vol. 18, No. 9 (September, 1955), p. 22, table 12.

mental conditions all indicate the need for more than the average hospitalization, nursing care, and other medical services. Existing arrangements in most places are clearly inadequate to provide the quality and quantity of medical services which the aged require. Voluntary private insurance is nonexistent for the assistance group. There is a wide range in what is now available in medical services to aged persons. This variation in services and the wide variation in costs indicates that much more can and should be done to make medical services in some states and localities more available.

This means more and better nursing homes, specialized services for the chronically ill . . . trained personnel in the whole field of geriatrics and the development and co-ordination of community services which relate to adult education, recreation, and rehabilitation, to help keep old people as independent as possible and functioning on their own.

We feel that the existing federal grants to the states for meeting the medical care needs of assistance recipients is not adequate. Hence, we have recommended to Congress that there be separately earmarked financing of the medical care costs of assistance recipients.

The eighty-fourth Congress accepted this proposal. Experience with the reimbursement formula will determine its sufficiency for the growth of high-standard state programs. When the same Congress made social insurance provisions for some classes of disabled persons it recognized the supplementary characteristics of public assistance and social insurance for disabled persons. It is inevitable that in the near future there will be significant developments in medical income maintenance programs of the public-assistance and social insurance types.

CHAPTER 24

Old-age and Survivors Insurance and Disability Insurance

(SOCIAL SECURITY ACT)

INTRODUCTION

Earlier, we pointed out that President Roosevelt's Committee on Economic Security was convinced that the program for improvement of assistance techniques and the participation of the federal government in their financing and operation would, if left alone, encourage reliance on public assistance in old age and accelerate the growth of federal and state assistance expenditures.[1] It concluded that a system of old-age contributory insurance should be established in order to curtail government expenditures for relief and as a means of encouraging thrift. Under an insurance scheme where benefits were received as a matter of right and based on contributions related to wages, workers would be encouraged to maintain the best possible employment record in order to earn the right to a high rate of benefits. The certainty and regularity of insurance benefit payments would increase the feeling of security. The aging person would not fear wage loss because of retirement. Nor would he be tempted to retain his job after sixty-five and thus possibly displace a younger person. These and other arguments pertaining to the social and economic benefits to be derived from an insurance scheme were sufficiently convincing to Congress to secure the passage of Title II, "Federal Old-Age Benefits," presently "Federal Old-Age and Survivors Insurance and Disability Insurance Benefits," and Title VIII, "Taxes with Respect to Employment," now contained in the Internal Revenue Code.[2]

---

[1] The author is greatly indebted to Sydney S. Miller, manager of the District Office of the Social Security Administration, Madison, Wis., who has carefully scrutinized this chapter. He made many corrections in, and additions to, the manuscript with respect to technical provisions of the old-age and survivors insurance and disability insurance programs.

[2] *Compilation of the Social Security Laws, Including the Social Security Act, as Amended, and Related Enactments Through December 31, 1954,* 83d Cong., 2d sess., S. Doc. 157 (Washington, D.C., G.P.O., 1955); Public Law 880, 84th Cong., 2d sess., ch. 836, H.R. 7225 (Washington, D.C., G.P.O., 1956); Public Law 271, 74th Cong., 2d sess., H.R. 7260 (Washington, D.C., G.P.O., 1935).

PROVISIONS FOR OLD-AGE AND SURVIVORS INSURANCE AND DISABILITY INSURANCE [3]

ADMINISTRATION

The administrative functions of OASI, a wholly federally operated program, are carried on by two agencies, the Treasury Department and the Social Security Administration of the Department of Health, Education, and Welfare. The treasury collects taxes, which are automatically appropriated to the federal Old-Age and Survivors Insurance Trust Fund and, since 1956, also to the federal Disability Insurance Trust Fund. With respect to these two trust funds there is the Board of Trustees of the Trust Funds, which is composed of the secretary of the treasury, who is the managing trustee, the secretary of labor, and the secretary of health, education, and welfare. The commmissioner of social security serves as secretary of the Board of Trustees. On certification from the Department of Health, Education, and Welfare, the Treasury Department issues benefit checks and makes payments from the fund to cover its own and the administration's operating expenses. Except in the case of public employees, the Treasury Department, through the director of internal revenue, also collects all the social security taxes. Because the federal government cannot tax states or their political subdivisions, the "taxes" of employer and employee become "contributions" and are imposed by the secretary of health, education, and welfare. However, even these contributions go into the trust funds and are distributed as benefits are due by the Treasury Department. Except for determination of disability, all other administrative functions are carried on by the Department of Health, Education, and Welfare.

Amendments to the Social Security Act in 1956 established the Advisory Council on Social Security Financing for the purpose of reviewing the status of the trust funds in relation to the long-term commitments of the old-age and survivors insurance and disability insurance programs.

---

[3] Much of the material for this chapter comes from U.S. Department of Health, Education, and Welfare, Social Security Administration, Bureau of Old-Age and Survivors Insurance, *Your Social Security*, (Washington, D.C., G.P.O., 1956), OASI 35; and Social Security Administration, *Social Security in the United States* (Washington, D.C., G.P.O., 1953). The second of these references contains a good bibliography, particularly of government documents; it also includes a chronology of "Significant Events in Social Security and Related Fields" by the federal government from 1785 through 1953. The monthly issues of the *Social Security Bulletin* contain invaluable factual materials concerning this and the other programs of the Social Security Administration. For comprehensive bibliography on problems of the aging, see *Selected References on Aging, an Annotated Bibliography: 1955,* compiled for the Committee on Aging by the Library of the U.S. Department of Health, Education, and Welfare (Washington, D.C., G.P.O., 1955).

The council consists of the commissioner of social security, chairman, and twelve other persons representing employers and employees, self-employed persons, and the public.

Since this entire system is wage related, it is administratively essential that centralization of wage records occur. This is done in the Accounting Operations Division of the Bureau of Old-Age and Survivors Insurance in Baltimore, Md. That office, upon request, renders reports to workers of the amount of their total wage credits, and it furnishes necessary wage information from its records to the district offices in connection with claims for benefits.

The field organization comprises 6 area offices, 532 district offices, and over 2,000 stations with itinerant service. Area offices review all claims, adjudicate those presenting unusual difficulties, maintain a roll of current beneficiaries, and certify to the treasury the amount of payments to be made to eligible claimants. This last responsibility includes terminating or reinstating or adjusting benefits as the circumstances of claimants change. The district and itinerant offices have numerous functions one of which is issuance of account numbers. If an individual is employed or self employed in any kind of work covered by the Social Security Act he must have an account number. The social security card shows the account number which is used to identify a record of earnings. Each worker should use the same account number all of his life. In November, 1956, there were some 158,000,000 names in the social security records. Other duties of district and itinerant offices include aid to applicants in filing claims, determination of entitlement to benefits, assisting applicants in filing requests for recomputation of benefits made possible in some instances by additional work, and dispersal of information on all matters related to the program.

If claimants are dissatisfied with the bureau's determination of their eligibility and the amounts of their benefit awards, they may make a request to the Bureau of Old-Age and Survivors Insurance for reconsideration, or they may ask through the bureau for a hearing before a referee of the Appeals Council. These hearings are informal and without cost to the applicant except for travel. They are under the supervision of the Appeals Council, which constitutes a separate unit of the Social Security Administration. If the applicant is dissatisfied with the decision of the referee he may request review by the Appeals Council. A further recourse from the council's decision is the United States District Court.

Each payday every worker in a covered job has deducted from his pay a percentage of his wages, not counting, since 1954, wages over $4,200 a year, as a premium on his old-age and survivors insurance and disability insurance. The employer contributes a like amount. The self-employed pay one-and-a-half times the amount of the employee's or employer's contribution. The present tax rates and the scheduled increases are shown in Table 14: [4]

Table 14

CALENDAR YEAR	TAX RATES PERCENTAGE		
	Employer	*Employee*	*Self-employed*
1956	2	2	3
1957–59	2¼	2¼	3⅜
1960–64	2¾	2¾	4⅛
1965–69	3¼	3¼	4⅞
1970–74	3¾	3¾	5⅝
1975 and after	4¼	4¼	6⅜

This schedule of tax rates is intended to meet the future obligations of the program, including the disability program for which tax rates were raised in 1957. The revenue derived from these new taxes for the disability program is kept in a separate trust fund. In other words, and we repeat, the entire program is designed to run on a self-supporting basis.

As mentioned previously, benefits are based on average monthly earnings. They are computed from individual accounts and are payable to:

a. Retired workers at age sixty-five or over if a man, or sixty-two if a woman, or at age seventy-two, regardless of retirement.

b. Wife of retired worker if she is age sixty-two or over, or regardless of age if entitled child under age eighteen is eligible and under her care. Dependent husband of retired worker if he is age sixty-five or over.

c. Widow aged sixty-two or over or dependent widower, age sixty-five or over, of deceased workers.

d. Children (under age eighteen) of retired worker, and children of deceased worker and their mother (the worker's widow or, in some cases, his divorced wife), regardless of her age, if there are children under her care.

e. Disabled children after reaching eighteen years of age if they became disabled before reaching eighteen and have remained so and were dependent on the retired or deceased insured worker.

f. Dependent parents (women at sixty-two and men at sixty-five), of deceased worker, if no surviving widow, widower, or child who could receive benefits.

g. In addition, a lump-sum payment upon death of an insured worker.

h. Monthly cash benefits on or after July, 1957, to a person aged fifty or over if permanently and totally disabled.

In effect, no individual can receive more than one type of monthly benefit, but rather the largest for which he is eligible.

INSURED STATUS

The provisions of the Social Security Act concerning insured status and benefits are involved and technical and we shall only summarily describe them. The yardstick for measuring whether or not an individual

---

[4] *Your Social Security*, p. 18.

is insured under the law is the quarter of coverage, meaning a three months' period, beginning January 1, April 1, July 1, or October 1, in which wages or self-employment income of a stipulated minimum amount are received. The number of quarters of coverage is used only in figuring whether or not a payment can be made. For the various kinds of benefits to be paid, the worker must be fully and/or currently insured.

Insured status means that to establish eligibility for benefits a person must have a certain number of quarters of coverage. The exact meaning of a quarter of coverage differs for different kinds of work. (1) The self-employed individual receives four quarters of coverage for each year in which he has $400.00 or more in net earnings from self-employment. (2) A farm worker gets one quarter of coverage for each $100.00 of cash wages from any one employer paid in a year as a farm employee but no more than four in a year. (3) An individual can also earn quarters of coverage through railroad employment and active military service. (4) For all other kinds of covered employment a worker receives one quarter of coverage for each calendar quarter in which he is paid $50.00 or more in wages. Quarters of coverage may be earned by working in covered employment as an employee at any time after 1936 and by most self-employment after 1950. Quarters of coverage need not be consecutive. Having acquired a certain number of these quarters of coverage, a person becomes insured.

There are two kinds of insured status, *fully insured* and *currently insured.* The male worker will be fully insured when he reaches sixty-five or at death, and the female worker when she reaches sixty-two or at death, and the worker when he reaches fifty and is disabled, if the total number of quarters of coverage (earned any time after 1936) is at least half as many as the number of calendar quarters since December 31, 1950, or since reaching age twenty-one, whichever is later. If the worker does not have enough quarters under this rule, but does have at least six quarters of coverage after 1954, he may become fully insured under a special provision of the law. Under this provision the worker will be fully insured if he has quarters of coverage in all but four of the calendar quarters after 1954 and up to retirement age, sixty-two for women and sixty-five for men. The worker will be currently insured if he has at least six quarters of coverage within the three years preceding retirement, disability, or death. Fully insured status applies primarily to retired workers and currently insured status to deceased workers. However, for certain types of benefits the worker must have been both fully and currently insured. It is important to bear in mind that being fully or currently insured means only that a benefit is payable, not the amount of the benefit. At least six quarters of coverage are necessary in every case. When the worker has forty quarters of coverage he is fully insured for life.

Table 15 indicates the quarters of coverage needed.[5]

Table 15

QUARTERS OF COVERAGE NEEDED

Year in which worker reaches retirement age	*January–June*	*July–December*
1953 or earlier	6	6
1954	6	7
1955	8	9
1956	10	11
1957	12	13
1958	14	15
1959	16	17
1960	18	19
1961	20	21
1962	22	23
1963	24	25
1964	26	27
1965	28	29
1966	30	31
1967	32	33
1968	34	35
1969	36	37
1970	38	39
1971 or later	40	40

Table 16 shows for each type of retirement, survivors, and disability insurance benefit whether the worker must be fully or currently insured or both.[6]

Table 16

RETIREMENT PAYMENTS

Monthly payments to—	*If worker is—*
Retired worker	Fully insured
And monthly payments to worker's—	
Wife 62 or over	Fully insured
Dependent child (under 18 or disabled)	Fully insured
Wife (regardless of age) if caring for child	Fully insured
Dependent husband 65 or over	Both fully and currently insured

SURVIVORS PAYMENTS

Monthly payments to—	*If at death worker was—*
Widow 62 or over	Fully insured
Widow or dependent divorced wife (regardless of age) if caring for child	Either fully or currently insured
Dependent child (under 18 or disabled)	Either fully or currently insured
Dependent widower 65 or over	Both fully and currently insured
Dependent parent (mother 62 or father 65)	Fully insured
Lump-sum payment to worker's—	
Widow or widower, or to the person who paid his burial expenses (may be made in addition to monthly benefits)	Either fully or currently insured

[5] *Ibid.*, p. 8.
[6] *Ibid.*, p. 9.

DISABILITY PAYMENTS

Monthly payments to—	*If worker is both fully and currently insured and has—*
Worker at age 50–65 if he is totally disabled for work	20 quarters of coverage in the 40 calendar quarters before the beginning date of disability

RETIREMENT AGE FOR WOMEN [7]

The provision enabling women to get monthly benefits at age sixty-two, instead of sixty-five as originally provided in the Social Security Act, went into effect in November, 1956. If a *working* woman she can choose to take payments before reaching sixty-five, but the amount of the monthly benefit will be permanently reduced. If she starts as soon as she reaches sixty-two, the amount of payment each month will be 80 per cent of what she would have received at sixty-five. If she is the *wife* of a man who is getting social security retirement payments and she chooses to receive wife's insurance benefits at age sixty-two, the amount of benefit will be 75 per cent of what she would have received at sixty-five. If her husband dies, she may become entitled to social security payments as a *widow* when she reaches age sixty-two, and her benefits based on her husband's social security account will not be reduced. If the *mother* of an insured worker who dies leaving no widow, widower, or child who could get monthly social security payments and the worker was furnishing at least half her support, she may become entitled at sixty-two, and her benefits will not be reduced.

BENEFITS [8]

The amount of a worker's social security benefit is determined by his average monthly earnings over a certain period of time. The period of time over which earnings are figured can start with January 1, 1937, or with January 1, 1951. In some instances, in averaging the income, the worker may use the year in which he reached the age of twenty-two instead of January 1, 1937, or January 1, 1951. Most people will receive higher benefits under the formula using average monthly earnings after 1950. The worker can drop out up to five calendar years after 1950 in which his earnings were lowest or in which he had no earnings. In dropping low years he ordinarily needs to keep at least two years on which to base his average. Benefits payable to the worker's dependents are

[7] *Ibid.*, pp. 11–12.
[8] *Ibid.*, pp. 13–17.

determined from the amount of his benefit in the proportions indicated in Table 17.[9]

Table 17

The monthly payment to worker's—	*Is this part of worker's monthly amount *—*
Wife	One half
Child	One half
Dependent husband	One half
Widow	Three fourths
Each child (after worker's death)	One half (plus an additional one fourth divided equally among all the children)
Dependent widower	Three fourths
Dependent parent	Three fourths

* Except where dependents' or survivors' benefits must be reduced to keep the total family payment within the maximum provided in the law.

Table 18 gives examples of amounts of benefits paid to workers with stipulated average monthly earnings and to their dependents.[10]

If a person becomes entitled to monthly benefits based on the social security accounts of more than one insured worker, the amount he will receive each month will be no more than the largest of the benefits. Upon the death of an insured person a lump-sum payment in addition to monthly payments may be paid to the widow or widower. If there is no eligible widow or widower, then the persons who paid the burial expenses can be repaid up to the amount of the burial expense not exceeding $255.00. The lump sum may be as much as three times the insured person's benefit if he were sixty-five but not more than $255.00.

A person does not need to retire completely in order to draw benefits.[11] Under a provision called the "work clause," or the "retirement test," a worker can earn $1,200 in a year in any employment, covered or noncovered, without loss of any benefits. For each $80.00 (or fraction thereof) of covered or noncovered earnings in excess of $1,200 in any one calendar year one month's benefit is withheld. In no case, however, are benefits withheld for any month in which the beneficiary's remuneration as an employee was $80.00 or less and in which he rendered no substantial services in self-employment. For workers over seventy-two years of age there is no limitation on the amount they may earn.

When a beneficiary under age seventy-two works outside the United States, his benefit cannot be paid for any month in which he works on seven or more calendar days in employment or self-employment not covered by the Social Security Act.[12] If his work is covered by the law, the same rules apply as to his earnings in the United States. Social security payments being made to a person who is not a citizen or national of the

[9] *Ibid.*, p. 16.
[10] *Ibid.*, p. 15.
[11] *Ibid.*, pp. 21–22.
[12] *Ibid.*, pp. 22–23.

United States may be stopped even if he is not working if he remains outside the United States for more than six months. If the payments are stopped for this reason, they cannot be started again unless he returns to this country and remains here for at least a full calendar month.

Table 18

EXAMPLES OF SOCIAL SECURITY BENEFITS

	Average monthly earnings after 1950 *						
	$50	$100	$150	$200	$250	$300	$350
Retirement and Disability Insurance Payments:							
Monthly retirement benefit at 65 or later, or disability benefit at 50	$30.00	$55.00	$68.50	$78.50	$88.50	$98.50	$108.50
Monthly retirement benefit for woman worker, starting at: †							
62	24.00	44.00	54.80	62.80	70.80	78.80	86.80
63	26.00	47.70	59.40	68.10	76.70	85.40	94.10
64	28.00	51.40	64.00	73.30	82.60	92.00	101.30
Monthly retirement benefit for couple, man 65 or over, wife starting at: †							
62	41.30	75.70	94.30	108.00	121.80	135.50	149.30
63	42.50	78.00	97.10	111.30	125.50	139.60	153.80
64	43.80	80.30	100.00	114.60	129.20	143.70	158.30
65	45.00	82.50	102.80	117.80	132.80	147.80	162.80
Survivors Insurance Payments:							
Widow, widower, child, or parent (monthly)	30.00	41.30	51.40	58.90	66.40	73.90	81.40
Widow and 1 child (monthly)	45.00	82.60	102.80	117.80	132.80	147.80	162.80
Widow and 2 children (monthly)	50.20	82.60	120.00	157.10	177.20	197.10	200.00
Lump-sum death payment	90.00	165.00	205.50	235.50	255.00	255.00	255.00

* In figuring average monthly earnings after 1950, worker may omit
- As many as 5 years in which he had low earnings.
- Any period in which his earnings record was frozen because he was disabled.

† Payments to women workers and wives are permamently reduced if started before age 65.

The benefit scale of the old-age and survivors insurance and disability insurance provisions of the Social Security Act is designed to give greater weight to the earnings of lower-paid and older workers who have not had the opportunity to contribute to the scheme over a considerable period of time. The system makes no commitment with respect to repaying any individual an amount comparable to his contributions. There is no guarantee of "a return of premium." In this respect OASI differs from many private insurance contracts, which guarantee the insured a return commensurate with his contributions.

DISABILITY BENEFITS [13]

By a 1954 amendment to the Social Security Act periods of disability of at least six months' duration may be excluded in determining insured status and average monthly wage. This is called "freezing" the social security record. In other words, by freezing the record benefits are protected. The period of disability during which there were little or no earnings will not count against the worker when the amount of benefits payable to him and his family is figured. To have his records frozen on the beginning date of the disability the worker must have six quarters of coverage within the last thirteen calendar quarters and twenty quarters of coverage within the last forty calendar quarters.

By 1956 amendments to the Social Security Act if a worker becomes so severely disabled that he is unable to work, he may be eligible to receive monthly disability insurance benefits if he is between fifty and sixty-five years of age. The first month for which payments could be made was July, 1957. To qualify for disability insurance benefits at age fifty the worker must be both fully and currently insured and have twenty quarters of coverage in the forty calendar quarters before the beginning date of his disability. Not all disabled workers who meet these work requirements are eligible to receive disability insurance benefits or to have their social security records frozen. Medical evidence must be submitted to show that the worker has a physical or mental condition so serious that it prevents him from any substantial gainful work and that the disability has lasted six months and is expected to continue indefinitely. The worker is not eligible if he is temporarily or only partly disabled, if he is able to work but cannot find a job, or if he is unable to do the kind of work he has done in the past but is able to do some kinds of work. The determination, in most cases, as to whether a person is permanently and totally disabled, is made by state agencies, usually vocational rehabilitation agencies. The actual determination is made by a team consisting of a qualified professional worker and a physician.

The amount of disability benefit the worker can receive between fifty and sixty-five years of age depends on his average monthly wage. The benefit is the same as the amount of OASI benefit for which he would be eligible if he were sixty-five on the official "beginning date" of his disability.

By 1956 amendments to the act a disabled child of a retired insured worker, or of an insured worker who has died, may receive child's benefits after reaching eighteen years of age if (1) he or she is determined to be disabled under the Social Security Act, became disabled before reaching 18 years of age, and has remained so ever since; (2) is dependent upon a

---

[13] *Ibid.*, pp. 25–31.

parent, stepparent or adopting parent who is entitled to old-age insurance benefits under the act or was dependent upon a parent who died after 1939 and was insured at the time of his or her death; (3) and is unmarried. January, 1957, was the first month for which a disabled child eighteen or over could receive benefits. They stop when the disabled child recovers from the disability, marries, is able to do substantial work, or is adopted by someone other than a stepparent, grandparent, uncle or aunt.

The amount of any disability insurance benefit or disabled child's benefit payable under the social security laws must be reduced by the amount of any other federal benefit payable because of disability and by the amount of any state or federal workmen's compensation benefit to which the person is entitled.

If an individual applies for a disability insurance benefit, a disability freeze, or disabled child's benefit, his name or that of his child will be referred to the vocational rehabilitation agency of his state. That agency may be able to provide rehabilitation services that will help the applicant prepare for and find suitable work. The worker can have his earnings record frozen whether or not he accepts rehabilitation services which may be offered. Disability insurance benefits and disabled child's benefits, however, must be withheld if the person refuses without good cause to accept rehabilitation services offered by the state agency. Among the opponents to extensive disability insurance benefits are those who fear that this type of insurance will encourage malingering. That argument has no more relevance to this kind of program than it has to workmen's compensation, veterans' pensions, and railroad worker schemes. It is legitimate, however, for Congress to require that disabled persons do everything reasonably within their power to become self-supporting.

EMPLOYMENT COVERED

Most employment is covered, including that which takes place in the forty-eight states, the District of Columbia, Alaska, Hawaii, Puerto Rico, the Virgin Islands, or which is performed outside the United States by American citizens employed by an American employer or on American ships and aircraft outside the United States. Individuals engaged in the following types of employment are covered: [14]

1. Virtually all employees in industry and commerce other than long-service railroad workers.
2. Farm and nonfarm self-employed (other than doctors of medicine) with $400.00 or more of net earnings from covered self-employment. Earnings of self-employed lawyers, dentists, osteopaths, veterinarians, chiropractors, naturopaths, and optometrists after 1955 count toward social security benefits.
3. State and local government employees not covered by a retirement system and those covered by a retirement system (excluding, generally, firemen

[14] *Ibid.*, pp. 6, 32–42.

and policemen) on a referendum basis conducted by the state and in which a majority eligible to vote are in favor of coverage.

4. Nonfarm domestic workers (based on $50.00 in cash wages from one employer in a quarter).

5. Farm workers, including farm domestic workers (based on $100.00 or more in cash wages from any one employer in a calendar year).

6. Ministers and members of religious orders (other than those who have taken a vow of poverty), either employed by nonprofit institutions or self-employed, on individual elective basis as self-employed. Other employees of nonprofit institutions are covered on elective basis; employer must elect coverage and at least two thirds of employees must concur.

7. Federal employees not now covered by retirement systems established by law of the United States other than a few specifically excluded small categories.

8. Individuals performing active duty or active duty for training as a member of the uniformed services of the United States after 1956 and, under some circumstances, those on active military duty during World War II (September 15, 1940, through July 24, 1947), or in the period following World War II (July 25, 1947, through December 31, 1956).

Any work performed as an employee by a parent for his son or daughter, by a child under twenty-one for his parent, by a husband for his wife, or by a wife for her husband is not covered by social security. Nor is work for an organization which is registered or has received a final order to register under the Internal Security Act of 1950 as a Communist-front, as a Communist-action, or as a Communist-infiltrated organization.

OASI TRUST FUND [15]

Congress, recognizing that costs of the program would rise tremendously over the years, provided in the original Social Security Act for long-period financing. It imposed a slowly rising tax on employer and employee designed to furnish a surplus over benefits currently paid sufficient to build up a large reserve for future costs. This plan for a rapidly growing reserve changed in 1939 with the amendments of that year. Congress became concerned over the effects of increasing taxes in a period of recession and alarmed at the economic implications of such a rapidly expanding reserve. It alleviated this anxiety by freezing the then tax at one per cent; by extending the scheme to dependents and survivors; and by setting up the Old-Age and Survivors Insurance Trust Fund. The law laid upon the trustees of the fund the duty to report immediately to Congress whenever the Board of Trustees was of the opinion that during the ensuing five fiscal years the trust fund would exceed three times the highest annual expenditures anticipated during that five-fiscal-year period, and whenever the Board of Trustees was of the opinion that the amount of the trust fund was unduly small.

Congress has encountered conflicts of opinion on the size of the reserve

[15] *Ibid.*, p. 19.

and the rapidity with which it should grow. It has never favored a pay-as-you-go program. The schedule of tax rates is designed to meet present and future obligations of the program and to keep it on a self-supporting basis. If larger benefits are paid, or if new programs and benefits are added, Congress intends that additional payroll taxes shall be levied or new sources of revenue found. Thus, when cash disability benefits were provided for in 1956, the tax rate was increased one fourth of one per cent on employer and employee effective January 1, 1957.

Table 19 shows the status of the trust fund as of June 30, 1955. Since the disability tax was not then in existence, this table reflects only OASI trust fund status.[16]

Table 19

STATUS OF THE OLD-AGE AND SURVIVORS INSURANCE TRUST FUND *
(Cumulative January, 1937–June, 1955)

Receipts	
Net contribution income and transfers	$35,635,237
Interest received	3,422,909
Expenditures	
Benefit payments	17,091,998
Administrative payments	825,505
Assets	
Net total U.S. government securities acquired	20,580,491
Unexpended balance at end of period	560,152
Total assets at end of period	21,140,643

* In thousands.

Receipts and expenditures of the funds are separated from all other accounts in the United States Treasury. Benefit payments and administrative costs of the old-age, survivors, and disability insurance system are the only expenditures made from the trust funds. Those parts of the funds not required for current expenditures must be invested in interest-bearing obligations of the United States or in obligations guaranteed as to both principal and interest by the United States. The interest from such investments is added to, and becomes a part of, the trust fund.

Doubts have been expressed concerning the investment of old-age and survivors insurance funds in government securities. It has sometimes been claimed that the government spends for general purposes the money received from the sale of securities to that fund and that people have been or will be taxed twice for the same benefits. These spurious arguments appear to have been reasonably answered by such conservative financial authorities as the *Wall Street Journal*. An article in that journal quotes favorably from a 1948 report of the Advisory Council on Social Security to the Senate Committee on Finance as follows: [17]

---

[16] *Social Security Bulletin*, Vol. 18, No. 9 (September, 1955), p. 18, Table 5.
[17] F. A. Korsmeyer, "Bonds in U.S. Pension Reserve," *Wall Street Journal* (February 9, 1950).

We do not agree with those who criticize this form of investment of the OASI reserve in government bonds on the ground that the government spends for general purposes the money received from the sale of securities to that fund. Actually such investment is as reasonable and proper as is the investment by life insurance companies of their own reserve funds in government securities. . . .

The investment of the old age and survivors insurance funds in government securities does not mean that people have been or will be taxed twice for the same benefits, as has been charged. The following example illustrates this point: Suppose some year in the future the out-go under the old age and survivors insurance system should exceed pay-roll tax receipts by $100 million. If there were then $5 billion of United States 2 per cent bonds in the trust fund, they would produce interest amounting to $100 million a year. This interest would, of course, have to be raised by taxation. But suppose there were no bonds in the trust fund. In that event, $100 million to cover the deficit in the old age and survivors insurance system would have to be raised by taxation; and, in addition, another $100 million would have to be raised by taxation to pay interest on $5 billion of government bonds owned by somebody else.

FACTS REGARDING OASI

In 1935, when the Social Security Act was passed, only about one worker in ten was covered by any retirement system and only about one in twenty by a public retirement system. Twenty years later, in 1955, about nine out of ten people who worked for a living could look forward to retirement benefits under the OASI program. They could also count on benefits for their dependents. Furthermore, nine out of ten mothers and children were assured of monthly insurance benefits in case of the death of the breadwinner.[18] In 1955 an estimated 69,000,000 workers were in covered employment. There were more than 5,500,000 men and women over the age of sixty-five who were neither employed nor drawing OASI benefits. Those in this group requiring help from other sources than savings and relatives had to look to old-age assistance. The 1956 amendments to the Social Security Act brought under the OASI system most of the balance of occupations and workers. The principle kinds of work not now covered are self-employment as a doctor of medicine, employment in most federal jobs covered by a retirement system, and teachers.

In October, 1955, monthly benefits paid under the OASI program totaled $424,100,000.[19] About 7,500,000 persons were receiving these benefits, 130,000 more than for the previous month of September. The number of retired workers receiving old-age benefits exceeded 4,400,000.

---

[18] U.S. Department of Health, Education, and Welfare, Social Security Administration, *Twenty Years of Social Security* (Washington, D.C., G.P.O., 1955), OASI26C (August, 1955).

[19] *Ibid.*, and U.S. Department of Health, Education, and Welfare, Social Security Administration, Bureau of Old-Age and Survivors Insurance, Division of Program Analysis, Actuarial Branch, *Old-Age and Survivors Insurance Summary: Benefit Data* (October, 1955).

It took eleven years from the time monthly benefits were first payable to reach the 2,000,000 mark. It took only four years to double that total. This rapid growth was largely due to liberalized insured status and the extension of coverage under the 1950 amendments and to liberalizations in the retirement test provided in the 1950 and successive amendments.

The average old-age benefit paid at the end of 1940 (the first year in which monthly payments were made) was $22.60. In October, 1955, the average monthly old-age benefit paid was $61.64 and for aged widows or widowers $47.89. Lump-sum death payments totaling $9,700,000 were awarded in April to 50,351 persons.

The year 1953 was the first in which the number of recipients of public assistance in the nation was less than the number of beneficiaries of old-age and survivors insurance. President Roosevelt's Committee on Economic Security recognized that many persons would never qualify for insurance benefits because they were already the victims of the hazards of old-age dependency and premature death of the breadwinner or because of limitations in insurance coverage or inability to work. The committee conceived the long-time role of the public-assistance provisions of the Social Security Act as residual rather than primary. However, it was not until almost twenty years after the passage of the act that the number of recipients of public assistance was less than the number of beneficiaries of old-age and survivors insurance. Although aged insurance beneficiaries outnumbered recipients of old-age assistance as early as 1951, the total number of assistance recipients under all programs still exceeded the total number of beneficiaries under old-age and survivors insurance by nearly half a million at the beginning of 1953. By the end of that year a declining trend in the number of assistance recipients, together with substantial month-to-month increases in the number of insurance beneficiaries, resulted in a reversal in the position of the two programs. This occurred in spite of the fact that the number of aged persons in the United States was increasing so rapidly.

In 1956 it could be said that the expanding OASI program had (1) reduced the number of recipients of public assistance by removing from the rolls some who had become eligible for OASI benefits; (2) reduced substantially the number of aged individuals who otherwise would have applied for OAA; and (3) gradually increased the number of old-age assistance recipients who were also insurance beneficiaries. The full impact on public assistance of the OASI program has yet to be felt. With the insurance program extended to practically all gainfully employed persons, including farmers and farm workers, the OAA program will become predominantly one supplying necessary supplementary cash payments to old-age and survivors insurance and disability insurance beneficiaries whose benefits do not meet all their needs, and furnishing financial aid to persons who have high medical care costs or other special needs. The growth of the OASI program, accelerated by the 1954 and 1956 amendments, will continue to decrease the need for public assistance of many people, especially the aged and dependent children.[20]

SUGGESTIONS FOR CHANGE

As we have already pointed out, the conspicuous gap in social security protection in the United States is lack of insurance against wage losses from, and costs of, disability and sickness.[21] On an average day of the year about 4,000,000 persons between the ages of fourteen and sixty-four are too sick or otherwise disabled to go about their usual pursuits in jobs, at home, or at school. About half of these have been disabled for seven months or more.[22] These figures do not include patients in mental or other hospitals. The number of disabled persons is increasing and will continue to do so as more of the population live to reach middle or later years. State workmen's compensation laws cover only work-connected disabilities, which are perhaps 5 to 10 per cent of all permanent or temporary disabilities at a given time. Railroad workers have social insurance against permanent and temporary disabilities, and other designated groups have some protection under retirement programs for public employees. Veterans' programs provide hospital and medical care and cash benefits for veterans with service-connected disabilities and sometimes also for their dependents.[23] Under some circumstances veterans receive similar benefits for non-service-connected disabilities. In three states all workers insured under the state unemployment insurance laws, and in a fourth state substantially all such workers, may receive benefits for temporary periods of unemployment due to disability. Except for the limited and very recent disability insurance program provided through the Social Security Act there are still no general and universal social insurance provisions for loss of wages due to permanent or temporary disability.

A similar situation exists for social insurance programs against costs

---

[20] Sue Ossman, "Concurrent Receipt of Public Assistance and Old-Age and Survivors Insurance," *Social Security Bulletin*, Vol. 19, No. 10 (October, 1956), pp. 11–16.

[21] Oscar R. Ewing, *The Nation's Health—A Ten Year Program* (Washington, D.C., G.P.O., 1948); Federal Security Agency, Social Security Board, Bureau of Research and Statistics, *Need for Medical Care Insurance*, 2d ed. (Washington, D.C., G.P.O., 1946), Bureau Memorandum No. 57; *Health Insurance Plans in the United States*, 82d Cong., 1st sess., S. Report 359 (Washington, D.C., G.P.O., 1951), 3 vols.; Agnes W. Brewster and Dorothy McCamman, *Health Costs of the Aged*, U.S. Department of Health, Education, and Welfare, Social Security Administration, Division of Research and Statistics (Washington, D.C., G.P.O., 1956), Report No. 20, includes a good bibliography of studies on this subject.

[22] *Social Security in the United States*, pp. 12–13.

[23] *Social Legislation Information Service*, 84th Cong. (December 31, 1955), No. 39.

of medical care. Although millions of persons in the United States belong to such private organizations as Blue Cross and Blue Shield, are protected by company and union health insurance schemes, are in receipt of veterans' hospital and medical care, or are provided medical care through public assistance, there is no universal public health insurance scheme. Surely before too many more administrations Congress will find ways of encouraging health insurance programs under federal, state, and private auspices.

Former commissioner for social security, Arthur J. Altmeyer, in 1955, proposed raising the top wage on which OASI benefits are based beyond the $4,200 level enacted into law in 1954.[24] He pointed out that the original maximum of $3,000 covered the full earnings of 94 per cent of regular male workers. In 1955, due to the rise in wage level, a maximum of $7,500 was necessary to include 94 per cent of such earnings.

Although Congress in 1954 rejected reactionary proposals such as those of the United States Chamber of Commerce and accepted the liberalizing provisions of the Eisenhower administration, we include a brief statement about them. We do so as a warning to those who believe that the principles of our present social insurance programs are no longer controversial. The Chamber of Commerce in summary recommended: [25]

1. Covering all gainful workers under Old-Age and Survivors Insurance.
2. Blanketing into the system all retired workers not then benefiting under Old-Age and Survivors Insurance or other public retirement plans. These would receive "minimum benefits" payable under Old-Age and Survivors Insurance financed by current receipts of the system.
3. Abolishing federal grants to states for old-age assistance.
4. Collecting only enough contributions under OASI to meet current costs.

The effect of these proposals would be to transfer the federal financing of old-age assistance from general taxes to payroll taxes. Further, the minimum insurance payment (then $25.00) to be paid to those blanketed-in would not cover what the states had determined to be the minimum needs of most old-age assistance recipients. In addition, the pay-as-you-go proposal would not cover the liabilities the system is building up. The Chamber of Commerce did not offer any long-range plan to finance higher future costs but merely left it to Congress to make annual appropriations. It seemed to forget that the interest on the accumulated reserves of the trust fund serve permanently to pay part of the annual cost of the system.

The old-age insurance provisions of the Social Security Act have been

[24] Arthur J. Altmeyer, *Your Stake in Social Security*, Public Affairs Pamphlet (New York, Public Affairs Committee, 1954), No. 206, pp. 17–18, and "The Struggle over Social Security," *The Progressive*, Vol. 18, No. 5 (May, 1954), pp. 7–9. Mr. Altmeyer has written extensively on various aspects of social security. See especially, *Social Security Bulletin* and annual reports of the Social Security Administration prior to 1953.

[25] Altmeyer, *Your Stake in Social Security*, pp. 20–22.

extensively modified since passage. The formulators of the original act intended that experience should be the foundation for expansion of coverage and benefits. Further experience and analysis of facts and figures will provide the basis for future modifications. In the words of Mr. Altmeyer, "Social security will always be a goal, never a finished thing, because human aspirations are infinitely expansible—just as human nature is infinitely perfectible." [26]

For Selected References, see those following Chapter 25.

[26] Arthur J. Altmeyer, "Ten Years of Social Security," in William Haber and Wilbur Cohen, eds., *Readings in Social Security* (Englewood Cliffs, N.J., Prentice-Hall, 1948), p. 88.

CHAPTER 25

Unemployment Compensation

(SOCIAL SECURITY ACT)

INTRODUCTION

UNEMPLOYMENT INSURANCE BEFORE 1935

Thomas Carlyle wrote, "A man willing to work and unable to find work is perhaps the saddest sight that fortune's inequality exhibits under the sun." It took the depression of the 1930's to convince the American people that such might well be true and that there were things which could be done to prevent and to alleviate this situation.

Consideration of legislation for unemployment compensation in the United States began twenty and more years before the appointment of the Committee on Economic Security. In 1916 an unemployment insurance bill was unsuccessfully introduced into the Massachusetts legislature. During the 1920's bills were introduced in several states, but no legislature ventured to enact a law, principally because of fear that such a law would put employers of the state at competitive disadvantage with employers in states that did not have an unemployment compensation law. In 1921 the Huber bill, drafted by John R. Commons, late professor of economics at the University of Wisconsin, was introduced into the Wisconsin legislature. For ten years, or five sessions of the legislature, it was reintroduced with modifications. A bill was finally passed in 1932, making Wisconsin the first state to enact a compulsory unemployment compensation law.

Inability to procure state unemployment insurance laws naturally led to consideration of a federal law. Several bills were introduced into Congress by the late Senator Robert Wagner (N.Y.) and others, but they got nowhere. Recognizing the need for thorough study of unemployment along with other matters of economic security, President Roosevelt referred this problem to his Committee on Economic Security.[1] At that

[1] Edwin E. Witte, "The Development of Unemployment Compensation," in William Haber and Wilbur Cohen, eds., *Readings in Social Security* (Englewood Cliffs, N.J., Prentice-Hall, 1948), pp. 160–172; Edwin E. Witte, "An Historical Account of Unemployment Insurance in the Social Security Act," 3 *Law and Contemp. Prob.* 157–169 (1936).

time there were extremely limited data on the phenomena of unemployment in this country. Many of the figures at hand were estimates. Despite inaccuracies and inadequacies in the available information, two facts were irrefutable: (1) millions of persons were unemployed through no fault of their own, and (2) some plan of compensation for unemployment was essential.

The committee assumed responsibility for aggregating and assimilating masses of information on the nature and extent of unemployment.[2] The assembled data established the following findings:

1. Unemployment varies among industrial groups; within an industry there is great dissimilarity among the different branches; individual establishments within a branch vary; and there is variation by region and state.
2. There are distinct trends in employment in different industries over a period of years which are the result of shifts in consumer demand, new products, displacement of labor by technological achievements, and changes in tariff policies.
3. Unemployment fluctuates widely from year to year, a large proportion of the total volume of unemployment appearing in depressions.
4. There is considerable fluctuation in many industries from month to month during any year; for example, in the automobile, construction, textile, railroading, mining, and retailing industries.
5. The record of total unemployment does not represent the entire picture since there is much part-time employment.
6. The duration of unemployment changes, the curve varying with the degree of unemployment.

OBJECTIVES AND PRINCIPLES OF AN UNEMPLOYMENT COMPENSATION PLAN

With so little accurate material available, it was difficult for the committee to work out predictions and actuarial tables for an unemployment insurance plan. However, it proceeded with the task of formulating a program built upon insurance concepts and methods. This was to be an insurance program based on the rights of qualified covered individuals to receive benefits and not an assistance or relief program based on the exercise of administrative discretion.

The principles upon which the committee based its recommendations to Congress included the following: [3]

---

[2] U.S. Committee on Economic Security, *Social Security in America: The Factual Background of the Social Security Act as Summarized from Staff Reports to the Committee on Economic Security by the Social Security Board*, Social Security Board Publication (Washington, D.C., G.P.O., 1937), No. 20, ch. 3; see also, Corrington Gill, *Wasted Man Power* (New York, Norton, 1939), chs. 1–4.

[3] *Social Security in America*, pp. 92–95: Edwin E. Witte, "The Essentials of Unemployment Compensation," *National Municipal Review* (March, 1936), pp. 1–7; *Unemployment Compensation: What and Why?* Social Security Board Publication (Washington, D.C., G.P.O., 1937), No. 14.

1. Reduction of competition between employers in different states by the imposition of a uniform federal tax.

2. Assurance that the unemployment reserves be so invested as not to affect adversely the credit situation.

3. Federal financial assistance to the states in the administration of their unemployment compensation acts.

4. Formulation of a program that would induce, even compel, the states to enact unemployment compensation laws.

The committee rejected the principle that the unemployment insurance program be exclusively federal and accepted instead a federal-state system.[4] The former had the advantages of affording a plan which would permit uniform protection, the pooling of risk over a wide area, and the provision of an easy method of handling the problems of interstate employees. The latter had the advantages of not centralizing administrative functions in Washington, of permitting wide latitude for experimentation, and, hence, of not fixing too quickly upon methods which might later be found unsound. The second principle prevailed. It has continued to be criticized by those who believe that the unemployed would have greater advantages under a federally administered program.

When Congress passed the Social Security Act, the unemployment compensation sections included the above four principles. Although other parts of the omnibus bill were radically changed by congressional committees, the unemployment compensation provisions became law almost as introduced.[5] Despite what appeared to be unanimity of thought, experts disagreed then, as they do now, on the merits and significance of various aspects of the program. In general they agree that unemployment compensation furnishes a measure of economic security to unemployed workers and their families, contributes to the stabilization of employment, helps maintain consumer purchasing power, helps preserve the skills of workmen, helps prevent depression of wages, and gives workmen some feeling of security. But they differ on the degree of importance assigned to each of these accomplishments. There is further disagreement on many technological aspects of the program. For example, there is great diversity of opinion regarding qualifications, disqualifying conditions, and the extent of disqualification; the proportion of benefits as related to wages; dependents' allowances; duration of benefits; means of financing the program; and whether or not the program shall be so financed as to withstand a long and heavy period of unemployment if and when it occurs.

---

[4] *Social Security in America*, chs. 4 and 5.

[5] Edwin E. Witte, "The Development of Unemployment Compensation," in Haber and Cohen, *op. cit.*, p. 169.

FEDERAL PROVISIONS FOR UNEMPLOYMENT COMPENSATION [6]

TAX PROVISIONS

Title III of the Social Security Act, "Grants to States for Unemployment Compensation Administration," Title VIII, "Taxes with Respect to Employment" (now contained in the Internal Revenue Code), Title IX, "Miscellaneous Provisions Relating to Employment Security," and Title XII, "Advances to State Unemployment Funds" constitute the charter of the unemployment compensation program. The unemployment insurance titles provide for a type of federal-state co-operation not tried in any other governmental activity. The law does not provide a federal system of benefits comparable to old-age and survivors insurance; nor does it provide matching grants, as in public-assistance payments. Instead, it levies a tax on employers in commerce and industry who employ eight or more workers (beginning in 1956 the number of workers was four) for at least twenty weeks of each year. The tax is not levied on wages above $3,000 a year. When a state has an approved unemployment insurance law, its employers can credit the taxes they pay to the state against 90 per cent of the federal tax. The federal tax was 1 per cent of payrolls for 1936, 2 per cent for 1937, and 3 per cent thereafter. The federal law further provides that employers can get credit on the federal tax not only for the contributions they pay under a state law but for the contributions they are excused from paying under the state's experience-rating system.

From the beginning there have been great differences in schedules. In 1937 employers in twelve states had a zero rate when their reserve ratios reached a specified level, but in twenty-five states the minimum rate was 0.9 or 1 per cent, and in two states 1.5 per cent, of taxable wages. In

---

[6] The author is extremely grateful to Lawrence A. Burley, assistant to the director of the Unemployment Compensation Department, Industrial Commission of Wisconsin, for spending many hours reviewing the technical unemployment compensation sections of this book. The library materials regarding federal and state provisions for unemployment insurance came primarily from *Compilation of the Social Security Laws, Including the Social Security Act, as Amended, and Related Enactments Through December 31, 1954*, 83d Cong., 2d sess., S. Doc. 157 (Washington, D.C., G.P.O., 1955); U.S. Department of Labor, Bureau of Employment Security, *Comparison of State Unemployment Insurance Laws as of August, 1954* (Washington, D.C., G.P.O., 1954); U.S. Department of Labor, *Employment Security Review: Twenty Years of Unemployment Insurance in the USA: 1935–55*, Vol. 20, No. 8 (August, 1955), entire issue. For additional materials, see U.S. Department of Health, Education, and Welfare, Social Security Administration, *Social Security in the United States* (1953); monthly issues of *The Labor Market;* quarterly issues of *Employment and Wages;* monthly issues of *Employment Security Review;* Eveline M. Burns, *The American Social Security System* (Boston, Houghton Mifflin, 1949); Haber and Cohen, *op. cit.*

1955 minimum rates were much lower: twelve states had a zero rate in their most favorable schedule; 3 states had a minimum rate of 0.9 per cent or more; and twenty-seven states had rates of 0.1 to 0.3 per cent. In 1937 all but ten states had a maximum rate higher than 2.7 per cent to balance rates under 2.7 per cent. In most states the maximum rate was 3.6 per cent; in ten states it was higher. Three had no specified maximum but required an average contribution rate of 2.7 per cent, the reduced rates to be balanced by rates above 2.7 per cent. In 1955 only ten states had a maximum rate over 2.7 per cent, and in most of these states the maximum rate applied only in the least favorable of several schedules, which would go into effect when the state reserves were at a specified low level.

UNEMPLOYMENT TRUST FUND AND OTHER FINANCIAL PROVISIONS

The federal law safeguards the financial stability of the unemployment compensation system by requiring that each state deposit the taxes it collects under its unemployment compensation law in the Unemployment Trust Fund in the United States Treasury for investment in government bonds. A separate account is kept for each state. The state may withdraw funds at any time but only to pay benefits. So that employers can receive up to 90 per cent tax credit against the federal tax a state must also meet the following requirements: (1) compensation shall be paid solely through public employment offices or such other agencies as the secretary of labor approves; (2) compensation shall not be denied to any individual otherwise eligible because he refuses to accept work where there is a strike or lockout, where conditions of employment are unfavorable according to the standards of the locality, or where he is required to join a company union or to refrain from joining a bona fide labor union.

The act authorizes funds to be appropriated for federal and state administration of unemployment insurance. Until the passage of the Employment Security Administrative Financing Act of 1954, popularly called the Reed Bill, the federal tax paid by employers became a part of the general revenues of the United States Treasury.[7] In the past there was no direct connection between revenues collected under the Federal Unemployment Tax Act and the expenditures made for the operation of the federal-state employment security program. Since tax collections under the Federal Unemployment Tax Act consistently exceeded appropriations for the administration of the employment security program, this practice, in effect, meant that these taxes were lost to the program. The Employ-

[7] Public Law 567, 83d Cong. A part of this law became the new Title XII of the Social Security Act as amended.

ment Security Administrative Financing Act of 1954 changed this by earmarking the collections under the Federal Unemployment Tax Act for the unemployment compensation program. In essence it does three things: (1) it earmarks federal unemployment tax revenues collected in excess of employment security administrative expenses for any fiscal year, beginning with fiscal year 1954; (2) it appropriates the first $200,000,000 of these surplus collections to a federal unemployment account established in the Federal Unemployment Trust Fund for the sole purpose of making available repayable but interest-free advances to states with depleted unemployment reserves; and (3) it appropriates any further surplus federal unemployment tax collections over the first $200,000,000 for distribution to the states by crediting the states' accounts in the trust fund according to a formula. Surplus collections for the fiscal year 1956 were estimated at approximately $31,400,000.[8]

REQUIREMENTS FOR STATE PLANS

The federal act provides that the secretary of labor shall make no certification for payment to any state for administrative purposes unless he finds that the law of such state, approved by him under the Federal Unemployment Tax Act, includes among others the following provisions: (1) it must furnish such methods of administration, including the maintenance of personnel standards on a merit basis, as are found by the secretary of labor to be reasonably calculated to insure full payment of compensation when due; (2) it must provide opportunities for a fair hearing before an impartial tribunal for all individuals whose claims for unemployment compensation are denied; (3) it must make such reports as the department requires; (4) upon request, it must make available to any agency of the United States charged with the administration of public works or assistance the identifying data regarding recipients of unemployment compensation. If administration is not in substantial compliance with the requirements of the federal act, the secretary of labor shall notify the state that further payments will not be made to it until compliance occurs.

STATE LAWS FOR UNEMPLOYMENT COMPENSATION

COVERAGE [9]

Except for the above types of requirements, the states are free to set up any unemployment compensation system they wish. They may add

[8] George F. Rohlich, "Employment Security Administrative Financing Act of 1954," *The Labor Market and Employment Security* (July, 1955), pp. 1–4.

[9] *Comparison of State Unemployment Insurance Laws as of August, 1954,* pp. 1–13; U.S. Department of Labor, Bureau of Employment Security, *Significant Provisions of State Unemployment Insurance Laws: November 1, 1956* (Washington, D.C., 1956); *Employment Security Review,* Vol. 20, No. 8, pp. 21–24.

employee and state contributions to those of employers. They may have variations in the provisions concerning contributions, the groups covered, the conditions under which individuals may or may not receive benefits, the amount and duration of benefits, the administrative features for the operation of the system.

The coverage provisions of the federal and state unemployment insurance laws form the basic framework of the program since they determine which employers are liable for contributions and, in the case of state laws, which workers may acquire rights to benefits. Coverage is limited by the exclusion of certain employing units and certain kinds of services. In almost all states, however, there are provisions which permit voluntary election of coverage by excluded groups. In January, 1956, when the federal tax applied to employers with at least four workers in twenty weeks, the laws of twenty-three states already protected workers in firms with one to three individuals.

In addition to size-of-firm exclusions the federal act excludes certain employments from the tax. They are primarily agricultural and domestic labor, work performed for certain stipulated relatives, and work done for nonprofit institutions operated exclusively for religious, charitable, or educational purposes. Only a few states have covered services which are excluded under the federal act.

The relationship of a worker to the person for whom he performs his services also influences whether the employer must count him in figuring his tax payments. The common-law master-servant relationship is a consideration in the determination of coverage in several states. Most states have a broader concept of what constitutes an employer-employee relationship. They have incorporated strict tests of what constitutes such absence of control of an employer over a worker that the worker would be classed as an independent contractor rather than an employee. Most state laws do not cover employees of the state or its political subdivisions. Newsboys and insurance agents on commission are excluded in the majority of states; real estate agents on commission in about half the states; and casual labor not in the course of the employer's business in over half the states.

With fifty-one jurisdictions operating separate unemployment insurance laws it is essential to have a basis for coverage which will keep individuals who work in more than one state from falling between two or more laws and which will prevent the requirement of duplicate employer contributions on the services of one individual. To avoid these problems the states have adopted uniform language for ascribing such services to a particular state. The entire service of a multistate worker is covered in one state if it meets certain statutory conditions. Under these conditions all services are covered in one state if they are performed primarily in that state with only temporary or incidental transactions in other states.

FINANCING [10]

There is no federal tax on employees. In all but the two states of Alabama and New Jersey the employee makes no contribution. In the other forty-nine jurisdictions the employer makes the total contribution. State laws differ as to the details of their unemployment funds. Seven of the original state laws provided for separate employer reserves, although they included a "partial pool" or shortly added one. Most states, however, early adopted a pooled fund plan in which all moneys collected from employers are "commingled and undivided" and the cost of unemployment is spread over all employers. Only one state in 1955 did not have a pooled fund system, but it had a "partial pool." A separate bookkeeping account is maintained for each employer, but his workers have no special claim on the funds he has paid in. All benefits are paid from the unemployment fund, regardless of the balance of an individual employer's contributions and the benefits paid his workers.

All state laws provide for some system of experience rating by which individual employers' contribution rates are varied from the standard rate on the basis of their experience with unemployment. We shall not attempt to describe these extremely complicated arrangements but merely to list the present five distinct systems of experience rating usually identified as reserve ratio, benefit ratio, benefit-wage ratio, compensable separations, and payroll variation. Because of federal requirements no employer can be granted a reduced rate until the agency has a record of his experience with the factors used to measure unemployment. Without such a record there would be no basis for rate determination.

BENEFITS AND QUALIFICATIONS [11]

Under all state unemployment insurance laws a worker's benefit rights depend on his experience in covered employment in a past period of time called the base period. The period during which the weekly rate and the duration of benefits determined for a given worker apply to him is called his benefit year. To qualify for benefits as an insured worker, a claimant must have earned a specified amount of wages or must have worked a certain number of weeks or calendar quarters in covered employment within the base period or must have met some combination of wage and employment requirements. He must also be free from disqualifications. All states, with a few exceptions, require a claimant to serve a waiting period. All states determine an amount payable for a week of total unemployment as defined in the state law.

---

[10] *Comparison of State Unemployment Insurance Laws as of August, 1954,* pp. 14–41; *Employment Security Review,* Vol 20, No. 8, pp. 25–30.

[11] *Comparison of State Unemployment Insurance Laws as of August, 1954,* pp. 42–74; *Employment Security Review,* Vol. 20, No. 8, pp. 25–30.

One state after another has increased the maximum weekly benefit from the $15.00 with which most states started to $30.00 or more. Weekly benefits to unemployed workers averaged $10.66 in 1939, rose to $18.77 in 1945, and have increased each successive year from 1948 to 1954, with a peak of almost $25.00 in 1954. With the effectuation of the 1955 amendments to state laws, maximum basic weekly benefits ranged from $25.00 to $45.00, with nineteen states under $30.00, eighteen at $30.00, and fourteen above $30.00. Increases in weekly benefits, however, have lagged behind rising wages. The average payment in the country as a whole has dropped from 41 per cent of the average wage of covered workers in 1939 to about one third in 1955. The experience of individual states varies substantially from these national averages. In 1954 only one state ratio exceeded 41 per cent, and that was Wyoming, which pays dependents' allowances. Only a few states have adopted dependents' allowances. The enactments have been sporadic, and there seems to be little tendency to move in this direction. In 1954 eleven states provided dependents' allowances.

Since 1945 all states but one have provided benefits for weeks of partial unemployment. Generally, the weekly benefit amount is used as a measure of the existence of compensable partial unemployment. In most states a worker is partially unemployed in a week of less than full-time work when he earns less than his weekly benefit amount or a little more.

Duration of benefits is determined by various formulas. Regardless of the formulas for determining duration, the laws specify a maximum number of weeks of benefits for total unemployment. Along with increases in weekly benefits, the maximum number of weeks of benefits payable under state laws increased between 1937 and 1955. Maximum duration in the modal state moved from sixteen weeks in 1937 to twenty in 1945 and to twenty-six in 1955. As a result of changes in maximum duration and maximum weekly benefits, the maximum amounts payable in a benefit year have also increased. In October, 1940, maximum annual benefits ranged from $180.00 to $468.00. By December, 1945, the range was $210.00 to $650.00. By June, 1955, the range was $384.00 to $1,170. The median amount was $728.00, but the largest number of states (eleven) provided $780.00. Thirteen states had maximum basic benefits of more than $800.00.

DISQUALIFICATIONS [12]

Although coverage has been expanded and weekly benefits and duration have been increased, some of the conditions for the receipt of benefits

[12] *Comparison of State Unemployment Insurance Laws as of August, 1954*, pp. 75–106; *Employment Security Review*, Vol. 20, No. 8, pp. 41–46.

have been made more restrictive in most jurisdictions. This is particularly true with respect to disqualifications which deny benefits to unemployed workers for reasons other than lack of wage credits. Each state law contains a set of disqualification provisions. As a minimum, all laws deny benefits to claimants who are unavailable for work or unable to work; are involved in a labor dispute; or have caused their own unemployment by some disqualifying act, such as a quit or refusal of work without just cause, or have been discharged for misconduct. The adoption of experience rating, which became widespread in the 1940's, had its influence upon the development of strict qualification provisions. Under experience rating an employer's tax rate is increased or decreased according to his experience with unemployment. He has an interest, then, in avoiding the payment of compensation benefits to those who are unemployed through no fault of the place of employment and of the employer. This result has been one of the unfavorable consequences of experience-rating schemes.

The number of disqualifications imposed each year is considerable. During each of nine years following World War II disqualifications exceeded 1,000,000. In 1954 the total number of disqualifications was 1,616,000. Because claimants may wrongfully be disqualified from receiving benefits, provision is needed for an impartial review procedure. The Social Security Act requires each state to make such a provision. The unemployment insurance benefit appeals system has worked well. Over 2,000,000 administrative appeal decisions have been issued since the program began, and relatively few of these decisions have been taken to the courts.

ADMINISTRATIVE ORGANIZATION [13]

Because unemployment is a national problem, the federal government has a vital interest in the administration of the program. For this reason the federal act provides that the secretary of labor is responsible for paying to the states out of the funds appropriated by Congress the amounts which he finds necessary for the proper and efficient administration of these laws. We earlier indicated some of the administrative requirements that the federal act imposes upon the states, among which is the obligation to make reports to the secretary of labor. As a result of these and other reports made to him, information on employment and unemployment is far more complete in 1955 than in 1935.

There are no federal requirements concerning the form of state organizations administering unemployment insurance programs. The scheme is administered in close co-operation with the national public employ-

---

[13] *Comparison of State Unemployment Insurance Laws as of August, 1954,* pp. 107–118; *Employment Security Review,* Vol. 20, No. 8, pp. 47–54.

ment service system established by the Wagner-Peyser Act of 1933. The federal agency responsible for administering unemployment insurance is the Bureau of Employment Security (which also includes the United States Employment Service). In all states, administration of the entire unemployment insurance program, including both tax and benefit operations, has always been centered in a single agency. Also, under the prevailing pattern, the public employment service is consolidated with the unemployment compensation organization in a single agency. In 1954 the largest number of state employment security agencies, nineteen, were independent boards or commissions. In fourteen states the administrative agencies were independent departments of state government; in seventeen they were in state departments of labor; and in one in the state workmen's compensation agency. In 1955 there were fifty-one central offices and 1,700 local offices. All but four states provided for state-wide advisory councils. In forty-four states such a council was mandatory; in three it was permissive. These councils are for the purpose of aiding the agency in formulating policies and meeting problems relating to the administration of the employment security act.

Administration of unemployment compensation plans has changed greatly since the inauguration of the program. The routine operations involved in benefit payments and employer accounts have been simplified substantially. There has been increasing emphasis on the importance of the claims processing operation. At first this operation was considered to be a routine clerical one, but experience has shown that the claims-taking operation is the basic one in paying unemployment compensation benefits. Another major change has been the tendency to decentralize administration and to locate offices close to the problems. Despite experience and improvements, administration becomes more complex and technical.

ADDITIONAL SOCIAL INSURANCE PLANS

TEMPORARY DISABILITY INSURANCE [14]

Three states—Rhode Island, California, and New Jersey—provide state benefits for unemployment due to temporary disability, which are administered by the state employment security agencies in co-ordination with the unemployment insurance programs. New York provides such benefits, and they are administered by its Workmen's Compensation Board. Rhode Island passed its law in 1942, California in 1946, New Jersey in 1948, and New York in 1949. The three systems of disability insurance co-ordinated with unemployment insurance use the same wage-

[14] *Comparison of State Unemployment Insurance Laws as of August, 1954,* pp. 119–128.

record procedures for both programs, but claims procedures differ. Under all the laws medical certification of disability in connection with claims is required from the claimant's attending doctor. In the three state schemes co-ordinated with unemployment insurance the benefit formula is similar to that for unemployment insurance.

OTHER FEDERAL UNEMPLOYMENT INSURANCE PLANS [15]

In addition to the unemployment insurance scheme we have been describing, Congress since the 1940's has enacted legislation providing unemployment benefits for five special groups of persons. We shall refer to these programs but shall not describe them.

First, there is the Railroad Unemployment Insurance Act. Railroad workers originally were covered by state unemployment insurance laws. In July, 1939, they were transferred to a new federal railroad unemployment insurance program administered by the Railroad Retirement Board, which had been set up to administer the railroad retirement program. The states transferred to this board the balance of contributions they had collected from the railroads over the benefits they had paid to railroad workers. In July, 1947, the railroad unemployment insurance program was expanded to include payments to railroad workers out of work because of sickness.

Second, Title V of the Servicemen's Readjustment Act of 1944 provided veterans' readjustment allowances of $20.00 for each week of involuntary unemployment up to fifty-two weeks. In addition it provided benefits to self-employed veterans endeavoring to establish businesses or professions. The federal administration of this program was the responsibility of the Veterans' Administration. The state agencies paid the benefits as agents of the federal government. More than 9,500,000 of the 15,100,000 World War II veterans filed claims for these benefits in the five-year period of its major operations and were paid benefits totaling $3,800,000,000.

Third, in October, 1952, a program providing for unemployment compensation for veterans with military service between June 27, 1950, and January 31, 1955, became effective under the provisions of Title IV of the Veterans' Readjustment Assistance Act of 1952. This program is coordinated with existing state unemployment insurance laws. The 1944 act specified eligibility and disqualification requirements, but the 1952 act utilizes the states' eligibility and disqualification provisions, except that benefits are not subject to cancellation under state disqualification provisions. Between October, 1952, when the program began, and June 30, 1955, when 4,000,000 veterans had returned to civilian life, 650,000 re-

---

[15] *Comparison of State Unemployment Insurance Laws as of August, 1954,* pp. 129–131; *Employment Security Review,* Vol. 20, No. 8, pp. 55–60.

ceived at least one benefit payment. Nine million weeks of unemployment were compensated, and $207,000,000 were paid in benefits.

Fourth, in 1953 Congress made the Federal Unemployment Tax Act applicable to services performed on or after July 1, 1953, on vessels operated under agreements between private ship operators and general agencies of the United States government. This act permits the states to cover these seamen under the regular provisions of state laws.

Fifth, the newest unemployment insurance program is "Unemployment Compensation for Federal Employees," provided by Title XV, which was added to the Social Security Act in 1954. Its protection extends to 2,500,000 federal civilian workers when they are unemployed after January 1, 1955. Benefits are paid to federal employees "in the same amount, on the same terms, and subject to the same conditions as the compensation that would be payable" if their federal employment had been subject to the state employment security law. In general, the law assigns wages earned in federal service to the state in which a federal worker had his last official station before filing his claim. All jurisdictions have signed agreements with the secretary of labor and are paying unemployment benefits to federal employees. During the first six months of 1955 over 60,000 former federal employees were compensated for 625,000 weeks of unemployment. Payments totaled about $16,000,000.

SUPPLEMENTAL UNEMPLOYMENT BENEFIT PLANS [16]

No discussion of unemployment compensation should close without reference to so-called "Guaranteed Annual Wage Plans," more accurately titled "Supplemental Unemployment Benefit Plans." The plans developed by the Ford, General Motors, and other plants are in reality supplemental unemployment benefit plans. The Ford plan provides that the company shall set up a fund from which the unemployed worker can draw benefits additional to his unemployment compensation benefits to make his total benefit (state and company) equal to a specified percentage of his wages after tax deductions. He can draw not more than 65 per cent of his wages for the first four weeks and 60 per cent during the remaining weeks, up to a maximum of twenty-six weeks in a year. The plan did not go into effect in any state until assurance was received that the state benefits would not be canceled or reduced because of employer benefits. Experts are asking such questions as: What will be the long-time effect of these plans on public unemployment compensation benefits? How will this type of plan affect workers outside of the strong unions or not in unions at all? Will union members and employers be interested in improving benefits provided by law? At this juncture such questions can be asked but

[16] "Notes and Comments: The Guaranteed Annual Wage," *Social Service Review*, Vol. 29, No. 3 (September, 1955), pp. 294–295.

not answered. Gearing and reconciling these types of plans and public unemployment compensation programs will take time and patience.

FUTURE ISSUES [17]

The Bureau of Employment Security of the United States Department of Labor, which administers the federal aspects of the unemployment compensation program (except those financial aspects administered by the United States Treasury Department), has pointed out numbers of spots at which this federal-state program for unemployment compensation can be improved. According to the bureau there is need for:

1. Universal coverage.
2. Permanent protection for ex-servicemen.
3. Expanded protection against wage loss through increased size and duration of benefits.
4. Simplification of benefit formulas.
5. Modification of qualifying employment and wage provisions.
6. Relaxation of disqualification provisions.
7. Improvements in administration.
8. Analysis of financing to insure payment of benefits in bad as well as good years.
9. Inclusion of a scheme for temporary disability insurance.

It seems clear that these problems will need continued attention for many years to come.

Arthur J. Altmeyer, former commissioner for social security, has pointed out some of the modifications he is convinced are needed in federal and state unemployment compensation legislation. They include:

1. States that have sufficient reserves should continue to be permitted to choose whether they will reduce employer contribution rates on a uniform basis or through some other method of employer experience rating, but at the same time the federal act should require state laws to meet standards of adequacy specified in the federal law.

2. These standards should require that weekly benefits average at least 65 per cent of the weekly wage and that the average potential duration of benefits be at least twenty-six weeks.

3. In view of the large reserves most states have built up, the Federal Unemployment Tax Act should be amended to permit or even require use of funds for benefits in unemployment due to temporary disability.

4. The co-operative federal-state program should be kept, but a simple system of federal grants to states to cover the cost of both benefits and administration, financing these grants out of a straight 1 per cent federal payroll tax, might be substituted for the present complicated tax-offset plan.

Altmeyer believes that although his proposals offer improvements over the present program, only a straight federal system of unemployment insurance can assure maximum spreading of the risk of unemployment,

---

[17] *Employment Security Review,* Vol. 20, No. 8, pp. 61–66.

maximum consistency of contribution rates and benefits, and maximum simplicity in administration. The idea of a federal system may sound startling today, according to Altmeyer, when employment is relatively high and states have large reserves for benefits. It would not sound so startling if unemployment were to rise sharply.[18] Altmeyer's position on the desirability of expanded federal responsibility is in disharmony with that of the Eisenhower administration. In the language of the Bureau of Employment Security: [19]

> The administration is committed to the policy of no federal encroachment on the responsibility of the states to meet the social and economic needs of their own citizens. At the same time, the federal government has a definite interest in, and responsibility for, the successful operation of the unemployment insurance program.

SUMMARY AND CONCLUSIONS

In this and the preceding chapter we have attempted to highlight the growth and development of the two forms of social insurance included in the Social Security Act. We have made no effort to describe the evolution of Workmen's Compensation, the first social insurance program developed in this country. We have only mentioned the Railroad Retirement and Railroad Unemployment Insurance acts, other federal unemployment compensation systems, and the voluntary and private insurance schemes developed by employers, employees, and many other resources. Detailed description of all these programs has been made by experts in the social insurance field. We have intended only to round out the picture of government-assumed responsibility for persons with economic and social needs through the Social Security Act and its amendments and to indicate that numbers of other economic protective measures are in existence.

Prior to the depression of the 1930's, state governments had assumed more or less responsibility for those with pronounced economic needs through general assistance laws, and for special groups of needy persons through categorical assistance programs. With the enactment of the Emergency Relief and Construction Act of 1932, the principle that relief of the needy is a public responsibility at all government levels was established. In the early years of the depression interest developed in permanent methods of meeting the economic problems of the unemployed, the aged, dependent children, and so forth. Out of these concerns came the insurance, public-assistance, and social service provisions of the Social Security Act. In these two final chapters we have culled a limited number

[18] Arthur J. Altmeyer, *Your Stake in Social Security,* Public Affairs Pamphlet (New York, Public Affairs Committee, 1954), No. 206, pp. 22–24.

[19] *Employment Security Review,* Vol. 20, No. 8, p. 61.

of facts and figures concerning the old-age and survivors insurance and unemployment insurance schemes of the Social Security Act. We have briefly summarized past and present developments. We have somewhat anticipated future needs and enumerated some of the suggestions for improvements in programs. We trust we have adequately demonstrated that much has been accomplished in federal and state legislation for social security since the enactment of the Social Security Act in 1935. We have intended also to emphasize the amazing achievements of those who have learned how to administer these vast programs efficiently and wisely.

We conclude our discussion of social security by referring to the statements of two experts in this field, Professor Wilbur J. Cohen and Professor Edwin E. Witte. Both men emphasize accomplishments and unfinished business in social security; both share a belief in the possibility of progress toward a better life for all in a democratic society.

In an address honoring Professor Witte, Professor Cohen made the following observations: [20]

We face a much different task today in charting a course for social security than we did in 1935. Then we had the advantage of a relatively clean slate but with the great disadvantage that all the problems of the unknown were before us. We have gained "know-how" in administration, we have gained a reasonable degree of competence in our financial, actuarial, and economic planning of the programs. But, today, we have a pluralistic piecemeal system with many vested interests; a jigsaw puzzle of many parts and many diverse arrangements which we did not have in 1935. And with each passing year it becomes more difficult to make basic changes in the structure as institutionalization takes hold . . . Over the past twenty years our thinking on social security has tended to become compartmentalized. . . . It is indeed unfortunate that a kind of intellectual separatism has crept into the components of social security when the very needs of the time are for a more comprehensive approach and cross-fertilization . . .

After analyzing several current technical and controversial problems, such as benefit adequacy and the relation of public and private responsibilities in our social security programs "from a comprehensive approach," Mr. Cohen concluded:

Social legislation is borne in controversy, and those of us who work in this field must be willing to be criticized for our views and recommendations. However, we must be sure we have the facts to guide us and that we continuously undertake research to keep up with changing conditions. Although controversy is part of our daily work, we must ever be tolerant of differing points of view. None of us have the sole clue to truth. We change our point of view and so do others. We must be willing to work with others who have different points of view. In our democracy we try to emphasize the positive by finding those areas at any given time in which there is agreement. . . . Those of us in social security who were nurtured . . . in the Commons-Perlman-Witte philosophy

---

[20] Wilbur J. Cohen, "The Future of Social Security," an address given in honor of Professor Edwin E. Witte at the University of Wisconsin Symposium on Labor and Government, Madison, Wis., March 28, 1957.

believe in the idea of progress. We believe that there can be a better life for all. We believe that for all practical purposes, want can be abolished and poverty eradicated. We believe that human problems are capable of solution.

In a speech given at the twentieth-anniversary celebration of the Social Security Act, Professor Witte summarized the growth of the act and emphasized the need of the experts and the citizenry to keep a forward look on social security problems. He said: [21]

Of course, we have not attained the ideal. The possibility and need for continuous progress is one of the most distinctive features of the American way of life and our economic system of free enterprise. We cannot be satisfied with the social security protection now provided to Americans. Retirement benefits in our old-age and survivors insurance system supply only one third as much income, or less, to the workers no longer able to work than is enjoyed by older people still in employment. While the benefits under state laws to unemployed and injured workers are greater, our unemployment insurance and workmen's compensation laws also are very much in need of liberalization and improvement. None of our social insurance programs are as broad in coverage as they should be. Great risks, like early disability and prolonged sickness, lack all governmental protection; and the voluntary forms of insurance we have, although most valuable, do not protect many of those who most need protection. Even at this time of near full employment and unprecedented total and average incomes, there are millions of Americans who face a most uncertain economic future and many who barely have the minimum essentials of life. The great objective of social security—assurance of a minimum necessary income to all people in all personal contingencies of life, has not been attained even in this great country in which the common man fares better than in any other.

We have come a long way. Great tasks remain. But mindful of the progress that has been made and believing on the basis of their records that the people now in the driver's seat and their faithful and conscientious subordinates are sincere in their profession of belief in social security, I feel that we can view the future of social security in the United States with complete assurance. We have made great progress, and, in accordance with our American ideals, will do still better in the future.

Selected References

ALTMEYER, Arthur J., *Your Stake in Social Security,* Public Affairs Pamphlet (New York, Public Affairs Committee, 1954), No. 206.

BURNS, Eveline M., *The American Social Security System* (Boston, Houghton Mifflin, 1941).

———, *Social Security and Public Policy* (New York, McGraw-Hill, 1956).

COHEN, Wilbur J., "Social Insurance," *Social Work Year Book: 1957,* pp. 537–547.

Compilation of the Social Security Laws, Including the Social Security Act, as Amended, and Related Enactments Through December 31, 1954, 83d Cong., 2d sess., S. Doc. 157 (Washington, D.C., G.P.O., 1955).

---

[21] Edwin E. Witte, "Twenty Years of Social Security," mimeographed address given at the observance of the twentieth anniversary of the Social Security Act by the Department of Health, Education, and Welfare at Washington, D.C., on August 15, 1955.

CORSON, John J., and MCCONNELL, John W., *Economic Needs of Older People* (New York, The Twentieth Century Fund, 1956).

Employment and Wages, published quarterly by the U.S. Department of Labor.

GAGLIARDO, Domenico, *American Social Insurance* (New York, Harper, 1949).

HABER, William, and COHEN, Wilbur J., eds., *Readings in Social Security* (Englewood Cliffs, N.J., Prentice-Hall, 1948).

The Labor Market and Employment Security, published monthly by the U.S. Department of Labor.

LARSON, Arthur, *Know Your Social Security* (New York, Harper, 1955).

MERIAM, Lewis, and SCHLOTTERBECK, Karl, *Cost and Financing of Social Security* (Washington, D.C., Brookings Institution, 1950).

National Association of Manufacturers, Indiana Relations Division, *Unemployment Compensation in a Free Economy,* Economic Policy Division Series (July, 1952), No. 52.

Public Law 880, 84th Cong., 2d sess., ch. 836, H. R. 7225 (Washington, D.C., G.P.O., 1956).

Social Legislation Information Service, semimonthly report issued by the Social Legislation Information Service, Inc., 1346 Connecticut Ave., N.W., Washington, D.C.

Social Security Bulletin, published monthly by the U.S. Department of Health, Education, and Welfare.

SOMERS, Herman M., and RAMSEY, Anne, *Workmen's Compensation* (New York, Wiley, 1954).

A Symposium on Unemployment Insurance, 2 Vand. L. Rev. 179–494 (1955).

U.S. Department of Health, Education, and Welfare, Social Security Administration, *Basic Readings in Social Security, Social Welfare—Social Insurance* (Washington, D.C., G.P.O., 1956), Pub. No. 28.

U.S. Department of Health, Education, and Welfare, *Social Security Bulletin: Social Security Protection, 1935–55,* anniv. issue, Vol. 18, No. 8 (August, 1955).

U.S. Department of Health, Education, and Welfare, Social Security Administration, *Social Security in the United States* (Washington, D.C., 1953).

U.S. Department of Labor, Bureau of Employment Security, *Comparison of State Unemployment Insurance Laws as of August, 1954* (Washington, D.C., G.P.O., 1954).

U.S. Department of Labor, Bureau of Employment Security, *Employment Security Bulletin: Twenty Years of Unemployment Insurance in the U.S.A., 1935–55,* Vol. 22, No. 8 (August, 1955).

U.S. House of Representatives, *Analysis of the Social Security System: Appendix II, Miscellaneous Documents: Hearings before a Subcommittee of the Committee on Ways and Means,* 83d Cong., 1st sess. (1954).

U.S. Senate, *Social Security Amendments of 1954: Hearings before the Senate Committee on Finance,* 83d Cong., 2d sess., on *H.R. 9366* (June 24–July 9, 1954).

The student should also consult the annual reports of the U.S. Department of Health, Education, and Welfare and the U.S. Department of Labor; pertinent hearings and reports of congressional committees.

TABLE OF CASES

Aborn et al. v. Janis et al., 62 Misc. N.Y. 95 (1907) 267
Abrams v. U.S. Fidelity and Guaranty Co., 127 Wis. 579 (1906) 268
Ackley v. United States, 200 Fed. 217 (1912) 174
Adams v. Palmer, 51 Me. 480 (1863) 74
Aldrich v. Bennett, 63 N.H. 415 (1885) 235
Alexander v. Alexander, 140 Ind. 555 (1894) 122
Alexandria Twnsp. v. Bethlehem Twnsp., N.J.L. 119 (1837) 518
Anderson v. Anderson, 89 Neb. 570 (1911) 131
Anderson v. Anderson, 68 Calif. App. 218 (1924) 124
Anderson v. Miller, 120 Pa. (Sup. Ct.) 463 (1936) 510
Appeal of Woodward, 81 Conn. 152 (1908) 315
Arado v. Arado, 281 Ill. 123 (1918) 100
Arais v. Kalensnikoff, 10 Cal. 2d 428 (1937) 358
Armstrong v. Armstrong, 92 N.Y. Supp. 165 (1904) 130
Arnaboldi v. Arnaboldi, 101 N.J. Eq. 126 (1927) 126
Atkins v. Curtis, 66 S. 2d 455 (1953) 576
Auditor of Lucas Co. v. The State, 75 Ohio 114 (1906) 582
Austen v. Austen, 55 Eng. Rep. 634 (1865) 229

Back v. Back, 148 Iowa 223 (1910) 100
Bailey v. Bailey, 97 Mass. 373 (1867) 124
Bailey v. Drexel Furniture Co., 259 U.S. 20 (1922) 305
Bain v. Bain, 79 Neb. 711 (1907) 127
Baker v. Smith, 82 Eng. Rep. 729 (1651) 85
Ball v. Ball, 57 Eng. Rep. 703 (1827) 220
Barber v. Barber, 16 Calif. 378 (1860) 135
Barlog v. Board of Water Commissioners, City of Dunkirk, 267 N.Y. Supp. 822 (1933) 537
Barnardo v. McHugh, Law Rep. App. Cases 388 (1891) 264, 348
Barngrover v. Barngrover, 57 Calif. App. 43 (1922) 124
Basham v. Co. Court, Kanawah Co., 114 W.Va. 376 (1933) 536
Bast v. Bast, 82 Ill. 584 (1876) 132
Baughman v. Baughman, 32 Kan. 538 (1884) 135
Bazeley v. Forder, L.R. 3 Q.B. 559 (1867) 237
Beamish v. Beamish, 11 Eng. Rep. 735 (1861) 78
Bellmore v. McLeod, 189 Wis. 431 (1926) 267
Berry v. Chaplin, 74 Cal. App. 2d 652 (1946) 359
Bickford v. Bickford, 57 Wash. 639 (1910) 128
Blank v. Nohl, 112 Mo. 159 (1892) 134
Blankenship v. Blankenship, 52 Nev. 48 (1929) 132
Blodget v. Brinsmaid, 9 Vt. 27 (1837) 100
Boardman, Effie, v. Orton P. Ward, 40 Minn. 399 (1889) 268
Board of Commissioners of Summit County v. Board of Commissioners of Trumbull County, 116 Ohio 663 (1927) 517
Board of Commissioners of Tipton County v. Brown, 4 Ind. App. 288 (1892) 496
Bours v. United States, 229 Fed. 960 (1915) 175
Bradford v. Worcester, 184 Mass. 557 (1904) 518
Bradley v. Tweedy, 185 Wis. 393 (1925) 330

Brown v. Maryland, 12 Wheat. 419 (1827) 6
Brown v. Scott, 140 Md. 258 (1922) 106
Brown et al. v. Board of Education of Topeka et al., 347 U.S. 483 (1954) 250
Brown et al. v. Board of Education of Topeka et al., 349 U.S. 294 (1955) 251
Buck v. Bell, Superintendent, 143 Va. 310 (1925), 274 U.S. 200 (1927) 204
Burger, By His Next Friend v. Frakes, 67 Iowa 460 (1885) 266
Busser v. Snyder, 282 Pa. 440 (1925) 530

C_____ v. C_____, 158 Wis. 301 (1914) 107
Cain v. Milburn, 192 Iowa 705 (1921) 127
Cairns v. Cairns, 109 Mass. 408 (1872) 131
Carmichael v. Gulf States Paper Corp., 301 U.S. 495 (1937) 556–557
Carmichael v. Southern Coal & Coke Co., 301 U.S. 495 (1937) 556–557
Caswell v. Caswell, 64 Vt. 557 (1892) 126
Cerro Gordo County v. Boone County, 152 Iowa 692 (1911) 494
Champion v. Ames, 188 U.S. 321, 355, 359 *et seq.* 305
Chapsky v. Wood, 26 Kan. 650 (1881) 224–225
Cheney v. Arnold, 15 N.Y. 345 (1857) 83
Christensen v. Thornby, 192 Minn. 123 (1934) 206
Cinque v. Boyd, 99 Conn. 70 (1923) 411
City of Bangor v. Inhabitants of Veazie, 111 Me. 371 (1914) 517
City of Two Rivers v. Town of Wabeno, 221 Wis. 158 (1936) 508
City of Waycross v. Hayes, 48 Ga. 317 (1934) 537
Clague v. Clague, 46 Minn. 461 (1891) 131
Clinton, John, v. Benjamin H. Laning and Isaiah C. Laning, 61 Mich. 355 (1886) 497
Coe v. Coe, 68 U.S. Sup. Ct. 1094 (1948) 140
Coffeen v. Town of Preble, 142 Wis. 183 (1910) 489
Colebrook v. Stewartstown, 30 N.H. 9 (1854) 497
Coltman v. Hall, 31 Me. 196 (1850) 267
Commonwealth (Mass.) v. Bakeman, 131 Mass. 577 (1881) 123
Commonwealth (Mass.) v. Gardner, and three other cases, 300 Mass. 372 (1938) 179
Commonwealth (Pa.) v. Fisher, 213 Penn. 48 (1905) 410
Commonwealth (Pa.) v. McClelland, 70 Pa. Super. 273 (1918) 230
Commonwealth of Pa. ex rel. William A. Schnader, Attorney General v. Alice F. Liveright, Secretary of Welfare of the Commonwealth of Pa. et al., 308 Penn. 35 (1932) 530
Commonwealth (Pa.) ex rel. Smith v. Gilmore, 95 Pa. Sup. Ct. 557 (1929), 97 Pa. Sup. Ct. 303 (1929) 249
Conovar v. Cooper, 3 Barb. Ch. 115 (1848) 235
Cooper v. Cooper, 17 Mich. 205 (1868) 124
Cross v. Cross, 3 Paige 139 (Ch. N.Y. 1832) 346

Dalrymple v. Dalrymple, 2 Hagg. Const. 54 (1811) 78
Davis v. Davis, 75 N.Y. 221 (1878) 227
Davis v. United States, 62 Fed. 2d 473 (1933) 174–175
Davis, Warden v. Walton, 74 Utah 80 (1929) 204
de Jarnett, Polly A., v. Josiah Harper, 45 Mo. A. 415 (1891) 266
Delaney v. Delaney, 71 N.J. Eq. 246 (1906) 130
Densmore et al. v. County Court of Mercer County, 106 W.Va. 317 (1928) 594
Denver & Rio Grande Railroad Co. v. Grand County, 51 Utah 294 (1917) 593
Dillon v. Dillon, 60 Ga. 204 (1878) 104
Doeme v. Doeme, 89 N.Y. Supp. 215 (1904) 130
Doughty v. Engler, 112 Kan. 583 (1923) 361
Drum v. Miller, 135 N.C. 204 (1904) 233
Dumaresly v. Fishly, 10 Ky. 368 (1820) 82
Durrett v. Unemployment Relief Committee et al., 152 S. (La.) 138 (1934) 537

Edwards v. Edwards, 26 Ky. L. 1051 (1901) ... 225
Edwards, Fred S., v. The People of the State of California, 34 U.S. 160 (1941) ... 512, 513, 520
Estate of Duncan, Popham v. Duncan, 87 Colo. 149 (1930) ... 75
Esteb v. Esteb, 138 Wash. 174 (1926) ... 241
Eward v. Eward, 72 Ind. App. 638 (1919) ... 124
Ex parte Daniecki, 117 N.J. Eq. 527 (1935) ... 412
Ex parte Januszewski, 196 Fed. 123 (1911) ... 411
Ex parte Mei, 122 N.J. Eq. 125 (1936) ... 412–413
Ex parte Ralph, 27 Cal. 2d 866 (1944) ... 426
Ex parte Skinner, 9 Moore 278 (1824) ... 218
Ex parte Suzahana, D.C. 295 Fed. 713 (1924) ... 82
Eyre v. Shaftsbury, 24 Eng. Rep. 659 (1722) ... 218, 262–263, 373

Fayette v. Chesterville, 77 Me. 28 (1885) ... 517, 518
Fearon v. Treanor, 272 N.Y. 268 (1936) ... 87
Fenton v. Reed, 4 Johns 52 (N.Y. 1809) ... 81
Fisher v. Fisher, 2 Swab. and Tr. 410 (1861) ... 136
Fisher v. Fisher, 250 N.Y. 313 (1929) ... 82
Fletcher v. People, 52 Ill. 395 (1869) ... 232
Flower v. Allen, 5 Cowper 654 (N.Y. 1825) ... 493
Freeman v. Freeman, 31 Wis. 235 (1872) ... 124
French v. French, 4 Mass. 587 (1808) ... 124

G_____ v. G_____, 67 N.J. Eq. 30 (1903) ... 103
Gally et al., 329 Mass. 143 (1952) ... 322
Gard v. Gard, 204 Mich. 255 (1918) ... 107
Garrett v. Garrett, 252 Ill. 318 (1911) ... 127
German v. German, 137 Md. 424 (1921) ... 123
Gibbs v. Gibbs, 18 Kan. 419 (1877) ... 124
Glascott v. Bragg, 111 Wis. 605 (1901) ... 316
Goodright v. Moss, 2 Cowper 591 (1777) ... 346
Gordon v. Mace, 144 Me. 351 (1949) ... 359
Gordon v. Potter, 17 Vt. 348 (1845) ... 239
Gould v. Gould, 78 Conn. 246 (1905) ... 99
Gouldsborough v. Sullivan, 132 Me. 342 (1934) ... 507
Gray v. Spalding, 58 N.H. 345 (1878) ... 497
Great Northern R.R. Co. v. Johnson, 254 Fed. 683 (1918) ... 82
Green v. State, 58 Ala. 190 (1877) ... 104
Griest v. Griest, 154 Md. 696 (1927) ... 125
Griffiths v. Griffiths, 69 N.J. Eq. 689 (1905) ... 129
Grigsby v. Reib, 105 Tex. 597 (1913) ... 82
Guardianship of Bynum, 72 Calif. App. 2d 120 (1945) ... 324
Guardianship of Walsh, 100 Calif. App. 2d 194 (1950) ... 324
Guardians of the Poor v. William P. Smith, 6 Pa. L.J. 433 (1847) ... 497

Haddock v. Haddock, 201 U.S. 562 (1906) ... 141
Hahn v. Bettingen, 81 Minn. 91 (1900) ... 85
Hammer v. Dagenhart, 247 U.S. 251 (1918) ... 8, 304
Harrison v. Gilbert, 71 Conn. 724 (1899) ... 510
Harrison v. Harrison, 94 Mich. 559 (1893) ... 107
Hastings v. Hastings, 147 Md. 177 (1925) ... 124
Hawkins v. Hawkins, 142 Ala. 571 (1904) ... 106, 110
Hawksworth v. Hawksworth, L.R. 6 Ch. App. 538 (1871) ... 229
Hayes v. Strauss, 151 Va. 136 (1928) ... 355
Hedden v. Hedden, 21 N.J. Eq. 61 (1870) ... 130
Helvering and the Edison Electric Illuminating Co. of Boston v. Davis, 301 U.S. 619 (1937) ... 10, 556

Hempel v. Hempel, 174 Wis. 332 ... 97
Hendrickson, Della, v. Town of Queen, 149 Minn. 79 (1921) ... 496
Henicle, Adm'x. v. Flack, Guardian, 3 Ohio App. 444 (1914) ... 265
Herd v. Herd, 194 Ala. 613 (1915) ... 82
Hernandez v. Thomas, 50 Fla. 522 (1905) ... 230, 264, 324
Hilborn v. Briggs, 58 N.Dak. 612 (1929) ... 510
Hively v. Golnick, 123 Minn. 498 (1913) ... 85
Hoadley v. Hoadley, 244 N.Y. 424 (1927) ... 98
Hockaday v. Lynn, 200 Mo. 456 (1906) ... 308, 330
Hoff v. Hoff, 48 Mich. 281 (1882) ... 132
Holcroft v. Dickenson, 124 Eng. Rep. 933 (1672) ... 84
Holingsworth v. Swendenborg, 49 Ind. 378 (1875) ... 239
Holland v. Belgium, 66 Wis. 557 (1886) ... 508
Holt v. Baldwin, 46 Mo. 265 (1870) ... 239
Horning v. Horning, 107 Mich. 587 (1895) ... 225
Howard, Asa, v. The Trustees of Whetstone Township, 10 Ohio 365 (1841) ... 497
Hoyt v. Sprague, 103 U.S. 613 (1881) ... 266
Hulett v. Carey, 66 Minn. 327 (1896) ... 82
Hull v. Oneida Co., 19 Johns 259 (N.Y. 1821) ... 494
Humphries v. Davis, 100 Ind. 274 (1884) ... 331
Hylton v. U.S., 3 Dall. 171 (1796) ... 14

In re Agar-Ellis, L.R. 10 Ch. D. 69 (1878) ... 229
In re Anonymous, 157 Misc. N.Y. 95 (1936) ... 332
In re Ballou's Estate, 181 Calif. 61 (1919) ... 329
In re Barnes, 119 Pa. (Sup. Ct.) 553 (1935) ... 510
In re Chirillo, 283 N.Y. 417 (1940) ... 510
In re Clarke, L.R. 21 Ch. D. 817 (1882) ... 229
In re Danikas' Estate, 76 Colo. 191 (1924) ... 83
In re Del Genovese's Will, 120 N.Y. Supp. 1121 (1909) ... 109
In re Doyle, 16 Mo. App. 159 (1884) ... 229
In re Goldman, 331 Mass. 647 (1954) ... 323
In re Gregorson, 160 Calif. 21 (1911) ... 110
In re Havsgord's Estate, 34 S.D. 131 (1914) ... 316
In re Herrera, 23 Cal. 2d 206 (1943) ... 426
In re Johnson, 87 Iowa 130 (1893) ... 265
In re McConnon et al., 112 N.Y. Supp. 590 (1908) ... 230
In re Mead, 113 Wash. 504 (1920) ... 223
In re Moore, 97 Ind. A. 492 (1933) ... 536
In re O'Connell, 102 Iowa 355 (1897) ... 265
In re Peter's Estate, 73 Colo. 271 (1923) ... 82
In re Santillanes, 47 N.M. 140 (1946) ... 412
In re Schwab's Adoption, 355 Pa. 534 (1947) ... 319
In re Silva's Estate, 32 Ariz. 573 (1927) ... 355
In re Spence, 2 Phillips 247 (1847) ... 373
In re Stockman, 71 Mich. 180 (1888) ... 226
In re Story, 2 Ir. R. 328 (1916) ... 229
In re Thorne's Will, Brantingham v. Huff, 155 N.Y. 140 (1898) ... 315
In re Tschudy's Adoption, 267 Wis. 120 (1954) ... 327
In re Wittick's Estate, 164 Iowa 485 (1914) ... 82

Jacobs v. Jacobs, 136 Minn. 190 (1917) ... 227
Jacobs v. Jacobs, 146 Ark. 45 (1920) ... 107
Jarrard v. Jarrard, 116 Wash. 70 (1921) ... 130
Jensen v. Jensen, 168 Wis. 502 (1919) ... 228
Johnson v. Johnson, 80 N.H. 15 (1921) ... 124
Jones v. Bowman, 13 Wyo. 79 (1904) ... 231

Kellogg v. Kellogg, 203 N.Y. Supp. 757 (1924) 93
Kelly v. Neely, 12 Ark. 657 (1852) 100
Kerr v. Kerr, 118 N.Y. Supp. 801 (1909) 123
King v. Cannon, 221 Wis. 322 (1936) 99
King v. De Manneville, 102 Eng. Rep. 1054 (1804) 217
King v. Henrietta Lavinia Greenhill, 111 Eng. Rep. 922 (1836) 218
Kirschbaum v. Kirschbaum, 92 N.J. Eq. 1 (1920) 103
Koehler v. Koehler, 137 Ark. 302 (1919) 124
Koenig v. State, 215 Wis. 658 (1934) 347
Kolzer v. New York Telephone Co., 93 N.J.L. 279 (1919) 414
Kurtz v. Frank, 76 Ind. 594 (1881) 86

Lane v. Pippin, 110 W.Va. 357 (1931) 319
Lanktree v. Lanktree, 42 Calif. App. 648 (1919) 129
Lavery v. Crooke, 52 Wis. 612 (1881) 236
Lawrence v. Cook, 56 Me. 187 (1868) 85
Lawrence v. Thomas, 84 Iowa 362 (1892) 266
Lawton v. State, 52 U.S. 133 (1894) 7
Leonard v. Leonard, 174 Iowa 734 (1916) 125
Lewis v. Lewis, 44 Minn. 124 (1890) 97
Lindsay et al. v. Lindsay et al., 257 Ill. 328 (1913) 415
Lingner v. Lingner, 165 Tenn. 525 (1933) 122
Litchfield v. State, 8 Okla. Cr. 164 (1912) 244
Lowell v. Seeback, 45 Minn. 465 (1891) 510
Lufkin v. Harvey, 132 Minn. 238 (1915) 235
Lundy v. Lundy, 23 Ariz. 213 (1922) 131
Lyannes v. Lyannes, 171 Wis. 381 (1920) 102
Lyster v. Lyster, 111 Mass. 327 (1873) 126

Mabin v. Webster, 129 Ind. 430 (1891) 85
McCauley v. McCauley, 88 N.J. Eq. 392 (1918) 129
McKelvey v. McKelvey et al., 111 Tenn. 388 (1903) 232
McLaughlin v. Antrim Road Commission, 266 Mich. 73 (1934) 537
McNabb v. McNabb, 182 Iowa 1143 (1918) 127
Mappes v. Iowa Co., 47 Wis. 31 (1879) 495, 496, 497
Marbury v. Madison, 1 Cranch 137, 2 L. Ed. 16 (1803) 14
Mathewson v. Phoenix Iron Foundry, 20 Fed. 281 (1884) 82
Matter of Application of Paul Daedler, 194 Calif. 320 (1924) 411
Matter of Conklin, 78 Misc. N.Y. 269 (1912) 497
Matter of the Petition of Mrs. Rose Snyder, 93 Wash. 59 (1916) 593
Mayhew v. Mayhew, 61 Conn. 233 (1891) 125
Maynard v. Hill, 125 U.S. 190 (1887) 75, 88
Meier v. Paulus, 70 Wis. 165 (1887) 493
Meister v. Moore, 96 U.S. 76 (1877) 81–82
Mercein v. The People ex rel. Barry, 25 Wendell 64 (N.Y. 1840) 222
Middlebury College v. Chandler, 16 Vt. 683 (1844) 249
Miles v. Miles, 137 Mo. App. 38 (1909) 122
Miller v. Pennington, 218 Ill. 220 (1905) 354
Morgan Co. v. Seaton, 122 Ind. 521 (1890) 494
Morrison v. Morrison, 20 Calif. 431 (1862) 125
Morrison v. Morrison, 142 Mass. 361 (1886) 130
Mortimore v. Wright, 151 Eng. Rep. 502 (1840) 237

Neal v. State, 54 Ga. 281 (1875) 232
Neff v. Neff, 96 Conn. 273 (1921) 123
Newcomer v. Jefferson Township, 181 Ind. 1 (1914) 494
Nicholl v. Koster, 157 Calif. 416 (1910) 414

Niland v. Niland, 96 N.J. Eq. 438 (1924) . . . 92
Nonnemacher v. Nonnemacher, 159 Pa. 634 (1894) . . . 98
Nordlund v. Nordlund, 97 Wash. 475 (1917) . . . 125
Norris v. Harris, 15 Calif. 226 (1860) . . . 265
Norton v. Lord Melbourne, Hansard's *Parliamentary Debates* (London 1837–1838), Vol. 39, cols. 1082–1090 . . . 220

Ohrns v. Woodward, 134 Mich. 596 (1903) . . . 226
Oliver v. Oliver, 169 Mass. 592 (1897) . . . 126
Owens v. State, 6 Okla. Cr. 110 (1911) . . . 244
Oxford v. Oxford, Ont. L.R. 15, 58 D.L.R. 251 (1921) . . . 181

Palm v. Smith, 183 Ore. 617 (1948) . . . 324
Patrick v. Baldwin, 109 Wis. 342 (1901) . . . 494
Patrick v. Town of Preble, 142 Wis. 183 (1910) . . . 494
Payne v. Dunham, 29 Ill. 125 (1862) . . . 518
Pearson v. Pearson, 230 N.Y. 141 (1920) . . . 124
Pease v. Pease, 72 Wis. 136 (1888) . . . 132
People v. Lattimore, 362 Ill. 206 (1935) . . . 413
People v. Mercein, 3 Hill 399 (N.Y. 1842) . . . 222
People v. Sanger, 222 N.Y. 192 (1918) . . . 178
People ex rel. Sission v. Sission, 271 N.Y. 285 (1936) . . . 399
People ex rel. Wilcox, 22 Barb. Ch. 178 (1854) . . . 267
Perez et al. v. Lippold, 32 Calif. 2d 711 (1948) . . . 105
Peterson v. Widule, 157 Wis. 641 (1914) . . . 101
Pile v. Pile, 94 Ky. 308 (1893) . . . 127
Plessy v. Ferguson, 163 U.S. 537 (1896) . . . 250
Port v. Port, 70 Ill. 484 (1873) . . . 82
Porter v. Powell, 79 Iowa 151 (1890) . . . 240
Portland v. New Gloucester, 16 Me. 427 (1840) . . . 517
Pretzinger v. Pretzinger, 45 Ohio St. 452 (1887) . . . 243
Provast v. Provast, 71 N.J. Eq. 204 (1906) . . . 125
Purinton v. Jamrock, 195 Mass. 187 (1907) . . . 231, 315, 329

Quarles v. Quarles, 19 Ala. 363 (1851) . . . 131

R. v. Soper, 5 Term R 278 (1789) . . . 348
R. E. L. v. E. L., Probate 211 (1949) . . . 181
Regina v. Millis, 10 Clark and Finnelly 532 (1843) . . . 78
Regina v. Smith, 1 Cox C.C. 260 (1845) . . . 374
Reynolds v. Reynolds, 3 Allen 605 (Mass. 1862) . . . 106
Reynolds v. Reynolds, 224 Ky. 668 (1928) . . . 125
Reynolds v. U.S., 98 U.S. 145 (1878) . . . 108
Rhine v. Sheboygan, 82 Wis. 352 (1892) . . . 489
Riddle v. Riddle, 26 Utah 268 (1903) . . . 74
Rocke v. Washington, 19 Ind. 53 (1862) . . . 74
Rockford v. Bailey, 322 Mo. 1155 (1929) . . . 320
Roether v. Roether, 180 Wis. 24 (1923) . . . 97
Rogers v. Rogers, 122 Mass. 423 (1877) . . . 131
Rogers v. Rogers, 67 N.J. Eq. 534 (1904) . . . 131
Roote v. Roote, 33 App. D.C. 398 (1909) . . . 123
Ross v. Ross, 89 Colo. 536 (1931) . . . 224
Rowe v. Rugg, 117 Iowa 606 (1902) . . . 232
Ruben v. Klemer, 44 R.I. 4 (1921) . . . 85
Rummens v. Evans et al., 168 Wash. 527 (1932) . . . 495

Salem v. Lyme, 29 Conn. 74 (1860) . . . 507
Saxville v. Bartlett, 126 Wis. 655 (1906) . . . 497
Scott v. State, 39 Ga. 321 (1869) . . . 104

Seigmund v. Seigmund, 46 Wash. 572 (1907) ... 127
Selph v. Selph, 27 Ariz. 176 (1925) ... 137
Senator v. City of Lincoln, 124 Neb. 403 (1933) ... 537
Sheehan v. Sheehan, 77 N.J. Eq. 411 (1910) ... 129
Shelhart v. Shelhart, 195 Mich. 144 (1917) ... 127
Shelley v. Westbrooke, 37 Eng. Rep. 850 (1816) ... 219
Sheridan Co. v. Denebrink, 15 Wyo. 342 (1907) ... 494
Sherrer v. Sherrer, 68 Sup. Ct. 1087 (1948) ... 140
Shoro v. Shoro, 60 Vt. 268 (1888) ... 107
Simpson Garment Co. v. Schultz, 182 Wis. 506 (1924) ... 241
Skinner v. State, 189 Okla. 235 (1941) ... 195
Smith v. Smith, 172 Mich. 175 (1912) ... 127
Squier v. Squier, 99 Vt. 452 (1926) ... 129
Stanley v. National Union Bank, 115 N.Y. 122 (1889) ... 235
Staples v. Staples, 87 Wis. 592 (1894) ... 137
State v. Bittick, 103 Mo. 183 (1891) ... 74
State v. Dwyer, 108 Vt. 303 (1936) ... 495
State v. Hansbrough, 181 Mo. 348 (1904) ... 82
State v. Henderson, 84 Iowa 161 (1891) ... 123
State v. Jager, 19 Wis. 251 (1865) ... 360
State v. Jones, 95 N.C. 588 (1886) ... 232
State v. Juvenile Court of Wadena County, 188 Minn. 125 (1933) ... 594
State v. Langford, 90 Ore. 251 (1918) ... 243
State v. Nelson, 126 Conn. 412 (1940) ... 179
State v. Porterfield, 222 Mo. App. 553 (1927) ... 362
State v. R.R. Commission of Wisconsin, 174 Wis. 458 (1921) ... 18
State v. Smith, 101 S.C. 293 (1915) ... 110
State ex rel. Boxberger v. Burns et al., 132 Neb. 31 (1937) ... 495
State ex rel. Fowler v. Moore, 46 Nev. 65 (1922) ... 134
State ex rel. Scott v. Lowell et al., 78 Minn. 166 (1899) ... 95
State ex rel. Walton v. Edmonson, 89 Ohio 351 (1913) ... 582
State ex rel. Wood Co. v. Dodge Co., 56 Wis. 79 (1882) ... 507
Steber v. Norris, 188 Wis. 366 (1925) ... 232
Steward Machine Company v. Davis, 301 U.S. 548 (1937) ... 9, 10, 556
Stickles v. Reichardt, 203 Wis. 579 (1931) ... 329
Stokes v. Anderson, 118 Ind. 533 (1888) ... 129
Stretcher v. Parker, 1 Rollis Abr. 22 (1638) ... 84
Strnad v. Strnad, 78 N.Y. Supp. 2d 390 (1948) ... 181

Taft v. Taft, 80 Vt. 256 (1907) ... 123
Thurston Co. Chapter, American National Red Cross v. Department of Labor and Industries of Washington, 116 Wash. 488 (1932) ... 536
Tileston v. Ulman, 129 Conn. 84 (1942) ... 179
Town of Bristol v. Town of Fox, 159 Ill. 500 (1896) ... 510
Town of Fox v. Town of Bristol, 45 Ill. App. 330 (1892) ... 511
Town of Kankakee v. McGraw, 178 Ill. 74 (1899) ... 495
Town of Milford v. Town of Worcester, 7 Mass. 48 (1810) ... 81, 88
Town of Rolling v. Town of Antigo, 211 Wis. 220 (1933) ... 508
Town of Saukville v. Town of Grafton, 68 Wis. 192 (1887) ... 491
Tozeland v. West Ham Union, 1 K.B. 538 (1906) ... 493
Trenchard v. Trenchard, 245 Ill. 313 (1910) ... 122
Trustees of Cincinnati Township v. Ogden, 5 Hammond (Ohio) 23 (1831) ... 495
Tufts v. Tufts, 8 Utah 142 (1892) ... 133
Turner v. Turner, 187 Calif. 632 (1921) ... 125

United States v. Dr. Jose Belaval, D.C. Puerto Rico (1939) ... 177
United States v. Bott, 24 Fed. 1204 (1873) ... 174
United States v. Certain Magazines, Himes, Claimant, 97 Fed. 2d 510 (1938) ... 176
United States v. Clarke, 38 Fed. 732 (1889) ... 175

United States v. Currey, 206 Fed. 322 (1913) ... 176
United States v. Darby, 312 U.S. 100 (1941) ... 9, 306
United States v. Dennett ... 175
United States v. One Book Entitled "Conception," 51 Fed. 2d 525 (1931) ... 176
United States v. One Book, Nicholas, Claimant, 97 Fed. 2d 510 (1938) ... 176
United States v. One Obscene Book Entitled "Married Love," 48 Fed. 2d 821 (1931) ... 175
United States v. One Package, 86 Fed. 2d 737 (1936) ... 176
United States v. Pupke, 133 Fed. 243 (1904) ... 175–176
United States v. Whitehead, 24 Fed. 1204 (1873) ... 174

Vaivida v. City of Grand Rapids, 264 Mich. 204 (1933) ... 536
Van Valkinburgh v. Watson, 13 Johns 480 (N.Y. 1816) ... 239
Verser v. Ford et al., 37 Ark. 27 (1881) ... 223

Wade v. Kalbfleisch, 58 N.Y. 282 (1874) ... 75
Wagner v. Varner, 50 Iowa 532 (1879) ... 331
Wamsely v. People, 64 Colo. 521 (1918) ... 362
Warner v. King, 267 Ill. 82 (1915) ... 331
Warner v. Warner, 54 Mich. 492 (1884) ... 125
Warren v. Prescott, 84 Me. 483 ... 330
Washburn v. White, 140 Mass. 568 (1886) ... 329
Watts v. Watts, 160 Mass. 464 (1894) ... 123
Wellesley v. Beaufort, 38 Eng. Rep. 236 (1827) ... 219, 263, 373
Wells v. Wells, 117 S.W. 2d 700 (1938) ... 225
West Milwaukee v. Industrial Commission, 216 Wis. 29 (1934) ... 537
Whately v. Hatfield, 196 Mass. 39 (1907) ... 506
Wiemer v. Wiemer, 21 N.D. 371 (1911) ... 129
Wightman v. Wightman, 4 Johns 343 (Ch. N.Y. 1820) ... 98, 110
Wiley v. Wiley, 75 Ind. App. 456 (1920) ... 88
Williams v. North Carolina, 63 Sup. Ct. 207 (1942) ... 140
Williams v. North Carolina, 65 Sup. Ct. 1092 (1945) ... 140
Williams v. Williams, 130 N.Y. 193 (1891) ... 125
Williams v. Williams, 130 N.Y. Supp. 875 (1911) ... 107
Wissenberg v. Bradley, 209 Iowa 813 (1930) ... 411
Witter v. Cook County Commissioners et al., 256 Ill. 616 (1912) ... 414
Wood v. Boone Co., 153 Iowa 92 (1911) ... 493, 494
Woodward v. Woodward, 41 N.J. Eq. 224 (1886) ... 130

Young v. Corrigan, 208 Fed. 431 (1912) ... 86
Young v. Young, 94 N.J. Eq. 155 (1922) ... 132
Youngs Rubber Corp. v. C. I. Lee Co., 45 Fed. 2d 103 (1930) ... 174

Zilley v. Dunwiddie, 98 Wis. 428 (1898) ... 243

INDEX

Abbott, Edith, 465, 493
Abbott, Grace, 299, 303
Abortion, 157, 158, 163, 177, 180
Act of 1388 (12th Richard II), 467, 468, 509
Act of 1601 (43 Elizabeth I), 469, 471
Act of 1834 (Eng.), 473
Act of Apprenticeship (1562, Eng.), 469
Act of Submission of the Clergy (1532, Eng.), 55
Adamic, Louis, 340
ADC. *See* Aid to Dependent Children
Adolescent courts. *See* Juvenile courts, Youth Correction Authority, Youth courts
Adoption, 308-338; early history of, 308-310; in England, 313-316; in the United States, *see* Adoption legislation (U.S.). *See also* Custody of children, Guardianship of children
Adoption Act (1950, Eng.), 287, 313, 314
Adoption legislation (U.S.): annulment, 332; decree issuance, 326-329; jurisdiction, 316-317; records, 332-334; religious factors, 321-325; rights and duties, 329-331; social investigation, 320-321; statistics, 336; statutory provisions, 315-336; surrender and consent, 317-320; trial period, 325-326; uniform act on, 334-335
Adultery, 181; as grounds for divorce, 59-61, 62, 120, 122-123, 130; historical, 33, 34, 36
Advisory Council on Social Security Financing, 608-609
Affinity, as marriage impediment, 54, 100
Afghanistan, 69
Agricultural Marketing Administration, 546
Aid to Blind. *See* Blind
Aid to Dependent Children (ADC), 271, 578, 588-594; *see also* Child welfare services, Guardianship of children
Alabama: marriage legislation, 104-105; old-age assistance legislation, 576; settlement law, 506; unemployment insurance, 632; work relief in, 538
Alaska, 574
Alcoholism, 101, 126-127
Alexander, P. W., 149, 420-421
Alimony, 136-138; *see also* Divorce
All China Federation of Women, 158
Allowance, meaning of term, 443, 445
Almsgiving, 439-440
Almshouses, 285, 289-291, 439
Altmeyer, A. J., 623, 624, 638-639
American Association of Labor Legislation, 554
American Association of Old Age Security, 554
American Bar Association, 83, 149, 422
American Chemical Society, 154
American International Institute for the Protection of Children, 289
American Law Institute, 424
American Medical Association, 164, 585
American Neurological Association, 190, 198, 200
American Printing House for the Blind, 581
American Public Welfare Association, 506, 514
Ancestor worship, 30
Andrews, J. B., 23
Anglo-Saxons, 20, 40
Annulment of marriage, 49, 98, 119-120; law on, *see* Statutory regulation of marriage (U.S.); reasons for, 103-104, 106-107; void and voidable marriage and, 109-112
Ansty, de, Richard, 50
Apprenticeship, 284, 291-293, 471; *see also* Children, Labor
Aquinas, St. Thomas, 154, 160
Argentina: adoption legislation in, 310, 312; illegitimacy legislation in, 351; juvenile courts in, 381-382
Arizona: illegitimacy legislation, 355; old-age assistance, 554, 572; relief legislation, 529
Arkansas: blind relief, 584; dependent child assistance, 591; divorce in, 121
Artificial insemination, 180-183
Arts projects, WPA, 542-543
Assistance. *See* Social assistance

Atkinson, Brooks, 543
Augustus, 6, 39
Augustus, John, 398
Australia, 555
Ayers, J. C., Jr., 343

Babylonian social legislation, 5
Ball, Robert M., 272-273
Baltimore almshouse, 290
Banns, 47-48, 88
Barden-LaFollette Act (1943), 581
Barnardo's Homes, Dr., 285
Barton, Bruce, 169
Bastardy, 339, 341, 344-348, 353
Bath, Lord (1753), 56
Belgium: birth control in, 156, 158, 159; illegitimacy in, 351, 352; social security in, 446-447
Besant, Annie, 156
Beveridge, Sir William, 286, 444, 465, 483; social insurance report, 286, 479-481
Bible: on marriage, 43, 44, 45; on birth control, 160-161
Bigamy, in marriage law, 107-109
Bill of Rights, English, 12
Bill of Rights, United States, 13
Bills of rights, 13
Binding out, 284
Birth control, 152-155, 166; rhythm method, 160, 162; *see also* Planned parenthood
Bismarck, von, Otto, 4, 454
Blacker, C. P., 188
Blackstone, William, 22, 64, 73, 76, 77, 136, 215, 244, 246, 283-284, 339, 353, 374
Blind assistance, 580-584
Bloodgood, Ruth, 404
Blood tests, in paternity cases, 358-360
Board of Trustees of Trust Funds, 608
Bohemia, 156
Bolivia: adoption in, 310, 312; juvenile courts in, 382
Bombay conference (1952), 159-160
Booth, Charles, 474, 475
Borstal system, 379
Boston, almshouse in, 290
Boston University Law Review, 323-324
Bowler, Alida, 404
Boys' courts, 422-423; *see also* Juvenile courts
Brace, Charles Loring, 293
Bradlaugh, Charles, 156
Brandeis, Louis D., 304
Brazil: birth control in, 156; illegitimacy in, 351; juvenile courts in, 382
Breach-of-promise suits, 84-87
Breckinridge, Sophonisba, 317
Bridewell, 468, 472
Bristol, Eng., poor relief in, 469-470
Brock, L. G., 188
Bruges plan, 446-447
Bryce, James, 37
Buck, Carrie, 204
Buck, Pearl, 282
Buffalo, N.Y.: charity organization in, 474; domestic relations court in, 419
Bureau of Employment Security, 562, 635, 638-639
Bureau of Old-Age and Survivors Insurance, 609
Bureau of Public Assistance, 590
Burns, E. M., 571
Byrnes, Ethel, 177, 178
Byrnes, James F., 512

Caesar, 36
California: blind relief, 584; child welfare services, 294; exclusion law, 512-513; guardianship of children in, 269; illegitimacy in, 358-359; juvenile courts, 376, 411, 414, 426-427; marriage legislation, 105, 106; old-age assistance, 554, 570, 571, 579; relief legislation, 529; sterilization legislation, 194, 206-208; unemployment insurance, 635; vagrancy in, 502
California Youth Authority, 426-427
Cambodia, 69
Canada: adoption in, 310, 312; birth control in, 157; old-age assistance, 555
Capper, Arthur, 113
Cardozo, Benjamin N., 9-10, 557
Carlyle, Thomas, 625
Castberg, Johan, 350
Casti connubii (1931), 161
Castration, 187, 203
Catherine the Great, 5
Catholic church. *See* Roman Catholic church
Catholic Hospital Association, 164
Catholic Lay Organizations, Co-ordinating Committee of, 168
Catholic Union of Obstetricians, 162
Chalmers, Thomas, 474
Chamber of Commerce, U.S., 623
Chamberlain, Neville, 476
Characteristics of State Public Assistance Plans, SSA, 567, 583
Charity. *See* Poor relief
Charity Organization Society, 475
Charlemagne, 439
Charles II, 56, 469
Chicago: boys' court in, 422-423; domestic relations court in, 419-420
Chicago Bar Association, 144, 182
Child labor laws, 8-9, 284, 285, 303-306

Child marriage, 92-95
Children: adoption of, *see* Adoption; aid to dependent under Social Security, 588-594; custody of, *see* Custody of children; delinquent, *see* Juvenile courts, Juvenile delinquency; disability assistance, 597-601, 616-617; English acts, 287, 314, 377-378; in English law, 68-69; in Greek civilization, 31-32; guardianship of, *see* Guardianship of children; health concern, 597-599; Hebrew, 43; illegitimate, *see* Illegitimacy; of migratory workers, 517-518; rights and disabilities, 252-253; in Roman civilization, 34, 35, 37-38, 39; in Teutonic tribes, 41. *See also* Family, Social Security Act
Children's Aid Society, 293
Children's Bureau, 296, 304, 318, 320, 326, 335, 336, 361, 366, 368, 369, 561, 562, 590, 591, 596, 598, 603; establishing of, 298-299, 300; guardianship of children and, 269, 275-278; juvenile delinquency division, 428; on training schools, 404; stand on juvenile courts, 388, 391, 394, 400, 405-406, 407, 416, 422
Children's Charter (1930), 301
Child Welfare League of America, 300
Child welfare services, 280-307; almshouse care, 289-291; apprenticeship and, 291-293; child labor movement, 303-306; definitions, 280-282; English methods, 283-288; federal, 298-299; foster home care, 293-298; institutional care, 285, 293-298; interstate placement, 298; primitive methods, 282-283; principles concerning, 302-303; state supervision of, 297-298; statistics on, 296-297; White House Conferences, 299-301; world-wide, 288-289. *See also* Children, Social Security Act
Chile, 351
China: birth control in, 158; old-age assistance in, 555; population problem, 166
Christianity: illegitimacy attitudes, 342-344; influence on family custom and law, 70; marriage and, 39, 44-49; poor relief emphasis, 439-441; status of women and, 38; *see also* separate churches
Church of England, 47, 53-63, 79-80
Chute, Charles L., 415
Cincinnati, family court, 420
Civil Code (France), 310
Civilian Conservation Corps (CCC), 539-540, 546
Civil Marriage Act (1653, Eng.), 55-56
Civil Service Commission, 555
Civil Works Administration (CWA), 531, 537, 541
Clarke, Tom C., 304
Cleveland, planned parenthood in, 183
Code of Hammurabi, 5, 308
Code Napoléon, 342, 352
Cohen, Wilbur J., 605-606, 640-641
Collusion, in divorce actions, 128-130
Colorado: juvenile courts, 375, 413, 419; old-age assistance, 570, 579; relief legislation, 529, 532; settlement law, 506-507
Commentaries, Kent, 240
Commentaries on the Laws of England, Blackstone, 22
Commission to Codify and Revise the Laws of Ohio, etc., 302
Commissioners on Uniform Legislation. *See* National Conference of Commissioners on Uniform State Laws
Committee on Economic Security, 552-553, 554, 556, 588, 596-597, 607, 621, 625-627
Common law, history of the, 19-23
Common-law marriage. *See* Marriage
Commons, J. R., 23, 625
Compact, meaning of term, 516
Comstock, Anthony, 170-171, 172
Comstock Act (1873), 160, 170-172, 173
Conant, James, 154-155
Condonation, in divorce actions, 131
Conference on Children in a Democracy (1940), 301
Congress, U.S., 15-16, 428-429, 595-596
Congressional Record, 170
Connecticut: birth control in, 172, 178, 179, 180; child welfare services, 294; disabled assistance, 587; divorce in, 141; guardianship of children in, 269; juvenile courts, 385, 411; marriage of epileptics in, 99; old-age assistance, 571, 572, 579; relief legislation, 543
Connell, Francis J., 161
Consanguinity, in marriage law, 54, 100
Constantine, 342
Constitution (1919), German, 246
Constitution, U.S., 9-10, 12-19, 69, 112, 113, 139, 250, 304-306
Constitutional law, theories of, 12-19
Constitutions, written and unwritten, 12-13
Construction work, government sponsored, 541, 547-548
Contraception: meaning of term, 153; *see also* Birth control, Planned Parenthood
Coods, George, 468
Cook, Henry, 156
Cook, Robert, 165-166

Cook County, Ill., 376, 423
Council of Florence, 46
Council of Poitiers, 343
Council of Trent, 39, 46, 47, 51
Courts, *passim;* dual system of government and, 15-16; due process of law under, 16-17; ecclesiastical, 49-51, 84, 136, 146, 343; equal protection of the laws under, 17-18; family, 405, 419-422; full faith and credit provision, 18-19; judicial review and, 13-15; as lawmakers, 22. *See also* Juvenile courts
Crime, ground for divorce, 126
Crippled children, government services for, 599-601
Cromwell, Oliver, 55-56
Cruelty, ground for divorce, 123-125
Cuba, 156
Curia Regis, 20
Custody of children: common-law background, 216-220; in divorce and separation actions, 138-139, 226-228; English law on, 220-221; United States law on, 216, 221-228, 400-403. *See also* Guardianship of children

Darwin, Leonard, 188
Dean, G., 206
Death rate, birth control and, 166
Deceased Brother's Widow's Marriage Act (1921, Eng.), 43 *n.*
Deceased Wife's Sister Marriage Act (1907, Eng.), 43
Delaware: almshouses, 290; divorce in, 143; juvenile courts, 414; old-age assistance, 571, 579; sterilization legislation, 202
Delinquent child: meaning of term, 282. *See also* Children, Juvenile courts, Juvenile delinquency
Denmark: adoption in, 310, 312; birth control in, 157; illegitimacy in, 352; juvenile courts in, 381; sterilization legislation in, 191
Dennett, Mary Ware, 171, 175
Dependent child: meaning of term, 281. *See also* Children, Child welfare services
Depression (1930's), 489, 501, 625; relief legislation, 524-551
Desertion: as ground for divorce, 125-126; legislation, 147-148; uniform act on, 242
Destitution, 488-490
Detention, child, 392-393
Deutsch, Albert, 404
Diocletian, 5
Disability insurance, 616-617; limitations of, 622-624; temporary, 635-636. *See also* Old-Age and Survivors Insurance
Disability Insurance Trust Fund, 608
Disabled, aid to, 584-588, 597-601, 616
Diseases, marriage legislation and, 101-103
District of Columbia, 172, 571, 574
Divorce: in ancient Greece, 33; Christian influences, 48-49; counsel in, 133-135; Hebrew, 43-44; primitive, 29; in Roman civilization, 36, 38-39; among Teutonic peoples, 42
Divorce Act of 1857 (Eng.), 60-62, 68
Divorce legislation (Eng.), 55, 58-63, 118, 119, 146, 148; alimony, 136; by act of Parliament, 59-60; king's proctor, 134
Divorce legislation (U.S.), 117-151; absolute and partial divorce, 119; alimony, 136-138; annulments, 106; complaint, 122; conflict in laws, 139-146; counsel, 133-135; custody of children, 138-139, 226-228; defenses, 128-133; diversity of statutes, 120; family court plan, 149-150; grounds for action, 122-128; history of, 117-120; jurisdiction in, 120-122, 139; laches, 133; limited, 146-148; parental duties, 242-244; remarriage rights, 135-136; resumption of maiden name, 138; residence requirement, 120-121; service of process, 121-122; statistics, 148; statutes of limitation, 132-133; uniformity of laws, 142-146. *See also* Legislative regulation of divorce
Divorce and Matrimonial Causes, Court for (Eng.), 60
Dix, Dorothea, 291
Domestic relations courts, 419-422
Domicile, meaning of term, 121, 505-506
Dos, 37, 39
Douglas, William O., 512-513
Dower, 37, 40
Due process of law, 16-17
Duress, marriage law and, 106-107

Edlin, Sara B., 341
Education, 228-231, 245-252
Education Act of 1944 (Eng.), 247
Edward I, 58
Edward VI, 55, 58
Edward VII, 62
Edward VIII, 62
Egypt, 69, 154, 166
Eire, 148, 158, 166
Eisenhower, Dwight D., 623, 639
Elberfeld plan, 449
Eldon, Lord, 218
Eliot, Martha, 299, 366, 368

Ellenborough, Lord, 217
Emergency Conservation Work (1933), 539
Emergency relief. *See* Federal Emergency Relief Act, Relief legislation
Emergency Relief Appropriation Act (1935), 527, 537, 542
Emergency Relief and Construction Act (1932), 526, 639
Emergency Work Relief Program, 531
Employment Security Administrative Financing Act (1954), 629-630
Employment Service, U.S., 546-547
England: adoption in, 313-314; birth control in, 155; child welfare services, 283-288; common law, 20-23; constitutional government in, 12; custody of children in, 216-221, 226-227; divorce in, 148; due-process concept in, 17; duties of parents, 237; guardianship of children, 259-263; illegitimacy in, 344-348; old-age assistance in, 555; parliamentary action final in, 14; religious education in, 228-229; revolt from Catholic church, 54-55; sterilization in, 188; as welfare state, 11
Enoch Arden marriages, 108
Epilepsy, 97, 99, 199, 200
Equal protection of the laws, 17-18
Equal rights (of sexes) amendment, 69
Ethiopia, 69
Eugenics, 188, 193-194
Eugenics Society, 188
Exclusion laws, 512-514
Exposure, infant, 31, 32, 35

Fabian Society, 474-475
Fair Labor Standards Act (1938), 9, 306, 548-549
Family: Christian influences on, 44-51; English law on, 53-72; in Greek civilization, 30-33; Hebrew influences on, 42-44; legislation concerning, 23; primitive, 29-30; Reformation and, 51-52; in Roman civilization, 33-39; Teutonic peoples, 39-42. *See also,* Children, Divorce, Marriage
Family Allowance Act (1945, Eng.), 481
Farm relief program, 545-546
Farm Security Administration, 518, 545-546
Fascism, women under, 28
Federal Compensation Act (1916), 537
Federal Council of Churches of Christ in America, 162-163
Federal Emergency Administration of Public Works, 547
Federal Emergency Relief Act (1933) (FERA), 518, 526, 527, 531-545; allocation problems, 532-533; construction projects, 541; eligibility, 533; farm aid, 546; funds for, 528; labor issues, 535-537; nonconstruction projects, 541-543; research projects, 543-544; transient relief, 537-539. *See also* Relief legislation
Federal Emergency Relief Administration, 526-527
Federal Security Agency, 540, 562
Federal Surplus Commodity Corporation, 546
Federal Surplus Relief Corporation, 546
Federal Theatre, 543
Federal Unemployment Tax Act, 629, 630, 637
Federal Works Administration, 547
Feeble-mindedness, marriage laws and, 97-99
Fee simple, 64
Fertility, control of human. *See* Birth control
Final Report on the W.P.A. Program: 1935–43, The, 544-545
Fleet Prison, 56
Fletcher, Joseph, 196
Florida: divorce in, 121, 142; guardianship of children in, 269; juvenile courts, 414; religious education in, 230
Ford unemployed benefit plan, 637
Fosdick, Harry Emerson, 169
Foster home program, 285-286, 293-298
Fourteenth Amendment, 17, 87, 105, 250, 513
France, 166; adoption in, 309, 310, 312; birth control in, 156, 158; education legislation in, 240; illegitimacy in, 342, 351; juvenile courts in, 381; welfare policies, 454-458
Francis I, 455
Frankfurter, Felix, 142, 410
Fraternal Order of the Eagles, 554
Fraud, in marriage, 106-107
Frederick the Great, 5
Frederick William I, 246
Free-thought movement, 156
French Revolution, 456
Freund, Ernst, 23, 355
Full faith and credit, 18-19

Garnett, W. H. S., 237
General assistance, meaning of term, 443, 445
General assistance legislation, 486-500; destitution under, 488-490; eligibility, 498-500; legal remedies, 493-496; meaning of, 486; obligations of relatives, 496-498; "poor" and "pauper" under, 490-491; settlement provisions,

General assistance legislation (*cont.*) 503-522; right to relief, 492-493; statistics on, 487-488; units of administration, 487-488; vagrancy and, 501-503. *See also* Poor relief
General Services Administration, 547
Gentile, F. M., 490
George VI, 62
Georgia: child welfare services, 302; relief legislation, 529, 537, 543; sterilization legislation, 201
Germany: birth control in, 156, 159; education legislation, 246; illegitimacy in, 342; juvenile courts in, 379-380; social security in, 447-454; sterilization practice, 187, 189-190
Gilbert, Thomas, 470
Gillin, J. L., 441
Glasgow, Scotland, poor relief, 474
Glueck, Eleanor, 398
Glueck, Sheldon, 398
Gosney, E. S., 208
Greece (modern), 166; adoption in, 310, 312; illegitimacy in, 351, 352
Greek civilization (early), 5; adoption in, 308-309; birth control in, 153-154; marriage and the family in, 30-33, 282-283; poor relief in, 437-438
Greenwood, Arthur, 479
Guardianship of children, 256-279, 400-403; ADC and, 271; court resources, 257-258; in English law, 259-263; federal study of, 269-274; by judicial appointment, 265-266; kinds of guardians, 256, 260-263; by nature, 264-265; Old-Age and Survivors Insurance and, 272-273; rights and duties, 267-269; in Roman law, 258-259; temporary legal, 267; termination of, 269; testamentary, 265; *tutela,* 259; Veterans' Administration and, 273-274
Guardians of the Poor, 470, 476-477
Guatemala, 310, 312

Hall, Fred S., 89-90, 91
Hamburg, poor relief in, 448-449
Hamilton County Court of Domestic Relations, 420
Hammurabi, Code of, 5, 308
Hand, Justice, 176
Hankins, Frank H., 339, 342
Hardwicke, Lord, 56, 346
Hardwicke Act (1753, Eng.), 48, 53, 56-58, 77, 78
Harrington, F. C., 541
Hawaii, 568, 574
Health, Education, and Welfare, Department of, 299, 562, 582, 590, 596, 597, 602, 608
Health insurance, 623
Health law (Eng.), 482-483
Health and Morals of Apprentices Act (1802, Eng.), 5
"Heart-balm" suits, 84-87
Hebrew civilization, 5; early birth control, 154; marriage and the family in, 30, 42-44; poor relief in, 437
Hendrix, Lillie, 140
Henry II, 20
Henry VIII, 55, 58, 468
Herbert, Alan Patrick, 62
Herschell, Lord, 348
Himes, Norman E., 176, 210
Hindu law, illegitimacy under, 351, 352
Hitler, Adolph, 159, 452
Hoffman, Charles W., 420
Holdsworth, W. S., 260
Holland, 156
Holmes, John Haynes, 169
Holmes, Oliver W., 8, 9, 198, 204, 304, 306
Home Owners Loan Corporation (HOLC), 548
Honduras, 69
Hoover, Herbert, 300, 525
Hopkins, Harry, 443, 526, 531, 532, 539
Hospitals, 439, 455, 456
Houses of refuge, 375, 403
Housing and Home Finance Agency, 548
Housing programs, federal, 548
Howard, D. S., 490
Howard, G. E., 59, 83
Huber bill (1921), 625
Hughes, Charles E., 15
Human Betterment Association of America, Inc., 199, 208
Human Rights. *See* Universal Declaration of Human Rights
Hurley, T. D., 376
Hutchinson, Thomas, 118

Idaho: divorce in, 121; settlement law, 507; sterilization law, 202
Illegitimacy, 109, 311-312, 339-367; adulterine bastardy, 339, 345-348; English law on, 344-348; history of, 341-349; mother's right of custody, 348; world-wide attitudes, 349-351. *See also* Illegitimacy law (U.S.)
Illegitimacy law (U.S.), 353-365; blood tests in, 358-360; evidence, 357-360; guardianship of children, 264, 265, 271, 274; jurisdiction, 356-357; legitimization, 354-356; statistics and, 366; support under, 360-362; uniform acts, 364-365
Illinois: child welfare services, 298, 302;

federal relief aid to, 532; illegitimacy law, 354; juvenile courts, 375-376, 413-415, 422; old-age assistance, 572; poor relief, 495; settlement law, 507, 510-511; youth authority, 426
Illinois Juvenile Court Act (1899), 376
Impotency, 103-104, 126
Income-tax exemptions, 581
Indenture contracts, 291-293
India, 166; birth control in, 154, 157-158, 159; juvenile courts in, 383; old-age assistance in, 555; sterilization legislation, 191-192
Indiana: blind relief, 581; child welfare services, 294, 298; marriage legislation, 74, 88; sterilization legislation, 201; work relief legislation, 536
Indians, American, 154
Industrial Revolution, 5, 471
Infancy, privileges and disabilities of, 252-253, 256
Infertility, treatment of, 152
Innocent III, Pope, 47, 439
Insanity, 97-99, 127-128
Institutions, 293-298, 392-393, 403-405, 569-570
Insurance. *See* Social insurance
Interdepartmental Committee on Social Insurance and Allied Services (Eng.), 286
Intermarriage. *See* Miscegenation
Internal Revenue Code, 607
Internal Security Act (1950), 618
International Labor Organization (ILO), 289, 460-461
International Planned Parenthood Conference (1952), 168
International Planned Parenthood Federation, 159
International Social Service, Inc., 312
International Union for Children, 289
International Union for Child Welfare, 289
Interprofessional Commission on Marriage and Divorce Laws, 149
Iowa: guardianship of children in, 264; juvenile courts, 376, 411, 414; marriage legislation, 100; old-age assistance, 572; poor relief, 493, 494; sterilization legislation, 195, 202
Iraq, 69
Iran, 69
Ireland, 148, 158, 166
Italy: birth control in, 156, 158, 159; divorce in, 148

Japan, 166; birth control in, 157; juvenile courts in, 383; sterilization law in, 191-192
Jest, marriage law and, 106-107
Jews, 5, 30, 42-44, 57, 154, 283, 437, 442
Jordan, 69
Judicature Act of 1873 (Eng.), 22
Judicial Committee of the Privy Council (1722, Eng.), 22
Judicial review, theory of, 13-15
Judicial system, 13-14, 61
Justinian, 37, 38, 39, 342
Juvenile courts, 258, 368-433; in England, 373-375; historical background, 374-377; international aspects, 377-383; principles underlying, 372-374
Juvenile courts (U.S.), 368-372, 375-377, 379-433; administration of, 407-408; community and, 405-406; constitutional questions, 410-415; custody and guardianship, 400-403; defects, 415-416; detention care, 392-393; hearing, 395-397; informal adjustments, 391-392; intake service, 390-391; jurisdiction, 386-389; personnel, 406-407; petition, 393, 394; police procedures, 389-390; principles involved, 409-410; records, 407; referees, 406; social study, 394-395; standard acts, 282, 416; summons, 395; venue, 384-385; youth correction authority, 424-427; youth courts, 422-423. *See also* Probation
Juvenile delinquency, 368-372; causes of, 370-372; congressional studies, 428-429; federal offenders, 417-419; services for handling, 370, 403-405, 427, 428; statistics, 368-370, 418-419. *See also* Juvenile courts
Juvenile Delinquency Act (1938), 417

Kansas: custody of children in, 226; federal relief aid to, 532; illegitimacy legislation, 360-361
Katherine of Aragon, 55
Kelly, Florence, 298
Kent, James, 81, 221-222, 240
Kentucky: general assistance, 489-490; youth authority, 426
Kerby, William J., 440-441
Knatchbull, Sir Edward, 470
Knowlton, Charles, 155-156, 160
Kraus, Hertha, 450

Labor, child, 8-9, 284, 285, 303-306. *See also* Apprenticeship
Labor legislation. *See* Social Security Act, separate agencies and laws
Labor, Department of, 562
Labor Management Relations Act (Taft-Hartley Law), 548

Labour Exchange Act (1909, Eng.), 477
Laches. *See* Divorce legislation
Laos, 69
Lasker awards, 168
Lateran Council (1215), 47
Lathrop, Julia, 299, 376
Latz, Leo J., 162
Law: *passim;* common, 19-23; constitutional, 12-19; *laissez-faire* concept, 5-6; "law of the land" concept, 17; police power and, 6-10; purposes of, 3-5; in the social service state, 11-12
League of Nations Advisory Committee on Social Questions, 353
Lee, C. I., Company, 174
Legislative regulation of divorce (U.S.), 122-133; adultery, 122-123; collusion, 128-130; condonation, 131; connivance, 130-131; conviction for crime, 126; cruelty, 123-125; desertion, 125-126; drunkenness, 126-127; impotence, 126; insanity, 127-128; nonsupport, 127; recrimination, 131-132; statutes of limitation, 132-133. *See also* Divorce legislation
Lehman, Herbert, 429
Lenroot, Katharine, 299
Letchworth, William Pryor, 295
Libya, 69
Liechtenstein, 69
Life expectancy, 560
Lindsey, Ben, 375
Local Government Act (1929, Eng.), 477
Lombard, Peter, 46
London: early poor laws, 468; poverty in, 475
London Charity Society, 474
Long, Huey, 553
Lou, H. H., 372
Louis XI, 455
Louis XIV, 456
Louisiana: federal relief aid to, 532; guardianship of children, 269; juvenile courts, 414; old-age assistance, 571; relief legislation, 529; work relief, 537
Lucas County Domestic Relations and Juvenile Court, 420
Luce, Robert, 19
Luther, Martin, 47, 51-52, 54, 70, 447, 448
Lutheran church, 163

McKenna, Joseph, 304
McKenney, Charles R., 162
Magna Charta, 12, 17
Maine, 74, 359
Maitland, F. W., 83, 259-260
Malthus, Thomas R., 155, 166
Malthusian League, 156
Mansfield, Lord, 346
Markandaya, Kamala, 282
Marriage, 47; Christian influences, 39, 44-48; a civil contract, 73-76; counseling services, 183-184; court conflicts and, 49-51; *de facto,* 51; *de jure,* 51; education for, 152; effect on status of women (Eng.), 63-69; evasion of, 114; in Greek civilization, 30, 32-33; Hebrew influences, 42-44; levirate, 43; with *manus,* 35-36, 38; meaning of term, 27; origins of, 29; primitive peoples and, 29-30; private, 47-48, 53; Reformation and, 51-52; in Roman civilization, 33, 35-37; settlement law and, 517; social regulation of, 27-28; Teutonic, 39-42; voluntary choice in, 28. *See also* Marriage law
Marriage law (Eng.), 43, 48, 53-58; affinity in, 100; breach-of-promise suits, 84; child marriage, 54; common-law marriage, 76-78; court conflicts, 49-51, 53-54; under Cromwell, 55-56; legal disabilities, 76-77; multiple marriages, 108; private marriage, 55, 56-58; Reformation and, 55-57
Marriage law (U.S.), 73-95; age in, 92-95; annulment, 98; breach-of-promise suits, 84-87; colonial, 78-80; common-law doctrine, 81-84; marriage defined, 73-76, 82-83; multiple marriages, 107-109; premarital physical examination, 101-103; religious v. civil, 79-80; remarriage rights, 135-136; state conflicts in, 112-113; uniformity pressure, 113-114. *See also* Statutory regulation of marriage (U.S.)
Married Women's Property Act (1870, Eng.), 68
Marshall, John, 6, 14
Maryland: almshouses in, 290; child welfare services, 294; juvenile courts, 376; marriage laws, 80
Massachusetts: adoption, 316, 322-324; birth control in, 172, 178-179; blind relief, 584; child welfare services, 291-292, 295, 297; dependent child assistance, 591; disabled assistance, 587; divorce, 118, 121, 142; education law, 230-231, 248; foster home care, 294; juvenile courts, 375, 414; marriage law, 79, 81, 113; old-age assistance, 554, 571; probation, 398; settlement law, 503-505; unemployment insurance, 625; youth authority, 426, 427
Maternal Health Association of Cleveland, 183

Maternity and Infancy Act (1921), 597
Matrimonial Causes Act (1857, Eng.), 226
Maule, Justice, 60
Medical care programs, 604-606, 622-623
Menander, 32
Mensinga, W. P. J., 154
Mental cruelty, ground for divorce, 124
Mental deficiency. *See* Sterilization
Merton, statute of (20 Henry III), 343
Methodist church, 184
Mexico, birth control in, 156
Michigan: child welfare services, 294, 298; custody of children in, 226; divorce in, 124; guardianship of children in, 269; sterilization law, 202; workmen's compensation, 536, 537
Midcentury White House Conference on Children and Youth (1950), 301
Migrants, 502-503; child labor, 306; settlement law and, 517; work relief for, 537-539
Miller, J., 206
Milwaukee, old-age living costs in, 559
Minnesota: blind relief, 584; child welfare services, 294, 298; dependent child in, 594; illegitimacy legislation, 350, 362; old-age assistance, 573; sterilization law, 201, 206; youth authority, 426
Miscegenation, 18, 104-105
Mississippi: dependent child assistance, 591; disabled assistance, 587; education in, 250; general assistance, 488; old-age assistance, 572, 579; relief legislation, 529
Missouri: blind relief, 582; dependent child in, 319-320, 588; federal relief aid to, 532; guardianship of children in, 270; illegitimacy legislation, 362; juvenile courts, 376; marriage in, 74; relief legislation, 529; religious education in, 229
Mistake, marriage law and, 106-107
Mobility of population, 501-503
Montana: income-tax legislation, 529; old-age assistance, 554; relief legislation, 529
Mormons, 74, 108
Morning gift, 40, 41
Mortality rates, U.S., 560
Mosaic Code, 5, 42
Moslem law, 351
Mothers' aid legislation, 588-594
Moulins, edict of (1566), 455
Munich, poor relief in, 448-449
Murphy, Douglas J., 168
Mussolini, Benito, 159
Napoleon, 456
National Assistance Act (1948, Eng.), 286, 477, 478, 482
National Assistance Board (Eng.), 478-479
National Association of Broadcasters, 168
National Association for Mental Health, 199
National Association of Women Lawyers, 144
National Broadcasting Company, censorship of birth control, 168
National Child Labor Committee, 306
National Conference of Charities and Corrections, 295, 514
National Conference of Commissioners on Uniform State Laws, 83, 113-114, 143, 147, 274, 326, 334-335, 359, 364-365, 514
National Conferences on Family Life, 422
National Congress on Uniform Divorce Laws (1906), 142-143
National Council of Churches of Christ in America, 442
National Health Service Act (1946, Eng.), 189, 481
National Industrial Recovery Act, 547
National Insurance, Ministry of (Eng.), 481
National Insurance Act (1946, Eng.), 481, 482
National Insurance Code of 1911 (West Germany), 454
National Labor Relations Board (NLRB), 548
National Negro Advisory Council, 168
National Probation and Parole Association, 407, 415, 416, 422
National Woman's Party, 69
National Youth Administration (NYA), 540-541, 546
Nazis, 187, 189-190, 380, 452-453, 454
Nebraska: federal relief aid to, 532; poor relief, 495; sterilization legislation, 202; work relief legislation, 537
Neglected child, meaning of term, 281
Neo-Malthusianism, 155
Nevada: divorce in, 121, 140, 141, 148; old-age assistance, 571; sterilization legislation, 195
New England: divorce in colonial, 117-118; marriage law in, 79. *See also* Plymouth Colony
New Hampshire, old-age assistance, 559, 573
New Jersey: child welfare services, 297; divorce in, 129, 143; juvenile courts, 376, 412-413, 414, 427; sterilization

New Jersey (*cont.*)
legislation, 196; unemployment insurance, 632, 635
New Mexico: juvenile courts, 412; old-age assistance, 559, 571; relief legislation, 529
New Orleans, old-age living costs in, 559
New York: almshouse system, 290-291; birth control in, 172, 177-178; child welfare services, 293-297; custody of children in, 228; dependent child assistance, 591; divorce in, 118, 141; general assistance, 488; juvenile courts, 375, 376, 419-420, 423, 427-428; marriage legislation, 80, 87, 93, 106; old-age assistance, 554, 568, 570, 579; probation, 399-400; religious education of children, 230; settlement law, 509, 510; unemployment insurance, 635; work relief legislation, 537
New York City Youth Board, 428
New York Civil Code (1865), 316
Nicaragua, 69
Nicholls, Sir George, 463
Nicolas, Sir Harry, 345, 346
Nonsupport legislation, 127, 147-148; *see also* Desertion
Norman Conquest, 20
Norman law, on illegitimacy, 344
North, Cecil C., 442
Northampton, Lord, 59
North Carolina: divorce in, 140-141; federal relief aid to, 532; planned parenthood in, 183; relief legislation, 543; sterilization legislation, 208-209
North Dakota: illegitimacy legislation, 355; relief legislation, 529
North Shore Mothers' Health Office, 178
Norway: birth control in, 157; illegitimacy legislation in, 350, 352, 355
Nurseries and Child-Minders Regulation Act (1948, Eng.), 287, 314

Office of Vocational Rehabilitation, U.S., 561-562
Ohio: blind relief, 581-582; child welfare services, 302; county children's homes, 294; juvenile courts, 376, 420-421; old-age assistance, 572; settlement law, 517
Oklahoma, sterilization legislation, 195
Old-age assistance legislation, 10, 515, 530, 621; administration of, 573-574; age in, 568; citizenship, 568; eligibility, 571-572; fair hearings, 577-578; federal provisions, 562-567; institutional care, 569-570; international, 555-556; payments, 566-567, 572-573; pension and insurance schemes, 555-557; personnel, 578; population covered by, 554; punitive provisions, 578-579; recoveries, 573; residence, 568-569; responsibility of relatives, 574-576; standards of need, 570-571; state provisions for, 567-576; statistics, 557-560, 579. *See also* Old-Age and Survivors Insurance
Old-Age and Survivors Insurance (OASI), 592, 607-624; account numbers, 609; administration of, 608-610; benefits, 613-615; employments covered, 617-618; guardianship of children and, 272-273; insured status, 610-612; limitations of, 622-624; retirement age for women, 612-613; statistics, 620-622. *See also* Disability insurance
Old-Age and Survivors Insurance Trust Fund, 608, 618-620
Omaha, poor relief, 495
Ordinance for a Common Chest (1523), 448
Oregon: custody of children in, 242; settlement law, 507; sterilization legislation, 202
Osborn, Fairfield, 166, 167
Owen, Sir Robert, 284, 285
Owen, Robert Dale, 155, 156, 160

Pan American Child Congress, 289
Paraguay, 69
Parental duties, 237-254; in divorce actions, 242-244; education, 245-251; extent of liability, 252-253; protection, 244-245; support, 237-242
Parental rights, 215-237, 400-403; to custody, 216-228; to earnings and services of minors, 233-237; emancipation doctrine, 234-236; in marriage legislation, 94-95; of punishment, 231-233; in religious education, 228-231
Parenthood. *See* Planned parenthood
Parole, juvenile, 405
Passfield, Baron. *See* Sidney Webb
Paton, Alan, 282
Pauper, 490-492
Pauper's oath, 499
Pearl, Raymond, 164
Pennsylvania: adoption in, 318-319; child welfare services, 294, 297; divorce in early, 118, 119; education legislation, 249; juvenile courts, 376, 410, 414, 423, 427; marriage law, 80; old-age assistance, 572; relief legislation, 529-530
Pennsylvania League for Planned Parenthood, 163, 169
Pensions: meaning of term, 443, 444, 445; old-age, 555-557

Pensions Act (1908, Eng.), 479
Persia, birth control in, 154
Peru: adoption in, 310, 312; juvenile courts in, 382
Petition of Rights (Eng.), 12
Petri papyrus, 153
Philadelphia: almshouse, 290; youth courts, 423
Phillips, Marion, 476
Pius XI, Pope, 196
Place, Francis, 155
Planned parenthood, 152-186; artificial insemination, 180-183; background of, 153-155; centers and clinics, 183-184; federal legislation, 170-177; international conferences, 159; medical opinion, 163-164; among Negroes, 168; population problem and, 165-167; public attitudes toward, 167-168; religious positions on, 160-163; scope of, 152-153; social and economic aspects, 164-165, 169; state legislation, 172-173, 177-180
Planned Parenthood Federation, 154, 163, 169, 171, 183
Planned Parenthood League of Connecticut, 179
Plymouth Colony, 374; apprenticeship in, 291; settlement law, 503-505
Poland, adoption in, 310, 312
Police, meaning of term, 6
Police power, 5-10
Pollock, Sir Frederick, 83, 259-260
Polls, on birth control: *Fortune,* 167-168; Gallup, 167; *Ladies' Home Journal,* 167
Poor, the, 490-492
Poor Law of 1601 (Eng.), 248
Poor Law of 1834 (Eng.), 155
Poor laws (Eng.), 353; apprenticeship under, 471; deportation to colonies under, 504; history of, 465-472; post-1832 legislation, 472-483
Poor relief: church approaches to, 439-443; definitions of terms, 443-446; history of, 5, 437-443, 446-463; responsibility of state for, 442-443. *See also* General assistance legislation, Social legislation, separate programs
Popenoe, Paul, 207, 208
Population problem, 165-167
Pound, Roscoe, 372, 410
Poverty, definitions of, 489
Presidential Reorganization Plan. *See* Social Security Board
President's Emergency Committee for the Unemployed (1930), 525
Price-fixing, 5, 40
Primogeniture, 23
Private law, 4
Probation, juvenile, 374, 397-400, 407, 417-418, 425
Protestant church attitudes: on birth control, 162-163; on marriage, 51-52; on poor relief, 441-443; on religious education, 228-231; on sterilization, 196
Protestant Episcopal church, 47
Public assistance (U.S.). *See* General assistance, Poor laws
Public Assistance Act (RFV, 1924, Germany), 450, 451, 452-453
Public Health Service (U.S.), 561-562
Public Health Service Act, 604
Public law, 4
Public Works Administration (PWA), 545
Puerto Rico, 166; birth control in, 177; blind relief, 584; dependent child assistance, 591; disabled assistance, 587; old-age assistance, 568, 579; sterilization legislation, 192
Puerto Rico Maternal and Child Health Association, 177
Punic Wars, 36, 38
Punishment. *See* Parental rights

Quakers, 57, 80
Quincy, Josiah, 290

Races. *See* Miscegenation
Rating and Valuation Act (1925, Eng.), 476
Radhakrishnan, S., 159
Railroad Retirement Act (1934), 555
Railroad Retirement Board, 636
Railroad Unemployment Insurance Act, 636
Rama Rau, Lady, 159
Randolph-Sheppard Act (1936), 581
Reader's Digest, 168
Reconstruction Finance Corporation, 525, 526
Recrimination, in divorce actions, 131
Redfield, Justice, 239
Red Cross Societies, League of, 289
Reed Bill, 629
Referees. *See* Juvenile courts
Reformatio Legum, 58-59, 118
Reformation: marriage under, 51-52, 55, 56-57; poor relief under, 447
Reformatories, 375
Reform Bill (1832, Eng.), 155
Relief Act (1939), 541
Relief Appropriations Act (1939–1940), 533
Relief legislation, 524-551; constitutional aspects, 529-531; construction activities and, 547-549; employment office system and, 546-547; farm program, 545-

Relief legislation (*cont.*)
546; funds for, 528-529; state action, 527-531; youth programs, 539-541; work relief, 531-539, 541-545. *See also* separate agencies, acts, and programs
Remarriage, 135-136
Removal legislation, 509-513
Reports, of court decisions, 22
Reproduction, human, research in, 152, 154-155
Resettlement Administration, 545
Residence, 121, 505-506; legislation, 518-520
Revenue Act (1918), 305
Rhode Island: juvenile courts, 375, 376, 385; old-age assistance, 568; unemployment insurance, 635
Richard II, 467, 468
Richmond, Mary E., 89-90, 91
Robson, William A., 488-489
Roman Catholic church, 195, 196, 228-231; attitude on birth control, 160-162, 167-169; divorce under, 48-49, 58; England's revolt from, 54-55; marriage under, 44-51; poor relief, 439-441
Roman civilization, 5; adoption in, 308-309; birth control, 153-154; guardianship of children, 258-259; illegitimacy in, 341-342; marriage and the family in, 33-39; police system, 6; poor relief in, 437-438
Roosevelt, Eleanor, 169
Roosevelt, Franklin D., 301, 526, 540, 552, 553, 596, 607, 621, 625
Roosevelt, Theodore, 299
Rowntree, B. S., 474, 475
Royal Commission on the Poor Laws and Relief of Distress (1905–1909, Eng.), 474, 475-476
Royal Commission on Marriage and Divorce, 62
Rubin, Sol, 415
Ruga, Spurius Carvilius, 39
Rumford, Count, 448–449

Sanger, Margaret, 152, 153, 159, 168, 171, 177-178, 184
Sanger (Margaret) Research Bureau of New York, 183
Saudi Arabia, 69
Senate Subcommittee to Investigate Juvenile Delinquency, 368, 371, 428, 429
Separation: judicial, 61; legal, 119; magisterial, 61
Servicemen's Readjustment Act (1944), 636
Settlement, meaning of term, 505-506
Settlement legislation, 503-522; acquisition of settlement, 506-508; exclusion, 512-514; loss of settlement, 508-509; modification proposals, 518-520; remedial procedures, 514-516; removal, 509-512; wives and children, 517-518
Shakespeare, William, 339-340
Sharp, Harry, 201
Shaw, George Bernard, 475
Shelters, for children, 392-393
Sheppard-Towner Act, 299, 597
Smith, Adam, 513
Social (or special) assistance, meaning of term, 443, 445
Social insurance, 23-24; in England, 286-288, 479-483; in Germany, 453-454; meaning of term, 443, 445; in Soviet Russia, 458-460. *See also* Social Security Act (1935), Social legislation, separate insurance programs
Social legislation, *passim;* chronology table, 564-565; common law and, 23; constitutional standards applied to, 12; court decisions on, 14-15; due-process clause and, 16-17; historical aspects, 5-10; international, 446-464; meaning of term, 4; philosophical background, 6; registration function, 58
Social security, meaning of term, 443, 444
Social security (Eng.), 465-485; legislation since 1832, 472-483; social insurances, 479-483. *See also* Poor laws
Social Security Act (1935), 9-10, 465-466, 496, 497, 544, 552-579, 580-606, 607-624, 625-642; amendments to, 561, 578, 589, 595-596; blind assistance through, 580-584; child benefits under, 270, 271, 280-281, 299, 302, 588-597, 602-604; costs of, 595; disability provisions, 584-588; maternal welfare provisions, 596-604; medical care program, 597-599, 604-606; statistics influencing, 557-560; titles of, 560-561. *See also* Guardianship of children (U.S.), Old-Age and Survivors Insurance, Unemployment compensation
Social Security Administration, 147, 608-610, 561-562
Social Security Board, 553, 561, 562, 570
Social services, meaning of term, 443, 444
Social service state, 11-12
Social Welfare, Division of, U.N., 289
Social work, 474, 578
Society for the Prevention of Cruelty to Animals, 281
Society for the Prevention of Cruelty to Children, 281
Solon's reforms (621 B.C.), 5, 31
South Carolina, 302
Soviet Russia: adoption in, 310, 312; birth control in, 158; juvenile courts

in, 380; population problem, 166; unemployment insurance in, 555; welfare policies, 458-460; women in, 28
Spain: birth control in, 156; divorce in, 148
Speenhamland, (Eng.), poor relief in, 471
Standard Juvenile Court Act, 385, 386, 416
States (U.S.): constitution of, 12-13; interrelationships, 18-19; powers of, 15-16. *See also* separate states
Statute of Apprentices (1563, Eng.), 248
Statute of Labourers (1350, Eng.), 467
Statutes, formulation of, 19
Statutes of limitation. *See* Divorce legislation
Statutory regulation of marriage (U.S.), 88-95, 96-115; bigamy, 108-109; child marriages, 92-95; consanguinity and affinity, 100; license requirement, 88-90; mental disability, 97-99; miscegenation, 104-105; moral disabilities, 106-107; parental consent, 94-95; physical disability, 97, 99, 101-104; prohibitive conditions, 96, protection of children by, 109; recording, 91-92; solemnizing, 90-91; uniformity problems, 112-114; "void or voidable" confusion, 109-112
Steinbeck, John, 502
Steinbicker, Carl, 441, 446, 447-448
Stephen, King, 50
Sterilization, definition of, 193
Sterilization legislation, 187-212; civic liability, 206-207; compulsory and voluntary, 200-201; criminal liability, 205-206; for epilepsy, 199; international aspects, 188-192; judicial decisions, 203-204; for the mentally disabled, 197-200; for punishment, 194-195; religious positions, 195-196; studies on, 207-209
Stone, Abraham, 163, 176, 183
Stone, Harlan F., 557
Stopes, Marie, 175, 176
Strassburg (poor relief) system, 449
Supreme Court, U.S., 8, 14-15
Supreme courts, state, 14-15
Sweden, 166; birth control in, 156, 157, 381; illegitimacy in, 352; sterilization legislation in, 190-191
Swedish National League for Sex Education, 157
Switzerland, 69; adoption in, 310, 312; birth control in, 156

Taft, William Howard, 305
Taft-Hartley Law, 548
Talfourd, Serjeant-at-law, 220
Talmud, 42
Tappen, Paul, 394
Tariff Act of 1930, 176
Teachers, relief assistance to, 542
Tenant, by the curtesy, 65
TenBrock, Jacobus, 513
Tennessee: alimony in, 138; child marriage in, 93; relief legislation, 543
Teutonic peoples, marriage and the family among, 39-42
Texas: relief legislation, 529; settlement law, 507; youth authority, 426
Textile mills, child labor in, 284
Thompson, Benjamin (Count Rumford), 448-449
Tileston, Wilder, 179
Tolan, John H., 520
Tolan Congressional Committee, 502
Toledo, O., family court in, 405, 420-421
Torah, 42
Tosephta Niddah, 154
Trade unions (Soviet), insurance systems, 459
Training schools, 403
Transfer of dependents act (1935), uniform, 514
"Transportation agreement," 514
Treasury Department, U.S., 608
Truelove, Edward, 156
Truman, Harry S., 301, 503
Truman's Commission on Migratory Labor, 503
Tuberculosis, in marriage legislation, 101
Tutela. See Guardianship of children
Twelve Tables, Roman, 5, 34, 35

Ulman, Abraham S., 179
Ulman, Joseph N., 426
Unemployment Act (1934, Eng.), 478
Unemployment Assistance Act (1939, Eng.), 478
Unemployment compensation, 625-642; administration, 634-635; benefits, 632-633; coverage, 630-631; disability, 635-636; federal employees, 637; federal provisions, 628-630; financing, 632; objectives, 626-627; qualifications, 632-634; state laws for, 630-635; supplemental plans, 637-638. *See also* Social Security Act
Unemployment insurance (U.S.), 525, 555; disability assistance, 616-624; history of, 524-525, 555-557; old-age assistance, 607-624. *See also* Relief legislation, Social insurance, Unemployment compensation
Unemployment Insurance Act (1911, Eng.), 477
Unemployment Trust Fund, 629-630

Uniform Act on Desertion and Nonsupport. *See* Desertion
Uniform laws. *See* National Conference of Commissioners on Uniform State Laws
Uniform Marriage License Application Act, 114
Uniform Reciprocal Enforcement of Support Act, 242
Uniform Veterans' Guardianship Act, 274
United Kingdom: adoption in, 312-316; education legislation, 245-247; juvenile courts in, 377-379. *See also* England
United Nations: adoption-of-children studies, 309; illegitimacy studies, 352; population problem, 167; status of women under, 69; welfare activities, 288, 289, 460-462
United Nations Charter, 69
United Nations Children's Fund, 289
United States: adoption in, 312; birth control in, 160-185; as constitutional government, 12-13; doctrine of judicial review, 14-15; government organization, 15-16; marriage regulation, 28; public assistance statistics, 621; social service functions in, 11-12; status of women in, 69. See also specific agencies, laws, and programs
United States Employees Retirement Act (1920), 555
United States Employment Service, 635
United States Housing Act (1937), 548
Universal Declaration of Human Rights (U.N.), 460
Uruguay, adoption in, 310
Utah: dependent child assistance in, 593; divorce in, 121; juvenile courts, 385, 414; sterilization legislation, 202, 204, 207

Vagabondage, in England, 466-467
Vagrancy, relief laws and, 501-503
Venereal diseases, 101-103
Vermont: divorce in, 143; marriage legislation, 100; sterilization legislation, 201
Vernier, Chester C., 236
Veterans' Administration, 273-274, 581, 636
Veterans' insurance, 622
Veterans' Readjustment Assistance Act (1952), 636
Veterans' relief, 486
Vincent de Paul, St., 455
Vinson, Fred M., 142
Virginia: child welfare services, 298; colonial, 504; education legislation, 249; federal relief aid to, 532; illegitimacy law, 353-354; marriage law, 79-80; probation in, 399
Virgin Islands: disabled assistance in, 587; divorce in, 121; old-age assistance in, 568
Virtue, Maxine Boord, 405
Vives, cited, 446
Vocational Rehabilitation Act, 581, 604
Voght, von, Baron Kaspar, 448
Vogt, William, 166-167, 168
Void and voidable marriages, 109-112

Wages, guaranteed annual, 637
Wagner, Robert, 625
Wagner-O'Day Act (1938), 581
Wagner-Peyser Act (1933), 546, 547, 635
Wald, Lillian D., 298
Wales, divorce in, 148
Wallas, Graham, 475
Wall Street Journal, 619-620
Walsh, Mary Elizabeth, 440
War: influence on status of women, 38; population movement during, 502
Warning out, 510
Warren, Earl, 250, 251
Washington: dependent child aid, 593; divorce in, 128; poor relief, 495; settlement law, 507; sterilization legislation, 194-195; work relief legislation, 536
Watts, Charles, 156
Wayward Minors' Act (1923, N.Y.), 423
Webb, Beatrice, 465, 466-467, 472, 473, 475
Webb, Sidney, 465, 466-467, 472, 473, 475
Welfare and Health Council of New York City, 169
Welfare and Hygiene of Maternity and Infancy Act, 299
Welfare state, 11
Welles, Carlotta, 458
Westermarck, Edward, 27
West Virginia: adoption, 319; blind relief, 584; dependent child assistance, 594; old-age assistance, 579; work relief legislation, 536
White House Conferences, 249, 299-302, 588, 602
Wigmore, John Henry, 346-347
Wilde, F. A., 154
Wilde, Serjeant-at-law, 218
William II, 56
William the Conqueror, 20, 344
Williams, O. B., 140
Wilson, Woodrow, 300
Wisconsin: adoption, 327-329, 330, 332; apprenticeship in, 292; child welfare

services, 294; common law, 22; custody of children, 227-228; disabled relief, 584; divorce in, 143, 144; federal relief aid to, 532; general assistance, 489, 498; illegitimacy legislation, 347-348, 360; income tax, 529; juvenile courts, 376, 402-403, 427; marriage legislation, 97, 99, 101, 113; old-age assistance, 568-569, 570, 576; poor relief, 491, 495, 496; settlement law, 507, 508, 511-512, 515, 516; sterilization legislation, 196, 203, 205, 207; unemployment insurance, 555, 625; work relief, 536; youth authority, 426, 427
Witte, Edwin E., 553, 557, 640
Woman Rebel, The, 153, 171
Women: birth-control attitudes, 167; buying and selling of, 40; under Christianity, 38; under English law, 63-72; in Greek civilization, 31-33; Hebrew, 42-43; international status, 69; labor legislation for, 69; primitive, 29-30; in Roman civilization, 34-39; among Teutonic peoples, 41; under U.S. law, 64; wife-capture, 39-40. *See also* Divorce, Family, Marriage
Wood, A. H., 188
Woodside, Moya, 208, 209
Workhouses, 470, 472-474
Workmen's compensation, 482, 622, 639; relief legislation and, 535-537
Workmen's Compensation Act of 1897 (Eng.), 479
Workmen's Compensation Board (N.Y.), 635
Works Progress Administration (WPA), 525, 527, 531-545; allocation problems, 532-533; construction projects, 541; eligibility, 533; farm aid, 546; funds for, 528; labor issues, 535-537; nonconstruction projects, 541-543; research projects, 543-544; statistics on, 544-545; transients, 537-539
World Federation for Mental Health, 289
World Health Organization (WHO), 160, 289
World War I, 309, 310
World War II, 310, 347, 502-503
Writers projects, WPA, 543
Wyoming: divorce in, 121; relief legislation, 529; religious education in, 231; unemployment insurance in, 633

Yates, J. V. N., 290
Yemen, 69
Youngs Rubber Corporation, 174, 175
Youth Board, New York City, 428
Youth Commission, N.Y., 428
Youth Correction Authority Act (1940), 424
Youth Corrections Act (1950), 418
Youth Courts, 422-427; *see also,* Juvenile courts
Yugoslavia, adoption in, 310, 312
Ypres plan, 446-447